*The*
# WILEY
*advantage*

Dear Valued Customer,

We realize you're a busy professional with deadlines to hit. Whether your goal is to learn a new technology or solve a critical problem, we want to be there to lend you a hand. Our primary objective is to provide you with the insight and knowledge you need to stay atop the highly competitive and ever-changing technology industry.

Wiley Publishing, Inc., offers books on a wide variety of technical categories, including security, data warehousing, software development tools, and networking — everything you need to reach your peak. Regardless of your level of expertise, the Wiley family of books has you covered.

- For Dummies – The *fun* and *easy* way to learn
- The Weekend Crash Course –The *fastest* way to learn a new tool or technology
- Visual – For those who prefer to learn a new topic *visually*
- The Bible – The *100% comprehensive* tutorial and reference
- The Wiley Professional list – *Practical* and *reliable* resources for IT professionals

The book you hold now, *Microsoft SQL Server 2000 Bible,* is your 100% comprehensive guide to developing database projects for SQL Server 2000. If you are new to SQL Server, or client/server technology, *SQL Server 2000 Bible* is everything you need to incorporate best practices into your database development. Beginning with database design theory, Paul Nielsen and his team of experts guide you through developing SQL Server databases, developing data connections, administering SQL Server and keeping your databases performing at their peak with a section on performance tuning and optimization. Our commitment to you does not end at the last page of this book. We'd want to open a dialog with you to see what other solutions we can provide. Please be sure to visit us at www.wiley.com/compbooks to review our complete title list and explore the other resources we offer. If you have a comment, suggestion, or any other inquiry, please locate the "contact us" link at www.wiley.com.

Finally, we encourage you to review the following page for a list of Wiley titles on related topics. Thank you for your support and we look forward to hearing from you and serving your needs again in the future.

Sincerely,

*Richard K. Swadley*

Richard K. Swadley
Vice President & Executive Group Publisher
Wiley Technology Publishing

**15 HOUR WEEKEND CRASH COURSE**

**Visual**™

**Bible**

**DUMMIES** FOR

**WILEY**
Independent Thinkers

*more information
on related titles*

# The Next Level of SQL Server Books

## Available from Wiley Publishing

ADVANCED

INTERMEDIATE

# Microsoft® SQL Server™ 2000 Bible

# Microsoft® SQL Server™ 2000 Bible

**Paul Nielsen**

Wiley Publishing, Inc.

**Microsoft® SQL Server™ 2000 Bible**

Published by
**Wiley Publishing, Inc.**
909 Third Avenue
New York, NY 10022
www.wiley.com

Copyright © 2003 by Wiley Publishing, Inc., Indianapolis, Indiana

ISBN: 0-7645-4935-9

Library of Congress Control Number: 2002110311

Manufactured in the United States of America

10 9 8 7 6 5 4 3 2 1

1B/RT/RS/QS/IN

Published by Wiley Publishing, Inc., Indianapolis, Indiana
Published simultaneously in Canada

# About the Authors

**Paul Nielsen** has been a programmer since 1979 and has focused exclusively on database development since the early '80s. After serving a term with the US Navy Submarine Service as a Data Systems Technician Petty Officer, Paul became a computer trainer and consultant, which led to writing computer magazine articles.

Paul co-authored a book with Peter Norton in the early '90s and contributed several chapters to various programming and database books. He was the initial technical editor for *Access Advisor* Magazine, and has spoken at several computer conferences including Microsoft Tech-Ed, and ICCM.

Over the course of a couple decades, Paul has developed several database projects using a variety of database products and tools. Much of the work has centered on the manufacturing industry, and insurance regulation databases. Recently, Paul was the data modeler and SQL Server developer for a team that built an MRP/II inventory system.

Of the 98,000 who have taken the *BrainBench.com RDBMS Concepts* certification test, at the time of this writing, Paul ranks fifth in the United States.

Currently, Paul is a database developer with Compassion International, a Christian organization dedicated to releasing children from poverty in Jesus' name. He is also a part-time SQL Server instructor with Learning Tree. When not thinking about database development, Paul plays a Taylor guitar, reads the *New Living Translation,* listens to Natalie Cole, and watches his kids grow up way too fast.

**Brian Patterson** currently works as a software developer in central Illinois. Brian has been writing for various Visual Basic publications since 1994 and has co-authored several .NET related books, including *Migrating to Visual Basic .NET* and *C# Bible*. Brian is exceptionally well rounded and in his spare time he likes to program, write about programming, and read about programming. He can generally be found posting in the MSDN newsgroups and is reachable by e-mail at briandpatterson@msn.com.

**Pierre Boutquin** is a senior software architect in the treasury of a major Canadian bank, where he helps develop leading-edge market risk management software. He has more than a decade of experience implementing PC-based computer systems, along with an in-depth knowledge of distributed systems design, data warehousing, Visual Basic, Visual C++, and SQL. He has co-authored many programming books and has also contributed material on C#, VB, COM+, XML, and SQL for others. Koshka and Sasha, his two adorable Burmese cats, own most of Pierre's spare time. While petting them, he often thinks how nice it would be to find more time and get back into chess or keep up with news from Belgium, his native country. Pierre can be reached at boutquin@hotmail.com.

**Todd Meister** is a developer specializing in Microsoft technologies. He has been a developer for over 10 years and has published articles for both *ActiveWeb Developer* and *MSDN Magazine*. Todd can be reached at tmeister@tmeister.com.

# Credits

**Senior Acquisitions Editor**
Sharon Cox

**Project Editor**
Andy Marinkovich

**Technical Editor**
Bobbie Townsend

**Copy Editor**
Sarah Kleinman

**Editorial Manager**
Mary Beth Wakefield

**Vice President and Executive
Group Publisher**
Richard Swadley

**Vice President and Executive
Publisher**
Bob Ipsen

**Executive Editorial Director**
Mary Bednarek

**Project Coordinator**
Erin Smith

**Graphics and Production Specialists**
Sean Decker, Melanie DesJardins,
Carrie Foster, Heather Pope

**Quality Control Technicians**
John Tyler Connoley, Andy Hollandbeck

**Proofreading and Indexing**
TECHBOOKS Production Services,
Johana VanHoose

*This work is dedicated to the author of the true Bible,
our heavenly Father, "Hallowed be Thy Name."*

*My heart, love, and blessing goes to you my wife, Melissa,
not for anything you do but because of who you are and
how you complete me. God blessed me greatly the day we met.
I can't imagine any other life or any better life. Thank you
for your love, compassion, faithfulness, and sweetness.
I will never forget.*

# Preface

## Welcome to this Book

SQL Server is an incredible database product. I have personally developed with about a dozen different database products and I enjoy working with SQL Server more than any other. It offers an excellent mix of performance, reliability, and ease of administration, yet enables the developer to control minute details when desired. SQL Server is a dream system for a database developer. Developing with SQL Server is a pleasure. The first goal of this book is to share with you the fun of working with SQL Server.

SQL Server is a big product. To cover every nuance of every command would consume several thousand pages. With that in mind, the second goal for this book is to provide a concise yet comprehensive guide to SQL Server based on the information I have found most useful in my experience as a database developer, consultant, and instructor.

A wise database developer once showed a box to an apprentice and asked, "How many sides do you see?" The apprentice replied, "There are six sides to the box." The experienced database developer then said, "Users may see six sides, but database developers only see two sides, the inside and the outside. To the database developer, the cool code goes inside the box." This book is about thinking inside the box.

## The Writing Style

I don't like filler text, screen shots stepping through wizards, or page-length query results, so this book avoids them. If a result set is long, it is abbreviated with an ellipsis in the listing. Wizards are explained with a numbered list.

Chatty writing tends to get in the way of the facts. First person writing is generally reserved for when I want to write directly to you from my experience, or share my opinion. The goal for the writing style is that every sentence adds value to the book. I doubt I reached that goal, but that was my intent.

# Conventions

This book uses the following style guidelines:

- ✦ New terms are *italicized* as they are defined in the text.

- ✦ When code is referenced within the text, the code words are set in mono-space type. Sometimes those same SQL keywords are used as concepts. For example, `inner` join is used both as SQL code and in referring to the concept of a type of join.

- ✦ Some of the code samples are long. To draw attention to the main point of the code, important keywords in code are highlighted in **bold**.

- ✦ For consistency sake, the code conventions are similar to those used by Microsoft SQL Server Books online.

# Icons

The following icons are used in this book to offer additional tips and information about the topics in the book:

In several places in this book, material overlaps. For example, when installing SQL Server, one decision has to do with the authentication mode used for security. Rather than constantly refer you to other parts of the book, I've tried to provide enough information so that the immediate issue is covered without being too redundant. Even so, there are numerous cross-references throughout the book so more detail on a topic may be easily looked up.

Best Practice icons indicate where I add to the factual material in the book with my opinions and lessons I've learned from my own experience.

Note icons emphasize additional facts about the topic at hand.

Caution icons caution you about potential negative effects if a procedure or process is not precisely executed.

# Walking Through the Book

A well-designed database is born not in the code, but in the planning. The same is true for a book. There's a purpose to the organization of this book. So that you understand the direction and destination of this book, here's the reasoning behind its organization.

## Development Philosophy

This book is based on a certain client/server development philosophy. The following themes reverberate throughout the book.

+ Transactional Integrity (ACID) is fundamental to the database.

+ SQL is a set-oriented environment and SQL code should be set-oriented rather than procedural or row-based.

+ The physical database schema is designed to serve the query.

+ Processing should be moved as close to the data as possible.

+ Performance is designed into every aspect of the database; it's not a final optimization step. However, slow and right beats fast and wrong every time.

+ Excellent database development requires a thorough understanding of the underlying theory, the best practices, and the database tools.

## Organization

The chapter organization of the book went through several evolutions. The final chapter plan is designed to segment the chapters into the most logical sequence for study as well as reference.

### Part I — Laying the Foundation

Provides a foundation for developing database projects with SQL Server. If you're new to SQL Server 2000, this part introduces SQL Server and the theory behind database development.

### Part II — Developing SQL Server Databases

Covers actual database development from creating the database to advanced server-side code. The real fun of SQL Server development is writing server side code. This part explains how and provides some interesting code examples. If you're a server-side developer or a front-end developer who needs to learn more about SQL Server, this section is designed for you.

### Part III — Data Connectivity

The database is the center of a multitude of applications using multiple data connectivity methods. Depending on your particular environment, choose the chapter that applies to you.

### Part IV — Administering SQL Server

Every database requires administration, maintenance, and security. Whether administration is your primary responsibility or if it falls under the "other duties as assigned" part of your job description, this part of the book is for you.

### Part V — Advanced Issues

Tuning and optimization is always a hot topic. The final part presents a few advanced topics to take the book to the next level.

# The Sample Databases

This book is more than just the text on the pages. The CD-ROM includes the SQL DDL code to create the tables and stored procedures for the five sample databases, as well as the scripts to populate them with sample data. Appendix B contains more details about the sample databases.

Learning is a combination of new information and new experiences. To get the most out of this book, install the databases on your computer and work through the chapters' sample code. I had fun writing the book and developing these databases; I hope your experience is equally as enjoyable.

# www.IsNotNull.com

Paul Nielsen publishes the Web site www.IsNotNull.com, which contains a series of articles focused on SQL queries, database development, and optimization, in addition to sample code, on-line polls, recommended resources, and performance tips.

# Your Input

I want to hear from you. Which sections did you enjoy? What did you learn? What section did you skip over? There will be new editions of this book that follow the new versions of SQL Server. What should be added to the next edition of the book? Your comments matter so please e-mail me at pauln@IsNotNull.com.

# Acknowledgments

**A** special thank you to Dr. Breeze and everyone in the University Hospital Neuro ICU in Denver, Colorado for the gentle care given to my wife during her last two weeks with us.

To my daughter, Lauren, "Daddy loves his little girl." You are growing into an incredible young lady. And to my son, David, watching you develop in the family tradition of engineering brings me great joy. And, things are being put back together more often these days, too! I'm very proud of you both. Hey kids, the book's fi-na-lly done! Lauren, let's FedEx in some white pizza from Dante's in Hickory! Hey Dave! My multiplayer computer game suspension is over! Let's head to Best Buy and pick out a new game. I love you both.

To my friend, Kennedy Kinyanjui Wainaina in Kenya, I'm proud of you and your studies. Thank you for your prayers. Keep up the good work and God bless you.

Thank you Wess Stafford, Mark Ambrose, Margo Beaven, Chuck Boudreau, Tim Chambers, Jim Finwick, Kaye Garten, Laura Goins, Aravindan Gurumurthy, Greg Hollmann, Brian Houghtaling, Ragu Maddipati, Scott Noll, Jim Pruett, Rod Stricklin, Steve Thompson, Bob Towry, Anthony Virgil, Alan Werckle, and my other team members at Compassion International in Colorado Springs and around the world. I truly believe we are fighting the good fight against poverty and I'm grateful that I'm working with you.

I'm indebted to Phil Senn, one of the best programmers I know, for the many lunches discussing Dilbert, programming style, good database design, the conflict between innovation and stability, and the difficulty of finding good management these days.

Hoorays to the entire Microsoft SQL Server team for developing a set of software that's truly a database developer's dream. Go Bill!

I'm indebted to Bobbie Townsend for her efforts as technical editor. She is one of the most professional instructors I know and she knows SQL Server inside and out. She is a Microsoft Certified Professional and has owned her own consulting company since 1992. Her company provides customized software development and training. She is a book author and has served as the technical editor for multiple books and classes. If any of you need professional SQL Server assistance, I would not hesitate to recommend Bobbie. She can be reached via email at BobbieTownsend@Hotmail.com.

I have been greatly influenced and have learned significantly from a few select database heroes. Joe Celko is at the top of my list of people I listen to. Credit is also due to SQL authors E.F. Codd, Chris J. Date (even though you're wrong about nulls), Sharon Dooley, Kalen Delaney, Ken Henderson, B.P. Margolin, and Bill Vaughn. Thank you all. I'm no Isaac Newton, but his saying "If I have seen further than you, it is only by standing on the shoulders of giants," rings true for me.

Recognition and appreciation goes out to Gary Fletcher for his contributions to the early design of this book.

Thank you all to the Learning Tree SQL Server course authors: Jamie Beidleman, Sharon Dooley and her cats, Geoff Ballard, Efrem Perry, Dag Hoftun Knutsen; my fellow Learning Tree SQL Server instructors: Scott Whigham, Melinda King, Bobbie Townsend, Nathan Stevens; and professionals: Sandra Thayer, Robin Hunter, Colleen Harrison, and Pete Peterson. I've enjoyed working alongside the experts at "the Tree." Moreover, thank you to my students — your interest and questions contributed greatly to this book.

A hearty "thanks!" goes out to my fellow programming buddies who provided a peer review of this book, submitted questions/SQL problems, or from whom I've learned some best practices or tips: Gary Lail, Donny Beard, Lauck Benson, Steve Miller, Dave Catherman, Robin Jueschke, Carl Federl, Lynn Garten, David Scott, Pascal Gill, Dan Adamson, Hilary Cotter, Hirantha S. Hettiarachchi, Bill Carver, Tom Sallese, Todd Porter, and, of course, Dean Vrables U.S.M.C. To my other friends on the SQL Yahoo Groups, too many to list, Thank You. Your conversation and feedback made the solitary process of writing so much more enjoyable, and your questions and comments greatly improved this book.

Mark Ambrose did a final code walk-through on the sample databases and the chapter code. Thank you, Mark.

Thank you Master Chief Miller, U.S.N., C.S.T.S.C. Mare Island, CA., who 20 years ago started me on the database developer path. To any of my old Navy friends, please send me an e-mail at `pauln@IsNotNull.com`.

Appreciation and honors to Matt Wagner of Waterside Productions for handling the business side of writing. Without hesitation, I recommend Matt and Waterside Productions to anyone desiring to have their words actually read by others. Having a trustworthy agent who really works for you makes a world of difference.

A grand "thank you!" to the folks at Wiley Publishing (formerly Hungry Minds, formerly IDG). Thanks to Terri Varveris for first envisioning this book and working through the numerous outline revisions with me. It was a pleasure working with you. To Sharon Cox and Chris Webb, thank you for your management of the book. To Sarah Kleinman, I greatly appreciate you and your contribution to the quality of this book. And, thank you, Andy Marinkovich, for your style direction, excellent editing, and smoothing of the material. I am grateful for the way all of you handled the final issues with the book while I was focused on my wife during her medical crisis. Thank you.

Credit is shared with the other authors who contributed material to this book: Brian Patterson, who took over the final stages of the author review process while I tended to my wife during her illness; Anthony Virgil, who contributed material to Part III, "Administering SQL Server;" Joseph Gagliardo, who assisted with the writing of Chapter 20, "Replicating Databases," and Chapter 22, "XML and Web Publishing;" John Paul Mueller, who authored Chapter 21, "ADO and ADO.Net;" Pierre Boutquin, who wrote Chapter 25, "Automating Database Maintenance with SQL Server Agent;" and Todd Meister, who penned Chapter 31 "Analysis Services." I couldn't have done it without all of you.

Hazzah! to Microsoft/Ensemble Studios and LucasArts Entertainment for *Star Wars Galactic Battleground™: Clone Campaigns™*, aka "AOE-Star Wars." AOE is the chess of the digital age. Besides SQL Server, it's the most fun on a computer I've had since DEC-Trek.

# Contents at a Glance

# Contents

• • • • • • • • • • • • • • • • • • • • • • • • • • • • • • • • • • • • •

## Part I: Laying the Foundation     1

## Part IV: Administering SQL Server                                        623

# Laying the Foundation

**W**elcome to SQL Server! SQL Server is built to deliver the performance, scalability, and transactional integrity required for heavy-duty, high-visibility databases. If the data is critical to an organization, then a well-developed and maintained SQL Server based application is worthy of the task.

The goal of this book is to help you develop such an application. The foundation begins with a well-rounded understanding of SQL Server, relational database logical schema design, as well as a programmer-to-programmer introduction to Enterprise Manager, the graphical DBA tool, and Query Analyzer, the database developer's editor of choice.

If the server is "the box" and developing is thinking inside the box, then Part I of this book is the mental preparation of approaching the box.

# Introducing SQL Server

**A**s a database, SQL Server is all about efficiently storing data within tables built from rows and columns. At the center of SQL Server is the SQL Server engine, which processes the database commands. The process runs inside Windows and understands only connections and SQL commands. Enterprise Manager, Query Analyzer, every SQL Server–enabled Graphical User Interface (GUI), Application Programming Interface (API), and application makes a connection to SQL Server and sends SQL statements to SQL Server for processing.

As robust as the engine is, SQL Server is much more than just the engine: it includes a set of tools for administrating the server and preparing queries; add-on tools for converting and moving data, and for performing data warehousing and analysis; and services for managing the connection at both the server side and the client side.

SQL Server is based on the ANSI SQL 92 standard. SQL is the *de facto* standard for stating relational-database queries. Nearly every database product is based on some variation of SQL, even if the SQL code is not visible to the end user.

**Note**    There's some debate over the pronunciation of SQL. Most developers simply say "sequel." But there are a few purists who insist the proper pronunciation is "ess-cue-el," because there was another language called Sequel before SQL. The pronunciation affects sentence grammar — "a sequel" versus "an SQL." Personally, I prefer "sequel," but either pronunciation is OK.

SQL Server is a complete database system, and fully mastering its scope can take years. In terms of features, commands, subsystems, components, and possibilities, SQL Server is one of the largest and most complex software products on the market. Fortunately, Microsoft has gone the extra mile to improve the "out-of-the-box experience" by making SQL easier to use and administer than other client/server database systems (including previous version of SQL Server). The server administration can be so simple that I know of several databases in production that were set up using administrative wizards and have not required administrative attention in over two years, yet they're still running great. Nonetheless, the sheer number of SQL Server features can easily overwhelm a new developer.

This initial chapter provides a 28,000-foot view of the numerous SQL Server components and features. This big-picture overview will serve as a framework for understanding the details in the rest of the book and how those details fit into SQL Server. In addition, this chapter will help you decide which features are most important to you and will show you why SQL Server is so popular.

# The Client/Server Database Model

Technically, the term *client/server* refers to any two cooperating processes. The client process requests a service from the server process, which in turn handles the request for the client. The client process and the server process may be on different computers or on the same computer: It's the cooperation between the processes that is significant, not the physical location.

The term *client/server* applies to many aspects of computing. File servers, print servers, and Internet service providers (ISPs) are all client/server models. File servers provide files, print servers handle print requests, and ISPs handle requests for Internet service. In the area of client/server databases, a database server process handles database requests from the database client process.

## Desktop Databases

Desktop databases perform all the database tasks at the client. While a multi-user desktop database may use client/server file processing, it doesn't qualify as client/server database processing. Access' Jet Engine, for example, performs all database tasks at the client. In a multi-user Access application, the file server is merely providing file sharing—no database intelligence is contained in the file server. If an Access user requests a customer, the entire index comes across the network and the search and retrieval takes place within the client process. Multi-user desktop databases tend to make heavy demands on the network and, therefore, bog down as the demand grows.

To visualize a desktop database searching for a phone number, picture the entire telephone book moving through the network wire (Figure 1-1). Actually, some desktop databases try to optimize the operation by opening only a portion of the database file, such as an index or a data page. Once the client computer has the index, the client computer searches it and selects the correct row. It then opens the table and retrieves the row. All this work takes place on the client. If multiple clients are working with the database, portions of the database file are constantly flying across the network. In other words, the network is as busy as the I-485 loop in Atlanta at 5:30 pm, and each client has the opportunity to corrupt the file. Updates are even messier.

As the database file grows, or the number of clients increases, the amount of data being transported by the network increases. From my experience, as a rule of thumb desktop databases are good for about 20 users, or about 20MB. There are exceptions, but beyond these thresholds, they become slow and unstable.

## Client/Server Databases

In contrast to desktop databases, which make the clients do all the work, client/server databases are like research librarians who handle the request by finding the information, and then return a photocopy. The actual reference materials never leave the watchful eye of the research librarian.

In a client/server database, the database client prepares a SQL request—just a small text message—and sends it to the database server, which in turn reads and processes the request (Figure 1-2). Inside the server, the security is checked, the indexes are searched, the data is retrieved or manipulated, any server-side code is executed, and the final results are sent back to the client.

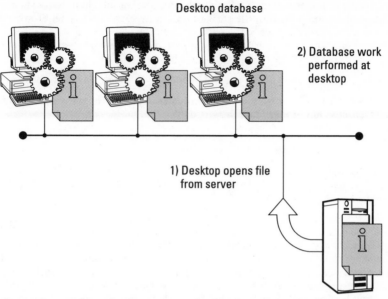

**Figure 1-1:** Desktop databases move the database file to the client, and the work is performed within the client.

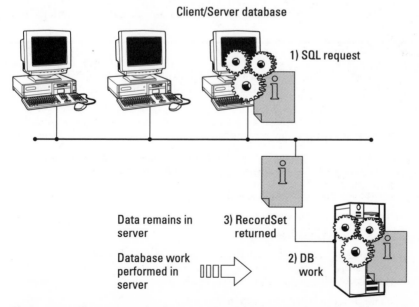

**Figure 1-2:** Client/server databases perform the work within the server process.

All the database work is performed within the database server. If the client requests a dataset, the dataset is prepared within the server and a copy of the data is sent to the client. The actual data and indexes never leave the server. When the client requests an insert, update, or delete operation, the server receives the SQL request and processes the request internally.

The client/server–database model offers several benefits over the desktop database model:

✦ Reliability is improved because the data is not spread across the network and several applications. Only one process handles the data.

✦ Data integrity constraints and business rules can be enforced at the server level, resulting in a more thorough implementation of the rules.

✦ Security is improved because the database keeps the data within a single server. Hacking into a data file that's protected within the server is much more difficult then hacking into a data file on a workstation.

✦ Performance is improved and better balanced among workstations because half of the workload, the database processing, is being handled by the server, and the workstations are only handling the user-interface half. Because the database server process has single-user rapid access to the data files, and much of the data is already cached in memory, database operations are much faster at the server than in a multi-user desktop-database environment. A database server is serving every user operating a database application; therefore it's easier to justify the cost of a beefier server.

✦ Network traffic is greatly reduced. Compared to a desktop database's rush-hour traffic, client/server traffic is like a single motorcyclist carrying a slip of paper with all 10 lanes to himself. This is no exaggeration! Upgrading a heavily used desktop database to a well-designed client/server database will reduce database-related network traffic by more than 95 percent.

✦ A byproduct of reducing network traffic is that well-designed client/server applications perform well in a distributed environment — even when using slower communications. So little traffic is required that even a 56KB dial-up line should be indistinguishable from a 100baseT Ethernet connection for a Visual Basic application connected to a SQL Server database.

## Client/Server Roles

In a client/server database configuration, each side plays a specific role. If the roles are confused, the performance and integrity of the client/server database application will suffer.

The database server is responsible for the following:

✦ Processing data modification and retrieval requests.

✦ Performing data-intensive processing.

✦ Enforcing all database rules and constraints.

✦ Enforcing data security.

The database client process should be responsible for:

✦ Presenting the data to the user in an easily recognizable, inviting, and useful format.

✦ Providing an interface to the various tools, data, and reports.

✦ Submitting requests to the server.

## *N*-Tier Design

Often, in a client/server application, more processes are involved besides the database client and the database-server process. Middle tiers are often employed to handle connection handling, connection pooling, and business logic, as shown in Figure 1-3.

Middle Tier

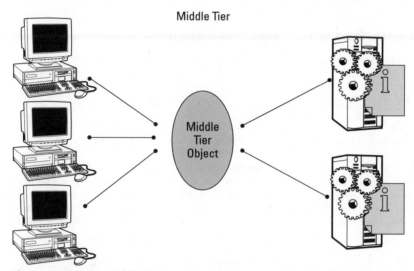

Middle
Tier
Object

**Figure 1-3:** *N*-tier middle layers can manage user connections between the client process and the database server.

A middle tier that handles connections is useful because multiple users can take advantage of a few constantly open connections to the database server. This type of connection, however, affects the way the database server can authenticate individual users. The database-security plan will have to take this into account.

In a situation in which more than one server may be available, a common connection object makes it easier to switch the users from Server A to Server B if Server A should go down. The connection object becomes a single point that could automatically detect the situation and switch to Server B.

Some developers argue that it's a good idea to place business rules in a middle-tier object because that makes modifying the business rules easier. I disagree. Business rules and database constraints should be enforced at the database server level so they can never be bypassed by any user application or process. Coding the business rules at the server level gives the code faster access to database lookups and improves performance. The only downsides to coding the business rules within the server are that the programmer must learn server-side programming, and that the database application is more difficult to port to other database products.

**Best Practice**

When you're considering the various roles within the client/server database application, the following rule is crucial: Move the processing as close to the data as possible.

# The Advantages of SQL Server

SQL Server is growing in popularity for good reason—it's a database with numerous compelling advantages. Microsoft marketing may offer a different set of reasons, but in the following sections I introduce what I think are the features that make SQL Server so great (in order of importance).

## ACID Properties and High Availability

Data integrity is the single most important feature of any significant database. To me, the single greatest benefit of SQL Server is its rock-solid implementation of the ACID properties—which means that transactions are Atomic, Consistent, Isolated, and Durable. Heavy-duty databases are judged by their implementation of the ACID properties.

This topic is so important that Chapter 11, "Transactional Integrity," is basically an explanation of ACID and how SQL Server meets the requirements with transactions and locks.

Closely related to ACID, the concept of *availability* in this context means that the data remains available even in the face of trouble. SQL Server uses a write-ahead transaction log, robust recovery methods, and high-end features such as log shipping and clustered servers to provide high availability. It will cost a pretty penny, but if it's important that the database always be available, regardless of the situation, SQL Server can do it. Even with standard server hardware, SQL Server data is highly available and easily recoverable.

Chapter 11, "Transactional Integrity," explains the write-ahead transaction log, and Chapter 29, "Advanced Availability," discusses developing databases that use the high-end availability features of SQL Server.

## SQL Server Has Become the Standard

If there's one thing I've learned in two decades of developing databases, it's that staying current in the software industry is like river rafting. Let me explain. The water in a river is constantly moving, but if you don't stay in the center of the current, you can get stuck in an eddy or hung up in the side of a rapid. Technology has to be more than cool to be desirable (remember NeXT computers?); it has to have momentum that will carry it through to tomorrow. The choice is to be in the current or to be caught in the debris.

SQL Server qualifies as a fast-moving current in five significant ways:

✦ SQL Server has the sales numbers to demonstrate it's a standard that's going to be here for a while. SQL Server sales surpassed the billion-dollar mark in mid-2001, and SQL Server is outselling the competition in both dollar volume and units of sales. SQL Server is the most popular Windows client/server database with 38 percent to 70 percent of market share (depending on whose figures are most believable), and Windows databases are growing twice as fast as UNIX databases. SQL Server holds a 68 percent market share of Web databases.

✦ Bill Gates recently identified SQL Server as one of Microsoft's most important products.

✦ SQL Server is a true relational database and is entry-level compliant with the SQL 92 ANSI standard.

✦ The database has won several significant industry awards, including the VARBusiness Annual Report Card Best Database.

✦ SQL Server is capable of supporting very large databases (VLDBs) having 1000s of users and terabytes of data. Several corporate success stories about very large databases running on SQL Server 2000 are detailed at www.microsoft.com/sql/evaluation/casestudies/2000/default.asp.

✦ A strong and healthy community of third-party tools, training, conferences, books, magazines, and user groups surrounds SQL Server. Microsoft claims there are over 85,000 trained SQL Server DBAs.

## SQL Server Security

Critical data must be secure. If there's a chance that any of the data has been compromised then all the data is suspect. When initially installed, SQL Server is wide open, which is OK because it makes learning SQL Server much easier. But when you want to secure the data, SQL Server has a very clean security model, which can be configured to meet the U.S. federal C2 security requirements.

Chapter 27, "Securing Databases," explains the SQL Server security model and provides advice about designing and implementing database security.

## SQL Server Performance and Scalability

Many developers are being introduced to SQL Server from Microsoft Access with the goal of improving performance for an existing database application. If that's you, you'll be pleased with SQL Server. It's fast and highly tunable. From my experience, a nice dual CPU server with a couple of RAID 5 disk subsystems and half a gig of RAM is incredibly fast.

While the performance of desktop databases will eventually max out, SQL Server performance will continue to scale with additional hardware. Scalability is the sustained performance as the database grows from a small database (under 10GB) to a large database (over 100GB), moving from Windows CE to multimillion-dollar 32-CPU clusters. It can take advantage of the hardware and add high-end features to handle very large databases.

Chapter 30, "Advanced Scalability," covers some of SQL Server's high-end features for scalability.

Database vendors compete with large-scale performance benchmarks. The Transaction Processing Council (TPC) is a not-for-profit organization that defines and monitors database-performance benchmarks such as the TPC-C, TPC-H, and TPC-W benchmarks.

The current benchmark results and the complete 130-page TPC-C specification is available on the TPC Web site at www.tpc.org.

The TCP-C benchmark is designed to simulate a typical online transaction processing (OLTP) database. The benchmark specifications detail the database schema and transactions for a standard order processing/inventory system, the way in which the costs must be calculated, and the auditing procedures for measuring the performance of the database. The TPC-C throughput measures how many new orders the database can accept while simultaneously handling four other types of transaction (payment, order-status, delivery, and stock-level).

The TCP competition is a cost-is-no-object free for all. A vendor submits a tuned configuration of hardware, operating system, and database, so the test isn't a database-only test and apples aren't compared with apples; nevertheless, TCP-C is the standard industry measure of database speed.

## Microsoft TerraServer

One of my favorite examples of the performance and scalability of SQL Server is Microsoft's TerraServer project (Figure 1). Microsoft purchased Russian surveillance photos of most of the populated world, augmented them with photos from the U.S. Geological Survey, loaded them all into SQL Server, and made them searchable for free on the Internet at `terraserver.microsoft.com`.

**Figure 1:** TerraServer's satellite view of the Cape Hatteras Light House (before it was moved in 2000) on the outer banks of North Carolina.

The TerraServer database includes several terrabytes of data, yet the Web site serves the images with an excellent response time. This performance demonstrates SQL Server's ability to scale from small databases to very large database and still perform well.

Database vendors are constantly trying to one-up one another in the benchmark wars. As of this writing, SQL Server 2000 holds several of the top positions including number one in performance and cost per transaction. And the margin isn't narrow. SQL Server's maximum number of transactions per minute is about three times that of fifth-place Oracle, and SQL Server costs half as much per transaction.

## Balanced and Complete

Several types of database applications exist. Transactional applications that handle the day-to-day work of a business are known as On-Line Transactional Processing Applications (OLTPs) and require the transactional-integrity aspects of the ACID properties mentioned earlier. Performance is critical for a database handling thousands of updates. SQL Server is well tuned for these applications, as are several other database products.

Another type of database application is intended to gather huge amounts of data history and perform amazing feats of analysis, data mining, and trend identification. These are On-Line Analysis Processing (OLAP) database applications. While several third-party analysis products are available, SQL Server includes tools for gathering data into SQL Server and performing the analysis.

The balanced and complete capabilities of SQL Server are one of its advantages. The numerous additional features, such as replication, DTS, Analysis Services, and jobs provide a future for a SQL Server–based project. A project started with SQL Server is not going to get locked into a limited feature set that restricts future growth.

## Out of the Box Experience

SQL Server is easy to install and use with little training. Microsoft has put considerable effort into simplifying the administrative tasks of a complex client/server database. SQL Server's copious controls enable fine-tuning and a high degree of developer control, but if that level of control isn't required, then SQL Server can be nearly self-administrating.

Other systems install with the assumption that security should be tight out of the box, and the administrator can choose to relax security as he or she comes to understand and require the various features. Believing that security shouldn't get in the way of the initial experience with the product, Microsoft takes the opposite approach. It's easy to install SQL Server so that it's fully open without any security.

Cross-Reference    Chapter 27, "Securing Databases," explains the SQL Sever security and object ownership model. Installing the SA account with a password is discussed in Chapter 3, "Installing and Configuring SQL Server."

## Developer Flexibility

SQL Server developers and DBAs enjoy a wide variety of interfaces and levels of detail (Figure 1-4). For many databases, SQL Server's automated default settings will work fine, but the control will be there when needed. As a developer or DBA, you decide the amount of control appropriate for the project. If you don't want to be bothered, SQL Server can handle most of the administration automatically.

SQL Server offers multiple interfaces. If you prefer down-and-dirty code, you can control almost every feature of SQL Server without ever seeing a graphical interface. At the other end of the spectrum, even complex tasks can be accomplished with one of the 22 major wizards. SQL Server offers you several ways to accomplish any task. Even within a SQL query there's the flexibility to state a request in the way that makes the most sense.

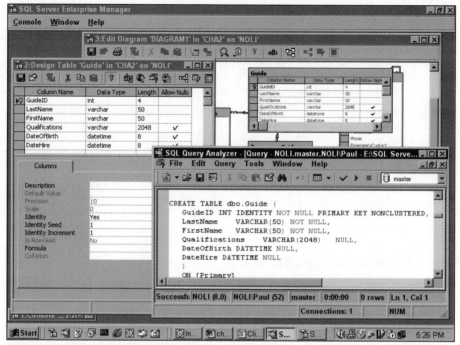

**Figure 1-4:** SQL Server offers unparalleled flexibility in terms of levels of control, tools, and connection technologies.

**Cross-Reference**
Chapter 4, "Using SQL Server's Developer Tools," covers both the GUI of Enterprise Manager and the command-line interface of Query Analyzer.

Beyond the SQL Server engine are multiple methods for importing data, analyzing data, connecting to SQL Server from code, publishing to the Web, and working with XML.

For the client-side programmer, connecting to SQL Server also presents several possibilities and multiple APIs.

Regardless of your preferences, SQL Server enables you to have it your way. At times, it may seem to the developer that SQL Server is *too* flexible. My recommendation is to begin with the graphical user interfaces and migrate to the command level as your needs and skills develop. Throughout this book I'll explain the multiple ways to accomplish a given task and make some recommendations as to the best developer interface for the task.

## Price and Performance

SQL Server is the cheapest of the high-end client/server databases based on the TCP benchmark cost per transaction (www.tcp.org). SQL Server 2000's cost per transaction is 44 percent less than the average cost per transaction of the other configurations in the TCP benchmark top-ten list.

Microsoft has priced SQL Server with a variety of editions and licensing models. You can select the edition with the features you need and spend appropriately. Licensing SQL Server for a cluster with eight computers with 16 CPUs each will cost about 2.5 million dollars, while the Desktop Engine is essentially free.

# Selecting the Right SQL Server 2000 Edition

SQL Server 2000 is available in several editions, which differ in terms of features, hardware, and cost. This section details the various editions and their respective features. Table 1-1 highlights the differences among the various editions.

## Enterprise (Developer) Edition

This is the high-end edition. It includes all the bells and whistles for very large corporate databases, including the advanced features Analysis Services, clustering and federated databases, and indexed views. In addition, Enterprise Edition supports the operating-system maximum for CPUs and memory, as detailed in Table 1-2. It installs only on server versions of Windows and not Windows 9x or Professional versions. The Enterprise Evaluation Edition is a full-featured copy of Enterprise Edition with a 120-day limit.

Here's a listing of the Enterprise Edition advanced features:

✦ *Clustering and system area network*: A grouping of several servers into a single virtual server, sharing a common high-performance disk subsystem. The client connects to the virtual server, and the cluster provides near instant failover recover.

✦ *Log shipping:* The transaction log is regularly backed up and the file sent to a warm backup server. If the primary server goes down, the warm backup server can be easily recovered and the clients can switch to the warm failover server lossing a minimum amount of work.

**For more details on SQL Server clusteriing and log shipping refer to Chapter 29, "Advanced Availability."**

✦ *Enhanced parallelism:* Complex queries may be processed using on multiple CPUs.

✦ *Indexed views:* An indexed view is actually a clustered index based on a view that denormalizes the data. Indexed views improve the performance of queries that read from very large tables.

✦ *Federated databases:* Databases that spread a single table's data over multiple servers using constraints and accessing the data through a union query speed performance by selecting smaller sets of data and improving the chance that the selected data pages will be in RAM.

**Indexed views and federated databases are explained in Chapter 30, "Advanced Scalability."**

The Developer Edition is the same as the Enterprise Edition, with two exceptions. First, the Developer Edition is licensed only for development and testing, so it can't legally be used in a production environment. Second, the Developer Edition runs on Windows NT Workstation, Windows 2000 Professional, and Windows XP Professional. To promote development and experimentation, Microsoft also grants Developer Edition licensees the right to download the CE Edition. The Developer Edition is included with MSDN Universal or may be purchased separately. When purchased, it is the lowest-cost edition of SQL Server.

## Table 1-1: SQL Server 2000 Editions Chart

| Feature | Enterprise Edition | Standard Edition | Personal Edition | MSDE Edition | CE Edition |
|---|---|---|---|---|---|
| Target Audience/ Intended Application | Very large enterprise databases | Mid-sized, department, workgroup databases | Mobile or remote user | Embedded within application | CE devices |
| **Engine Features** | | | | | |
| Multiple Instances | Yes | Yes | Yes | Yes | No |
| Clustering | Yes | No | No | No | No |
| Log Shipping | Yes | No | No | No | No |
| Enhanced Parallelism | Yes | No | No | No | No |
| Indexed Views | Yes | No | No | No | No |
| Federated Databases | Yes | No | No | No | No |
| **Data Analysis and DTS Features** | | | | | |
| Analysis Services | Yes | Yes | Yes | No | No |
| Data Mining | Yes | Yes | Yes | No | No |
| Advanced Analysis Services | Yes | No | No | No | No |
| DTS Packages | Yes | Yes | Yes | Deployment only | No |
| English Query | Yes | Yes | Yes | No | No |
| **Replication Features** | | | | | |
| Snapshot Replication | Yes | Yes | Yes | Yes | No |
| Transactional Replication | Yes | Yes | Subscriber only | Subscriber only | No |
| Merge Replication | Yes | Yes | Yes | Yes | Yes, anonymous subscriber only |
| Immediate Updating Subscribers | Yes | Yes | Yes | Yes | No |
| Queued Subscribers | Yes | Yes | Yes | Yes | No |

| Feature | Enterprise Edition | Standard Edition | Personal Edition | MSDE Edition | CE Edition |
|---|---|---|---|---|---|
| **Scaling Limitations** | | | | | |
| Database Size Limit | 1,048,516TB | 1,048,516TB | 1,048,516TB | 2GB | 2GB |
| CPUs Supported (may also be limited by the Windows version) | 32 | 4 | 2 | 2 | 1 |
| Memory Supported (also limited by the Windows version) | 64GB | 2GB | 2GB | 2GB | 2GB |

## Table 1-2: Physical Capabilities of the Operating System

| Windows Version | Clustering | CPUs Supported | Memory Supported |
|---|---|---|---|
| Windows 2000 DataCenter | Yes | 32 | 64GB |
| Windows 2000 Advanced Server | No | 8 | 8GB |
| Windows 2000 Server | No | 4 | 4GB |
| Windows 2000 / XP Professional | No | 2 | 2GB |
| Windows 9x | No | 1 | 2GB |
| Windows CE | No | 1 | 2GB |

# Standard Edition

The majority of database projects will be well served by the Standard Edition. This workhorse edition supports up to four CPUs and provides all the features required for most projects. Many IT departments consider purchasing Enterprise Edition, thinking they need the advanced features, but the Standard Edition will likely meet their needs and save them a considerable amount of money.

# Personal Edition

The Personal Edition may be purchased as a stand-alone product, and is also included with the Enterprise Edition and Standard Edition. The purpose of the Personal Edition is to enable you to extend the reach of SQL Server products by installing a mobile copy of SQL Server on desktops or notebooks that are not normally connected to the main server. Therefore, the Personal Edition lacks some high-end features. It is supported on Windows 98, and will run on Windows 95, but is not supported by Microsoft on this platform.

**Note**    Because full-text search (the ability to index words within character columns and then search the index) is implemented by Windows 2000, full-text search will not be available in the Personal Edition if it is running on Windows 98.

## MSDE/Desktop Engine

The Desktop Engine is a royalty-free, redistributable edition of SQL Server that's intended to serve as an embedded database within an application. It's included with MSDN Universal, Office Developer Edition 10, and a few other Microsoft developer products. It's basically the database engine from Personal Edition. MSDE does have some limitations: It may not publish transactional replications (a type of replication), does not include full-text search, and is limited to 2GB in size and five user logons.

MSDE does not include licenses for the client tools such as Enterprise Manager and Query Analyzer. MSDE is not simply a plug-in replacement for the Access Jet database engine. It's SQL Server and it requires administration. If an application is using MSDE as the embedded database, that application will need to provide administrative controls such as adding users, performing backups and restores, handling the transaction log, and so on. Throughout this book, the administrative tasks will be presented both in the GUI method and with code.

## SQL Server CE Edition

The CE edition of SQL Server is technically a different database engine that is fully compatible with SQL Server. Its small footprint of only 1MB of RAM means that it can actually serve well on a Pocket Windows handheld device. Other than the ability to subscribe to a merged replication, this edition lacks all other advanced features.

## Licensing SQL Server 2000

Microsoft offers two licensing structures for SQL Server 2000. Client Access Licenses (CALs) may be purchased on a per-seat basis. Per-seat licensing is intended for internal applications with a known, small number of users. Per-seat licensing may not be used for servers with users behind a firewall.

Alternately, SQL Server may be licensed on a per-CPU basis. The advantage of per-CPU licensing, besides ease of administration, is the flexibility of deploying a project or Web site when the number of future clients is completely unknown.

For configurations including both active servers and passive backup servers, a license is not required for the passive server.

## MSDN Universal

Microsoft Developer Network (MSDN) includes every server and development tool offered by Microsoft including the many editions of SQL Server, and will keep you in the loop with service packs and new releases. In total, over $48,000 worth of software is included for about $2500, depending on special pricing and volume discounts. The MSDN subscription provides quarterly (sometime monthly) updates on CD-ROM or DVD and many downloads in the private area of www.microsoft.com for MSDN subscribers.

If your IT shop develops applications internally, I highly suggest you investigate MSDN.

# Server Components

SQL Server is more than just a database engine. A complete set of tools, utilities, interfaces, and extensions round out its data-handling and analyzing features (Figure 1-5). Because SQL Server has so many components, it's worth the time to briefly see the role each plays and to get a sense of the breadth of features available.

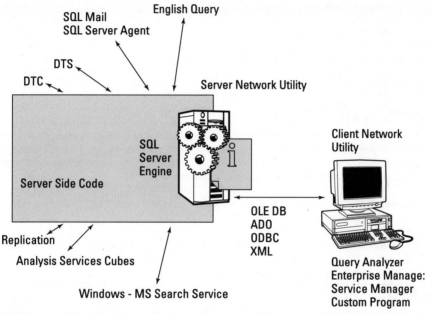

**Figure 1-5:** SQL Server is a collection of server and client components.

SQL Server's components are either server processes or client processes. The following four components are server processes for SQL Server.

## SQL Server Engine

The SQL Server engine is the core of SQL Server. It is the process that handles all the relational database work. SQL is a descriptive language, meaning that it describes to the engine only the query to be processed. SQL Server's query optimizer determines how to process the query based on the costs of different types of query-execution operations. The estimated and actual query-execution plans may be viewed graphically with the Query Analyzer.

SQL Server 2000 supports installation of multiple instances of the engine on a single server machine. Each instance is the same as a complete separate installation of SQL Server.

## SQL Server Agent

The agent is an optional process which, when running, executes the SQL jobs and handles other automated tasks. It can be configured to automatically run when the system boots, or may be started from the Service Manager or Enterprise Manager.

**Cross-Reference** Chapter 25, "Automating Database Maintenance with SQL Server Agent," details SQL agents, jobs, and mail, as well as the SQL Server Agent.

## Distributed Transaction Coordinator (DTC)

The Distributed Transaction Coordinator is a process that handles dual-phase commits for transactions that span multiple SQL Servers. DTC can be started from the Service Manager or from within Windows' Computer Administration/Component Services. If the application regularly uses distributed transactions, then I recommend you start DTC when the operating system starts.

**Cross-Reference** Chapter 18, "Working with Distributed Queries," explains dual-phase commitments and distributed transactions.

## Microsoft Search Service

The Microsoft Search Service is actually a component of the operating system that maintains text-search capabilities for files. SQL Server leverages the Search Service when performing full-text searches. The service may be started or stopped with the Service Manager or from within Windows' Computer Administration/Component Services.

**Cross-Reference** Chapter 8, "Searching Full-Text Indexes," explains how to create full-text catalogs and how to query them using the `contains` command.

The next three components are not considered core server processes for SQL Server. Nonetheless, they function within the server, so I've included them in this list.

## SQL Mail

The SQL Mail component enables SQL Server to send mail to an external mailbox through a mail profile. Mail may be generated from multiple sources within SQL Server, including T-SQL code, jobs, alerts, DTS packages, and maintenance plans.

**Cross-Reference** Chapter 25, "Automating Database Maintenance with SQL Server Agent," explains how to set up a mail profile for SQL Server and how to send mail.

## English Query

English Query is a very different sort of application. Using English Query, a developer can specify English words that a specific user population might use when discussing the data and the relationships among the data. Once these words are fully developed and tested, the developer can create a .dll that can translate English questions using these words into SQL queries. An application or Web page can then send these English questions through the DLL, and use the returned SQL query to fetch the answer from SQL Server. Popular questions are often stored in a list to help users get started. But let me warn you, English Query takes a lot of work to develop and implement and the results are sometimes questionable. English Query is an optional component and is installed separately from SQL Server.

# Data Transformation Services

Data Transformation Services (DTS) moves data among nearly any types of data sources. As shown in Figure 1-6, DTS uses a graphical tool to define how data can be moved from one connection to another connection. DTS packages have the flexibility to either copy data column for column or perform complex transformations, lookups, and exception handling during the data move. DTS is extremely useful during data conversions, collecting data from many dissimilar data sources, or gathering for data warehousing data that can be analyzed using Analysis Services.

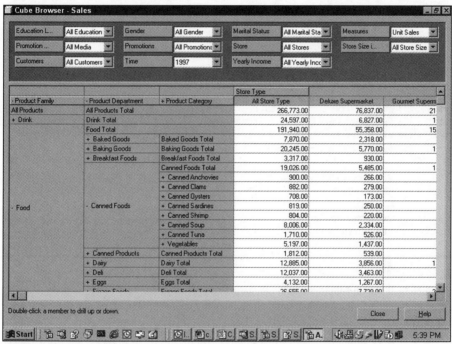

**Figure 1-6:** DTS graphically illustrates the data transformations within a planned data migration or conversion.

Data Transformation Services is located within Enterprise Manager. You can use SQL Agent to schedule a DTS package to run, and you can optionally save the package as a Visual Basic script.

DTS is very cool. If you have experience with other databases, but are new to SQL Server 2000, this is one of the tools that will most impress you. If any other company were marketing DTS it would be the flagship product, but instead we find it bundled inside SQL Server without much fanfare and at no extra charge. Be sure to find the time to explore DTS.

**Cross-Reference**    Chapter 19, "Migrating Data with DTS," describes how to create and execute a DTS package.

## Analysis Services

Analysis Services is the component within SQL Server that provides business intelligence or online analysis processing (OLAP). Essentially, Analysis Services enables the developer to define cubes that are similar to Excel pivot tables or Access crosstab queries, but with multiple dimensions. The cubes contain pre-calculated summary, or aggregate, data from very large databases. This enables the user to easily and quickly browse the cube's summarized totals and subtotals without having to query terabytes worth of data (Figure 1-7).

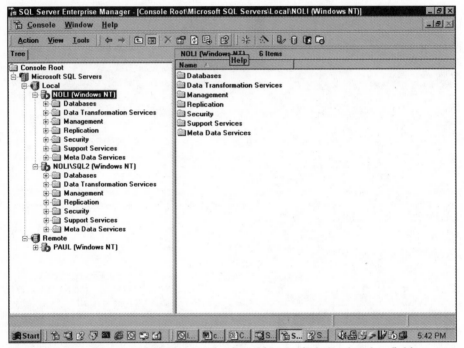

**Figure 1-7:** Browsing a multidimensional cube within Analysis Services is a fluid way to compare various aspects of the data.

Analysis Services is loaded separately from SQL Server and is considered a high-end data-warehousing feature.

**Cross-Reference**    Chapter 31, "Analysis Services," shows you how to create cubes and browse the work table's data based on the cube's dimensions.

# Client Components

The following components are client processes for SQL Server used to control, or communicate with, SQL Server.

## Server Network Utility

Since SQL Server is a client/server process, it's important that it be able to listen to the network and communicate with clients. SQL Server's Server Network Utility configures the way in which SQL Server communicates with clients. Technically this is a client component used to control the server.

## Client Network Utility

SQL Server's Client Network Utility is the client-side partner to the Server Network Utility. It establishes the protocols used to communicate from the client to the server.

## SQL Server Service Manager

When SQL Server is installed, a SQL Server icon appears in the system tray. This icon is sometimes confused as the icon for the SQL Server engine, but it actually represents the Service Manager, a client utility used to start and stop the major services of SQL Server and to indicate the current status.

Service Manager can control multiple servers and instances, and all the processes required to run SQL Server. By default it displays the first instance on the local server and polls the instance every 10 seconds, but it is configurable.

Running the Service Manager is completely optional. Many DBAs avoid loading Service Manager because of its sizable memory footprint (about 3MB), and instead choose to launch it from the Start menu when needed.

## Enterprise Manager

Enterprise Manager is often confused with the SQL Server engine, but Enterprise Manager is only a client application. Although Enterprise Manager often has trouble knowing when to automatically refresh, and must frequently be manually refreshed, nearly all of SQL Server may be easily controlled using the GUI controls and wizards (Figure 1-8). Tables and queries are easily created and browsed with the Query Designer. Enterprise Manager's weakness is in the area of code development, because of the poorly designed modal interface. On the other hand, Enterprise Manager is the only SQL Server interface that includes database diagrams. The bottom line is that Enterprise Manager is more useful for administrative tasks than for database development.

Cross-Reference: Chapter 4, "Using SQL Server's Developer Tools," discusses using the Service Manager, Enterprise Manager, and Query Analyzer.

## Query Analyzer

Although it might be mistaken for Notepad, there's actually a lot of intelligence within Query Analyzer. This lightweight tool is the perfect means of executing raw batches of T-SQL code. Editing, executing, and saving scripts of SQL code is what Query Analyzer does best. Its object browser enables the developer to easily view the existing database objects and to create or alter objects.

Where Query Analyzer really shines is in viewing query-optimization plans and execution statistics, as shown in Figure 1-9.

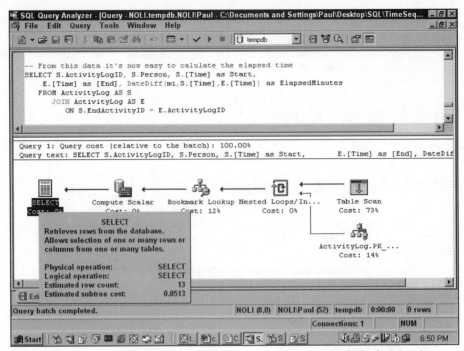

**Figure 1-8:** Enterprise Manager provides an easy graphical method of administering multiple SQL Servers from any workstation.

## Command-Line Utilities: Isql, osql, Bulk Copy

These command-line interfaces enable the developer to execute SQL code or perform bulk-copy operations from the DOS prompt or a command-line scheduler. DTS and SQL Server Agent have rendered these tools somewhat obsolete, but in the spirit of extreme flexibility, Microsoft still includes them.

## SQL Books On-Line

The SQL Server team did an excellent job with Books On-Line (BOL). The articles tend to be complete and include several examples. The indexing method provides a short list of applicable articles.

BOL is well integrated with the primary interfaces. Selecting a keyword within Query Analyzer and pressing Shift+F1 will launch BOL to the selected keyword The Enterprise Manager help buttons will also launch the correct BOL topic.

I have only two complaints about Books On-Line. First, while the articles are detailed, they don't often provide a sense of the big picture. If a developer understands SQL Server, BOL is a great place to find details quickly. But developers new to SQL Server sometimes complain that it's a steep learning curve. Using BOL can be like studying geography, one square foot at a time.

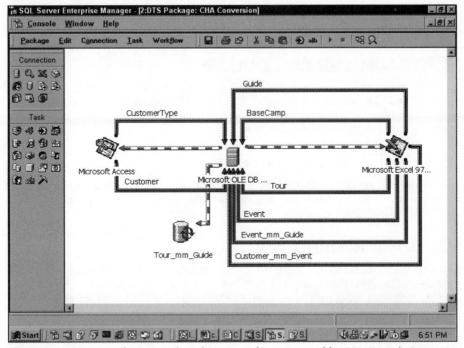

**Figure 1-9:** Query Analyzer can view the query plan generated by SQL Server's Query Optimizer.

My second comment is that the articles in BOL are not always indexed by the article title. For example, there's a great article entitled "Lock Compatibility," but it can't be found by searching the index for the title. Instead, search for "Update Lock" and then select "Lock Compatibility." Because of this problem, the Favorites tab is especially useful. This feature is a welcome improvement that stores the locations of articles for future reference.

Other than those two minor comments, SQL Books On-Line is far superior to any other developer-tool help I've used.

## SQL Profiler

SQL Profiler quietly watches SQL Server's traffic and events, recording the selected information to the screen, table, or file. Profiler is great for debugging an application or tuning the database. The Index Tuning Wizard can use the collected data to optimize the database.

## Performance Monitor

While Profiler records large sets of details concerning SQL traffic and SQL Server events, Performance Monitor is a visual window into the current status of the selected performance counters. Performance Monitor is found within Windows 2000's administrative tools. When SQL Server is installed it adds the SQL Server counters within Performance Monitor. And SQL Server has a ton of useful performance counters. It's enough to make a network administrator jealous.

**Cross-Reference**    Chapter 28, "Advanced Performance," covers SQL Profiler and Performance Monitor.

## MSDTC Administrative Console

Distributed transactions — those that update more than one server's data — are handled by the Distributed Transaction Coordinator (DTC). The best way to monitor distributed transactions is with the DTC administrative console. In Windows 2000, the console is found under Administrative Tools/Component Services.

## IIS Virtual Directory Manager

SQL Server 2000 supports XML queries directly from a browser. To make this happen, IIS needs to think of SQL Server as one of its virtual directories. The "Configure SQL XML support for IIS" Wizard initially sets up that virtual directory.

## SQL Server Resource Kit

Although the Resource Kit is a separate product from SQL Server, it includes several useful utilities, sample procedures, and white papers for SQL Server, Analysis Services, and DTS. It may be purchased separately, although it's included with MSDN Universal, and much of it can be downloaded from msdn.microsoft.com.

# Transact SQL

SQL Server is based on the SQL standard with some Microsoft-specific extensions. SQL was invented by E. F. Codd while he was working at the IBM research labs in San Jose in 1971. SQL Server 2000 is entry-level (Level 1) compliant with the ANSI SQL 92 standard. The complete specifications for the ANSI SQL standard are found in five documents that can be purchased from www.techstreet.com/ncits.html.

While the ANSI SQL definition is excellent for the common data-selection and data definition commands, it does not include commands with which to control SQL Server properties, or provide the level of logical control within batches required to develop a SQL Server–specific application. Therefore, the Microsoft SQL Server team has extended the ANSI definition with several enhancements and new commands, and has also left out a few commands because SQL Server implemented them differently. The final result is Transact-SQL or T-SQL — the dialect of SQL understood by SQL Server 2000.

Missing from T-SQL are very few ANSI SQL commands (the union join variants, minus and intersect, and certain foreign key cascade options, nullify and default) primarily because Microsoft implemented the functionality in other ways. T-SQL, by default, also handles nulls, quotes, and padding differently from the ANSI standard, although that behavior can be controlled. From my personal development experience, none of these differences affect the process of developing a database application using SQL Server. T-SQL adds significantly more to ANSI SQL than it lacks.

Understanding SQL Server requires understanding T-SQL. The SQL Server engine understands only one language — Transact-SQL. Every command sent to SQL Server 2000 must be a valid T-SQL command. Batches of stored T-SQL commands may be executed within the server as stored procedures. Other tools, like Enterprise Manager, which provide graphical user interfaces with which to control SQL Server, are at some level converting those mouse clicks to T-SQL for processing by the engine.

T-SQL commands are divided into the following three categories:

✦ *Data Manipulation Language (DML)*: Includes the common SQL `select`, `insert`, `update`, and `delete` commands. DML is sometimes mistakenly said to stand for *Data Modification Language*; this is misleading, because the `select` statement does not modify data. It does, however, manipulate the data returned.

✦ *Data Definition Language (DDL)*: Those commands that create and manage data tables, constraints, and other database objects.

✦ *Data Control Language (DCL)*: Security commands such as `grant`, `revoke`, and `deny`.

# Client Applications

A client/server database won't be used without client processes delivering the data to users. Several technologies (such as DB-Lib, ADO, ODBC) are available with which client applications can connect to SQL Server. Access, Excel, and Visio all leverage these technologies to display and edit SQL Server data. This section is a brief overview of some of the connection technologies available.

## DB-Lib

The original API to SQL Server was DB-Library. It was the native connection method for SQL Server 6.5 (and older), and intended for C programs. Although DB-Lib was fast, it's no longer supported. It exists only for the sake of backward capability.

## ODBC/DSN

Open Database Connectivity (ODBC) is the Microsoft standard for connecting to relational databases. Its strength is the number of OBDC drivers available; however, being "all things to all data formats" means that ODBC requires some internal compatibility layers and internal data types. The result is that ODBC works smoothly, but fails to set performance records.

ODBC is actually a C-language interface, but objects such as DAO (Data Access Objects) are available for most languages and for many years it was the most popular connectivity technology. Microsoft Jet Engine, built into Microsoft Access since version 1.0, uses ODBC to connect to nearly any data format.

ODBC references data source names (DSNs) to manage connection strings and settings. DSNs are organized within Windows 2000's Administrative Tools, in the Data Sources tool. Deploying ODBC connections to several workstations requires setting up the DSN on each individual computer. However, file DSNs make this process easier.

## OLE-DB/ADO

OLE-DB is the replacement for ODBC and features several improvements. But first, ignore the OLE in OLE-DB. OLE originally stood for Object Linking and Embedding, and back in the Windows 2 days it enabled a Microsoft Word document to point to live data in an Excel spreadsheet. Over the years, the term OLE came to mean, informally, "new cool technology." OLE-DB is superior to ODBC because it's a lighter-weight object intended to be wrapped within a data-source object that extends OLE-DB to meet the data source's capabilities.

This means that OLE-DB loses some of the unnecessary overhead of ODBC and at the same time gains the flexibility to handle data types other than relational data. Hence the name OLE—new cool technology.

As more data sources become available for OLE-DB, it will be able to work with as many databases as ODBC. (There's even an OLE-DB data source to ODBC, which lets OLE-DB go through ODBC to get to nearly any database.)

OLE-DB is important to SQL Server 2000 client-side developers because it's the native means of connecting to SQL Server. This means that it's the fastest possible connection technology.

ActiveX Data Objects, or ADO, is the object wrapper that exposes OLE-DB to developer languages such as Visual Basic (Figure 1-10). With .NET, ADO is being extended and will have an even faster direct connection to SQL Server.

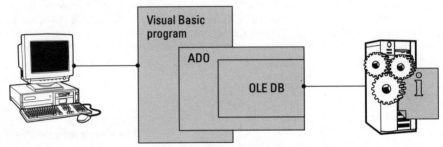

**Figure 1-10:** Connecting to SQL Server through ADO.

 **Cross-Reference**   Chapter 21, "ADO and ADO.Net," demonstrates how to construct and use an ADO connection.

## Microsoft Access

Microsoft Access is listed here because, since Access 2000, it has had the ability to work with two types of files: Access databases (.mdb) with the Jet Engine, and Access Projects (.adp). Access Projects don't include the traditional Access Jet Engine, but instead connect directly to SQL Server (Figure 1-11).

Many SQL Server developers have found that Access Projects make a fast and easy SQL Server client. While Access Projects may not be the final client interface for large databases, they make an excellent transition and data-management tool. For smaller databases, merging the reliability of SQL Server with the development ease of Access Forms is a winning combination.

Access includes an Upsizing Wizard that can automatically move tables and data to SQL Server to make it easier to convert from existing Access databases to SQL Server.

## Excel

Surprisingly, Excel integrates well with SQL Server. SQL Server includes a wizard to export data to Excel for analysis, and can directly connect to Excel spreadsheets using distributed queries. In return, Excel can view and edit data inside SQL Server.

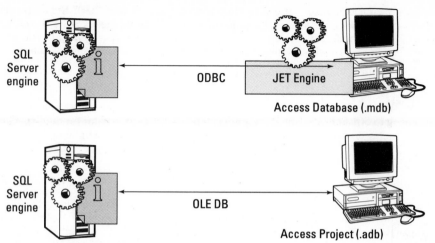

**Figure 1-11:** An Access Project leaves Jet behind and connects directly to SQL Server objects using OLE-DB.

As database developers, we tend to shun flat-file modes of working with data as uncivilized. However, denormalizing some data and preparing them for a manager to manipulate using his or her favorite data tool will likely reduce the report workload and free developer time for more noble pursuits, such as tuning indexes or testing the recovery plan.

## Visio

Enterprise Manager's database-diagramming tool is augmented by Visio's ability to import database schemas from SQL Server and create databases within SQL Server based on Visio drawings.

A large diagram of the database schema from a drafting plotter helps the whole team work with the database. I always try to get one posted on the wall.

## Data Analyzer

The Microsoft Data Analyzer, a new product in Microsoft Office, is designed for business intelligence (BI) analysis — much like the On-Line Analysis Processing (OLAP) cubes within SQL Server's Analysis Services, but with an emphasis on graphing.

# Certifications and Training

As a SQL Server DBA or developer, you may wish to pursue certification for two reasons. First, SQL Server 2000 has a board set of features. Typically, IT professionals are experts in the features they've had to employ to solve problems, but are less familiar with other portions of the software. Seeking certification will help shore up these deficiencies and round out your skills. A thorough knowledge of the capabilities of SQL Server will help you find the most appropriate solution to future problems.

The second compelling reason for certification is career advancement. SQL Server is selling very well, and the user interface, which hides many of the details, makes SQL Server 2000 seem simple to operate. Certification, along with your experience, can help differentiate you from Joe's brother-in-law who installed SQL Server last week. The following sections cover the available certification options.

## Microsoft MCP

The Microsoft Certified Professional program is intended to train you for product-specific certification. Passing any Microsoft exam qualifies you for MCP status. Completing a series of exams qualifies an MCP for a premium certification such as MCSE (System Engineer), MCSD (Solution Developer), or MCDBA (Database Administrator).

The following two MCP exams are aimed specifically at SQL server DBAs and developers:

✦ *Exam 70-228—SQL Server 2000 Administration* covers DBA skills including installation, configuration, creating databases, monitoring and troubleshooting, DTS, linked servers, replication, IIS and XML, security, and SQL Server Agent.

✦ *Exam 70-229—SQL Server 2000 Database Design and Implementation* covers logical and physical database design, retrieving and modifying data, T-SQL programming, database security, and tuning and optimization.

Both tests have a reputation for being difficult and taking the full allotment of time to complete (an hour and 45 minutes for 45 questions). The tests are skewed toward the details of new features and include several questions that are less than specific. Several times I've found myself thinking that a question provided a poor scenario, and then asked me to choose among four bad practices. Several questions present a complex story with four lengthy options and then ask which option best meets the story's requirements. Just reading the question carefully consumes much of the time allowed per question.

Microsoft also offers Microsoft Official Curriculum (MOC) courses taught by third-party education centers. I have personally used the Microsoft Press Readiness Review books, the Exam Cram books, and some online practice tests to prepare for Microsoft exams.

MCP exams may qualify for college credit with Regents University. For complete and current information on MCP exams go to `www.microsoft.com/MCP`.

## MCDBA

The Microsoft Certified DBA certification is a premier certification, with only 25,088 people meeting the qualification at the time of this writing. That's about 1.8 percent of those holding some type of Microsoft certification, but about a third of trained SQL Server DBAs. Qualifying for MCDBA within the SQL Server 2000 track requires passing four exams:

✦ One of the following Server Exams:

• Exam 70-215—Installing, Configuring, and Administering Microsoft Windows 2000 Server

or

• Exam 70-275—Installing, Configuring and Administering Microsoft Windows.NET Server

✦ Both SQL Server 2000 Exams:

- Exam 70-228 — SQL Server 2000 Administration
- Exam 70-228 — SQL Server 2000 Database Design and Implementation

✦ One elective exam from the following list:

- 70-015 — Designing and Implementing Distributed Applications with Microsoft Visual C++ 6.0
- 70-019 — Designing and Implementing Data Warehouses with Microsoft SQL Server 7.0
- 70-155 — Designing and Implementing Distributed Applications with Microsoft Visual FoxPro 6.0
- 70-175 — Designing and Implementing Distributed Applications with Microsoft Visual Basic 6.0
- 70-216 — Implementing and Administering a Microsoft Windows 2000 Network Infrastructure
- 70-276 — Implementing and Administering a Microsoft Windows .Net Server Network Infrastructure

As .Net and WindowsXP exams become available these requirements may change. I also expect to see SQL Server 2000 data-warehousing and DTS exams in the future.

MCDBA certification offers several excellent benefits, including discounts on MSDN Universal, the Tech-Ed conference, and discounted membership in the Professional Organization for SQL Server (PASS).

# Learning Tree SQL Server 2000 Certifications

As an alternative to the Microsoft test-based certifications, Learning Tree offers several classroom-based courses which lead to two SQL Server 2000 certifications, one for DBAs and one for developers. Each certification requires four hands-on classes and passing a straightforward test at the end of the week.

Learning Tree courses qualify as college credits with the American Council on Education (ACE). For more information on Learning Tree courses or the Learning Tree certification programs referred to here, go to www.learningtree.com.

# Brainbench.com

A third certification option is Brainbench.com, an on-line independent certification company with over 350 certifications. Brainbench tests are open book — referencing any resource, except another person, is encouraged. The results of the Brainbench tests are more detailed than Microsoft's and the transcript may be posted on-line within Brainbench.com.

If certification is important to you, my recommendation is to combine multiple certifications with hands-on experience.

## Conferences

If you want to stay on top of SQL Server developments and hear from the experts, two conferences demand your consideration:

✦ *Microsoft Tech-Ed* is an annual event held in over a dozen locations throughout the world. The U.S. Tech-Ed is typically held during the spring in a large southern city. It's the premier technical-education event for Microsoft. The products are explained by Microsoft developers and program managers. For complete information, visit `msdn.microsoft.com/events/teched`.

✦ *SQL PASS* is the annual conference of the Professional Association for SQL Server. The U.S. conference is held in the fall and the European conference is held in the spring. SQL PASS tends to attract independent experts as well as the Microsoft SQL Server development team. While Microsoft Tech-Ed covers all Microsoft IT technologies, SQL PASS focuses solely on developing with, administrating, and extending SQL Server. For more information about PASS and the PASS conference, visit `www.sqlpass.org`.

# SQL Server in a Brave New .Net World

SQL Server 2000 is marketed by Microsoft as a .Net Server. However, SQL Server 2000 was released before the .Net initiative was announced and almost a year and a half before the .Net languages shipped. Is the combination of SQL Server 2000 and .Net more than just Microsoft marketing hype? I think so, and here's why.:

## .Net and Application Development

.Net is a complete redesign of application development, built directly on top of Win32, and provides all languages with equal access to Win32 features.

Use of a Common Language Runtime (CLR) means that any .Net language can compile to the same MSIL intermediate language. COM+ used to be tacked onto objects to allow them to share data. The CLR now lets any object easily share with any other object without the overhead of COM+. Functions built in C.NET may mix with applications built with VB.NET. The language no longer divides the code.

.Net's Base Class Library provides a consistent library for all development, regardless of language or deployment — Windows or Web.

It has always been difficult to develop fully interactive applications because HTML is stateless. To the server every page redraw is handled as a new page request. The entire page must be completely rebuilt at the server based on the URL request.

ASP.Net takes much of the work out of developing ASP Web applications. The new Web Forms include methods that actually respond to events on the page. And because ASP.Net uses the same base-class library, the functionality is huge and Web Forms include many great controls. But wait, there's more. The ASP handler examines the client browser and automatically generates the correct code for that browser at runtime. Finally, thin-client development is as straightforward and as powerful as full GUI development.

Combine all these features with a new set of tools and developer interfaces, and .Net is the biggest initiative from Microsoft since Windows NT.

## .Net and XML

HTML is a presentation mark-up language. HTML data is polluted with presentation information and lacks a data protocol. At the heart of .Net is XML and the ability to mark up not only how data should appear, but also what the data mean. In addition to its inherent capabilities, several companion technologies enhance XML:

✦ XSLT—Business logic within XML

✦ XPath—XML query language

✦ XQuery—New way to query data

✦ SOAP—Simple Object Access Protocol

The purpose of XML is to allow any application on any platform to share data with any other application on any other platform. The idea is that your PC will share information with your handheld, alarm clock, cell phone, bank, travel agent, airline, and work scheduler.

**Cross-Reference**　Chapter 22, "XML and Web Publishing," includes a sample XML document from the Cape Hatteras Adventures database.

Some believe that XML is superior to the SQL language because XML handles a greater variety of data. The two are compared in Table 1-3.

### Table 1-3: SQL Data Versus XML Data

| Data feature | SQL Resultset | XML Dataset |
| --- | --- | --- |
| Level of data handled | Single table (rows and columns) | Multiple hierarchical data |
| Embedded data schema | No | Yes |
| Embedded business rules | No | Yes |
| Embedded data constraints | No | Yes |
| Format using stylesheets into HTML, WML, or other XML | No | Yes |

## Microsoft BizTalk and EDI

Electronic Data Interchange (EDI) has been the standard for companies exchanging data for over a decade. Nearly every industry has numerous complex data-file formats. These formats, developed by industry committees, include every possible data field including the kitchen sink, and are often tied to older, non-relational database structures (such as AS-400 flat-file). To make sense of this mess, several companies handle the EDI translation of data between business partners. This service is not cheap.

Microsoft is proposing to undo the EDI monopolies with BizTalk, a graphical data-mapping server that enables companies to easily exchange XML data. BizTalk can be envisioned as DTS for XML with multiple mapping capabilities. Using BizTalk, multiple companies will be able to share XML mappings and then swap data without paying the EDI translators.

## How SQL Server Fits into .Net

All these development tools need fast access to data. .Net is optimized to use SQL Server 2000 as its data store. SQL Server 2000 includes the ability to receive and send data in XML format. Because .NET is designed around SQL Server and XML, SQL Server is, by definition, a core .NET server.

## The Future

SQL Server 2000 is a cool product, but Microsoft isn't sitting still. The next version of SQL Server, code named Yukon, has been in development for a couple of years and is expected to ship in late 2003.

The future of databases is XML, and Yukon is being built to handle XML as well as it handles SQL. It would also seem logical for Microsoft to incorporate other .NET technologies, such as the Common Language Runtime, making it possible to program with languages other than T-SQL, work with objects, and share data with other .NET objects. In short, I expect Yukon to be a whole new world for SQL Server developers.

# Summary

SQL Server is indeed a large and complex product. It's important to have a solid understanding of the big picture concerning SQL Server before diving into its details. From here, the next chapter continues to build a foundation for SQL Server development as it drills into the theory of relational database design.

✦    ✦    ✦

# Modeling the Logical Database Schema

**W**hen I was in the U.S. Navy Submarine Service there was an on-going friendly debate between the sailors about who was most important. The nuclear power–plant engineers (glow-in-the-darks) seemed to think that the purpose of the boat was to transport their nuclear reactor. Although I was a Data System Tech, I thought the torpedo mates were the most important. Without them, the rest of us were just on an underwater cruise.

It's the same with information technology.

During the late 1980s, in keeping with the belief that the medium is the message, Sun Microsystems preached that the network is the computer. But, as the explosion of Web pages has demonstrated, it's content that brings people back to a site. The data is the computer.

Web-page designers may have the limelight, and the newest processors and hardware may get the headlines, but without the database the rest of the computer network only shares files and sends e-mail. If you have selected database development as your career, I think you've made a wise choice.

This concise chapter introduces the basic design skills required to design a database application. Volumes have been written on these topics; the goal here is to provide a concise introduction and the background you need in order to develop with SQL Server. Without dealing specifically with SQL Server, this chapter explains the skills and methods used to develop the logical design, which is then implemented with SQL Server.

**On the CD-ROM** Some of the examples in this chapter refer to the sample database on the CD. For more information on these databases, see Appendix B, "Sample Databases."

# Database Basics

The purpose of a database is to store the day-to-day operational information required by an organization. Any means of collecting and organizing data is a database. Prior to the Information Age, information was primarily stored on cards, in file folders, or in ledger books. Before the adding machine, offices employed dozens of workers who spent all day adding columns of numbers and double-checking the math of others. The title of those who had that exciting career was *computer*.

As the number crunching began to be handled by digital machines, human labor, rather than being eliminated, shifted to other tasks. Analysts, programmers, managers, and IT staff have replaced the human "computers" of days gone by.

## Benefits of a Digital Database

The Information Age and the relational database brought several measurable benefits to organizations:

✦ Increased data consistency and better enforcement of business rules

✦ Improved sharing of data, especially across distances

✦ Faster searches for and retrieval of data

✦ Improved generation of comprehensive reports

✦ Improved ability to analyze data trends

The general theme is that a computer database originally didn't save time in the entry of data, but rather in the retrieval of data and in the quality of the data retrieved. However, with automated data collection in manufacturing, bar codes in retailing, databases sharing more data, and consumers placing their own orders on the Internet, the effort required to enter the data has also decreased.

## Tables, Rows, Columns

A relational database collects common, or related, data in a single list. For example, all the product information may be listed in one table and all the customers in another table.

A table appears similar to a spreadsheet and is constructed of columns and rows. The appeal of the spreadsheet is its informal development style, which makes it easy to modify and add to as the design matures. In fact, managers tend to store critical information in spreadsheets, and many databases started as informal spreadsheets.

In both a spreadsheet and a database table, each row is an item in the list and each column is a specific piece of data concerning that item. So each cell should contain a single piece of data about a single item. While a spreadsheet tends to be free-flowing and loose in its design, database tables should be very consistent as to the meaning of the data in a column. Because row and column consistency is so important to a database table, the design of the table is critical.

Over the years different development styles have referred to these columns with various different terms, listed in Table 2-1.

**Table 2-1: Comparing Database Terms**

| Development Style | The Common List | An Item in the List | A Piece of Information in the List |
|---|---|---|---|
| Spreadsheet | Spreadsheet/ worksheet/ named range | Row | Column/cell |
| Historic software | File | Record | Field |
| Relational algebra/ logical design | Entity | Tuple (rhymes with couple) | Attribute |
| SQL/physical design | Table | Row | Column |
| Object-oriented design | Class | Object instance | Property |

SQL Server developers generally refer to database elements as tables, rows, and columns when discussing the physical schema, and sometimes use the terms entity, tuple, and attribute when discussing the logical design. While the rest of this book will use the physical-schema terms, this chapter is devoted to the theory behind the design, and so it will use the relational-algebra terms (entity, tuple, and attribute).

## Transaction Processing Databases

A database that's used for day-to-day processing with frequent data inserts, updates, and searches is referred to as an *online transaction processing* (OLTP) database. OLTP databases typically have multiple purposes, with several front-end applications accessing the data for searches, modification, and reporting.

Data integrity is a high priority for OTLP because the data change frequently. Therefore, OTLPs use a normalized data schema and several methods of enforcing data-integrity rules and business rules (this chapter will explain the various forms of normalization). For performance, OLTP databases are tuned for a balance of data retrieval and updating for both indexing and locking.

## Decision Support Databases

Another type of database is one that's used primarily for analysis: this is the *online analysis processing* (OLAP) database. These databases generally receive large amounts of data from several OLTP databases in a process called *extract-transform-load* (ETL).

The primary task of an OLAP database is data retrieval and analysis, so the data-integrity concerns present with an OLTP database don't apply. Analysis databases are designed for fast retrieval and aren't as normalized as OLTP databases. OLAP databases use a basic star schema design. Locks generally don't apply and the indexing is applied without risk of slowing down inserts or updates.

The analysis process is usually more than SQL queries, and also uses data cubes that consolidate gigabytes of data into dynamic pivot tables. Data warehousing is the combination of the ETL process, the OLAP database, and the acts of creating and browsing cubes.

## Digital Nervous System

Bill Gates has promoted the concept of a "digital nervous system" in the past few years. The idea is that vital information is collected and made available throughout the organization. While his book, *Business @ the Speed of Thought* (Warner Books, 2000), is about using data to improve the effectiveness of an organization, a data analyst will read it as a series of database case studies.

The OLTP database is part of a digital nervous system brain. It's the portion that collects all the information from every nerve and organizes the information so that it can be processed by the rest of the brain. The OLTP database is used for quick responses and instant recognition of the surroundings. For example, by quickly solving an order-handling problem, the OLTP database serves as the autonomic nervous system, or the reflexes, of an organization.

In contrast, the OLAP database (the data warehouse) is the memory of the organization. It stores history and is used for trend analysis, such as finding out where (and why) an organization is doing well or is failing. The portion of the digital nervous system that used by an organization for thoughtful musings — slowly turning over a problem and gaining wisdom — is the OLAP database and a cube.

# Data Modeling

The goal of data modeling is to define a data structure that logically represents certain objects and events. The foundation of data modeling is careful observation and understanding of reality. Based on those insights, the data modeler constructs a logical system — a new virtual world — that models reality.

The basic data element is a single container for data — the intersection of a tuple (row) and an attribute (column) — a single cell in a spreadsheet visualization. Data modeling is the art of fitting that single unit of data in the right place inside hundreds of entities and millions of tuples so that the entire system of data units is logically correct, properly models reality, is easily searchable, and is utterly consistent. To be a data modeler is to see every scene, situation, and document from the viewpoint of data elements and relational design.

The role of the data modeler is arguably the most critical role in any software project, because the data modeler designs the foundation, or structure, of the artificial reality the rest of the code must survive, or die within. Any feature the project is going to offer must be designed within the data schema.

Actually doing data modeling involves several processes. Because each step of the design process is so dependent on the other steps, and discovery continues throughout the process to some degree, designing a data schema isn't a only a sequential process; rather the data modeler moves among these processes as the design takes shape.

1. Observation and requirements gathering

2. Logical representation of reality

3. Visible entity identification and design

4. Schema design (secondary and supporting entities)

5. Application-structure design

No schema can perfectly model reality. Each data schema is designed to meet the requirements of the project at a given stage of the project's life cycle. Discerning the actual requirements, balancing the trade-offs between reality and the design, and building a data schema that supports the current version and allows room to grow are skills learned not from a book, but from experience.

# Gathering Project Requirements

The success of any project is based on meeting the requirements of the client. This leads to the following two questions:

1. Who are the clients?

2. What do they need?

Various people in the client organization may have different and competing needs in terms of software features, timelines, and interfaces. The requirements must be understood at several levels, from the overall organizational structure down to the individual details.

Managing the requirement-gathering phase of the project is often the most difficult task, in part because it's so easy to satisfy one faction while missing other critical requirements.

Some of the means of learning client requirements are:

✦ Interviews with management, end users, and business analysts

✦ Existing forms and reports

✦ Project focus groups

The goal of the requirement-gathering phase is to reach a consensus on the following issues:

✦ The business objects to be modeled; how they are identified by the users; and how the objects are further described

✦ How the objects relate to one another

✦ The business rules for the objects

✦ The primary searches and forms required

✦ The primary reports required

✦ How the database will share data with the rest of the organization

# Logical Database Schema

The purpose of the logical design is to describe entities, relationships, and rules. The physical-schema design will take the logical design and implement it within the structure of a particular software product.

A mathematical approach to relational-database design involves several rules of normalization — rules that govern whether the database design is valid. While designing hundreds of normalized database designs, I have developed an approach to database design that follows the rules of normalization based on the concept of *visible* and *supporting* entities. Visible entities represent elements users would recognize, while supporting entities are abstract entities designed by the database modeler to physically support the logical design.

## Visible Entities

Visible entities generally represent objects that most people would recognize. Many objects are nouns — people, places, or things, such as a contact, a facility, an item, or an airplane. Visible entity might also represent actions, such as a material being assembled or an order being processed. Typically, a visible object is already represented in a document somewhere.

Some visible objects represent ways in which other primary objects are organized, or grouped. For example, clients recognize that groceries fall into several categories — dairy, bread, meats, canned goods, and so on. For another example, purchase orders might be categorized by their priority.

### Every Tuple (row) Is an Island

At the tuple level, each tuple must represent a complete logical thought, and each attribute in the tuple must belong specifically to that tuple and no other.

Every entity is based on the idea that each tuple represents, or models, a single noun or verb. Here's where the experience of data modeling pays off. The key is properly identifying the unique, yet generic, nouns and verbs. That's what is meant by the term *relational database system*. It's not that entities relate to other entities, but that similar, or related, data are assembled into a single entity.

Only data that describe the object belong in the entity. Some of the possible attributes, even though they are sometimes listed on paper documents for one object, may actually describe another object. An order form will often include the customer's name and address although the name belongs to the customer and not the order. The address also belongs to the customer. However, if the customer changes his or her address next year, the order should still show the old address. The point is that careful analysis of the objects and their properties is vital to data modeling.

Well-designed entities are generic so they can handle a variety of similar items. For example, a single grocery entity would contain a variety of grocery items, instead of there being an apple entity and a separate beef entity, and so on.

### Primary Keys

Every tuple in an entity has to represent a single unique object in reality. In the same way that there can't be two of the same airplane, there can't be two tuples that represent the same airplane. To logically prove that each tuple is unique, one attribute (the primary key) is assigned to be the primary way that a specific tuple is referenced for data-modification commands. The logical purpose of the primary key is only to uniquely identify or name the tuple. If you can demonstrate that each object in reality has a single primary key, and visa versa, then you've done your job well.

For an example of a primary key in the physical schema, each customer in the Cape Hatteras Adventures database is identified by their Customer ID. Using SQL Server's identity column option, a new integer is automatically generated for each customer row as the row is inserted in the table.

## Identifying Multiple Entities

While each entity must be a proper entity with all attributes dependent on the primary key, a single entity can't model very much. It takes several entities modeled together to represent an entire business function or organizational task.

Additional entities provide multiple additional pieces of information about the primary objects, group the primary objects, and connect them. While developing the logical data model, several types of logical scenarios within the requirements that will require multiple entities in the logical model are:

✦ Multiple objects

✦ Relationships between objects

✦ Organizing or grouping objects

✦ Consistent look-up values

✦ Complex objects

Sometimes the differentiation between objects, lookup values, and grouping objects blur. As long as all the previous scenarios are considered, the logical data model will be complete.

## Multiple Objects

Sometimes what appears to be a single object is in fact a list of multiple objects. For example:

✦ In the Cape Hatteras Adventures database, a tour may be offered several times. Each time is an event.

✦ In the Family database, each person may have several children.

✦ An employee timecard can include multiple timestamps. The employee timecard can be considered a single object, but upon closer examination it's really a list of time events.

✦ A daily calendar can include multiple appointments.

## Relationships Between Objects

The most common purpose of multiple entities is to describe some type of relationship between two different objects. For example:

✦ In the Cape Hatteras Adventures (CHA) sample database, customers participate in tours, and guides lead tours. These are relationships between customers and tours, and between guides and tours.

✦ A material can be built from multiple other materials.

✦ A health insurance policy can cover multiple family members; this is a relationship between the policy and the family members.

✦ For a software-quality tracking system, a software feature can have multiple bugs.

**Best Practice**

When examining objects and attributes, use the "none, one, or infinity" rule. Whenever it is possible that more than one of any object or attribute may exist, allow for an infinite number. If the user says that the object will always have a fixed number of related objects, just nod, say "I understand," and design for infinity anyway.

## Organizing or Grouping Objects

Objects are sometimes grouped into different categories. These categories should be listed in their own entities. For example:

✦ Customers may be grouped by their customer type in the CHA database.

✦ Materials are grouped by their state (raw materials, works in process, finished goods)

✦ In the Cape Hatteras Adventures sample database, the base camp groups the tours.

### Consistent Look-Up Values

Object attributes often require consistent look-up values. For example:

✦ The type of credit card used for a purchase

✦ The region for an address

✦ The department code for an item

### Complex Objects

Some objects in reality are too complex to model with a single entity. The information takes on more forms than a single primary key and a single tuple can contain. Usually this is because the object in reality includes some form of multiplicity. For example, an order can include multiple order lines. The order lines are part of the order, but the order requires a secondary entity to properly model the multiplicity of the order lines.

## Modeling Relationships

Once the nouns and verbs are organized, the next step is to determine the relationships among the objects. Each relationship connects two entities using their keys and has the following two main attributes:

✦ *Cardinality* — The number of objects that may exist on each side of the relationship.

✦ *Optionality* — Whether the relationship is mandatory or optional.

Clients or business analysts should be able to describe the common relationships between the objects using terms like *includes*, *has*, or *contains*. A customer may place many orders. An order may include many items. An item may be on many orders.

### Secondary Entities and Foreign Keys

When two objects relate, one entity is typically the primary entity and the other entity the secondary entity. One object in the primary entity will relate to multiple objects or tuples in the secondary entity, as shown in Figure 2-1.

The role of the foreign key is to hold the primary key's value so the secondary tuple can be matched with the relating primary tuple.

### Relationship Cardinality

The cardinality of the relationship describes the number of tuples on each side of the relationship. Either side of the relationship may either be restricted to a single tuple or allow multiple tuples. The type of key enforces the restriction of multiple tuples. Primary keys enforce the single-tuple restriction while foreign keys permit multiple tuples.

There are several possible cardinality combinations as shown in Table 2-2. Within this section, each of the cardinality possibilities is examined in detail.

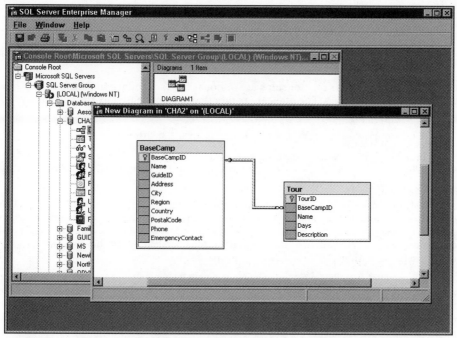

**Figure 2-1:** A one-to-many relationship consists of a primary entity and a secondary entity. The secondary entity's foreign key connects with the primary entity's primary key.

## Table 2-2: Relationship Cardinality

| Relationship Type | First Entity's Key | Second Entity's Key |
| --- | --- | --- |
| One-to-one | Primary entity–primary key–single tuple | Primary entity–primary key–single tuple |
| One-to-many | Primary entity–primary key–single tuple | Secondary entity–foreign key–multiple tuples |
| Many-to-many | Secondary entity–foreign key–multiple tuples | Secondary entity–foreign key–multiple tuples |

## Relationship Optionality

The second property of the relationship is its optionality. The difference between an optional and a mandatory relationship is critical to the data integrity of the database.

Some secondary tuples require that the foreign key point to a primary key. The secondary tuple would be incomplete or meaningless without the primary entity. It's critical in these cases that the relationship be enforced as a mandatory relationship, for the following reasons:

✦ An order-line item without an order is meaningless.

✦ An order without a customer is invalid.

✦ In the Cape Hatteras Adventures database, an event without an associated tour tuple is a useless event tuple.

On the other hand, some relationships are optional. The secondary tuple can stand alone without the primary tuple. The object in reality that is represented by the secondary tuple would exist with or without the primary tuple. For example:

✦ A customer without a discount code is still a valid customer.

✦ In the OBX Kites sample database, an order may or may not have a priority code. Whether the order's `PriorityID` points to a valid tuple in the order priority entity or not, it's still a valid order.

Some database developers prefer to avoid optional relationship and so they design all relationships as mandatory and point tuples that wouldn't need a foreign key value to a surrogate tuple in the primary table. For example, rather than allow nulls in the discount attribute for customers without discounts, a "no discount" tuple is inserted into the discount entity and every customer without a discount points to that tuple.

There are two reasons to avoid surrogate null tuples; the design adds work when work isn't required (additional inserts and foreign key checks), and it's easier to locate works without the relationship by selecting `where column is not null`. The null value is a useful design element. Ignoring the benefits of nullability only creates additional work for both the developer and the database.

Some rare situations call for a complex optionality based on a condition. Depending on a rule, the relationship must be enforced as follows:

✦ If an organization sometimes sells *ad hoc* items that are not in the item entity, the relationship may, depending on the item, be considered optional. The `orderdetail` entity can use two attributes for the item. If the `ItemID` attribute is used then it must point to a valid `item` entity primary key.

✦ However, if the `temext` attribute is used instead, the `ItemID` attribute is left null.

How the optionality is implemented is up to the physical schema. The only purpose of the logical design is to model the organization's objects, their relationships, and their business rules.

## Data-Model Diagramming

Data modelers use several methods to graphically work out their data models. The Chen ER diagramming method is popular, and Visio Professional includes it and five others. The method I prefer is rather simple and works well on a whiteboard, as shown in Figure 2-2. The cardinality of the relationship is indicated by a single line or by three lines (chicken feet). If the relationship is optional, a circle is placed near the foreign key.

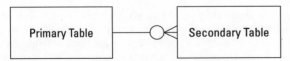

**Figure 2-2:** A simple method for diagramming logical schemas.

Another benefit of this simple diagramming method is that it doesn't require an advanced version of Visio.

## One-to-Many Relationships

By far the most common relationship is a one-to-many relationship. Several tuples in the secondary entity relate to a single tuple in the primary entity. The relationship is between the primary entity's primary key and the secondary entity's foreign key, as in the following examples:

✦ In the Cape Hatteras Adventures database, each base camp may have several tours that originate from it. Each tour may originate from only one base camp. So the relationship is modeled as one base camp relating to multiple tours. The relationship is made between the BaseCamp's primary key and the Tour entity's BaseCampID foreign key, as diagrammed in Figure 2-3. Each Tour's foreign-key attribute contains a copy of its BaseCamp's primary key.

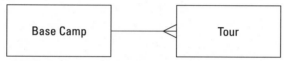

**Figure 2-3:** The one-to-many relationship relates a primary key to a foreign key.

✦ Each customer may place multiple orders. While each order has its own unique OrderID primary key, the Order entity also has a foreign-key attribute that contains the CustomerID of the customer who placed the order. The Order entity may have several tuples with the same CustomerID that defines the relationship as one-to-many.

✦ A non-profit organization has an annual pledge drive. As each donor makes an annual pledge, the pledge goes into a secondary entity that can store several years' worth of pledges. An entity structure of donor name, 2001pledge, 2002pledge, 2003pledge is an amateurish design.

✦ One order may have several order lines. The Order primary key is duplicated in the OrderDetail entity's foreign key. This constrains each order to a single tuple in the Order entity, but allows multiple associated tuples in the OrderDetail entity.

## One-to-One Relationships

One-to-one relationships connect two entities with primary keys at both entities. Because a primary key must be unique, each side of the relationship is restricted to one tuple.

One-to-one relationships are sometimes used to expand the tuple in one entity with additional, but optional or separate, attributes. For instance, an Employee entity can store general information about the employee. However, more sensitive information is stored in a separate entity. While security can be applied on an attribute-by-attribute basis, or a view can project selected attributes, many organizations choose to model sensitive information as two one-to-one entities.

## Super-Type/Sub-Type Relationship

A design element that leverages the one-to-one relationship is the super-type/sub-type relationship. This relationship connects a single super-type entity with multiple sub-type entities to extend the tuple with flexible attributes depending on the type of tuple. The super-type entity has a one-to-one optional relationship with each sub-type.

This design is useful when some objects share a majority of attributes but differ in a few attributes such as customers, vendors, and shippers. All three share name and address attributes, but each has specific attributes. For example, only customers have credit limits and only suppliers have purchase order-related attributes.

While it's possible to use separate entities for customers and suppliers, a better design is to use a single `Contact` entity to hold the common attributes and separate entities for the attributes unique to customers and suppliers.

If the contact is a customer, additional customer information is stored in the `Customer` entity. If the contact is a supplier, supplier-related information is stored in the `Supplier` entity. All three entities (`Contact`, `Customer`, `Supplier`) share the same primary key. One tuple in the `Contact` entity can optionally relate to one tuple in the `Customer` entity, and to one tuple in the `Supplier` entity, as shown in Figure 2-4.

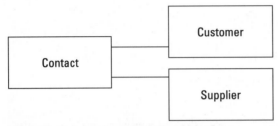

**Figure 2-4:** A one-to-one relationship relates a primary key to a primary key.

Most super-type/sub-type designs permit only a single sub-type tuple for each super type tuple. The contact example, however, could permit a contact to be both a customer and a supplier by adding tuples in each of the sub-type entities.

There's a performance hit for using this design. Inserts must insert into two entities and selects must join the super-type and sub-type entities. Therefore, don't use the super-type/sub-type design to categorize tuples; use this design only when there are several columns that are unique to each sub-type, and it reduces the workload when selecting only tuples from one of the sub-types.

## Many-to-Many Relationships

In a many-to-many relationship both sides may relate to multiple tuples on the other side of the relationship. The many-to-many relationship is common in reality, as shown in the following examples:

✦ In the OBX Kites sample database an order may have multiple items, and each item may be sold on multiple orders.

✦ In the Cape Hatteras Adventures sample database a guide may qualify for several tours, and each tour may have several qualified guides.

✦ In the Cape Hatteras Adventures sample database a customer may participate in several events, and each tour/event hopefully has several customers.

Referring to the previous example in the logical model, the many-to-many relationship between customers and tours is modeled by signifying multiple cardinality at each side of the relationship, as shown in Figure 2-5. The many-to-many relationship is optional because the customer and the tour/event are each valid without the other:

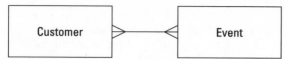

**Figure 2-5:** The many-to-many logical model shows multiple tuples on both ends of the relationship.

The one-to-one and the one-to-many relationship may be constructed from objects from their organizations that users can describe and understand. In the physical schema, a many-to-many relationship can't be modeled with just the visible objects.

A resolution table (Figure 2-6), sometimes called an associative or junction table, is required to resolve the many-to-many relationship. This supporting table artificially creates two one-to-many relationships between the two entities.

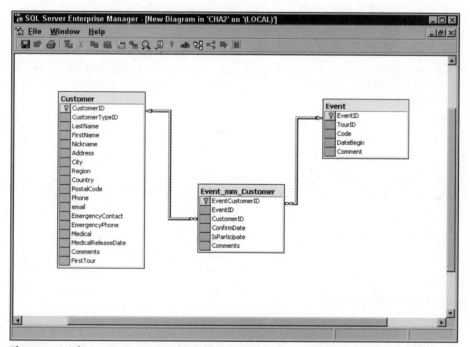

**Figure 2-6:** The many-to-many physical model includes a resolution table providing artificial one-to-many relationships for both tables.

In some cases, additional information may describe the many-to-many relationship. Such information belongs in the resolution entity. For example, in the bill of materials example, the material-to-material relationship might include a quantity attribute in the resolution entity to describe the amount of one material used in the construction of the second material.

The relationship between each primary entity and the resolution entity is mandatory because the relationship is invalid without the primary object. If either the customer or the tour/event were to be deleted, the tuple representing the resolution relationship would become invalid.

## Category Entities

Another type of supporting entity is the *category* entity, sometimes called a *look-up table*. These entities provide consistency in terms of the way tuples are organized. An excellent example of this consistency is a state table. Instead of `Customer` tuples containing inconsistent references in the `Region` attribute to Florida, such as `FL`, `Fl`, `Fla`, and `Florida`, any tuples referencing Florida simply point to the Florida tuple in the state entity. Searching and sorting is faster and easier because of the consistency.

Visible entities typically relate to category entities in a one-to-many relationship. The relationship can be optional or mandatory.

## Reflexive Relationships

In some cases a relationship is between two items of the same type, as in the following examples:

✦ An organizational chart represents a person reporting to another person.

✦ A bill of materials details how a material is constructed from other materials.

✦ Within the Family sample database a person relates to his or her mother and father.

These are examples of *reflexive relationships*, also referred to as *recursive*, *unary*, or *self-join* relationships. Because of the way it's diagrammed, it's sometimes informally called an *elephant-ear* relationship.

To use the Family database as an example, each tuple in the `Person` entity represents one person. Each person has both a mother and a father, who are also in the `Person` entity. So the `MotherID` foreign key and the `FatherID` foreign key point to the mother and father tuples in the same person entity.

Because `PersonID` is a primary key and `MotherID` is a foreign key, the relationship cardinality is one-to-many, as shown in Figure 2-7. One mother may have several children, but each child may have only one mother.

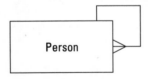

**Figure 2-7:** The reflexive, or recursive, relationship is a one-to-many relationship between two tuples of the same entity.

A bill of materials is more complex because a material may be built from several source materials, and the material may be used to build several materials in the next step of the manufacturing process. This many-to-many reflexive relationship is illustrated in Figure 2-8.

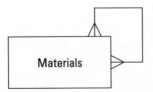

**Figure 2-8:** The logical schema of a many-to-many reflexive relationship shows multiple cardinality at each end of the relationship.

A resolution entity is required to resolve the many-to-many relationship, just as with the previous many-to-many relationship. In the material-specification sample database, the BillOfMaterials resolution entity has two foreign keys that both point to the Material entity, as shown in Figure 2-9.

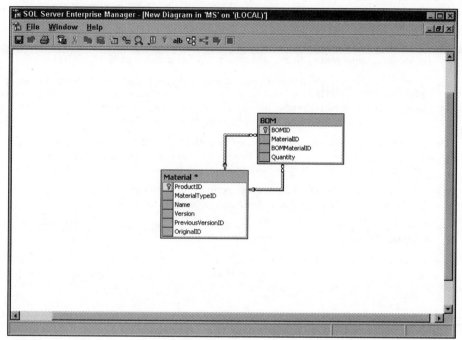

**Figure 2-9:** The physical database schema of the many-to-many reflexive relationship must include a resolution entity, just like the many-to-many two-entity relationship.

The first foreign key points to the material being built. The second foreign key points to the source material.

## Normalization

When creating the logical design, *normalization* is the mathematical method of evaluating the relational quality of the data model. The opposite of a relational-database model, a flat-file or non-normalized data model, tends to exhibit certain problems with data updates, generally caused by duplicate data. Each progressive form of normalization removes another type of flat-file problem.

A normalized database design has the following advantages over flat-file databases:

✦ Improved data integrity owing to the elimination of duplicate storage locations for the same data

✦ Reduced locking contention and improved multiple-user concurrency

✦ Smaller files

A data model does not begin un-normalized and then move through the normal forms. Instead, a data modeler usually initially designs the logical schema in at least a third normal form, and may choose to take a portion of the schema to a higher form.

## First Normal Form (1NF)

The first normalized form means the data is in an entity format, such that the following three conditions are met:

✦ *Every unit of data is represented within scalar attributes*. A scalar value is a value "capable of being represented by a point on a scale," according to Merriam-Webster.

Every attribute must contain one unit of data, and each unit of data must fill one attribute. Designs that embed multiple pieces of information within an attribute violate the first normal form. Likewise, if multiple attributes must be combined in some way to determine a single unit of data, the attribute design is incomplete.

✦ *All data must be represented in unique attributes*. Each attribute must have a unique name and a unique purpose. An entity should have no repeating attributes. If the attributes repeat, or the entity is very wide, the object is too broadly designed.

A design that repeats attributes, such as an order entity that includes item1, item2, and item3 attributes to hold multiple line items, violates the first normal form.

✦ *All data must be represented within unique tuples*. If the entity design requires or permits duplicate tuples, that design violates the first normal form.

For an example of the first normal form in action, consider the listing of base camps and tours from the Cape Hatteras Adventures database. Table 2-3 shows base camp data in a model that violates the first normal form. The repeating tour attribute is not unique.

### Table 2-3: Violating the First Normal Form

| *BaseCamp* | *Tour1* | *Tour2* | *Tour3* |
|---|---|---|---|
| Ashville | Appalachian Trail | Blue Ridge Parkway Hike | |
| Cape Hatteras | Outer Banks Lighthouses | | |
| Freeport | Bahamas Dive | | |
| Ft. Lauderdale | Amazon Trek | | |
| West Virginia | Gauley River Rafting | | |

To redesign the data model so that it complies with the first normal form, resolve the repeating group of tour attributes into a single unique attribute, as shown in Table 2-4, and then move any multiple values to a unique tuple. The BaseCamp entity contains a unique tuple for each base camp, and the Tour entity's BaseCampID refers to the primary key in the BaseCamp entity.

## Table 2-4: Conforming to the First Normal Form

| Tour Entity | | BaseCamp Entity | |
|---|---|---|---|
| BaseCampID(FK) | Tour | BaseCampID (PK) | Name |
| 1 | Appalachian Trail | 1 | Ashville |
| 1 | Blue Ridge Parkway Hike | 2 | Cape Hatteras |
| 2 | Outer Banks Lighthouses | 3 | Freeport |
| 3 | Bahamas Dive | 4 | Ft. Lauderdale |
| 4 | Amazon Trek | 5 | West Virginia |
| | Gauley River Rafting | | |

Another example of a data structure that desperately needs to adhere to the first normal form is a corporate product code that embeds the department, model, color, size, and so forth within the code. I've even seen product codes that were so complex they included digits to signify the syntax for the following digits.

In a theoretical sense this type of design is wrong because the attribute isn't a scalar value. In practical terms, it has the following problems:

✦ Using a digit or two for each data element means that the database will soon run out of possible data values.

✦ Databases don't index based on the internal values of a string so searches require scanning the entire table and parsing each value.

✦ Business rules are difficult to code and enforce.

Entities with non-scalar attributes need to be completely redesigned so that each individual data attribute has its own attribute.

## The Second Normal Form (2NF)

The second normal form ensures that each attribute is in fact an attribute of the entity. It's an issue of dependency. Every attribute must require its primary key, or it doesn't belong in the database.

If the entity's primary key is a single value, this isn't too difficult. Composite primary keys can sometimes get into trouble with the second normal form if the attributes aren't dependent on every attribute in the primary key. If the attribute depends on one of the primary key attributes but not the other, that is a partial dependency that violates the second normal form.

An example of a data model that violates the second normal form is one in which the base-camp phone number is added to the BaseCampTour entity, as shown in Table 2-5. Assume that the primary key (PK) is a composite of both the BaseCamp and the Tour, and that the phone number is a permanent phone number for the base camp, not a phone number assigned for each tour.

### Table 2-5: Violating the Second Normal Form

| PK-BaseCamp | PK-Tour | Base Camp PhoneNumber |
|---|---|---|
| Ashville | Appalachian Trail | 828 -555-1212 |
| Ashville | Blue Ridge Parkway Hike | 828 -555-1212 |
| Cape Hatteras | Outer Banks Lighthouses | 828 -555-1213 |
| Freeport | Bahamas Dive | 828 -555-1214 |
| Ft. Lauderdale | Amazon Trek | 828 -555-1215 |
| West Virginia | Gauley River Rafting | 828 -555-1216 |

The problem with this design is that the phone number is an attribute of the base camp but not the tour. So, the phone number attribute is only partially dependent on the entity's primary key. (A more significant problem is that the composite primary key does not uniquely identify the base camp.)

An obvious practical problem with this design is that updating the phone number requires either updating multiple tuples or risking having two phone numbers for the same phone.

The solution is to remove the partially dependent attribute from the entity with the composite keys, and create an entity with a unique primary key for the base camp, as shown in Table 2-6. This new entity is then an appropriate location for the dependent attribute.

### Table 2-6: Conforming to the Second Normal Form

| Tour Entity | | Base Camp Entity | |
|---|---|---|---|
| PK-Base Camp | PK-Tour | PK-Base Camp | PhoneNumber |
| Ashville | Appalachian Trail | Ashville | 828 -555-1212 |
| Ashville | Blue Ridge Parkway Hike | Cape Hatteras | 828 -555-1213 |
| Cape Hatteras | Outer Banks Lighthouses | Freeport | 828 -555-1214 |
| Freeport | Bahamas Dive | Ft. Lauderdale | 828 -555-1215 |
| Ft. Lauderdale | Amazon Trek | West Virginia | 828 -555-1216 |
| West Virginia | Gauley River Rafting | | |

The PhoneNumber attribute is now fully dependent on the entity's primary key. Each phone number is stored in only one location, and no partial dependencies exist.

## The Third Normal Form (3NF)

The third normal form checks for transitive dependencies. A *transitive dependency* is similar to a partial dependency in that they both refer to attributes that are not fully dependent on a primary key. A dependency is transient when attribute1 is dependent on attribute2, which is dependent on the primary key.

Just as with the second normal form, the normal form is resolved by moving the non-dependent attribute to a new entity.

Continuing with the Cape Hatteras Adventures example, a guide is assigned as the lead guide responsible for each base camp. The `BaseCampGuide` attribute belongs in the `BaseCamp` entity. But it is a violation of the third normal form if other information describing the guide is stored in the base camp, as shown in Table 2-7.

### Table 2-7: Violating the Third Normal Form

*Base Camp Entity*

| *BaseCampPK* | *BaseCampPhoneNumber* | *LeadGuide* | *DateofHire* |
|---|---|---|---|
| Ashville | 1- 828 -555-1212 | Jeff Davis | 5/1/99 |
| Cape Hatteras | 1- 828 -555-1213 | Ken Frank | 4/15/97 |
| Freeport | 1- 828 -555-1214 | Dab Smith | 7/7/2001 |
| Ft. Lauderdale | 1- 828 -555-1215 | Sam Wilson | 1/1/2002 |
| West Virginia | 1- 828 -555-1216 | Lauren Jones | 6/1/2000 |

The `DateofHire` describes the guide not the base, so the hire-date attribute is not directly dependent on the BaseCamp entity's primary key. The `DateOfHire`'s dependency is transitive in that it goes through the `LeadGuide` attribute.

Creating a `Guide` entity and moving its attributes to the new entity resolves the violation of the third normal form and cleans up the logical design, as demonstrated in Table 2-8.

### Table 2-8: Conforming to the Third Normal Form

| *Tour Entity* | | *LeadGuide Entity* | |
|---|---|---|---|
| *BaseCampPK* | *LeadGuide* | *LeadGuidePK* | *DateofHire* |
| Ashville, NC | Jeff Davis | Jeff Davis | 5/1/99 |
| Cape Hatteras | Ken Frank | Ken Frank | 4/15/97 |
| Freeport | Dab Smith | Dab Smith | 7/7/2001 |
| Ft. Lauderdale | Sam Wilson | Sam Wilson | 1/1/2002 |
| West Virginia | Lauren Jones | Lauren Jones | 6/1/2000 |

**Best Practice**

If the entity has a good primary key and every attribute is scalar and fully dependent on the primary key then the logical design is in the third normal form. Most database designs stop at the third normal form.

The additional forms prevent problems with more complex logical designs. If you tend to work with mind-bending modeling problems and develop creative solutions, then understanding the advanced forms will prove useful.

### The Boyce-Codd Normal Form (BCNF)

The Boyce-Codd normal form occurs between the third and fourth normal forms, and it handles a problem with an entity that might have two sets of primary keys. The Boyce-Codd normal form simply stipulates that in such a case the entity should be split into two entities, one for each primary key.

### The Fourth Normal Form (4NF)

The fourth normal form deals with problems created by complex composite primary keys. If two independent attributes are brought together to form a primary key along with a third attribute, but the two attributes don't really uniquely identify the entity without the third attribute, then the design violates the fourth normal form.

For example, suppose the following conditions:

**1.** The BaseCamp and the base camp's LeadGuide were used as a composite primary key.

**2.** An Event and the Guide were brought together as a primary key.

**3.** Because both used a guide all three were combined into a single entity.

The preceding example violates the fourth normal form.

The fourth normal form is used to help identify entities that should be split into separate entities. Usually this is only an issue if large composite primary keys have brought too many disparate objects into a single entity.

### The Fifth Normal Form (5NF)

The fifth normal form provides the method for designing complex relationships that involve multiple (three or more) entities. A *three-way* or *ternary* relationship, if properly designed, is in the fifth normal form. The cardinality of any of the relationships could be one or many. What makes it a ternary relationship is the number of related entities.

As an example of a ternary relationship, consider a manufacturing process that involves an operator, a machine, and a bill of materials. From one point of view, this could be an operation entity with three foreign keys. Or it could be thought of as a ternary relationship with additional attributes.

Just like a two-entity many-to-many relationship, a ternary relationship requires a resolution entity in the physical schema design to resolve the many-to-many into multiple artificial one-to-many relationships. But, in this case the resolution entity has three or more foreign keys.

In such a complex relationship, the fifth normal form requires that each entity, if separated from the ternary relationship, remains a proper entity without any loss of data.

# Data Integrity

The purpose of the relational database is to model reality. Toward that end, the rules and methods of enforcing data integrity are important to both the theory and the practice of developing databases.

One of the keys to enforcing data integrity is educating the owners of the data so that they will value data integrity and "own" not only the job and the project, but the data integrity as well.

Data integrity seldom occurs by accident. It must be planned for from day one of the project.

One of the most difficult factors in a project's data integrity is legacy data. When legacy data meet relational-data integrity some serious problems with the legacy data are often revealed.

**Best Practice**

It's easy for those who were responsible for the legacy system to feel personally threatened by the new project. Getting the legacy developers to feel that they own the data integrity and to participate in the development of the project is far better than presenting the new project so that they are cornered and react defensively. One way to do this is to enable them to set goals and then help them see how best to meet those goals.

## Entity Integrity

*Entity integrity* involves the structure (primary key, and its attributes) of the entity. If the primary key is unique, and all attributes are scalar and fully dependent on the primary key then the integrity of the entity is good. Essentially, entity integrity is normalization.

In the physical schema, the table's primary key enforces entity integrity.

## Domain Integrity

In relational theory terms, a domain is a set of possible values for an attribute, such as integers, bit values, or characters. *Domain integrity* enforces that only valid data is permitted in the attribute. Nullability (whether a null value is valid for an attribute) is also a part of domain integrity. In the physical schema, the data type and nullability of the row enforce entity integrity.

## Referential Integrity

A subset of domain integrity, *referential integrity* refers to the domain integrity of the foreign key. If the foreign key attribute has a value that value must be in the domain. In the case of the foreign key, the domain is the list of values in the related primary key.

Referential integrity is therefore not an issue of the integrity of the primary key, but of the foreign key.

Several methods of enforcing referential integrity at the physical-schema level exist. Within a physical schema, a foreign key can be enforced by declarative referential integrity (DRI) or by a custom trigger attached to the table.

## User-Defined Integrity

Besides the relational theory–integrity concerns, the user-integrity requirements must also be enforced, as follows:

✦ Simple business rules, such as a restriction to the domain, limit the list of valid data entries. Check constraints are commonly used to enforce these rules in the physical schema.

✦ Complex business rules limit the list of valid data based on some condition. For example, certain tours may require a medical waiver. Inplementing these rules in the physical schema generally requires stored procedures or triggers.

Some other of data-integrity concerns can't be checked by constraints or triggers. Invalid, incomplete, or questionable data may pass all the standard data-integrity checks. For example, an order without any order detail tuples is not a valid order, but no automatic method traps such an order. SQL queries can locate incomplete orders and can also help in identifying other less measurable data-integrity issues, including the following:

✦ Wrong data

✦ Incomplete data

✦ Questionable data

✦ Inconsistent data

The quality of the data depends upon the people modifying the data. Data security, controlling who can view or modify the data, is also an aspect of data integrity.

Another aspect of data integrity is knowing the history of the data. A database that requires a very high level of integrity would benefit from a data-audit trail that maintains an automatic and secure record of every data modification.

 **Cross-Reference** Chapter 16, "Advanced Server-Side Programming," includes examples of implementing such a data-audit trail.

# Object-Oriented Database Design

Object-oriented development has revolutionized the software industry. The basic concepts of object-oriented development may also be applied to database development resulting in an object-oriented database management system (OODBMS).

Object-oriented development is based on the concept that an object is an instance of an object class. The class defines the properties and methods of the object, and contains all the code for the object. Each instance of the object can have its own internal variables and can interact with the software world outside the object on its own.

The real power of object-oriented development is building a class based on another class. The new class inherits all the properties and methods of its base class and can add new properties and methods. For example, a base class of vehicle may have certain properties and methods common to all vehicles. An automobile class based on vehicle would include all of the vehicle properties and methods as well as new properties and methods specific to the automobile class. A Dodge Intrepid object, therefore, will have the properties of an automobile, including the vehicle properties.

Some database systems are designed to specifically implement all the features of object-oriented development. Microsoft SQL Server 2000 is a relational database system (RDBMS) and not an OODBMS. However, the basic concepts of class, inheritance, objects, properties, and methods may be implemented within a data structure design using SQL Server 2000.

The process of building an OODBMS using SQL Server 2000 begins with a data schema supporting object classes, properties, and inheritance, as shown in Figure 2-10.

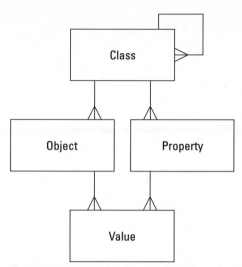

**Figure 2-10:** A basic object-oriented–
database schema from the sample database OOD.

The class entity drives the database schema. The class entity includes a reflexive relationship to support object class inheritance. As with a hierarchical structure or organizational chart, this relationship permits each object class to have multiple subclasses and each object class to have one base class. For example, the vehicle object class would be one tuple in the object class entity. Because it is a base class, it would not have a value in the InheritedClassID attribute. The vehicle class would also be a tuple in the object entity and its InheritedClassID attribute would refer back to the vehicle class.

The property entity is a secondary entity to the object entity and enables each object class to contain multiple properties. To determine all the properties for a specific object class, a stored procedure would have to navigate the inherited classes.

An object is a specific instance of an object class. As such, it needs to have its own specific values for every property of its object class and all inherited object classes.

Although the result can be impressive, many complications are involved in this process. Many-to-many relationships, which exist in real life, are simulated within object-oriented databases by means of object collections. Properties must meet data-type and validation rules, which must be simulated by the data schema rather than by SQL Server's built-in data-type and validation rules.

So, building an object-oriented database on top of SQL Server means creating an entirely new database system using SQL Server as a tool. Every data-modification command (insert, update, delete, or select) must be coded with stored procedures to handle the class inheritance.

**On the CD-ROM** OODBMS is a small sample database that includes an example book object, and related properties. Also check www.IsNotNull.com for any additional sample files.

# Dynamic/Relational Database Design

Some database requirements state that the attributes must be dynamic. A manufacturing material-specifications system, for example, would require different attributes for nearly every material type. To further complicate matters, the attributes that are tracked frequently change based on the Total Quality Management (TQM) or ISO 9000 process (TQM) within the company. A purely relational database might use an entity for each material type and would require constant schema changes to keep current with the material tracking requirements.

Gary Lail and I have designed several databases using a data-driven method we call *dynamic/relational database design*, which implements some of the flexibility of an object-oriented design without completely discarding the familiar relational-database methods. The dynamic/relational design is not used exclusively within a database, only for some of the user recognizable objects being modeled. The dynamic/relational design method applies an object-oriented method to a portion of the relational design.

The basic idea behind a dynamic/relational database is that the attributes are vertical instead of horizontal.

One way to picture a dynamic/relational database is to compare it to the basic spreadsheet table. Instead of storing the data as an entity with tuples and attributes, the dynamic/relational method involves building an entity with three attributes: tuple, attribute, and value. A traditional entity uses tuples and attributes, as shown in Table 2-9.

### Table 2-9: A Relational Entity

| Primary Key | Color | Speed | Size |
|---|---|---|---|
| 1 | Red | Fast | Medium |
| 2 | Green | Slow | Small |
| 3 | Yellow | Average | Petite |

A dynamic/relational representation of the same data is shown in Table 2-10. The new entity uses only three attributes: primary key, property, and value. Each spreadsheet cell is represented in its own tuple. The entity is the same width regardless of the number of properties, but easily grows vertically with additional objects or properties.

### Table 2-10: A Dynamic/Relational Entity

| Primary Key | Property | Value |
|---|---|---|
| 1 | Color | Red |
| 1 | Speed | Fast |
| 1 | Size | Medium |
| 2 | Color | Green |
| 2 | Speed | Slow |

| Primary Key | Property | Value |
| --- | --- | --- |
| 2 | Size | Small |
| 3 | Color | Yellow |
| 3 | Speed | Average |
| 3 | Size | Petite |

The basic example is much too free-form and footloose to serve as an actual database model. But by incorporating an entity design that "goes vertical," some object-oriented concepts, and relational normalization, the concept becomes as robust as it is flexible.

## Basic Dynamic/Relational Design

Within a dynamic/relational database design the relational entity is redesigned using four entities, as shown in Figure 2-11. Theoretically, the Object entity stores only the identifying data about each item being represented in the entity. The objects are organized by ObjectType entity. Each object type may have multiple properties, or attributes stored in the Property entity, also organized by object type. The actual attribute values for each object are stored in the Value entity, a many-to-many resolution entity between Object and Property.

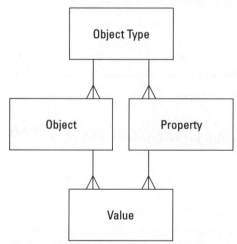

**Figure 2-11:** The basic dynamic/relational design uses four entities to dynamically model a single object.

To continue with the material-specifications example, a material type can be plastic, wood, or steel. Each material type can have multiple properties or attributes stored in the properties secondary entity. If a material type has 50 specifications that must be tracked, instead of listing each specification in an attribute (which makes for a wide table), the dynamic/relational design lists the 50 specifications as 50 tuples in the property entity.

Each specific material is listed in the object entity, and the `ObjectTypeID` foreign key points to the object type. This portion of the `Object` entity adheres to a standard normalized design. Where it differs is in the descriptive attributes, which are not attributes in the `Object` entity, but are tuples in the `Property` entity. The descriptive data is placed vertically in the `Value` entity.

## Dynamic/Relational Front-End Programming

Most front-end applications use forms with fixed controls for data attributes. But a dynamic/relational database doesn't have predefined data attributes. Two user work surfaces are required. The first gives administrators access to the `ObjectType`, `Type`, and `Property` entities with which to manage the dynamic nature of the database. The second application is used by users to enter and examine the objects and the property values.

The user application typically uses grids that are populated on the fly with the current appropriate properties for the object being examined.

While it admittedly requires more work to develop a front-end application that's designed for a dynamic/relational database than a front-end application for a traditional relational database, the result is very flexible and will have a long life. Unlike a fixed-control application that requires a programmer to add new attributes, the dynamic/relational database enables the user to add new properties as required without additional programming.

## Advanced Dynamic/Relational Database Design

The basic dynamic/relational concept may be extended to handle more complex designs by expanding the features of the properties.

Properties often apply to multiple object types. Therefore, a many-to-many relationship between `ObjectType` and `Property` entities allows properties to serve multiple object types.

The business rules for each property, such as data type, must be stored in a entity. The business rules for each property as it applies to each object type can be stored in a secondary entity.

The material-specification sample database is a dynamic/relational database that includes the following advanced features, as shown in Figure 2-12:

✦ The database uses a material state entity — raw material, work in progress (wip), finished goods, and so on — to further group material types.

✦ Each property may be aligned with multiple material types.

✦ Because material specifications are version-specific, the material entity supports multiple versions of each material. Each version includes a pointer to the version it's based upon. The original material is stored in every subsequent version to make it easy to locate each material in the version hierarchy.

✦ Materials are associated with other materials as parts within an assembly. The multiple reflexive relationship built with the `BOM` (bill of material) entity enables each material to be constructed from many other materials, and to be used in the construction of many other materials.

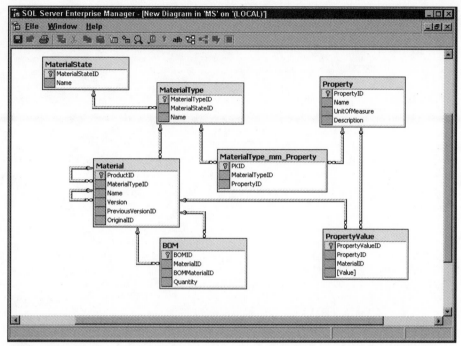

**Figure 2-12:** The material-specification database is an advanced dynamic/relational database.

**On the CD-ROM**

The script `MS_Create.sql`, on the CD, creates the entity structure for the material-specification database and populates it with a small sampling of data. While the material-specification database could work for any industry, the sample database is populated for a neighborhood computer-company.

Microsoft uses integers for primary keys to make it easy to examine the sample data. However, a production dynamic/relational database would likely use GUIDs for primary keys for two reasons. First, the value entity would likely outgrow an integer-based primary key. Second, any significant flexible database will likely be replicated, and that requires GUIDs.

The dynamic/relational database method pushes database design to the limit, but for certain applications it can provide a database design that's flexible and useful.

# Summary

Data modeling merges reality with the abstract. This chapter presents a method of thinking about that merger. Normalization is a good thing, but the point is not the form by form process, but the resulting data model. Part one of this book is an introduction to developing databases with SQL Server. The next chapter continues this introduction as it deals with installing SQL Server.

✦　　✦　　✦

# Installing and Configuring SQL Server

**W**hile SQL Server is relatively easy to install, this chapter handles the exceptions and explains why certain installation options are preferable to others. As with most tasks in life, extra time spent in preparation pays off during execution, so I include additional hardware recommendations and planning suggestions for a SQL Server installation.

Very few database projects are virgin endeavors; most are upgrades from previous implementations. In light of that reality, this chapter includes not only information about the server upgrade but advice about moving existing projects to SQL Server 2000's client/server environment.

While a freshly installed server will not contain any user databases, it will contain several system databases, sample databases, and system views.

## Planning Your Installation

You should experience no complications when installing a default installation of SQL Server — but you will have to make a few decisions, and it's best to think those decisions through before performing the installation. The areas that you need to think about prior to installation are:

✦ A security plan

✦ Disk configuration and file locations

✦ Collations or sort methods

✦ Network protocols used to communicate with clients

### Operating System

SQL Server 2000 is not restricted to running on Windows 2000. It installs and runs fine on Windows NT, Windows 2000, and Windows XP Professional or Server. However, some limitations exist concerning which operating system edition is supported by which SQL Server edition, as detailed in Table 3-1.

**Table 3-1: Operating System Editions Supported by SQL Server 2000**

| SQL Server Edition | Windows 98, ME, XP Home | Windows NT Workstation, 2K Workstation, or XP Professional | Windows NT, 2K, or XP: Server, Advanced Server, Data Center |
|---|---|---|---|
| Enterprise Edition/120-day Evaluation Edition | No | No | OK |
| Developer Edition | No | OK | OK |
| Standard Edition | No | OK | OK |
| Personal Edition | OK | OK | OK |
| Desktop Engine (MSDE) | OK | OK | OK |

## Planning the Security Accounts

Setting up SQL Server security may be confusing because it includes two separate questions. First, which types of user logins will SQL Server recognize—Windows user accounts only, or also SQL Server accounts?

Second, which Windows account will SQL Server and its services use to log on to Windows?

Cross-Reference    Chapter 27, "Securing Databases," discusses SQL Security in detail.

SQL Server runs as a process on the server's operating system, and as such it needs permission to get to the SQL Server files regardless of the permission of the person who is currently using SQL Server. In fact, typically, no users will be logged on at the server. So the service security account is the logon that SQL Server uses to access Windows resources—not a login for users connecting to SQL Server.

The SQL Server engine and the services (SQL Server Agent and the Distributed Transaction Controller) will both need to log on. By default they share the same Windows logon account, but a separate logon can be provided for SQL Server Agent.

Two options exist for this account. The first option is *local system account*, which does not require a password and will provide SQL Server with the required system permissions without any maintenance. However, the local system account does not allow network access, which will cause problems for backups to network drives, SQL Mail, and distributed queries.

The second, and recommended, option is to use a named Windows logon account on the server or domain. This option has the benefit of providing better tracking and logging of activities. I recommend creating a specific account just for SQL Server rather than share a general network system administrator account. This will help reduce the chance that a network-system administrator will one day delete the account or change the password, causing SQL Server to fail.

Windows accounts are created and maintained in Window's Setup/Administrative Tools/Computer Management application. To manage user accounts, you must be logged on with administrator privileges.

A created local account must be

✦ A local administrator

✦ Able to log on as a service

✦ Able to access and update the SQL Server program directory

✦ Able to read and write registry keys

If the installation will include multiple servers which will need to communicate and perform distributed queries or replication, then the logon account must be a domain level account. The domain account must be a member of the Windows Administrators group.

The SQL Server account settings may be changed later in the Security tab of the Server Properties page within Enterprise Manager.

## Planning the File Locations

During installation, file locations are selected for the SQL Server program files and the default location is selected for the data files. For the program files this location is permanent. The data-file locations will be used for the system databases.

**Best Practice**

To ensure-up-to-the-minute recovery, always create the database data file and the transaction log in different disk subsystems.

The transaction log is a write-ahead log of all data changes and is used for up-to-the-minute restoration in case of failure. It's vital that the log not fail at the same time the data file fails. The installation process only creates a single default location for database files. However, after the installation, the server properties include two default file locations — one for data files and one for transaction logs. These are only the defaults, as file locations may be configured for individual databases.

Typically the default location for the program files is adequate. You will probably need to change the data-file locations to reflect your server's disk-subsystem configuration. There's more on disk-drive configurations and hardware recommendations later in this chapter.

## Planning the Sort Collation

SQL Server is an international product. As such, it includes the ability to sort data in various languages. The *collation setting* determines the language and sensitivity of the sort. By default, SQL Server will choose the language based on the language selected within Windows. Optionally, the collation can determine the case and accent sensitivity of the sort. In all, there are 753 available collations available within SQL Server.

The default collation for U.S. English installations is SQL_Latin1_General_CP1_CI_AS, which means Latin characters, case insensitive, accent sensitive.

Unlike the security settings, collation is difficult to change after installation. Changing the default collation involves exporting all the data, rebuilding the master database, specifying the new collation setting, and importing all the data.

The permanence of the choice of collation is lessened by SQL Server 2000's ability to set the collation on a database and column level, and during any query.

ASCII characters are one byte in length, which limits the number of possible ASCII characters. This causes problems for international applications, and for languages with a large number of characters. The collation determines which characters are represented by which ASCII values.

Unicode makes it easier to develop international databases by using two bytes per character and bypassing the ASCII character limitation at the cost of disk space. Unicode is not available as a collation, but may be used on a column and variable basis as tables are created by using a Unicode-enabled data type, such as `nvarchar`. The relative merits of Unicode versus ASCII characters is an ongoing debate among SQL Server developers. The question of flexibility versus disk space is similar to the question of global unique identifiers versus identity columns as primary keys.

Using Unicode does not make the collation setting moot. While the collation does not determine the character set, it still determines the accents, case sensitivity, and sort order of the alphabet.

## Planning the Network Protocols

When a client connects to SQL Server, the connection is not with the Windows operating system on the server but is rather a direct connection between the client and SQL Server. Therefore, SQL Server and every client must use the same network protocol.

SQL Server supports several network protocol libraries, as detailed in Table 3-2.

### Table 3-2: SQL Server Network Libraries

| Protocol | Supports Routing | Supports Named Instances |
|----------|------------------|--------------------------|
| Named Pipes | No | Yes |
| TCP/IP sockets | Yes | Yes |
| Multiprotocol | Yes | No |
| NWLink IPX/SPX | Yes | Yes |
| AppleTalk | Yes | No |
| BanyanVines | Yes | No |

Named Pipes is based on netbios. The default pipe is \\.\pipe\sql\query. There's no reason to change the pipe name, but it must match between server and client. If the client and server are on the same physical computer Named Pipes can use shared memory. Named Pipes is not available on Windows 98/ME.

When configuring SQL Server's TCP/IP properties the TPC/IP firewall port may be specified. The default port is 1433 for the first instance and randomly determined for additional instances the first time the instance is run. Encryption may be forced on a client-by-client basis by setting the option in the Client Network Utility.

The Multiprotocol option will automatically select from among the Named Pipes, TCP/IP, and NWLInk IPX/SPX protocols. This option does not support named instances of SQL Server, so it may only be used with the default instance. Multiprotocol encryption is for backward compatibility — it's different from the Secure Socket Layer Encryption.

NWLink IPX/SPX is the native network protocol for Novell networks. You specify the server using the service name and port. NWLink is not available if the server is running on Windows 98/ME.

AppleTalk and BanyanVines are included only for backward compatibility. They will likely be dropped in a future version of SQL Server.

Secure Socket Layer Encryption may be enabled using any protocol, but it requires a digital certificate.

SQL Server will listen for traffic on WinSock Proxy if the WinSock Proxy option is selected and the required address and port are supplied.

The network protocols selected during installation are not fixed in stone; they may be changed later using Enterprise Manager, the Server Network Utility, or the Client Network Utility. Keep in mind that the network protocol is set for each instance of SQL Server, and for each client workstation.

## Planning the Authentication Mode

SQL Server can use two methods to authenticate users, a Windows User account or a SQL Server account. The option selected during installation determines the methods that will be available later, as shown in Table 3-3.

### Table 3-3: Security-Authentication Modes

| Login Method | Windows Authentication Mode | Mixed Mode |
| --- | --- | --- |
| Users may authenticate using their Windows User logon | Yes | Yes |
| SQL Server–specific accounts | No | Yes |

Each SQL authentication method includes Windows User Accounts. The question is whether to also allow SQL Server–specific accounts. These accounts are created within SQL Server. I recommend SQL Server Mixed Mode: You can still require all users to log in to SQL Server using Windows authentication, and Mixed Mode also enables you, as the DBA, to easily create test users in order to test the security permissions.

If you enable Mixed Mode, the sa account may be assigned a password during installation. An sa account with no password is the most common security hole. I strongly suggest that you apply a password to the account.

 **Cross-Reference** SQL Server authentication and the sa account is discussed in more detail in Chapter 27, "Securing Databases."

## Planning the Server Instances

SQL Server 2000 supports up to 16 instances of SQL Server running on the same physical server. The multiple SQL Server instances may be of different editions (Enterprise, Standard, or MSDE).

There are several reasons why multiple instances might be desired:

✦ For developing and testing databases on a platform identical to production, but with separate server options and protection if something should go wrong.

✦ For testing replication scenarios or distributed transactions.

✦ For testing different editions of SQL Server.

✦ For applying service packs in order to test applications with the service packs before applying the service packs to the production instance.

✦ For disaster-recovery testing using the actual hardware used for production. What's the point of a backup if the restore doesn't recover smoothly?

✦ For running SQL Server 7 concurrently with SQL Server 2000. However, the database compatibility mode, which forces SQL Server 2000 to run T-SQL code from earlier SQL Server versions, makes this reason less compelling.

**Caution**    Don't use multiple instances to support multiple databases. A single instance of SQL Server running multiple databases will be more efficient than multiple instances running a single database each.

The first installation is normally the default instance and will have the same name as the server. Each additional instance must have an instance name that will then be referenced as [server\instance]. The instance name may be up to 16 characters long, cannot include spaces or reserved words, and must begin with a letter, underscore, or ampersand (but a mixing of special characters into an instance name is a poor practice).

Each instance is a complete installation of SQL Server with separate program files, registry entries, network connectivity, server options, and databases.

The default instance location is:

```
C:\Program Files\Microsoft SQL Server\MSSQL
```

The location for the additional instance named SQL2 is:

```
C:\Program Files\Microsoft SQL Server\MSSQL$ SQL2
```

Certain non-engine components, such as English Query, net libraries, client tools, Service Manager, and so on, are shared among all instances on a server.

Each instance is started and stopped independently and consumes memory according to the specifications of the server-memory properties. This could be an issue in a memory-starved server, because one instance is not going to release memory to another instance. Servers with multiple instances should have each instance's maximum SQL Server memory set to accommodate the multiple instances.

Performance is also affected because every running instance will also demand CPU cycles to check connections and the like. On a single CPU server, multiple instances will cause each instance to run slower.

If multiple instances are used for testing purposes, don't set the test instance to automatically start when the OS starts. Instead, start the instance when it's needed and stop it when the test is complete.

# Hardware Recommendations

Hardware is quickly out-of-date. The good news is that SQL Server runs well on most servers, but hardware does make a difference. Ignoring Microsoft's minimum hardware requirements, this section provides some design guidelines for planning a server.

The big decision you make when designing a server for SQL Server is deciding how much to invest in each of the server components. While a server should be fairly balanced in the performance of its subsystems, I've prioritized this list according to my opinion of the relative importance of each.

## Dedicated Server

SQL Server is a demanding server application, so running other server tasks (Domain Controller, SMS, Exchange Server, Proxy Server, file or printer server functions, for example) on the same server will degrade SQL Server performance. When SQL Server wants to run a large query it needs the CPU cycles. When it needs to perform, don't make it share the CPU with another process.

Running other software can also cause troubles when the other software requires service packs, hot patches, or the like, and needs to be rebooted or develops some type of conflict.

Buying a single mega-server (read: mini-empire) and running several processes spread across multiple CPUs doesn't work in the real world and only renders the server obsolete faster. It's better to spread the work across multiple dedicated servers.

## Copious Memory

SQL Server 2000 reads the data pages from the disk into memory and then performs the database work in memory. If a `select` statement needs to perform a table scan the entire table is read into memory. To perform updates, SQL Server 2000 reads the data pages into memory, performs the update, and then writes the data back to disk as a background process.

Caching as much of the database as possible in memory not only saves the time required to fetch the data page from the disk but also saves the CPU time in determining which pages must be fetched.

Having plenty of memory will help compensate for CPU and hard disk limitations; conversely, memory starvation will kill SQL Server performance. So how much memory is required? A simple answer is the size of the largest database times two, since Windows doesn't like to give too much memory to any single process. Realistically speaking, though, considering the falling prices of memory and the SIMM-slot limitations on the motherboard, it's not worth it to calculate a memory requirement of 448MB and then put in one 256MB SIMM, 1x128MB SIMM, and 1x64MB SIMM. A better plan is to buy a single 512MB memory SIMM and save the other SIMM slots for expansion. Memory is the cheapest component and provides the best bang for the buck.

## Using Multiple CPUs

Tradition holds that databases are disk-bound. I've even been told by a computer salesperson that CPU performance has no effect on the performance of a database application. I disagree. Joins are performed by the CPU. Query optimization plans are calculated by the CPU. Code is executed by the CPU. And, because the plan is to have the data pages already cached in memory, the CPU along with the memory drives the performance.

When planning the hardware, balance CPU performance, quantity of RAM, and speed throughput of the disk subsystems.

SQL Server is a smooth multitasking and multi-threading program, so SQL Server performance naturally benefits from servers with multiple CPUs. While it's true that there's some overhead for the operating system required to control multiple CPUs, the overhead is small compared to the gain. The additional multitasking performance helps because SQL Server queries must share time not only with other queries and connections, but also with Windows itself. The cost of dual CPUs has come down to the point that it's worth the extra performance. Personally, I prefer a dual Pentium server as a starting point for SQL Server servers.

Moving up the scale, quad-CPU and eight-way servers have also become more reasonable and more reliable than ever before. Be careful to avoid justifying the purchase by consolidating servers. Keep the server dedicated to SQL Server. Also, when considering CPUs, remember that a large CPU L2 cache is very important.

Another factor is that per-CPU licensing will increase the cost of servers with additional CPUs. A single faster CPU may serve as well as a dual slower CPU and save several thousand dollars in software costs.

## Disk-Drive Subsystems

Although I've placed the memory and CPU higher in my list of priorities than the disk subsystem, disk performance is still vital for SQL Server. Fortunately, disks are faster, more reliable, and available in more intelligent subsystems than in previous years. Of course, you should buy the fastest SCSI drives your budget will allow.

### RAID Disk Subsystems

High-performance disk subsystems nearly always involve some type of RAID, listed in Table 3-4. RAID was originally an acronym for "*Redundant Array of Inexpensive Disks*," however, vendors are now referring to it as a "*Redundant Array of Individual Disks.*"

### Table 3-4: RAID Levels

| RAID Level | Redundancy Percentage | Description |
| --- | --- | --- |
| 0 | 0% | *Data Striping* — Data is written to multiple drives, speeding up data writes and reads. No parity or redundancy is available. |
| 1 | 50% | *Data Mirroring* — Data is written to two drives and read from either drive. |
| 5 | Depends on number of drives, if five drives and last is for parity then 20% | Data striping with a parity bit written to one of the drives. Because of the parity bit, any single drive can fail, and the disk subsystem can still function even if any single drive fails. When the failed disk drive is replaced, the disk subsystem can recreate the data on the failed drive it contained. |
| | | RAID 5 is popular because it offers excellent protection, and good speed, and at the lowest cost. |
| 1/0 | 50% | *Mirrored striped drives*, which offer the speed of data stripping and the protection of data mirroring. This is the most expensive option. |

**Caution**

Windows' Disk Management utility enables you to define a mirrored or striped disk. Although this technique might prove useful for a workstation or a low- volume file server, it trades CPU cycles for disk redundancy and is not suitable for a SQL Server server. And because the disk writes are typically sequential through the same controller, disk performance is halved.

In the same vein, enabling Windows file compression or encryption for SQL Server data files or the transaction file is not a recommended practice.

If you are using anti-virus protection (and you are, right?) then disable the automatic virus check for the directory storing SQL Server files, or specify no virus checking for .mfd, .ndf, and .ldf files.

Most RAID controllers support hot-swappable drives, meaning that if a drive fails, the failed drive may be pulled and a new drive inserted in its place while the computer is running. During the failure, the RAID controller (if configured for RAID 5) calculates the data that was on the failed drive by comparing the remaining data with the parity bits. Once a new drive is inserted, the controller rebuilds the drive's data automatically. Whether or not you need this capability depends on your organization's tolerance for down time. If you maintain the spare drive on hand, swapping a failed drive and rebuilding the data could take a few hours.

RAID controllers also typically include some amount of physical memory that serves as a hardware disk cache and greatly improves the throughput of the disk subsystem. Even though these controllers generally include a battery back-up to maintain the cache memory in case of power failure or computer crash, I recommend that you disable caching the write and force the controller to perform the disk write immediately. I'm not willing to sacrifice consistency for performance. The ACID properties of the database are much more critical than a split-second gain of in performance.

## Disk Subsystem Design

When you're considering disk subsystems, the two most important aspects are redundancy and throughput. You want some level of redundancy to ensure the reliability of the drives and throughput for raw performance.

When planning the disk subsystems and file distributions for a server, consider spreading the files across different disk subsystems, as described in Table 3-5, using the RAID levels listed in Table 3-4.

### Table 3-5: File/Disk Configuration

| Files | Description | Ideal RAID level |
|---|---|---|
| Windows and SQL Server program files | Locate these on the primary bootable drive local to the server. | 1 or 5 |
| Windows Swap file and Temp directory | Some designers put the Swap file on its own high-speed drive, although they could easily remain on the same drive as the Windows and SQL Server program files. If the operating system is Windows XP then the swap file can be disabled, which is my favorite course of action. | None or 1 |

*Continued*

**Table 3-5** *(continued)*

| *Files* | *Description* | *Ideal RAID level* |
|---|---|---|
| Transaction log | SQL Server writes all data-modification operations to the transaction log and then reads the log as part of the process of committing a transaction. Therefore, the transaction log must be on a high-speed write and read drive. | 1/0<br><br>You can perform a restore to any point in time by combining the data-file backups, the transaction-log backups, and the current transaction log. Therefore, the transaction log is the single most critical point of failure. |
| Tempdb file | SQL Server uses Tempdb internally as a scratch pad for temporary work when sorting or hashing data. Application code may use Tempdb for cursor temporary storage.<br><br>One way to balance the disk I/O load is to locate Tempdb on its own a drive subsystem. | 0 or 1<br><br>Tempdb is a high-volume read/write file. Data striping is recommended, and data mirroring is optional. Tempdb is cleared every time SQL Server is restarted; however, a tempdb failure causes major problems. |
| Primary and secondary data files | If the database is defined with multiple data files, SQL Server will spread the data pages among the files, attempting to evenly balance the disk I/O load. Alternately, using filegroups, individual tables, and indexes can be manually positioned on a specific data file. | 5 |

When planning these file/disk separations the first priority is to ensure that the transaction log is separate from the data files. Never, ever store the transaction log on the same drive as the data file for a production application; doing so would compromise the recovery. Next, separate the data files onto multiple drive subsystems. Lastly, consider separating the Swap and Tempdb files.

## Network Performance

Well-written client/server applications by their nature require less network bandwidth than other software technologies, so the *network interface card*, or NIC, is often overlooked during the planning of a server. The NIC supplied by the server vendor, or the corporate standard workstation NIC, is often used by default. The NIC card, however, plays an important role in the processing of client requests.

Every transaction includes communication over network, generally TCP/IP over Ethernet. NIC cards that include some portion of the TPC/IP stack processing, or encryption/decryption, in their hardware can increase the NIC throughput by as much as 800 percent while reducing the CPU load. The Alacritech Server NICs offload 99 percent of TPC/IP processing. Because the goal is to free up as many CPU cycles for SQL Server as possible, including a new NIC intended for servers is a wise investment. Server-quality NICs are available from Intel, 3Com, and Alacritech.

If you are building clustered servers, a federated database, or a failsafe system, a direct dedicated high-speed fiber network connection between the servers may be required or recommended.

# Performing the Installation

Once you have chosen your installation plan, set up the server machine, and loaded Windows, it's time to perform the installation.

## Attended Installations

Performing an attended installation should be familiar to Windows users and IT professionals. The SQL Server CD-ROM should automatically launch the installation program. If the program fails to launch, execute the `autorun.exe` program on the SQL Server CD.

Prior to installing SQL Server, make sure that the following conditions are met:

✦ The SQL Server account in Windows is configured

✦ Directories are created for the data files.

✦ The Windows Event viewer and Registry viewer have been shut down

✦ Any services or programs dependent on SQL Server have been shut down, if you're reinstalling SQL Server 2000.

If SQL Server 7.0 is already installed on the computer, the installation program will offer to upgrade SQL Server to SQL Server 2000.

SQL Server 2000 Database Server, Analysis Services, and English Query are all separate installations as shown in Figure 3-1. Optionally, the installation/upgrade help is available from the installation welcome screen. SQL Server may be installed to the local computer or to a remote server.

When you are installing a new instance, keeping the default option is appropriate, as shown in Figure 3-2. However, if an existing instance is being modified, as in the case of a 120-day Evaluation Edition being upgraded to a Standard Edition, that option is available as well. The advanced options pertain to unattended installations.

**Figure 3-1:** SQL Server, Analysis Services, and English Query install separately.

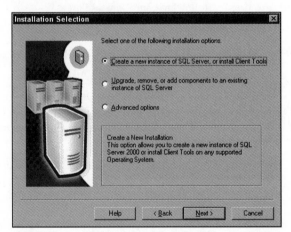

**Figure 3-2:** Set-up can install a new instance of SQL Server, modify an installation, or create an unattended install.

When you are installing SQL Server 2000, the primary component selections include, respectively:

✦ Server processes, client tools, and connectivity

✦ Client tools and connectivity

✦ Only connectivity

If this is the first installation of SQL Server on the server, then it's likely that the default instance will suffice. If SQL Server has already been installed at least once, the additional instances will require a name.

The three types of installation are Typical, Minimum, and Custom, as listed in Table 3-6. In most cases the typical installation will work fine.

### Table 3-6: Installation Type

| Installation Type | Description |
| --- | --- |
| Typical | Everything installed with defaults. |
| Minimum | Appropriate when SQL Server must run with limited disk space: Upgrade tools, client-management tools, Books On Line, and Development Tools are not installed. Appropriate for large "server farms." |
| Custom | All options installed as specified by the user. |

If you select Custom installation, you will be asked to select the specific components and features you wish to install.

As the installation progresses, the Windows account for SQL Server and its services must be identified. The authentication mode configures SQL Server to accept SQL Server user logins as well as Windows user logins.

When the installation program has gathered enough information, SQL Server will be installed onto the computer. The installer may shut down some tasks during the installation process.

## Unattended Installations

You may have to deploy SQL Server throughout the world, at hundreds of client sites, or on 200 servers in a server farm. Fortunately, you can install SQL Server using a predefined unattended-installation script. Performing unattended installations is basically a two-step process: The first step is creating the unattended script file, and the second is performing the unattended installation.

The unattended installation file, or Setup.IIS file, may be created manually, but the easiest way to generate the file is by letting the SQL Server setup program create it from a sample "mock" installation. Setup.IIS is automatically created during every installation. Selecting Record Unattended .IIS File in the Advanced Options inside setup will only create the required file and not actually install SQL Server. Setup.IIS is about two pages long; the first 10 lines run as follows:

```
[InstallShield Silent]
Version=v5.00.000
File=Response File
[File Transfer]
OverwriteReadOnly=NoToAll
[DlgOrder]
Dlg0=DlgW2kReboot-0
Count=13
Dlg1=SdWelcome-0
Dlg2=DlgMachine-0
...
```

Once the `setup.iis` file is created, a batch file can install SQL Server automatically from the command prompt. The SQL Server CD-ROM contains sample `.iis` and batch files.

## Installing Multiple Instances

SQL Server 2000 permits up to 16 instances of SQL Server running on a single physical server. To install additional instances, simply rerun the setup program. Instead of installing the default instance in the dialog page that asks for the server name, unselect the default instance checkbox and enter the instance name.

## Testing the Installation

The best way to test the installation is to connect to the SQL Server instance using Enterprise Manager or Query Analyzer, and browse the Northwind or Master databases.

# Installing Service Packs

Microsoft's practice is to release minor upgrades and fixes in the form of service packs. SQL Server 7.0 saw three service packs. At the time of this writing the first service pack has been made available for SQL Server 2000. You can download it from `www.microsoft.com/sql`.

You can determine the current version of SQL Server by selecting the @@Version system variable within T-SQL code, or by viewing the server properties in Enterprise Manager, as listed in Table 3-7.

### Table 3-7: SQL Server 2000 Service-Pack Versions

| SQL Server Service-Pack Version | @@Version |
| --- | --- |
| SQL Server 2000 RTM (release to manufacturing) | 8.00.194 |
| Database Components SP1 (released May 30, 2001) | 8.00.384 |
| SP2 | 8.00.534 |

Service Pack 1 only gives you the options of selecting a server and instance. If the server has multiple instances the service pack must be applied to each individually. The service pack upgrades the database engine, the client tools, and MDAC.

Service Pack 2 upgrades the database engine, the client tools, and Analysis Services.

When installing the service packs be sure to back up all databases, including system databases, users databases, and Analysis Services data, and stop SQL Server. Microsoft Knowledgebase article Q290211 includes a links to the list of SP2 fixes and the readme file.

# Upgrading from Previous Versions

Upgrading to a new database platform is potentially a major step in the life cycle of an application. An upgrade to SQL Server 2000 is an opportunity to review other aspects of the application and upgrade those as well.

## Upgrading from SQL Server 7

As of this writing SQL Server 7 is even with SQL Server 2000 in the number of installations, but many organizations are moving to SQL Server 2000.Because the two versions are architecturally so similar, the upgrade from SQL Server 7 to SQL Server 2000 is relatively straightforward.

SQL Server 2000 can even coexist with SQL Server 7 on the same physical server. When you're installing SQL Server 2000 on a server that is already running SQL Server 7, the installation routine will enable you to either overwrite SQL Server 7 or add SQL Server 2000. If both versions are installed on the same physical server, SQL Server 7 will have to be the default instance, because it does not understand instance names. You can install multiple instances of SQL Server 2000: Each will be installed as a named instance.

Only one version of each of the client tools (Enterprise Manager, Query Analyzer, and so on) may be installed. This does not present a problem because the SQL Server 2000 client tools will work fairly well with the SQL Server 7 engine. However, if you are supporting clients who use SQL Server 7 tools, the differences may prove frustrating.

There are several methods available to upgrade the server or databases from SQL Server 7 to SQL Server 2000:

✦ Upgrade an entire SQL Server 7 server and all databases during installation

✦ Back up databases from SQL Server 7 and restore on SQL Server 2000

✦ Detach a database from SQL Server 7 and attach it to SQL Server 2000

✦ Use the Copy Database Wizard

## Upgrading from SQL Server 6.5

At the time of this writing, about 5 percent of SQL Server installations are still running SQL Server Version 6.5. A wizard is available to aid in the move from SQL Server Version 6.5 to SQL Server 2000.

The SQL Server Upgrade Wizard will perform the upgrade from SQL Server 6.5 to SQL Server 2000. The wizard can upgrade on the same server or from a different server. To upgrade on the same server you need SQL Server 6.5 Service Pack 5a. You need Service Pack 3 or later to upgrade from a different server. Both servers must use Named Pipes communication.

The wizard can move the databases using a direct pipeline or using multiple tapes. The tape method is very slow. If at all possible, choose the direct pipeline.

The SQL Server Upgrade Wizard can move a significant amount of information during the upgrade, including:

✦ All or selected databases

✦ Logins

✦ Server-configuration properties (not recommended)

✦ SQL Executive settings (tasks, alerts, and jobs)

✦ Replication configuration (not recommended)

While moving the databases is the point of the upgrade, and moving logins may be a good idea if you're keeping the same login scheme, I urge you not to move the server and replication configurations. You're much better off reconfiguring the server and taking advantage of the increased administrative flexibility of SQL Server 2000.

It is possible to run SQL Server 6.5 and 2000 on the same server but not at the same time. SQL Server 6.5 and SQL Server 2000 are not compatible services and will not run concurrently. The Switch application (from the Start menu) will shut down whichever SQL Server version is running, and start the other version. The client tools, menus, and engine will all be switched. While this process is clumsy, at least it's possible so you can develop SQL Server 2000 databases and maintain SQL Server 6.5 databases on one computer.

## Upgrading from Versions Previous to 6.5

There is no direct path from SQL Server 4.2 or 6.0 to SQL Server 2000. A 4.2 database will need to be upgraded to 6.5 and then upgraded to 2000. A 6.0 database can be upgraded to SQL Server 6.5 or SQL Server 7.0 via the SQL Server Upgrade Wizard, and then upgraded to SQL Server 2000 via the tools within SQL Server 2000.

## After Upgrading

After upgrading from any previous SQL Server version, there are a few options that need to be manually configured:

✦ Perform a full population on any full text search catalog

✦ Update the statistics for all indexes using the `sp_updatestats` system stored procedure

✦ Re-establish replication using SQL Server 2000 replication

✦ Re-check all server-configuration properties

## Database Compatibility Level

During a conversion cycle, each database's compatibility level may be set to an earlier version so that older code will still function. The compatibility level affects only the T-SQL code syntax; all other SQL Server 2000 performance gains are still realized, even if the database is executing version 6.5 T-SQL code.

Within Enterprise Manager you may set, or check, the compatibility level by viewing the database properties, as shown in Figure 3-3. The compatibility level may also be set within code by using the `sp_dbcmptlevel` system stored procedure. The following code will set the OldOrderEntry database so that its T-SQL 7.0 code works correctly:

```
Exec sp_dbcmptlevel 'OldOrderEntry', 70
```

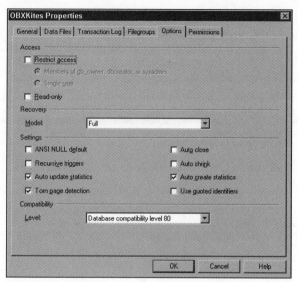

**Figure 3-3:** Setting the compatibility level in Enterprise Manager.

# Upsizing from Access

Many businesses and developers are moving from Access to a combination of Access and SQL Server. Moving to a client/server environment and taking advantage of the reliability of SQL Server is a wise move for users with applications that use business-critical data. To make the transition easier, Microsoft has included an Upsizing Wizard within Access.

I've heard developers say that Access is good for prototyping a database before moving it to SQL Server. I disagree. Good development practices in Access do not make good client/server applications. A working Access application must be rewritten for SQL Server.

Despite the ease of using the Upsizing Wizard, the conversion from Access to SQL Server is a major process.

## Converting to a Client/Server Design

From my experience, moving from Access to SQL Server is an opportunity to strengthen the design of the database.

Access applications tend to be form-centric. Code is executed on the form level, and forms are fed by queries, which often reference the form for filtering. Both of these practices make poor client/server applications. The goal of a smooth-upsizing project is to morph the application from an Access style into one that complies with the best practices of client/server design by doing the following:

✦ Moving the process as close to the data as possible

✦ Returning only the data that is strictly required

Specifically, consider the following issues when moving from Access to SQL Server:

✦ Moving code from forms to stored procedures or triggers

✦ Moving form-based data validation to SQL Server constraints

✦ Checking the normalization of the data schema

✦ Checking the integrity of the data and beginning to enforce referential integrity with DRI (Access applications often do not include referential integrity)

✦ Moving data-import and -export procedures from Access code or macros to DTS packages

✦ Moving Access crosstab queries to stored procedures or Analysis Services cubes

✦ Completely reevaluating indexing using the guidelines for SQL Server indexing

✦ Checking all form queries to eliminate selecting all rows (Access `.adp` project forms that select a single row based on the value of a combo box are very fast)

✦ Applying SQL Server security

✦ Moving Access action queries to stored procedures

Having performed several Access upsizing projects, I have found that no aspect of the project is untouched in the transition. I have used the following methodology when performing Access to SQL Server conversion:

1. Re-analyze the current project requirements

2. Prepare the SQL Server server

3. Move the Access schema using the Access Upsizing Wizard

4. Modify the SQL Server database

5. Create SQL Server stored procedures, triggers, and constraints

6. Build a reusable DTS package to convert the Access data to the new SQL Server database design

7. Build a new Access `.adp` file front end

8. Repeatedly convert the data and test the new database and front end during the development and testing process. During this time, there's nothing wrong with using the 120-day Evaluation Edition of SQL Server to test your database with less financial risk.

9. Perform the final data conversion to SQL Server

10. Tune the SQL Server database

## Using the Access Upsizing Wizard

The Access Upsizing Wizard is a slick utility that moves the data schema, data, rules, and referential integrity from Access to SQL Server. It can also build a client/server Access `.adp` project as a new front end. While it can't replace the database developer in making design modifications and improving the application, it does a good job of handling the drudgery and is a good start to upsizing a project.

The Access Upsizing Wizard (Figure 3-4) must be installed with the Advanced Wizards option during Access installation and is then located within Access under the Tools menu. The Upsizing Wizard will move data and objects from a single Access database (not a split database) to an Access/SQL Server client/server database. Tables and queries will be moved to a SQL Server database. Access forms, reports, and code will be moved to a new Access database project.

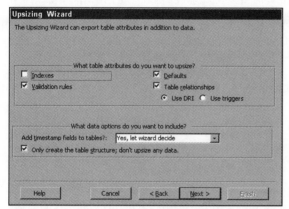

**Figure 3-4:** The Access Upsizing Wizard can move the schema and data to a SQL Server database.

Because Access 2000 shipped before SQL Server 2000, Access 2000 is unaware of new features in SQL Server 2000. The Upsizing Wizard in Access 2000 is intended to upsize the database to SQL Server 7.0. A patch, located at `http://office.Microsoft.com/2000/downloaddetails/Accsql.htm`, will modify an Office SR-1 copy of Access so that the Upsizing Wizard can upsize to SQL 2000.

To run the Upsizing Wizard, select the wizard from within the Access database to be upsized. The wizard will progress through the following options:

1. Create a new SQL Server database or upsize to an existing database. In organizations with tight security, it may be easier to ask a DBA to create a database than to request the necessary rights to permit the Upsizing Wizard to create the database.

2. Select the SQL Server/database and provide a SQL Server user name and password. To use Windows Authentication mode, leave the user name and password blank.

   If the Upsizing Wizard is unable to log in to SQL Server with the user name and password, a second login dialog box will appear and ask you to re-enter the user name and password. This second dialog box includes an option for a trusted connection to SQL Server that explicitly uses Windows Authentication.

3. Select the tables to upsize and the table upsizing options you want, including specifying which table attributes to upsize (Indexes, Validation Rules, Defaults, and Referential Integrity).

   SQL Server 2000 indexing is dramatically more complex than Access indexing. I recommend not moving the indexes from Access to SQL Server, and instead creating the indexes manually in SQL Server.

Referential integrity within the Access database can be transferred to the new SQL Server database via one of two methods. The Upsizing Wizard can either create triggers or SQL Server DRI (foreign keys) to enforce referential integrity. If Access referential integrity includes cascading deletes it can present a problem. SQL Server 7.0 DRI did not support cascading deletes and the Wizard will not move the cascading deletes even though SQL Server 2000 can implement DRI with cascading deletes.

Therefore, the only way to move cascading deletes using the Upsizing Wizard is to use triggers to enforce referential integrity in SQL Server 2000. I strongly recommend that you do not move the cascading deletes to triggers. The trigger code will be difficult to manage and slower than SQL Server 2000 DRI. Let the Wizard create DRI and recreate the cascading deletes in SQL Server 2000 after the upsizing process.

The Wizard can add timestamps to the tables during the upsizing, which can aid in detecting lost updates (see Chapter 11, "Transactional Integrity," for more information on lost updates).

By default the Wizard will move the data, but it can optionally move only the data structure.

4. The final set of options concerns the resulting front-end application used to connect to the new SQL Server database. The first option is to do nothing.

The second option is to modify the tables within the Access database so that they are linked tables pointing to the new tables within SQL Server. This option retains the Access .mdb file and Jet database. While this option keeps the Access queries that reference form controls intact, it fails to fully take advantage of client/server architecture.

Creating a new Access client/server project is the best option because it will create a new Access .adp project front-end file sans Jet database engine.

When complete, the Upsizing Wizard will present an Access report of its success and failures, including several warnings. This report can be very long, and it represents a one-time opportunity to see the issues the Upsizing Wizard didn't handle. Don't just close the report, review it carefully or print it.

## Access .adp Front-End Applications

Access 2000 introduced Access projects (.adp) as an alternative to Access databases (.mdb). The primary difference between the two is that the Access project drops the Jet database engine and becomes a relatively thin client on top of SQL Server, as shown in Table 3-8. I have personally found Access projects to be fast and efficient, providing the proper connection to SQL Server with the ease of Access form development.

### Table 3-8: Access Projects versus Databases

| Aspect | Access Database | Access Project |
|---|---|---|
| Database engine/architecture | Jet/desktop database. Unless queries are specifically written as pass-through queries, the Jet Engine retrieves all the data from SQL Server and performs the query locally. | SQL Server/client/server. A thin OLE DB layer passes all query work to SQL Server. |

| Aspect | Access Database | Access Project |
|---|---|---|
| File type | `.mdb` | `.adp` |
| Table relationships | A single Relationship diagram used to display and edit referential integrity. | Referential integrity established at the table level with foreign keys, or within multiple database diagrams. |
| Heterogeneous data | Yes, the JET engine may link to other data sources and tables outside the database. | Yes, SQL Server may link to other data sources and then the forms may access the data through SQL Server. |
| Stored SQL statements | Access Queries, precompiled, are stored in the `.mdb` and may reference form controls. | SQL Server Views, not precompiled, are stored in the server and may not reference any front-end forms or parameters. |
| Working with server-side code | Unable to expose SQL Server views, stored procedures, or functions for development use. | All server-side code is available to the developer. |

## Coding Efficient Access Project Forms

The key to building fast Access Projects is to code efficient forms that retrieve single rows from SQL Server. Whereas an Access Database might open a form with the entire table and permit the user to browse the data using the form, doing so works poorly in a client/server environment.

The best way to build an Access Project form is to code the form to retrieve only the selected row. Here's how to code such a form:

1. Enable the user to select a row by either entering a value into a textbox, selecting a row from a combo box, or selecting a row from a separate search list box.

2. From the value entered or selected by the user, determine the primary key of the row to be viewed in the form.

3. Update the form's `recordsource` property to retrieve the selected row, using code similar to the following in the `after update` event of the control used to select the row:

```
Private Sub cboSelectCustomer_AfterUpdate()
  Form.RecordSource =
    "Select * from Customer
       where CustomerID = " & Str(cboSelectCustomer)
End Sub
```

In this example from the CHA2 sample database, when the user selects a customer in the `cboSelectCustomer` dropdown list, the form quickly goes to that customer row and returns only the required columns. Access Project forms developed in this manner produce very fast database applications.

The Cape Hatteras Adventurers Access Project, `CHA2.adp`, demonstrates this form technique. Refer to Appendix B, "Sample Databases," for more information on the sample databases.

# Migrating to SQL Server

A recurring theme in database development is that most data has a history, and that baggage comes along with any conversion project. If you're moving to SQL Server from MySQL or Oracle, here are a few thoughts on the differences and the conversion process.

## Upgrading from MySQL

If you're moving from MySQL to SQL Server, I think you'll like what you find. Although MySQL is a nice database, it lacks some of the server-side functionality expected in a client/server database—namely stored procedures and triggers. For this reason, many of the same principles that apply to an Access conversion also apply to a MySQL conversion.

The most prominent conversion opportunity with the greatest gains in performance and data integrity is to master T-SQL and move code from the front-end client or middle tier to the server. You'll also find that SQL Server provides more flexibility, and complexity, in its administration options than MySQL.

## Migrating from Oracle

SQL Server and Oracle are comparable databases, and projects sometimes move from one to another. If you're moving a project from Oracle to SQL Server, here are a few differences you'll want to keep in mind:

✦ Oracle 7 and Oracle 8 do not recognize ANSI SQL 92 joins and are limited to ANSI SQL 89 syntax. As you move code to SQL Server you may want to begin writing in the newer, more readable style. Neither style provides a performance gain over the other.

✦ The two databases handle transaction-isolation levels differently. Oracle avoids dirty reads and non-repeatable reads with a read log, which ensures that other transactions will read the data as it was prior to changes. This method encourages developers to code with a style that permits long transactions.

SQL Server handles transaction isolation with the full set of four isolation levels, as opposed to Oracle's two levels; however, SQL Server takes a much more cautious position than Oracle and prevents cross-transaction problems with locks instead of a read log. For this reason, applications that are ported from Oracle to SQL Server tend to perform poorly, as they create lock contention.

Cross-Reference

Be sure to read the chapter 11, "Transactional Integrity," for guidelines on avoiding performance problems related to lock contention.

✦ Oracle's PL-SQL is different from SQL Server's Transact-SQL. One of the first differences you'll encounter is that transactions are implicit in Oracle but, by default, explicit in SQL Server. SQL operations occur when they are issued and don't require an explicit `commit trans`.

✦ SQL Server triggers fire once per operation, not once per row, while Oracle triggers may fire either per statement or per row. Be sure to write your code to handle the entire multi-row set of inserts or updates. Additionally, Oracle triggers may fire on more events (DDL commands) than SQL Server, and may be attached to system tables.

✦ It's much easier to return record sets from T-SQL stored procedures than from Oracle PL-SQL stored procedures.

✦ Oracle sequences are more robust than SQL Server identity columns.

✦ Of course, SQL Server and Oracle have different data types. In most cases SQL Server offers greater variety and precision than Oracle, and so moving from Oracle to SQL Server opens up more possibilities and resolves problems. Moving from SQL Server to Oracle can create data-type problems.

If you're migrating a serious project from Oracle to SQL Server, I recommend reading the 104-page Microsoft white paper, *Migrating Oracle Databases to SQL Server 2000*, available at http://www.microsoft.com/SQL/techinfo/deployment/2000/MigrateOracle.asp. The paper is also published within the SQL Server 2000 Resource Kit.

As with any other conversion project, I recommend creating a DTS package to handle the data transfer so that it's a repeatable process.

# Removing SQL Server

To remove SQL Server, use the Add/Remove Programs option in Window's Control Panel. Each instance of SQL Server is listed separately and may be uninstalled without affecting the other instances. If you remove the default instance, any named instances will continue to function properly.

User databases will not be deleted by the uninstall. If the databases are in the default data directory under SQL Server's program directories, those directories are left intact.

Copying a database to another server prior to removing an instance of SQL Server enables continued access to the data. If that's not possible, backup and restore the database to another server or attach the orphaned database to another server.

# Client Connectivity

In a client/server database, the server and client must be able to communicate. SQL Server communicates directly with the client without depending on the operating system. The twin network tools enable you to view and edit the current network protocol.

## Server Network Utility

The network protocol used by the server is initially set during installation and may be adjusted later via the SQL Server Network Utility (Figure 3-5). The utility may be launched from either the Start menu or Enterprise Manager. To launch it from Enterprise Manager, select the server and use the Action ⇨ All Tasks ⇨ Server Properties menu, or the right mouse menu. In the General tab, click the Network Configuration button.

The Server Network Utility presents a list of all the available protocols and communication options. The server must be restarted if the protocols are changed.

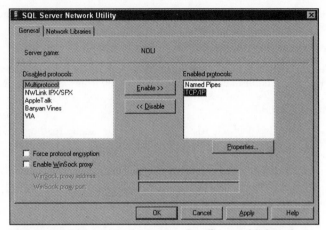

**Figure 3-5:** The SQL Server Network Utility establishes the connectivity protocols used by SQL Server to communicate with clients.

### Client Network Utility

The Client Network Utility establishes the protocol for the client. For nearly all installations the default protocol will work fine and this utility isn't necessary. But if the protocol varies from the default then this utility establishes the protocol at the client side of the connection. Its operation is similar to the Server Network Utility.

## Exploring System Databases and Tables

When SQL Server is initially installed, it already contains several system and user objects. Four system databases are used by SQL Server for self-management, two sample user databases are available for experimentation, and every database includes several system objects, including tables, views, stored procedures, and functions.

Within Enterprise Manager, the system objects might be hidden. In the Registered SQL Server Properties page you can choose what to display using the "Show system database and system objects" option, as shown in Figure 3-6.

### System Databases

SQL Server uses three system databases to store system information, track operations, and provide a temporary work area. In addition, the model database is a template for new user databases. These four system databases are:

✦ *Master*—Contains information about the server's databases. In addition, objects in Master are available to other databases. For example, stored procedures in Master may be called from a user database.

✦ *MSDB*—Maintains lists of activities, such as backups and jobs, and tracks which database backup goes with which user database.

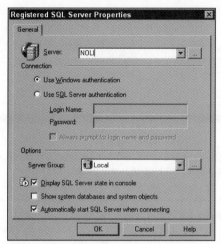

**Figure 3-6:** Choosing if system objects are hidden or displayed in the Registered SQL Server Properties dialog box.

✦ *Model* — The template database from which new databases are created. Any object placed in the Model database will be copied into any new database.

✦ *Tempdb* — Used for ad-hoc tables by all users, batches, stored procedures (including Microsoft stored procedures), and the SQL Server engine itself. If SQL Server needs to create temporary heaps or lists during query execution, it creates them in Tempdb. Tempdb is completely cleared when SQL Server is restarted.

## Pubs and Northwind

SQL Server ships with two small sample databases, Pubs and Northwind. Pubs, a database of fictional authors, books, and publishers has been with SQL Server since the beginning. Northwind, the database of a fictional distributor of fine foods, has been a sample database within Access since Access version 1. It joined SQL Server with version 7.0.

These two Microsoft databases are valuable for three reasons:

✦ They are frequently referred to by Books On Line and other instructional publications.

✦ They are commonly installed on every server, and easy to rebuild, making them well suited for experimentation. A SQL script to rebuild each sample database, `instnwnd. sql` and `instpubs.sql`, is located in `C:\Program Files\Microsoft SQL Server\ MSSQL\Install`.

✦ They demonstrate numerous database features, relationships, and possible practices.

The last benefit listed is also a hindrance. In demonstrating a variety of possibilities, Northwind includes several questionable database design practices. For example, the table `[Order Details]` includes a space thus requiring the brackets, the tables have plural names, no global unique identifies are used as primary keys, and the `Customers` table even uses a meaningful char column as a primary key! In addition, the `Region` column exists in the `Customers`, `Employees`, `Orders`, and `Suppliers` tables, yet none of these include foreign keys to the `Region` table.

While Pubs has a better relational model than Northwind, it is inconsistent and uses unfamiliar column names.

Aside from these issues, Northwind and Pubs are so commonly used for examples that it is worth your while to become familiar with them and to keep them loaded on your server.

## System Tables

Each database is defined by the information within the system tables listed in Table 3-9. SQL Server, as a relational database, maintains information about the database in relational tables. It's generally considered a dangerous practice to directly update the system tables; however, reading from the system tables can be useful. For example, DDL code commonly references SysObjects code prior to creating or dropping an object to see if the object exists.

### Table 3-9: SQL Server System Tables

| System Table | Description |
| --- | --- |
| SysColumns | Table/column definitions |
| SysComments | Code from views, stored procedures, triggers, and functions |
| SysDepends | Dependencies between objects based on foreign keys |
| SysFilegroups | Information about filgroups used by the database |
| SysFiles1 | The files for the database |
| SysFiles | The additional information about the database tables, including size |
| SysForeignKeys | Listing of the foreign keys |
| SysFulltextCateglogs | Listing of the full-text search catalogs |
| SysFullTextNotify | Additional information required by full-text search |
| SysIndexes | Information on the indexes within a table |
| SysIndexKeys | Primary keys |
| SysMembers | Users assigned to roles |
| SysObjects | Listing of all objects in the database |
| SysPermissions | Information about permissions granted and denied to users, groups, and roles in the database for the tables, views, stored procedures, etc. Also contains information about which users, groups, and roles have been granted or denied the various CREATE statements. |
| Sysproperties | Information on the processes currently running (only in the Master database) |
| Sysprotects | User object permissions (similar to SysPermissions) |
| Sysreferences | Foreign-key listings for each table |
| Systypes | System and user-defined data types |
| Sysusers | Database users (Windows or SQL Server users) |

# Information Schema Views

The design of system tables has changed before, and it's likely that Microsoft will revise the design in the future. Compounding the problem of future instability is the Microsoft-specific design of SQL Server's system tables. Building a system to read a database schema from any relational database would require a standard and permanent method of getting to the system tables.

The ANSI SQL 92 standard specifies several non-proprietary schema views with which to examine the schema of a database. Views are stored SQL statements that enable the user to refer to a complex SQL statement using the name of the view. The Information Schema views, listed in Table 3-10, extract database-design information from SQL Server's system tables.

## Table 3-10: ANSI Information Schema Views

| System Table | Description |
| --- | --- |
| CHECK_CONSTRAINTS | Check constraints in the database |
| COLUMN_DOMAIN_USAGE | Columns in the database that reference user-defined data types |
| COLUMN_PRIVILEGES | Column-security information |
| COLUMNS | All columns in the database |
| CONSTRAINT_COLUMN_USAGE | Columns with constraints |
| CONSTRAINT_TABLE_USAGE | Table constraints |
| DOMAIN_CONSTRAINTS | User-defined data types with bound rules |
| DOMAINS | User defined data types |
| KEY_COLUMN_USAGE | Primary keys |
| PARAMETERS | Stored procedure and user-defined function parameters |
| REFERENTIAL_CONSTRAINTS | Foreign keys |
| ROUTINE_COLUMNS | Table-function columns |
| ROUTINES | Stored procedures and functions |
| SCHEMATA | Databases available to the current user |
| TABLE_CONSTRAINTS | Table constraints including check constraints, unique constraints, primary keys, and foreign keys |
| TABLE_PRIVILEGES | User permissions and ownership for tables |
| TABLES | All tables |
| VIEW_COLUMN_USAGE | Table columns used in views |
| VIEW_TABLE_USAGE | Tables used in views |
| VIEWS | Views |

The Information Schema views are stored in the Master database and owned by information schema. Because they are in the Master database they are available from any database and will present the schema for the current database from which they are accessed.

The Information Schema views are strongly influenced by the permissions of the current user. Nearly every view presents not all the information from the system tables, but only the information the current user has permission to access.

## Summary

SQL Server 2000 is easy to install; the work is in the planning. Most projects have a history and the installation is probably another upgrade in the life of the project rather than a fresh new database. Nevertheless, SQL Server installation and configuration are relatively smooth processes.

With SQL Server installed, the next chapter examines SQL Server's developer tools, Service Manager, Enterprise Manager, and Query Analyzer.

✦　　✦　　✦

# Using SQL Server's Developer Tools

SQL Server provides a wealth of developer interfaces. The three interfaces most commonly used by SQL developers and DBAs are Service Manager, Enterprise Manager, and Query Analyzer. These client tools enable the developer or DBA to control SQL Server and develop database projects with either a GUI interface or T-SQL code.

This chapter's purpose is not to explain the use of every option within the tools, but to point out a few of the interesting features and to help you get comfortable with navigating, exploring, and using the developer interfaces.

## Using Service Manager

Although the Service Manager is physically loaded on the server, it is actually a client process that can start or stop several server processes, as shown in Figure 4-1. Service Manager's functionality comes in addition to the operating-system interfaces within Administrative Tools that can also start and stop services. SQL Server's Service Manager is nothing more than an additional tool for controlling SQL Server. SQL Server does not require Service Manager to be loaded or running; it is only an extra convenience.

By default, SQL Server adds Service Manager to the start-up menu group so that it loads when the operating system starts. If Service Manager is removed from the start-up menu group, SQL Server's server processes will still start and function normally.

Service Manager provides the following benefits:

✦ A DBA interface with which to define the SQL Server instances and processes to start when the operating system loads.

✦ An easy method of starting and stopping any SQL Server process, on any server.

✦ A visual indication of the run status of a process.

However, these minor benefits come at a high cost:

✦ The process `sqlmanager.exe` occupies about 3MB of memory.

✦ SQL Manager regularly polls the service, a cost which is insignificant compared to the memory footprint.

My personal practice is to remove Service Manger from the start-up menu group and launch it from the Start menu when I need it.

**Figure 4-1:** Service Manager can control any server process for any SQL Server instance.

Every server process may be controlled within Service Manager. The system tray displays the selected service (listed in Table 4-1). The default service may be selected within the options.

## Table 4-1: SQL Server Processes

| Server Process | Description | Count |
| --- | --- | --- |
| SQL Server | The database engine | 1 per instance |
| SQL Server Agent | Executes jobs | 1 per instance |
| Microsoft Search | Executes full-text searches | 1 per physical server |
| Distributed Transaction Coordinator | Controls multi-server transactions | 1 per physical server |
| MSSQLServerOLAP Service | Analysis Services | 1 per physical server |

SQL Server Service Manager will display the current running state of any server process in the dialog box and in the system tray icon. By default, it displays the local server's default instance, but that may be changed in the options.

Service Manager has four tasks for SQL Server: starting SQL Server, pausing SQL Server, resuming SQL Server, and stopping SQL Server:

✦ Starting a SQL Server instance — This action launches the SQL Server engine and performs a recovery.

✦ Pausing a SQL Server instance — A paused SQL Server instance will continue to complete any current work; the only restriction is that new connections are prohibited. Depending on the method used to program it, a pooled connection might be open for a long time. The intention is that a paused server will allow time for a controlled shut-down of the server and for notification to be sent to the users, perhaps by means of a net send command.

✦ Resuming a paused SQL Server instance.

✦ Stopping a SQL Server instance — initiates the following shut-down procedure within SQL Server:

1. All logins are disabled except for those of users assigned to the system-administrator role.

2. Any running SQL transactions or stored procedures are allowed to finish execution. This is important for maintaining the ACID properties of the database.

3. A checkpoint is performed for every database. Checkpoints are important to the recovery model.

4. The SQL Service stops execution.

To manage the processes, the user must be a Windows local administrator (or domain admin) to start and stop processes.

SCM.exe is a command-line companion to Service Manager and, like Service Manager, can start, pause, or stop services.

# Using Enterprise Manager

Perhaps no other feature has welcomed more new DBAs to SQL Server more than Enterprise Manager. Its well-organized, inviting, and powerful interface feels familiar and its very structure helps a new DBA explore and become familiar with the various aspects of SQL Server.

A common misconception among new DBAs is that Enterprise Manager *is* SQL Server. It's not. Enterprise Manager is a client front-end tool used to manage SQL Server. Enterprise Manager sends T-SQL commands to SQL Server. It also inspects SQL Server and presents the data and configuration for viewing. An important feature to organizations with multiple servers is that Enterprise Manager can connect to, or register, multiple instances of SQL Server, reducing the travel required to manage disparate servers.

**Cross-Reference**  It's very interesting to watch the commands sent by Enterprise Manager to SQL Server. Chapter 28, "Advanced Performance," includes information about configuring SQL Profiler, which can display nearly any detail of the traffic between the engine and its clients.

## The Microsoft Management Console Add-In

The Microsoft Management Console (MMC) is employed throughout Windows operating systems as a standard plug-and-play container for several utilities and administrative tools. Its familiar tree-and-list interface brings consistency to the look and feel of various system administrative tasks. To experiment with MMC, try launching it as an empty shell with the following command: Run mmc.exe

You can build your own custom MMC console, one that includes the add-ins you use frequently, with the Console ➪ Add/Remove Snap-in menu command and the Add button. Figure 4-2 shows a custom MMC. Additional menus will appear in the MMC depending on the current add-in.

Interestingly, the SQL Server MMC add-in is also installed inside Administrative Tools/Computer Management/Services, and Applications.

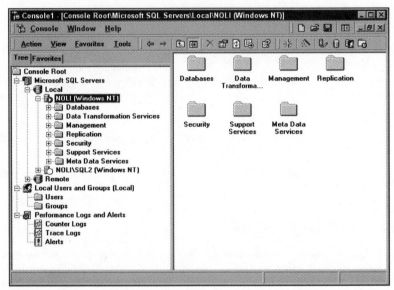

**Figure 4-2:** This custom MMC tree includes Enterprise Manager, Windows users, and Performance Monitor.

## Connecting to a Server

The first step in connecting to a server instance from Enterprise Manager is to register the instance within Enterprise Manager. An instance may be registered using the Register Server Wizard, or from the right-mouse menu under Server Groups.

Registering the server establishes the connection and user-authentication information so Enterprise Manager can access the server, as shown in Figure 4-3. A key option in the Registered SQL Server Properties dialog box is the "Show system databases and system objects" checkbox, which enables or disables the display of system objects when viewing tables, views, and stored procedures.

Within the Enterprise Manager tree, servers may be organized by server groups. There's no meaning whatsoever to these groups; their only purpose is to visually group the servers within the tree.

**Caution** Because Enterprise Manager and SQL Server are communicating as client and server, the two processes are not always in sync. Changes on the server are often not reflected in Enterprise Manager unless Enterprise Manager is refreshed. Even then, Enterprise Manager will rarely catch every change in SQL Server. The last resort is to disconnect from the server and reconnect, which forces a complete refresh.

## Server Properties

Right-clicking on a server and selecting Properties will open the Server Property dialog. This dialog collects in one location the necessary server-configuration options.

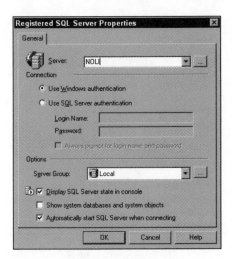

**Figure 4-3:** Registering a SQL Server within Enterprise Manager so it can connect to the server.

## Navigating the Tree

In keeping with the Explorer metaphor, the tree on the left side of Enterprise Manager (Figure 4-4) is a hierarchical, expandable view of the objects available within the registered servers. A tree is built of roots and nodes. For example, within the Windows Explorer tree, the desktop is the root and all folders or devices expand under the desktop as nodes. Enterprise Manager's tree structure is standardized, or fixed, within a server. However, additional tree nodes are added as servers are enabled for replication and articles are published.

The first two levels of the tree present the registered SQL Server instances and their relative statuses, organized by server groups. The icons representing the server indicate the current SQL Server instance status, as follows:

✦ Green indicates the server is running

✦ Green circle indicates Enterprise Manager is connected to the server

Under each server is a node for the server's databases, DTS packages, server management, replication, security, support services, and metadata services.

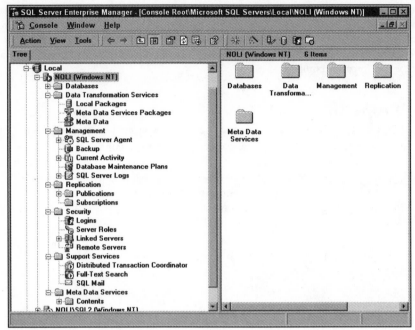

**Figure 4-4:** Enterprise Manager's tree structure invites the DBA to explore the various components of SQL Server management.

The database node contains all the server's databases. When you right-click on a database, the menu includes a host of options and commands. If the database is in Taskpad view, the right-side pane will provide the three Taskpad options of the database. Under each database are standard nodes (Figure 4-5), which manage the following database objects:

✦ *Diagrams* — Illustrate several tables and their relationships. A database may contain multiple diagrams, and each diagram does not need to display all the tables. This makes it easy to organize large databases into modular diagrams.

✦ *Tables* — Used to create and modify the design of tables, view and edit the contents of tables, and work with the tables' indexes, permissions, and publications. Triggers, stored procedures that respond to data-modification operations (insert, update, and delete), may be created and edited here. The only way to launch the Query Designer is from the table listing.

✦ *Views* — Stored SQL statements. They are listed, created, and edited, and the results viewed, from this node.

✦ *Stored procedures* — Pre-compiled batches of T-SQL statements that are the fastest means of programming SQL Server applications.

✦ *Users* — First declared as authorized within the server, but must be specifically authorized for any given database in order to use it.

✦ *Roles* — Similar to security groups, roles are used to assign database-object permissions to sets of users in a consistent security design.

✦ *Rules* — May be predefined and then bound to table columns providing methods of organizing rules. Alternately, table constraints may be used to restrict data entry.

✦ *Defaults* — Defined under this node and then bound to a data column. Default constraints may also be assigned directly within the tables.

✦ *User-defined data types* — SQL Server data types with pre-assigned lengths, nullability, default, and data validation rules may be named as user-defined data types and then consistently employed within data schemas.

✦ *User-defined functions* — New to SQL Server 2000, custom functions are extremely powerful, compiled, and way cool. Chapter 14, "Building User-Defined Functions," explains how to create and reference user-defined Functions.

✦ *Full-text catalogs* — Full-text searches use catalogs, which are maintained by Search Engine in Windows. This node helps organize those catalogs.

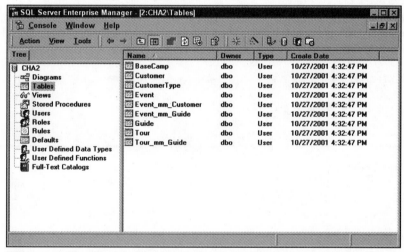

**Figure 4-5:** The simpler view of only the Cape Hatteras Adventures database.

Continuing on with the first level of the tree (refer back to Figure 4-4):

✦ *Data Transformation Services* — Lists the DTS packages for the server and the metadata services used with DTS.

✦ *Management* — DBA functions, including SQL Server Agent's alerts, operators, and jobs, backup devices, processes and locks, maintenance plans, and logs, are organized under this node.

✦ *Replication* — Articles (tables, views, and stored procedures) that are published for replication or subscribed to, are organized under this node.

✦ *Security*—User logins and server roles are organized under this node, as well as standing connections to linked servers and remote servers.

✦ *Support services*—The Distributed Transaction Coordinator, Full-Text Search Engine, and SQL Mail item are organized under this node.

✦ *Meta Data Services*—Metadata are an advanced means of identifying the design of the database, or information about the data, for data sharing. Metadata is defined and maintained in this node.

The tree can be very busy on a server with multiple databases. To create a new tree with nodes pertinent to your current task, right-click the node of interest and select New Window from Here. Figure 4-5 shows Enterprise Manager displaying only the Cape Hatteras Adventurers sample database in the window.

## Taskpad

The Taskpad view (Figure 4-6), available for servers and databases, is enabled by selecting Taskpad from the View menu. To turn off the Taskpad, reselect an icon or list view. The Taskpad is turned on or off on a server-by-server, or database-by-database, basis.

While the Taskpad contains many excellent features, I have found it to be error-prone. If the Taskpad begins to generate errors (often indicating that it can't find its own internal variables), the only solution is to close and restart Enterprise Manager.

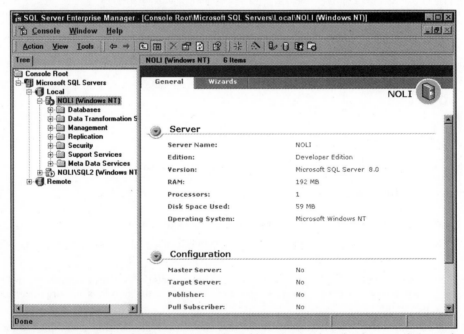

**Figure 4-6:** The Taskpad offers a means of quickly reviewing key database statistics and launching common tasks.

## Menus and Toolbars

Enterprise Manager's Toolbar interface consists of a menu bar and two toolbars. From left to right, the interface contains:

✦ *Action menu* — Essentially the same as the right-click menu.

✦ *View menu* — Changes the view style (icon, detail list, and so on) of the item in the right-hand pane.

✦ *Tool menu* — Presents many tasks and tools pertaining to SQL Server administration.

✦ *Previous Item/Next Item/Up Level buttons* — Performs the same tree navigation functions as in Windows Explorer.

✦ *Show/Hide Console Tree button* — Shows or hides the left-hand pane containing the console tree.

✦ *Delete button* — No surprises here: This button deletes the currently selected item.

✦ *Properties button* — Opens the Properties page for the selected item.

✦ *Refresh button* — The right-click menu of most tree nodes includes a refresh command. This button also refreshes the currently selected tree node.

✦ *Export button* — Not a Database Export Wizard tool. Instead, it exports to a text file the contents of the Enterprise Manager list in the left-hand pane.

✦ *Help button* — Provides context-sensitive help.

✦ *Wizards button* — Opens the Wizards dialog box, which contains 23 wizards.

✦ *New button* — Creates a new object of whichever object type is selected in the tree.

The following four buttons launch wizards that perform basic "new installation" tasks. They aren't very useful for experienced DBAs or developers:

✦ *Register Server*

✦ *New Database*

✦ *New Login*

✦ *New Job*

## The Right-Click Menu

In keeping with the Microsoft Windows interface standards, the right-click menu is the primary means of selecting actions or viewing properties throughout Enterprise Manager. The right-click menu for a server or database includes submenus for new objects, and `all tasks`. These are the workhorse menus within Enterprise Manager.

## The Wizards

Enterprise Manager includes 23 wizards, most of which are available from the Wizards button on the toolbar or the Wizards command in the Tools menu. Both bring up a Select Wizard dialog box (Figure 4-7) that lists the wizards that are appropriate for the currently selected object in the console tree in a tree structure. While the database wizards are not particularly useful, the DTS, maintenance, and replication wizards are.

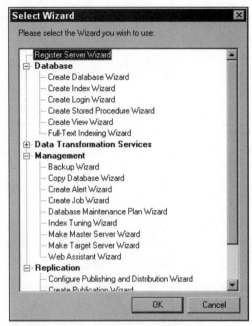

**Figure 4-7:** The Select Wizard dialog box presents a tree containing 23 wizards.

The Taskpad view (discussed previously in this chapter), includes a tab that lists the appropriate wizards for the server or database selected, as well as other tasks suitable for the currently selected item. Several of the wizards are also available from individual actions.

An advantage of the Wizards dialog box is that a wizard is still available through it even if the wizard's "don't use this wizard again" checkbox has been enabled, causing the standard dialogs to open instead of the wizards.

Wizards of note include:

✦ *DTS Import/Export Wizard* — Creates a simple DTS package with which to move data between SQL Server and an external database. Using this wizard is a good way to begin exploring DTS.

✦ *Copy Database Wizard* — One of the best means of moving a database along with all logins, permissions, and so on to another server.

✦ *Database Maintenance Plan Wizard* — Generates a complete database-maintenance plan including optimizations, backups, and integrity checks.

✦ *Index Tuning Wizard* — Analyzes a single query, or a full set of traffic captured by the Profiler, and suggests useful indexes.

✦ *Web Assistant Wizard* — Creates a simple HTML page that lists data. The wizard can set up a job or trigger to automatically recreate the HTML page when the underlying data is changed.

✦ All the replication wizards are useful. Since setting up replication is probably not a daily process, the wizards walk through what can be a complex task. Also, in my experience, disabling replication is nearly impossible without the assistance of the wizard.

## The Table Design View

Creating a new table, or editing the design of an existing table, is easy with the Table Design view. The Table Design view (Figure 4-8) is very similar to Access's Relationship view and other database design tool interfaces. A new table may be created by selecting the table node in the tree, and then selecting New table from the right-click menu. The design of existing tables may be edited by selecting the table, right-clicking, and selecting Design view from the right-click menu.

Columns may be individually selected and edited in the top pane. The column properties for the selected column are listed in the bottom pane.

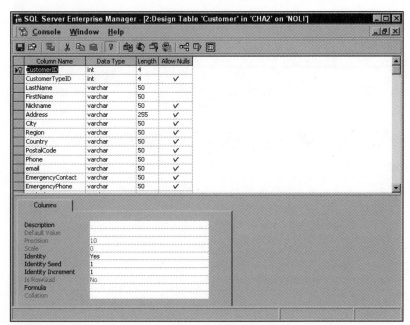

**Figure 4-8:** Tables may be created or their designs edited using the Table Design tool.

# Building Database Diagrams

The Database Designer takes the Table Design view up a notch by adding custom table design views (Figure 4-9) and a multi-table view of the foreign-key relationships. The Database Designer has its own node under each database. Each database may contain multiple diagrams, which makes working with very large databases easier because each module, or section, of the database may be represented by a diagram.

Personally, I like the Database Designer, but some developers think it's clumsy in two areas. The major complaint is that the relationship lines connect the tables without pointing to the primary- and foreign-key columns. This problem is compounded by another: the frustrating tendency of the lines to become pretzels when tables or lines are moved. However, I find that the Database Designer is most useful for working with very large databases. In this situation, primary tables often have dozens of connecting lines. If the lines were automatically linked to the primary key, the result would be an unreadable mess.

A major advantage to using the Database Designer, as I see it, is the customizable table-design views (Figure 4-10), which are far superior to the standard Enterprise Manager Table Design view. Different styles of database design require different column properties. The custom view (available from the right mouse menu) presents only the selected column properties.

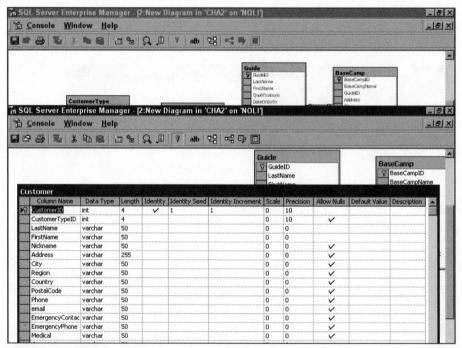

**Figure 4-9:** The Cape Hatteras Adventures database relationships viewed with the Database Designer.

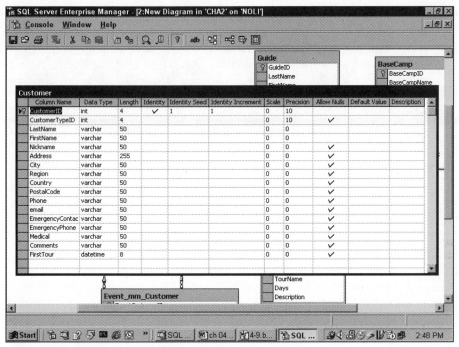

**Figure 4-10:** The custom table view within Database Designer is one of the highlights of Enterprise Manager.

## The Query Designer

The Query Designer is a popular tool for data retrieval and modification, even though it's nearly hidden within Enterprise Manager. The only way to open the Query Designer is to drill into the table listing under a database, select a table, and then select Open Table from the Action menu or right-click menu. The Query Designer always opens with a single table, and there's no way to simply open the Query Designer without a table.

Unlike other query tools that alternate among a graphic view, a SQL text view, and the query results, Enterprise Manager's Query Designer simultaneously displays multiple panes (Figure 4-11) as selected with the view buttons in the toolbar:

✦ *Diagram pane* — Multiple tables or views may be added to the query and joined together in this graphic representation of the select statement's from clause.

✦ *Grid pane* — Lists the columns being displayed, filtered, or sorted.

✦ *SQL pane* — The raw SQL select statement may be entered or edited in this pane.

✦ *Results pane* — When the query is executed with the Run button (!), the results are captured in the Results pane. If the results are left untouched for too long, Enterprise Manager will request permission to close the connection.

The Query Designer can perform DML (Data Manipulation Language — select, insert, update, delete) queries besides select. Unlike Query Analyzer, it cannot perform batches or non-DML commands.

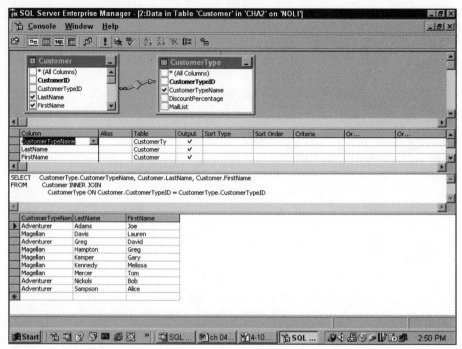

**Figure 4-11:** Enterprise Manger's Query Designer.

The Query Designer may be used to edit data directly in the Results pane—a quick and dirty way to correct or mock up data. Occasionally, you'll see an error message that says, "Cannot edit data while in Firehose mode." This means that the Query Designer is still retrieving data. Waiting a few seconds to give Enterprise Manager a chance to catch up with SQL Server will normally resolve the error.

Navigating the Query Designer should feel familiar to experienced Windows users. While Books On Line lists several pages of keyboard shortcuts, most are standard Windows navigation commands. The one that is worth repeating here is Control+zero, which enters a `null` into the result pane.

## Top 10 Enterprise Manager Annoyances

Every SQL Server developer spends a significant portion of his or her life using these tools. Since programmers tend to think in terms of design and development, I imagine most developers have their own pet peeves about whichever development tool they use. Here's my Top 10 list of things I hate about SQL Server's development tools:

**10.** Query Analyzer and Enterprise Manager's Query Designer are inconsistent in how common developer tasks are performed, for example:

✦ QA will execute a query with F5; QD won't.

✦ QA permits changing the font; QD doesn't.

✦ QD automatically renders SQL keywords in caps; QA color-codes them.

✦ QA will save the code; QD won't.

9. Launching Enterprise Manager's Query Designer is clumsy. It's a good tool and should be promoted to the top layer of the interface, instead of being buried five clicks under the database. It should be available directly from the database level with a dialog box for selecting the first table in the query.

8. Double-clicking a table in Enterprise Manager should open either the design view or the Query Designer. Opening a non-editable property page is useless, non-intuitive, and inconsistent with the Windows standard that the double-click performs a task.

7. The Database Designer should have the option of connecting the relationship lines to the columns. The connector style should be configurable (ER diagrams, Chen diagrams, etc.).

6. The Taskpad is incorrectly located in the menu. A check indicates that you can turn it off by clicking the option again. But Taskpad is not an on-off option; it's one of a series of exclusive options including the icons. The Taskpad should be a Windows radio button instead of a checkbox. This is a novice design flaw and causes developers to avoid the Taskpad, thinking that it won't go away when it's turned off.

5. Enterprise Manager needs to handle automatic refreshes better. Often, Enterprise Manager must be manually refreshed before it will show current information.

4. Enterprise Manager, in conjunction with the SQL Profiler, needs a wizard that performs a consistency check to locate unused code or columns.

3. Enterprise Manager should provide developers with a way to view the security permissions for any user or object that properly combines all the permissions a user might have for an object or task and displays the effective permission level.

2. Other programming editors include code beautifiers that automatically aid developers in formatting code according to the formatting options. SQL statements tend to be long and consistent formatting improves the readability. I love a good formatting tool.

1. XML is becoming so important that DTS needs an XML import/export connector, and both Query Analyzer and Enterprise Manager need a good XML viewer.

In addition to the current problems there are two issues that are solved with third-party tools. It's difficult to recommend that Microsoft incorporate features from third-party utilities, because it's healthy for us as a community for the add-on market to flourish. However, these utilities fill obvious voids in the SQL Server feature set:

✦ Enterprise Manager desperately needs a good database schema–reporting tool like FMS's *Total SQL Server Analyzer*.

✦ Viewing or understanding the Transaction Log is vital to T-SQL programming. A feature similar to Lumigent's *Log Explorer* to illuminate the T-Log would be wonderful.

Evaluation editions of both of these utilities are on the book's CD.

# Using Query Analyzer

Query Analyzer (often called QA) is a dream tool for a SQL developer. I know several well-respected SQL Server developers who make it their practice never to use Enterprise Manager. They do all their work in Query Analyzer. While I use both tools and tend to like graphical interfaces, I must admit to being fond of SQL Server 2000's Query Analyzer. It is a well-polished developer's tool.

## Connecting to a Server

Query Analyzer can maintain multiple open windows and connections, as demonstrated in Figure 4-12. In fact, different windows may be connected as different users, which is very useful for testing security.

When Query Analyzer first opens it will prompt for an initial login. To make further connections, use the File ➪ New Connection menu command. The window title displays the current SQL Server and login user.

In Figure 4-12, the top window is logged in as Paul using Windows Authentication and the code can `select` from the customer table. However, the second window is logged in as James, who has been denied permission to select from the customer table.

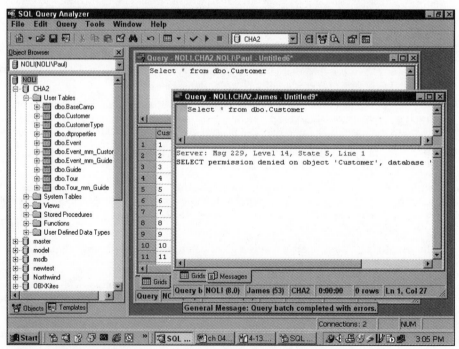

**Figure 4-12:** Query Analyzer can open multiple connections to SQL Server.

## Executing SQL Batches

As a developer's tool, QA is designed to execute T-SQL batches, which are collections of multiple T-SQL statements. To submit a batch to SQL Server for processing, use Query ➪ Execute Query, click on the Run Query toolbar button, use the F5 key, or press control-E.

Because batches tend to be long, and it's often desirable to execute a single T-SQL command or a portion of the batch for testing or stepping through the code, the SQL Server team provides you with a convenient feature. If no text is highlighted, the entire batch is executed. If text is highlighted, only that text is executed.

It's worth pointing out that the Parse Query menu command and toolbar button only checks the SQL code. It does not check object names (tables, columns, stored procedures, and so on). This actually is a feature, not a bug. By not including object name–checking in the syntax check, SQL Server permits batches that create objects and then references them.

The T-SQL batch will execute within the context of a database. The current database is displayed, and may be changed, within the database combo box in the toolbar. While each SQL Server user may be assigned a default database, this is often ignored along with the current Query Analyzer database. The result is that the user's initial current database is the Master system database, and it tends to collect junk that's created in the Master database by accident by T-SQL commands running in Query Analyzer.

The results of the query are displayed in the bottom pane. The format may be either text or grid; you can switch using Ctrl-T or Ctrl-D, respectively. The new format will be applied to the next batch execution.

While working with T-SQL code in Query Analyzer, you can get Books On Line (BOL) keyword help by pressing Shift+F1.

## Opening and Saving Scripts

The development style based on Query Analyzer, as opposed to Enterprise Manager graphic tools, tends to work heavily with saved scripts. It's the repeatability of the code as it goes through multiple iterations of improvement that draws developers to Query Analyzer.

As you would expect, the File Open, Save, and Save as commands open or save T-SQL scripts as `.sql` files. These files are simple text files. The sample databases on the CD-ROM are stored in this manner.

I recommend that you configure Windows file associations to open `.sql` files using `C:\Program Files\Microsoft SQL Server\80\Tools\Binn\isqlw.exe`. This will enable you to double-click an `.sql` file in Windows Explorer and open it with QA.

## Object Browser

One of the exciting new features of SQL Server 2000 is the QA Object Browser, previously shown in the left-hand side of Figure 4-12. This tree representation of the database objects includes three significant features:

- ✦ The ability to generate scripts that modify objects. For example, the right-click menu for a stored procedure enables you to launch a new window and generate the `alter` command for that stored procedure.

- ✦ The stored-procedure debugger, also launched from the right-click menu inside the Object Browser, is useful for tracing T-SQL code.

- ✦ Object names and functions can be dragged from the Object Browser to a batch window.

## Templates

The Query Analyzer templates (Figure 4-13) are worth mentioning even though they have received mixed reviews. The ability to create a new object from a template is a good idea. It helps make the code consistent.

Microsoft must love templates, because there's a menu command and two buttons on the toolbar for creating an object using a template. The first button, New Query, includes a dropdown arrow that lists templates. The fourth button in the toolbar opens a template browser that may be used to select a template file.

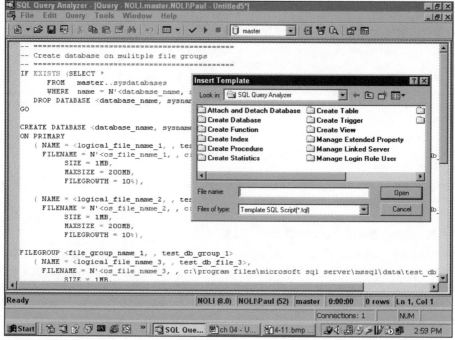

**Figure 4-13:** The Query Analyzer templates provide all of the syntax and code you need to create an object.

Once the template is selected and the code is pasted into a Query Analyzer window, the code options may be manually edited. Alternately, the Edit ⇨ Replace Template Parameters menu opens a dialog box with the code options for that current template.

The templates are simply stored SQL scripts within a directory structure, which means that it's easy to create your own templates or to modify the existing ones. The template directory is specified in the General tab of the Options dialog box. This let's several developers share a common set of templates on a network drive.

For developers or organizations desiring consistency in their own development styles or standards, I highly recommend taking advantage of Query Analyzer templates.

## Viewing Query Execution Plans

Since the name of the tool is Query Analyzer, one of the most significant features is the ability to graphically view Query Execution Plans (Figure 4-14).

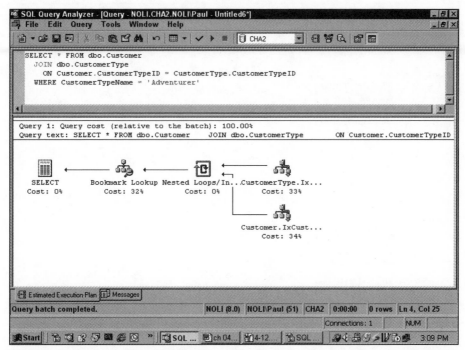

**Figure 4-14:** Query Analyzer's ability to graphically display the execution plan of a query is perhaps its most useful feature.

What makes the Query Execution Plans even more important is that SQL is a descriptive language and does not tell the Query Optimizer exactly how to go get the data but only which data to retrieve. While some performance tuning can be applied to the way the query is stated, most of the tuning is accomplished by adjusting the indexes, which greatly affect how the Query Optimizer can compile the query. The Query Execution Plan reveals how SQL Server will optimize the query, take advantage of indexes, pull data from other data sources, and perform joins. Reading the Query Execution Plans and understanding their interaction with the database schema and indexes is both a science and an art.

**Cross-Reference**    Chapter 28, "Advanced Performance," includes a full discussion on reading the Query Execution Plan and tuning the underlying indexes.

Query Analyzer can display either an estimated Query Execution Plan prior to executing the query, or the actual plan after the query is run.

# Summary

Enterprise Manager and Query Analyzer are the two primary DBA and developer interfaces for SQL Server. Mastering the navigation of both of these tools is vital to success with SQL Server.

With this understanding of the development interfaces as a foundation, the next part of the book discusses building the database, manipulating data, and coding T-SQL procedures, functions, and triggers.

✦      ✦      ✦

# Developing SQL Server Databases

◆ ◆ ◆ ◆

◆ ◆ ◆ ◆

When I was in the Navy, I learned more from Master Chief Miller than he or I probably realized at the time. One of his theories was that an application was half program and half data. In my twenty some odd years of developing databases, my experience agrees with the Master Chief.

The data, both the schema and the data itself, is often more critical to the success of a project than the application code. The primary features of the application are designed at the data schema level. If the data schema supports a feature then the code will readily bring the feature to life. But, if the feature is not designed in the tables, then the front-end forms can jump through as many hoops as can be coded and it will never work right.

Part II is all about developing the database, thinking inside the box, and moving the processing as close to the data as possible.

# Implementing the Physical Database Schema

**D**atabase performance begins with the design of the physical database schema. This chapter could have been called, "Advanced Performance - Step 1."

The logical database schema, discussed in Chapter 2, "Modeling the Logical Database Schema," is a purely academic exercise designed to ensure the business requirements are understood. A logical design has never stored nor served up any data. In contrast, the physical database schema is an actual data store, that must consider not only data integrity and the user requirements, but also performance, agility, query paths, and maintainability as the database is implemented within the nitty-gritty syntax of the particular database platform.

Every project team develops the physical database schema drawing from these two disciplines (logical data modeling and physical schema design) in one of the following possible combinations:

✦ A logical database schema is designed and then implemented without the benefit of physical schema development.

This plan is a sure way to develop a slow and unweildy database schema. The application code will be frustrating to write and the code will not be able to overcome the performance limitations of the design.

✦ A logical database schema is developed to ensure the business requirements are understood. Based on the logical design, the database development team develops a physical database schema. This method can result in a fast, usable schema.

Developing the schema in two stages is a good plan if the development team is large enough and one team is designing and collecting the business requirements and a subsequent team is developing the physical database schema. An area of caution is to be sure that having a completed logical database schema does not squelch the team's brainstorming as the physical database schema is designed.

✦ The third combination of logical and physical design methodologies combines the two into a single development step as the database development team develops a physical database schema directly from the business requirements.

This method can work well providing that the team fully understands both logical database modeling, physical database modeling, and advanced query design.

The key task in designing a physical database schema is brainstorming multiple possible designs that each meet the user requirements and ensure data integrity. Each design is evaluated based on its simplicity, performance of possible query paths, flexibility, and maintainability.

This chapter discusses designing the physical database schema and then focuses on the data-definition language commands `create`, `alter`, and `drop`. These three commands are used to build the physical database schema.

The actual implementation of the physical design involves these six components:

✦ Creating the database files.

✦ Creating the tables.

✦ Creating the primary and foreign keys.

✦ Creating the data columns.

✦ Adding data-integrity constraints.

✦ Creating indexes.

Translating the logical database schema into a physical database schema may involve the following changes:

✦ Converting complex logical designs into simpler, more agile table structures.

✦ Converting composite primary keys to computer-generated single-column primary keys.

✦ Converting the business rules to constraints.

✦ Converting logical many-to-many relationships to two one-to-many relationships with a junction table.

# Designing the Physical Database Schema

When designing the physical design, the design team should begin with a clean logical design and/or well-understood and documented business rules, and then brainstorm until a simple, flexible design emerges that performs great.

## The Designing for Simplicity and Agility

The great truths in life are simple. And the same is true of great database designs. To quote Albert Einstein, *"Things should be made as simple as possible — but no simpler."*

### Complexity

Complexity tends to require additional complexity until it grows into an unwieldy mess. Complex designs also tend to handle data as a series of exceptions, which limits the flexibility and usefulness of those designs in the future.

Tax codes are a perfect example of a system that handles every question as a complex series of exceptions. We all know the additional frustration and cost of a system filled with unnecessarily excessive complexity.

## Simplicity

The goal is to invent a flexible design that handles every case with a single simple method. This type of design dramatically improves nearly every other aspect of the database including the development cost. Because the design is simple, the data integrity constraints are more easily understood, implemented, and evaluated.

A simple design shows its agility as the business requirements evolve. A single method design will likely handle a new requirement with a slight change in the look-up data or a single modification to the formula. A complex, by-exception, design will require a new set of exception tables added to the database and/or a significant amount of new code.

**Best Practice**

I can't overemphasize the benefit of the database development team brainstorming the physical database structure. The goal of a simple, elegant, powerful design can be difficult to achieve without numerous refinements to the design.

As an example of complexity versus simplicity, a complex manufacturing material specification design might have a table for each type of material. As new material types were developed the design would require additional tables. Changes to how a material is specified would necessitate altering the table structure and the application code. The front-end application would have to examine different tables depending on the material, and maybe even the material version. Such a design is more expensive to develop and maintain, and less agile for the business.

On the other hand, a simple design creates a single method to describe any material regardless of its type or changes to how the materials are being specified. The cost of developing the application is a fraction of the complex method. The business can alter the way it specifies materials instantly.

**On the CD-ROM**

The Material Specification database on the book's CD includes a material specification design populated with sample computer hardware data.

## Simplicity and Normalization

Simplicity doesn't mean violating data integrity. The forms of normalization are as basic to database design as grammar is to writing. Good writing doesn't have to break the rules of grammar. In a manner of thinking, the primary principle of Strunk and White's *The Elements of Style* (be concise) is as fundamental to database design as it is to writing.

## Refining the Data Patterns

The key to simplicity is refining the entity definition with lots of team brainstorming so that each entity does more work—rearranging the data patterns until an elegant and simple pattern emerges. This is where a broad repertoire of database experience aids the design process.

Often the solution is to view the data from multiple angles, finding the commonality between them. Users are too close to the data and they seldom correctly identify the true entities. What a user might see as multiple entities, a database design team might model as a single entity with dynamic roles.

Combining this quest for simplicity with some dynamic/relational design methods can yield normalized databases with higher data integrity, more flexibility/agility, and dramatically fewer tables.

## Designing for Performance

A normalized logical database design without the benefit of physical database schema optimization will perform poorly, because the logical design alone doesn't consider performance. Issues like lock contention, composite keys, excessive joins for common queries, and table structures that are difficult to update are just some of the problems a logical design might bring to the database.

The key to designing a physical schema that performs well is to approach the database design from the query point of view and to identify areas of the schema that require overly complex or clumsy queries. As the team brainstorms multiple possible designs, it's critical that the team is able to see how queries could be built for each design.

The physical database schema is the foundation for the queries. Building a database without planning for query performance is like building a foundation for a home without any idea of the shape of the home.

Designing for performance is greatly influenced by the simplicity or complexity of the design. Each unnecessary complexity requires additional code, extra joins, and breeds even more complexity.

One particular decision regarding performance concerns the primary keys. Logical database designs tend to create composite meaningful primary keys. The physical schema benefits from redesigning these as single-column surrogate (computer-generated) keys. The section on creating primary keys later in this chapter discusses this in more detail.

## Designing for Security

Well-designed databases tend to split data vertically into several normalized tables. Unfortunately, clients are prone to feeling possessive of their data on a row-by-row horizontal basis. For example, a database might put all materials in a material table, but the various department heads want exclusive rights to the materials in their own departments.

SQL Server security takes place on a vertical basis, by tables or columns. While replication can publish data on a view basis, that's a messy option. Views can provide row-level security, but that option will either be complex and slow or hard-coded and troublesome to maintain. If the requirement is to provide row-level security, I recommend building the security into stored procedures or triggers.

The logical design does not deal with data security, but the physical design must include the security requirements, which may affect the table design, the coding method, or both.

## Designing for Maintainability

Maintenance over the life of the application will cost more than the initial development. Therefore, during the initial development process you should consider as a primary objective making it as easy as possible to maintain the physical design, code, and data. The following techniques may reduce the cost of database maintenance:

✦ Use a consistent naming convention.

✦ Avoid data structures that are overly complex, as well as unwieldy data structures, when a simpler data structures will suffice.

✦ Develop with scripts instead of Enterprise Manager.

✦ Avoid non-portable non-ANSI T-SQL extensions.

✦ Enforce the data integrity constraints from the beginning. Polluted data is a bear to clean up after a few years of loose data integrity rules.

✦ Develop the core feature first, and once that's working then add the bells and whistles.

✦ Document not only how the procedure works, but also why it works.

## Responsible Denormalization

Interestingly, the Microsoft Word spell checker suggests replacing "denormalization" with "demoralization." Within an OLTP database, I couldn't agree more.

Denormalization is the technique of duplicating data within the data to make it easier to retrieve the data. It's purposefully breaking the normal forms described in Chapter 2, "Modeling the Logical Database Schema."

For some examples of denormalizing a data structure, including the customer name in an [Order] table would allow retrieving the customer name when querying an order without joining to the Customer table. Or, including the CustomerID in a ShipDetail table would allow joining directly from the ShipDetail table to the Customer table while bypassing the OrderDetail and [Order] tables. Both of these examples violate the normalization because the attributes don't depend on the primary key.

Some developers regularly denormalize portions of the database in an attempt to improve performance. While it can reduce the number of joins required for a query, such a technique can slow down an OLTP database overall because additional triggers must keep the duplicated data in sync and the data integrity checks become more complex.

The reason for normalization is to ensure data consistency as data is entered. The recommendation to denormalize a portion of the database therefore depends on the purpose of that data within the database:

✦ If the data is being used in an OLTP manner — that is, the data is original and data integrity is a concern. Never denormalize original data.

✦ Denormalize aggregate data, such as account balances, or inventory on-hand quantities within OLTP databases for performance even though such data could be calculated from the inventory transaction table or the account transaction ledge table.

✦ If the data is not original and is primarily there for OLAP or reporting purposes, data consistency is not the primary concern. For performance, denormalization is a wise move.

The architecture of the databases and which databases or tables are being used for which purpose is the driving factor in any decision to denormalize a part of the database.

If the database requires both OLTP and OLAP, the best solution course might just be to create a few tables that duplicate data for their own distinct purposes. The OLTP side might need its own tables to maintain the data. But the reporting side might need that same data in a single, wide, fast table from which it can retrieve data with any joins or locking concerns. The trick is to correctly populate the denormalized data in a timely manner.

As part of one project I worked on, several analysts entered and massaged data to produce a database that was published quarterly. The published database was static for a quarter and used only for searches — a perfect example of a project that includes both OLTP and OLAP requirements. As a way to improve search performance, a denormalized database was created expressly for reporting purposes. A procedure ran for several hours to de-normalize all the data and populated the OLAP database. Both sides of the equation were satisfied.

Indexed views are basically denormalized clustered indexes. Chapter 30, "Advanced Scalability," discusses setting up an indexed view. Chapter 31, "Analysis Services," includes advice on creating a de-normalized reporting database and data warehouse.

# Creating Databases

The database is the physical container for all database schema, data, and all the server-side programming. SQL Server's database is a single logical unit, even though it may exist in several files.

Database creation is one of those areas in which SQL Server can run fine with little administrative work, but you may decide instead to tune the database files with more sophisticated techniques.

Creating a database using the default parameters is very simple. The following Data Definition Language (DDL) command is taken from the Cape Hatteras Adventures sample database:

```
CREATE DATABASE CHA2
```

The create command will create a data file with the name provided and a .mdf file extension, as well as a transaction log with a .ldf extension.

Of course, more parameters and options exist than the previous basic create command suggests. By default, the database is created as follows:

✦ **Default collation:** Server collation

✦ **Initial size:** 1MB

✦ **Location:** Both database and transaction log file in the same default directory

While these defaults might be acceptable for a sample or development database, they are inadequate for a production database. Better alternatives will be explained as the create database command is covered.

Using Enterprise Manager, creating a new database requires only that the database name be entered in the new database form, as shown in Figure 5-1. You open the form by right-clicking the database node under a server and selecting New Database.

**Figure 5-1:** The simplest way to create a new database is by entering the database name in Enterprise Manager's new database form and clicking OK.

## Database-File Concepts

A database consists of two files (or two sets of files): the data file and the transaction log. The data file contains all system and user tables, indexes, views, stored procedures, user-defined functions, triggers, and security permissions. The write-ahead transaction log is central to SQL Server's design. All updates to the data file are first written and verified in the transaction log ensuring that all data updates are written to two places.

**Best Practice**

Never, ever store the transaction log on the same disk subsystem as the data file. For the sake of the transactional-integrity ACID properties and the recoverability of the database, it's critical that a failing disk subsystem not be able to take out both the data file and the transaction file.

The transaction log contains not only user writes but also system writes such as index writes, page splits, table reorganizations, and so on. After one intensive update test, I inspected the log using Lumigent's Log Explorer and was surprised to find that about 80 percent of all entries represented system activities, not user updates. Because the transaction file contains not only the current information but also all updates to the data file, it has a tendency to grow and grow.

**Cross-Reference**

Administering the transaction log involves backing up and truncating it as part of the recovery plan, discussed in Chapter 26, "Recovery Planning." How SQL Server uses the transaction log within transactions is covered in Chapter 11, "Transactional Integrity."

## Configuring File Growth

Prior to SQL Server version 7, the data files required manual size adjustment to handle additional data. Fortunately, SQL Server today can automatically grow thanks to the following options (see Figure 5-2):

✦ *Automatically grow file (auto-grow)* — As the database begins to hold more data, the file size must grow. If auto-grow is not enabled, an observant DBA will have to manually adjust the size. If auto-grow is enabled, SQL Server automatically adjusts the size according to the following growth parameters:

   • *File growth in megabytes* — When the data file needs to grow, this option will add the specified number of megabytes to the file. Growing by a fixed size is a good option for larger data files. Once file growth is predictable, setting this option to a fixed number equal to the amount of growth per week is probably a sound plan.

   • *File growth by percent* — When the data file needs to grow, this option will expand it by the percent specified. Growing by percent is the best option for smaller databases. With very large files, this option may add too much space in one operation and hurt performance while the data file is being resized. For example, adding 10 percent to a 5GB data file will add 500MB; writing 500MB could take a while.

✦ *Maximum file size* — Setting a maximum size can prevent the data file or transaction log file from filling the entire disk subsystem, which would cause trouble for the operating system.

**Figure 5-2:** With Enterprise Manager's New Database form, NewDB is configured for automatic file growth and a maximum size of 2GB.

Automatic file growth can be specified in code by adding the file options to the create database DDL command. The file sizes can be specified in kilobytes (KB), megabytes (MB), gigabytes (GB), or terabytes (TB). Megabytes is the default. The file growth can be set to a size or a percent. The following code creates the NewDB database with an initial data-file size of 10MB, a maximum size of 2GB, and a file growth of 10MB. The Transaction Log file is initially 5MB with a maximum size of 1GB and a growth of 10 percent:

```
CREATE DATABASE NewDB
ON
PRIMARY
  (NAME = NewDB,
    FILENAME = 'c:\SQLData\NewDB.mdf',
      SIZE = 10MB,
      MAXSIZE = 2Gb,
      FILEGROWTH = 20)
LOG ON
  (NAME = NewDBLog,
    FILENAME = 'd:\SQLLog\NewDBLog.ldf',
      SIZE = 5MB,
      MAXSIZE = 1Gb,
      FILEGROWTH = 10%)
```

If auto-grow is not enabled then the files will require manual adjustment if they are to handle additional data. The file size can be adjusted in Enterprise Manager by editing it in the database properties form.

The file sizes and growth options can be adjusted in code with the alter database DDL command and the modify file option. The following code sets NewDB's data file to manual growth and sets the size to 25MB:

```
ALTER DATABASE NewDB
  MODIFY FILE
    (Name = NewDB,
    SIZE = 25MB,
    MAXSIZE = 2Gb,
    FILEGROWTH = 0)
```

## Using Multiple Files

Both the data file and the transaction log can be stored on multiple files for improved performance and to allow for growth. Any additional, or *secondary*, data files have a .ndf file extension by default. If the database uses multiple data files, then the first, or *primary*, file will contain the system tables.

While it does not enable control over the location of tables or indexes, this technique does reduce the I/O load on each disk subsystem. SQL Server attempts to balance the I/O load by splitting the inserts among the multiple files according to the free space available in each file. As SQL Server balances the load, rows for a single table may be split among multiple locations. If the database is configured for automatic growth, all of the files will fill up before SQL Server increases the size of the files.

## Creating a Database with Multiple Files

To create a database with multiple files using Enterprise Manager, add the file name to the file grid in either the Data Files tab or the Transaction Log tab in the Database Properties dialog box (Figure 5-3).

**Figure 5-3:** Creating a database with multiple files using Enterprise Manager.

To create a database with multiple data files from code, add the file locations to the create database DDL command using the on option:

```
CREATE DATABASE NewDB
ON
PRIMARY
  (NAME = NewDB,
    FILENAME = 'e:\SQLData\NewDB.mdf'),
  (NAME = NewDB2,
    FILENAME = 'f:\SQLData\NewDB2.ndf')
LOG ON
  (NAME = NewDBLog,
    FILENAME = 'g:\SQLLog\NewDBLog.ldf'),
  (NAME = NewDBLog2,
    FILENAME = 'h:\SQLLog\NewDBLog2.ldf')
```

Result:

```
The CREATE DATABASE process is allocating
  0.63 MB on disk 'NewDB'.
The CREATE DATABASE process is allocating
  1.00 MB on disk 'NewDB2'.
```

```
The CREATE DATABASE process is allocating
  1.00 MB on disk 'NewDBLog'.
The CREATE DATABASE process is allocating
  1.00 MB on disk 'NewDBLog2'.
```

## Modifying the Files of an Existing Database

The number of files for an existing database may be easily modified. If the data is filling the drive, another data file can be added to the database by adding it to the files grid. Add the new file name and location to the database properties file grid in the same way that the files were initially created.

**Best Practice**

I highly recommend spreading the data file over multiple disk subsystems. It improves the effective throughput without replacing the server and requires less administrative overhead than filegroups (our next topic). Just remember to separate the data files from the Transaction Log files.

In code, a file can be added to an existing database using the `alter database` DDL command and the `add file` option. The file syntax is identical to that which was used to create a new database. The following code adds a third file to the NewDB:

```
ALTER DATABASE NewDB
  ADD FILE
    (NAME = NewDB3,
      FILENAME = 'i:\SQLData\NewDB3.ndf',
      SIZE = 10MB,
      MAXSIZE = 2Gb,
      FILEGROWTH = 20)
```

Result:

```
Extending database by 10.00 MB on disk 'NewDB3'.
```

If a file is no longer desired because the disk subsystem is being retired or designated for another use, one of the data or Transaction Log files can be deleted by shrinking the file using `DBCC ShrinkFile` and then deleting it in Enterprise Manager by selecting the file and pressing Delete.

Using T-SQL code, you can remove additional files with the `alter database remove file` DDL command. The following code removes the data file you added earlier:

```
DBCC SHRINKFILE (NewDB3, EMPTYFILE)
ALTER DATABASE NewDB
  REMOVE FILE NewDB3
```

Result:

```
DbId FileId CurrentSize MinimumSize UsedPages EstimatedPages
---- ------ ----------- ----------- --------- --------------
12   5      1280        1280        0         0

The file 'NewDB3' has been removed.
```

## Planning Multiple Filegroups

A *filegroup* is an advanced means of organizing the database objects. By default the database has a single filegroup—the *primary* filegroup. By configuring a database with multiple filegroups, new objects (tables, indexes, and so on) can be created on a specified filegroup. This technique can support two main strategies:

✦ Using multiple filegroups can increase performance by separating heavily used tables or indexes onto different disk subsystems.

✦ Using multiple filegroups can organize the backup and recovery plan by containing static data in one filegroup and more active data in another filegroup.

**Note**     An easy way to determine the files and file sizes for all databases from code is to query Master.sysaltfiles.

### Creating a Database with Filegroups

To create a database with multiple filegroups in Enterprise Manager, create a database with multiple files and enter or select the filegroup in the rightmost column. You can also create a filegroup in the Filegroup tab (Figure 5-4), but to assign a file to a filegroup requires that you use the Data File tab. The Filegroups tab is available from the Database Properties dialog box, but only after the database is created.

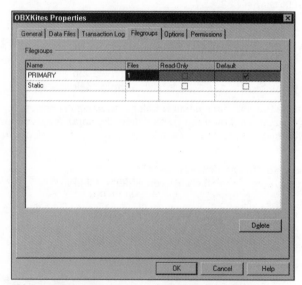

**Figure 5-4:** You can create a new group with the Filegroups tab, which also reports the status of current filegroups.

Using T-SQL, you can specify filegroups for new databases using the Filegroups option. The following code creates the NewDB database with two data filegroups:

```
CREATE DATABASE NewDB
ON
PRIMARY
  (NAME = NewDB,
    FILENAME = 'd:\SQLData\NewDB.mdf',
      SIZE = 50MB,
      MAXSIZE = 5Gb,
      FILEGROWTH = 25MB),
FILEGROUP GroupTwo
  (NAME = NewDBGroup2,
    FILENAME = 'e:\SQLData\NewDBTwo.ndf',
      SIZE = 50MB,
      MAXSIZE = 5Gb,
      FILEGROWTH = 25MB)
LOG ON
  (NAME = NewDBLog,
    FILENAME = 'f:\SQLLog\NewDBLog.ndf',
      SIZE = 100MB,
      MAXSIZE = 25Gb,
      FILEGROWTH = 25MB)
```

## Modifying Filegroups

You modify filegroups in the same way that you modify files. Using Enterprise Manager, you can add new filegroups, add or remove files from a filegroup, and remove the filegroup if it is empty. Emptying a file group is more difficult than shrinking a file. If there's data in the filegroup, shrinking a file will only move the data to another file in the filegroup. The tables and indexes must be dropped from the filegroup before the filegroup can be deleted.

With Query Analyzer and T-SQL code, you can add or drop filegroups using the `alter database add filegroup` or `alter database remove filegroup` command, much as you would use the add or remove file command.

## Dropping a Database

You can remove a database from the server by selecting the database in Enterprise Manager and selecting Delete Database from the right-click menu or Action menu.

In code, you can remove a database with the `drop database` command:

```
DROP DATABASE NewDB
```

# Creating Tables

Like all relational databases, SQL Server is table-oriented. Once the database is created the next step is to create the tables. A SQL Server database may include up to 2,147,483,647 objects, including tables, so there's effectively no limit to the number of tables you can create.

# Designing Tables Within Enterprise Manager

If you prefer working in a graphical environment, Enterprise Manager provides two primary work surfaces for creating tables, both of which you can use to create new tables or modify existing ones:

✦ The Table Designer tool (Figure 5-5) lists the table columns vertically and places the column properties below the column grid.

✦ The Database Designer tool (Figure 5-6) is more flexible than the Table Designer form, can display the properties for all columns in a grid, and can display foreign-key constraints as well.

**Cross-Reference** Chapter 4, "Using SQL Server's Developer Tools," explains how to launch and navigate these tools.

Each of these tools presents a graphical design of the table. Once the design is complete, Enterprise Manager generates a script that applies the changes to the database. Often the script must save the data in a temporary table, drop several items, create the new tables, and reinsert the data.

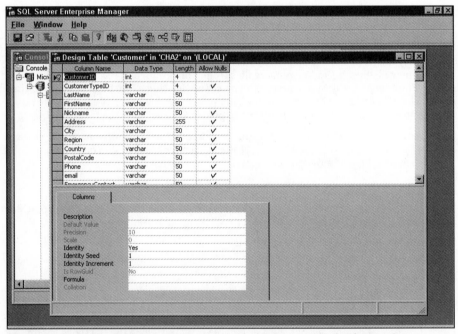

**Figure 5-5:** Developing the customer table in the CHA2 sample database using Enterprise Manager's Table Designer.

Table Designer displays only the column name, data type, and length, and allows nulls in the column grid. While these are the main properties of a column, I personally find it annoying to have to select each column in order to inspect or change the rest of the properties.

Each data type is explained in detail later in this chapter. For some data types the length property sets the data length while other data types have fixed lengths. Nulls are discussed in the "Creating User-Data Columns" section, later in this chapter.

Once an edit is made to the table design, the Save Change Script toolbar button is enabled. This button displays the actual code that the Table Designer will run if the changes are saved. In addition, the Save Change Script button can save the script to a .sql file so the change can be repeated on another server.

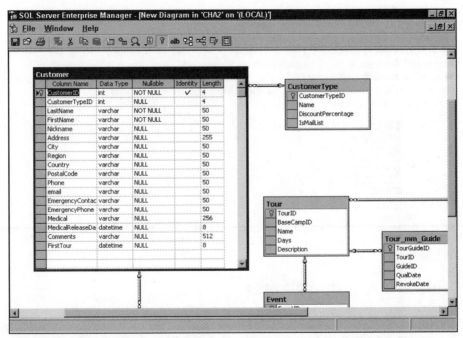

**Figure 5-6:** Developing the Customer table in the CHA2 sample database using Enterprise Manager's Database Designer.

# Working with SQL Scripts

If you are developing a database for mass deployment or repeatable installations, the benefits of developing the database schema in scripts become obvious:

✦ The code is all in one location. Working with SQL scripts is similar to developing an application with Visual Basic or C.

✦ The script may be stored in Microsoft *SourceSafe* or another change-management system.

✦ The most current version of the database may be installed without running change scripts or restoring a backup.

✦ An installation is a fresh new database as opposed to a backup or detached database that may have residual test data.

Working with scripts does have its drawbacks, however:

✦ The T-SQL commands may be unfamiliar and the size of the script may become overwhelming.

✦ If the foreign-key constraints are embedded within the table, the table-creation order is very picky. If the constraints are applied after the tables are created, the table-creation order is no longer a problem; however, the foreign keys are distanced from the tables in the script.

✦ Enterprise Manager database diagrams are not part of the script.

The T-SQL commands for working with objects, including tables, are create, alter, and drop. The following create table DDL command from the Outer Banks Kite Store sample database creates the ProductCategory table. The table name, including the name of the owner (dbo), is provided, followed by the table's columns. The final code directs SQL Server to create the table on the primary filegroup:

```
CREATE TABLE dbo.ProductCategory (
  ProductCategoryID UNIQUEIDENTIFIER NOT NULL
    ROWGUIDCOL DEFAULT (NEWID()) PRIMARY KEY NONCLUSTERED,
  ProductCategoryName NVARCHAR(50) NOT NULL,
  ProductCategoryDescription NVARCHAR(100) NULL
  )
  ON [Primary]
```

For extensive examples of building databases and tables with scripts, you can reference this book's sample databases, which are all developed with scripts and are available on the book's CD-ROM.

## Table and Column Names

SQL Server is very liberal with table and column names, allowing up to 128 Unicode characters and spaces, as well as both upper- and lowercase letters. Of course, taking advantage of that freedom with wild abandon will be regretted later when typing the lengthy column names and having to place brackets around columns with spaces. It's more dangerous to discuss naming conventions with programmers than it is to discuss politics in a mixed crowd. Nevertheless, you paid for this book so here's my two cents.

There is a huge debate over whether table names should be singular or plural. I've seen well-meaning developers ask reasonable questions in the newsgroups and receive a barrage of attacks over their table names.

The plural camp believes that a table is a set of rows and as such it should be named with a plural name. The reasoning often used by this camp is, "A table of customers is a set of customers. Sets include multiple items so the table should be named the Customers table, unless you only have one customer, in which case you don't need a database."

From my informal polling, the singular-name view is held by about three-fourths of SQL Server developers. These developers hold that the customer table is the customer set, rather than the set of customers. A set of rows is not called a *rows set*, but a *row set*. And because tables are generally discussed as singular items, saying, "the Customer table" sounds cleaner than "the Customers table."

Most (but not all) developers would agree that consistency is more important than the naming convention itself.

**Best Practice**

Consistency is the database developer's holy grail. The purpose of naming conventions, constraints, referential integrity, relational design, and even column data type is to bring order and consistency to the data we use to model reality. Whenever you're faced with a database decision, asking, "which choice is the most consistent?" is a good step toward a solution.

Personally, I think that developers choose their naming conventions as a way to distance themselves from sloppy designs they've had to work with in their past. Having worked on poorly designed flat-file databases with plural names, I prefer singular names.

If a database is large enough that it will encompass several logical groupings of tables, I prefix a two- or three-letter abbreviation to the table name to make it easier to navigate the database. I've seen a system of numbering modules and tables that I don't recommend. InvItem is a good name for the item table in the inventory module. 0207_Item is too cryptic.

Another issue involving differences in naming is the use of underscores to indicate words within the name. For example, some IT shops insist that the order-detail table be named ORDER_DETAIL. Personally, I avoid underscores except in many-to-many resolution tables. Studies have shown that the use of mixed case, such as in the name OrderDetail, is easier to read than all lower- or all uppercase words. However, some databases do not permit lowercase letters in names.

Here are the database-naming conventions I use when developing databases:

✦ Use singular table names with no numbers, and a module prefix if useful.

✦ For many-to-many resolution tables use table_mm_table.

✦ Set all names in MixedCase with no underscores or spaces.

✦ For the primary key, use the table name + ID. For example, the primary key for the Customer table is CustomerID.

✦ Give foreign keys the same name as their primary key, unless the foreign key enforces a reflexive/recursive relationship such as MotherID referring back to PersonID in the Family sample database, or the secondary table has multiple foreign keys to the same primary key, such as the many-to-many reflexive relationship in the Material sample database (BillofMaterials.MaterialID to Material.MaterialID and BillofMaterials.SourceMaterialID to Material.MaterialID).

✦ Avoid abbreviation.

✦ Use consistent table and column names across all databases. For example, always LastName followed by FirstName.

## Filegroups

Apart from the columns, the only information you normally supply when creating a table is the name. However, you can create the table on a specific filegroup if the database has multiple filegroups.

The OBX Kites database uses two filegroups for data-organization purposes. All data that are modified on a regular basis go into the `primary` filegroup. This filegroup is backed up frequently. Data that are rarely modified (such as the order priority look-up codes) go into the `static` filegroup:

```
CREATE TABLE OrderPriority (
    OrderPriorityID UNIQUEIDENTIFIER NOT NULL
        ROWGUIDCOL DEFAULT (NEWID()) PRIMARY KEY NONCLUSTERED,
    OrderPriorityName NVARCHAR (15) NOT NULL,
    OrderPriorityCode NVARCHAR (15) NOT NULL,
    Priority INT NOT NULL
    )
    ON [Static]
```

# Creating Keys

The primary and foreign keys are the links that bind the tables into a working relational database. I treat these columns as a domain separate from the user's data column. The design of these keys has a critical effect on the performance and usability of the physical database.

The database schema must transform from a theoretical logical design into a practical physical design, and the structure of the primary and foreign keys is often the crux of the redesign. Keys are very difficult to modify once the database is in production. Getting the primary keys right during the development phase is a battle worth fighting.

## Primary Keys

The relational database depends on the primary key—the cornerstone of the physical database schema. A physical-layer primary key has only two purposes:

✦ To uniquely identify the row

✦ To serve as a useful object for a foreign key

With these two purposes in mind, these are my rules for primary keys at the physical layer:

✦ The primary key should be meaningless to users. If a user sees the raw data of a many-to-many junction table and complains that it's useless, that's one clue that the primary keys are well designed.

✦ Primary keys should be single columns for fast joins and where clauses.

Two reasons are commonly given for a composite primary key and both are wrong. The first reason is that some piece of meaningful data must be part of the primary key. Adding meaning to a primary key is a sure way to invite humans to foul the data.

The second justification given for building a composite primary key is that it enables the use of two foreign keys in a many-to-many junction table as the primary key. I'm opposed to this practice. Composite primary keys make vicious foreign keys. As the junction table becomes the primary key to another secondary table, and so on, the bottom table requires several columns in the primary keys.

I was asked to look at a database a client had purchased from a vendor, which was performing unusually slowly. Besides some major indexing errors, I found secondary tables with seven columns in the primary key! The SQL statements were over a page long, and included horrendous joins on seven conditions. Avoiding such queries is the reason for the primary key's second purpose.

✦ Primary keys should never need updating. If a primary key in fact has no purpose other than to uniquely identify the row, then there's no reason to ever change the value. An update to a primary key is a sure clue that the rule that the primary key should be meaningless is being violated. An exception to this rule is that data often needs massaging during data conversions or multiple-database mergers.

✦ Primary keys should not contain data that dynamically change, such as a timestamp column, a date-created column, or a date-updated column.

✦ Primary keys should be computer-generated. If a human manages the creation of the primary key, it will soon serve a purpose other than simply uniquely identifying the row. Once that line is crossed the human will want to modify the primary key, and the system used to link rows and manage relationships will be in the hands of people who don't understand database design.

## Natural Primary Keys

Every week or so, someone in the SQL Yahoo Groups (where I often hang out) posts a message saying, "I have a table with duplicate primary keys, how can I clean it up?" The root cause of this problem is that someone used a natural, or reality-based, value for the primary key. Probably what happened is that the database began with the primary key constraint that was enforced, but one day the constraint objected to new data so it was removed.

There are values in reality that seem to uniquely identify a row, such as national identification numbers, vehicle-identification numbers, and ID-badge numbers. Logical database schemas tend to use these natural primary keys, although none of these natural keys are foolproof. Given enough time and human involvement, each of these systems will fail. U.S. Social Security numbers are not unique. However, they are excellent data columns, they should obviously be indexed and used for searches in the user interface, and they may be candidates for a unique constraint. But even though a Social Security number may look like a natural primary key, don't use it as such. Let the user think it's the primary column for finding and naming a row, but don't make it an actual primary key.

If you must use a natural primary key, be sure to enable cascading updates on every foreign key that refers to a natural primary key so that primary key modifications will not break referential integrity.

## SQL Server Primary-Key Constraints

SQL Server implements primary keys and foreign keys as constraints. The purpose of a constraint is to ensure that new data meets certain criteria, or to block the data-modification operation.

A primary-key constraint is effectively a combination of a unique constraint (not a null constraint) and either a clustered or non-clustered unique index.

**Best Practice**

Primary keys should be meaningless, single-column, computer-generated, non-editable, and protected from users.

Divide each table into two discreet logical parts. The first part should contain the keys and belong to you, the database developer. It's the part of the database that links the rows and keeps the relationships in line. It is the domain of the database developer and DBA. The second part should consist of the columns containing user data. Users should be free to view and manipulate those data. But if users think that they need to see or edit the keys, the project is in big trouble. Defending the keys from the users is one of the primary goals of a successful database developer.

## Creating Primary Keys

Setting a column, or columns, as the primary key in Enterprise Manager is as simple as selecting the column and clicking the primary-key toolbar button, as previously shown in Figures 5-5 and 5-6. To build a composite primary key, select all the participating columns and press the primary-key button.

**Best Practice**

Enterprise Manager creates primary keys with clustered indexes. This is a poor index choice and a waste of the one clustered index (described in the index section later in this chapter) available for a table. If you use the graphic tools to create the physical schema, you should manually reset the primary-key index to non-clustered.

In code, you set a column as the primary key in one of two ways:

✦ Declare the primary-key constraint in the `create table` statement. The following code from the Cape Hatteras Adventures sample database uses this technique to create the `Guide` table and set `GuideID` as the primary key with a non-clustered index:

```
CREATE TABLE dbo.Guide (
  GuideID INT IDENTITY NOT NULL PRIMARY KEY NONCLUSTERED,
  LastName  VARCHAR(50) NOT NULL,
  FirstName  VARCHAR(50) NOT NULL,
  Qualifications  VARCHAR(2048) NULL,
  DateOfBirth  DATETIME NULL,
  DateHire  DATETIME NULL
  )
  ON [Primary]
```

✦ Declare the primary-key constraint after the table is created using an `alter table` command. Assuming the primary key was not already set for the Guide table, the following DDL command would apply a primary-key constraint to the `GuideID` column:

```
ALTER TABLE dbo.Guide ADD CONSTRAINT
  PK_Guide PRIMARY KEY NONCLUSTERED(GuideID)
  ON [PRIMARY]
```

Two data types are excellent for primary keys: identity columns and unique identifier columns. So you can experience sample databases with both methods, the Family, Cape Hatteras Adventures, and Material Specification sample databases use identity columns and the Outer Banks Kite Store sample database uses unique identifiers.

## Using Identity Columns

By far the most popular method for building primary keys involves using an identity column. Like an auto-number column or sequence column in other databases, the identity column generates consecutive integers as new rows are inserted into the database. Optionally, you can specify the initial seed number and interval.

Identity columns offer two advantages:

✦ Integers are easier to manually recognize and edit than GUIDs.

✦ Integers are small and fast. My informal testing shows that integers are about 10 percent faster than GUIDs. Other published tests show integers as 10 to 33 percent faster. However, this performance difference only shows up when you're looping through a thousand selects. A single `select` statement, retrieving a few rows from a large table as a single operation, should show no performance benefit.

An identity column used as a primary key with a clustered index (a common, but poor, practice) may be extremely fast when retrieving a single row with a single user. However, that configuration will cause lock-contention hot spots on the database and the effect will be like pouring molasses into the hard drive. There's more to performance than column width.

Identity-column values are created by SQL Server as the row is being inserted. Attempting to insert a value into an identity column or update an identity column will generate an error unless `set insert_identity` is set to true.

**Cross-Reference**  Chapter 10, "Modifying Data," includes a full discussion of the problems of modifying data in tables with identity columns.

The following DDL code from the Cape Hatteras Adventures sample database creates a table that uses an identity column for its primary key (abbreviated code listing):

```
CREATE TABLE dbo.Event (
  EventID INT IDENTITY NOT NULL PRIMARY KEY NONCLUSTERED,
  TourID INT NOT NULL FOREIGN KEY REFERENCES dbo.Tour,
  EventCode VARCHAR(10) NOT NULL,
  DateBegin DATETIME NULL,
  Comment NVARCHAR(255)
  )
  ON [Primary]
```

## Using GUIDs

The `uniqueidentifier` data type is SQL Server's counterpart to COM's global unique identifier (GUID, pronounced GOO-id or gwid). It's a 16-byte hexadecimal number that is essentially unique among all tables, all databases, all servers, and all planets. While both identity columns and GUIDs are unique, the scope of the uniqueness is greater with GUIDs than identity columns, so while it is grammatically incorrect, GUIDs are more unique than identity columns. The uniqueness is due to the GUID generator using several factors, including the computer NIC code, the MAC address, the CPU internal ID, and the current tick of the CPU clock. The last 6 bytes are from the node number of the NIC card.

GUIDs offer several advantages:

✦ A database using GUID primary keys can be replicated without a major overhaul. Replication will add a unique identifier to every table without a `uniqueidentifier` column. While this makes the column globally unique for replication purposes, the application code will still be identifying rows by the integer primary key only, and therefore merging replicated rows from other servers will cause an error because there will be duplicate primary key values.

✦ The randomness of the GUID helps reduce database hot spots by spreading new rows around the table or index and avoiding lock contention.

✦ GUIDs discourage users from working with or assigning meaning to the primary keys.

✦ GUIDs eliminate join errors caused by joining the wrong tables but returning data regardless, because rows that should not match share the same integer values in key columns.

✦ GUIDs are forever. The table based on a typical integer-based identity column will hold only 2,147,483,648 rows. Of course, the data type could be set to bigint or numeric, but that lessens the size benefit of using the identity column.

✦ Because the GUID can be generated by either the column default, the `select`-statement expression, or code prior to the `select` statement, it's significantly easier to program with GUIDs than with identity columns. Using GUIDs circumvents the data-modification problems of using identity columns.

The Product table in the Outer Bank Kite Store sample database uses a `uniqueidentifier` as its primary key. In the following script, the `ProductID` column's data type is set to `uniqueidentifier`. Its nullability is set to false. The column's `rowguidcol` property is set to true, enabling replication to detect and use this column. The default is a newly generated `uniqueidentifier`. It's the primary key, and it's indexed with a non-clustered unique index.

```
CREATE TABLE dbo.Product (
  ProductID UNIQUEIDENTIFIER NOT NULL
    ROWGUIDCOL DEFAULT (NEWID())
    PRIMARY KEY NONCLUSTERED,
  ProductCategoryID UNIQUEIDENTIFIER NOT NULL
    FOREIGN KEY REFERENCES dbo.ProductCategory,
  ProductCode CHAR(15) NOT NULL,
  ProductName NVARCHAR(50) NOT NULL,
  ProductDescription NVARCHAR(100) NULL,
  ActiveDate DATETIME NOT NULL DEFAULT GETDATE(),
  DiscountinueDate DATETIME NULL
  )
  ON [Static]
```

## Creating Foreign Keys

A secondary table that relates to a primary table uses a foreign key to point to the primary table's primary key. *Referential integrity* (RI) refers to the fact that the references have integrity, meaning that every foreign key points to a valid primary key. Referential integrity is vital to the consistency (from the ACID database principles discussed in Chapter 11, "Transactional Integrity") of the database. The database must begin, and end, every transaction in a consistent state. This consistency must extend to the foreign-key references.

SQL Server tables may have up to 253 foreign-key constraints. The foreign key can reference primary keys, unique constraints, or unique indexes of any table except a temporary table.

That referential integrity is an aspect of the primary key is a common misconception. It's the foreign key that is constrained to a valid primary-key value, so the constraint is an aspect of the foreign key, not the primary key.

## Declarative Referential Integrity

SQL Server's *Declarative Referential Integrity* (DRI) can enforce referential integrity without writing custom triggers or code. DRI is handled inside the SQL Server engine, which executes significantly faster than custom RI writing in triggers.

SQL Server implements referential integrity with foreign-key constraints. You can establish a foreign-key constraint in Enterprise Manager in two ways:

✦ Using the Database Diagrammer, select the primary-key column and drag it to the foreign-key column. A Create Relationship dialog box very similar to the Foreign Key Table Properties dialog box will appear. Figure 5-7 shows a diagram from the Cape Hatteras Adventures sample database with completed relationships.

You can modify the foreign key in the Database Diagrammer by right-clicking the relationship line and selecting Properties from the pop-up menu. This opens the table properties to the selected relationship.

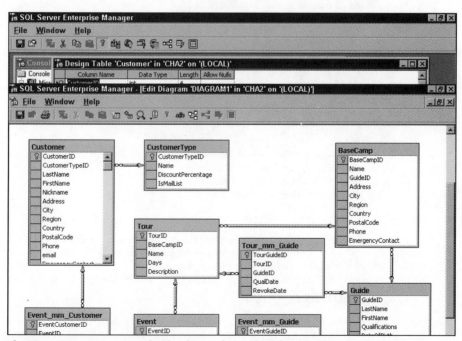

**Figure 5-7:** You can create foreign keys relationships by dragging the primary key to the foreign key in the Database Diagrammer.

✦ Using the Table Properties dialog box, available from the Table Designer or the Database Diagrammer, you can use the Relationships tab to create or modify a DRI foreign key. The Relationships tab, shown in Figure 5-8, displays the relationship settings for the currently selected foreign key. You can create other relationships using the New button, or select them using the "Selected relationship" combo box. The relationship's tables and columns are then presented in the column grid.

The foreign key can either check or ignore existing and replicated data. The important option for declarative referential integrity is the "Enforce relationship for INSERTS and UPDATES" option. If this option is not checked the foreign key has no effect. If DRI is enforced, cascading deletes and cascading updates (described later in this section) are available.

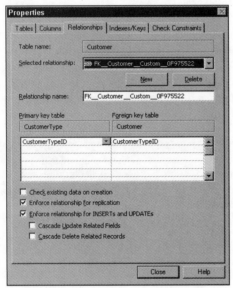

**Figure 5-8:** Enterprise Manager's table properties—you can use the Relationships tab to define and maintain foreign-key constraints.

Within a T-SQL script, you can declare foreign-key constraints are declared by either including the foreign-key constraint in the table-creation code or applying the constraint after the table is created. After the column definition, the phrase `foreign key references`, followed by the primary table, and optionally the column(s), creates the foreign key, as follows:

```
ForeignKeyColumn FOREIGN KEY REFERENCES PrimaryTable(PKID)
```

The following code from the CHA sample database creates the `tour_mm_guide` many-to-many junction table. As a junction table, `tour mm guide` has two foreign-key constraints: one to the `Tour` table, and one to the `Guide` table. For demonstration purposes, the `TourID` foreign key specifies the primary-key column, but the `GuideID` foreign key simply points to the table and uses the primary key by default.

```
CREATE TABLE dbo.Tour_mm_Guide (
  TourGuideID INT
```

```
      IDENTITY
      NOT NULL
      PRIMARY KEY NONCLUSTERED,
   TourID INT
      NOT NULL
      FOREIGN KEY REFERENCES dbo.Tour(TourID)
      ON DELETE CASCADE,
   GuideID INT
      NOT NULL
      FOREIGN KEY REFERENCES dbo.Guide
      ON DELETE CASCADE,
   QualDate DATETIME NOT NULL,
   RevokeDate DATETIME NULL
   )
   ON [Primary]
```

Some database developers prefer to include foreign-key constraints in the table definition, while others prefer to add them after the table is created. If the table already exists, you can add the foreign-key constraint to the table using the `alter table add constraint` DDL command, as shown here:

```
ALTER TABLE SecondaryTableName
  ADD CONSTRAINT ConstraintName
    FOREIGN KEY (ForeignKeyColumns)
    REFERENCES dbo.PrimaryTable (PrimaryKeyColumnName)
```

The person table in the family database must use this method because it uses a reflexive relationship, also called a *unary* or *self-join* relationship. A foreign key can't be created before the primary key exists. Since a reflexive foreign key refers to the same table, that table must be created prior to the foreign key.

This code, copied form the `family_create.sql` file, creates the `Person` table and then establishes the `MotherID` and `FatherID` foreign keys, as shown here:

```
CREATE TABLE dbo.Person (
  PersonID  INT NOT NULL PRIMARY KEY NONCLUSTERED,
  LastName  VARCHAR(15) NOT NULL,
  FirstName  VARCHAR(15) NOT NULL,
  SrJr  VARCHAR(3) NULL,
  MaidenName VARCHAR(15) NULL,
  Gender CHAR(1) NOT NULL,
  FatherID INT NULL,
  MotherID INT NULL,
  DateOfBirth  DATETIME  NULL,
  DateOfDeath  DATETIME  NULL
  )
go
ALTER TABLE dbo.Person
  ADD CONSTRAINT FK_Person_Father
    FOREIGN KEY(FatherID) REFERENCES dbo.Person (PersonID)
ALTER TABLE dbo.Person
  ADD CONSTRAINT FK_Person_Mother
    FOREIGN KEY(MotherID) REFERENCES dbo.Person (PersonID)
```

## Optional Foreign Keys

An important distinction exists between optional foreign keys and mandatory foreign keys. Some relationships require a foreign key, as with an OrderDetail row that requires a valid order row. But other relationships don't require a value. The data are valid with or without a foreign key, as determined in the logical design.

In the physical layer, the difference is the nullability of the foreign-key column. If the foreign key is mandatory, the column should not allow nulls. An optional foreign key allows nulls. A relationship with complex optionality will require either a check constraint or a trigger to fully implement the relationship.

## Cascading Deletes

A complication created by referential integrity is that RI will prevent you from deleting a primary row being referred to by secondary rows until those secondary rows have been deleted. If the primary row is deleted and the secondary rows' foreign keys are still pointing to the now-deleted primary keys, referential integrity is violated.

The solution to this problem is to cascade the delete operation from the primary row down to the related secondary rows, effectively deleting the secondary rows before deleting the primary rows and maintaining referential integrity. You can do this in code from the client application; however, SQL Server DRI gives you the option of performing the secondary-row delete as a step within the primary-row delete. If cascading delete is enabled, deleting a primary row also deletes all related secondary rows. For example, if the order-detail foreign-key constraint that points to the order table has cascading delete enabled, deleting an order will also delete that order's order-detail rows.

**Cross-Reference**     Cascading deletes are also discussed in the "Deleting Data" section in Chapter 10, "Modifying Data."

Cascading deletes may be enabled within Enterprise Manager by selecting the cascade delete option in the Relationship tab of the Database Diagrammer Properties dialog shown previously in Figure 5-8. Within T-SQL code, adding the on delete cascade option to the foreign-key constraint enables the cascade operation. The following code, extracted from the OBXKites sample database's OrderDetail table, uses the cascading delete option on the OrderID foreign-key constraint:

```
CREATE TABLE dbo.OrderDetail (
  OrderDetailID UNIQUEIDENTIFIER
    NOT NULL
    ROWGUIDCOL
    DEFAULT (NEWID())
    PRIMARY KEY NONCLUSTERED,
  OrderID UNIQUEIDENTIFIER
    NOT NULL
    FOREIGN KEY REFERENCES dbo.[Order]
      ON DELETE CASCADE,
  ProductID UNIQUEIDENTIFIER
    NULL
    FOREIGN KEY REFERENCES dbo.Product,
```

**Cross-Reference** Chapter 16, "Advanced Server-Side Programming," shows how to create triggers that handle custom referential integrity and cascading deletes for non-standard data schemas or cross-database referential integrity.

Generally, cascading deletes are a part of the physical schema, not the logical schema. To determine if cascading deletes are appropriate to a foreign key, use these rules of thumb:

✦ If the secondary table's data is meaningless apart from the primary table's data, cascading the delete is useful.

✦ If the secondary table's data has meaning on its own, cascading the delete is dangerous.

✦ If the foreign key is optional, cascading the delete should never be applied.

# Creating User-Data Columns

A user-data column stores user data. These columns typically fall into two categories: columns users use to identify a person, place, thing, event, or action, and columns that further describe the person, place, thing, event, or action.

SQL Server tables may have up to 1,024 columns, but well-designed relational-database tables seldom have more than 25, and most have only a handful.

Data columns are created during table creation by listing the columns as parameters to the create table command. The columns are listed within parentheses as column name, data type, and any column attributes such as constraints, nullability, or default value:

```
CREATE TABLE TableName (
ColumnName DATATYPE Attributes,
ColumnName DATATYPE Attributes
)
```

Data columns can be added to existing tables using the alter table add column command:

```
ALTER TABLE TableName
   ADD ColumnName DATATYPE Attributes
```

An existing column may be modified with the alter table alter column command:

```
ALTER TABLE TableName
   ALTER COLUMN ColumnName
      NEWDATATYPE Attributes
```

## Column Data Types

The column's data type serves two purposes:

✦ It enforces the first level of data integrity. Character won't be accepted into a datetime or numeric column. I have seen databases with every column set to nvarchar to ease data entry. What a waste. The data type is a valuable data-validation tool that should not be overlooked.

✦ It determines the amount of disk storage allocated to the column.

## Character Data Types

SQL Server supports several character data types, listed in Table 5-1.

### Table 5-1: Character Data Types

| Data Type | Description | Size in Bytes |
|---|---|---|
| char | Fixed-length character data up to 8,000 characters length using collation character set | Defined length * 1 byte |
| nchar | Unicode fixed-length character data | Defined length * 2 bytes |
| varchar | Variable-length character data up to 8,000 length using collation character set | 1 byte per character |
| nvarchar | Unicode variable-length character data up to 8,000 length using collation character set | 2 bytes per character |
| text | Variable-length character data up to 2,147,483,647 length | 1 byte per character |
| ntext | Unicode variable-length character data up to 1,073,741,823 length | 2 bytes per character |
| sysname | A Microsoft user-defined data type used for table and column names that is the equivalent of nvarchar(128) | 2 bytes per character |

Unicode data types are very useful for storing multilingual data. The cost, however, is the doubled size. Some developers use nvarchar for all their character-based columns, while others avoid it at all costs. I recommend using Unicode data if the database might use foreign languages; otherwise use char, varchar, or text.

## Numeric Data Types

SQL Server supports several numeric data types, listed in Table 5-2.

### Table 5-2: Numeric Data Types

| Data Type | Description | Size in Bytes |
|---|---|---|
| bit | 1 or 0 | 1 bit |
| tinyint | Integers from 0 to 255 | 1 byte |
| smallint | Integers from -32,768 to 32,767 | 2 bytes |
| int | Integers from -2,147,483,648 to 2,147,483,647 | 4 bytes |
| bigint | Integers from $-2^{63}$ to $2^{63}-1$ | 8 bytes |
| decimal or numeric | Fixed-precision numbers up to $-10^{38} + 1$ | Varies according to length |

| Data Type | Description | Size in Bytes |
|---|---|---|
| money | Numbers from -2^63 to 2 ^63, accuracy to one ten-thousandths (.0001) | 8 bytes |
| smallmoney | Numbers from -214,748.3648 through +214,748.3647, accuracy to ten thousandths (.0001) | 4 bytes |
| float | Floating-point numbers ranging from -1.79E + 308 through 1.79E + 308, depending on the bit precision | 4 or 8 bytes |
| real | Float with 24-bit precision | 4 bytes |

**Best Practice**

When working with monetary values, be very careful with the data type. Using float or real data types for money will cause rounding errors. The data types money and small-money are accurate to one hundredth of a U.S. penny. For some monetary values, the client may request precision only to the penny, in which case decimal is the more appropriate data type.

## Date/Time Data Types

SQL Server stores both the date and the time in a single column using the datetime and smalldatetime data types, listed in Table 5-3. The primary differences between the two are accuracy and history. If the column is to hold only the date and will not contain historical data from before the twentieth century, smalldatetime is appropriate. If time is included in the requirement, the precision of smalldatetime is usually insufficient.

### Table 5-3: Date/Time Data Types

| Data Type | Description | Size in Bytes |
|---|---|---|
| datetime | Date and time values from January 1, 1753, through December 31, 9999, accurate to three milliseconds | 8 bytes |
| smalldatetime | Date and time values from January 1, 1900, through June 6, 2079, accurate to one minute | 4 bytes |

The Julian calendar took effect on January 1, 1753. Since SQL Server doesn't want to decide which nation's or religion's calendar system to use for data from before 1753, it avoids the issue and simply won't accept any dates prior to 1753. While this is normally not a problem, some historical and genealogy databases require earlier dates. As a workaround, I recommend creating a date column from a char data type and using a trigger or stored procedure to verify the date's formatting and validity upon insertion.

**Caution**

Some programmers (non-DBAs) choose character data types for date columns. This can cause a horrid conversion mess. Use the IsDate() function to sort through the bad data.

## Other Data Types

Other data types, listed in Table 5-4, fulfill the needs created by unique values, binary large objects, and variant data.

### Table 5-4: Other Data Types

| Data Type | Description | Size in Bytes |
|---|---|---|
| rowversion, timestamp | Database-wide unique random value generated with every update | 8 bytes |
| uniqueidentifier | System-generated 16-byte value | 16 bytes |
| binary | Fixed-length data up to 8,000 bytes | Defined length |
| varbinary | Variable-length binary data up to 8,000 bytes | Bytes used |
| image | Variable-length binary data up to 2,147,483,647 1bytes | Bytes used |
| sql_variant | Can store any data type up to 2,147,483,647 bytes | Depends on data type and length |

Rowversion is the new name for the SQL Server timestamp data type. It's good that Microsoft is changing to rowversion because the ANSI SQL standard uses timestamp as a datetime data type. Rowversion is not used for datetime data; it's simply a column that's updated to a new value every time the row is updated. This is useful for detecting lost updates, as discussed in Chapter 11, "Transactional Integrity."

The uniqueidentifier is a significant data type and it serves well as a primary key, especially when the database might be replicated. Uniqueidentifiers are discussed in detail in the "Creating Keys" section earlier in this chapter.

## Calculated Columns

A calculated column is powerful in that it presents the results of a predefined expression the way a view (a stored SQL select statement) does, but without the overhead of a view. Such a column does not actually store any data; instead the data is calculated when queried.

Calculated columns also improve data integrity by performing the calculation at the table level rather than trusting that each query developer will get the calculation correct. They may even be indexed.

The syntax is the opposite of that of a column alias:

```
ColumnName as Expression
```

The OrderDetail table from the OBX Kites sample database includes a calculated column for the extended price (abbreviated code listing):

```
CREATE TABLE dbo.OrderDetail (
...
  Quantity NUMERIC(7,2) NOT NULL,
  UnitPrice MONEY NOT NULL,
  ExtendedPrice AS Quantity * UnitPrice,
...
```

```
    )
    ON [Primary]
Go
```

# Column Constraints and Defaults

The database is only as good as the quality of the data. A constraint is a high-speed data-validation check or business-logic check performed at the database-engine level. Besides the data type itself, SQL Server includes five types of constraints:

✦ Primary-key constraint: Ensures a unique non-null key.

✦ Foreign-key constraint: Ensures value points to a valid key.

✦ Nullability: Whether the column can accept a null value.

✦ Check constraint: Custom Boolean constraint.

✦ Unique constraint: Ensures a unique value.

SQL Server also includes the column option:

✦ Column Default: Supplies a value if none is specified in the `insert` statement.

The column default is referred to as a type of constraint on one page of SQL Server SQL Server Books Online, but not listed in the constraints on another page. I call it a column option because it does not constrain user-data entry, nor does it enforce a data-integrity rule. However, it serves the column as a useful option.

## Column Nullability

A null value is an unknown value; typically it means that the column has not yet had a user entry.

**Cross-Reference** Chapter 6, "Retrieving Data with Select," explains how to define, detect, and handle nulls.

Whether or not a column will even accept a null value is referred to as the nullability of the column and is configured by the `null` or `not null` column attribute.

New columns in SQL Server default to not null, meaning that they do not accept nulls. However, this option is normally overridden by the connection property `ansi_null_dflt_on`. The ANSI standard is to default to `null`, which accepts nulls, in table columns that aren't explicitly created with a `not null` option.

**Best Practice** Because the default column nullability differs between ANSI SQL and SQL Server, it's best to avoid relying on the default behavior and explicitly declare null or not null when creating tables.

The following code demonstrates the ANSI default nullability versus SQL Server's nullability. The first test uses the SQL Server default by setting the database `ansi null` option to false and the `ansi_null_dflt_off` connection setting to on:

```
USE TempDB
EXEC sp_dboption 'TempDB', ANSI_NULL_DEFAULT, 'false'
SET ANSI_NULL_DFLT_OFF ON
```

The `NullTest` table is created without specifying the nullability:

```
CREATE TABLE NullTest(
  PK INT IDENTITY,
  One VARCHAR(50)
  )
```

The following code attempts to insert a null:

```
INSERT NullTest(One)
  VALUES (NULL)
```

Result:

```
Server: Msg 515, Level 16, State 2, Line 1
Cannot insert the value NULL into column 'One',
table 'TempDB.dbo.NullTest';
column does not allow nulls. INSERT fails.
The statement has been terminated.
```

Because the nullability was set to the SQL Server default when the table was created, the column does not accept null values. The second sample will rebuild the table with the ANSI SQL nullability default:

```
EXEC sp_dboption 'TempDB', ANSI_NULL_DEFAULT, 'true'
SET ANSI_NULL_DFLT_ON ON

DROP TABLE NullTest

CREATE TABLE NullTest(
  PK INT IDENTITY,
  One VARCHAR(50)
  )
```

Attempting to insert a null:

```
INSERT NullTest(One)
  VALUES (NULL)
```

Result:

```
(1 row(s) affected)
```

## Unique Constraints

A unique constraint is similar to a unique index or a primary-key constraint. Its purpose is to ensure that every value is a unique value. This option is likely to be used when a column has meaning to a user and is perceived as unique, such as an SSN or ID number.

In Enterprise Manager, a unique constraint is applied in the Index tab of the Table Properties dialog box in the same way that an index is created, except that the unique constraint is selected instead of index.

In code, a unique constraint may be applied to a column by specifying `unique` after the column definition, as follows:

```
CREATE TABLE Employee (
  EmployeeID INT PRIMARY KEY NONCLUSTERED,
  EmployeeNumber CHAR(8) UNIQUE,
  LastName NVARCHAR(35),
```

```
    FirstName NVARCHAR(35)
    )
Insert Employee (EmployeeID, EmployeeNumber, LastName, FirstName)
    Values( 1, '1', 'Wilson', 'Bob')

Insert Employee (EmployeeID, EmployeeNumber, LastName, FirstName)
    Values( 2, '1', 'Smith', 'Joe')
```

Result:

```
Server: Msg 2627, Level 14, State 2, Line 1
Violation of UNIQUE KEY constraint 'UQ__Employee__68487DD7'.
Cannot insert duplicate key in object 'Employee'.
The statement has been terminated.
```

To add a unique constraint to an existing table, use the `alter table` DDL command:

```
ALTER TABLE Employee
    ADD CONSTRAINT EmpNumUnique
        UNIQUE (EmployeeNumber)
```

## Check Constraints

The check constraint is a fast row-level integrity check. It's basically a small formula that ultimately must return a Boolean true or false. A check constraint may access any data local to the current row. It can't check other table values or perform look-ups. Scalar functions (covered in Chapter 6, "Retrieving Data with Select") may be included in the check constraint.

**Cross-Reference**

A check constraint can contain a user-defined scalar function, covered in Chapter 14, "Building User-Defined Functions," and the function can perform a range of T-SQL code. As a result, calling a user-defined scalar function within a check constraint opens up a world of possibilities, including the possiblity for complex look-ups. However, complex business-rule checks are more commonly performed within after triggers.

Check constraints are useful for ensuring the enforcement of general data-validation rules or simple business rules, such as checking that the termination date is greater than or equal to the hire date, and that the hire date is greater than the birthdate plus 18 years.

**Best Practice**

A check constraint is significantly faster than a table trigger. If the data-validation rule can be performed by a check constraint, use the check constraint instead of a trigger.

The following code applies the constraint that the `EmployeeNumber` must be other than "1":

```
Drop Table Employee

CREATE TABLE Employee (
    EmployeeID INT PRIMARY KEY NONCLUSTERED,
    EmployeeNumber CHAR(8) CHECK (EmployeeNumber <> '1'),
    LastName NVARCHAR(35),
    FirstName NVARCHAR(35)
    )

Insert Employee (EmployeeID, EmployeeNumber, LastName, FirstName)
    Values( 2, '1', 'Smith', 'Joe')
```

Result:

```
Server: Msg 547, Level 16, State 1, Line 1
INSERT statement conflicted with COLUMN CHECK constraint
'CK__Employee__Employ__5FB337D6'.
The conflict occurred in database 'tempdb',
table 'Employee', column 'EmployeeNumber'.
The statement has been terminated.
```

Use the `alter database` command to add a check constraint to an existing table:

```
ALTER TABLE Employee
  ADD CONSTRAINT NoHireSmith
    CHECK (Lastname <> 'SMITH')
```

## Default Option

The default is the value SQL Server will insert into the table if no value is supplied by the `insert` DDL command. Defaults become more important when the column does not permit nulls, because failing to specify a value when inserting into a non-nullable column without a default will cause the insert to be rejected.

The default value may be one of the following:

✦ A valid static numeric or character value, such as 123, or 'local'

✦ A scalar system function, such as GetDate(), or newID()

✦ A user-defined scalar function

✦ A null

The default value must a data type compatible with the column.

If the table is being created using Enterprise Manager, the default is easily specified as one of the column properties.

From code, the default is added as one of the column options as the table is first created, or later as an `alter table add constraint` DDL command.

The following truncated code sample is taken from the product table of the OBX Kite Store sample database. The `ActiveDate` column's default is set to the current date:

```
CREATE TABLE dbo.Product (
...
  ActiveDate DATETIME NOT NULL DEFAULT GETDATE(),
...
  )
```

The same default can be set after the table is created. The following code runs `sp_help` to determine the existing default constraint name, `drop` the constraint, and then re-establish the default constraint using `alter table`:

```
sp_help Product
```

Result (abbreviated):

```
constraint_type          constraint_name
------------------------  ------------------
DEFAULT on column ActiveDate
                          DF__Product__ActiveD__7F60ED59
```

The `alter table` command removes the existing default constraint:

```
ALTER TABLE Product
  DROP CONSTRAINT DF__Product__ActiveD__7F60ED59
```

The `add constraint` command re-applies the default:

```
ALTER TABLE Product
  ADD CONSTRAINT ActiveDefault
  DEFAULT GetDate() FOR ActiveDate
```

# Data Catalog

While SQL Server lacks a formal data-catalog feature, the user-defined data types can serve as a substitute. A user-defined data type is basically a named object with the following additional features:

✦ Defined data type and length

✦ Defined nullability

✦ Predefined rules that may be bound to the user-defined data types

✦ Predefined user-defaults that may be bound to the user-defined data types

For highly normalized databases that don't have the same basic data in different tables, the data-catalog concept may seem to be irrelevant. However, a good data-type standard within an IT shop is very useful. For example, if every database shares the same specs for a last-name column, coding at all levels becomes easier and less error-prone. To create a data catalog of rules, defaults, and user-defined data types, and apply it to multiple databases, the best plan would be to create a `DataCatalog.sql` script and then run that script in each database, or place them within the Model database.

## User-Defined Rules

A rule is similar to a check constraint, except it's created independently and then bound to a column. Once a rule is created it may be bound to multiple columns or user-defined data types. The rule consists only of a name and a Boolean expression. The Boolean expression can refer to data using the @ character followed by the name of a data column.

The following code demonstrates creating a rule that tests the birthday column and makes sure that future births aren't entered:

```
-- User Defined Rules
CREATE RULE BirthdateRule AS @Birthdate <= Getdate()
```

To apply the rule to a table column or user-defined data type, use the `sp_bindrule` stored procedure. The first parameter is the name of the rule and the second parameter is the object to which the rule is being bound. This code applies `BirthdateRule` to the `BirthDate` column in the person table:

```
EXEC sp_bindrule
  @rulename = 'BirthdateRule',
  @objname =  'Person.Birthdate'
```

**Best Practice**

Rules are considered a backward-compatibility feature, are not recommended by Microsoft and might not be supported in a future version of SQL Server. Check constraints are placed directly on the column, and using them is considered better coding practice than using Rules.

Within Enterprise Manager, rules are created and bound within the Rules node under each database. However, most developers who use rules will want to create them in a reusable script.

### User-Defined Default

Defaults are easily created directly in the table definition, although, like rules, they exist primarily for backward compatibility. However, the default object is a named value that may be consistently applied across multiple tables. The defaults may be created and bound to columns in Enterprise Manager in the Defaults node under each database.

The following code creates a user-defined default of the current date. The default is then bound to the Hiredate column:

```
CREATE DEFAULT HireDefault AS Getdate()
go
sp_bindefault 'HireDefault', 'Contact.Hiredate'
```

### User-Defined Data Type

A user-defined data type assigns a name to a system data type and nullability setting. The named user-defined data type may then be used like a system data type within any table definition.

The SysName data type is actually a Microsoft-supplied user-defined data type that should be used whenever you are storing system names (table names, column names) in columns.

Using Enterprise Manager, user-defined data types may be created under the User-Defined Data Type node under each database. User-defined data types may be defined with the sp_addtype system stored procedure by passing the name, data type, and nullability as parameters. The following example creates a user-defined data type, adds a default and a rule, and then binds that rule to a table:

```
EXEC sp_addtype
  @typename = Birthdate,
  @phystype = SmallDateTime,
  @nulltype = 'NOT NULL'
go
EXEC sp_bindefault
  @defname = 'BirthdateDefault',
  @objname = 'Birthdate',
  @futureonly = 'futureonly'

EXEC sp_bindrule
  @rulename = 'BirthdateRule',
  @objname = 'Person.Birthdate'
```

# Creating Indexes

The Aesop's Fable sample database, on the book's CD, contains 25 very short stories. The database is small enough that if you read through the stories, you can find any story within a few seconds. SQL Server Books-Online (BOL) is a different matter. I have several BOL articles in my Favorites tab, but my primary means of finding an article is the index.

The same is true of databases. Scanning the raw data is fine for small tables, but as the data grow, you need indexes to navigate quickly.

Indexing is one area where I really appreciate SQL Server. If you're moving to SQL Server from Access, you'll be amazed at the level of control SQL Server gives you over indexes. If you're moving to SQL Server from another client/server database, I think you'll like the administrative features that make working with indexes enjoyable. But my favorite feature of SQL Server indexes is their speed.

**Cross-Reference**

When creating indexes there's a tension between improving search performance and improving update performance. Indexes are great for reading data, but they cause extra work in terms of writing data.

While this section explains the various types of indexes and the mechanics of creating them, Chapter 28, "Advanced Performance," covers the SQL Server Profiler, the Index Tuning Wizard, and strategies for tuning indexes and queries.

SQL Server's indexes are fast balanced-tree (b-tree) style indexes. In one test that I performed at a client site several years ago, we used SQL Server 6.5 to set up two tables, one with a thousand rows of sample data, and one with a million rows, both properly indexed. The client didn't know which table was which. From the query execution speed when retrieving a single row the client was unable to tell the difference between the two tables. We got permission to do the job in SQL Server.

As I wrote this chapter, I ran *dbgencon,* a utility included with the SQL Server Resource Kit that generates random data, in the background, with the priority set to below average, for about 24 hours to populate two tables. The first table now has 25,583,733 rows; Enterprise Manager's Taskpad reports 8.63GB in it. The second table has a thousand rows at 376KB. Other than the number of rows, both tables have the same schema. With a non-clustered index on each table, retrieving a single row from each table requires three logical reads and 0 milliseconds. The number of logical hits needed to navigate through the b-tree was identical, and the performance difference was insignificant! Performing a join between the two tables was equally impressive. (And it's not my hardware — believe me.)

**Cross-Reference**

You can create an index on views; however this feature should be reserved for specific situations that require denormalizing. See Chapter 30, "Advanced Scalability," for more information on index views.

## Creating Indexes with Enterprise Manager

Three main methods exist for creating and managing indexes graphically:

✦ The Create Index Wizard

✦ The Index tab of the Table Properties page

✦ The Index Manager

Creating indexes using T-SQL code is demonstrated as each type of index is explained in the "Understanding Indexes" section later in this chapter.

### The Create Index Wizard

The Create Index Wizard is launched from the Wizards list. It doesn't add any functionality or value; it simply breaks down the decisions into the following separate pages:

✦ Choose a database name and table.

✦ Select a current index or create a new index.

✦ Select the columns to be included in the index.

✦ Set the index as clustered and/or unique. Select the fill factor.

✦ Enter the name of the index and position the columns in the correct order.

✦ Finished.

## Using the Index Manager

In contrast to the wizard, Enterprise Manager's Index Manager (Figure 5-9) is an excellent tool for viewing and administrating all the indexes on a table.

To open the Index Manager, select a table. From the right-mouse menu or the Action menu, choose All Tasks ⇨ Manage Indexes.

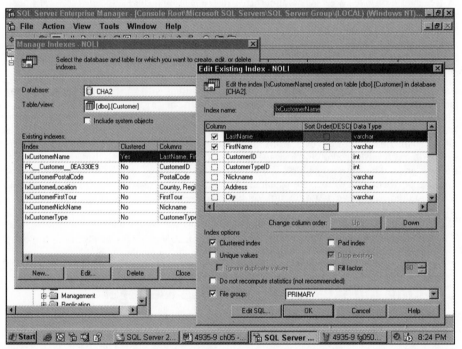

**Figure 5-9:** Enterprise Manager's Index Manager is the best graphic tool for working with indexes.

The Index Manager has two work surfaces. The first lists the current indexes, the index type (clustered or non-clustered), and the columns in the index. The New and Edit buttons open the Index dialog box with every index option available. The options are explained in the upcoming "Understanding Indexes" section.

## Table-Design Properties

The most common method of working with indexes graphically is by using the Table Properties dialog box in the Table Designer and Database Diagrammer. The Indexes/Keys tab does the job, as shown in Figure 5-10, but the interface is slightly clumsy. The top combo box is used to select an index to modify. There's no OK or Apply button. Whatever is entered is applied along with any changes in the table designer. Also, the New button instantly creates a new index. If the index isn't complete, the new index must be deleted before the dialog can be closed.

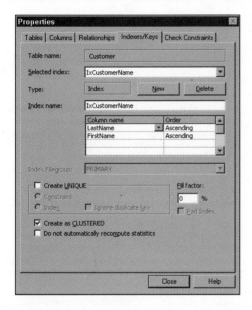

**Figure 5-10:** The Indexes/Keys tab of the Table Properties dialog box is the most commonly used indexing tool.

Once the clumsy interface is conquered, the rest of the Indexes/Keys tab is useful. It may be used to rename the index, assign any columns, and enable the options.

# Understanding Indexes

SQL Server uses two basic types of indexes, clustered and non-clustered. Both types of indexes may have multiple columns, in which case they are also considered composite indexes. And depending on how the index is used by a query, it may be a covering index.

## Non-Clustered Indexes

A typical desktop database uses a *non-clustered* index. The index is sorted and each index node points to an unsorted data row, as illustrated in Figure 5-11. A SQL Server 2000 table may have up to 255 non-clustered indexes.

The index in the back of this book is a good example of a non-clustered index. Any topic may be easily found in the text by first finding the topic in the book index and then using the index to point to a page in the book.

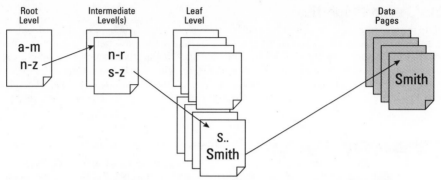

**Figure 5-11:** A non-clustered index is a fast b-tree structure that points to the data page.

To create a non-clustered index in code, use the `create index` DDL command followed by the index name. The index is created on a table and columns. This DDL command creates a non-clustered index on the `OrderNumber` column of the `[Order]` table in the OBXKites sample database:

```
CREATE NONCLUSTERED INDEX IxOrderNumber
  ON dbo.[Order] (OrderNumber)
```

An index may be created on a calculated column. The `quoted_identifier setting` must be on to create or modify indexed views or indexes on calculated columns.

## Clustered Indexes

A *clustered index* keeps the data in the same physical order as the index. A perfect example of a clustered index is a telephone book. The data and the index are one and the same. Inside a clustered index, SQL Server merges the leaf node of the index page with the data page, as shown in Figure 5-12. The data can have only one physical order, and therefore only one clustered index.

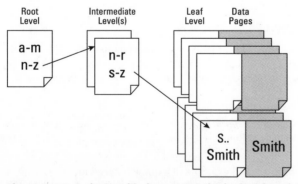

**Figure 5-12:** A clustered index merges the leaf nodes of the index page with the data page keeping the data in the same order as the index.

The fact that the clustered-index leaf nodes are merged with the data page has two effects. First, retrieving data via the clustered index requires one fewer logical read. Second, any other non-clustered index will point to the clustered-index ID instead of to the data page.

**Best Practice**

Clustered indexes gather rows with the same index value to the smallest possible number of data pages, thus reducing the number of data pages required to retrieve a set a rows. Clustered indexes are therefore excellent for columns that are often used to select a range of rows, such as secondary table foreign keys like OrderDetail.OrderID. For the same reason, a clustered index adds no significant performance benefits for single-row searches.

Clustered indexes tend to be misunderstood. Common misconceptions are:

✦ *A clustered index slows inserts because half the data must be moved down to make room for the inserted row.* This is false. The fill percentage allows room in the index page for inserts. If a page does fill, SQL Server performs a page split, with the result that only the first page is affected.

✦ *A clustered index on a primary key with an identity column is the fastest possible table design.* This is false. It's a waste of the clustered index. And, this method bunches every new row into the same data page at the end of the table, thus causing database hot spots and lock contention. A database I've seen with this scheme made customer-service reps wait several minutes to confirm every new order.

Although row locking (introduced with SQL Server version 7) partially relieves the hot spot problem (common with SQL Server 6.5 and earlier), depending on the number of rows being locked, the number of rows on the page, and the number of users, the lock manger may escalate rows locks to a page lock, and the hot spot is still a problem.

✦ *Clustered indexes are like magic. If any search is slow, set that column to the clustered index and the table will be fast.* This is false. Clustered indexes are ever-so-slightly faster than non-clustered indexes. Since each table can have only one clustered index, it's a precious performance resource and should be reserved for columns referenced by searches that look for a range or group of rows.

Clustered indexes are created in code with the create index command, much like non-clustered indexes. The following command creates a clustered index on the OrderID foreign key of the OrderDetail table:

```
CREATE CLUSTERED INDEX IxOrderID
  ON dbo.OrderDetail (OrderID)
```

To remove an index use the drop index command with both the table and index name:

```
DROP INDEX OrderDetail.IxOrderID
```

## Composite Indexes

A *composite index* is a clustered or non-clustered index that is based on multiple columns. Because composite indexes include multiple columns, they must be declared in a create index DDL statement after the table is created. The following code sample creates a composite clustered index on the guide table in the CHA2 database:

```
CREATE CLUSTERED INDEX IxGuideName
    ON dbo.Guide (LastName, FirstName)
```

The order of the columns in a composite index is important. For a search to take advantage of a composite index it must include the index columns from left to right. If the composite index is lastname, firstname, a search for firstname will not use the index, but a search for lastname, or lastname and firstname, will.

## Index Options

SQL Server indexes may have several options, including uniqueness, space allocation, and performance options.

### Unique Indexes

A `unique index` option is more than just an index with a unique constraint; index optimizations are available to unique indexes. A primary key or a unique constraint automatically creates a unique index.

In Enterprise Manager you create a unique index by checking the Unique option in the Create Index wizard, the Index Manager, or the Indexes/Keys tab of the Table Properties dialog box.

In code, you set an index as unique by adding the unique keyword to the index definition, as follows:

```
CREATE UNIQUE INDEX OrderNumber
  ON [Order] (OrderNumber)
```

### The Index Fill Factor and Pad Index

An index needs a little free space in the tree so that new entries don't require restructuring of the index. The fill factor is the percentage of space to be filled with data.

Because the index is a binary tree, each page must hold at least two rows. The fill factor and the pad index affect both the intermediate pages and the leaf node, as listed in Table 5-5.

### Table 5-5: Fill Factor and Pad Index

| Fill Factor | Intermediate Page(s) | Leaf Node |
|---|---|---|
| 0 | One free entry | 100% full |
| 1-99 | One free entry or <= fill factor if pad index | <= Fill factor |
| 100 | One free entry | 100% full |

The fill factor only applies to the detail, or leaf, node of the index, unless the `pad index` option is applied to the fill factor. The `pad index` option directs SQL Server to apply the looseness of the fill factor to the intermediate levels of the b-tree as well.

**Best Practice**

The best fill factor depends on the purpose of the database. If the database is primarily for data retrieval, a high fill factor will pack as much as possible in an index page. However, if the table sees lots of inserts, leaving some space open will improve update-operation performance. If the table will see a dramatic number of inserts, a mid-range fill factor and the `pad index` option are appropriate.

You specify the fill factor and index pad as options after the `create index` command. The following code example creates the OrderNumber index with 15 percent free space in both the leaf nodes and the intermediate pages:

```
CREATE NONCLUSTERED INDEX IxOrderNumber
  ON dbo.[Order] (OrderNumber)
  WITH FILLFACTOR = 85, PAD_INDEX
```

### The Index Sort Order

SQL Server can create the index as a descending index although I don't recommend changing from the default ascending-index order. You won't see a performance benefit and it can only cause confusion later. Any query using an `order by` clause will still be sorted ascending unless the query's `order by` specifically states `desc`.

The `asc` or `desc` option follows the column name in the `create index` DDL command.

### The Ignore Dup Key Index Option

The `ignore duplicate key` option doesn't affect the index, but rather how the index affects data modification operations later.

Normally, transactions are atomic, meaning that the entire transaction either succeeds or fails as a logical unit. However, the `ignore duplicate key` option directs `insert` transactions to succeed for all rows accepted by the unique index, and to ignore any rows that violate the unique index.

This option does not break the unique index. Duplicates are still kept out of the table, so the consistency of the database is intact, but the atomicity of the transaction is violated. Although this option might make importing a zillion questionable rows easier, I personally don't like any option that weakens the ACID properties of the database.

The following command is the same as the previous `create unique index` command, but with the `ignore_duplicate_key` option:

```
CREATE UNIQUE INDEX OrderNumber
   ON [Order] (OrderNumber)
   WITH IGNORE_DUP_KEY
```

### The Drop Existing Index Option

The `drop existing` option directs SQL Server to drop the current index and rebuild the new index from scratch. This may cause a slight performance improvement over rebuilding every index if the index being rebuilt is a clustered index and the table also has non-clustered indexes, because rebuilding a clustered index forces a rebuild of any non-clustered indexes.

### The Statistics Norecompute Index Option

The SQL Server query optimizer depends on data-distribution statistics to determine which index is most significant for the search criteria for a given table. Normally SQL Server updates these statistics automatically. However, some tables may receive large amounts of data just prior to being queried, and the statistics may be out of date. For situations that require manually initiating the statistics update, the `statistics norecompute` index option disables automatic statistics. But for nearly all indexes, this option should be ignored.

### Sort in Tempdb

This option modifies the only index-creation method by forcing it to use tempdb as opposed to memory. If the index is routinely dropped and recreated, this option may shorten the index-creation time. For most indexes, this option is neither required nor important.

### Filegroup

If the database was created with multiple named filegroups, the index may be created on a certain filegroup with the `on filegroupname` option:

```
ON filegroupname
```

This option is useful for spreading the disk I/O throughput for very heavily used databases. For example, if a Web page is hit by a million users per minute, and the main pages use a query that involves two tables and three indexes, and several disk subsystems are available, then placing each table and index on its own disk subsystem will improve performance. Remember that a clustered index must be in the same location as the table because the clustered index pages and the data pages are merged.

## Documenting the Database Schema

Several development errors can be averted by clearly documenting the database schema. I recommend the following five documentation methods:

✦ To list information about an object run `sp_help` *objectname*. To report the indexes and their sizes use `sp_spaceused`.

✦ Examine the information schema views (listed in Chapter 4, "Using SQL Server's Developer Tools") and develop your own views to list the column attributes that interest you.

✦ Organize the tables by module, creating a separate database diagram for each module. If done correctly these diagrams will fit on an 8-1/2 by 11 page for inclusion in a project binder.

✦ Use *Total SQL Analyzer* from FMS. This program loads information about your SQL Server database into another database and then produces dozens of excellent reports, lists of possible errors, performance suggestions, and more.

**On the CD-ROM** A 30-day trail version of *Total SQL Analyzer Pro* is on the book's CD.

✦ And my personal favorite: Use Visio to reverse-engineer the database and produce a database diagram that, once plotted, will cover the wall.

## Summary

The logical database schema often requires tweaking in order to serve as a physical schema. It's in the nitty-gritty of the physical-database schema that the logical design takes shape and becomes a working database within the restrictions of the data types, keys, and constraints of the database product. Knowing the table-definition capabilities of SQL Server means that you can implement some project features at the server-constraint level rather than in T-SQL code in a trigger or stored procedure.

With the physical layer in place, the next tasks typically involve establishing a recovery plan, moving the database to other servers, and securing the database. With that as the goal, the next chapter tackles recovery models, backup, and restore.

✦         ✦         ✦

# Retrieving Data with Select

**S**elect is the most powerful word in SQL. Because select is so common, it's easy to take it for granted; however, no keyword in any language I can think of is so flexible. Select can retrieve, twist, shape, join, and group data in nearly any way imaginable, and it's easily extended with the insert, update, and delete verbs for data modification.

A lot can be said about select, the premier data-manipulation language (DML) command. This chapter will first walk through the single table select command in its syntax order. From this foundation, advanced features are explained that add to the power of select, incorporating complex expressions, multiple types of joins, subqueries, and groupings.

Admittedly, this is a huge chapter; however, understanding the multiple options and creative techniques available with the select command is key to becoming a successful SQL Server developer or DBA.

One of the first things to understand is that SQL is a *declarative* language. This means that the SQL code describes the SQL query to the SQL optimizer, which then determines the best way to execute the query. As you'll see in this chapter, many ways of stating the query often exist, but each method is usually optimized to the same query-execution plan. This means you are free to express the SQL query in the way that makes the most sense to you. In some cases one method is considered cleaner or faster than another: I'll point those instances out as well.

## Choosing Your Tool

SQL statements may be issued from multiple sources: Enterprise Manger, Query Analyzer, MS Access, or one of many other user interfaces, including custom-written applications. Any of these graphic tools, or a programming interface such as ADO, sends SQL-modification statements to SQL Server for processing. From SQL Server's point of view, it doesn't matter where the statement originates; each statement is evaluated and processed as a SQL statement.

Regardless of which client tool you're using, the command you send to SQL Server to retrieve data is the select command. The two primary user interfaces within SQL Server, Enterprise Manager and the Query Analyzer, are both excellent tools for developing and testing select statements.

# Selecting Data with Enterprise Manager

Follow these steps to retrieve data using Enterprise Manager:

1. Open a database.

2. Select the Tables node.

3. Select a table.

4. Right-click the table.

5. Choose Open Table ➪ Return all rows.

The Enterprise Manager Query Designer (Figure 6-1) is comprised of four panes (descending):

✦ The Diagram pane is a graphical representation of the SQL from clause, including the data sources and joins.

✦ The Grid pane is used to choose the specific columns for output, update, where conditions, or sort order.

✦ The SQL pane uses the first two graphic panes to display the SQL statement as it is created. You can edit the SQL code here to build the SQL statement directly. This pane will prove to be an excellent transition tool as you become comfortable with SQL code.

✦ The Results pane displays the result set(s).

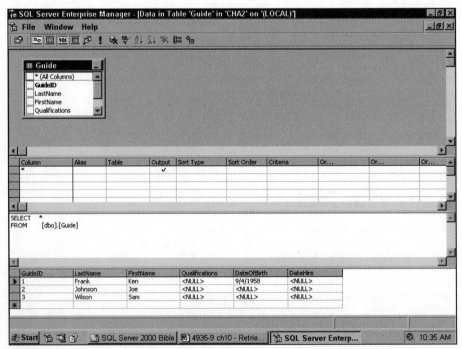

**Figure 6-1:** Building a select query in the Enterprise Manager Query Designer.

The panes may be enabled or hidden by selecting the desired pane in the toolbar. By default, the Query Designer opens to a `select` query. To execute the SQL statement, click the exclamation-mark button (!) on the toolbar.

This is just a quick overview for the purpose of retrieving data. For more information about using Enterprise Manger or Query Analyzer, refer to Chapter 4, "Using SQL Server's Developer Tools."

Don't rely too heavily on Enterprise Manger if you intend to master T-SQL and write stored procedures. Coding stored procedures requires SQL code with embedded variables, clean formatting, and joins arranged in a readable order. Enterprise Manager won't generate suitable SQL code for cutting and pasting into complex stored procedures and triggers.

## Retrieving Data with Query Analyzer

Query Analyzer is an excellent tool for ad-hoc data retrieval because it gets out of the way and lets the developer work as close to the SQL code as possible.

When selecting data using Query Analyzer, you enter the SQL statements as raw code in the top pane, as shown in Figure 6-2. The bottom pane displays the results in Grid mode or Text mode, and also displays any messages. The Object Browser presents a tree of all the objects in SQL Server, as well as templates for creating new objects with code.

If text is highlighted in Query Analyzer, then QA will execute only that text when you hit the Execute Query command button or the F5 key. This is an excellent way to test portions of SQL code.

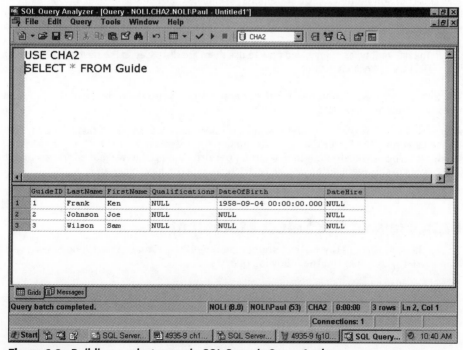

**Figure 6-2:** Building a select query in SQL Server's Query Analyzer.

Tip

Though it may vary depending on the user-security settings, the default database is probably the Master database. Be sure to change to the appropriate user database using the Database selector combo box in the toolbar, or the USE database command.

# Selecting Data from a Single Table

In its basic form, the select statement tells SQL Server what data to retrieve, including which columns, rows, and tables to pull from, and how to sort the data. This chapter begins by describing the basic flow of the select statement and then adds options as the chapter progresses.

Here's an abbreviated syntax for the select command:

```
SELECT *, columns, or expressions
  [FROM table]
    [JOIN table
      ON condition]
  [WHERE conditions]
  [GROUP BY columns]
  [HAVING conditions]
  [ORDER BY Columns]
```

The select statement begins with a list of columns or expressions. At least one expression is required — everything else is optional. The simplest possible valid select statement is:

```
select 1
```

The from portion of the select statement assembles all the data sources into a result set, which is then acted upon by the rest of the select statement. Within the from clause multiple tables may be referenced by using one of several types of joins.

Cross-
Reference

The different types of joins and how to use them are discussed in the next chapter, "Merging Data Using Relational Algebra."

The where clause acts upon the record set assembled by the from clause to filter certain rows based upon conditions.

Aggregate functions perform summation-type operations across the dataset. The group by clause can group the larger dataset into smaller datasets based upon the columns in the group by. The aggregate functions are then performed on the new smaller groups of data. The results of the aggregation can be restricted using the having clause.

And finally, the order by clause determines the sort order of the result set.

## Basic Flow of the Select Statement

To see the basic flow of the select statement, open Query Analyzer, turn on Show Execution Plan (Ctrl+K), and then run the following query:

```
SELECT LastName, FirstName
  FROM Guide
  WHERE Qualifications LIKE '%first aid%'
  ORDER BY LastName, FirstName
```

On the
CD-ROM

All the code for this chapter is on the CD in the file, \SQLServerBible\ChapterCode\ Ch 06 - Retreiving Data with Select.sql.

As illustrated in Figure 6-3, from right to left, the basic flow of the select statement is as follows:

1. The query begins with an Index Scan, which assembles the result set as specified in the from portion of the select statement.

2. The filter process is actually the where clause selecting only those rows of which the qualification includes the phrase "%First Aid%".

3. Once the rows are available and filtered they are sorted according to the order by.

4. The final process exports the select columns, which presents the result set to the client.

As more complexity is added to the SQL select, the flow will also become more complex. The indexes and tables available to the SQL Server Query Optimizer also affect the Query Execution Plan.

As you begin to think in terms of the SQL select statement rather than in terms of the graphical user interface, understanding the flow of select and how to read the Query Execution Plan will help you think through and debug difficult queries.

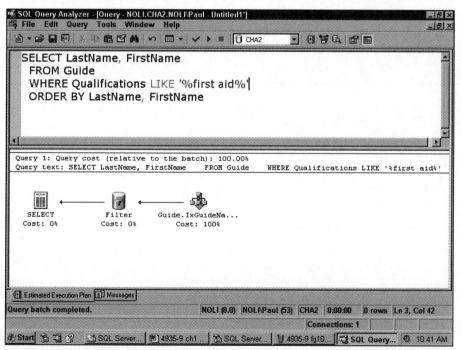

**Figure 6-3:** The Query Execution plan, read from right to left, shows the flow of the select statement.

## Select Distinct

The first predicate option in the `select` command is the keyword `distinct`, which eliminates duplicate rows from the result set of the query. The duplications are based only on the output columns, not the underlying tables.

The opposite of `distinct` is `all`. Because `all` is the default, it is typically ignored.

The following code sample demonstrates the `distinct` predicate. Joins are explained in the next chapter, "Merging Data Using Relational Algebra," but here the `join` between `tour` and `event` is generating a row for each time a tour is run as an event. Because this `select` statement returns only the `tourname` column, it's a perfect example of duplicate rows for the `distinct` predicate.

```
SELECT ALL TourName
  FROM Event
    JOIN Tour
      ON Event.TourID = Tour.TourID
```

Result:

```
TourName
-------------------------------------------------
Amazon Trek
Amazon Trek
Appalachian Trail
Appalachian Trail
Appalachian Trail
Bahamas Dive
Bahamas Dive
Bahamas Dive
Gauley River Rafting
Gauley River Rafting
Outer Banks Lighthouses
Outer Banks Lighthouses
Outer Banks Lighthouses
Outer Banks Lighthouses
Outer Banks Lighthouses
Outer Banks Lighthouses
```

With the `distinct` predicate:

```
SELECT DISTINCT TourName
  FROM Event
    JOIN Tour
      ON Event.TourID = Tour.TourID
```

Result:

```
TourName
-----------------------------------
Amazon Trek
Appalachian Trail
Bahamas Dive
Gauley River Rafting
Outer Banks Lighthouses
```

While the first query returned 16 rows, the `distinct` predicate in the second query eliminated the duplicate rows and retuned only the 5 unique rows.

**Note**  SQL Server's `distinct` is different from MS Access's `distinctrow`, which eliminates duplicates based on data in the source table(s), not duplicates in the result set of the query.

`Select distinct` functions as if a `group by` clause (discussed later in this chapter, in the "Summing and Grouping Data" section) exists on every output column. Examining the Query Execution Plan for the two previous queries (Figure 6-4), you can clearly see the `distinct` as a Stream Aggregate operation. So `distinct` does require another step in the Query Execution Plan. The performance hit, however, is small, (the details of the operation reveal that only .000006% of the query-execution time is used performing the Stream Aggregate operation); if `distinct` is logically necessary, you should not avoid it because of its effect on performance.

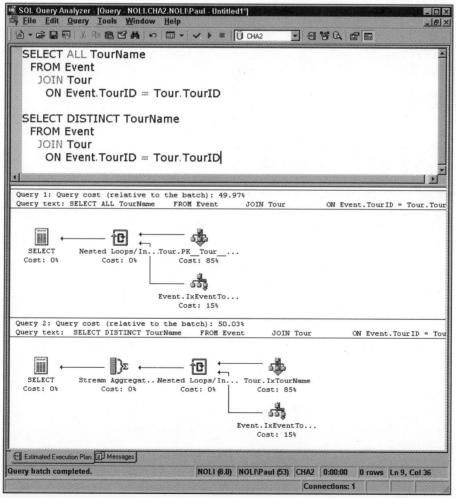

**Figure 6-4:** Comparing the Query Execution Plan for the two queries reveals the Stream Aggregate operation, which performs the distinct predicate and eliminates duplicate rows.

## Returning the Top Rows

By default, SQL Server will return all the rows from the select statement. The optional top predicate tells SQL Server to return only a few rows (either a fixed number or a percentage), based upon the options specified, as shown in Figure 6-5.

Top works hand in hand with order by. It's the order by clause that determines which rows are first. If the select statement does not have an order by clause, the top predicate still works by returning an unordered sampling of the result set.

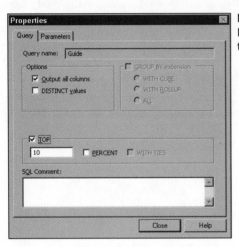

**Figure 6-5:** The top predicate is set within Enterprise Manager's Query Designer inside the query's Properties page.

The OBXKites sample database is a good place to test the top predicate. The following query finds the most expensive 3 percent of prices in the price table. The price table allows each product to have multiple prices, according to the effective date:

```
SELECT TOP 3 PERCENT Code, ProductName, Price,
    CONVERT(VARCHAR(10),EffectiveDate,1) AS PriceDate
  FROM Product
    JOIN Price ON Product.ProductID = Price.ProductID
  ORDER BY Price DESC
```

Result:

```
ProductCode  ProductName            Price      PriceDate
-----------  ---------------------  ---------  ----------
1018         Competition Pro 48"    284.9500   05/01/01
1018         Competition Pro 48"    264.9500   05/01/02
1017         Competition 36"        245.9500   05/20/03
1017         Competition 36"        225.9500   05/01/01
```

The next query locates the three cheapest prices in the price table:

```
SELECT TOP 3 Code, ProductName, Price,
    CONVERT(VARCHAR(10),EffectiveDate,1) AS PriceDate
  FROM Product
    JOIN Price ON Product.ProductID = Price.ProductID
  ORDER BY Price
```

Result:

```
ProductCode   ProductName              Price        PriceDate
-----------   --------------------     ----------   ----------
   1044       OBX Car Bumber Sticker   .7500        05/01/01
   1045       OBX Car Window Decal     .7500        05/20/01
   1045       OBX Car Window Decal     .9500        05/20/02
```

The query looks clean, and the answers look good; unfortunately, it's wrong. If you look at the raw data sorted by price, you'll see that there are actually three rows with a price of 95 cents. The with ties option will solve this problem.

**Best Practice**

> By the very nature of the formatting, computer-generated data tends to appear correct. Testing the query against a subset of data and known results is the best way to check its quality.

## The With Ties Option

The with ties option is important to the top predicate. It allows the last place to include multiple rows if those rows have equal values in the columns used in the order by clause. The following version of the previous query includes the with ties option and correctly results in five rows from a top 3 predicate:

```
SELECT TOP 3 WITH TIES ProductCode,
    ProductName, Price,
    CONVERT(varchar(10),EffectiveDate,1) AS PriceDate
  FROM Product
    JOIN Price ON Product.ProductID = Price.ProductID
  ORDER BY Price
```

Result:

```
ProductCode   ProductName              Price        PriceDate
-----------   --------------------     ----------   ----------
   1044       OBX Car Bumber Sticker   .7500        05/01/01
   1045       OBX Car Window Decal     .7500        05/20/01
   1045       OBX Car Window Decal     .9500        05/20/02
   1041       Kite Fabric #6           .9500        05/01/01
   1042       Kite Fabric #8           .9500        05/01/01
```

**Note**

> If you are moving from Access to SQL Server, you should be aware that, by default, Access adds the with ties option to the top predicate for you automatically.

## Dynamic Top

The number or percentage of rows returned by the top predicate must be hard-coded into the select statement. The top predicate won't accept a variable or expression in place of the number or percentage. As a workaround, the rowcount global variable may be used to set the number of rows affected for all following DML statements. To turn off the rowcount restriction, set rowcount to 0 and all rows will again be affected. In the following code sample, the rowcount variable is set to 3 to limit the rows returned by the select statement:

```
SET ROWCOUNT 3

SELECT  ProductCode, ProductName, Price,
  CONVERT(varchar(10),EffectiveDate,1) AS PriceDate
  FROM Product
    JOIN Price ON Product.ProductID = Price.ProductID
  ORDER BY Price
```

Result:

```
ProductCode  ProductName             Price      PriceDate
-----------  ----------------------  ---------  ----------
1044         OBX Car Bumber Sticker  .7500      05/01/01
1045         OBX Car Window Decal    .7500      05/20/01
1045         OBX Car Window Decal    .9500      05/20/02

SET ROWCOUNT 0
```

While rowcount gives you the luxury of dynamically setting the number of rows returned, it lacks the with ties option and can produce incomplete results.

**Caution**    Top is a Microsoft T-SQL extension to ANSI SQL and is not portable. If the database must be migrated to another database platform, the use of top will become a conversion problem. In contrast, the rowcount variable is portable. For more information about portability turn to Chapter 32, "Advanced Portability."

**Cross-Reference**    Alternately, you can code a dynamic SQL statement to handle the dynamic top value. Dynamic SQL is discussed in Chapter 12, "Programming with Transact SQL."

## Columns, Stars, Aliases, and Expressions

The title of this section may read like a bad tabloid headline, but in all seriousness it refers to the fact that the SQL select statement will return the columns in the order in which they're listed in the select statement. The source of a result column may be any expression or table column.

### The Star

The *, commonly called "star," is a special wildcard that includes all columns in their table order. If the query pulls from multiple tables, the * will include all columns from every table. Alternately, *tablename*.* will include only the columns from the named table.

**Best Practice**    It's better to list the columns returned by a select statement than to use the * and return all rows. This is true for two reasons. First, it reduces the amount of data returned. Second, specifying the columns prevents future errors that might otherwise be caused by table-schema changes, and which would then break code expecting *n* columns but receiving *n*+1 columns.

### Aliases

The name of the column in the underlying table will become the name of the column in the result set. Optionally, you can provide a column alias. If two underlying table columns have the same name, an alias will be required. Expressions and constants will have a blank column heading in the result set unless an alias is provided.

The as keyword is optional, however using it is a good practice that improves the readability of the code and helps prevent errors.

To use an alias that's identical to a SQL Server keyword or that includes a space, enclose the alias in square brackets, single quotes, or double quotes. Although the square brackets are not technically required if the alias is the same as an object name (that is, table or column name), I prefer to explicitly specify that the alias is not a keyword.

The following code demonstrates adding aliases to columns:

```
SELECT ProductName AS Product,
    'abc',
    ActiveDate + 365 AS OneYearSalesDate
  FROM Product
```

Result:

```
Product                     OneYearSalesDate
--------------------------- ---- ------------------------
Basic Box Kite 21 inch      abc  2003-07-22 20:59:53.967
Dragon Flight               abc  2003-07-22 20:59:54.000
Sky Dancer                  abc  2003-07-22 20:59:54.000
...
```

The first column's name is changed from `ProductName` to `Product` by means of an alias. The second column is an expression without an alias, so it has no column name. A better practice is to name expression columns using an alias, as demonstrated in the third column.

## Expressions

You can construct SQL expressions from a nearly limitless list of constants, operators, and functions, as detailed in Table 6-1. Figure 6-6 illustrates an expression and an alias.

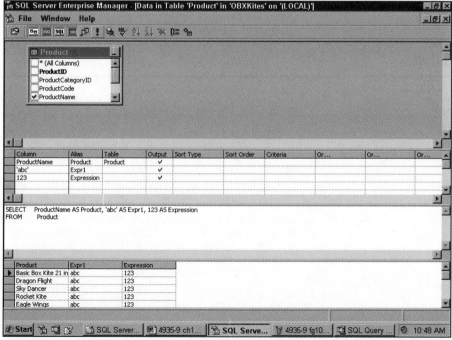

**Figure 6-6:** Building an expression and assigning an alias with Enterprise Manager's Query Designer.

### Table 6-1: Building Expressions

| Expression Components | Examples |
| --- | --- |
| Numeric constants | `1, 2, 3` |
| String literals | `'LastName', 'Employee: ', 'Life''s Great!'` |
| Dates | `'1/6/80', 'Jan 6, 1980', '19800106'` |
| Mathematical operators (in order of precedence) | `*, /, % (remainder), +, -` |
| String operator (concatenation) | `+` |
| Bitwise operators | `and &, or |, exclusive or ^, not ~` |
| Columns | `LastName, PrimaryKeyID` |
| Case Expressions | `CASE Column1`<br>`    WHEN 1 THEN 'on'`<br>`    ELSE 'off'`<br>`END AS Status` |
| Subqueries | `(Select 3)` |
| User-defined variables | `@MyVariable` |
| Global variables | `@@Error` |
| Scalar functions | `GetDate(), SysUser()` |
| User-defined functions | `dbo.MyUDF()` |

**Cross-Reference**    Case expressions are explained later in this chapter. Subqueries are covered in the next chapter, Merging Data using Relational Algebra." Variables are discussed in Chapter 12, "Programming with Transact-SQL." User-defined functions are detailed in Chapter 14, "Building User-Defined Functions."

While the meaning of many of these expression constants, operators, and expressions is obvious and common to other programming languages, a few deserve special mention:

✦ The Modulo mathematical operator (`%`) returns only the remainder of the division. The `floor()` (that's "deck" for sailors) and `ceiling()` mathematical functions, which return the integer rounded down or up, are related to it. The `floor` function is the SQL Server equivalent of the Basic `int()` function:

```
SELECT 15%4 as Modulo,
    FLOOR(1.25) as [Floor], CEILING(1.25) as [Ceiling]
```

Result:

```
Modulo       Floor Ceiling
----------- ----- -------
3            1     2
```

✦ The + operator is used for both mathematical expressions and string concatenation. This operator is different from the MS-DOS symbol for string concatenation, the ampersand (&).

```
SELECT 123 + 456 as Addition,
  'abc' + 'defg' as Concatenation
```

Result:

```
Addition     Concatenation
-----------  -------------

579          abcdefg
```

Data from table columns and string literals may be concatenated together to return custom data:

```
Select 'Product: ' + ProductName as [Product]
  From Product
```

Result:

```
Product
---------------------------------
Product: Basic Box Kite 21 inch
Product: Dragon Flight
Product: Sky Dancer
...
```

✦ When working with string literals, it's generally difficult to insert a quote into the string without ending the string and causing a syntax error. SQL Server handles this situation by accepting two single quotes and converting them into one single quote within the string:

```
'Life''s Great!' is stored as: Life's Great!
```

## Bitwise Operators

The bitwise operators are useful for binary manipulation. For example, one way to determine which columns were updated in a trigger is to inspect the `columns_updated()` function, which returns a binary representation of those columns. The trigger code can test `columns_updated()` using bitwise operations and respond to updates on a column-by-column basis.

Boolean bit operators (and, or, and not) are the basic building blocks of digital electronics and binary programming. While digital-electronic Boolean gates operate upon single bits, these bitwise operators work across every bit of the integer family data type (`int`, `smallint`, `tinyint`, and `bit`) values.

### Boolean And

A Boolean and, represented by the ampersand character (&), returns a value of `true` only if both inputs are true. If either or both are false, the "and" will return a value of `false`, as follows:

```
SELECT 1 & 1
```

Result:

```
1
```

Another "and" example:

```
SELECT 1 & 0
```

Result:

```
0
```

"And"ing two integers:

```
-- 3 = 011
-- 5 = 101
-- AND ---
-- 1 = 001

SELECT 3 & 5
```

Result:

```
1
```

## Boolean Or

The Boolean "or" operator, the vertical pipe character (|), returns true if either input is true:

```
SELECT 1 | 1
```

Result:

```
1
```

The following select statement combines a set and a cleared bit using the bitwise or operator:

```
SELECT 1 | 0
```

Result:

```
1
```

"Or"ing two integers:

```
-- 3 = 011
-- 5 = 101
-- OR  ---
-- 7 = 111

SELECT 3 | 5
```

Result:

```
7
```

## Boolean Exclusive Or

The "exclusive or" bitwise operator, the carat (^), returns a value of true if either input is true, but not if both are true. Using it is the same as "or"ing two "and"s, each with a "not" on one input. While that's simple to build in digital electronics, in code the operator is much easier to use, as shown here:

```
SELECT 1^1
```

Result:

```
0
```

A set bit "exclusive or"ed with a cleared bit results in a set bit:

```
SELECT 1^0
```

Result:

```
1
```

### Bitwise Not

The last bitwise operator, denoted by the tilde (~), is a bitwise "not" function. Traditionally, the "not" operates on a single bit and is used to alter the input of an "or" or "and" digital gate. This bitwise "not" is a little different. The "not" performs a logical bit reversal for every bit in the expression. The result depends on the data length of the expression. For example, the bitwise "not" of a set bit is a cleared bit:

```
DECLARE @A BIT
SET @A = 1
SELECT ~@A
```

Result:

```
0
```

The bitwise "not" is not suitable for use with Boolean expressions such as if conditions. The following code, for example, is invalid:

```
SELECT  * FROM Product WHERE ~(1=1)
```

Note that the "not" operator also serves as the "one's complement" operator.

## Case Expressions

SQL Server's case command is a flexible and excellent means of building dynamic expressions. If you're a programmer, no doubt you use the case command in other languages. This case command, however, is different. It's not used for programmatic flow of control, but rather to logically determine the value of an expression based on a condition, much like the iif() function in other programming languages.

Like any other expression, a case expression won't automatically have a column name. Therefore, as a rule, always provide an alias for any case expression.

**Best Practice**

When programmers write procedural code, it's often because part of the formula changes depending on the data. To a procedural mind-set, the best way to handle this is to loop through the rows and use multiple if statements to branch to the correct formula. However, using a case expression to handle the various calculations and executing the entire operation in a single query allows SQL Server to optimize the process and is dramatically faster.

Since the case expression returns an expressions, it may be used anywhere in the SQL DML statement where an expression may be used, including, column expression, join condition, where condition, having condition, or in the order by.

The case statement has two forms, simple and Boolean, described in the following sections.

### Simple Case

With the simple case the value is presented first and then each test value is listed. However, this case is limited in that it can perform only equal comparisons. The case expression sequentially checks the when conditions and returns the then value of the first true when condition.

In the following example, based on the OBX Kite Store database, one customertype is the default for new customers and is set to true in the isdefault column. The case expression compares the value in the default column with each possible bit setting and returns the character string 'default type' or 'possible' based on the bit setting.

```
USE OBXKites
SELECT CustomerTypeName,
    CASE [IsDefault]
      WHEN 1 THEN 'default type'
      WHEN 0 THEN 'possible'
      ELSE '-'
    End as AssignStatus
  From CustomerType
```

Result:

```
CustomerTypeName          AssignStatus
------------------------- ------------
Preferred                 possible
Wholesale                 possible
Retail                    default type
```

The case expression concludes with an end and an alias. In this example, the case expression evaluates the isdefault column, but produces the AssignStatus column in the SQL select result set.

### Boolean Case

The Boolean form of case is more flexible than the simple form in that each individual case has its own Boolean expression. So not only can each when condition include comparisons other than =, but the comparison may also reference different columns:

```
SELECT
  CASE
    WHEN 1<0 THEN 'Reality is gone.'
    WHEN GetDate() = '11/30/2005'
      THEN 'David gets his driver''s license.'
    WHEN 1>0 THEN 'Life is normal.'
  END AS RealityCheck
```

Result of the query when executed on David's 16th birthday:

```
RealityCheck
--------------------------------
David gets his driver's license.
```

As with the simple case, the first true then condition halts evaluation of the case and returns the when value. In this case (Ha! A pun!), if 1 is ever more than 0 the RealityCheck case will accurately report 'reality is gone.' When my son turns 16, the realitycheck will again accurately warn us of his legal driving status. If neither of these conditions is true, and 1 is still greater than 0, all is well with reality and 'Life is normal.'

The point of the preceding code is that the Boolean case expression offers more flexibility than the simple case. This example mixed various conditional checks (<, =, >), and differing data was checked by the when clause.

The Boolean case expression can handle complex conditions including Boolean and and or operators. The following code sample uses a batch to set up the case expression (including T-SQL variables which are explained in Chapter 12, "Programming with Transact SQL"), and the case includes an and and a between operator:

```
DECLARE @b INT, @q INT

SET @b = 2007
SET @q = 25

Select CASE
   WHEN @b = 2007 AND @q BETWEEN 10 AND 30 THEN 1
   ELSE NULL
END AS Test
```

Result:

```
Test
---------
1
```

# From Datasets

The first component of the execution of a typical SQL select statement is the from clause. In a simple SQL select statement the from clause will contain a single table. However, the from clause can contain multiple joined tables, subqueries as derived tables, and views. The maximum number of tables that may be accessed within a single SQL select statement is 256.

The from clause is the foundation of the rest of the SQL statement. For a table column to be in the output, or accessed in the where conditions, or in the order by, it must be in the from clause.

## Named Ranges

A table may be assigned a named range, or table alias, within the from clause. Once the table has an alias, the table must be referred to by this new name. The keyword as is optional and is commonly ignored. The following code accesses the Guide table, but refers to it within the query as table G:

```
-- From Table [AS] Range Variable
USE CHA2
SELECT G.lastName, G.FirstName
  FROM Guide AS G
```

## [Table Name]

If the name of a database object, such as a table or column name, conflicts with a SQL keyword, you can let SQL know that it's the name of an object by placing it inside square brackets. The [Order] table in the OBX Kites sample database is a common example of a table name that's also a keyword:

```
USE OBXKites
SELECT OrderID, OrderDate
  FROM [Order]
```

Although it's considered poor practice to include spaces within the names of database objects, some database developers don't follow this guideline. If this is the case, square brackets are required when specifying the database object. The `Order Details` table in the Northwind sample database illustrates this:

```
USE Northwind
SELECT OrderID, ProductID, Quantity
  FROM [Order Details]
```

### Four-Part Table Names

The full and proper name for a table is not just the table name but what's called a *four-part* name:

```
Server.Database.Owner.Table
```

If the table is in the current database, the server and database name are not required. Although it is not required, it's still good practice to specify the table's owner, and here's why. It's possible for a database to have multiple tables with the same name if the tables have different owners. In this case the tables have scope to their respective owner. If the database owner creates a table called `Customer`, and Mary creates a table called `Customer` with herself as the owner, then Mary will see `Mary.Customer` and everyone else will see `dbo.Customer`. If the owner is not specified, SQL Server must check to see which table is actually being referenced.

The use of the four-part name enables the reusability of the query-execution plan. Therefore, it's not only a cleaner programming practice; performance benefits also result from specifying the table's owner. Now that the four-part name has been explained, from here on sample code in this book will include the owner in the name.

Chapter 28, "Advanced Performance," discusses Query Execution Plan re-use in more detail.

The `from` clause is not limited to tables only in the current database or even on the current server. Chapter 18, "Working with a Distributed Queries," explains the many methods of retrieving data from, and updating the data outside, the local database, and even outside SQL Server.

## Where Conditions

The `where` conditions filter the output of the `from` clause and restrict the rows that will be returned in the result set. The conditions can refer to the data within the tables, expressions, built-in SQL Server scalar functions, or user-defined functions. The `where` conditions can make use of several possible comparison operators and wildcards, as listed in Table 6-2. Also, you can specify multiple `where` conditions with Boolean `and`, `or`, and `not` operators.

One sure way to improve the performance of a client/server database is to let the database engine do the work of restricting the rows returned rather than making the calling application wade through unnecessary data. However, if the database design requires the use of functions within the `where` clause to locate rows, the function will seriously degrade performance, because the function is performed on each row. Because of this, well-written `where` conditions, based on well-planned database designs, are some of the best performance tools available to the SQL Server developer.

## Table 6-2: Standard Comparison Operators

| Description | Operator | Example |
|---|---|---|
| Equals | = | Quantity = 12 |
| Greater than | > | Quantity > 12 |
| Greater than or equal to | >= | Quantity >= 12 |
| Less than | < | Quantity < 12 |
| Less than or equal to | <= | Quantity<= 12 |
| Not equal to | <> , != | Quantity <> 12 , Quantity != 12 |
| Not less than | !< | Quantity !< 12 |
| Not greater than | !> | Quantity !> 12 |

**Caution**

The comparison operators that include an exclamation point are not ANSI standard SQL. <> is portable; != is not.

In addition to the standard comparison operators, which are no doubt familiar, SQL provides four special comparison operators: between, in, like, and is. The first three are explained in this section. Testing for nulls using the is keyword, and handling nulls, are explained in the next section.

**Best Practice**

The best way to find a thing is to look for it, rather than to first eliminate everything it isn't. It's far easier to locate a business in a city than it is to prove that the business doesn't exist somewhere in a city. The same is true of database searches. Proving that a row meets a condition is faster than first eliminating every row that doesn't meet that condition. As a guideline, restating a negative where condition as a positive condition will improve performance.

## Using the Between Search Condition

The between search condition tests for values within a range. The range can be deceiving, because the range is inclusive. For example, between 1 and 10 would test for 1 and 10. When using the between search condition the first value must be less than the latter value because in actuality, the between search condition is shorthand for "greater than or equal to the first value, and less than or equal to the second value."

The between search condition is commonly used with dates. The following code sample, also shown in Figure 6-7, locates all events from the Cape Hatteras Adventures sample database occurring during July 2001:

```
USE CHA2

SELECT EventCode, DateBegin
  FROM dbo.Event
  WHERE DateBegin BETWEEN '07/01/01' AND '07/31/01'
```

Result:

```
EventCode   DateBegin
----------  -------------------------
01-006      2001-07-03 00:00:00.000
01-007      2001-07-03 00:00:00.000
01-008      2001-07-14 00:00:00.000
```

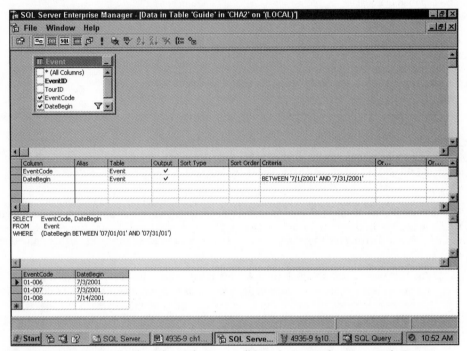

**Figure 6-7:** You can set the where clause conditions in Enterprise Manager's Query Designer in the Grid or SQL pane.

The previous query returns an accurate result if the dates are stored without a time value. But most applications grab the data and time using SQL Server's GetDate() function, with the time captured to within three milliseconds. If this is the case, every row has the date and time stored. Therefore, the previous query would miss every row after the time 00:00:00.000 on '07/31/01'. If rows are to be properly selected by full date and time, the end parameter must include the last time for the day. As the next code sample demonstrates, the last time the SQL Server knows about is 12:59:59.998 pm:

```
CREATE TABLE dbo.DateTest(
  PK INT IDENTITY,
  OrderDate DATETIME
  )
go
INSERT dbo.DateTest(OrderDate)
  VALUES('1/1/01 00:00')
INSERT dbo.DateTest(OrderDate)
  VALUES('1/1/01 23:59')
```

```
INSERT dbo.DateTest(OrderDate)
  VALUES('1/1/01 11:59:59.995 pm')
INSERT dbo.DateTest(OrderDate)
  VALUES('1/2/01')
```

The following query demonstrates the last valid time for the day:

```
SELECT *
  FROM dbo.DateTest
  WHERE OrderDate BETWEEN '1/1/1' AND '1/1/1 11:59:59.998 PM'
```

Result:

```
PK           OrderDate
----------- ------------------------
1            2001-01-01 00:00:00.000
2            2001-01-01 23:59:00.000
3            2001-01-01 23:59:59.997
```

SQL Server automatically adjusts this query to the next nearest three milliseconds, causing it to return erroneous results:

```
SELECT *
  FROM dbo.DateTest
  WHERE OrderDate BETWEEN '1/1/1' AND '1/1/1 11:59:59.999 PM'
```

Result:

```
PK           OrderDate
----------- ------------------------
1            2001-01-01 00:00:00.000
2            2001-01-01 23:59:00.000
3            2001-01-01 23:59:59.997
4            2001-01-02 00:00:00.000

DROP TABLE DateTest
```

The second query's end time is adjusted to the nearest three-millisecond mark and incorrectly selects any rows for the next day without a time.

The same issue is present with `smalldatetime` data-type columns, which are accurate only to the minute. Selecting `where column <= 11:59:30 pm` rounds up to 12:00 am the next day.

The following query from the `Family_Queries.sql` script uses the `between` search condition to find mothers who bore children less than nine months after marrying.

Beginning with the `from` clause, the query gathers information about the mother, the marriage, and the children, all from the `person` table. The `where` clause then restricts the results to those with the child's `DateOfBirth` within a certain time frame.

```
SELECT Person.FirstName + ' ' + Person.LastName AS Mother,
   Convert(Char(12), Marriage.DateOfWedding, 107) as Wedding,
   Child.FirstName + ' ' + Child.LastName as Child,
   Convert(Char(12), Child.DateOfBirth, 107) as Birth
  FROM Person
   JOIN Marriage
     ON Person.PersonID = Marriage.WifeID
   JOIN Person Child
     ON Person.PersonID = Child.MotherID
```

```
WHERE Child.DateOfBirth
   BETWEEN Marriage.DateOfWedding
     AND DATEADD(mm, 9, Marriage.DateOfWedding)
```

Result:

```
Mother            Wedding        Child             Birth
----------------  -------------  ----------------  ------------
Alysia Halloway   Jan 01, 1975   James Halloway    May 24, 1975
```

## Using the In Search Condition

The in search condition is similar to the equals comparison operator, but the in search condition searches for an exact match from a list. If the value is in the list, the comparison is true. For instance, if region data was entered into the database, the following code finds any Cape Hatteras Adventures' base camps in North Carolina or West Virginia:

```
USE CHA2
SELECT BaseCampname
  FROM dbo.BaseCamp
  WHERE Region IN ('NC', 'WV')
```

Result:

```
BaseCampName
-----------
West Virginia
Cape Hatteras
Ashville NC
```

Effectively, the in search condition is the equivalent of multiple equals comparisons "or"ed together:

```
USE CHA2
SELECT BaseCampname
  FROM dbo.BaseCamp
  WHERE Region = 'NC'
    OR Region = 'WV'
```

Result:

```
BaseCampName
-----------
West Virginia
Cape Hatteras
Ashville NC
```

The in operator may be combined with not to exclude certain rows. For example, where not in ('NC', 'SC') would return all rows except those in the Carolinas:

```
USE CHA2
SELECT BaseCampname
  FROM dbo.BaseCamp
  WHERE Region NOT IN ('NC', 'SC')
```

Result:

```
BaseCampName
-----------
FreePort
Ft Lauderdale
West Virginia
```

It's difficult to prove a negative. Especially when a null value is involved. Since the meaning of null is "unknown," the value being searched for could be in the list. The code sample demonstrates how a null in the list will make it impossible to prove that 'A' is not in the list.

```
SELECT 'IN' WHERE 'A' NOT IN ('B',NULL)
```

There's no result, because the unknown null value just might be an "A." Since SQL can't logically prove that "A" is not in the list, the where clause returns a false. Any time a not in condition is mixed with a null in the list, every row will be evaluated as false.

In is very powerful. Although the previous query used a hard-coded list of states, when combined with a subquery (explained in the next chapter) to generate a dynamic list, in solves a world of problems.

## Using the Like Search Condition

The like search condition uses wildcards to search for patterns within the string. The wildcards, however, are very different from the MS-DOS wildcards you may be familiar with, as shown in Table 6-3.

### Table 6-3: SQL Wildcards

| Description | SQL Wildcard | MS/DOS Wildcard | Example |
|---|---|---|---|
| Multiple characters | % | * | 'Able' LIKE 'A%' |
| Single character | _ | ? | 'Able' LIKE 'Abl_' |
| Match in range of characters | [ ] | n/a | 'a' LIKE '[a-g]' |
| | | | 'a' LIKE '[abcdefg]' |
| Match not in range of characters | [^ ] | n/a | 'a' LIKE '[^w-z]' |
| | | | 'a' LIKE '[^wxyz] ' |

The next query uses the like search condition located all products that begin with "air" followed by any number of characters:

```
USE OBXKites

SELECT ProductName
  FROM dbo.Product
  WHERE ProductName LIKE 'Air%'
```

Result:

```
ProductName
-------------------
Air Writer 36
Air Writer 48
Air Writer 66
```

The following query finds any `productname` beginning with a letter between *a* and *d* inclusive:

```
SELECT ProductName
  FROM Product
  WHERE ProductName LIKE  '[a-d]%'
```

Result:

```
ProductName
-------------------------------------------------
Basic Box Kite 21 inch
Dragon Flight
Chinese 6" Kite
Air Writer 36
Air Writer 48
Air Writer 66
Competition 36"
Competition Pro 48"
Black Ghost
Basic Kite Flight
Advanced Acrobatics
Adventures in the OuterBanks
Cape Hatteras T-Shirt
```

To search for a pattern that contains a wildcard, there are two possible methods: Either enclose the wildcard in square brackets, or put an escape character before it. The trick to the latter workaround is that the escape character is defined within the `like` expression.

The following two examples search for the phrase "F-15" in the OBX Kites `product` table. The first query encloses the hyphen, which is normally a wildcard, in square brackets, while the second query defines the ampersand as the escape character:

```
SELECT ProductCode, ProductName
  FROM Product
  WHERE ProductName LIKE '%F[-]15%'

SELECT ProductCode, ProductName
  FROM Product
  WHERE ProductName LIKE '%F&-15%' ESCAPE '&'
```

Both queries produce the same Result:

```
ProductCode      ProductName
---------------  -----------
1013             Eagle F-15
```

**Caution**      Of the two methods of searching for wildcard characters, the square bracket method is T-SQL specific and is not ANSI SQL standard. The escape method, however, is SQL standard and is portable.

When using the `like` operator, be aware that the database collation's sort order will determine both the case sensitivity and the sort order for the range of characters. You can optionally use the keyword `collate` to specify the collation sort order used by the `like` operator.

**Best Practice**

While the `like` operator can be very useful, it can also cause a performance hit. Indexes are based on the beginning of the column, not on phrases in the middle of the column. If you find that the application requires frequent use of the `like` operator, you should enable full-text indexing—a powerful indexing method that can even take into consideration weighted words and variations of inflections, and can even return the result set in table form with ranking for joining. See Chapter 8, "Searching Full-Text Indexes," for more details.

## Multiple Where Conditions

You can combine multiple `where` conditions within the `where` clause using the Boolean logical operators: `and`, `or`, and `not`. Just as with the mathematical operators of multiplication and division, an order of precedents exists with the Boolean logical operators: `and` comes first, then `or`, and then `not`:

```
SELECT ProductCode, ProductName
  FROM dbo.Product
  WHERE
      ProductName LIKE 'Air%'
    OR
      ProductCode between '1018' AND '1020'
    AND
      ProductName LIKE '%G%'
```

Result:

```
ProductCode       ProductName
---------------   ----------------------
1009              Air Writer 36
1010              Air Writer 48
1011              Air Writer 66
1019              Grand Daddy
1020              Black Ghost
```

With the addition of parentheses, the result of the query is radically changed:

```
SELECT ProductCode, ProductName
  FROM Product
  WHERE
    (ProductName LIKE 'Air%'
    OR
      ProductCode between '1018' AND '1020')
    AND
      ProductName LIKE '%G%'
```

Result:

```
ProductCode       ProductName
---------------   ----------------------
1019              Grand Daddy
1020              Black Ghost
```

While the two preceding queries are very similar, in the first query the natural precedence of Boolean operators caused the and to be evaluated before the or. The or included the Air Writers in the results.

The second query used parentheses to explicitly dictate the order of the Boolean operators. The or collected the Air Writers and products with a ProductCode of 1018, 1019, or 1020. This list was then anded with the Products that included the letter g in their names. Only Products 1019 and 1020 passed both of those tests.

**Best Practice**

When coding complex Boolean or mathematical expressions, explicitly stating your intentions with parentheses or detailed code reduces misunderstandings and errors based on assumptions.

## Select...Where

Amazingly, using the where clause in a select statement does not require you to use a from clause, or any table reference at all. A select statement without a from clause operates as a single row:

```
SELECT 'abc'
```

Result:

```
abc
```

A where clause on a non-table select statement serves as a restriction to the entire select statement. If the where condition is true, the select statement will function as expected:

```
SELECT 'abc' WHERE 1>0
```

Result:

```
abc
```

If the where condition is false, the select statement is not executed:

```
DECLARE @test NVARCHAR(15)
SET @test = 'z'
SELECT @test = 'abc' WHERE 1<0
SELECT @test
```

Result:

```
z
```

Functionally, a where clause on a non-table select statement is shorthand for an if condition like the one that follows:

```
DECLARE @test NVARCHAR(15)
SET @test = 'z'
IF 1<0
  SELECT @test = 'abc'
SELECT @test
```

Result:

```
z
```

## Ordering the Result Set

Data in a SQL table takes the form of an unsorted list. The primary key's purpose is to uniquely identify the row, not sort the table. Other desktop databases may present the table in the order of the primary key if no order by clause exists. However, it is not a good practice to depend on that behavior. If you do not specify an order by clause, the order of the rows in the result set will have no defined meaning.

Having said that, if no order by clause exists, SQL Server will return the rows in the order in which they are fetched. If a table has a clustered index, the rows will likely be returned according to the clustered index. Other logical operations within the query may sort the data to support the logical operation. For example, some joins will sort the data to make the join easier to perform. So even without an order by clause the data result may appear to be sorted, but this is merely a coincidence. Again, if the rows are required to be in that order, good practice is to specify such within an order by clause, as demonstrated in Figure 6-8.

SQL can sort by multiple columns, and the sort columns don't have to be columns that are returned by the select, so there's lots of flexibility in how the columns are specified.

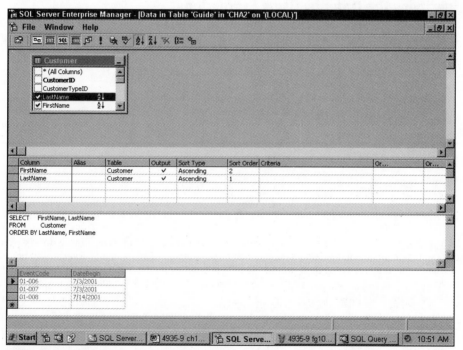

**Figure 6-8:** Within Enterprise Manager's Query Designer, you can define the sort order by clicking the Ascending or Descending button on the toolbar, or by setting the sort order in the Grid Pane.

## Specifying the Order by Using Columns Names

The simplest way to sort the result set is to completely spell out the order by columns:

```
USE CHA2

SELECT FirstName, LastName
  FROM dbo.Customer
  ORDER BY LastName, FirstName
```

Result:

```
FirstName      LastName
-------------  --------------------
Joe            Adams
Missy          Anderson
Debbie         Andrews
Dave           Bettys
...
```

## Specifying the Order by Using Expressions

In the case of sorting by an expression, the entire expression can be repeated in the order by clause. This does not cause a performance hit, because the SQL Server query optimizer is smart enough to avoid recomputing the expression.

```
SELECT LastName + ', ' + FirstName
  FROM dbo.Customer
  ORDER BY LastName + ', ' + FirstName
```

Result:

```
FullName
---------------------
Adams, Joe
Anderson, Missy
Andrews, Debbie
Bettys, Dave
...
```

Using an expression in the order by clause can solve some headaches. Some database developers store titles in two columns, one column includes the full title, and the duplicate column stores the title stripped of the leading "The." For performance, such denormalization might be a good idea. But using a case expression within the order by clause will sort correctly without duplicating the title.

The Aesop's Fables sample database includes a list of titles. If the Title includes a leading "The" then the case expression removes it from the data and passes to the order by:

```
USE Aesop
SELECT Title, Len(FableText) AS TextLength
  FROM Fable
  ORDER BY
    CASE
      WHEN SubString(Title, 1,3) = 'The'
        THEN SubString(Title, 5, Len(Title)-4)
      ELSE Title
    END
```

Result:

```
FableName                              TextLength
-------------------------------------  -----------
Androcles                              1370
The Ant and the Chrysalis              1087
The Ants and the Grasshopper           456
The Ass in the Lion's Skin             465
The Bald Knight                        360
The Boy and the Filberts               435
The Bundle of Sticks                   551
The Crow and the Pitcher               491
...
```

## Specifying the Order by Using Column Aliases

Alternately, a column alias may be used to specify the columns used in the order by clause. This is the preferred method for sorting by an expression, because it makes the code easier to read. In addition, this example sorts in descending order rather than the default ascending order:

```
SELECT LastName + ', ' + FirstName as FullName
  FROM dbo.Customer
  ORDER BY FullName DESC
```

Result:

```
FullName
-------------
Zeniod, Kent
Williams, Larry
Valentino, Mary
Spade, Sam
...
```

Notice that an alias is allowed in the order by clause, but not the where clause. That's because the where clause is logically executed near the beginning of the query execution, while the order by clause is the last logical operation and follows the assembling of the columns and aliases.

## Specifying the Order by Using Column Ordinal Positions

The ordinal number (column position number) of the column can be used to indicate the order by columns. I don't recommend this method because if the columns are changed at the beginning of the select statement the order by will function differently. However, I have used the ordinal number to specify the sort for complex union queries, which are discussed in the next chapter. The following query demonstrates sorting by ordinal position:

```
SELECT LastName + ', ' + FirstName as FullName
  FROM dbo.Customer
  ORDER BY 1
```

Result:

```
FullName
--------------------
Adams, Joe
Anderson, Missy
Andrews, Debbie
Bettys, Dave
...
```

## Order by and Collation

SQL Server's collation order is vital to sorting data. Besides determining the alphabet, the collation order also determines whether accents, case, and other alphabet properties are considered in the sort order. For example, if the collation is case-sensitive, the uppercase letters are sorted before the lowercase letters. The following functions report the installed collation options and the current collation server property:

```
SELECT * FROM ::fn_helpcollations()
```

Result:

```
name                    description
--------------------    --------------------------
Albanian_BIN            Albanian, binary sort
Albanian_CI_AI          Albanian, case-insensitive,
                        accent-insensitive,
                        kanatype-insensitive, width-insensitive
Albanian_CI_AI_WS       Albanian, case-insensitive,
                        accent-insensitive,
                        kanatype-insensitive, width-sensitive
...
SQL_Latin1_General_CP1_CI_AI
                        Latin1-General, case-insensitive,
                        accent-insensitive,
                        kanatype-insensitive, width-insensitive
                        for Unicode Data, SQL Server Sort Order
                        54 on Code Page 1252 for non-Unicode
                        Data
...
```

The following query reports the current server collation:

```
SELECT SERVERPROPERTY('Collation') AS ServerCollation
```

Result:

```
ServerCollation
------------------------
SQL_Latin1_General_CP1_CI_AS
```

While the server collation setting was determined during setup, the collation property for a database or column can be set using the collate keyword. The following code changes the Family database collation so that it becomes case-sensitive:

```
ALTER DATABASE Family
   COLLATE SQL_Latin1_General_CP1_CS_AS
```

```
SELECT DATABASEPROPERTYEX(Family,'Collation')
  AS DatabaseCollation
```

Result:

```
DatabaseCollation
----------------------------------
SQL_Latin1_General_CP1_CS_AS
```

Not only can SQL Server set the collation at the server, database, and column levels, but the collation can even be set at the individual query. The following query will be sorted according to the Danish collation without regard to case or accents:

```
SELECT *
  FROM dbo.Product
  ORDER BY ProductName
    COLLATE Danish_Norwegian_CI_AI
```

Not every query needs to be sorted, but for those that do, the order by clause combined with the many possible collations yields tremendous flexibility in sorting the result set.

# Working with Nulls

The relational database model represents missing data using null. Technically, null means "value unknown." In practice, null can indicate that the data has not yet been entered into the database, or the column does not apply to the particular row.

Because null is unknown, the result of any expression that includes null will also be unknown. If the contents of a bank account are unknown, and its funds are included in a portfolio, the total value of the portfolio is also unknown. The same concept is true in SQL, as the following code demonstrates. Phil Senn, a database developer, puts it this way: "Nulls zap the life out of any other value."

```
SELECT 1 + NULL
```

Result:

```
NULL
```

Because they have such a devastating effect on expressions, some developers detest the use of nulls. They develop their databases so that nulls are never permitted and column defaults supply surrogate nulls (blanks, 0's, or 'n/a') instead. Other database developers argue that an unknown value shouldn't be represented by a zero or a blank just to make coding easier. I fall in the latter camp. Nulls are valuable in a database because they provide important information about the status of the data, so it's worth your while to write code that checks for nulls and handles them appropriately.

## Testing for Null

Because null is unknown, null is not even equal to null. Going back to the bank account example, if the value of account 123 is unknown and the value of account 234 is unknown, then it's logically impossible to prove that the two accounts are equal. Because the equal operator can't check for nulls, SQL includes a special operator, is, to test for equivalence to special values, as follows:

```
WHERE Expression IS NULL
```

The `is null` SQL search condition is used to test for a null value:

```
IF NULL = NULL
  SELECT '='
ELSE
  SELECT '!='
```

Result:

```
!=
```

The `is` search condition, however, works as advertised:

```
IF NULL IS NULL
  SELECT 'Is'
ELSE
  SELECT 'Is Not'
```

Result:

```
Is
```

The `is` search condition may be used in the `select` statement's `where` clause to locate rows with null values. Most of the Cape Hatteras Adventures customers do not have a nickname in the database. The following query retrieves only those customers with a null in the `Nickname` column:

```
USE CHA2
SELECT FirstName, LastName, Nickname
  FROM dbo.Customer
  WHERE Nickname IS NULL
  ORDER BY LastName, FirstName
```

Result:

```
FirstName     LastName        Nickname
------------  --------------  ----------------
Debbie        Andrews         NULL
Dave          Bettys          NULL
Jay           Brown           NULL
Lauren        Davis           NULL
...
```

The `is` operator may be combined with `not` to test for the presence of a value by restricting the result set to those rows where `Nickname is not null`:

```
SELECT FirstName, LastName, Nickname
  FROM dbo.Customer
  WHERE Nickname IS NOT NULL
  ORDER BY LastName, FirstName
```

Result:

```
FirstName     LastName        Nickname
------------  --------------  ----------------
Joe           Adams           Slim
Melissa       Anderson        Missy
Frank         Goldberg        Frankie
Raymond       Johnson         Ray
...
```

One exception to the rule that adding a null to a value results in null concerns nulls within columns being added by an aggregate function. Aggregate functions (Sum(), Avg(), and so on) tend to ignore nulls. Aggregates are covered in the "Summing and Grouping Data" section later in this chapter.

# Handling Nulls

When you are supplying data to reports, to end users, or to some applications, a null value will be less than welcome. Often a null must be converted to a valid value so the data may be understood, or so the expression won't fail.

Nulls require special handling when used within expressions, and SQL includes a few functions designed specifically to handle nulls. Isnull() and coalesce() convert nulls to usable values, and nullif() will create a null if the specified condition is met.

To complicate matters further, SQL Server uses three-state logic when dealing with Boolean expressions. Comparing a null with a true will yield null.

## Using the IsNull() Function

The most common null-handling function is isnull(), which is different from the is null search condition. This function accepts a single column or expression, and a substitution value. If the source is a valid value (not null), the isnull() function passes the value on. However, if the source is a null, the second parameter is substituted for the null, as follows:

```
IsNull(source_expression, replacement_value)
```

Functionally, isnull() is the same as the following case expression:

```
CASE
  WHEN source_expression IS NULL THEN replacement_value
  ELSE source_expression
END AS ISNULL
```

The following code sample builds on the previous queries by substituting the string ('none') for a null for customers without a nickname:

```
SELECT FirstName, LastName, ISNULL(Nickname,'none')
  FROM Customer
  ORDER BY LastName, FirstName
```

Result:

```
FirstName     LastName        Nickname
------------  --------------  -----------------
Joe           Adams           Slim
Melissa       Anderson        Missy
Debbie        Andrews         none
Dave          Bettys          none
. . .
```

If the row has a value in the Nickname column, that value is passed though the isnull() function untouched. However, if the nickname is null for a row, the null is handled by the isnull() function and converted to the value "none."

**Caution**   The isnull() and nullif() functions are a T-SQL specific and are not ANSI standard SQL.

## Coalesce()

Coalesce() is rarely used, perhaps because it's not well known. However, it's a cool function. Coalesce() accepts a list of expressions or columns and returns the first non-null value, as follows:

```
Coalesce(expression, expression, ...)
```

Coalesce() is derived from the Latin words *co + alescre,* which mean to unite toward a common end, to grow together, or to bring opposing sides together for a common good. The SQL keyword however, is derived from the alternate meaning of the term – "to arise from the combination of distinct elements." In a sense, the coalesce() function brings together multiple, differing values of unknown usefulness, and from them emerges a single valid value.

Functionally, coalesce() is the same as the following case expression:

```
CASE
  WHEN expression1 IS NOT NULL THEN expression1
  WHEN expression2 IS NOT NULL THEN expression2
  WHEN expression3 IS NOT NULL THEN expression3
  ...
END AS COALESCE
```

The following code sample demonstrates the coalesce() function returning the first non-null value. In this case it's 1+2:

```
SELECT Coalesce(NULL, 1+NULL, 1+2, 'abc')
```

Result:

```
3
```

Coalesce() is excellent for merging messy data. For example, if a table has partial data in several columns, the coalesce() function can help pull the data together. In one project I worked on, the client had collected names and addresses from several databases and applications into a single table. The contact name and company name made it into the proper columns, but some addresses were in Address1, some in Address2, and some in Address3. Some rows had the second line of the address in Address2. If the address columns had an address, then the SalesNote was a real note. But in many cases the addresses were in the SalesNote column. Here's the code to extract the address from such a mess:

```
SELECT Coalesce(
     Address1 + str(13)+str(10) + Adress2,
     Address1,
     Address2,
     Address3,
     SalesNote) AS NewAddress
   FROM TempSalesContacts
```

For each row in the TempSalesContacts table, the coalesce() function will search through the listed columns and return the first non-null value. The first expression returns a value only if there's a value in both Address1 and Address2, because a value concatenated with a null produces a null. So if a two-line address exists, it will be returned. Otherwise, a one-line address in Address1, Address2, or Address3 will be returned. Failing those options, the SalesNote column will be returned. Of course, the result from such a messy source table will still need to be manually scanned and verified.

You won't use the coalesce() function every day, but it's a useful tool to have in your developer's bag.

## Nullif()

There are instances when a null should be created in place of surrogate null values. If a database is polluted with n/a, blank, or ‐ values where it should contain nulls, you can use the nullif() function to replace the inconsistent values with nulls and clean the database.

The nullif() function accepts two parameters. If they are equal, it returns a null; otherwise it returns the first parameter. Functionally nullif() is the same as the following case expression:

```
CASE
  WHEN Expression1 = Expression2 THEN NULL
  ELSE Expression1
END AS NULLIF
```

The following code will convert any blanks in the Nickname column into nulls. The first statement updates one of the rows to a blank for testing purposes.

```
UPDATE Customer
  SET Nickname = ''
  WHERE LastName = 'Adams'

SELECT LastName, FirstName,
    CASE NickName
      WHEN '' THEN 'blank'
      ELSE Nickname
    END AS Nickname,
    NullIf(Nickname,'') as NicknameNullIf
  FROM dbo.Customer
  WHERE LastName IN ('Adams', 'Anderson', 'Andrews')
  ORDER BY LastName, FirstName
```

Result:

```
LastName    FirstName    Nickname    NicknameNullIf
----------- ------------ ----------- --------------
Adams       Joe          blank       NULL
Anderson    Melissa      Missy       Missy
Andrews     Debbie       NULL        NULL
```

The third column uses a case expression to expose the blank value as "blank," and indeed, the nullif() function converts the blank value to a null in the fourth column. To test the other null possibilities, Melissa's Nickname was not affected by the nullif() function, and Debbie's null Nickname value was still in place.

## Non-Default Null Behavior

Everything so far in discussing nulls is based on SQL Server's default behavior with nulls. However, SQL Server is highly flexible, and the null behaviors may be altered.

By all logic, concatenating a null with a value should produce a null. But that behavior can be changed. The connection setting, concat_null_yields_null, determines the outcome of concatenating a value with a null. The connection setting is initially determined by the database default with the same name (`concat_null_yields_null`). Changing the null behavior can be difficult to test because Query Analyzer also has a default set of connection settings, which it applies with every new connection.

The following code sets the database option and the connection option to disable the default behavior:

```
-- set database option
sp_dboption 'CHA2',  CONCAT_NULL_YIELDS_NULL, 'false'
-- examine the database option
SELECT DATABASEPROPERTYEX('CHA2', 'IsNullConcat')
```

Result:

```
0
```

Setting the connection setting:

```
SET CONCAT_NULL_YIELDS_NULL OFF
```

Concatenating a null:

```
SELECT NULL + 'abc'
```

Result:

```
abc
```

Normally in ANSI SQL (and SQL Server), a comparison to null will yield null. For example evaluating (`1>null`) results in a null. However, you can change that behavior by setting ANSI nulls off in the connection. The greatest affect of this change is that nulls may be tested with an `equals` condition instead of only with an `is` operator.

As with the previous concatenation option, the connection setting is the one that counts. The following code sample sets the database default option and the connection settings to disable ANSI null behavior:

```
-- set database option
sp_dboption 'CHA2',  ANSI_NULLS, 'false'
-- examine the database option
SELECT DATABASEPROPERTYEX('CHA2','IsAnsiNullsEnabled')
```

Result:

```
0
```

Concatenating a null:

```
SET ANSI_NULLS OFF
```

Testing for a null with an equals sign:

```
SELECT 'true' WHERE (NULL = NULL)
```

Result:

```
true
```

# Scalar Functions

A *scalar function* returns a single value. They are commonly used in expressions within the select columns, the where clause, or T-SQL code. SQL Server includes dozens of functions, as illustrated in Figure 6-9. In this section I'll explain the functions I find most useful.

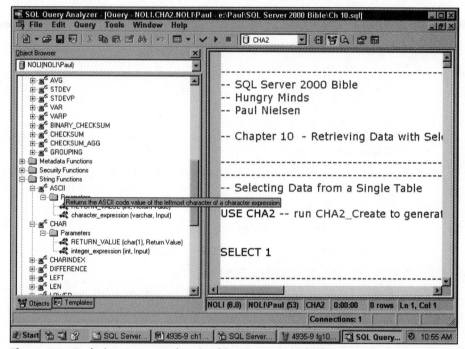

**Figure 6-9:** Exploring Query Analyzer's Object Browser is the best way to discover all of SQL Server's functions.

**Best Practice**

Performance is as much a part of the data-schema design as it is a part of the query. Plan on storing the data in the way they will be searched by a where condition, rather than depending upon manipulating the data with functions at query time. While using a function in an expression in a result-set column may be unavoidable, using a function in a where condition forces the function to be calculated for every row.

**Cross-Reference**

With SQL Server 2000 you can develop three types of user-defined functions, as explained in Chapter 14, "Building User-Defined Functions."

## Server Environment Information

System functions return information about the current environment. The section covers the more commonly used system functions.

✦ GetDate(): Returns the current server date and time to the nearest three milliseconds.

✦ Db_name(): Returns the name of the current database, as in the following example:

```
SELECT GETDATE() AS 'Date',
  DB_NAME() AS 'Database'
```

Result:

```
Date                     Database
------------------------ -------
2001-11-15 18:38:50.250  CHA2
```

✦ GetUTCDate(): Returns the current Universal Time Coordinate time, or Greenwich Mean Time. This is very useful for consistently recording times for applications that span multiple time zones.

✦ ServerProperty(): Several useful pieces of information about the server may be determined from the serverproperty (*property*) function, including:

- Collation: The collation type

- Edition: Enterprise, Developer, Standard, and so on

- EngineEdition: 1 — Personal or Desktop Engine, 2 — Standard, 3 — Enterprise

- InstanceName: Null if default instance

- ProductVersion: The version number of the SQL Server

- ProductLevel: "RTM" for the initial release-to-manufacturing version, "SP*n*" for service packs, "B*n*" for beta software

- ServerName: The full server and instance name

For example, the following code returns the engine edition and the product level for my current instance of SQL Server:

```
SELECT
  SERVERPROPERTY ('ServerName') AS ServerName,
  SERVERPROPERTY ('Edition') AS Edition,
  SERVERPROPERTY ('EngineEdition') AS EngineEdition,
  SERVERPROPERTY ('ProductLevel') AS ProductLevel
```

Result:

```
ServerName  Edition            EngineEdition  ProductLevel
----------  -----------------  -------------  ------------
NOLI        Developer Edition  3              SP2
```

## User Information Functions

In a client/server environment, it's good to know who the client is. Toward that end, the following four functions are very useful, especially for gathering audit information.

✦ User_name(): Returns the name of the current user as he or she is known to the database. When a user is granted access to a database, the user name different than the server login name may be assigned.

✦ Suser_sname(): Returns the login name by which the user was authenticated to SQL Server. If the user was authenticated as a member of a Windows user group, this function still returns the user's Windows login name.

✦ Host_name(): Returns the name of the user's workstation.

✦ App_name(): Returns the name of the application connected to SQL Server, as follows:

```
SELECT
  USER_NAME() AS 'User',
  SUSER_SNAME() AS 'Login',
  HOST_NAME() AS 'Workstation',
  APP_NAME() AS 'Application'
```

Result:

```
User     Login            Workstation   Appllication
-------  ---------------  ------------  ------------------
dbo      NOLI\Paul CHA2   NOLI          SQL Query Analyzer
```

## Data-Time Functions

Databases must often work with date-time data and SQL Server includes several useful date-time functions. SQL Server stores both the data and the time in a single data type. For more about data types refer to Chapter 5, "Implementing the Physical Database Schema." The following four SQL Server date-time functions handle extracting or working with a specific portion of the date or time stored within a datatime column:

✦ DateName(*date portion, date*): Returns the proper name for the selected portion of the datetime value. The portions for datename() and datepart() are listed in Table 6-4:

```
SELECT DATENAME(Year, GetDate()) as Year
```

Result:

```
Year
--------
2001
```

The following code example assigns to Mr. Frank a date of birth and then retrieves the proper names of some of the portions of that date of birth using the datename() function:

```
UPDATE Guide
  SET DateOfBirth = '9/4/58'
  WHERE lastName = 'Frank'
```

Result:

```
SELECT LastName,
    DATENAME(yy,DateOfBirth) AS [Year],
    DATENAME(mm,DateOfBirth) AS [Month],
    DATENAME(dd,DateOfBirth) AS [Day],
    DATENAME(weekday, DateOfBirth) AS BirthDay
  FROM dbo.Guide
  WHERE DateOfBirth IS NOT NULL

LastName  Year   Month        Day   BirthDay
--------- ------ ------------ ----- ----------------
Frank     1958   September    4     Thursday
```

## Table 6-4: Datetime Portions Used by Date Functions

| Portion | Abbreviation |
| --- | --- |
| Year | yy, yyyy |
| Quarter | qq, q |
| Month | mm, m |
| DayofYear | dy, d |
| Day | dd, d |
| Week | wk, ww |
| Weekday | dw |
| Hour | hh |
| Minute | mi, n |
| Second | ss, s |
| Millisecond | ms |

✦ DatePart(*date portion, date*): Returns the selected portion of the datetime value. The following example retrieves the day of the year and the day of the week as integers:

```
SELECT DATEPART(DayofYear, GetDate()) AS DayCount
```

Result:

```
DayCount
-----------
321
```

```
SELECT DATEPART(dw, GetDate()) AS DayWeek
```

Result:

```
DayWeek
-----------
7
```

The easiest way to get just the date – stripping off the time, is to use a couple string functions:

```
Select Cast(Char(10), GetDate(), 101) as DateTime
```

✦ DateAdd(*date portion, amount, beginning date*) and DateDiff(*date portion, amount, beginning date*): **Performs addition and subtraction on** date-time **data. Databases must often perform addition and subtraction on** datetime **data. The** datediff() **and the** dateadd() **functions are designed expressly for this purpose. The** datediff() **doesn't look at the complete date but just the date part being extracted.**

The following query calculates the number of years and days that my wife Melissa and I have been married:

```
SELECT
  DATEDIFF(yy,'1984/5/20', Getdate()) AS MarriedYears,
  DATEDIFF(dd,'1984/5/20', Getdate()) AS MarriedDays
```

Result:

```
MarriedYears MarriedDays
------------ -----------
17           6390
```

The next query adds 100 hours to the millisecond of this writing:

```
SELECT DATEADD(hh,100, GETDATE()) AS [100HoursFromNow]
```

Result:

```
100HoursFromNow
-----------------------
2001-11-21 18:42:03.507
```

The following query is based on the Family sample database and calculates the mother's age at the birth of each child using the datediff() function:

```
USE Family
SELECT Person.FirstName + ' ' + Person.LastName AS Mother,
    DATEDIFF(yy, Person.DateOfBirth,
    Child.DateOfBirth) AS Age,Child.FirstName
  FROM Person
    JOIN Person Child
      ON Person.PersonID = Child.MotherID
  ORDER By Age DESC
```

The datediff function in this query returns the year difference between Person. DateOfBirth, which is the mother's birthdate, and the child's date of birth. Because the function is in a column expression, it's calculated for each row in the result set:

```
Mother                           Age         FirstName
-------------------------------- ----------- ---------------
Audry Halloway                   33          Corwin
Kimberly Kidd                    31          Logan
Elizabeth Campbell               31          Alexia
Melanie Campbell                 30          Adam
Grace Halloway                   30          James
...
```

## String Functions

Like most modern programming languages, T-SQL includes many string-manipulation functions:

✦ SubString(*string, starting position, length*): Returns a portion of a string. The first parameter is the string, the second parameter is the beginning position of the substring to be extracted, and the third parameter is the length of the string extracted.

```
SELECT SUBSTRING('abcdefg', 3, 2)
```

Result:

```
cd
```

✦ Stuff(*string, insertion position, delete count, string inserted*): The inverse of substring(), the stuff() function inserts one string into another string. The inserted string may delete a specified number of characters as it is being inserted.

```
SELECT STUFF('abcdefg', 3, 2, '123')
```

Result:

```
ab123efg
```

The following code sample uses nested stuff() functions to format a U.S. Social Security Number:

```
SELECT STUFF(STUFF('123456789', 4, 0, '-'), 7, 0, '-')
```

Result:

```
123-45-6789
```

✦ CharIndex(*search string, string, starting position*): Returns the character position of a string within a string:

```
SELECT CHARINDEX('c', 'abcdefg', 1)
```

Result:

```
3
```

The TitleCase() user defined function later in this section uses the CharIndex() to locate the spaces separating words.

✦ PatIndex(*%pattern%, string*): Searches for a pattern, which may include wildcards, within a string. The following code locates the first position of either a c or d in the string:

```
SELECT PATINDEX('%[cd]%', 'abdcdefg')
```

Result:

```
3
```

✦ Right(*string, count*) and Left(*string, count*): Return the right- or leftmost part of a string:

```
SELECT Left('Nielsen',2) AS '[Left]',
  RIGHT('Nielsen',2) AS [Right]
```

**Result:**

```
Left   Right
-----  ----
Ni     en
```

✦ Len(*string*): **Returns the length of a string:**

```
SELECT LEN('Supercalifragilisticexpialidocious') AS Len
```

**Result:**

```
Len
-----------
34
```

✦ Rtrim(*string*) **and** Ltrim(*string*): **Remove leading or trailing spaces. While it's diffi-cult to see in print, the three leading and trailing spaces are removed from the follow-ing string. I adjusted the column-header lines with the remaining spaces to illustrate the functions.**

```
SELECT RTRIM('   middle earth   ') AS [RTrim],
  LTRIM('   middle earth   ') AS [LTrim]
```

**Result:**

```
RTrim           LTrim
--------------- ---------------
   middle earth middle earth
```

✦ Upper(*string*) **and** Lower(*string*): **Convert the entire string to upper- or lowercase. Minuscules, or lowercase letters, were first used in the ninth century to facilitate hand-writing. With the advent of the printing press in the fifteenth century, printers manually set the type for each page printed. They stored the letters in cases above the page box. The uncials (capital letters) were stored above the minuscules. The terms "uppercase" and "lowercase" stuck. Other than the history, there's not much to know about these two functions.**

```
Select UPPER('one TWO tHrEe') as [UpperCase],
  LOWER('one TWO tHrEe') as [LowerCase]
```

**Result:**

```
UpperCase     LowerCase
------------- -------------
ONE TWO THREE one two three
```

✦ **Replace(string, string): The** replace() **function operates as a global search and replace within a string. Using** replace() **within an** update **DML command can quickly fix problems in the data such as removing extra tabs, or correcting string patterns. The following code sample removes apostrophes from the** LastName **column in the** OBXKites **database's** Contact **table:**

```
USE OBXKites

UPDATE Contact
  SET LastName = 'Adam''s'
  WHERE LastName = 'Adams'
```

```
SELECT LastName, REPLACE(LastName, '''', '')
  FROM Contact
  WHERE LastName LIKE '%''%'

UPDATE Contact
  SET LastName = REPLACE(LastName, '''', '')
  WHERE LastName LIKE '%''%'
```

✦ pTitleCase(*source, search, replace*): **T-SQL lacks a function to convert text to title case (first letter of each word in uppercase, and the remainder in lowercase). Therefore the following user-defined function accomplishes this task:**

```
CREATE FUNCTION pTitleCase (
  @StrIn NVARCHAR(1024))
RETURNS NVARCHAR(1024)
AS
  BEGIN
    DECLARE
      @StrOut NVARCHAR(1024),
      @CurrentPosition INT,
      @NextSpace INT,
      @CurrentWord NVARCHAR(1024),
      @StrLen INT,
      @LastWord BIT

    SET @NextSpace = 1
    SET @CurrentPosition = 1
    SET @StrOut = ''
    SET @StrLen = LEN(@StrIn)
    SET @LastWord = 0

    WHILE @LastWord = 0
      BEGIN
        SET @NextSpace =
          CHARINDEX(' ',@StrIn, @CurrentPosition+ 1)
        IF  @NextSpace = 0 -- no more spaces found
          BEGIN
            SET @NextSpace = @StrLen
            SET @LastWord = 1
          END
        SET @CurrentWord =
          UPPER(SUBSTRING(@StrIn, @CurrentPosition, 1))
        SET @CurrentWord = @CurrentWord +
          LOWER(SUBSTRING(@StrIn, @CurrentPosition+1,
                  @NextSpace - @CurrentPosition))
        SET @StrOut = @StrOut +@CurrentWord
        SET @CurrentPosition = @NextSpace + 1
      END
    RETURN @StrOut
  END
```

Running a user-defined function requires including the owner name in the function name:

```
Select dbo.pTitleCase('one TWO tHrEe') as [TitleCase]
```

Result:

```
TitleCase
-----------------------
One Two Three
```

**Note** The pTitleCase function does not take into consideration surnames with nonstandard capitalization, such as McDonald, VanCamp, or de Jonge. It would be inadequate to hard-code a list of exceptions. Perhaps the best solution is to store a list of exception phrases (Mc, Van, de, and so on) in an easily updateable list. Keep checking www.isnotnull.com to see if I've updated the function, or if you'd like to submit further enhancements.

The code for the pTitleCase user-defined function is on the book's CD in the SQLServerBible\Utility directory.

## Soundex Functions

Soundex is a phonetic pattern-matching system created for the American census. Franklin Roosevelt directed the United States Bureau of Archives to develop a method of cataloging the population that could handle the variations in spelling of similar surnames. Margaret K. Odell and Robert C. Russell developed Soundex and were awarded U.S. patents 1261167 (1918) and 1435663 (1922) for their efforts. The census filing card for each household was then filed under the Soundex method. Soundex has been applied to every census since and has been post-applied to census records back to 1880.

The purpose of Soundex is to sort similar-sounding names together, which is very useful for dealing with contact information in a database application. For example, if I call a phone bank and give them my name (Nielsen), they invariably spell it "Nelson" in the contact look-up form. But if the database uses Soundex properly I'll still be in the search-result list box.

For more information concerning Soundex and its history, refer to the following Web sites:

✦ http://www.nara.gov/genealogy/coding.html

✦ http://www.amberskyline.com/treasuremaps/uscensus.html

✦ http://www.bluepoof.com/soundex/

Here's how Soundex works. The first letter of a name is stored as the letter, and the following three Soundex phonetic sounds are stored according to the following code:

```
1 - B, F, P, V
2 - C, G, J, K, Q, S, X, Z
3 - D, T
4 - L
5 - M, N
6 - R
```

Double letters with the same Soundex code, *A*, *E*, *I*, *O*, *U*, *H*, *W*, *Y*, and some prefixes are disregarded. So "Nielsen" becomes "N425" via the following method:

1. The *N* is stored.

2. The *i* and *e* are disregarded.

3. The *l* sound is stored as the Soundex code 4.

4. The *s* is stored as the Soundex code 2.

5. The *e* is ignored.

6. The *n* is stored as the Soundex code 5.

By boiling them down to a few consonant sounds, Soundex assigns "Nielsen," "Nelson," and "Neilson" the same code: "N425."

Additional Soundex name examples:

✦ Brown = B650 (*r*—6, *n*—5)

✦ Jeffers = J162 (*ff*—1, *r*—6, *s*—2)

✦ Letterman = L365 (*tt*—3, *r*—6, *m*—5)

✦ Nelson = N425 (*l*—4, *s*—2, *n*—5)

✦ Nicholson = N242 (*c*—2, *l*—4, *s*—2)

✦ Nickols = N242 (*c*—2, *l*—4, *s*—2)

## Using the Soundex() Function

SQL Server includes two Soundex-related functions, `soundex()` and `difference()`. The `soundex(string)` function calculates the Soundex code for a string as follows:

```
SELECT SOUNDEX('Nielsen') AS Nielsen,
  SOUNDEX('Nelson') AS NELSON,
  SOUNDEX('Neilson') AS NEILSON
```

Result:

```
Nielsen NELSON NEILSON
------- ------ -------
N425    N425   N425
```

> **Note**    Other, more refined, soundex methods exist. Ken Henderson, in his book *The Guru's Guide to Transact SQL* (Addison-Wesley Pub Co; ISBN: 0201615762), provides an improved soundex algorithm and stored procedure. If you are going to implement Soundex in a production application, I recommend exploring his version. Alternately, you can research one of the other refined Soundex methods on the Web sites listed previously and write your own custom stored procedure.

There are two possible ways to add Soundex searches to a database. The simplest method is to add the `soundex()` function within the `where` clause, as follows:

```
USE CHA2
SELECT LastName, FirstName
  FROM dbo.Customer
  WHERE SOUNDEX('Nikolsen') = SOUNDEX(LastName)
```

Result:

```
LastName        FirstName
-------------   -------------------
Nicholson       Charles
Nickols         Bob
```

While this implementation has the smallest impact on the data schema, it will cause performance issues as the data size grows because the soundex() function must execute for every row in the database. A faster variation of this first implementation method pre-tests for names with the same first letter, thus enabling SQL Server to use any indexes to narrow the search, so the soundex() function must only be performed for a rows selected by the index:

```
SELECT LastName, FirstName
  FROM dbo.Customer
  WHERE SOUNDEX('Nikolsen') = SOUNDEX(LastName)
    AND LastName LIKE 'N%'
```

The first query executes in 37.7 milliseconds on my test server, while the improved second query executes in 6.5 milliseconds. I suspect that the performance difference would increase with more data.

The second implementation method is to write the Soundex value in a column and index it with clustered index. Because the Soundex value for each row is calculated during the write the soundex() function does not need to be called for every row read by the select statement. This is the method I would recommend for a database application that heavily depends on Soundex for contact searches.

The OBX Kites sample database demonstrates this method. The pContact_AddNew stored procedure calculates the Soundex code for every new contact and stores the result in the SoundexCode column. Searching for a row, or all the matching rows, based on the stored Soundex code is extremely fast:

First determine the Soundex for "Smith":

```
USE OBXKites
SELECT SOUNDEX('Smith')
-------
S530
```

Knowing the Soundex value for "Smith," the Soundex search is now a fast index seek without ever calling the soundex() function for the row being read during the select statement:

```
SELECT LastName, FirstName, SoundexCode
  FROM Contact
  WHERE SoundexCode = 'S530'
```

Result:

```
LastName        FirstName        SoundexCode
-------------   ----------------  -----------
Smith           Ulisius          S530
Smith           Oscar            S530
```

## Using the Difference() Soundex Function

The second SQL Server Soundex function, `difference()`, returns the Soundex difference between two strings in the form of a ranking from 1 to 4, with 4 representing a perfect soundex match:

```
USE CHA2
SELECT LastName, DIFFERENCE ('Smith', LastName) AS NameSearch
  FROM Customer
  ORDER BY DIFFERENCE ('Smyth', LastName) DESC
```

Result:

```
LastName              NameSearch
--------------------  -----------
Smythe                4
Spade                 3
Zeniod                3
Kennedy               3
Kennedy               3
Quinn                 2
...
Kemper                1
Nicholson             0
...
```

The advantage of the `difference()` function is that it broadens the search beyond the first letters. The problem with the function is that it wants to calculate the Soundex value for both parameters, which prevents it from taking advantage of prestored Soundex values.

# Data-Type Conversion Functions

Converting data from a one data type to another data type is often handled automatically by SQL Server. Many of those conversions are implicit, or automatic. (The exceptions are detailed in Table 6-5.)

### Table 6-5: Data-Type Conversion Exceptions

| From Data Type(s) | To Data Type(s) | Conversion Issue |
|---|---|---|
| binary, varbinary | float, real, ntext, text | Conversion not allowed |
| char, varchar, nchar, nvarchar | binary, varbinary, money, smallmoney, timestamp | Explicit conversion required |
| nchar, nvarchar | image | Conversion not allowed |
| datetime smalldatatime | decimal, numeric, float, real, bigint, int, smallint, tinyint, money, smallmoney, bit, timestamp | Explicit conversion required |
| datetime smalldatatime, decimal, numeric, float, real bigint, int, smallint, tinyint, money, smallmoney, bit | uniqueidentifier, image, ntext, text | Conversion not allowed |

| From Data Type(s) | To Data Type(s) | Conversion Issue |
|---|---|---|
| decimal, numeric | decimal, numeric | Requires explicit cast to handle numeric precision without data loss |
| float, real | timestamp | Conversion not allowed |
| money. smallmoney | char, varchar, nchar, nvarchar | Explicit conversion required |
| timestamp | nchar, nvarchar, float, real, uniqueidentifier, ntext, text sql_variant | Conversion not allowed |
| uniqueidentifier | datetime smalldatatime, decimal, numeric, float, real bigint, int, smallint, tinyint, money, smallmoney, bit, timestamp, image, ntext | Conversion not allowed |
| image | char, varchar, nchar, nvarchar, datetime smalldatatime, decimal, numeric, float, real bigint, int, smallint, tinyint, money, smallmoney, bit, ntext, sql_variant | Conversion not allowed |
| ntext, text | binary, varbinary, datetime smalldatatime, decimal, numeric, float, real bigint, int, smallint, tinyint, money, smallmoney, bit, timestamp, uniqueidentifier, image, sql_variant | Conversion not allowed |
| ntext | char, varchar | Explicit conversion required |
| text | nchar, nvarchar | Conversion not allowed |
| sql_variant | timestamp, image, ntext, text | Conversion not allowed |

Those conversions that are explicit require a cast() or convert() function.

✦ Cast(*Input* as *data type*): The ANSI standard SQL means of converting from one data type to another. Even if the conversion can be performed implicitly by SQL Server, using the cast() function forces the desired data type.

Cast is actually programmed slightly differently from a standard function. Rather than separating the two parameters with a comma (as most functions do), the data passed to the cast function is followed by the as keyword and the requested output data type:

```
SELECT CAST('Away' AS NVARCHAR(5)) AS 'Tom Hanks'
```

**Result:**

```
Tom Hanks
---------
Away
```

Another example:

```
SELECT CAST(123 AS NVARCHAR(15)) AS Int2String
```

Result:

```
Int2String
---------------
123
```

✦ Convert(`datatype, expression, style`): **Returns a value converted to a different data type with optional formatting. The first parameter of this non-ASNI SQL function is the desired data type to be applied to the expression.**

```
Convert (data type, expression[, style])
```

The style parameter refers to be optional date styles listed in Table 6-6. The style is applied to the output during conversion from datetime to a character-based data type, or to the input during conversion from text to datetime. Generally the one- or two-digits style provides a two-digit year and its three-digit counterpart provides a four-digit year. For example, style 1 provides 01/01/03, while style 101 provides 01/01/2003. The styles marked with an asterisk (*) in Table 6-6 are the exceptions to this rule.

SQL Server also provides numeric formatting styles, however, numeric formatting is typically the task of the user interface, not the database.

### Table 6-6: Convert Function Date Styles

| Style | Description | Format |
|-------|-------------|--------|
| 0 / 100* | Default | `mon dd yyyy hh:mi` AM (or PM) |
| 1 /101 | USA | `mm/dd/yy` |
| 2 /102 | ANSI | `yy.mm.dd` |
| 3 / 103 | British/French | `dd/mm/yy` |
| 4 / 104 | German | `dd.mm.yy` |
| 5 / 105 | Italian | `dd-mm-yy` |
| 6 / 106 | - | `dd mon yy` |
| 7 / 107 | - | `mon dd, yy` |
| 8 / 108 | - | `hh:mm:ss` |
| 9 or 109* | Default+milliseconds | `mon dd yyyy hh:mi:ss:mmm`AM (or PM) |
| 10 or 110 | USA | `mm-dd-yy` |
| 11 or 111 | Japan | `yy/mm/dd` |
| 12 or 112 | ISO | `yymmdd` |
| 13 or 113* | Europe default+milliseconds | `dd mon yyyy hh:mm:ss:mmm` (24h) |
| 14 or 114 | - | `hh:mi:ss:mmm` (24h) |
| 20 or 120* | ODBC canonical | `yyyy-mm-dd hh:mi:ss` (24h) |

| Style | Description | Format |
|-------|-------------|--------|
| 21 or 121* | ODBC canonical + milliseconds | *yyyy-mm-dd hh:mi:ss.mmm* (24h) |
| 126 | ISO8601 for XML use | *yyyy-mm-dd Thh:mm:ss:mmm* (no spaces) |
| 130 | Kuwaiti | *dd mon yyyy hh:mi:ss:mmm*AM (or PM) |
| 131 | Kuwaiti | *dd/mm/yy hh:mi:ss:mmm*AM (or PM) |

\* Both styles return dates with centuries.

**Best Practice**

In a clean client/server design, the server provides the data without formatting and the client application formats the data as required by the user. Unformatted data are more independent than formatted data and can be used by more applications.

The following code demonstrates the convert() function:

```
SELECT  GETDATE() AS RawDate,
    CONVERT (NVARCHAR(25), GETDATE(), 100) AS Date100,
    CONVERT (NVARCHAR(25), GETDATE(), 1) AS Date1
```

Result:

```
RawDate                     Date100                 Date1
--------------------------- ----------------------- ----------
2001-11-17 10:27:27.413     Nov 17 2001 10:27AM     11/17/01
```

Two additional data-type conversion functions provide fast ways to move data between text and numeric:

✦ Str(*number, length, decimal*): Returns a string from a number.

```
SELECT STR(123,5,2) AS [Str]
```

Result:

```
Str
-----
123.0
```

# Summing and Grouping Data

Turning raw lists of data and keys into useful information often involves summarizing data and grouping them in meaningful ways. While a certain amount of summarization and analysis can be performed with other tools, such as a report writer or Analysis Services, SQL is a set-based language and a fair amount of summarizing and grouping can be performed very well right inside the SQL select statement.

## Aggregate Functions

SQL includes a set of *aggregate functions* that can perform a calculation across an entire set of data producing a single row that summarizes the original data set, as illustrated in Figure 6-10.

SQL aggregate functions are listed in Table 6-7.

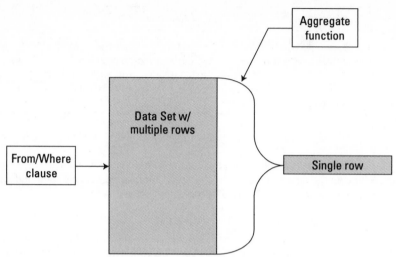

**Figure 6-10:** The aggregate function produces a single row result from a data set.

## Table 6-7: Aggregate Functions

| Aggregate Function | Data Type Supported | Description |
|---|---|---|
| sum() | Numeric | Totals all the non-null values in the column. |
| avg() | Numeric | Averages all the non-null values in the column. Input data type will be returned by avg(), so the input is often converted to a higher precision, such as avg(cast *col* as float). |
| min() | numeric, string, datetime | Returns the smallest number or the first datetime or the first string according to the current collation from the column. |
| max() | numeric, string, datetime | Returns the largest number or the last datetime or the last string according to the current collation from the column. |
| count ([distinct] *) | Any data type (row-based) | Performs a simple count of all the rows in the result set up 2,147,483,647. Will not count uniqueidentifiers, or blobs. |
| count_big ([distinct] *) | Any data type (row-based) | Similar to the count() function, but the bigint datatype can handle up to 2^63-1 rows. |

Using the aggregate functions within a `select` statement is pretty straightforward. Here are a few rules to keep in mind while using aggregate functions:

✦ Because SQL is now returning information from a set rather than building a record set of rows, as soon as a query includes an aggregate function every column (in the column list, expression, or in the order by) must participate in an aggregate function. This is logical because if a query returned the total number of order sales it could not return a single order number on the same row.

✦ The aggregate (`distinct`) option serves the same purpose as `select distinct` except that it eliminates duplicate values instead of duplicate rows — so it's of questionable usefulness when used with `sum()` and `avg()`.Count(`distinct *`) is invalid; a column must be specified.

✦ Count(`*`) counts all the rows, but count(`column`) counts all the rows with a value in that column.

✦ Because aggregate functions are expressions, an alias will provide a column name.

✦ Developers often use a primary key as the parameter in the count() function. However, if the primary key is a `uniqueidentifier`, the count() function will fail. Also, counting by all rows (using an asterisk) allows SQL Server's Query Optimizer to select the column or index counted, which could result in a performance enhancement.

Aggregate functions are enabled in Enterprise Manager's Query Designer with the Group By toolbar button, as illustrated in Figure 6-11. In SQL code, the following example counts the number of contacts in the OBXKites database:

```
USE OBXKites
SELECT Count(*)
   FROM dbo.Contact
```

Result:

```
21
```

The previous query ran because every column participated in the aggregate purpose of the query. To test the rule, the next query adds a data column from the table:

```
SELECT LastName, Count(*)
   FROM Contact
```

As expected, including LastName in the column list causes the query to return an error message:

```
Server: Msg 8118, Level 16, State 1, Line 2
Column 'Contact.LastName' is invalid in the select list
because it is not contained in an aggregate function and
there is no GROUP BY clause.
```

To include non-aggregate descriptive columns either include the additional columns in the group by clause (next topic), or perform the aggregate function in a subquery (explained in the next chapter, "Merging Data Using Relational Algebra") and include the additional columns in the outer query.

The following query, still from the OBXKites database, uses the sum() function to calculate the total quantity of products sold and the total dollar volume sold in the year 2001. The query has to do a join to fetch the order date, but the point of the query is the sum() function:

```
SELECT SUM(Quantity) AS QuantitySold,
    SUM(Quantity*UnitPrice) AS DollarSold
  FROM dbo.OrderDetail
    JOIN [Order]
      ON [Order].OrderID = OrderDetail.OrderID
    WHERE OrderDate
      Between '1/1/2001' AND '12/31/2001 11:59.998PM'
```

Result:

```
QuantitySold    DollarSold
---------------  ----------------------
206.00           1729.895000
```

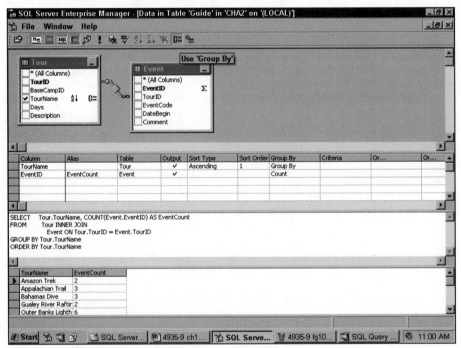

**Figure 6-11:** Performing an aggregate query within Enterprise Manager's Query Designer.

## Grouping Within a Result Set

Aggregate functions are all well and good, but how often do you need a total for an entire table? Most aggregate functions will be like the previous query and will use some kind of condition to limit the aggregation to a certain date range, department, type of sale, region, or the like. That presents a problem. If the only tool to restrict the aggregate function were the where clause, database developers would waste hours replicating the same query, or writing lots of dynamic SQL queries and the code to execute the aggregate queries in sequence.

Fortunately, aggregate functions are complemented by the group by function, which automatically partitions the dataset into subsets based upon the values in certain columns. Once the dataset is divided into subgroups, the aggreagate functions are performed on each subgroup. The final result is one summation row for each group as shown in Figure 6-12.

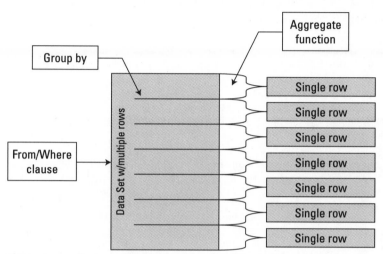

**Figure 6-12:** The group by clause slices the dataset into multiple subgroups.

For example, while the previous query uses the where clause, grouping the dataset by year would automatically answer the question and prevent the query from becoming obsolescent over time, as follows:

```
SELECT DatePart(yy,OrderDate) AS [Year], SUM(Quantity) AS QuantitySold,
   SUM(Quantity*UnitPrice) AS DollarSold
  FROM dbo.OrderDetail
   JOIN dbo.[Order]
    ON [Order].OrderID = OrderDetail.OrderID
  GROUP BY DatePart(yy,OrderDate)
```

The first column of this query returns the year from the OrderDate column. While this column does not have an aggregate function, it still participates within the aggregate because that's the column the query is being grouped by. The result set lists every year with orders. The aggregate sum function now calculates the quantity and dollar sold for each group subset, in this case each year:

```
Year      QuantitySold     DollarSold
--------  ---------------  ------------------
2001      152.00           612.600000
2002      54.00            1235.495000
```

SQL is not limited to grouping by one column. The previous query is enhanced with the addition of a grouping by `ProductCategoryName,` as follows:

```
SELECT DatePart(yy,OrderDate)  AS [Year],
    ProductCategoryName, SUM(Quantity) AS QuantitySold,
    SUM(Quantity*UnitPrice) AS DollarSold
  FROM dbo.OrderDetail
    JOIN dbo.[Order]
      ON [Order].OrderID = OrderDetail.OrderID
    JOIN dbo.Product
      ON OrderDetail.ProductID = Product.ProductID
    JOIN dbo.ProductCategory
      ON Product.ProductCategoryID =
          ProductCategory.ProductCategoryID
   GROUP BY DatePart(yy,OrderDate),ProductCategoryName
```

Result:

```
Year   ProductCategoryName    QuantitySold     DollarSold
------ -------------------- ---------------- -----------
2001   Accessory            6.00             10.530000
2001   Clothing             9.00             113.600000
2001   Kite                 59.00            1499.902500
2001   Material             3.00             5.265000
2001   OBX                  127.00           64.687500
2001   Video                2.00             35.910000
```

For the purposes of a `group by` nulls are considered equal to other nulls and will be grouped together.

The `group by all` option passes through every group by output row, even if the where clause eliminated all the rows for that group. For example, the eliminated group will be in the result set with a `count(*)` of zero.

## Filtering Grouped Results

Filtering, when combined with grouping, can be a problem. Are the row restrictions applied before the `group by` or after the `group by`? Some databases use nested queries to properly filter before or after the `group by`. SQL, however, uses the `having` clause to filter the groups. At the beginning of this chapter you saw the simplified order of the SQL `select` statement's execution. A more complete order is as follows:

1. The `from` clause assembles the data from the data sources.

2. The `where` clause restricts the rows based on the conditions.

3. The `group by` clause assembles subsets of data.

4. Aggregate functions are calculated.

5. The `having` clause filters the subsets of data.

6. Any expressions are calculated.

7. The `order by` sorts the results.

Continuing to improve upon the previous OBX Kites sales-analysis aggregate query, the following query removes any employee sales from the analysis and requires that any group reported must have sold more than two items during the year.

Relational databases segment data into multiple tables, and to retrieve a complete answer, multiple joins are often required. To restrict the sales and remove the employee sales, the `contact` table must now become involved in the `from` clause. The next chapter is dedicated to exploring SQL `select` statements that work with multiple tables and data sources.

The polished sales analysis query also sorts by dollar volume sold:

```
SELECT DatePart(yy,OrderDate)  AS [Year],
    ProductCategoryName, SUM(Quantity) AS QuantitySold,
    SUM(Quantity*UnitPrice) AS DollarSold
  FROM dbo.OrderDetail
    JOIN dbo.[Order]
      ON [Order].OrderID = OrderDetail.OrderID
    JOIN dbo.Product
      ON OrderDetail.ProductID = Product.ProductID
    JOIN dbo.ProductCategory
      ON Product.ProductCategoryID =
            ProductCategory.ProductCategoryID
    JOIN dbo.Contact
      ON [Order].ContactID = Contact.ContactID
  WHERE Contact.IsEmployee = 0
  GROUP BY DatePart(yy,OrderDate),ProductCategoryName
  HAVING SUM(Quantity) > 2
  ORDER BY SUM(Quantity*UnitPrice) DESC
```

Result:

```
Year   ProductCategoryName   QuantitySold   DollarSold
------ --------------------- -------------- -----------
2001   Kite                  59.00          1499.902500
2001   Clothing              9.00           113.600000
2001   OBX                   127.00         64.687500
2001   Accessory             6.00           10.530000
2001   Material              3.00           5.265000
```

Not surprisingly, the majority of products sold are in the Kite category.

Moving to a real-life example of using the `having` clause, my grocery store holds seasonal promotions — "Spend at least $40 a week in one shopping trip for 14 of the next 15 weeks and get a free turkey and stuffing!" Every shopper who qualifies is given a coupon each week he or she qualifies. When the 15 weeks are up, shoppers must turn in 14 coupons to win the prize. My problem with this is that every shopper has a VIC card with a bar code, and the card is scanned at the checkout counter so the customer can receive any special prices. I asked the store manager why the VIC numbers couldn't automatically track who had purchased $40 for 14 of 15 weeks. He said he had previously checked with the IT department and had been told that setting this up would be too difficult.

Because I hate to keep track of coupons for 15 weeks, here's the answer. The `Vic` table contains the VIC card number, the date, and the amount of purchase:

```
USE Tempdb

DROP TABLE Vic
go
CREATE TABLE Vic (
    VICNumber INT,
    PurchaseDate SMALLDATETIME,
```

```
    Amount MONEY
    )
go
INSERT Vic (VICNumber, PurchaseDate, Amount)
  VALUES (123, '1/3/2003', 55.24)
INSERT Vic (VICNumber, PurchaseDate, Amount)
  VALUES (123, '1/12/2003', 74.24)
INSERT Vic (VICNumber, PurchaseDate, Amount)
  VALUES (123, '1/18/2003', 102.24)
INSERT Vic (VICNumber, PurchaseDate, Amount)
  VALUES (123, '1/23/2003', 47.24)
INSERT Vic (VICNumber, PurchaseDate, Amount)
  VALUES (123, '1/29/2003', 55.24)
INSERT Vic (VICNumber, PurchaseDate, Amount)
  VALUES (123, '2/3/2003', 55.24)
INSERT Vic (VICNumber, PurchaseDate, Amount)
  VALUES (123, '2/12/2003', 74.24)
INSERT Vic (VICNumber, PurchaseDate, Amount)
  VALUES (123, '2/18/2003', 102.24)
INSERT Vic (VICNumber, PurchaseDate, Amount)
  VALUES (123, '2/23/2003', 47.24)
INSERT Vic (VICNumber, PurchaseDate, Amount)
  VALUES (123, '2/28/2003', 55.24)
INSERT Vic (VICNumber, PurchaseDate, Amount)
  VALUES (123, '3/3/2003', 75.24)
INSERT Vic (VICNumber, PurchaseDate, Amount)
  VALUES (123, '3/12/2003', 64.24)
INSERT Vic (VICNumber, PurchaseDate, Amount)
  VALUES (123, '3/18/2003', 62.24)
INSERT Vic (VICNumber, PurchaseDate, Amount)
  VALUES (123, '3/23/2003', 67.24)
INSERT Vic (VICNumber, PurchaseDate, Amount)
  VALUES (123, '3/29/2003', 65.24)
INSERT Vic (VICNumber, PurchaseDate, Amount)
  VALUES (123, '4/3/2003', 55.24)
INSERT Vic (VICNumber, PurchaseDate, Amount)
  VALUES (123, '4/12/2003', 74.24)
```

With the data loaded, the following query displays the week for each qualifying row:

```
SELECT DISTINCT VICNumber, DatePart(ww,PurchaseDate) AS [Week]
  FROM Vic
  WHERE Amount >=40
```

Result (abridged):

```
VICNumber   Week
----------- -----------
123         1
123         3
123         4
...
```

With a where clause, a group by, and a having clause, the seasonal contest winners are easy to produce. The where condition filters out any purchases of less than $40 prior to the group by operation. The group by partitions the results by VIC number. Finally, the count() aggregate function restricts the grouped results to those with at least 14 distinct weeks:

```
SELECT VICNumber AS Winner
  FROM Vic
  WHERE Amount >= 40
  GROUP BY VICNumber
  HAVING Count(Distinct DatePart(ww,PurchaseDate)) >= 14
```

And the winner is:

```
Winner
-----------
123
```

That's not much code to solve the problem. Maybe my grocery store's IT department will buy this book and we won't have to keep a bunch of coupons under a large magnet on our refrigerator door.

## Generating Totals

I'll admit that I'm not very excited about any of these last three options. I believe that subtotals and totals are best calculated in the client-side reporting tool or client application form and should not be a part of the result set passed from SQL Server to the client application. Nonetheless, certification tests tend to ask about these functions, so I'll include them here for your benefit.

The compute, cube, and rollup aggregate functions all generate subtotals and grand totals, and supply a null in the group by column to indicate the grand total. They are all similar in syntax. Rollup generates subtotal and total rows for the group by columns. Cube extends the capabilities by generating subtotal rows for every group by column. A special function grouping() is true when the row is a subtotal, or total row. Here I'll demonstrate the rollup function.

The rollup option, placed after the group by clause, instructs SQL Server to generate an additional total row. In this example, the grouping() function converts the total row to something understandable. The order by clause uses an insull() function to sort the total row to the end of the results:

```
USE OBXKites
SELECT
    CASE Grouping(ProductCategoryName)
      WHEN 0 THEN ProductCategoryName
      WHEN 1 THEN 'All Products'
    END AS ProductCategory,
    SUM(Quantity) AS QuantitySold,
    SUM(Quantity*UnitPrice) AS DollarSold
  FROM dbo.OrderDetail
    JOIN dbo.[Order]
      ON [Order].OrderID = OrderDetail.OrderID
    JOIN dbo.Product
      ON OrderDetail.ProductID = Product.ProductID
    JOIN dbo.ProductCategory
      ON Product.ProductCategoryID =
           ProductCategory.ProductCategoryID
  GROUP BY ProductCategoryName
    WITH ROLLUP
  ORDER BY ISNULL(ProductCategoryName, 'zzz')
```

The result includes the generated row with the grand total:

```
ProductCategory      QuantitySold      DollarSold
-------------------  ----------------  ---------------
Accessory            6.00              10.530000
Clothing             9.00              117.050000
Kite                 59.00             1614.652500
Material             3.00              5.265000
OBX                  127.00            64.687500
Video                2.00              35.910000
All Products         206.00            1848.095000
```

If you choose to pass back to the application programmer an additional row that includes the total dollars and then expect the application program to filter out the total row and place the value into a control below the grid, well, you're on your own.

As useful as these aggregate functions are, they don't eliminate the need for a good client-side report writer. Besides being the wrong place in the client-server paradigm for generating totals and subtotals, the aggregate functions just don't do certain tasks very well by themselves, such as:

✦ *Including descriptive data* — Because every column must participate in the average aggregate function, some developers simply slap group bys on additional descriptive columns not needed for the group by, such as names, when grouping by customer ID. A better solution is to perform the group by and aggregate functions in a subquery and then reference the descriptive columns in the outer query. The next chapter talks about subqueries.

✦ *Running sums* — While requesting running sums is not an uncommon topic on the SQL Server Internet forums, I believe the task is better handled by the client report writer than by SQL Server, which must use a cursor to step through the data to generate a running sum.

✦ *Crosstabs* — While it's possible to build crosstab result sets using cursors and stored procedures, it's inefficient. Several client-analysis tools, including access, perform crosstab analysis very easily. Browsing an Analysis Services cube is by far the ultimate crosstab. Any time spent developing a crosstab in a stored procedure would be much better spent developing the OLAP cube.

## Summary

While SQL contains several other keywords and commands, the heart of SQL is in its ability to manipulate data, and the select command excels in this area. While this chapter did include a few joins in some of the examples, every technique may be used in a single table join. A wealth of power and flexibility is hidden in the simple select command. SQL is declarative — you're only phrasing a question. The query optimizer figures out how to execute the query, so you have some flexibility in the development style of the query.

The next chapter takes the basic idea of the select statement and runs with it by adding multiple types of joins, unions, and subqueries. By combining some of the cooler functions of the select with subqueries, you can build some very creative and powerful queries.

✦    ✦    ✦

# Merging Data Using Relational Algebra

CHAPTER

7

In This Chapter

Understanding
relational algebra

Using inner, outer,
complex, and Θ (theta)
joins

Building simple and
correlated subqueries

Merging data vertically
with unions

Using relational division

In my introduction to this book I said that my purpose was to share the fun of developing in SQL Server. This chapter is it. Making data twist and shout, pulling an answer out of data with a creative query, replacing a few hundred lines of slow looping VB code with a single lightning fast SQL query — it's all pure fun and covered here.

Relational databases, by their very nature, segment data into several narrow, but long, tables. Seldom does looking at a single table provide meaningful data. Therefore, merging data from multiple tables is an important task for SQL developers. The theory behind merging data sets is *relational algebra*, as defined by E. F. Codd in 1970.

Relational algebra consists of eight relational operators:

+ *Restrict* — Returns the rows that meet a certain criterion

+ *Project* — Returns selected columns from a data set

+ *Product* — Relational multiplication that returns all possible combinations of data between two data sets

+ *Union* — Relational addition and subtraction that merges two tables vertically by stacking one table above another table and lining up the columns

+ *Intersection* — Returns the rows common to both data sets

+ *Difference* — Returns the rows unique to one data set

+ *Join* — Returns the horizontal merger of two tables, matching up rows based on common data

+ *Divide* — Returns exact matches between two data sets

In addition, as a method of accomplishing relational algebra, SQL has developed:

+ *Subqueries* — Similar to a join, but more flexible; the results of the subquery are used in place of an expression, list, or data set within an outer query.

In the formal language of relational algebra:

+ A table, or data set, is a *relation* or *entity*

+ A row is a *tuple*

+ A column is an *attribute*

I'll use these terms throughout this chapter.

Relational theory is now thirty-something and has become better defined over the years as the database vendors compete with extensions and database theorists further define the problem of representing reality within a data structure. However, E. F. Codd's original work is still the foundation of relational-database design and implementation.

**Note**    To give credit where credit is due, this entire chapter is based on work of E. F. Codd and C. J. Date. For information on relational theory, my library includes books by C. J. Date and Joe Celko. You can find a complete listing of recommended resources in the Appendix or online at www.isnotnull.com.

This chapter explains the multiple types of joins, simple and correlated subqueries, a few types of unions, relational division, and more.

## Using Joins

In relational algebra, a *join* is the multiplication of two data sets and a restriction of the result so that only the intersection of the two data sets is returned. The whole purpose of the join is to horizontally merge two data sets (usually tables) and produce a new result set from the combination by matching rows in one data source to rows in the other data source, as illustrated in Figure 7-1. This section explains the various types of joins and how to use them to select data.

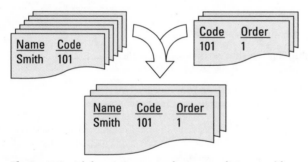

**Figure 7-1:** A join merges rows from one data set with rows from another data set, and creates a new set of rows that includes columns from both.

By merging the data using the join, the rest of the SQL select statement, including the column expressions, aggregate groupings, and where clause conditions, can access any of the columns or rows from the joined tables. These abilities are the core and power of SQL.

I apologize if this sounds too much like your teenager's math homework, but joins are based on the idea of intersecting data sets. As Figure 7-2 illustrates, a relational join deals with two sets of data that have common values, and it's these common values that define how the tables intersect.

**Note**    These set diagrams are a type of Venn diagram. For more information about Venn set diagrams, visit http://www.combinatorics.org/Surveys/ds5/VennEJC.html.

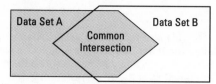

**Figure 7-2:** Relational joins are based on the overlap or common intersection of two data sets.

The intersection simply represents the fact that some common attribute can connect a row from the first data set to data in the second data set. The common values are typically a primary key and a foreign key, such as these examples from the OBX Kites sample database:

✦ CustomerID between the Customer and [Order] tables

✦ OrderID between the [Order] and OrderDetail tables

✦ ProductID between the Product and OrderDetail tables

SQL includes many types of joins that determine how the rows are selected from the different sides of the intersection. Table 7-1 lists the join types (each is explained in further detail later in this section).

## Table 7-1: Join Types

| Join Type | Query Designer Symbol | Definition |
|---|---|---|
| Inner join | | Includes only matching rows. |
| Left outer join | | Includes all rows from the left table regardless of whether a match exists, and matching rows from the right table. |
| Right outer join | | Includes all the rows from the right table regardless of whether a match exists, and matching rows from the left table. |
| Full outer join | | Matches rows using a non-equal condition. |
| Θ (theta) join | | Includes all the rows from both tables regardless of whether a match exists. |
| Cross join | No join connection | Produces a cartisian product — a match between each row in data source one with each row from data source two without any conditions or restrictions. |

# Inner Joins

The *inner join* is by far the most common join. In fact, it's also referred to as a *common join*, and was originally called a *natural join* by E. F. Codd. The inner join returns only those rows that represent a match between the two data sets. An inner join is well named because it extracts only data from the inner portion of the intersection of the two overlapping data sets, as illustrated in Figure 7-3.

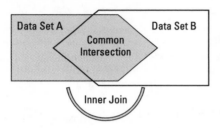

**Figure 7-3:** The inner join includes only those rows from each side of the join that are contained within the intersection of the two data sources.

Inner joins are easily constructed within Enterprise Manager using the graphical Query Designer tool, as shown in Figure 7-4. Once both tables have been placed in the Diagram pane using the Add Table function, or by dragging the tables from the table list, the join is created by dragging the common column from the first table to the second table. By default the join is an inner join.

The Query Designer uses a different symbol for each type of join, as shown in Table 7-1. The symbol for an inner join, the *join diamond*, is an accurate illustration of that type of join.

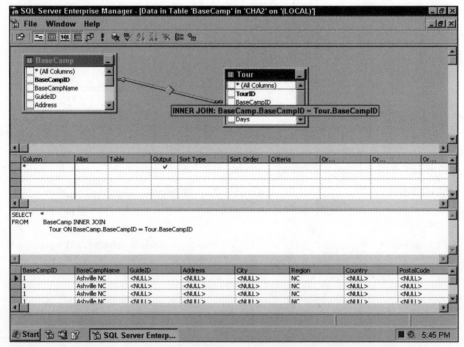

**Figure 7-4:** Building an inner join within Enterprise Manager's Query Designer.

## Creating Inner Joins Within SQL Code

Within SQL code, joins are specified within the `from` portion of the `select` statement. The keyword `join` identifies the second table, and `on` defines the common ground between the two tables. The default type of join is an inner join, so the keyword `inner` is optional:

```
SELECT *
  FROM Table1
    [INNER] JOIN Table2
      ON Table1.column = Table2.column
```

Because joins pull together data from two data sets, it makes sense that SQL needs to know how to match up rows from those sets. SQL Server merges the rows by matching a value common to both tables. Typically, a primary key value from one table is being matched with a foreign key value from the secondary table. Whenever a row from the first table matches a row from the second table, the two rows are merged into a new row containing data from both tables.

The following code sample joins the `Tour` (secondary) and `BaseCamp` (primary) tables from the Cape Hatteras Adventures sample database:

```
USE CHA2

SELECT Tour.TourName, Tour.BaseCampID,
    BaseCamp.BaseCampID, BaseCamp.BaseCampName
  FROM dbo.Tour
    JOIN dbo.BaseCamp
      ON Tour.BaseCampID = BaseCamp.BaseCampID
```

The query begins with the `Tour` table. For every `Tour` row, SQL Server will attempt to identify matching `BaseCamp` rows by comparing the `BasecampID` columns in both tables. The `Tour` table rows and `BaseCamp` table rows that match will be merged together into a new result:

| Tour.<br>TourName | Tour.<br>BaseCampID | Basecamp.<br>BaseCampID | Basecamp.<br>BaseCampName |
| --- | --- | --- | --- |
| Appalachian Trail | 1 | 1 | Ashville NC |
| Outer Banks Lighthouses | 2 | 2 | Cape Hatteras |
| Bahamas Dive | 3 | 3 | Freeport |
| Amazon Trek | 4 | 4 | Ft Lauderdale |
| Gauley River Rafting | 5 | 5 | West Virginia |

## Number of Rows Returned

In the preceding query every row in both the `Tour` and `BaseCamp` tables had a match. No rows were excluded from the join. However, in real life this is seldom the case. Depending upon the number of matching rows from each data source and the type of join, it's possible to reduce or increase the final number of rows in the result set.

To see how joins can alter the number of rows returned, look at the `Contact` and `[Order]` tables of the OBX Kites databases. The initial row count of contacts is 21, yet when the customers are matched with their orders, the row count changes to 10. The following code sample compares the two queries and their respective results side by side:

```
USE OBXKites

SELECT LastName                SELECT ContactCode, OrderNumber
  FROM dbo.Contact               FROM dbo.Contact
```

```
ORDER BY ContactCode                    JOIN dbo.[Order]
                                          ON [Order].ContactID
                                             = Contact.ContactID
                                        ORDER BY ContactCode
```

Results from both queries:

| ContactCode | LastName | | ContactCode | OrderNumber |
| --- | --- | --- | --- | --- |
| 101 | Smith | | 101 | 1 |
| | | | 101 | 2 |
| | | | 101 | 5 |
| 102 | Adams | | 102 | 6 |
| | | | 102 | 3 |
| 103 | Reagan | | 103 | 4 |
| | | | 103 | 7 |
| 104 | Franklin | | 104 | 8 |
| 105 | Dowdry | | 105 | 9 |
| 106 | Grant | | 106 | 10 |
| 107 | Smith | | | |
| 108 | Hanks | | | |
| 109 | James | | | |
| 110 | Kennedy | | | |
| 111 | Williams | | | |
| 112 | Quincy | | | |
| 113 | Laudry | | | |
| 114 | Nelson | | | |
| 115 | Miller | | | |
| 116 | Jamison | | | |
| 117 | Andrews | | | |
| 118 | Boston | | | |
| 119 | Harrison | | | |
| 120 | Earl | | | |
| 121 | Zing | | | |

Only contacts 101 through 106 have matching orders. The rest of the contacts are excluded from the join because they have no matching orders.

Joins can also appear to multiply rows. If a row on one side of the join matches with several rows on the other side of the join, the result will include a row for every match. In the preceding query, some contacts (Smith, Adams, and Reagan) are listed multiple times because they have multiple orders.

**Best Practice**

Depending on the nullability of the keys and the presence of rows on both sides of the join, joins tend to miss rows because one table or the other produces incorrect data. When retrieving data from multiple tables, it's a best practice to carefully select the correct type of join (inner, left outer, or right outer) for the query, so that every valid row is returned.

## Legacy Joins

A join is really nothing more than the act of selecting data from two tables for which a condition of equality exists between common columns. Join conditions are similar to where clauses. In fact, before ANSI-92 standardized the join...on syntax, *legacy style joins* accomplished the same task by listing the tables within the from clause and specifying the join condition in the where clause. SQL Server retains this legacy syntax for backward compatibility.

The previous sample join between `Contact` and `[Order]` could be written as a legacy join, as follows:

```
SELECT Contact.ContactCode, [Order].OrderNumber
  FROM dbo.Contact, dbo.[Order]
  WHERE [Order].ContactID = Contact.ContactID
  ORDER BY ContactCode
```

Personally, I prefer to write joins using the ANSI SQL-92 join...on syntax. I believe it's cleaner to specify the join completely within the `from` clause. Legacy joins break up the join so that the joined tables are in the `from` clause and the join condition is in the `where` clause, and that seems error-prone to me. However, neither style results in a performance benefit because SQL Server will create the exact same query execution plan regardless of whether the join is constructed using the ANSI standard join or the legacy `where` clause method.

## Multiple Table Joins

As some of the examples have already demonstrated, a select statement isn't limited to one or two tables; a SQL Server select statement may refer to up to 256 tables. That's a lot of joins. Because SQL is a declarative language, the order of the data sources is not important. Multiple joins may be combined in multiple paths, or even circular patterns (A joins B joins C joins A). Here's where a large whiteboard and a consistent development style really pay off.

An interesting thing happens when joins across multiple tables are combined with a where-clause restriction (that is, when the joins carry with them the where-clause restriction). A restriction in any one table means that only those rows that meet the restriction condition participate in the join.

The following query (first shown in Figure 7-5 and then worked out in code) answers the question "Who purchased kites?" The answer must involve five tables:

1. The `Contact` table for the "who"

2. The `[Order]` table for the "purchased"

3. The `OrderDetail` table for the "purchased"

4. The `Product` table for the "kites"

5. The `ProductCategory` table for the "kites"

The following SQL `select` statement begins with the "who" portion of the question and specifies the join tables and conditions as it works through the required tables. The query that is shown graphically in Enterprise Manager (Figure 7-5) is listed as raw SQL in the following code sample. Notice how the `where` clause restricts the `ProductCategory` table rows and yet affects the contacts selected.

```
USE OBXKites
SELECT LastName, FirstName, ProductName
  FROM dbo.Contact
    JOIN dbo.[Order]
      ON Contact.ContactID = [Order].ContactID
    JOIN dbo.OrderDetail
      ON [Order].OrderID = OrderDetail.OrderID
    JOIN dbo.Product
      ON OrderDetail.ProductID = Product.ProductID
    JOIN dbo.ProductCategory
      ON Product.ProductCategoryID = ProductCategory.ProductCategoryID
  WHERE ProductCategoryName = 'Kite'
  ORDER BY LastName, FirstName
```

Results:

```
LastName              FirstName                ProductName
----------------      --------------------     ----------------
Adams                 Terri                    Dragon Flight
Dowdry                Quin                     Dragon Flight
...
Smith                 Ulisius                  Rocket Kite
```

Compared with the SQL code generated by Enterprise Manager's Query Designer, the SQL code in the previous query is easier to decipher. While the Query Designer makes queries easier to initially develop, the code is more difficult to read. Sometimes the Query Designer places the on conditions away from the join table, and the formatting is atrocious.

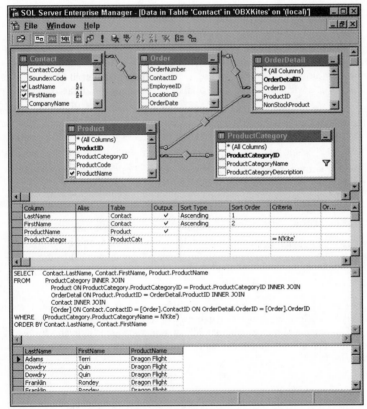

**Figure 7-5:** Answering the question "Who purchased kites?" using Enterprise Manager's Query Designer.

## Outer Joins

While an inner join contains only the intersection of the two data sets, an *outer join* extends the inner join by adding the non-matching data from the left or right data set, as illustrated in Figure 7-6.

Outer joins solve a significant problem for many queries by including all the data regardless of a match. The previous customer-order query demonstrates this problem well. If the requirement is to build a query that lists all customers plus their recent orders, an inner join between customers and orders would miss every customer who had not placed a recent order. This type of error is very common in database applications.

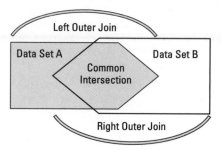

**Figure 7-6:** An outer join includes not only rows from the two data sources with a match but also unmatched rows from outside the intersection.

Some of the data in the result set produced by an outer join will look just like the data from an inner join. There will be data in columns that come from each of the data sources. But any rows from the outer-join table that do not have a match in the other side of the join will return data only from the outer-join table. In this case, columns from the other data source will have null values.

When building queries using Query Designer, you can change the join type from the default, inner join, to outer join via either the right-click mouse menu or the properties of the join, as shown in Figure 7-7. The Query Designer, in my opinion, does an excellent job of illustrating the types of joins with the join symbol (as previously detailed in Table 7-1).

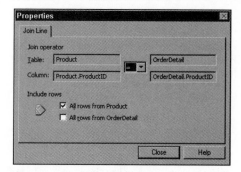

**Figure 7-7:** The join Properties dialog box displays the join columns, and is used to set the join condition (=, >, <, etc.) and add the left or right side of an outer join (all rows from Product, all rows from OrderDetail).

In SQL code, an outer join is declared by the keywords left outer or right outer before the join (technically, the keyword outer is optional):

```
SELECT *
  FROM Table1
    LEFT|RIGHT [OUTER] JOIN Table2
      ON Table1.column = Table2.column
```

**Best Practice**

Although several keywords in SQL are optional (such as inner and outer) or may be abbreviated (such as proc for procedure), explicitly stating the intent by spelling out the full syntax improves the readability of the code. However, most developers omit the optional syntax.

There's no trick to telling the difference between left and right outer joins. In code, left or right refers to the table that will be included regardless of the match. The outer-join table (sometimes called the driving table) is typically listed first, so left outer joins are more common than right outer joins. I suspect any confusion between left and right outer joins is caused by the use of graphical-query tools to build joins, because the left and right refers to the table's listing in the SQL text, and the tables' positions in the graphical-query tool are moot.

To modify the previous contact-order query so that it returns all contacts regardless of any orders, changing the join type from inner to left outer is all that's required, as follows:

```
SELECT ContactCode, OrderNumber
  FROM dbo.Contact
    LEFT OUTER JOIN dbo.[Order]
      ON [Order].ContactID = Contact.ContactID
  ORDER BY ContactCode
```

The `left outer join` will include all rows from the `Contact` table and matching rows from the `[Order]` table. The abbreviated result of the query is as follows:

```
Contact.          [Order].
ContactCode       OrderNumber
---------------   -----------
101               1
101               2
...
106               10
107               NULL
108               NULL
...
```

Because contact 107 and 108 do not have corresponding rows in the `[Order]` table, the columns from the `[Order]` table return a null for those rows.

The T-SQL legacy join syntax uses a trick to specify an outer join — an asterisk is added to the equals sign in the where clause condition:

✦ Left outer join: *=

✦ Right outer join: =*

For example, the previous outer-join query is written as follows using the legacy join style:

```
SELECT ContactCode, OrderNumber
  FROM dbo.Contact, dbo.[Order]
  WHERE Contact.ContactID *= Contact.ContactID
  ORDER BY ContactCode
```

**Best Practice**

If you are maintaining existing code you may see some legacy-style joins. However, I advise using the ANSI-style join syntax for all current development.

## Outer Joins and Optional Foreign Keys

Outer joins are often employed when a secondary table has a foreign-key constraint to the primary table and also permits nulls in the foreign key column. The presence of this optional foreign key means that if the secondary row refers to a primary row, the primary row must exist. However, it's perfectly valid for the secondary row to refrain from referring to the primary table at all.

Another example of an optional foreign key is an order alert or priority column. Many order rows will not have an alert or special-priority status. However, those that do must point to a valid row in the order-priority table.

The OBX Kite store uses a similar order-priority scheme, so reporting all the orders with their optional priorities requires an outer join:

```
SELECT OrderNumber, OrderPriorityName
  FROM dbo. [Order]
    LEFT OUTER JOIN dbo.OrderPriority
    ON [Order].OrderPriorityID =
      OrderPriority.OrderPriorityID
```

The left outer join retrieves all the orders and any matching priorities. The OBXKites_Populate.sql script sets two orders to rush priority:

```
OrderNumber OrderPriorityName
----------- -----------------
1           Rush
2           NULL
3           Rush
4           NULL
5           NULL
6           NULL
7           NULL
8           NULL
9           NULL
10          NULL
```

Reflexive relationships (also called recursive or self-joins relationship) also use optional foreign keys. In the Family sample database, the MotherID and FatherID are both foreign keys that refer to the PersonID of the mother or father. The optional foreign key allows persons to be entered without their father and mother already in the database. But if a value is entered in the MotherID or FatherID columns, the data must point to valid persons in the database.

## Full Outer Joins

A *full outer join* returns all the data from both data sets regardless of the intersection, as shown in Figure 7-8. It is functionally the same as a union distinct operation from a left outer join and a right outer join (unions are explained later in this chapter).

In real life, referential integrity reduces the need for a full outer join because every row from the secondary table should have a match in the primary table (depending on the optionality of the foreign key), so left outer joins are typically sufficient. Full outer joins are most useful for cleaning up data that has not had the benefit of clean constraints to filter out bad data.

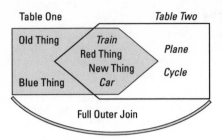

**Figure 7-8:** The full outer join returns all the data from both data sets, matching the rows where it can and filling in the holes with nulls.

The following example mocks up such a situation and compares the full outer join with an inner and a left outer join. Table One is the primary table. Table Two is a secondary table with a foreign key that refers to table One. There's no foreign-key constraint, so there may be some non-matches for the outer join to find:

```
CREATE TABLE dbo.One (
  OnePK INT,
  Thing1 VARCHAR(15)
  )

CREATE TABLE dbo.Two (
  TwoPK INT,
  OnePK INT,
  Thing2 VARCHAR(15)
  )
```

The sample data includes rows that would normally break referential integrity. The foreign key (OnePK) for the plane and the cycle in table Two do not have a match in table One. And two of the rows in table One do not have related secondary rows in table Two. The following batch inserts the eight sample data rows:

```
INSERT dbo.One(OnePK, Thing1)
  VALUES (1, 'Old Thing')
INSERT dbo.One(OnePK, Thing1)
  VALUES (2, 'New Thing')
INSERT dbo.One(OnePK, Thing1)
  VALUES (3, 'Red Thing')
INSERT dbo.One(OnePK, Thing1)
  VALUES (4, 'Blue Thing')

INSERT dbo.Two(TwoPK, OnePK, Thing2)
  VALUES(1,0, 'Plane')
INSERT dbo.Two(TwoPK, OnePK, Thing2)
  VALUES(2,2, 'Train')
INSERT dbo.Two(TwoPK, OnePK, Thing2)
  VALUES(3,3, 'Car')
INSERT dbo.Two(TwoPK, OnePK, Thing2)
  VALUES(4,NULL, 'Cycle')
```

An inner join between table One and table Two will return only the two matching rows:

```
SELECT Thing1, Thing2
  FROM dbo.One
    JOIN dbo.Two
      ON One.OnePK = Two.OnePK
```

Result:

```
Thing1            Thing2
---------------   ---------------
New Thing         Train
Red Thing         Car
```

A `left outer join` will extend the inner `join` and include the rows from table `One` without a match:

```
SELECT Thing1, Thing2
  FROM dbo.One
    LEFT OUTER JOIN dbo.Two
      ON One.OnePK = Two.OnePK
```

All the rows are now returned from table `One`, but two rows are still missing from Table two:

```
Thing1            Thing2
---------------   ---------------
Old Thing         NULL
New Thing         Train
Red Thing         Car
Blue Thing        NULL
```

A `full outer join` will retrieve every row from both tables, regardless of a match between the tables:

```
SELECT Thing1, Thing2
  FROM dbo.One
    FULL OUTER JOIN dbo.Two
      ON One.OnePK = Two.OnePK
```

The plane and cycle from table `Two` are now listed along with every row from table `One`:

```
Thing1            Thing2
---------------   ---------------
NULL              Plane
New Thing         Train
Red Thing         Car
NULL              Cycle
Blue Thing        NULL
Old Thing         NULL
```

As this example shows, full outer joins are an excellent tool for finding all the data, even bad data. Set difference queries, explored later in this chapter, build on outer joins to zero in on bad data.

## Placing the Conditions Within Outer Joins

When working with inner joins a condition has the same effect whether it's in the join clause or the where clause, but that's not the case with outer joins. When the condition is in the join clause, SQL Server includes all rows from the outer table and then uses the condition to include rows from the second table. When the restriction is placed in the where clause, the join is performed and then the where clause is applied to the joined rows. The following two queries demonstrate the effect of the placement of the condition.

## A Join Analogy

When I teach how to build queries, I often use this story to explain the different types of joins. Imagine a Pilgrim church in the 17th Century segmented by gender. The men all sit on one side of the church and the women on the other. Imagine that each side of the church is a database table and the combinations that leave the church represent the different types of joins.

If all the married couple stood up, joined hands and left the church, that would be an inner join between the men and women. The result set leaving the church would include only matched pairs.

If all the men stood, those who were married held hands with their brides, and they left as a group that would be a left outer join. The line leaving the church would include some couples and some bachelors.

Likewise, if all women with their husbands left the church that would be a right outer join. All the bachelors would be left alone in the church.

A full outer join would be everyone leaving the church, but only the married couples could hold hands.

In the first query, the `left outer join` includes all rows from table `One` and then joins those rows from table `Two` with an equal `OnePK` column and `Thing1`'s value is New Thing. The result is the same rows from table `One`, but fewer rows from table `Two`:

```
SELECT Thing1, Thing2
  FROM dbo.One
    LEFT OUTER JOIN dbo.Two
      ON One.OnePK = Two.OnePK
        AND One.Thing1 = 'New Thing'
```

Result:

```
Thing1            Thing2
---------------   ---------------
Old Thing         NULL
New Thing         Train
Red Thing         NULL
Blue Thing        NULL
```

The second query performs the `left outer join` producing four rows. The `where` clause then restricts that result to those rows where Thing1 is equal to New Thing1.

```
SELECT Thing1, Thing2
  FROM dbo.One
    LEFT OUTER JOIN dbo.Two
      ON One.OnePK = Two.OnePK
    WHERE One.Thing1 = 'New Thing'
```

Result:

```
Thing1            Thing2
---------------   ---------------
New Thing         Train
```

# Self-Joins

A *self-join* is a join that refers back to the same table. This type of unary relationship is often used to extract data from a reflexive (also called a recursive) relationship, such as a manufacturing databases with bill of materials data (build-from-material to material) and human-resource databases (employee to boss).

The Family sample database uses two self-joins between a child and his or her parents, as shown in the database diagram in Figure 7-9. The mothers and fathers are also people, of course, and are listed in the same table. They link back to their parents and so on. The sample database is populated with five fictitious generations that can be used for sample queries.

The key to constructing a self-join is to include a second reference to the table using a named range or table alias. Once the table is available twice to the select statement, the self-join functions much like any other join.

The following query locates the children of Audry Halloway:

```
USE Family

SELECT Person.PersonID, Person.FirstName,
   Person.MotherID, Mother.PersonID
  FROM dbo.Person
    JOIN dbo.Person Mother
      ON Person.MotherID = Mother.PersonID
  WHERE Mother.LastName = 'Halloway'
    AND Mother.FirstName = 'Audry'
```

The query uses the `Person` table twice. The first reference without a named range is joined with the second reference, which is restricted by the `where` clause to only Audry Halloway. Only the rows with a `MotherID` that points back to Audry will be included in the inner join. Audry's `PersonID` is 6 and her children are as follows:

| PersonID | FirstName | MotherID | PersonID |
|----------|-----------|----------|----------|
| 8 | Melanie | 6 | 6 |
| 7 | Corwin | 6 | 6 |
| 9 | Dara | 6 | 6 |
| 10 | James | 6 | 6 |

While the previous query adequately demonstrates a self-join, it would be more useful if the mother weren't hard-coded in the `where` clause, and if more information were provided about each birth, as follows:

```
SELECT CONVERT(NVARCHAR(15),Person.DateofBirth,1) AS Date,
    Person.FirstName AS Name, Person.Gender AS G,
    ISNULL(F.FirstName + ' ' + F.LastName, ' * unknown *')
      as Father,
    M.FirstName + ' ' + M.LastName as Mother
  FROM dbo.Person
    Left Outer JOIN dbo.Person F
      ON Person.FatherID = F.PersonID
    INNER JOIN dbo.Person M
      ON Person.MotherID = M.PersonID
  ORDER BY Person.DateOfBirth
```

This query makes three references to the person table: the child, the father, and the mother. The result is a better listing:

```
Date      Name      G   Father              Mother
--------  --------  --- ------------------  ----------------
5/19/22   James     M   James Halloway      Kelly Halloway
8/05/28   Audry     F   Bryan Miller        Karen Miller
8/19/51   Melanie   F   James Halloway      Audry Halloway
8/30/53   James     M   James Halloway      Audry Halloway
2/12/58   Dara      F   James Halloway      Audry Halloway
3/13/61   Corwin    M   James Halloway      Audry Halloway
3/13/65   Cameron   M   Richard Campbell    Eizabeth Campbell
...
```

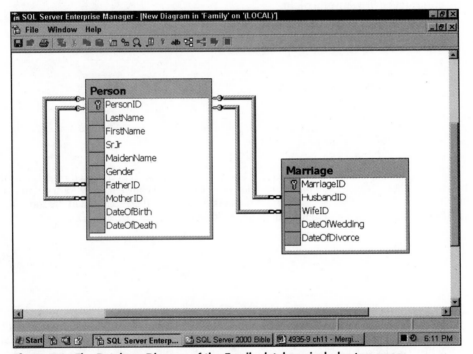

**Figure 7-9:** The Database Diagram of the Family database includes two unary relationships (children to parents) on the left and a many-to-many unary relationship (husband to wife) on the right.

## Cross (Unrestricted) Joins

The *cross join*, also called an unrestricted join, is a pure relational algebra multiplication of the two source tables. Without a join condition restricting the result set, the result set includes every possible combination of rows from the data sources. Each row in data set one is matched with every row in data set two, for example, if the first data source has five rows and second data source has four rows, a cross join between them would result in 20 rows. This type of result set is referred to as a *Cartesian product*.

Using the one/two sample tables, a cross join is constructed in Enterprise Manager by omitting the join condition between the two tables, as shown in Figure 7-10.

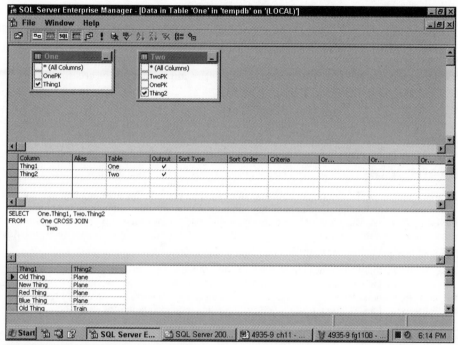

**Figure 7-10:** A graphical representation of a cross join is simply two tables without a join condition.

In code, this type of join is specified by the keywords `cross join` and the lack of an on condition:

```
SELECT Thing1, Thing2
  FROM dbo.One
    CROSS JOIN dbo.Two
```

The result of a join without restriction is that every row in table One matches with every row from table Two:

```
Thing1          Thing2
--------------- ---------------
Old Thing       Plane
New Thing       Plane
Red Thing       Plane
Blue Thing      Plane
Old Thing       Train
New Thing       Train
Red Thing       Train
Blue Thing      Train
Old Thing       Car
```

```
New Thing      Car
Red Thing      Car
Blue Thing     Car
Old Thing      Cycle
New Thing      Cycle
Red Thing      Cycle
Blue Thing     Cycle
```

Most cross joins are the result of forgetting to draw the join in a graphical-query tool; however, they are useful for populating databases with sample data, or for creating empty "pidgin hole" rows for population during a procedure.

Understanding how a cross join multiplies data is also useful when studying relational division, the inverse of a relational multiplication. Relational division requires subqueries, shown in Figure 7-12, so it's explained later in this chapter.

# Exotic Joins

Nearly all joins are based on a condition of equality between the primary key of a primary table and the foreign key of a secondary table, which is why the inner join is sometimes called an *equijoin*. But while it's commonplace to base a join on a single equal condition, it is not a requirement. The condition between the two columns is not necessarily equal, nor is the join limited to one condition.

The on condition of the join is in reality nothing more than a where condition restricting the product of the two joined data sets. where-clause conditions may be very flexible and powerful, and the same is true of join conditions. This reasoning enables the use of three powerful techniques; Θ *(theta) joins, multiple-condition joins*, and *non-key joins*.

## Θ (theta) Joins

A Θ (theta) join is a join based on a non-equal on condition. In relational theory conditional operators (=, >, <, >=, <=, <>) are called Θ operators. While the equals condition is technically a Θ operator, it is commonly used; only joins that deviate from the equi-join are referred to as Θ joins.

The Θ condition may be set within Enterprise Manager's Query Designer using the Join Properties dialog box, as previously shown in Figure 7-7.

Θ joins are often combined with multiple condition joins involving non-key columns, the rest of the code samples in this section all use Θ joins.

## Multiple-Condition Joins

If a join is nothing more than a condition between two data sets, it makes sense that multiple conditions are possible at the join. In fact, multiple-condition joins and Θ joins go hand-in-hand. Without the ability to use multiple-condition joins, Θ joins would be of little value.

Join conditions can refer to any table in the from clause, enabling interesting three-way joins. For example:

```
From A
  JOIN B
    ON A.col = B.col
  JOIN C
    ON B.col = C.col
    AND A.col = C.col
```

## Non-Key Joins

Joins are not limited to primary and foreign keys. The join can match a row in one data source with a row in another data source using any column, as long as the columns share compatible data types and the data match.

For example, an inventory allocation system would use a non-key join to find products that are expected to arrive from the supplier before the customer's required ship date. A non-key join between the PurchaseOrder and OrderDetail tables with a Θ condition between PO.DateExpected and OD.DateRequired will filter the join to those products that can be allocated to the customer's orders. The following code demonstrates the non-key join (this is not in a sample database):

```
SELECT OD.OrderID, OD.ProductID, PO.POID
FROM OrderDetail OD
  JOIN PurchaseOrder PO
    ON OD.ProductID = PO.ProductID
      AND OD.DateRequired > PO.DateExpected
```

When working with inner joins, non-key join conditions can be placed in the where clause or in the join. Because the conditions compare similar values between two joined tables, I often place these conditions in the join portion of the from clause rather than the where clause. The critical difference lies in whether you view the conditions as a part of creating the record set the rest of the SQL select statement is acting upon, or as a filtering task that follows the from clause. Either way, the query-optimization plan is identical, so use the method that is most readable and seems most logical to you. Note that when constructing outer joins the placement of the condition in the join or in the where clause yields different results, as is explained in the section on outer joins.

Looking at the Family sample database, the question "Who are twins?" uses all three exotic join techniques in the join between person and twin. The join contains three conditions. The Person.PersonID <> Twin.PersonID condition is a Θ join that prevents a person from being considered his or her own twin. The join condition on MotherID, while a foreign key, is non-standard because it's being joined with another foreign key. The DateOfBirth condition is definitely a non-key join condition. The where condition check for DateOfBirth is not null simply removes from the query those who married into the family and thus have no recorded parents:

```
SELECT Person.FirstName + ' ' + Person.LastName,
    Twin.FirstName + ' ' + Twin.LastName as Twin,
    Person.DateOfBirth
  FROM dbo.Person
    JOIN dbo.Person Twin
      ON Person.PersonID <> Twin.PersonID
        AND Person.MotherID = Twin.MotherID
        AND Person.DateOfBirth = Twin.DateOfBirth
  WHERE Person.DateOfBirth IS NOT NULL
```

The following is the same query, this time with the exotic join condition moved to the where clause. Not surprisingly, SQL Server's query optimizer produces the exact same query-execution plan for each query.

```
SELECT Person.FirstName + ' ' + Person.LastName AS Person,
    Twin.FirstName + ' ' + Twin.LastName as Twin,
    Person.DateOfBirth
  FROM dbo.Person
```

```
        JOIN dbo.Person Twin
          ON Person.MotherID = Twin.MotherID
            AND Person.DateOfBirth = Twin.DateOfBirth
      WHERE Person.DateOfBirth IS NOT NULL
        AND Person.PersonID != Twin.PersonID
```

Results:

```
Person           Twin             DateOfBirth
---------------  ---------------  ------------------------
Abbie Halloway   Allie Halloway   1979-08-14 00:00:00.000
Allie Halloway   Abbie Halloway   1979-08-14 00:00:00.000
```

In Microsoft's Northwind database, a non-key join could be created comparing the Region columns of the Customers, Shippers, and Orders tables.

The difficult query scenarios at the end of this chapter also demonstrate exotic joins often used with subqueries.

# Using Subqueries

A *subquery* is an imbedded select statement within an outer query. The subquery provides an answer to the outer-query in the form of a scalar value, a list of values, or a dataset, and may be substituted for an expression, list, or table, respectively, within the outer-query. The matrix of subquery types and select-statement usage is shown in Table 7-2. Because a subquery may only contain a select query, and not a data-modification query, subqueries are sometimes referred to as *subselects*.

The subquery comes in two forms, *simple* and *correlated*. The simple subquery can be a stand-alone query and can run by itself. It is executed once and the result is passed to the outer query. A correlated subquery references at least one column in the outer query and so it cannot run separately by itself. The outer query runs first and the correlated subquery runs once for every row in the outer query.

## Simple Subqueries

Simple subqueries are executed in the following order:

1. The simple subquery is executed once.

2. The results are passed to the outer query.

3. The outer query is executed once.

The most basic simple subquery returns a single (scalar) value, which is then used as an expression in the outer query, as follows:

```
SELECT (SELECT 3) AS SubqueryValue
```

Result:

```
SubqueryValue
-------------
3
```

## Table 7-2: Subquery Usage

| Select-Statement Element | Subquery Returns: | | |
|---|---|---|---|
| | **Expression** Subquery returns scalar value | **List** Subquery returns list of values | **Data Set** Subquery returns data source |
| Select (subquery) | The subquery result is used as an expression supplying the value for the column. | X | X |
| From (data source) as SQ | X | X | The subquery's data set is accepted as a derived table source within the outer-query. |
| Where x {=, >, <, >=, <=, <>} (subquery) | The where clause is true if the test value compares true with the subquery's scalar value. | X | X |
| Where x In (subquery) | The where condition is true if the test value is equal to the scalar value returned by the subquery. | The where condition is true if the test value is found within the list returned by the subquery. | X |
| Where Exists (Subquery) | The where condition is true if the subquery returns at least one row. | The where condition is true if the subquery returns at least one row. | The where condition is true if the subquery returns at least one row. |

The subquery (select 3) returns a single value of 3, which is passed to the outer select statement. The outer select statement is then executed as if it were the following:

```
SELECT 3 AS SubqueryValue
```

Of course, a subquery with only hard-coded values is of little use. A useful subquery fetches a date from a table, as follows:

```
USE OBXKites

SELECT ProductName
  FROM dbo.Product
  WHERE ProductCategoryID
    = (Select ProductCategoryID
         FROM dbo.ProductCategory
         Where ProductCategoryName = 'Kite')
```

To execute this query, SQL server first evaluates the subquery and returns a value to the outer query (your unique identifier will be different from the one in this query):

```
Select ProductCategoryID
        FROM dbo.ProductCategory
        Where ProductCategoryName = 'Kite'
```

Result:

```
ProductCategoryID
------------------------------------
C38D8113-2BED-4E2B-9ABF-A589E0818069
```

The outer query then executes as if it were the following:

```
SELECT ProductName
  FROM dbo.Product
  WHERE ProductCategoryID
    = 'C38D8113-2BED-4E2B-9ABF-A589E0818069'
```

Result:

```
ProductName
--------------------------------------------------
Basic Box Kite 21 inch
Dragon Flight
Sky Dancer
Rocket Kite
...
```

If you think subqueries seem similar to joins, you're right. Many joins may be rewritten as subqueries.

## Using Scalar Subqueries

If the subquery returns a single value it may then be used anywhere inside the SQL select statement where an expression might be used, including column expressions, join conditions, where conditions, or having conditions. Normal operators (+, =, between, and so on) will work with single values returned from a subquery; data-type conversion using the cast() or convert() function may be required, however.

The previous example used a subquery within a where condition. The following sample query uses a subquery within a column expression to calculate the total sales so each row can calculate the percentage of sales:

```
SELECT ProductCategoryName,
     SUM(Quantity * UnitPrice) AS Sales,
     Cast(SUM(Quantity * UnitPrice) /
        (SELECT SUM(Quantity * UnitPrice)
            FROM dbo.OrderDetail) *100 AS INT)
        AS PercentOfSales
  FROM dbo.OrderDetail
    JOIN dbo.Product
      ON OrderDetail.ProductID = Product.ProductID
    JOIN dbo.ProductCategory
      ON Product.ProductCategoryID = ProductCategory.ProductCategoryID
  GROUP BY ProductCategoryName
  ORDER BY Count(*) DESC
```

The subquery, `select sum(Quantity * UnitPrice) from OrderDetail`, returns a value of 1729.895, which is then passed to the outer query's `PercentageOfSales` column. The result lists the product categories, sales amount, and percentage of sales:

```
ProductCategoryName    Sales            PercentOfSales
---------------------  ---------------  --------------
Kite                   1499.902500      86.70
OBX                    64.687500        3.74
Clothing               113.600000       6.57
Accessory              10.530000        0.61
Material               5.265000         0.30
Video                  35.910000        2.08
```

The following `select` statement is extracted from the `fGetPrice()` user-defined function in the OBXKites sample database. The OBXKites database has a price table that allows each product to have a list of prices, each with an effective date. The OBX Kite store can pre-define several price changes for a future date rather than enter all the price changes the night before the new prices goes into effect. As an additional benefit, this data model maintains a price history.

The `fGetPrice()` function returns the correct price for any product, any date, and any customer-discount type. To accomplish this, the function must determine the effective date for the date submitted. For example, if a user needs a price for July 16, 2002, and the current price was made effective on July 1, 2002, then in order to look up the price the query needs to know the most recent price date using `max(effectivedate)` where `effectivedate` is = `@orderdate`. Once the subquery determines the effective date, the outer query can look up the price. Some of the function's variables are replaced with static values for the purpose of this example.

```
SELECT @CurrPrice = Price * (1-@DiscountPercent)
  FROM dbo.Price
    JOIN dbo.Product
      ON Price.ProductID = Product.ProductID
  WHERE ProductCode = '1001'
    AND EffectiveDate =
      (SELECT MAX(EffectiveDate)
        FROM dbo.Price
          JOIN dbo.Product
            ON Price.ProductID = Product.ProductID
        WHERE ProductCode = '1001'
          AND EffectiveDate <= '6/1/2001')
```

Calling the function,

```
Select dbo.fGetPrice('1001','5/1/2001',NULL)
```

the subquery determines that the effective price date is '05/01/2001'. The outer query can then find the correct price based on the `ProductID` and effective date. Once the `fGetPrice()` function calculates the discount, it can return `@CurrPrice` to the calling `select` statement:

```
14.9500
```

## Using Subqueries as Lists

Subqueries begin to shine when used as lists. A single value, commonly a column, in the outer query is compared with the list by means of the in operators. The subquery must return only a single column.

The in operator returns a value of true if the column value is found anywhere in the list supplied by the subquery, in the same way that where ... in returns a value of true when used with a hard-coded list:

```
SELECT *
  FROM dbo.Contact
  WHERE HomeRegion IN ('NC', 'SC', 'GA', 'AL', 'VA')
```

A list subquery serves as a dynamic means of generating the where ... in condition list:

```
SELECT *
  FROM dbo.Contact
  WHERE Region IN (Subquery that returns a list of states)
```

The following query answers the question "When OBXKites sells a kite, what else does it sell with the kite?" To demonstrate the use of subqueries, this query will use only subqueries — no joins. All of these subqueries are simple queries, meaning that each can run as a stand-alone query.

The subquery will find all orders with kites and pass those OrderID's to the outer query. Four tables are involved in providing the answer to this question: ProductCategory, Product, OrderDetail, and Order. The nested subqueries are executed from the inside out, so they read in the following order:

1. The subquery finds the one ProductCategoryID for the kites.

2. The subquery finds the list of products that are kites.

3. The subquery finds the list of orders with kites.

4. The subquery finds the list of all the products on orders with kites.

5. The outer query finds the product names.

```
SELECT ProductName
  FROM dbo.Product
  WHERE ProductID IN
    -- 4. Find all the products sold in orders with kites
    (SELECT ProductID
      FROM dbo.OrderDetail
      WHERE OrderID IN
      -- 3. Find the Kite Orders
      (SELECT OrderID  -- Find the Orders with Kites
        FROM dbo.OrderDetail
        WHERE ProductID IN
          -- 2. Find the Kite Products
          (SELECT ProductID
            FROM dbo.Product
            WHERE ProductCategoryID =
              -- 1. Find the Kite category
              (Select ProductCategoryID
                FROM dbo.ProductCategory
                Where ProductCategoryName
                  = 'Kite' ) ) ) )
```

**Tip**    You can highlight any of these subqueries and run it as a stand-alone query in Query Analyzer by selecting the subquery and pressing F5.

Subquery 1 finds the ProductCategoryID for the kite category and returns a single value.

Subquery 2 uses subquery 1 as a where clause expression subquery that returns the kite ProductCategoryID. Using this where-clause restriction, subquery 2 finds all products of which the ProductCategoryID is equal to the value returned from subquery 2.

Subquery 3 uses subquery 2 as a where-clause list subquery by searching for all OrderDetail rows that include any one of the productIDs returned by subquery 2.

Subquery 4 uses subquery 3 as a where clause list subquery that includes all orders that include kites. The subquery then locates all OrderDetail rows for which the orderID is in the list returned by subquery 3.

The outer query uses subquery 4 as a where clause list condition and finds all products of which the ProductID is in the list retuned by subquery 4, as follows:

```
ProductName
--------------------------------------------------
Falcon F-16
Dragon Flight
OBX Car Bumper Sticker
Short Streamer
Cape Hatteras T-Shirt
Sky Dancer
Go Fly a Kite T-Shirt
Long Streamer
Rocket Kite
OBX T-Shirt
```

Drat! There are kites in the list. They'll have to be eliminated from the query. To fix the error, the outer query needs to find all the products where:

✦ The ProductID is in order that included a kite

and

✦ The ProductID is not in the list of kites

Fortunately, subquery 2 returns all the kite products. Adding a copy of subquery 2 with the not in operator to the outer query will remove the kites from the list, as follows:

```
SELECT ProductName
  FROM dbo.Product
  WHERE ProductID IN
    -- 4. Find all the products sold in orders with kites
    (SELECT ProductID
      FROM dbo.OrderDetail
      WHERE OrderID IN
      -- 3. Find the Kite Orders
      (SELECT OrderID  -- Find the Orders with Kites
        FROM dbo.OrderDetail
        WHERE ProductID IN
          -- 2. Find the Kite Products
          (SELECT ProductID
            FROM dbo.Product
```

```
                    WHERE ProductCategoryID =
                      -- 1. Find the Kite category
                      (Select ProductCategoryID
                        FROM dbo.ProductCategory
                        Where ProductCategoryName
                          = 'Kite' ) ) )
              -- outer query continued
              AND ProductID NOT IN
                (SELECT ProductID
                  FROM dbo.Product
                  WHERE ProductCategoryID =
                     (Select ProductCategoryID
                       FROM dbo.ProductCategory
                       Where ProductCategoryName
                          = 'Kite' ) ) )
```

**Result:**

```
ProductName
--------------------------------------------------
OBX Car Bumber Sticker
Short Streamer
Cape Hatteras T-Shirt
Go Fly a Kite T-Shirt
Long Streamer
OBX T-Shirt
```

For comparison purposes, the following queries answer the exact same question but are written with joins. The `Product` table is referenced twice, so the second reference that represents only the kites has a named range of `Kite`. As with the previous subqueries, the first version of the query locates all products and the second version eliminates the kites:

```
SELECT Distinct Product.ProductName
  FROM dbo.Product
    JOIN dbo.OrderDetail OrderRow
      ON Product.ProductID = OrderRow.ProductID
    JOIN dbo.OrderDetail KiteRow
      ON OrderRow.OrderID = KiteRow.OrderID
    JOIN dbo.Product Kite
      ON KiteRow.ProductID = Kite.ProductID
    JOIN dbo.ProductCategory
      ON Kite.ProductCategoryID
            = ProductCategory.ProductCategoryID
  Where ProductCategoryName  = 'Kite'
```

The only change necessary to eliminate the kites is the addition of another condition to the `ProductCategory` join. Previously, the join was a equi-join between `Product` and `ProductCategory`. Adding a Θ-join condition of `!=` between the `Product` table and the `ProductCategory` table removes any products that are kites, as shown in the following code sample:

```
SELECT Distinct Product.ProductName
  FROM dbo.Product
    JOIN dbo.OrderDetail OrderRow
      ON Product.ProductID = OrderRow.ProductID
```

```
JOIN dbo.OrderDetail KiteRow
  ON OrderRow.OrderID = KiteRow.OrderID
JOIN dbo.Product Kite
  ON KiteRow.ProductID = Kite.ProductID
JOIN dbo.ProductCategory
  ON Kite.ProductCategoryID
     = ProductCategory.ProductCategoryID
  AND Product.ProductCategoryID
      != Kite.ProductCategoryID
Where ProductCategoryName = 'Kite'
```

These two sets of queries, written using dramatically different syntax, provide the exact same answers. So which is the best query? That's up to you. Depending on complexity, subqueries can be faster because they select fewer rows from step to step. More complex subqueries tend to perform better than large join queries.

**Best Practice**

SQL is very flexible—there are often a dozen ways to express the same question. Your choice of SQL method should be made according to your style and to which method enables you to be legibly and logically correct, and then according to performance considerations. Slow and correct beats fast and wrong every time.

Here's another example of how a creative subquery can solve a problem. SQL handles finding the top rows from a result set easily, but it's a little trickier to find a middle range of rows. In this day of Web searches that return hundreds of hits, finding rows 101 through 125 is a useful, and frequently required, ability.

This example, based on the OBX Kite Store sample database, finds five products beginning with the 26th product. The subquery finds the first 25 products, which are then skipped by the outer query because of the where not in clause:

```
USE OBXKites
SELECT TOP 5 ProductName, ProductCode
  FROM dbo.Product
  WHERE ProductID NOT IN
    (SELECT TOP 25 ProductID
      FROM dbo.Product
      ORDER BY ProductCode)
  ORDER BY ProductCode
```

Result:

```
ProductName            ProductCode
---------------------- ---------------
Handle                 1026
Third Line Release     1027
High Performance Line  1028
Kite Bag               1029
Kite Repair Kit        1030
```

## Using Subqueries as Tables

In the same way that a view may be used in the place of a table within the from clause of a select statement, a subquery in the form of a *derived table* can replace any table, provided the subquery has a named range. This technique is very powerful and is often used to break a difficult query problem down into smaller bite-sized chunks.

Using a subquery as a derived table is an excellent solution to the aggregate-function problem. When you are building an aggregate query, every column must participate in the aggregate function in some way, either as a group by column or as an aggregate function (sum(), avg(), count(), max(), or min()). This stipulation makes returning additional descriptive information difficult. However, performing the aggregate functions in a subquery and passing the rows found to the outer query as a derived table enables the outer query to then return any columns desired.

The question "How many of each product have been sold?" is easy to answer if only one column from the Product table is included in the result:

```
SELECT ProductCode, SUM(Quantity) AS QuantitySold
  FROM dbo.OrderDetail
    JOIN dbo.Product
      ON OrderDetail.ProductID = Product.ProductID
  GROUP BY ProductCode
```

Result:

```
ProductCode    QuantitySold
-------------- ---------------------------------------
1002           47.00
1003           5.00
1004           2.00
1012           5.00
```

The result includes ProductCode, but not the name or description. Of course it's possible to simply group by every column to be returned, but that's sloppy. The following query performs the aggregate summation in a subquery that is then joined with the Product table so that every column is available without additional work:

```
SELECT Product.ProductCode, Product.ProductName,
    Sales.QuantitySold
  FROM dbo.Product
  JOIN (SELECT ProductID, SUM(Quantity) AS QuantitySold
          FROM dbo.OrderDetail
          GROUP BY ProductID) Sales
    ON Product.ProductID = Sales.ProductID
  ORDER BY ProductCode
```

The query is fast and efficient, it provides the required aggregate data, and all the product columns can be added to the output columns. The result is as follows:

```
ProductCode ProductName          QuantitySold
----------- -------------------- -------------------
1002        Dragon Flight        47.00
1003        Sky Dancer           5.00
1004        Rocket Kite          2.00
1012        Falcon F-16          5.00
...
```

Another example of using a derived table to solve a problem answers the question "How many children has each mother borne?" from the Family sample database:

```
USE Family
SELECT PersonID, FirstName, LastName, Children
  FROM dbo.Person
```

```
      JOIN (SELECT MotherID, COUNT(*) AS Children
              FROM dbo.Person
              WHERE MotherID IS NOT NULL
              GROUP BY MotherID) ChildCount
    ON Person.PersonID = ChildCount.MotherID
  ORDER BY Children DESC
```

The subquery performs the aggregate summation, and the columns are joined with the Person table to present the final results, as follows:

```
PersonID     FirstName         LastName          Children
-----------  ----------------  ----------------  -----------
6            Audry             Halloway          4
8            Melanie           Campbell          3
12           Alysia            Halloway          3
20           Grace             Halloway          2
```

## Correlated Subqueries

Correlated subqueries sound impressive, and they are. They are used in the same ways that simple subqueries are used, the difference being that correlated subqueries reference columns in the outer query. This ability to limit the subquery by the outer query makes these queries powerful and flexible. Because correlated subqueries can reference the outer query, they are especially useful for complex where conditions.

The ability to reference the outer query also means that correlated subqueries won't run by themselves because the reference to the outer query would cause the query to fail. The logical execution order is as follows:

1. The outer query is executed once.

2. The subquery is executed once for every row in the outer query, substituting the values from the outer query into each execution of the subquery.

3. The subquery's results are integrated into the result set.

If the outer query returns 100 rows, SQL Server will execute the logical equivalent of 101 queries — one for the outer query, and one subquery for every row returned by the outer query. In practice, the SQL Server query optimizer will likely figure out a way to perform the correlated subquery without actually performing the 101 queries. In fact, I've sometimes seen correlated subqueries outperform other query plans. If they solve your problem don't avoid them for performance reasons.

To explore correlated subqueries, the next few queries, based on the Outer Banks Adventures sample database, use them to compare the locations of customers and tour base camps. First, the following data-modification queries set up the data:

```
USE CHA2
UPDATE dbo.BaseCamp SET Region = 'NC' WHERE BaseCampID = 1
UPDATE dbo.BaseCamp SET Region = 'NC' WHERE BaseCampID = 2
UPDATE dbo.BaseCamp SET Region = 'BA' WHERE BaseCampID = 3
UPDATE dbo.BaseCamp SET Region = 'FL' WHERE BaseCampID = 4
UPDATE dbo.BaseCamp SET Region = 'WV' WHERE BaseCampID = 5

UPDATE dbo.Customer SET Region = 'ND' WHERE CustomerID = 1
UPDATE dbo.Customer SET Region = 'NC' WHERE CustomerID = 2
UPDATE dbo.Customer SET Region = 'NJ' WHERE CustomerID = 3
```

```
UPDATE dbo.Customer SET Region = 'NE' WHERE CustomerID = 4
UPDATE dbo.Customer SET Region = 'ND' WHERE CustomerID = 5
UPDATE dbo.Customer SET Region = 'NC' WHERE CustomerID = 6
UPDATE dbo.Customer SET Region = 'NC' WHERE CustomerID = 7
UPDATE dbo.Customer SET Region = 'BA' WHERE CustomerID = 8
UPDATE dbo.Customer SET Region = 'NC' WHERE CustomerID = 9
UPDATE dbo.Customer SET Region = 'FL' WHERE CustomerID = 10
```

This sample set of data produces the following matrix between customer locations and base-camp locations:

```
SELECT DISTINCT Customer.Region, BaseCamp.Region
  FROM dbo.Customer
    JOIN dbo.Event_mm_Customer
      ON Customer.CustomerID = Event_mm_Customer.CustomerID
    JOIN dbo.Event
      ON Event_mm_Customer.EventID = Event.EventID
    JOIN dbo.Tour
      ON Event.TourID = Tour.TourID
    JOIN dbo.BaseCamp
      ON Tour.BaseCampID = BaseCamp.BaseCampID
  WHERE Customer.Region IS NOT NULL
  GROUP BY Customer.Region, BaseCamp.Region
  ORDER BY Customer.Region, BaseCamp.Region
```

Result:

```
Customer   BaseCamp
Region     Region
-------    --------

BA         BA
BA         FL
BA         NC
FL         FL
FL         NC
FL         WV
NC         BA
NC         FL
NC         NC
NC         WV
ND         BA
ND         FL
ND         NC
NE         FL
NE         WV
NJ         FL
NJ         NC
NJ         WV
```

With this data foundation, the first query asks, "Who lives in the same region as one of our base camps?" The query uses a correlated subquery to locate base camps that share the same Region as the customer. The subquery is executed for every row in the Customer table. If a BaseCamp match exists for that row, the exists condition is true and the row is accepted into the result set.

```
SELECT C.FirstName, C.LastName, C.Region
  FROM dbo.Customer C
  WHERE EXISTS
    (SELECT * FROM dbo.BaseCamp B
      WHERE B.Region = C.Region)
```

The same query written with joins requires a distinct predicate to eliminate duplicate rows. However, it can refer to columns in every referenced table — something a correlated subquery within a where exists can't do.

```
SELECT DISTINCT C.FirstName, C.LastName, C.Region, B.Region
  FROM Customer C
    JOIN dbo.BaseCamp B
      ON C.Region = B.Region
```

The result:

```
FirstName          LastName             Region
----------------   ------------------   -------------------
Jane               Doe                  BA
Francis            Franklin             FL
Melissa            Anderson             NC
Lauren             Davis                NC
Wilson             Davis                NC
John               Frank                NC
```

A more complicated comparison asks, "Who has gone on a tour in his or her home region?"

The answer lies in the Event_mm_Customer table — a resolution (or junction) table between the Event and Customer tables that serves to store the logical many-to-many relationship between customers and events (multiple customers may attend a single event, and a single customer may attend multiple events). The Event_mm_Customer table may be thought of as analogous to a customer's ticket to an event.

The outer query logically runs though every Event_mm_Customer row to see if there exists any result from the correlated subquery. The subquery is filtered by the current EventID and customer RegionID from the outer query.

In an informal way of thinking, the query checks every ticket and creates a list of events in a customer's home region that that customer has attended. If anything is in the list, the where exists condition is true for that row. If the list is empty, where exists is not satisfied and the customer row in question is eliminated from the result set:

```
USE CHA2
SELECT DISTINCT C.FirstName, C.LastName, C.Region AS Home
  FROM dbo.Customer C
    JOIN dbo.Event_mm_Customer E
      ON C.CustomerID = E.CustomerID
  WHERE C.Region IS NOT NULL
    AND EXISTS
        (SELECT *
          FROM dbo.Event
            JOIN dbo.Tour
              ON Event.TourID = Tour.TourID
            JOIN dbo.BaseCamp
              ON Tour.BaseCampID = BaseCamp.BaseCampID
          WHERE BaseCamp.Region = C.Region
            AND Event.EventID = E.EventID)
```

Result:

```
FirstName LastName    Home

code:Francis    Franklin    FL
Jane      Doe         BA
John      Frank       NC
Lauren    Davis       NC
Melissa   Anderson    NC
```

The same query can be written using joins. Although it might be easier to read, the following query took 131 milliseconds compared to only 80 milliseconds taken by the previous correlated subquery:

```
SELECT Distinct C.FirstName, C.LastName, C.Region AS Home,
    Tour.TourName, BaseCamp.Region
  FROM dbo.Customer C
    JOIN dbo.Event_mm_Customer
      ON C.CustomerID = Event_mm_Customer.CustomerID
    JOIN dbo.Event
      ON Event_mm_Customer.EventID = Event.EventID
    JOIN dbo.Tour
      ON Event.TourID = Tour.TourID
    JOIN dbo.BaseCamp
      ON Tour.BaseCampID = BaseCamp.BaseCampID
      AND C.Region = BaseCamp.Region
      AND C.Region IS NOT NULL
  ORDER BY C.LastName
```

The join query has the advantage of including the columns from the Tour table without having to explicitly return them from the subquery. The join also lists Lauren and Frank twice, once for each in-region tour. And yes, the Amazon Trek tour is based out of Ft. Lauderdale:

```
FirstName LastName    Home  TourName                  Region
er Banks  Lighthouses NC
Lauren    Davis       NC    Appalachian Trail         NC
Lauren    Davis       NC    Outer Banks Lighthouses   NC
Jane      Doe         BA    Bahamas Dive              BA
John      Frank       NC    Appalachian Trail         NC
John      Frank       NC    Outer Banks Lighthouses   NC
Francis   Franklin    FL    Amazon Trek               FL
```

Although correlated subqueries can be mind-bending, the flexibility and potential performance gains are worth it. Be careful that the correlated subquery returns the correct answer.

# Using Unions

The union operation is different from a join. In relational algebra terms, a union is addition, whereas a join is multiplication. Instead of extending a row horizontally as a join would, the union stacks multiple result sets into a single long table, as illustrated in Figure 7-11. These few rules must be followed when constructing a union query:

✦ The column names, or aliases, must be determined by the first select.

✦ Every select must have the same number of columns and each lineup of columns must share the same data-type family.

✦ Expressions may be added to the select statements to identify the source of the row so long as the column is added to every select.

✦ The union may be used as part of a select into (a form of the insert verb covered in Chapter 10, "Modifying Data") but the into keyword must go in the first select statement.

✦ While the select command will default to all unless distinct is specified, the union is the opposite. By default, the union will perform a distinct; if you wish to change this behavior you must specify the keyword all. (I recommend that you think of the union as "union all" in the same way that the you might think of top as "top with ties.")

✦ The order by clause sorts the results of all the selects and must go on the last select, but uses the column names from the first select.

**Cross-Reference** Unions are also used within partitioned views (explained in Chapter 30, "Advanced Scalability"), a means of segmenting large tables into several smaller tables while retaining the ability to insert or update data through the union.

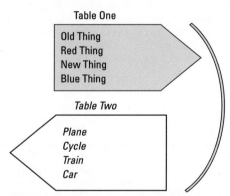

**Figure 7-11:** A union vertically appends the result of one select statement to the results of another select statement.

In the following union query the order by clause references the Thing1 column in the first select statement:

```
SELECT OnePK, Thing1, 'from One' as Source
  FROM dbo.One
UNION ALL
SELECT TwoPK, Thing2, 'from Two'
  FROM dbo.Two
ORDER BY Thing1
```

The resulting record set uses the column names from the first `select` statement:

```
OnePK          Thing1             Source
-----------    ----------------   --------
4              Blue Thing         from One
3              Car                from Two
4              Cycle              from Two
2              New Thing          from One
1              Old Thing          from One
1              Plane              from Two
3              Red Thing          from One
2              Train              from Two
```

Unions aren't limited to two tables. The largest I've personally worked with had about 90 tables (I won't try that again anytime soon). As long as the total number of tables referenced by a query is 256 or less, SQL Server handles the load.

## Intersection Union

An *intersection union* finds the rows common to both data sets. An inner join finds common rows horizontally, while an intersection union finds common rows vertically. SQL Server doesn't handle intersection or difference unions natively, so they take a little work. To set up the intersection query, these first two statements add rows to table Two so there will be an intersection:

```
INSERT dbo.Two(TwoPK, OnePK, Thing2)
  VALUES(5,0, 'Red Thing')
INSERT dbo.Two(TwoPK, OnePK, Thing2)
  VALUES(6,0, 'Blue Thing')
```

The intersection union query wraps a `group by` around a `union` in a subquery. If the `count()` is greater than 1, the row must be in both `select` statements. The `select distinct` eliminates duplicates within each `select` statement that would skew the intersection union query. It's important that the union be a `union all` and not a `union distinct`; otherwise the union itself would eliminate duplicates and the intersection would be eliminated before it could be counted:

```
SELECT DISTINCT U.Thing1
FROM
(SELECT DISTINCT Thing1
  FROM dbo.One
UNION ALL
SELECT DISTINCT Thing2
  FROM dbo.Two) U
GROUP BY Thing1
HAVING Count(*) > 1
```

Result:

```
Thing1
---------------
Blue Thing
Red Thing
```

To include more columns in the intersection query, you must add the columns to both the union and the `group by`.

## Difference Union

The *difference union* is similar to the intersection union, but the `having` restriction permits only those rows found in only one of the two data sets.

A difference union is similar to a *set difference query* (covered later in this chapter) in that it locates all rows that are in one data set but not the other. While a set difference query is interested only in the join conditions (typically the primary and foreign keys) and joins the rows horizontally, a difference union is looking at the entire row (or, more specifically, all the columns that participate in the union's `select` statements) vertically.

This query is the first step in building a difference union query. It locates any row that is in table `One` or in table `Two`, but not in both — sort of like a data set "exclusive or," if there were such a thing. Any row found by the `union` with a row `count()` of 1 must only exist in one of the source tables.

```
SELECT Thing1
FROM
(SELECT DISTINCT Thing1
   FROM dbo.One
UNION ALL
SELECT DISTINCT Thing2
   FROM dbo.Two) U
GROUP BY Thing1
HAVING Count(*) =1
```

Result:

```
Thing1
---------------
Car
Cycle
New Thing
Old Thing
Plane
Train
```

A small adjustment to this technique locates the rows in table `One` that are not in table `Two`. Because the result set is restricted to those rows `having` a `count()` of 2, the rows must be in table `One`. If they were only in table `Two` the `count()` would be 1. If the row were in both tables, the count would be 3.

```
SELECT DISTINCT Thing1
FROM
(SELECT DISTINCT Thing1
   FROM dbo.One
UNION ALL
 SELECT DISTINCT Thing1
   FROM dbo.One
UNION ALL
SELECT DISTINCT Thing2
   FROM dbo.Two) U
GROUP BY Thing1
HAVING Count(*) = 2
```

The final difference union query solution now produces only those rows in table One that are not found in table Two:

```
Thing1
---------------
New Thing
Old Thing
```

# Relational Division

A cross join, discussed previously in this chapter, is relational multiplication—two data sets are multiplied to create a Cartesian product. In theory, all joins are cross joins with some type of conditional restriction. Even an inner join is the relational-multiplication product of two tables restricted to those results that match keys.

*Relational division* complements relational multiplication just as basic math division complements multiplication. If the purpose of relational multiplication is to produce a product set from two multiplier sets, the purpose of relational division is to divide one data set (the *dividend data set*) by another data set (the *divisor data set*) to find the *quotient data set*, as shown in Figure 7-12. In other words, if the Cartesian product is known, and one of the multiplier data sets is known, relational division can deduce the missing multiplier set.

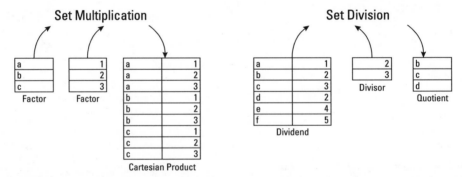

**Figure 7-12:** Relational division is the inverse of relational multiplication and deduces the quotient set by dividing the dividend set by the divisor set.

While this may sound academic, relational division can be very practical. The classic example of relational division answers the question "Which students have passed every required course?" An *exact relational division* query would list only those students who passed the required courses and no others. A *relational division with a remainder*, also called an *approximate divide*, would list all the students who passed the required courses and include students who passed any additional courses. Of course, that example was both practical and academic.

Relational division is more complex than a join. A join simply finds any matches between two datasets. Relational division finds exact matches between two datasets. Joins/subqueries and relational division solve different types of questions. For example, the following questions apply to the sample databases and compare the two methods:

✦ Joins/subqueries:

- **CHA2:** Who has ever gone on a tour?
- **CHA2:** Who lives in the same region as a base camp?
- **CHA2:** Who has attended any event in his or her home region?

✦ Exact relational division:

- **CHA2:** Who has gone on every tour in his or her home state, but no tours outside it?
- **OBXKites:** Who has purchased every kite but nothing else?
- **Family:** Which women (widows or divorcees) have married the same husbands as each other, but no other husbands?

✦ Relational division with remainders:

- **CHA2:** Who has gone on every tour in his or her home state, and possibly other tours as well?
- **OBXKites:** Who has purchased every kite and possibly other items as well?
- **Family:** Which women have married the same husbands and may have married other men as well?

## Relational Division with a Remainder

Relational division with a remainder essentially extracts the quotient while allowing some leeway for rows that meet the criteria but contain additional data as well. In real-life situations this type of division is typically more useful than an exact relational division.

The previous OBX Kites sales question ("Who has purchased every kite and possibly other items as well?") is a good one to use to demonstrate relational division. Because it takes five tables to go from contact to product category, and because the question refers to the join between `OrderDetail` and `Product`, this question involves enough complexity that it simulates a real-world relational-database problem.

The toy category will make a good example category because it contains only two toys and no one has purchased a toy in the sample data. So the query will answer the question "Who has purchased at least one of every toy sold by OBX Kites?" (And yes, my kids volunteered to help test this query.)

First, the following data will mock up a scenario in the OBX Kites database. The only toys are `ProductCode` 1049 and 1050. The OBX Kites database uses unique identifiers for primary keys and therefore uses stored procedures for all inserts. The first `Order` and `OrderDetail` inserts will list the stored procedure parameters so the following stored procedure calls are easier to understand:

```
USE OBXKites
DECLARE @OrderNumber INT
```

The first person, ContactCode 110, orders exactly all toys:

```
EXEC pOrder_AddNew
   @ContactCode = '110',
   @EmployeeCode = '120',
   @LocationCode = 'CH',
   @OrderDate= '6/1/2002',
   @OrderNumber = @OrderNumber output

EXEC pOrder_AddItem
   @OrderNumber = @OrderNumber,
   @Code = '1049',
   @NonStockProduct = NULL,
   @Quantity = 12,
   @UnitPrice = NULL,
   @ShipRequestDate = '6/1/2002',
   @ShipComment = NULL


EXEC pOrder_AddItem
   @OrderNumber, '1050', NULL, 3, NULL, NULL, NULL
```

The second person, ContactCode 111, orders exactly all toys — toy 1050 twice:

```
EXEC pOrder_AddNew
   '111', '119', 'JR', '6/1/2002', @OrderNumber output
EXEC pOrder_AddItem
   @OrderNumber, '1049', NULL, 6, NULL, NULL, NULL
EXEC pOrder_AddItem
   @OrderNumber, '1050', NULL, 6, NULL, NULL, NULL

EXEC pOrder_AddNew
   '111', '119', 'JR', '6/1/2002', @OrderNumber output
EXEC pOrder_AddItem
   @OrderNumber, '1050', NULL, 6, NULL, NULL, NULL
```

The third person, ContactCode 112, orders all toys plus some other products:

```
EXEC pOrder_AddNew
   '112', '119', 'JR', '6/1/2002', @OrderNumber output
EXEC pOrder_AddItem
   @OrderNumber, '1049', NULL, 6, NULL, NULL, NULL
EXEC pOrder_AddItem
   @OrderNumber, '1050', NULL, 5, NULL, NULL, NULL
EXEC pOrder_AddItem
   @OrderNumber, '1001', NULL, 5, NULL, NULL, NULL
EXEC pOrder_AddItem
   @OrderNumber, '1002', NULL, 5, NULL, NULL, NULL
```

The fourth person, ContactCode 113, orders one toy:

```
EXEC pOrder_AddNew
   '113', '119', 'JR', '6/1/2002', @OrderNumber output
EXEC pOrder_AddItem
   @OrderNumber, '1049', NULL, 6, NULL, NULL, NULL
```

So only customers 110 and 111 order all the toys and nothing else. Customer 112 purchases all the toys as well as some kites. Customer 113 is an error check because she only bought one toy.

At least a couple of methods exist for coding a relational-division query. The original method, proposed by Chris Date, involves using nested correlated subqueries to locate rows in and out of the sets. A more direct method has been popularized by Joe Celko: it involves comparing the row count of the dividend and divisor datasets.

Basically, Celko's solution is to rephrase the question as "For whom is the number of toys ordered equal to the number of toys available?"

The query then is asking two questions. The outer query will group the orders with toys for each contact and the subquery will count the number of products in the toy product category. The outer query's having clause will then compare the distinct count of contact products ordered that are toys against the count of products that are toys:

```
-- Is number of toys ordered...
SELECT Contact.ContactCode
  FROM dbo.Contact
    JOIN dbo.[Order]
      ON Contact.ContactID = [Order].ContactID
    JOIN dbo.OrderDetail
      ON [Order].OrderID = OrderDetail.OrderID
    JOIN dbo.Product
      ON OrderDetail.ProductID = Product.ProductID
    JOIN dbo.ProductCategory
      ON Product.ProductCategoryID = ProductCategory.ProductCategoryID
  WHERE ProductCategory.ProductCategoryName = 'Toy'
  GROUP BY Contact.ContactCode
  HAVING COUNT(DISTINCT Product.ProductCode) =
-- equal to number of toys available?
      (SELECT Count(ProductCode)
        FROM dbo.Product
          JOIN dbo.ProductCategory
            ON Product.ProductCategoryID
              = ProductCategory.ProductCategoryID
          WHERE ProductCategory.ProductCategoryName = 'Toy')
```

Result:

```
ContactCode
---------------
110
111
112
```

# Exact Relational Division

*Exact relational division* finds exact matches without any remainder. It takes the basic question of relational division with remainder and tightens the method so that the divisor will have no extra rows that would cause a remainder.

In practical terms it means that the example question now asks, "Who has ordered only every toy?"

If you address this query with a modified form of Joe Celko's method, the pseudocode becomes, "For whom is the number of toys ordered equal to the number of toys available, and also equal to the total number of products ordered?" If a customer has ordered additional products other than toys, the third part of the question eliminates that customer from the result set.

The SQL code contains two primary changes to the previous query. The first change is that the outer query must find both the number of toys ordered and the number of all products ordered. It does this by finding the toys purchased in a derived table and joining the two datasets. The second change is modifying the `having` clause to compare the number of toys available with both the number of toys purchased and the number of all products purchased, as follows:

```
-- Exact Relational Division
-- Is number of all products ordered...
SELECT Contact.ContactCode
  FROM dbo.Contact
    JOIN dbo.[Order]
      ON Contact.ContactID = [Order].ContactID
    JOIN dbo.OrderDetail
      ON [Order].OrderID = OrderDetail.OrderID
    JOIN dbo.Product
      ON OrderDetail.ProductID = Product.ProductID
    JOIN dbo.ProductCategory P1
      ON Product.ProductCategoryID = P1.ProductCategoryID

    JOIN
        -- and number of toys ordered
      (SELECT Contact.ContactCode, Product.ProductCode
        FROM dbo.Contact
          JOIN dbo.[Order]
            ON Contact.ContactID = [Order].ContactID
          JOIN dbo.OrderDetail
            ON [Order].OrderID = OrderDetail.OrderID
          JOIN dbo.Product
            ON OrderDetail.ProductID = Product.ProductID
          JOIN dbo.ProductCategory
            ON Product.ProductCategoryID =
                  ProductCategory.ProductCategoryID
        WHERE ProductCategory.ProductCategoryName = 'Toy'
      ) ToysOrdered

    ON Contact.ContactCode = ToysOrdered.ContactCode

  GROUP BY Contact.ContactCode

  HAVING  COUNT(DISTINCT Product.ProductCode) =
-- equal to number of toys available?
    (SELECT Count(ProductCode)
      FROM dbo.Product
        JOIN dbo.ProductCategory
          ON Product.ProductCategoryID
            = ProductCategory.ProductCategoryID
      WHERE ProductCategory.ProductCategoryName = 'Toy')
```

```
-- AND equal to the total number of any product ordered?
  AND COUNT(DISTINCT ToysOrdered.ProductCode) =
     (SELECT Count(ProductCode)
       FROM dbo.Product
         JOIN dbo.ProductCategory
           ON Product.ProductCategoryID
             = ProductCategory.ProductCategoryID
       WHERE ProductCategory.ProductCategoryName = 'Toy')
```

The result is a list of contacts containing the number of toys purchased (2), and the number of total products purchased (2), both equal to the number of products available (2):

```
ContactCode
---------------
110
111
```

## Set Difference

A similar query type that's useful for analyzing the correlation between two datasets is a *set difference* query, which finds the difference between the two datasets based on the conditions of the join. In relational-algebra terms it removes the divisor from the dividend, leaving the difference. This type of query is the inverse of an inner join. Informally, it's called a *find unmatched rows* query.

Set difference queries are great for locating out-of-place data or data that doesn't match, such as rows that are in dataset one and not in dataset two (Figure 7-13).

**Note**    The ANSI SQL standard implements the set difference query with the keyword `except`, which SQL Server does not support.

The set difference query is the same as the difference union, except that the difference union is a row-based operation between tables with the same column definitions while a set difference query is concerned only with the columns in the join condition. In a sense, the set difference query is a difference union of only the join-condition columns.

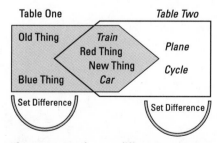

**Figure 7-13:** The set difference query finds data that are outside the intersection between the two datasets.

Using the One/Two sample tables, the following query locates all rows in table One without a match in table Two, removing set two (the divisor) from set one (the dividend). The result will be the rows from set one that do not have a match in set two.

The outer join already includes the rows outside the intersection, so to construct a set difference query use an outer join with an is null restriction on the second dataset's primary key. This will return all the rows from table One that do not have a match in table Two:

```
USE Tempdb

SELECT Thing1, Thing2
  FROM dbo.One
    LEFT OUTER JOIN dbo.Two
      ON One.OnePK = Two.OnePK
  WHERE Two.TwoPK IS NULL
```

Table One's difference is as follows:

```
Thing1            Thing2
---------------   ---------------
Old Thing         NULL
Blue Thing        NULL
```

Taking the theory to a real-world scenario from the OBX Kites sample database, the following code is a set difference query that locates all contacts who have not yet placed an order. The Contact table is the divisor and the set difference query removes the contacts with orders (the dividend). The left outer join produces a dataset with all contacts and matching orders. The where condition restricts the result set to only those rows without a match in the [Order] table.

```
USE OBXKites
SELECT LastName, FirstName
  FROM dbo.Contact
    LEFT OUTER JOIN dbo.[Order]
      ON Contact.ContactID = [Order].ContactID
  WHERE OrderID IS NULL
```

The result is the difference between the Contact table and the [Order] table—that is, all contacts who have not placed an order:

```
LastName        FirstName
------------    ----------------
Andrews         Ed
Boston          Dave
Earl            Betty
Hanks           Nickolas
Harrison        Charlie
...
```

The set difference query could be written using a subquery. The where not in condition removes the subquery rows (the divisor) from the outer query (the dividend), as follows:

```
SELECT LastName, FirstName
  FROM dbo.Contact
  WHERE ContactID NOT IN
    (SELECT ContactID FROM dbo.[Order])
  ORDER BY LastName, FirstName
```

Either form of the query (left outer join or not in subquery) works well. The query optimization plans and performance of the two are very similar, though the subquery form is slightly faster, as shown in Figure 7-14.

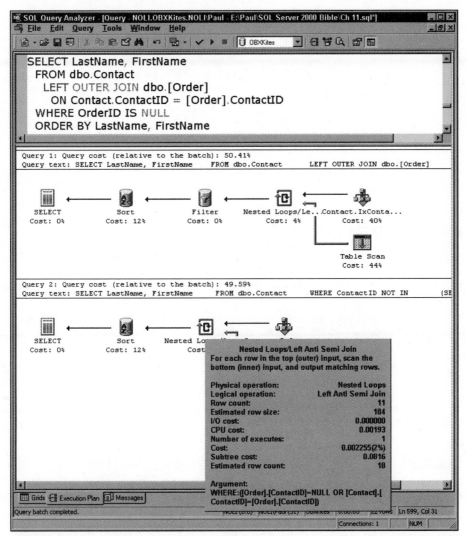

**Figure 7-14:** The subquery form of the set difference join uses a left anti semi join, which proves faster than the left outer join.

I often use a modified version of this technique to clean up bad data during conversions. A *full set difference query* is the logical opposite of an inner join. It identifies all rows outside the intersection from either data set by combining a `full outer join` with a `where` restriction that accepts only nulls in either primary key:

```
SELECT Thing1, Thing2
  FROM One
    FULL OUTER JOIN Two
      ON One.OnePK = Two.OnePK
  WHERE Two.TwoPK IS NULL
    OR One.OnePK IS NULL
```

The result is every row without a match in the One/Two sample tables:

```
Thing1            Thing2
---------------   ---------------
NULL              Plane
NULL              Cycle
Blue Thing        NULL
Old Thing         NULL
```

# Three Query Scenarios

I like to teach by example, so while writing this book I asked a few of the SQL-oriented Yahoo! groups to send me some interesting query problems (without solutions). Their contributions helped produce some of the queries in this book, as well as these three stimulating query problems.

**Best Practice**

Traditional programming tends to involve handling problems with loops performing the same calculation on each record one row at a time. Unlearning this style of programming is the single most important hurdle for a programmer moving to SQL.

SQL wants to work with sets so that the entire query is solved in one large "kachunka." SQL Server can be programmed with cursors to loop through the rows, and sometimes (rarely) that's necessary, but most problems can be solved with a single creative SQL query. In one consulting project I compared a row-based cursor with a set-based query, and found the cursor to be 77 times slower than the query.

## Scenario #1: Northwind's Inventory Problem

Northwind (a sample database that installs with SQL Server 2000) has an inventory problem. The warehouse personnel frequently attempt to pull a product for shipment only to find the product is out of stock. They'd like to discover out-of-stock situations from the database instead of the shelf so that the purchasing agent can solve the problem before the ship date.

Asking the question, "Of what product is there not enough inventory to fill current orders?" of the Microsoft Northwind database can include a Θ join to compare the quantity available with the quantity required.

The first step is to determine the demand for the product. A simple aggregate query can sum() the total demand. The where clause filters out all orders that have been shipped prior to the grouping and summation:

```
USE Northwind
SELECT ProductID, sum(Quantity)
  FROM dbo.Orders
    JOIN dbo.[Order Details]
      ON Orders.OrderID = [Order details].OrderID
    Where ShippedDate Is Null
    GROUP BY ProductID
```

Once the demand query is known, it may be joined with the availability using a derived table and a Θ join. By joining on ProductID to line up the rows and also join on the condition that demand is greater than available stock, the join returns only those products with a shortfall in inventory.

```
SELECT Products.ProductName,
    Demand.TotalDemand
      - (Products.Unitsinstock + Products.UnitsOnOrder)
        AS Short
  FROM dbo.Products
  JOIN (SELECT ProductID, SUM(Quantity) AS TotalDemand
          FROM dbo.Orders
            JOIN dbo.[Order Details]
              ON Orders.OrderID = [Order details].OrderID
            WHERE ShippedDate IS NULL
            GROUP BY ProductID) Demand
      ON Products.ProductID = Demand.ProductID
        AND Demand.TotalDemand
          > Products.Unitsinstock + Products.UnitsOnOrder
      ORDER BY Short DESC
```

Northwind's purchasing agent needs to restock the following products ASAP:

```
ProductName                               Short
----------------------------------------- -----------
R!!ssle Sauerkraut                        72
Camembert Pierrot                         54
Wimmers gute Semmelkn!!del                30
Konbu                                     20
Pavlova                                   17
Alice Mutton                              12
Guaranã Fantãstica                        10
Perth Pasties                             10
Ipoh Coffee                               9
Chang                                     5
Steeleye Stout                            4
Manjimup Dried Apples                     4
Audit Test                                1
Uncle Bob's Organic Dried Pears           1
```

# Scenario #2: Denormalizing Time Sequences

It's common to store time-clock records or manufacturing-activity data with the current time. Because SQL is set-based, calculating the duration between two time events a can be difficult.

The goal is to develop a system that can easily join the begin time with the end time so that the activity data can be handled as datasets rather than sequentially calculated row by row. A self-join optional foreign key that connects each end-event row with its corresponding begin-event row is a perfect solution.

The following example activity log sets up an excellent test scenario. Each row in the Event table represents Joe or Sue starting or ending an activity. The Start bit and the time is the only information Joe and Sue are providing to the database:

```
USE Tempdb

DROP TABLE Event

CREATE TABLE dbo.Event (
    EventID INT Identity(1,1) PRIMARY KEY NONCLUSTERED,
    Person CHAR(3),
    Start BIT, -- true if begin, false if end
    [Time] DATETIME,
    EndEventID INT
    )
go

ALTER TABLE dbo.Event ADD CONSTRAINT
  FK_Event_End FOREIGN KEY (EndEventID)
    REFERENCES dbo.Event (EventID)
```

To make the data easier to follow, the comments at the start entry indicate the start and end EventIDs for that entry.

Day one:

```
INSERT dbo.Event(Person, Start, [Time]) -- start 1 end 2
    VALUES ('Sue', 1, '20011029 8:00')
INSERT dbo.Event(Person, Start, [Time])
    VALUES ('Sue', 0, '20011029 13:10')
INSERT dbo.Event(Person, Start, [Time]) -- 3, 4
    VALUES ('Joe', 1, '20011029 8:01')
INSERT dbo.Event(Person, Start, [Time])
    VALUES ('Joe', 0, '20011029 11:58')
INSERT dbo.Event(Person, Start, [Time]) -- 5, null
    VALUES ('Joe', 1, '20011029 12:41')
```

Notice that Joe forgot to record an end-activity entry.

Day two:

```
INSERT dbo.Event(Person, Start, [Time]) -- 6, 9
    VALUES ('Joe', 1, '20011030 8:00')
    -- Joe forgot to logout last night
```

```
INSERT dbo.Event(Person, Start, [Time]) -- 7, 8
   VALUES ('Sue', 1, '20011030 8:00')
INSERT dbo.Event(Person, Start, [Time])
   VALUES ('Sue', 0, '20011030 12:00')
INSERT dbo.Event(Person, Start, [Time])
   VALUES ('Joe', 0, '20011030 12:00')
INSERT dbo.Event(Person, Start, [Time]) -- 10, 12
   VALUES ('Sue', 1, '20011030 12:36')
INSERT dbo.Event(Person, Start, [Time]) -- 11, 13
   VALUES ('Joe', 1, '20011030 13:05')
INSERT dbo.Event(Person, Start, [Time])
   VALUES ('Sue', 0, '20011030 16:30')
INSERT dbo.Event(Person, Start, [Time])
   VALUES ('Joe', 0, '20011030 15:15')
```

Check the inserts:

```
SELECT * FROM dbo.Event
```

Result:

```
EventID Person Start Time                   EndEventID
------- ------ ----- ---------------------- ----------
1       Sue    1     2001-10-29 08:00:00.000 NULL
2       Sue    0     2001-10-29 13:10:00.000 NULL
3       Joe    1     2001-10-29 08:01:00.000 NULL
...
```

This join begins the process of building the solution query by matching all starts with ends for each person. It's a beginning but there's still more to work out. This query matches *every* start with *every* end for each person, so Sue's first start time is matched with every one of Sue's end times:

```
SELECT *
  FROM dbo.Event A
    JOIN (SELECT *
            FROM dbo.Event
            WHERE Start = 0) B
      ON A.Person = B.Person
  WHERE A.Start = 1
```

Adding a Θ join condition to the query filters only those ends that are after the corresponding start:

```
SELECT A.EventID, MIN(B.EventID) as MinEvent
  FROM dbo.Event A
    JOIN (
      SELECT *
        FROM dbo.Event
        WHERE Start = 0) B
    ON A.Person = B.Person
      AND A.[Time] <= B.[Time]
  WHERE A.Start = 1
  GROUP BY A.EventID
```

Result:

```
EventID     MinEvent
----------- -----------
1           2
3           4
5           9
6           9
7           8
10          12
11          13
```

There's still a problem: start events 5 and 6 both end with event 9. Only the last start event before an end should have an end event. Another group by will select the max() from the previous query, now nested as a subquery:

```
SELECT MAX(C.StartID) AS MaxStart, C.EndID
  FROM (
    SELECT A.EventID AS StartID, Min(B.EventID) AS EndID
      FROM dbo.Event A
        JOIN  (SELECT *
                 FROM dbo.Event
                 WHERE Start = 0) B
          ON A.Person = B.Person
            AND A.[Time] <= B.[Time]
          WHERE A.Start = 1
          GROUP BY A.EventID) C
    GROUP BY C. EndID
```

Result:

```
MaxStart    EndID
----------- -----------
1           2
3           4
7           8
6           9
10          12
11          13
```

This is the solution to the problem. But repeatedly performing this query on thousands of rows is a waste. Writing the end-event row's EventID to the start-event row provides two benefits. First, the matched start and end rows are known and can be ignored in future calculations. Secondly, it becomes trivial to join the start rows with the end rows for more calculations.

The update command will be covered in Chapter 10, "Modifying Data," but here the previous query is modified to match only events without an entry in EndeventID. The query is then joined as a derived table with the Event table, and the Update command writes the end EventID into the start-event row:

```
UPDATE dbo.Event
  SET EndEventID = D.EndID
  FROM dbo.Event
    JOIN (SELECT MAX(C.StartID) AS StartID, C.EndID
          FROM (SELECT A.EventID AS StartID,
```

```
                Min(B.EventID) AS EndID
            FROM dbo.Event A
            JOIN (SELECT *
                    FROM dbo.Event
                    WHERE Start = 0 ) B
              ON A.Person = B.Person
                AND A.[Time] <= B.[Time]
            WHERE A.Start = 1
              AND A.EndEventID IS NULL
            GROUP BY A.EventID) C
        GROUP BY C.EndID) D
    ON Event.EventID = D.StartID
```

Check the effect of the update by selecting the start rows:

```
SELECT * FROM dbo.Event where Start = 1
```

Result:

```
EventID Person Start Time                    EndEventID
------- ------ ----- ----------------------- ----------
1       Sue    1     2001-10-29 08:00:00.000 2
3       Joe    1     2001-10-29 08:01:00.000 4
5       Joe    1     2001-10-29 12:41:00.000 NULL
6       Joe    1     2001-10-30 08:00:00.000 9
7       Sue    1     2001-10-30 08:00:00.000 8
10      Sue    1     2001-10-30 12:36:00.000 12
11      Joe    1     2001-10-30 13:05:00.000 13
```

From this data it's now easy to calculate the elapsed time:

```
SELECT S.EventID, S.Person, S.[Time] as Start,
    DateDiff(mi,S.[Time],E.[Time]) as ElapsedMinutes
  FROM dbo.Event AS S
    JOIN dbo.Event AS E
        ON S.EndEventID = E.EventID
```

Solution:

```
EventID     Person Start                   ElapsedMinutes
----------- ------ ----------------------- --------------
1           Sue    2001-10-29 08:00:00.000 310
3           Joe    2001-10-29 08:01:00.000 237
6           Joe    2001-10-30 08:00:00.000 240
7           Sue    2001-10-30 08:00:00.000 240
10          Sue    2001-10-30 12:36:00.000 234
11          Joe    2001-10-30 13:05:00.000 130
```

Of course, Joe is upset because he didn't get credit for one of his days. The following cooperative query finds open start times:

```
SELECT *
  FROM dbo.Event
  WHERE EndEventID IS NULL
    AND Start = 1
```

Result:

```
EventID      Person Start Time                    EndEventID
----------   ------ ----- ----------------------- ----------
5            Joe    1     2001-10-29 12:41:00.000 NULL
```

Once Joe learns to punch out on time, this technique will run flawlessly.

## Scenario #3: The Stockbroker Problem

A stock firm combines information from multiple places. The programmers are faced with several tables of daily buy-sell-hold recommendations from multiple sources. Each table holds the day's recommendations for one broker. Not every broker makes a recommendation for every stock. The goal is to build a cross-tab–type view across these tables so the recommendations may be easily viewed.

To set up the story, the following three tables hold sample data:

```
CREATE TABLE dbo.RatingsBroker1(
  PK INT IDENTITY,
  Ticker VARCHAR(10),
  Rating  VARCHAR(10)
  )

CREATE TABLE dbo.RatingsBroker2(
  PK INT IDENTITY,
  Ticker VARCHAR(10),
  Rating  VARCHAR(10)
  )

CREATE TABLE dbo.RatingsBroker3(
  PK INT IDENTITY,
  Ticker VARCHAR(10),
  Rating  VARCHAR(10)
  )

INSERT dbo.RatingsBroker1(Ticker, Rating)
  VALUES('ABC', 'Buy')
INSERT dbo.RatingsBroker1(Ticker, Rating)
  VALUES('MSFT', 'Buy')
INSERT dbo.RatingsBroker1(Ticker, Rating)
  VALUES('UAL', 'Sell')
INSERT dbo.RatingsBroker2(Ticker, Rating)
  VALUES('ABC', 'Buy')
INSERT dbo.RatingsBroker2(Ticker, Rating)
  VALUES('GENE', 'Hold')
INSERT dbo.RatingsBroker3(Ticker, Rating)
  VALUES('ABC', 'Hold')
INSERT dbo.RatingsBroker3(Ticker, Rating)
  VALUES('MSFT', 'Buy')
INSERT dbo.RatingsBroker3(Ticker, Rating)
  VALUES('GENE', 'Sell')
```

**Note**     The data presented here are completely useless and should not be read as secret insider tips or recommendations. If you buy or sell based on this sample data, you'll earn what you deserve.

The key to achieving this goal is building a common list of all brokers. By default, union is distinct and eliminates duplicate rows, so the following union query generates a useable list of brokers:

```
SELECT Ticker
   FROM dbo.RatingsBroker1
UNION
SELECT Ticker
   FROM dbo.RatingsBroker2
UNION
SELECT Ticker
   FROM dbo.RatingsBroker3
```

Result:

```
Ticker
----------
ABC
GENE
MSFT
UAL
```

The union is the center of the following query even though it's a subquery as a derived table with the named range U. Each broker table is left outer joined with the union list of brokers. This allows each stock rating to be listed under each broker:

```
SELECT U.Ticker,
    RatingsBroker1.Rating AS B1,
    RatingsBroker2.Rating AS B2,
    RatingsBroker3.Rating AS B3
  FROM (SELECT Ticker
          FROM dbo.RatingsBroker1
        UNION
        SELECT Ticker
          FROM dbo.RatingsBroker2
        UNION
        SELECT Ticker
          FROM dbo.RatingsBroker3) U
    LEFT JOIN RatingsBroker1
      ON U.Ticker = RatingsBroker1.Ticker
    LEFT JOIN RatingsBroker2
      ON U.Ticker = RatingsBroker2.Ticker
    LEFT JOIN RatingsBroker3
      ON U.Ticker = RatingsBroker3.Ticker
  ORDER BY U.Ticker
```

The result is exactly what the client was looking for:

```
Ticker      B1           B2           B3
----------  ----------   ----------   ----------
ABC         Buy          Buy          Hold
GENE        NULL         Hold         Sell
MSFT        Buy          NULL         Buy
UAL         Sell         NULL         NULL
```

**Note**    For a known set of values such as this, the union left outer join solution is workable. For a more dynamic crosstab solution, I recommend an Analysis Services cube, an Access crosstab, or another client-application pivot table. Having said that, Chapter 12, "Programming with Transact SQL," shows several ways to generate a crosstab dataset.

## Summary

Merging data is the heart of SQL, and it shows in the depth of relational algebra as well as the power and flexibility of SQL. From natural joins to correlated subqueries, SQL is excellent at selecting sets of data from multiple data tables. The challenge for the SQL Server database developer is to master the theory of relational algebra and the many T-SQL techniques to effectively manipulate the data. The reward is the fun.

You are now over the hump of this book's explanation of the techniques of retrieving data using SQL Server. The previous chapter covered the select statement, while this chapter expanded the select with joins, unions, and subqueries, including some advanced techniques. The next chapter continues to describe the repertoire of data-retrieval techniques with full-text search. Leveraging the full-text search engine built into Windows, full-text search indexes every significant word and provides powerful search capabilities far beyond those of the simple SQL-like operator.

✦    ✦    ✦

# Searching Full-Text Indexes

**S**everal years ago I wrote a word search for a large database of legal texts. For word searches, the system parsed all the documents and built a word-frequency table as a many-to-many junction between the word table and the document table. It worked well, and word searches became lightning-fast. While I found coding the string manipulation fun, fortunately, you have a choice.

The server versions of Windows include a structured word/phrase indexing system called MS Search. More than just a word parser, MS Search actually performs linguistic analysis by determining base words, word boundaries, and conjugating verbs for different languages. SQL Server leverages MS Search on a row and column basis as full-text search catalogs.

ANSI Standard SQL uses the `like` operator to perform basic word searches and even wildcard searches. For example, the following code uses the `like` operator to query the Aesop's Fables sample database:

```
-- SQL Where Like
SELECT Title
  FROM Fable
  WHERE Fabletext LIKE '%lion%'
    AND Fabletext LIKE '%bold%'
```

Result:

```
Title
---------------------------------------------
The Hunter and the Woodman
```

**On the CD-ROM** All the code samples in this chapter use the Aesop's Fables sample database. The `Aesop_Create.sql` script will create the database and populate it with 25 of Aesop's fables. All the code within this chapter is in `Ch08.sql`.

The main problem with performing SQL Server `where...like` searches is the slow performance. Indexes are searchable from the beginning of the word, so searching for `like 'word%'` is fast, but `like '%word%'` is terribly slow. Searching for strings within a string can't use the b-tree structure of an index to perform a fast index seek so it must perform a table scan instead, as demonstrated in Figure 8-1. It's like looking for all the "Paul"s in the telephone book. The phone book isn't indexed by first name, so each page must be scanned.

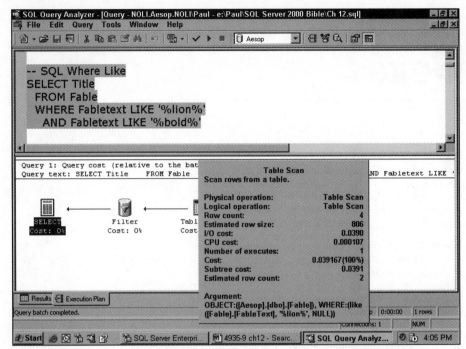

**Figure 8-1:** A search for words in the middle of the FableText column using Like requires a table scan logical operation, which consumes 99.9999 percent of the resources used to solve this query.

Full-text indexing builds an index of every significant word and phrase and thus solves the performance problem. In addition, the full-text search engine adds advanced features such as the following:

✦ Searching for one word near another word

✦ Searching with wildcards

✦ Searching for inflectional variations of a word (such as run, ran, running)

✦ Weighting one word or phrase as more important to the search than another word or phrase

✦ Performing fuzzy word/phrase searches

✦ Searching character data with embedded binary objects stored with SQL Server

Since full-text search exists in a service separate from SQL Server, it takes a little work to set up a full-text search catalog. And because the indexes are external to SQL Server, MS Search doesn't automatically know about data written to SQL Server, so the full-text search catalog must be initially populated and then periodically updated.

# Configuring Full-Text Search Catalogs

A *full-text search catalog* is a collection of full-text indexes for a single SQL Server database. Each catalog may store multiple full-text indexes for multiple tables, but each table is limited to only one catalog. Typically a single catalog will handle all the full-text searches for a database, although dedicating a single catalog to a very large table (one with over a million rows) will improve performance.

Catalogs may only index user tables, not views, temporary tables, table variables, or system tables.

## Enabling Full-Text Search on the Server

Full-text search uses the MS Search service included with workstation-class and server-class operating systems but not with home versions of Windows. MS Search may not be installed, although it is possible to force an install of MS Search on professional editions from the SQL Server installation by using add/remove components and selecting the full-text search option.

Full-text search is not included with the Personal Edition of SQL Server, nor can it be installed on any version of Windows 9*x* or Windows XP Home.

If the MS Search service is installed, it can be managed (start, stop, view status, set to automatically start) with either the Windows Services/Components tool or SQL Server's Service Manager.

To configure a catalog you must belong to the database-owner or system-administrator role.

## Creating a Catalog with the Wizard

Although creating and configuring a full-text search catalog with code is relatively easy, the task is usually done once and then forgotten. Unless the repeatability of a script is important for redeploying the project, the Full-Text Wizard is sufficient for configuring full-text search.

Once the wizard is launched it will begin with the database and table based on the selected database or table in Enterprise Manager, and may skip the first one or two steps. So it's a good idea to select the database or table prior to launching the wizard.

The wizard may be launched from within Enterprise Manager by any of these locations:

✦ From the Tools menu, select Full-Text Indexing.

✦ Select Wizards on the toolbar, open the database wizards, and then select the Full-Text Indexing Wizard.

✦ In a database Taskpad view, select the Wizards page and then select the Full Text Indexing Wizard.

If the Full-Text Indexing Wizard is not available, it means either that the MS Search service is not installed, or that the edition of SQL Server you are using does not support full-text search.

The Full-Text Indexing Wizard works through multiple steps to configure the full-text catalog, as follows:

1. A catalog must belong to a single database.

2. Select the table to add to the catalog.

3. Specify a unique index that MS Search can use to identify the rows indexed with MS Search. The primary key is typically the best choice for this index; however, any non-nullable, unique, single-column index is sufficient. If the table uses composite primary keys, another unique index must be created to use full-text search.

4. Choose the columns to be full-text indexed, as shown in Figure 8-2. Valid column data types are character data types (`char`, `nchar`, `varchar`, `nvarchar`, `text`, and `ntext`) and `image`. (Indexing binary images is an advanced topic covered later in this chapter.) You may need to specify the language used for parsing the words, although the computer default will likely handle this automatically. Computed columns may not be full-text indexed.

   Full-text search can also read documents stored in `image` columns. (Using full-text search with embedded blobs is covered later in this chapter.)

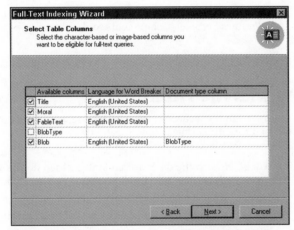

**Figure 8-2:** Any valid columns are listed by the Full-Text Indexing Wizard and may be selected for indexing.

5. Select a catalog or opt to create a new catalog.

6. Skip creating a population schedule, there's a better way to keep the catalog up to date. (The strategies for maintaining a full-text index are discussed later in the chapter.)

7. Finish.

When the wizard is finished, the catalog is created but still empty. To initially populate the catalog, right-click on the table and select Full-Text Index Table ➪ Start Full Population. This directs SQL Server to begin passing data to MS Search for indexing. Depending on the amount of data in the indexed columns, the population will take a few seconds, a few minutes, or a few hours to complete.

# Creating a Catalog with T-SQL Code

To implement full-text search using a method that can be easily replicated on other servers, your best option is to create a SQL script. Creating a catalog with code means following the same steps as the Full-Text Indexing Wizard. A set of system-stored procedures handles configuring and maintaining full-text indexes. The following steps configure a full-text search catalog for the Aesop's Fables sample database:

1. Enable the database for full-text search:

```
USE AESOP
EXEC sp_fulltext_database 'enable'
```

**Note**　Every one of these steps will take a few seconds to complete. SQL Server is the client initiating the process, but it doesn't wait for the conclusion. If the configuration is being written as a script, the waitfor delay T-SQL command can insert the required pause.

2. Create the full-text catalog:

```
EXEC sp_fulltext_catalog 'AesopFable', 'create'
```

3. Mark a table for full-text search:

```
EXEC sp_fulltext_table
   'Fable', 'create', 'AesopFable', 'FablePK'
```

4. Add columns to the full-text catalog:

```
EXEC sp_fulltext_column 'Fable', 'Title', 'add'
EXEC sp_fulltext_column 'Fable', 'Moral', 'add'
EXEC sp_fulltext_column 'Fable', 'FableText', 'add'
```

The sp_fulltext_column stored procedure has two other parameters, which specify the word-parsing language and image-indexing information, respectively. The full syntax of the stored procedure is as follows:

```
sp_fulltext_column
   @tabname ='table_name',
   @colname ='column_name',
   @action = 'action',
   @Language = 'language',
   @type_colname ='type_column_name'
```

The action parameter indicates 'add' or 'drop'.

Full-text search can automatically parse the following languages:

- Neutral—0

- Chinese_Simplified—0x0804, 2052

- Chinese_Traditional—0x0404, 1028

- Dutch—0x0413, 1043

- English_UK—0x0809, 2057

- English_US—0x0409, 1033

- French — 0x040c, 1036

- German — 0x0407, 1031

- Italian — 0x0410, 1040

- Japanese — 0x0411, 1041

- Korean — 0x0412, 1042

- Spanish_Modern — 0x0c0a, 3082

- Swedish_Default — 0x041d, 1053

The language determines the word break points and how the words are parsed for inflections (run, ran, running) and phrases. (Use Neutral for multiple languages or an unsupported language.) The corresponding hex code or integer is passed as a parameter to `sp_fulltext_columns`. All columns in a table must use the same language.

**5.** Activate the full-text catalog:

```
EXEC sp_fulltext_table 'Fable','activate'
```

Although the full-text catalog has been defined, it's not yet populated. To initially populate the catalog with code, run the following stored procedure:

```
EXEC sp_fulltext_table 'Fable', 'start_full'
```

## Pushing Data to the Full-Text Index

Full-text indexes are off-line indexes maintained by an external service and are updated only when SQL Server passes new data to MS Search. That's both a benefit and a drawback. On one hand it means that updating the full-text index doesn't slow down large-text updates. On the other hand, it means that the full-text index is not real-time the way SQL Server data are. If a user enters a résumé and then searches for it using full-text search before the full-text index has been updated, the résumé won't be found.

Every full-text index begins empty, and if data already exist in the SQL Server tables they must be *pushed* to the full-text index by means of a *full population*. A full population re-initializes the index and passes data for all rows to the full-text index. A full population may be performed with Enterprise Manager or T-SQL code. Because the data push is driven by SQL Server, data is sent from one table at a time regardless of how many tables might be full-text indexed in a catalog. If the full-text index is created for an empty SQL Server table, a full population is not required.

Two primary methods of pushing ongoing changes to a full-text index exist:

✦ *Incremental populations* — An incremental population uses a timestamp to pass any rows that have changed since the last population. This method can be performed manually from Enterprise Manager or by means of T-SQL code, or scheduled as a SQL Server Agent job (typically for each evening). Incremental population requires a `rowversion` (`timestamp`) column in the table.

Incremental populations present two problems. First, a built-in delay occurs between the time the data are entered and the time the user can find the data using full-text search. Second, incremental populations consolidate all the changes into a single process that consumes a significant amount of CPU time during the incremental change. In a heavily used database the choice is between performing incremental populations each evening and forcing a one-day delay each time, or performing incremental populations at scheduled times throughout the day and suffering performance hits at those times.

✦ *Change tracking and background population*—SQL Server can watch for data changes in columns that are full-text indexed and then send what is effectively a single-row incremental population every time a row changes. While this method seems costly in terms of performance, in practice the effect is not noticeable. The full-text update isn't fired by a trigger, so the update transaction doesn't need to wait for the data to be pushed to the full-text index. Instead, the full-text update occurs in the background slightly behind the SQL DML transaction. The effect is a balanced CPU load and a full-text index that appears to be near real-time.

**Best Practice**

If the database project incorporates searching for words within columns, using full-text search with change tracking and background population is the best overall way to balance search performance with update performance.

## Maintaining a Catalog with Enterprise Manager

Within Enterprise Manager, the full-text search catalogs are maintained with the right-click menu for each table. The menu offers the following maintenance options under Full-Text Index Table:

✦ Define Full-Text Indexing on Table...: Launches the Full-Text Indexing Wizard to create a new catalog as described earlier in the chapter.

✦ Edit Full-Text Indexing...: Launches the Full-Text Indexing Wizard to modify the catalog for the selected table.

✦ Remove Full-Text Indexing from a Table...: Drops the selected table from its catalog.

✦ Start Full Population: Initiates a data push of all rows from the selected SQL Server table to its full-text index catalog.

✦ Start Incremental Population: Initiates a data push of rows that have changed since the last population in the selected table from SQL Server to the full-text index.

✦ Stop Population: Halts any currently running full-text population push.

✦ Change Tracking: Performs a full or incremental population and then turns on change tracking so that SQL Server can update the index.

✦ Update Index in Background: Pushes updates of rows that have been flagged by change tracking to the full-text index as the changes occur.

✦ Update Index: Pushes an update of all rows that change tracking has flagged to the full-text index.

## Maintaining a Catalog in T-SQL Code

Each of the previous Enterprise Manager full-text maintenance commands can be executed from T-SQL code. The following examples demonstrate full-text catalog-maintenance commands applied to the Aesop's Fables sample database:

✦ Full population:

```
EXEC sp_fulltext_table 'Fable', 'start_full'
```

✦ Incremental population:

```
EXEC sp_fulltext_table 'Fable', 'start_incremental'
```

✦ Remove a full-text catalog:

```
EXEC sp_fulltext_catalog 'AesopFable', 'drop'
```

✦ Change tracking and background updating:

```
EXEC sp_fulltext_table Fable, 'Start_change_tracking'
EXEC sp_fulltext_table Fable,
    'Start_background_updateindex'
```

In addition, T-SQL stored procedures include the following enhanced maintenance features:

✦ *Rebuild*—This command essentially drops and redefines the full-text catalog, but does not repopulate the new full-text index. Rebuilding should be followed with a full population. The benefit of rebuilding the catalog is that it automatically reconfigures the table and columns, ensuring that the internal structure of the full-text catalog is clean.

```
EXEC sp_fulltext_catalog 'AesopFable', 'rebuild'
```

✦ *Clean up unused full text catalogs* — This stored procedure removes any vestiges of unused catalogs:

```
EXEC sp_fulltext_service 'clean_up'
```

Throughout SQL Server 2000, the sp_help stored procedure is a welcome means of reporting system information. The full-text search versions of sp_help are as follows:

✦ sp_help_fulltext_catalogs — This system-stored procedure returns information about a catalog, including the current population status:

```
EXEC sp_help_fulltext_catalogs 'AesopFable'
```

Result:

```
                                              NUMBER
                                              FULLTEXT
ftcatid NAME        PATH                 STATUS TABLES
------- ----------- -------------------- ------ ------
5       AesopFable  C:\Program Files     0      1
                    \Microsoft SQL Server
                    \MSSQL\FTDATA
```

The population status column returns the current activity of the catalog as follows:

- 0 - Idle
- 1 - Full population in progress
- 2 - Paused
- 3 - Throttled
- 4 - Recovering
- 5 - Shutdown
- 6 - Incremental population in progress
- 7 - Building index
- 8 - Disk is full. Paused
- 9 - Change tracking

✦ `sp_help_fulltext_tables` — Information about the tables included in the catalog is returned by this variation of sp_help:

```
EXEC sp_help_fulltext_tables 'AesopFable'
```

Result (formatted):

| TABLE OWNER | TABLE NAME | FULLTEXT KEY INDEX NAME | FULLTEXT KEY COLID | FULLTEXT INDEX ACTIVE | FULLTEXT CATALOG NAME |
|-------|-------|---------|--------|---------|-----------|
| dbo | Fable | FablePK | 1 | 1 | AesopFable |

✦ `sp_help_fulltext_columns` — Information about the columns included in the full-text catalog:

```
EXEC sp_help_fulltext_columns 'fable'
```

Result (formatted and truncated):

| TABLE_ OWNER | NAME | FULLTEXT COLUMNNAME | BLOBTP COLNAME | LANGUAGE |
|-------|-------|------------|---------|----------|
| dbo | Fable | Title | NULL | 1033 |
| dbo | Fable | Moral | NULL | 1033 |
| dbo | Fable | FableText | NULL | 1033 |

## Noise Files

When I built my custom word-search procedure several years ago, one of the optimizations that dramatically improved performance was the exclusion of common words such as a, the, and of. As soon as a word was parsed, the first check was to see if the word was in what I called the "weed list." If it was, the procedure parsed the next word without any handling of the weed word. The time required to parse a legal cite was reduced by more than half, and the size of the word-frequency table was significantly smaller.

MS Search uses a similar technique by storing lists of ignored words in a *noise file*. Noise words are completely ignored by full-text search; in fact, if a query's search depends on noise words it generates an error.

The decision to include a word in the noise list is made according to its frequency of use and its relative search importance. If a word is very common it's not a good search candidate and the frequency of its occurrence will hurt performance, so it should be in the noise list.

Alternately, the project may need to search for words in the noise list. For example, if a search for "C language" is important to the database, the letter "C" should be removed from the noise file.

Because noise files are plain-text files, they may be tweaked to meet the needs of certain applications. The file name is `noise`, and the file extension designates the language: `.enu` is U.S. English. You must stop MS Search prior to editing the noise file. The difficulty is locating the correct noise file. On my system, a Windows Explorer search for `noise.enu` found seven copies with at least three variations of the file.

Assuming a default installation directory, the copy used by SQL Server's full-text search is located in:

```
C:\Program Files\Microsoft SQL Server
    \MSSQL\FTDATA\SQLServer\Config\noise.enu
```

To test the noise file, stop MS Search using SQL Server Service Manager, add a word to the file, and then try a full-text search for that word. If the query produces the following error, the word was added to the correct noise file:

```
Server: Msg 7619, Level 16, State 1, Line 1
A clause of the query contained only ignored words
```

# Word Searches

Once the catalog is created, full-text search is ready for word and phrase queries. Word searches are performed with the `contains` keyword. The effect of `contains` is to pass the word search to MS Search and await the reply. Word searches can be used within a query in one of two means, `contains` and `ContainsTable`.

## The Contains Function

`Contains` operates within the `where` clause, much like a `where in (subquery)`. The parameters within the parentheses are passed to MS Search, which returns a list of primary keys that meet the criteria.

The first parameter passed to MS Search is the column name to be searched, or an asterisk for a search of all columns from one table. If the `from` clause includes multiple tables, the table must be specified in the `contains` parameter. The following basic full-text query searches all indexed columns for the word "Lion":

```
USE Aesop
SELECT Title
  FROM Fable
  WHERE CONTAINS (Fable.*,'Lion')
```

The following fables contain the word "Lion" in either the fable title, moral, or text:

```
Title
-------------------------------------------------
The Dogs and the Fox
The Hunter and the Woodman
The Ass in the Lion's Skin
Androcles
```

## ContainsTable

Not only will full-text search work within the `where` clause, but the `ContainsTable` function operates as a table or subquery and returns the result set from MS Search. This SQL Server feature opens up the possibility of powerful searches.

`ContainsTable` returns a result set with two columns. The first column, `Key`, identifies the row using the unique index that was defined when the catalog was configured.

The second column, Rank, reports the ranking of the rows using values from 1 (low) to 1000 (high). There is no high/median/low meaning or fixed range to the rank value; the rank only compares the row with other rows with regard to the following factors:

✦ The frequency/uniqueness of the word in the table

✦ The frequency/uniqueness of the word in the column

Therefore, a rare word will be ranked as statistically more important than a common word.

The same parameters that define the full-text search for contains also define the search for ContainsTable. The following query returns the raw data from MS Search:

```
SELECT *
  FROM CONTAINSTABLE (Fable, *, 'Lion')
```

Results:

```
KEY           RANK
-----------   -----------
3             86
4             80
20            48
14            32
```

The key by itself is useless to a human, but joining the ContainsTable results with the Fable table, as if ContainsTable were a derived table, allows the query to return the Rank and the fable's Title, as follows:

```
SELECT Fable.Title, FTS.Rank
  FROM Fable
    JOIN CONTAINSTABLE (Fable, *, 'Lion') FTS
    ON Fable.FableID = FTS.[KEY]
  ORDER BY FTS.Rank DESC
```

Result:

```
Title                                 Rank
----------------------------------    -----------
Androcles                             86
The Butt in the Lion's Skin           80
The Hunter and the Woodman            48
The Dogs and the Fox                  32
```

A fourth ContainsTable parameter, top *n* limit, reduces the result set from the full-text search engine much as the SQL select top predicate does. The limit is applied assuming that the result set is sorted descending by rank so that only the highest ranked results are returned. The following query demonstrates the top *n* limit throttle:

```
SELECT Fable.Title, Rank
  FROM Fable
    JOIN CONTAINSTABLE (Fable, *, 'Lion', 2) FTS
    ON Fable.FableID = FTS.[KEY]
  ORDER BY FTS.Rank DESC
```

Result:

```
Title                            Rank
-------------------------------  -----------
Androcles                        86
The Ass in the Lion's Skin       80
```

The advantage to using the top *n* limit option is that the full-text search engine can pass fewer data back to the query. It's more efficient than returning the full result set and then performing a SQL `top` in the `select` statement. It illustrates the principle of performing the data work at the server instead of the client. In this case, MS Search is the server process and SQL Server is the client process.

**Best Practice**

Since MS Search is a separate component from SQL Server, it competes for CPU cycles. Therefore, the addition of a serious full-text search feature to a SQL Server database project is a compelling justification for using a multiple-CPU server. MS Search is also memory- and Windows–swap-file intensive. A heavily used database that sees regular updates and searches of full-text–enabled columns should run on a stout server.

# Advanced Search Options

Full-text search is powerful, and you can add plenty of options to the search string. These options work with `contains` and `ContainsTable`.

## Multiple Word Searches

Multiple words may be included in the search by means of the `or` and `and` conjunctions. The following query finds any fables containing both the word "Tortoise" and the word "Hare" in the text of the fable:

```
SELECT Title
  FROM Fable
  WHERE CONTAINS (FableText,'Tortoise AND Hare')
```

Result:

```
Title
--------------------------------------------------
The Hare and the Tortoise
```

One significant issue pertains to the search for multiple words: While full-text search can easily search across multiple columns for a single word, it only searches for multiple words if those words are in the same column. For example, the fable "The Ants and the Grasshopper" includes the word "thrifty" in the moral and the word "supperless" in the text of the fable itself. But searching for "thrifty and supperless" across all columns yields no results, as shown here:

```
SELECT Title
  FROM Fable
  WHERE CONTAINS (*,' "Thrifty AND supperless" ')
```

Result:

```
(0 row(s) affected)
```

Two solutions exist, and neither one is pretty. The query can be reconfigured so the and conjunction is at the where-clause level rather than within the contains parameter. The problem with this solution is performance. The following query requires two remote scans to the full-text search engine, as shown in Figure 8-3, each of which requires 363 milliseconds of the total 811-millisecond query-execution time:

```
SELECT Title
  FROM Fable
  WHERE CONTAINS (*,'Thrifty')
    AND CONTAINS(*,'supperless')
```

Result:

```
Title
--------------------------------------------------
The Ants and the Grasshopper
```

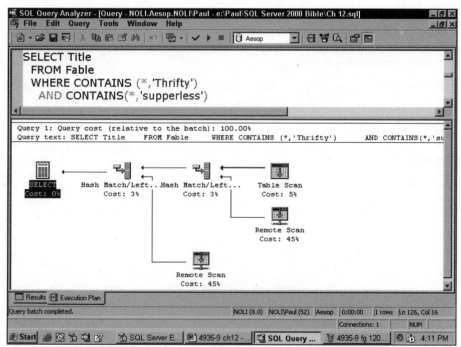

**Figure 8-3:** Each contains function requires a separate remote call to MS Search; the result from the full-text search engine is then scanned by SQL Server.

The other solution to the multiple-column search problem consists of adding an additional column to hold all the text to be searched and duplicating the data from the original columns to a FullTextSearch column within an after trigger. This solution is not smooth either. It duplicates data and costs performance time during inserts and updates. The crux of the decision on how to solve the multiple-column is the conflict between fast reads and fast writes — OLAP versus OLTP.

## Searches with Wildcards

Because MS Search is part of the OS and not a SQL Server–developed component, its wildcards use the standard DOS conventions (asterisks and double quotes) instead of SQL-style wildcards.

The other thing to keep in mind about full-text wildcards is that they only work at the end of a word, not at the beginning. Indexes search from the beginning of strings, as shown here:

```
SELECT Title
  FROM Fable
  WHERE CONTAINS (*,' "Hunt*" ')
```

Result:

```
Title
--------------------------------------------------
The Hunter and the Woodman
The Ass in the Lion's Skin
The Bald Knight
```

If the phrase search includes a wildcard, the wildcard applies to every word in the phrase. For example, the query

```
CONTAINS (*,'He pulled out the thorn*')
```

is the equivalent of the query

```
CONTAINS (*,'He* pulled* out* the* thorn*')
```

## Phrase Searches

Full-text search can attempt to locate full phrases if those phrases are surrounded by double quotes. For example, to search for the fable about the boy who cried wolf, searching for "Wolf! Wolf!" does the trick:

```
SELECT Title
  FROM Fable
  WHERE CONTAINS (*,' "Wolf! Wolf!" ')
```

Result:

```
Title
--------------------------------------------------
The Shepherd's Boy and the Wolf
```

## Word-Proximity Searches

When searching large documents it's nice to be able to specify the proximity of the search words. Full-text search implements a proximity switch by means of the near option. The relative distance between the words is calculated and, if the words are close enough (within about 30 words, depending on the size of the text), full-text search returns a true for the row.

The story of Androcles, the slave who pulls the thorn from the lion's paw, is one of the longer fables in the sample database, so it's a good test sample.

The following query attempts to locate the fable "Androcles" based on the proximity of the words "pardoned" and "forest" in the fable's text:

```
SELECT Title
  FROM Fable
  WHERE CONTAINS (*,'pardoned NEAR forest')
```

Result:

```
Title
--------------------------------------------------
Androcles
```

The proximity switch can handle multiple words. The following query tests the proximity of the words "lion," "paw," and "bleeding":

```
SELECT Title
  FROM Fable
  WHERE CONTAINS (*,'lion NEAR paw NEAR bleeding')
```

Result:

```
Title
--------------------------------------------------
Androcles
```

The proximity feature can be used with `ContainsTable` to return a rank from 0–64, which indicates relative proximity. The following query ranks the fables that mention the word "life" near the word "death" in order of proximity:

```
SELECT Fable.Title, Rank
  FROM Fable
    JOIN CONTAINSTABLE (Fable, *,'life NEAR death') FTS
    ON Fable.FableID = FTS.[KEY]
  ORDER BY FTS.Rank DESC
```

Result:

```
Title                            Rank
-------------------------------- -----------
The Serpent and the Eagle        7
The Eagle and the Arrow          1
The Woodman and the Serpent      1
```

# Word-Inflection Searches

The full-text search engine can actually perform linguistic analysis and base a search for different words on a common root word. This enables you to search for words without worrying about number or tense. For example, the inflection feature makes possible a search for the word "flying" that finds a row containing the word "flew." The language you specify for the table is critical in a case like this. Something else to keep in mind is that the word base will not cross parts of speech, meaning that a search for a noun won't locate a verb form of the same root. The following query demonstrates inflection by locating the fable with the word "flew" in "The Crow and the Pitcher":

```
SELECT Title
  FROM Fable
  WHERE CONTAINS (*,'FORMSOF(INFLECTIONAL,fly)')
```

Result:

```
Title
------------------------------------------------------
The Crow and the Pitcher
The Bald Knight
```

 **Note**   A nice front-end client program will give the user the option of highlighting the search words in the display of the found documents. Inflection searches will create a difficulty: If the user enters "fly" and the word that was found is "flew," a simple find-and-replace with HTML formatting will miss the found word. The `webhits.dll` script in Index Server can help solve this problem.

## Variable-Word–Weight Searches

In a search for multiple words the relative weight may be assigned, making one word critical to the search and another word much less important. The weights are set on a scale of 0.0 to 1.0.

The `isabout` option enables weighting and any hit on the word allows the rows to be returned, so it functions as an implied Boolean `or` operator.

The following two queries use the `weight` option with `ContainsTable` to highlight the difference between the words "lion," "brave," and "eagle" as the weighting changes. The query will examine only the `fabletext` column to prevent the results from being skewed by the shorter lengths of the text found on the title and moral columns. The first query weights the three words evenly:

```
SELECT Fable.Title, FTS.Rank
  FROM Fable
    JOIN CONTAINSTABLE
    (Fable, FableText,
        'ISABOUT (Lion weight (.5),
          Brave weight (.5),
          Eagle weight (.5))',20) FTS
    ON Fable.FableID = FTS.[KEY]
    ORDER BY Rank DESC
```

Result:

```
Title                               Rank
----------------------------------- --------
Androcles                           92
The Eagle and the Fox               85
The Hunter and the Woodman          50
The Serpent and the Eagle           50
The Dogs and the Fox                32
The Eagle and the Arrow             21
The Ass in the Lion's Skin          16
```

When the relative importance of the word "eagle" is elevated, it's a different story:

```
SELECT Fable.Title, FTS.Rank
```

```
FROM Fable
  JOIN CONTAINSTABLE
  (Fable, FableText,
     'ISABOUT (Lion weight (.2),
      Brave weight (.2),
      Eagle weight (.8))',20) FTS
  ON Fable.FableID = FTS.[KEY]
  ORDER BY Rank DESC
```

Result:

| Title | Rank |
|-------|------|
| The Eagle and the Fox | 102 |
| The Serpent and the Eagle | 59 |
| The Eagle and the Arrow | 25 |
| Androcles | 25 |
| The Hunter and the Woodman | 14 |
| The Dogs and the Fox | 9 |
| The Ass in the Lion's Skin | 4 |

When all the columns participate in the full-text search, the small size of the moral and the title make the target words seem relatively more important within the text. The next query uses the same weighting as the previous query but includes all columns (*):

```
SELECT Fable.Title, FTS.Rank
  FROM Fable
    JOIN CONTAINSTABLE
    (Fable, *,
       'ISABOUT (Lion weight (.2),
        Brave weight (.2),
        Eagle weight (.8))',20) FTS
    ON Fable.FableID = FTS.[KEY]
    ORDER BY Rank DESC
```

Result:

| Title | Rank |
|-------|------|
| The Wolf and the Kid | 408 |
| The Hunter and the Woodman | 408 |
| The Eagle and the Fox | 102 |
| The Eagle and the Arrow | 80 |
| The Serpent and the Eagle | 80 |
| Androcles | 25 |
| The Ass in the Lion's Skin | 23 |
| The Dogs and the Fox | 9 |

The ranking is very relative and is based on word frequency, word proximity, and the relative importance of a given word within the text. "The Wolf and the Kid" does not contain an eagle or a lion, but two factors favor bravado. First, "brave" is a rarer word than "lion" or "eagle" in both the column and the table. Secondly, the word "brave" appears in the moral as one of only 10 words. So even though "brave" was weighted less, it rises to the top of the list. It's all based on word frequencies and statistics (and sometimes, I think, the phase of the moon!).

# Fuzzy Searches

While the contains predicate and ContainsTable-derived table perform exact word searches, the freetext predicate expands on the contains functionality to include *fuzzy*, or approximate, full-text searches from free-form text.

Instead of searching for two or three words and adding the options for inflection and weights, the fuzzy search handles the complexity of building searches that make use of all the MS Search options and tries to solve the problem for you. Internally, the free-form text is broken down into multiple words and phrases and the full-text search with inflections and weighting is then performed on the result.

## Freetext

Freetext works within a where clause just like contains, but without all the options. The following query uses a fuzzy search to find the fable about the big race:

```
SELECT Title
  FROM Fable
  WHERE FREETEXT
   (*,'The tortoise beat the hare in the big race')
```

Result:

```
Title
--------------------------------------------------
The Hare and the Tortoise
```

## FreetextTable

Fuzzy searches benefit from the freetext-derived table that returns the ranking in the same way that ContainsTable does. The two queries shown in this section demonstrate a fuzzy full-text search using the freetext-derived table. Here is the first query:

```
SELECT Fable.Title, FTS.Rank
  FROM Fable
    JOIN FREETEXTTABLE
      (Fable, *, 'The brave hunter kills the lion',20) FTS
      ON Fable.FableID = FTS.[KEY]
  ORDER BY Rank DESC
```

Result:

```
Title                               Rank
----------------------------------- ----------
The Hunter and the Woodman          257
The Ass in the Lion's Skin          202
The Wolf and the Kid                187
Androcles                           113
The Dogs and the Fox                100
The Goose With the Golden Eggs      72
The Shepherd's Boy and the Wolf     72
```

Here is the second query:

```
SELECT Fable.Title, FTS.Rank
  FROM Fable
    JOIN FREETEXTTABLE
      (Fable, *, 'The eagle was shot by an arrow',20) FTS
      ON Fable.FableID = FTS.[KEY]
    ORDER BY Rank DESC
```

Result:

```
Title                             Rank
--------------------------------- -----------
The Eagle and the Arrow           288
The Eagle and the Fox             135
The Serpent and the Eagle         112
The Hunter and the Woodman        102
The Father and His Two Daughters  72
```

# Binary Object Indexing

SQL Server can store any binary object up to 2GB, which definitely qualifies as a binary large object (blob) in an image column. Full-text search can index words from within those binary objects if the following criteria are met:

✦ Windows must have a filter installed for the object type. SQL Server installs the filters for file types .doc, .xls, .ppt, .txt, and .htm in the file offfilt.dll.

✦ A separate column, char(3), must store the document extension for the blob stored in that row.

✦ The column must be added to the full-text search catalog as a blob search and the document type (eg. .txt, .doc, .xls) must be stored in an accompanying column.

✦ The full-text search catalog must be populated with full and incremental populations. The Change-tracking and Update-in-the-background options will not support indexing the blobs.

✦ The object must be properly initialized as it is loaded into SQL Server using the Bulk Image Insert program.

Even when full-text search is carefully setup for blobs, I have found that this technology is less than perfect and it takes some tinkering to make it work.

The following stored-procedure call sets up the blob column for full-text search:

```
EXEC sp_fulltext_column
    'Fable','Blob','add',0x0409,'BlobType'
```

The parameters are the same as those for adding a text column, except that the last parameter identifies the column used to specify the blob document type.

SQL Server includes Bulk Image Insert or BII.exe, a modified version of the Bulk Copy Program that initializes the blob files and loads them into SQL Server. It's zipped in the file unzip_util.zip in the C:\Program Files\Microsoft SQL Server\80\Tools\DevTools\Samples\utils directory. Once unzipped, it creates the bii subdirectory and unzips the utility files.

The Bulk Image Insert utility copies data from a text file into SQL Server. The text file must be semicolon-delimited (despite the documentation's claim that it must be comma-delimited). Within the text file, an at sign (@) indicates the blob name.

The following sample text file loads the MS Word document fox.doc into the Aesop's Fables sample database. The sixth column loads the blobtype and the seventh column points to fox.doc (the single line is word-wrapped to fit on the page):

```
Sample.txt:
26; Test Fable; Persistence Pays Off;
                    Try, try again.;doc;@fox.doc
```

Calling the bii utility at the command prompt, the utility will move data into the fable table from sample.txt. The other parameters specify the server name, the database, the user name (using SQL Server users), and the password. The -v parameter directs bii.exe to report the details of the operation as follows (formatted to fit):

```
>bii "fable" in "sample.txt"
      -S"Noli" -D"Aesop" -U"sa" -P"sa" -v
```

Result:

```
BII - Bulk Image Insert Program for Microsoft SQL Server.
Copyright 2000 Microsoft Corporation, All Rights Reserved.
Version: V1.0-1
Started at 2001-12-07 16:28:09.231 on NOLI
Table Noli.Aesop.sa.fable
        FableID int (4)
        Title varchar (50)
        Moral varchar (100)
        FableText varchar (1536)
        BlobType char (3) null
        Blob image (16) null
Inserted 1 rows Read 1 rows 0 rows with errors
   Total Bytes = 19508 inserted 19456 File Bytes
 Total Seconds = 0.02  Kb Per Second = 952.539063
BII - Bulk Image Insert Program for Microsoft SQL Server.
Copyright 2000 Microsoft Corporation, All Rights Reserved.
Version: V1.0-1
Finished at 2001-12-07 16:28:09.332 on NOLI
```

Once the twenty-sixth fable is loaded into the database and the full-text catalog is populated you can use the following command to search the Word document within SQL Server:

```
EXEC sp_fulltext_table 'Fable', 'start_full'
```

The following query looks for the word "jumped," which is found in the twenty-sixth fable:

```
SELECT Title, BlobType
  FROM Fable
  WHERE CONTAINS (*,'jumped')
```

Result:

```
Title                             BlobType
--------------------------------- -----------
Test Fable                        doc
```

# Summary

SQL Server indexes are not designed for searching for words in the middle of a column. If the database project requires flexible word searches, full-text search is the best tool, even though it requires additional development and administrative work.

The second part of this book, "Developing SQL Server Databases," deals with managing data, beginning with a description of the basic `select` statement. This chapter explained how to make retrieving data with the `select` statement even better by adding full-text search. The next chapter also addresses the subject of data retrieval, by describing how to store predefined SQL statements as views.

✦     ✦     ✦

# Creating Views

**A** *view* is a stored SQL select statement that may be referenced as a table — no more, no less. Microsoft Access programmers who move up to SQL Server tend to develop using views, thinking of them as the SQL Server equivalent to Access Queries. This makes sense because using pre-compiled Queries is a best practice in Access. While SQL Server views are similar to Access Queries, they bring with them both new features and a new set of performance problems.

Views are sometimes described as "virtual tables." This isn't an accurate description, because views don't store data, and no actual data is stored anywhere specifically for a standard view. Views merely refer to the data stored in tables.

With this in mind, it's important to fully understand how views work, and the pros and cons of using views, before you plan your project architecture.

## Why Use Views?

When it comes to views three general opinions, or development styles, prevail. The first and most popular opinion is that views should be avoided like the plague. Developers in this camp cite performance issues and problems with updating, and their applications tend to be clean and fast, but their users miss out on the benefits of views.

At the other extreme, some developers love views and will develop a project based entirely on them. Every access from the client application hits a view. These applications work well in development but begin to fail as the database sees heavier usage.

I recommend a moderate approach. Views can play a useful role in a database project, but overusing them will cause problems.

**Best Practice**

Use views to simplify complex joins or aggregate queries, denormalize data, or rename columns to support ad hoc queries and reports. When used in this way, views add to the consistency of the database. But don't use views to support the main user application, or to simulate security.

**Cross-Reference** SQL Server includes two advanced forms of views: *partitioned views* and *federated databases (distributed partition views)*. Both of these types of views enable you to split, or partition, huge tables across multiple smaller tables or separate servers to improve performance. The partitioned view then spans the multiple tables or servers and even enables updates to the correct underlying table. These advanced views are explained in Chapter 30, "Advanced Scalability."

## Creating Views

Since a view is nothing more than a saved SQL `select`, the creation of a view begins with a working `select` statement. A SQL `select` statement, as long as it's a valid SQL `select` statement (with a few minor exceptions), can be cut and pasted from nearly any other tool into a view.

### Creating Views with Enterprise Manager

Views are listed in their own node under each database. The right-click menu for a view is similar to the right-click menu for a table. The New View command in the right-click menu will launch the View Designer in a mode that creates views, as shown in Figure 9-1.

Tables or other views can be added to the new view by means of dragging them to the Diagram pane from Enterprise Manager's main window, or using the Add Table toolbar button. (The actual placement of the table or view in the Diagram pane is not saved, so there's little point in making it look great.)

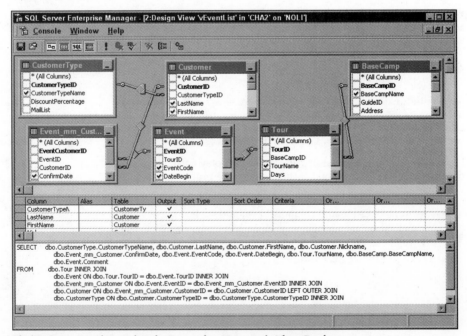

**Figure 9-1:** Creating a view in Enterprise Manager's View Designer.

The View Designer functions similarly to Enterprise Manager's Query Designer, which is also used to query tables. Columns may be added to the view by means of the Diagram pane, the Grid pane, or the SQL pane. Editing the raw SQL query in the SQL pane will extend the SQL query beyond the graphic capabilities of the diagram pane and in this manner the view may include subqueries.

**Cross-Reference** For more details on using Enterprise Manager's Query Designer, refer to Chapter 4, "Using SQL Server's Developer Tools."

The Verify SQL button in the toolbar only verifies the SQL syntax and does not verify the names of tables, views, or columns in the SQL `select` statement.

The Run right-click menu item, or the `!` toolbar button, executes the query and displays the answer in the Result pane. Because the view will be executed again from other code, testing is imperative.

The Save toolbar button, or the Save item or Save As item in the right-click menu, actually creates the view. Unlike other Enterprise Manager save features, these do not offer the option of previewing the script used to actually create or alter the view. Note that the view must be a valid, error-free SQL `select` statement in order to be saved.

Once the view is created, it may be edited within Enterprise Manager by means of selecting the view and selecting the Design item from the right-click menu.

The view can be run from within Enterprise Manger in the same way that a table's contents can be viewed. Select the view and select one of the Open items from the right-click menu. Because the view is now being executed, or *called*, from a `select` statement, the view itself now appears within the Diagram pane as a data source.

The SQL pane will show the view in the `from` clause of the `select` statement. This is how the view will be referenced by users:

```
SELECT * FROM dbo.vEventList
```

When views are called from user applications, a `where` condition is typically used to retrieve the correct data from the view. The `where` condition may be entered in the Grid pane or the SQL pane. For example:

```
SELECT * FROM dbo.vEventList WHERE (EventCode = '101')
```

Views may be deleted from the database using Enterprise Manager by selecting the view and deleting it.

## Creating Views with DDL Code

Views may be managed within Query Analyzer or SQL scripts with the Data Definition Language (DDL) commands: `create`, `alter`, and `drop`. The basic syntax for creating a view is as follows:

```
CREATE dbo.ViewName
As
SQL Select Statement
```

For example, to create the view `vEventList` in code, the following command would be executed in Query Analyzer:

```
CREATE VIEW dbo.vEventList
AS
SELECT dbo.CustomerType.CustomerTypeName,
    dbo.Customer.LastName, dbo.Customer.FirstName,
    dbo.Customer.Nickname,
    dbo.Event_mm_Customer.ConfirmDate, dbo.Event.EventCode,
    dbo.Event.DateBegin, dbo.Tour.TourName,
    dbo.BaseCamp.BaseCampName, dbo.Event.Comment
    FROM dbo.Tour
        INNER JOIN dbo.Event
            ON dbo.Tour.TourID = dbo.Event.TourID
        INNER JOIN dbo.Event_mm_Customer
            ON dbo.Event.EventID = dbo.Event_mm_Customer.EventID
        INNER JOIN dbo.Customer
            ON dbo.Event_mm_Customer.CustomerID
                = dbo.Customer.CustomerID
        LEFT OUTER JOIN dbo.CustomerType
            ON dbo.Customer.CustomerTypeID
                = dbo.CustomerType.CustomerTypeID
        INNER JOIN dbo.BaseCamp
            ON dbo.Tour.BaseCampID = dbo.BaseCamp.BaseCampID
```

Attempting to create a view that already exists will cause an error. Once a view has been created, the SQL select statement may be easily edited by means of the alter command:

```
ALTER dbo.ViewName
As
SQL Select Statement
```

The alter command supplies a new SQL select statement for the view.

Here's where the Query Analyzer's Object Browser earns its keep. To automatically generate an alter statement from an existing view, drill down to the list of views in the Object Browser and select "Script Object to New Windows As... Alter" from the right-click menu.

Altering a view is preferable to dropping and re-creating it, because dropping the view will also drop any security-object permissions that have been established.

To remove a view from the database, use the drop command:

```
Drop View dbo.ViewName
```

## View Restrictions

Although a view can contain nearly any valid select statement, a few basic restrictions do apply:

✦ Views may not include the select into option that creates a new table from the selected columns. Select into fails if the table already exists, and it does not return any data, so it's not a valid view.

```
SELECT * INTO Table
```

✦ Views may not refer to a temporary table (one with a # in the name) or a table variable, because these types of tables are very transient.

✦ Views may not contain compute or compute by columns. Instead use standard aggregate functions and groupings. (Compute and computer by are obsolete and included for backward compatibility only.)

# Creating Views for Ad Hoc Queries

Based on the premise that views are best used for ad hoc queries, and not as a central part of the application, here are some ideas for building ad hoc–query views:

✦ *Use views to denormalize or flatten complex joins and hide the mysterious keys used to link data within the database schema.* A well-designed view will invite the user to get right to the data of interest.

Without views to pre-build some of the complex joins, ad hoc queries pose a potential data integrity problem. Even if users understand joins, they rarely understand when to use an inner join versus an outer join. Getting that aspect of the join wrong will lead to incorrect results. The vEventList view created earlier in this chapter is a good example of a six-table join turned into a single-user recognizable record set.

✦ *Save complex aggregate queries as views.* Because every column must participate in an aggregate function or group by, many complex aggregate queries tend to involve subqueries so they will be able to present non-aggregated columns. Ad hoc query users might be grateful to you for composing these complex queries in advance.

✦ *Use aliases to change cryptic column names to recognizable column names.* Just as the SQL select statement can use column aliases or named ranges (table aliases) to modify the names of columns or tables, these features may be used within a view to present a more readable record set to the user. For example, the column au_lname in the Microsoft Pubs database could use the alias LastName:

```
SELECT au_lname AS LastName FROM Pubs.dbo.Author
```

A view based on the previous select statement would list the author's last name column as LastName instead of au_lname.

✦ *Include only the columns of interest to the user.* When columns that don't concern users are left out of the view the view is easier to query. The columns that are included in the view are called *projected columns*, meaning that they project only the selected data from the entire underlying table.

✦ *Plan generic, dynamic views that will have long, useful lives; single-purpose views will quickly become obsolete and clutter the database.* Build the view intending that it be used with a where clause to select a subset of data. The view should return all the rows if the user does not supply a where restriction. For example, the vEventList view returns all the events; the user should use a where clause to select the local events, or the events in a certain month.

If a view is needed to return a restricted set of data, such as the next month's events, then the view should calculate the next month so that it will continue to function over time. Hard-coding values such as = Dec would be poor practice.

The goal when developing views is two-fold — to enable users to get to the data easily, and to protect the data from the users. By building views that provide the correct data, you are protecting the data from mis-queries and misinterpretation.

# The With Check Option

The `with check option` causes the `where` clause of the view to check the data being inserted or updated through the view in addition to the data being retrieved. In a sense, it makes the `where` clause a two-way restriction.

This option is useful when the view should limit inserts and updates with the same restrictions applied to the `where` clause.

To understand the need for the `with check option`, it's important to first understand how views function without the `check option`. The following view will generate a list of tours for the Cape Hatteras base camp:

```
CREATE VIEW dbo.vCapeHatterasTour
AS
SELECT TourName, BaseCampID
   FROM dbo.Tour
   WHERE BaseCampID = 2


SELECT * FROM dbo.vCapeHatterasTour


TourName                         BaseCampID
----------------------------     -----------
Outer Banks Lighthouses             2
```

If the Ashville base camp adds a Blue Ridge Parkway Hike tour and inserts it through the view without the `check option`, the `insert` is permitted:

```
INSERT dbo.vCapeHatterasTour (TourName, BaseCampID)
   VALUES ('Blue Ridge Parkway Hike', 1)
(1 row(s) affected)
```

The `insert` worked and the new row is in the database, but the row is not visible through the view because the `where` clause of the view filters out the inserted row. This is a phenomenon called *disappearing rows*.

```
SELECT * FROM dbo.vCapeHatterasTour


TourName                         BaseCampID
----------------------------     -----------
Outer Banks Lighthouses          2
```

If the purpose of the view was to give the users at the Cape access to their tours alone, the view failed. Although they can see only the Cape's tours, they successfully modified another base camp's tours.

The `with check option` would have prevented this fault. The following code will back out the `insert` and redo the same scenario, but this time the view will include the `with check option`:

```
DELETE dbo.vCapeHatterasTour
   WHERE TourName = 'Blue Ridge Parkway Hike'

ALTER VIEW dbo.vCapeHatterasTour
   AS
   SELECT TourName, BaseCampID
      FROM dbo.Tour
```

```
        WHERE BaseCampID = 2
   WITH CHECK OPTION

INSERT dbo.vCapeHatterasTour (TourName, BaseCampID)
   VALUES ('Blue Ridge Parkway Hike', 1)
```

```
Server: Msg 550, Level 16, State 1, Line 1
The attempted insert or update failed because the target view either
specifies WITH CHECK OPTION or spans a view that specifies WITH CHECK
OPTION and one or more rows resulting from the operation did not qualify
under the CHECK OPTION constraint.
The statement has been terminated.
```

This time the insert failed and the error message attributed the cause to the with check option in the view, which is exactly the effect desired.

Some developers will employ views and the with check option as a means of providing row-level security — a technique called *horizontally positioned views*. As in the base-camp–view example, they will create a view for each department, or each sales branch, and then give users security permission to the view that pertains to them. While this method does achieve row-level security it also has a high maintenance cost.

**Cross-Reference**      A better way to achieve row-level security is to build the security into user-access tables and stored procedures, as demonstrated in Chapter 16, "Advanced Server-Side Programming."

Within Enterprise Manager's View Designer, the with check option can be enabled within the View Properties page, which is available from the right-click menu.

## Order By and Views

Views don't normally include a sort order. The order by clause is typically added to the SQL statement that refers to the view. For example, the following code selects data from the vEventList view and orders it by EventCode and name. The order by is not a part of vEventList, but is applied to the view by the calling SQL statement.

```
SELECT EventCode, LastName, FirstName, IsNull(NickName,'')
   FROM dbo.vEventList
   ORDER BY EventCode, LastName, FirstName
```

However, SQL Server permits the top predicate in views and the top predicate is generally useless without an order by. So if the view includes top 100 percent, it can include an order by:

```
ALTER VIEW dbo.vCapeHatterasTour
   AS
   SELECT TOP 100 PERCENT TourName, BaseCampID
      FROM dbo.Tour
      WHERE BaseCampID = 2
      ORDER BY TourName
```

I like this capability because it fits perfectly with my reason for recommending that you use views in your project. Managers and other users who typically create ad hoc queries and reports tend to be unfamiliar with SQL syntax. Even if they use a graphic tool to select from the view, your performing the most likely sort in the view means one less thing for them to worry about.

If the SQL select statement referring to the view does include an order by clause, the calling order by overrides the view's order by.

## Protecting the View

Two final options protect views from data-schema changes and prying eyes. These options are simply added to the create command and applied to the view, much as the with check option is applied.

Database code is fragile and tends to break when the underlying data structure changes. Because views are nothing more than stored SQL select queries, changes to the referenced tables will break the view. Even adding new columns to an underlying table may cause the view to break.

Creating a view with schema binding locks the underlying tables to the view and prevents changes, as demonstrated in the following code sample:

```
CREATE TABLE Test (
    [Name] NVARCHAR(50)
    )
go

CREATE VIEW vTest
WITH SCHEMABINDING
AS
SELECT [Name] FROM dbo.Test
Go

ALTER TABLE Test
    ALTER COLUMN [Name] NVARCHAR(100)

Server: Msg 4922, Level 16, State 1, Line 1
ALTER TABLE ALTER COLUMN Name failed
because one or more objects access this column.
```

Some restrictions apply to the creation of schema-bound views. The select statement must include the owner name for any referenced objects, and select all columns (*) is not permitted.

The with encryption option is another simulated-security feature. When views or stored procedures are created the text is stored in the SysComments system table. The code is therefore available for viewing. The view may contain a where condition that should be kept confidential, or some other reason for encrypting the code. The with encryption option encrypts the code in SysComments and prevents anyone from viewing the original code.

In the following code example, the text of the view is inspected within SysComments, the view is encrypted, and SysComments is again inspected. As you would expect, the select statement for the view is then no longer readable.

```
SELECT Text
    FROM SysComments
    JOIN SysObjects
        ON SysObjects.ID = SysComments.ID
    WHERE Name = 'vTest'
```

The result is the text of the `vText` view:

```
Text
```

```
------------------------------
CREATE VIEW vTest
WITH SCHEMABINDING
AS
SELECT [Name] FROM dbo.Test
```

The following `alter` command rebuilds the view `with encryption`:

```
ALTER VIEW vTest
WITH ENCRYPTION
AS
SELECT [Name] FROM dbo.Test
```

Rerunning the previous select from `SysComments` returns unreadable text:

```
Text
```

```
------------------------------

_____

_____
```

Be careful with this option. Once the code is encrypted, the Query Analyzer Object Browser can no longer produce a script to alter the view, and will instead generate this message:

```
/****** Encrypted object is not transferable,
and script cannot be generated. ******/
```

 **Cross-Reference** Just as with stored procedure encryption, view encryption is easily broken. Refer to Chapter 13, "Developing Stored Procedures," for more information.

Within Enterprise Manager's View Designer, the `with schema binding` and `with encryption` options can be enabled within the View Properties page.

# Updatable Views

One of the main complaints concerning views as that they are often not updatable. In fact, if the view is much more than a simple `select`, chances are that data can't be updated through the view.

Any of these factors may cause a view to be non-updatable:

 **Cross-Reference** Of course the other standard potential difficulties with updating and inserting data still apply. The next chapter, "Modifying Data," discusses modifying data in more detail.

✦ Only one table may be updated. If the view includes joins, the update statement that references the view must attempt to update only one table.

✦ An instead of trigger on the view or an underlying table will modify the data-modification operation. The code inside the instead of trigger will be executed instead of the submitted data update.

✦ Aggregate functions or group bys in the view will cause the view to be non-updatable. SQL Server wouldn't be able to determine which of the summarized rows should be updated.

✦ If the view includes a subquery as a derived table, none of the derived table's columns may be in the output of the view. However, aggregates are permitted in a subquery that is being used as a derived table.

✦ If the view includes the with check option, the insert or update operation must meet the view's where-clause conditions.

✦ The update or insert columns must refer to a single column in the underlying tables. If the same column name appears in two tables, use the designation *table.column* in the column list.

As you can see, it's easy to create a non-updatable view. However, if the project is using views for ad hoc queries and reporting only, updatability isn't a serious issue.

**Cross-Reference**

One way to work around non-updatable views is to build an instead of trigger that inspects the modified data and then performs a legal update operation based on that data. Chapter 15, "Implementing Triggers," explains how to create an instead of trigger.

# Performance Problems with Views

By far the most critical problem with views is one of performance. Developers who shun views rightly point out that views are not pre-compiled and that they cause a performance hit.

When a view is referenced by a SQL select statement several steps are taken to resolve the query:

1. The calling SQL select statement and the referenced view are combined into a new single query.

2. The new query's tables must be resolved. If the table name does not indicate an owner, the proper table must be determined. For example, if there are two tables, dbo.Client and bob.Client, then Client will mean bob.Client to Bob's query and dbo.Client to everyone else's query.

3. Security must be processed and checked. If the ownership chain from the view to the underlying tables is consistent, the user may reference the tables through the view (assuming that the view's owner has permission to the tables) if he or she has permission to the view regardless of the permission to the table. However, if the ownership chain is broken or changes from the view to the underlying tables, the user must have permission to every object in the chain. So checking security may extract a performance hit.

4. If a previous query with the same types of parameters has been executed, and the query and view included the owner name, the query can take advantage of auto-parameterization, and the stored query-execution plan may be reused.

   If either the query or the view includes a table without the owner's name, or it is the first time the query-and-view combination has been executed, the query optimizer must determine a query-execution plan.

5. The query is executed.

So how much of a performance hit is exacted by a view? From my experience, a well-written stored procedure will be about 10–20 percent faster than a well-written view. Of course, many variables exist.

The following batch will retrieve data through the `vEventList` view created previously in a 1,000-iteration loop:

```
DECLARE @pCounter INT
SET @pCounter = 0

WHILE @pCounter < 1000
BEGIN
  SET @pCounter = @pCounter + 1
  SELECT * FROM vEventlist
END
```

On my computer the view batch took 99 seconds to complete. The following code will create a version of the same `select` statement as a stored procedure and then run the same loop:

```
CREATE PROC GetEventList
AS
SET NOCOUNT ON
SELECT dbo.CustomerType.CustomerTypeName,
    dbo.Customer.LastName, dbo.Customer.FirstName,
    dbo.Customer.Nickname,
    dbo.Event_mm_Customer.ConfirmDate, dbo.Event.EventCode,
    dbo.Event.DateBegin, dbo.Tour.TourName,
    dbo.BaseCamp.BaseCampName, dbo.Event.Comment
    FROM dbo.Tour
        INNER JOIN dbo.Event
            ON dbo.Tour.TourID = dbo.Event.TourID
        INNER JOIN dbo.Event_mm_Customer
            ON dbo.Event.EventID = dbo.Event_mm_Customer.EventID
        INNER JOIN dbo.Customer
            ON dbo.Event_mm_Customer.CustomerID
                = dbo.Customer.CustomerID
        LEFT OUTER JOIN dbo.CustomerType
            ON dbo.Customer.CustomerTypeID
                = dbo.CustomerType.CustomerTypeID
        INNER JOIN dbo.BaseCamp
            ON dbo.Tour.BaseCampID = dbo.BaseCamp.BaseCampID

SP_SQLEXEC GetEventList -- test the proc

DECLARE @pCounter INT
```

```
SET @pCounter = 0

WHILE @pCounter < 1000
BEGIN
  SET @pCounter = @pCounter + 1
  EXEC GetEventList
END
```

The stored procedure loop completed in 88 seconds. That's a 12 percent increase in performance. Is that significant? Only you can decide.

Whether the overhead associated with views is acceptable in a project depends on the load and the frequency with which the view will be called. If the view is supporting a form used to update a look-up table once a month, a view is sufficient. However, if the majority of users are constantly reviewing and updating the data, such as in an order-processing form, you'll want to use a stored procedure to instead of a view.

**Cross-Reference**

*Indexed views*, discussed in Chapter 30, "Advanced Scalability," and included with the Enterprise Edition of SQL Server 2000, are a powerful feature that creates an index over a denormalized set of data as defined by a view. The index may then be applied when executing queries that join across that set of data, regardless of whether the view is in the query, so the name is slightly confusing.

A related performance issue involving views concerns the locks that views can place on the data. There's nothing inherently wrong with the way views lock the data, and if data is selected through a view and the select is immediately completed the locks will be immediately dropped. The problem is that users have a tendency to use views to browse data using a front-end application that opens all the data and keeps it open for the length of the browse session. For this reason views have garnered an undeservedly poor reputation for holding locks. The issue is not the view, but the front-end code or tool. I mention it here in defense of views and to alert you to this potential performance problem.

## Nested Views

Since a view is nothing more than a SQL select statement, and a SQL select statement may refer to a view as if it were a table, then views may themselves refer to other views. Views referred to by other views are sometimes called *nested views*.

The following view uses vEventList and adds a where clause to restrict the results to those events taking place in the next 30 days:

```
CREATE VIEW dbo.vEventList30days
   AS
   SELECT dbo.vEventList.EventCode, LastName, FirstName
      FROM dbo.vEventList
      JOIN dbo.Event
         ON vEventList.EventCode = Event.EventCode
      WHERE Event.DateBegin
         BETWEEN GETDATE() and GETDATE() + 30
```

In this example, the view vEventList is nested within vEventList30Days. Another way to express the relationship is to say that vEventList30Days depends on vEventList. (Within Enterprise Manager, the dependencies of an object may be viewed by means of selecting All Tasks ➪ Display Dependencies from the right-click menu for the object.) Figure 9-2 shows the Dependencies dialog boxes for both of the views.

## Alternatives to Views

If your development style involves a lot of views, this may have been a depressing chapter. Fortunately, SQL Server 2000 provides several other cool alternatives.

Stored procedures and functions, assuming a well-designed security scheme, skip directly to Step 4 (of the five steps mentioned previously to execute a view) the first time they are executed and to Step 5 thereafter. Stored procedures do not offer schema binding (a very attractive benefit), while views do; however, user-defined functions provide the compiled speed and input parameters of a stored procedure with the schema binding of a view. If you like building modular SQL statements such as views, as I do, you'll find user-defined functions to your liking.

Chapters 12 – 14 discuss T-SQL, stored procedures, and functions.

If you are using views to support ad hoc queries, as I suggest you do, you may also want to explore providing Analysis Services cubes for those users who need to perform complex explorations of the data. Cubes *pre-aggregate,* or summarize, the data along multiple dimensions. The user may then browse the cube and compare the different data dimensions. For the developer, providing one cube can often eliminate several queries or reports.

Chapter 31, "Analysis Services," explains creating cubes.

(a)

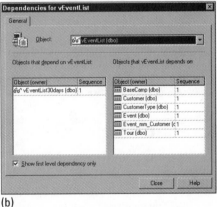
(b)

**Figure 9-2:** The dependency chain for the nested views is easily discerned from the Dependencies dialog boxes for the calling view: (a) vEventList30Days, and (b) the nested view vEventList.

**Cross-Reference**  Another high-end specialized view is a partitioned view that unions data that has been split into several segmented tables for performance reasons. Partitioned views are explained in Chapter 30, "Advanced Scalability."

Views aren't the only means of nesting `select` statements. Subqueries supplying data as if they were tables, or derived tables, may also be nested, which will likely improve performance. The nested view in the preceding code sample could be rewritten as nest-derived tables, as follows (the subquery is the code enclosed in parentheses):

```
SELECT E.EventCode, LastName, FirstName
  FROM
  (SELECT dbo.CustomerType.CustomerTypeName,
     dbo.Customer.LastName, dbo.Customer.FirstName,
     dbo.Customer.Nickname,
     dbo.Event_mm_Customer.ConfirmDate, dbo.Event.EventCode,
     dbo.Event.DateBegin, dbo.Tour.TourName,
     dbo.BaseCamp.BaseCampName, dbo.Event.Comment
   FROM dbo.Tour
     INNER JOIN dbo.Event
       ON dbo.Tour.TourID = dbo.Event.TourID
     INNER JOIN dbo.Event_mm_Customer
       ON dbo.Event.EventID = dbo.Event_mm_Customer.EventID
     INNER JOIN dbo.Customer
       ON dbo.Event_mm_Customer.CustomerID
          = dbo.Customer.CustomerID
     LEFT OUTER JOIN dbo.CustomerType
       ON dbo.Customer.CustomerTypeID
          = dbo.CustomerType.CustomerTypeID
     INNER JOIN dbo.BaseCamp
       ON dbo.Tour.BaseCampID = dbo.BaseCamp.BaseCampID
   ) E
   JOIN dbo.Event
     ON E.EventCode = Event.EventCode
   WHERE Event.DateBegin BETWEEN GETDATE()
     and GETDATE() + 30
```

The subquery is given the names range, or table alias, of E. From then on it's referred to by the outer query as E. Granted, this is not a suitable technique for end-user ad hoc queries, but if you're a developer who has been using nested views and you want to regain some lost performance, nested derived tables are worth trying.

**Cross-Reference**   Chapter 7, "Merging Data Using Relational Algebra," explains using subqueries.

## Summary

Views are nothing more than stored SQL select queries. There's no magic in a view. Any valid SQL select statement may be saved as a view including subqueries, complex joins, and aggregate functions.

The previous chapters have discussed retrieving data using the powerful select statement. Views store the select statement for ad hoc queries. The next chapter will show you how to add data-modification verbs to insert, update, and delete data.

✦      ✦      ✦

# Modifying Data

Things change. Life moves on. Since the purpose of a database is to accurately represent reality, the data must change along with reality. For SQL programmers, that means inserting, updating, and deleting rows — using the basic Data Manipulation Language (DML) commands. But these operations aren't limited to writing single rows of data. Working with SQL means thinking in terms of datasets. The process of modifying data with SQL draws upon the entire range of SQL Server data-retrieval capabilities — the powerful `select`, joins, full-text searches, subqueries, and views.

**Best Practice**

**The SQL `insert`, `update`, and `delete` commands are really verb extensions of the basic `select` command. The full potential of the `select` command lies within each data-modification operation. Even when modifying data, you should think in terms of sets rather than single rows.**

This chapter is all about modifying data within SQL Server using the `insert`, `update`, and `delete` SQL commands. Modifying data raises issues that need to be addressed, or at least considered. Inserting primary keys requires special methods. Table constraints may interfere with the data modification. Referential integrity demands that some `delete` operations cascade to other related tables. This chapter will help you understand these concerns and offer some ways of dealing with them. Because these potential obstacles affect `insert`s, `update`s, and, to some degree, `delete`s, they are addressed in their own sections after the sections devoted to the individual commands.

The ACID database properties (Atomic, Consistent, Isolated, and Durable) are critical to the modification of data. Within the big picture of SQL Server, the next chapter, "Transactional Integrity," continues with the data-modification theme as it digs into SQL Server's architecture and explains how data modifications occur within transactions to meet the ACID requirements, and how SQL Server manages data locks.

Data-modification commands may be submitted to SQL Server from any one of several interfaces. This chapter is concerned more with the strategy and use of the `insert`, `update`, and `delete` commands than with the interface used to submit a given command to SQL Server.

Two main interfaces are provided with SQL Server for submitting SQL commands: Query Analyzer and Enterprise Manager's Query Designer. Query Analyzer, while lacking the visual representation of joins and columns, has a richer set of features for working with T-SQL commands. Query Designer has the advantage of enabling you to build data-manipulation commands both visually and in code, as shown in Figure 10-1. Either interface is suitable for learning data-modification

## In This Chapter

Inserting data from expressions, other result sets, and stored procedures

Updating data

Deleting data

Avoiding and solving data-modification problems

SQL commands, but because Query Analyzer is better for working with SQL scripts, I recommend you use Query Analyzer as you work through this chapter.

**Cross-Reference**    For more details on using Enterprise Manager's Query Designer and Query Analyzer, see Chapter 4, "Using SQL Server's Developer Tools."

# Inserting Data

SQL offers four forms of `insert` and `select/into` as the primary methods of inserting data (as shown in Table 10-1). The most basic method simply inserts a row of data, while the most complex builds a dataset from a complex `select` statement and creates a table from the result.

## Table 10-1: Insert Forms

| Insert Form | Description |
| --- | --- |
| `insert/values` | Inserts a single row of values; commonly used to insert data from a user interface. |
| `insert/select` | Inserts a result set; commonly used to manipulate sets of data. |
| `insert/exec` | Inserts the results of a stored procedure; used for complex data manipulation. |
| `insert default` | Creates a new row with all defaults; used for pre-populating pigeonhole data rows. |
| `select/into` | Creates a new table from the result set of a `select` statement. |

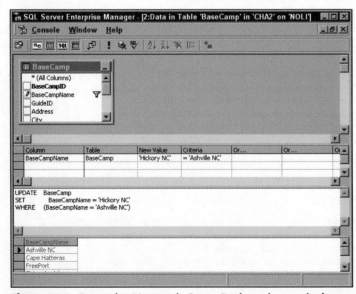

**Figure 10-1:** Enterprise Manager's Query Designer is amazingly well-suited to modifying data.

Each of these `insert` forms is useful for a unique task, often depending on the source of the data being inserted.

**Cross-Reference**

SQL Server complements the SQL `insert` commands with other tools to aid in moving large amounts of data or in performing complex data conversions. The venerable Bulk Copy and the Copy Database Wizard are introduced in Chapter 17, "Transferring Databases." The Copy Database Wizard actually creates a simple Data Transformation Service (DTS) package. Chapter 19, "Migrating Data with DTS," details DTS, a very powerful tool that can move and manipulate large sets of data between/among nearly any data sources.

When inserting new data, primary keys must be generated to identify the new rows. While identity columns and GUIDs both make excellent primary keys, each requires special handling during the insertion of rows. This section covers how to create identity-column values and GUIDs.

## Inserting One Row of Values

The simplest and most direct method of inserting data is the `insert/values` method. Because this form accepts a single set of values, it's limited to inserting data one row at a time. Since user interfaces tend to accept one row of data at a time, this is the preferred method for inserting data from a user interface.

```
INSERT [INTO] owner.Table [(columns,...)]
    VALUES (value,...)
```

Building an `insert/values` statement is pretty straightforward, although you do have a few options. The `into` keyword is optional and is commonly ignored. The key to building an `insert` statement is getting the columns listed correctly and ensuring that the data type of the value is valid for the inserting column.

When the values are inserted into a new row, each value corresponds to an insert column. The insert columns may be in any order — the order of the columns within the table is irrelevant — as long as the insert columns and the value columns in the SQL insert command are in the same order.

**On the CD-ROM**

The file `Ch 10 - Modifying Data.sql` on this book's CD contains all the sample code for this chapter. Additional examples of data-modification statements may be found in any of the sample database "populate" scripts, or in the stored procedures of the OBX Kites sample database.

The following `insert` commands reference the columns in varying order:

```
USE CHA2

INSERT INTO dbo.Guide (LastName, FirstName, Qualifications)
    VALUES ('Smith', 'Dan', 'Diver, Whitewater Rafting')

INSERT INTO dbo.Guide (FirstName, LastName, Qualifications)
    VALUES ('Jeff', 'Davis', 'Marine Biologist, Diver')

INSERT INTO dbo.Guide (FirstName, LastName)
    VALUES ('Tammie', 'Commer')
```

The following select command verifies the insert:

```
SELECT * FROM dbo.Guide
```

Result (your listing may be different depending on the data loaded into the database):

```
GuideID  LastName    FirstName    Qualifications
-------- ----------  -----------  ----------------------------
1        Smith       Dan          Diver, Whitewater Rafting
2        Davis       Jeff         Marine Biologist, Diver
3        Commer      Tammie       NULL
```

Not every column in the table has to be listed, but if the column is listed, then a value has to be available for the insert command. The third insert statement in the previous sample code left off the qualifications column. The insert operation worked nonetheless, and inserted a null into the omitted column.

If the Qualifications column had default constraint, the default value would have been inserted instead of the null. When a column has both no default and a Not Null constraint, and when no value is provided in the insert statement, the insert operation will fail. (There's more about inserting defaults and nulls in the "Potential Data-Modification Obstacles" section later in this chapter.)

It's possible to explicitly force the insert of a default without knowing the default value. If the keyword DEFAULT is provided in the value-column list, SQL Server will store the default value for the column. This is a good practice because it documents the intention of the code rather than leaving the code blank and assuming the default.

Explicitly listing the columns is a good idea. It prevents an error if the table schema changes, and it helps document the insert. However, the insert-column list is optional. In this case, the values are inserted into the table according to the order of the columns in the table (ignoring an identity column). It's critical that every table column receive valid data from the value list. Omitting a column in the value list will cause the insert operation to fail.

Just as when the columns are explicitly listed within the insert/values command, an identity column can't receive a value, so the identity column is also ignored in the value list when the columns are assumed. The rest of the values are in the same order as the columns of the Guide table, as follows:

```
INSERT Guide
  VALUES ('Jones', 'Lauren',
      'First Aid, Rescue/Extraction','6/25/59','4/15/01')
```

To view the inserted data, the following select command pulls data from the Guide table:

```
SELECT GuideID, LastName, FirstName, Qualifications
  FROM dbo.Guide
```

Result:

```
GuideID  LastName    FirstName    Qualifications
-------- ----------  -----------  ----------------------------
1        Smith       Dan          Diver, Whitewater Rafting
2        Davis       Jeff         Marine Biologist, Diver
3        Commer      Tammie       NULL
4        Jones       Lauren       First Aid, Rescue/Extraction
```

So far in the sample code, values have been hard-coded string literals. Alternately, the value could be returned from an expression. This is useful when a data type requires conversion, or when data need to be altered, calculated, or concatenated:

```
INSERT dbo.Guide (FirstName, LastName, Qualifications)
  VALUES ('Greg', 'Wilson',
          'Rock Climbing' + ', ' + 'First Aid')
```

The next select statement verifies Greg's insert:

```
Select * FROM dbo.Guide
```

Result:

```
GuideID  LastName    FirstName    Qualifications
-------- ----------  -----------  ------------------------------
1        Smith       Dan          Diver, Whitewater Rafting
2        Davis       Jeff         Marine Biologist, Diver
3        Commer      Tammie       NULL
4        Jones       Lauren       First Aid, Rescue/Extraction
5        Wilson      Greg         Rock Climbing, First Aid
(5 row(s) affected)
```

When the data to be inserted, usually in the form of variables sent from the user interface, are known, inserting using the insert/values form is the best insert method. But this method isn't very dynamic. If data already exists in the database, the most efficient and flexible method is using the insert/select form.

## Inserting a Result Set from Select

Data may be moved and massaged from one result set into a table by means of the insert/select statement. The real power of this method is that the select command can pull data from nearly anywhere and reshape it to fit the current needs. It's this flexibility the insert/select statement exploits. Because select can return an infinite number of rows, this form can insert an infinite number of rows. The syntax is as follows:

```
INSERT [INTO] owner.Table
  SELECT columns
    FROM data sources
    [WHERE conditions]
```

**Cross-Reference** For a comprehensive discussion of the select portion of this command, turn to Chapter 6, "Retrieving Data with Select."

As with the insert/values statement, the data columns must line up and the data types must be valid. If the optional insert columns are ignored, every table column (except an identity column) must be populated in the table order.

The following code sample uses the OBX Kites database. It selects all the guides from the Cape Hatteras Adventures database and inserts them into the OBX Kites' Contact table. The name columns are pulled from the Guide table, while the company name is a string literal. (Note that the Guide table is specified by means of a three-part name: *database. owner.table*.)

```
USE OBXKites
-- Using a fresh copy of OBXKites without population

INSERT dbo.Contact (FirstName, LastName, CompanyName)
  SELECT FirstName, LastName, 'Cape Hatteras Adventures'
    FROM CHA2.dbo.Guide
```

To verify the insert, the following `select` statement reads the data from the `Contact` table:

```
SELECT FirstName AS First, LastName AS Last, CompanyName
  FROM dbo.Contact
```

Result:

```
First      Last       CompanyName
---------  ---------  -----------------------
Dan        Smith      Cape Hatteras Adv.
Jeff       Davis      Cape Hatteras Adv.
Tammie     Commer     Cape Hatteras Adv.
Lauren     Jones      Cape Hatteras Adv.
Greg       Wilson     Cape Hatteras Adv.

(5 row(s) affected)
```

The key to using the `insert/select` statement is selecting the correct result set. It's a good idea to run the `select` statement by itself to test the result set prior to executing the insert. Measure twice, cut once.

## Inserting the Result Set from a Stored Procedure

The `insert/exec` form of the `insert` operation pulls data from a stored procedure and inserts them into a table. Behind these inserts are the full capabilities of T-SQL. The basic function is the same as that of the other insert forms. The columns have to line up between the `insert` columns and the stored-procedure result set. Here's the basic syntax of the `insert/exec` command:

```
INSERT [INTO] owner.Table [(Columns)]
  EXEC StoredProcedure Parameters
```

Be careful though, because stored procedures can easily return multiple record sets. In which case, the `insert` attempts to pull data from each of the result sets, and the columns from every result set must line up with the insert columns.

**Cross-Reference** For more about programming stored procedures, refer to Chapter 13, "Developing Stored Procedures."

The following code sample builds a stored procedure that returns the first and last names of all guides from both the Cape Hatteras Adventures database and Microsoft's Northwind sample database. Next, the code creates a table as a place to insert the result sets. Once the stored procedure and the receiving table are in place, the sample code performs the `insert/exec` statement:

```
Use CHA2

CREATE PROC ListGuides
AS
  SET NOCOUNT ON
```

```
-- result set 1
SELECT  FirstName, LastName
  FROM dbo.Guide
-- result set 1
SELECT  FirstName, LastName
  FROM northwind.dbo.employees
RETURN
```

When the ListGuides stored procedure is executed, two result sets should be produced:

```
Exec ListGuides
```

Result:

```
FirstName                  LastName
----------------------     ----------------------
Dan                        Smith
Jeff                       Davis
Tammie                     Commer
Lauren                     Jones
Wilson                     Greg

FirstName   LastName
----------  ----------------------
Nancy       Davolio
Andrew      Fuller
Janet       Leverling
Margaret    Peacock
Steven      Buchanan
Michael     Suyama
Robert      King
Laura       Callahan
Anne        Dodsworth
```

The following DDL command creates a table that matches the structure of the procedure's result sets:

```
CREATE TABLE dbo.GuideSample
  (FirstName VARCHAR(50),
   LastName VARCHAR(50) )
```

With the situation properly setup, here's the insert/exec command:

```
INSERT dbo.GuideSample (FirstName, LastName)
  EXEC ListGuides
```

A select command can read the data and verify that 14 rows were inserted:

```
SELECT * FROM dbo.GuideSample
```

Result:

```
FirstName              LastName
--------------------   --------------------
Dan                    Smith
Jeff                   Davis
Tammie                 Commer
Lauren                 Jones
```

```
Wilson          Greg
Nancy           Davolio
Andrew          Fuller
Janet           Leverling
Margaret        Peacock
Steven          Buchanan
Michael         Suyama
Robert          King
Laura           Callahan
Anne            Dodsworth
```

Insert/exec does require more work than insert/values or insert/select, but because the stored procedure can contain complex logic, it's the most powerful of the three.

**Caution**  The insert/exec and select/into forms will not insert data into table variables. Table variables are covered in Chapter 12, "Programming with Transact SQL."

## Creating a Default Row

SQL includes a special form of the insert command that creates a new row with only default values. The only parameter of the new row is that the table name, data, and column names are neither required nor accepted. The syntax is very simple as this code sample shows:

```
INSERT owner.Table DEFAULT VALUES
```

I have never used this form of insert in any real-world applications. Nevertheless, if you ever need to pre-populate a table with numerous default rows, insert default may be of use.

## Creating a Table While Inserting Data

The last method of inserting data is a variation on the select command. The into select option will take the results of a select statement and create a new table containing the results. Select/into is often used during data conversions and within utilities that must dynamically work with a variety of source-table structures. The full syntax includes every select option. Here's an abbreviated syntax to highlight the function of the into option:

```
SELECT Columns
  INTO NewTable
  FROM DataSources
  [WHERE conditions]
```

The data structure of the newly created table might be less of an exact replication of the original table structure than expected because the new table structure is based on a combination of the original table and the result set of the select statement. String lengths and numerical digit lengths may change. If the select/into command is pulling data from only one table and the select statement contains no data-type conversion functions, there's a good chance that the table columns and null settings will remain intact. However, keys, constraints, and indexes will be lost.

Select/into is a bulk-logged operation, similar to bulk insert and bulk copy. Bulk-logged operations may enable SQL Server to quickly move data into tables by skipping the transaction-logging process (depending on the database's recovery model). Therefore, the database options and recovery model affect `select/into` and the other bulk-logged operations. If the database-recovery model is other than full, the `select/into` operation will not be logged.

**Cross-Reference**

For more about `bulk insert` **and** `bulk copy`, **refer to Chapter 17, "Transferring Databases." For details on recovery models refer to Chapter 26, "Recovery Planning."**

The following code sample demonstrates the `select/into` command as it creates the new table `GuideList` by extracting data from `Guide` (some results abridged):

```
USE CHA2

-- sample code for setting the bulk-logged behavior
Alter DATABASE CHA2 SET RECOVERY FULL
SP_DBOPTION 'CHA2', 'select into/bulkcopy', 'TRUE'

-- the select/into statement
SELECT *
  INTO dbo.GuideList
  FROM dbo.Guide
  ORDER BY Lastname, FirstName
```

The `sp_help` command can display the structure of a table. Here it's being used to verify the structure that was created by the `select/into` command:

```
sp_help GuideList
```

Results (some columns abridged):

```
Name          Owner     Type          Created_datetime
-----------   --------  ------------  -----------------------
GuideList     dbo       user table    2001-08-01 16:30:02.937


Column_name         Type        Length    Prec  Scale Nullable
-----------------   ----------  --------- ----- ----- --------
GuideID             int         4         10    0     no
LastName            varchar     50                    no
FirstName           varchar     50                    no
Qualifications      varchar     2048                  yes
DateOfBirth         datetime    8                     yes
DateHire            datetime    8                     yes

Identity        Seed      Increment   Not For Replication
--------------  --------  ----------  -----------------------
GuideID         1         1           0

RowGuidCol
---------------------------
No rowguidcol column defined.

Data_located_on_filegroup
---------------------------
```

```
PRIMARY

The object does not have any indexes.

No constraints have been defined for this object.

No foreign keys reference this table.
No views with schema binding reference this table.
```

The following insert adds a new row to test the identity column that was created by the select/into:

```
INSERT Guidelist (LastName, FirstName, Qualifications)
  VALUES('Nielsen', 'Paul', 'trainer')
```

To view the data that was inserted using the select/into command and the row that was just added with the insert/values command, the following select statement extracts data from the GuideList table:

```
SELECT GuideID, LastName, FirstName
  FROM dbo.GuideList
```

Result:

```
GuideID     LastName     FirstName
----------- ------------ --------------------------
12          Nielsen      Paul
7           Atlas        Sue
11          Bistier      Arnold
3           Commer       Tammie
2           Davis        Jeff
10          Fletcher     Bill
5           Greg         Wilson
4           Jones        Lauren
1           Smith        Dan
```

In this case, the select/into command retained the column lengths and null settings. The identity column was also carried over to the new table, although this may not always be the case. I recommend that you build tables manually, or at least carefully check the data structures created by select/into.

Select/into can serve many useful functions, such as:

✦ If zero rows are selected from a table, select/into will create a new table with only the data schema.

✦ If select reorders the columns, or includes the cast() function, the new table will retain the data within a modified data schema.

✦ When combined with a union query, select/into can combine data from multiple tables vertically. The into goes in the first select statement of a union query.

✦ Select/into is especially useful for de-normalizing tables. The select statement can pull from multiple tables and create a new flat-file table.

✦ Select/into can create a copy of the inserted and deleted tables with a trigger, to pass them to a stored procedure or dynamic SQL statement. This technique is one way to build a dynamic audit trigger, and is demonstrated in Chapter 16, "Advanced Server-Side Programming."

## Developing a Data Style Guide

There are potential data troubles that go beyond data types, nullability, and check constraints. Just as MS Word's spelling checker and grammar checker can weed out the obvious errors but also create poor (or libelous) literature, a database can only protect against gross logical errors. Publishers use manuals of style and style guides for consistency. For example, should Microsoft be referred to as MS, Microsoft Corp., or Microsoft Corporation in a book or article? The publisher's chosen style manual provides the answer.

Databases can also benefit from a data style guide that details your organization's preferences about how data should be formatted. Do phone numbers include parentheses around the area codes? Are phone extensions indicated by "x." or "ext."?

One way to begin developing a style guide is to spend some time just looking at the data and observing the existing inconsistencies. Having done that, try to find consensus about a common data style. Picking up a copy of *The Chicago Manual of Style, 14th Edition* will also provide some ideas. There's no magical right or wrong style — the goal is simply data consistency.

 **Caution**  One caveat concerning `select/into` and development style is that the `select/into` statement should not replace the use of joins or views. When the new table is created it's a snapshot in time — a second copy of the data. Databases containing multiple copies of old datasets are a sure sign of trouble. If you need to de-normalize data for ad-hoc analysis, or to pass to a user, creating a view is likely a better alternative.

# Updating Data

Without being overly dramatic, SQL's `update` command is an incredibly powerful tool. What used to take dozens of lines of code with multiple nested loops now takes a single statement. What's even cooler is that SQL is not a true command language; it's a declarative language. The SQL code is only describing to the Query Optimizer what you want to do. The Query Optimizer then develops a cost-based optimized query-execution plan to accomplish the task. It figures out which tables to fetch and in which order, how to merge the joins, and which indexes to use. And it does this based on several factors, including the current data-population statistics, the indexes available and how they relate to the data population within the table, and table sizes. The Query Optimizer even considers the current CPU performance, memory capacity, and hard-drive performance when designing the plan. Writing code to perform the update row by row could never result in that level of optimization.

## Updating a Single Table

The `update` command in SQL is straightforward and simple. The `update` command can update one column of one row in a table, or every column in every row in the updated table, but the optional `from` clause enables that table be a part of a complete complex data source with all the power of the SQL `select`.

Here's how the `update` command works:

```
UPDATE dbo.Table
  SET column = value or expression or column,
    column = value...
```

```
[FROM  data sources]
[WHERE conditions]
```

The update command can update multiple rows, but only one table. The set keyword is used to modify data in any column in the table to a new value. The new value can be a hard-coded string literal, a variable, an expression, or even another column from the data sources listed in the from portion of the SQL update statement.

 **Cross-Reference**  For a comprehensive listing of expression possibilities see Chapter 6, "Retrieving Data With Select."

The where clause is vital to any update statement. Without it the entire table is updated. If a where clause is present, every row not filtered out by the where clause is updated. Be sure to check and double-check the where clause. Measure twice, cut once.

The following sample update resembles a typical real-life operation and will alter the value of one column for a single row. The best way to perform a single-row update is to filter the update operation by referencing the primary key.

```
USE CHA2

UPDATE dbo.Guide
  SET Qualifications = 'Spelunking, Cave Diving,
First Aid, Navigation'
  Where GuideID = 6
```

The following select statement confirms the previous update command:

```
SELECT GuideID, LastName, Qualifications
  FROM dbo.Guide
  WHERE GuideID = 6
```

Result:

```
GuideID     LastName                 Qualifications
----------- ------------------------ ---------------
6           Bistier                  Spelunking, Cave Diving,
                                       First Aid, Navigation
```

## Performing Global Search and Replaces

Cleaning up bad data is a common database developer task. Fortunately, SQL includes a replace() function, which when combined with the update command can serve as a global search and replace.

In this code sample, which references the Family sample database, every occurrence of "ll" in the LastName column is updated to "qua":

```
Use Family

Update Person
  Set LastName = Replace(Lastname, 'll', 'qua')
```

The following select statement examines the result of the replace() function:

```
Select lastname from Person
```

Result (abbreviated):

```
lastname
---------------
Haquaoway
Haquaoway
Miquaer
Miquaer
Haquaoway
...
```

## Referencing Multiple Table While Updating Data

A more powerful function of the SQL update command is setting a column to an expression that can refer to the same column, other columns, or even other tables.

While expressions are certainly available within a single-table update, expressions often need to reference data outside the updated table. The optional from clause enables joins between the table being updated and other data sources. Only one table can be updated, but when the table is joined to the corresponding rows from the joined tables the data from the other columns are available within the update expressions.

One way to envision the from clause is to picture the joins merging all the tables into a new super-wide result set. Then the rest of the SQL statement sees only that new result set. And while that's what's happening in the from clause, the actual update operation is functioning not on the new result set, but only on the declared update Table.

**Caution**

The update   from **syntax is a T-SQL extension and not standard ASNI SQL 92. If the database will possibly be ported to another database platform in the future, use a subquery to update the correct rows:**

```
DELETE FROM Table1 a
  WHERE EXISTS (SELECT *
                 FROM Table2 b
                 WHERE
                     EMPL_STATUS = 'A'
                 AND
                     a.EMPLID = b.EMPLID
               )
```

For a real-life example, all employees will soon be granted a generous across-the-board raise (OK, I confess, it's not real life) based on department, time in position, performance rating, and time with the company. If the percentage for each department is stored in the Department table, SQL can adjust the salary for every employee with a single update statement by joining the Employee table with the Department table and pulling the Department raise factor from the joined table. Assume the formula is as follows:

```
2 + (((Years in Company * .1) + (Months in Position * .02)
  + ((PerformanceFactor * .5 ) if over 2))
  * Department RaiseFactor)
```

The sample code will set up the scenario by creating a couple of tables, populating them, and testing the formula before the code finally performs the update:

```
CREATE TABLE dbo.Dept (
  DeptID INT IDENTITY NOT NULL PRIMARY KEY NONCLUSTERED,
  DeptName VARCHAR(50) NOT NULL,
  RaiseFactor NUMERIC(4,2)
    )
  ON [Primary]
go

Create  TABLE dbo.Employee (
  EmployeeID INT IDENTITY NOT NULL PRIMARY KEY NONCLUSTERED,
  DeptID INT FOREIGN KEY REFERENCES Dept,
  LastName VARCHAR(50) NOT NULL,
  FirstName VARCHAR(50) NOT NULL,
  Salary INT,
  PerformanceRating NUMERIC(4,2),
  DateHire DATETIME,
  DatePosition DATETIME
    )
  ON [Primary]
go
 -- build the sample data
INSERT dbo.Dept VALUES ('Engineering', 1.2)
INSERT dbo.Dept VALUES ('Sales',.8)
INSERT dbo.Dept VALUES ('IT',2.5)
INSERT dbo.Dept VALUES ('Manufacturing',1.0)
go
INSERT dbo.Employee
  VALUES( 1,'Smith','Sam',54000, 2.0,'1/1/97','4/1/2001' )
INSERT dbo.Employee
  VALUES( 1,'Nelson','Slim',78000,1.5,'9/1/88','1/1/2000' )
INSERT dbo.Employee
  VALUES( 2,'Ball','Sally',45000,3.5,'2/1/99','1/1/2001' )
INSERT dbo.Employee
  VALUES( 2,'Kelly','Jeff',85000,2.4,'10/1/83','9/1/1998' )
INSERT dbo.Employee
  VALUES( 3,'Guelzow','Jo',120000,4.0,'7/1/95','6/1/2001' )
INSERT dbo.Employee
  VALUES( 3,'Anderson','Missy',95000,1.8,'2/1/99','9/1/97' )
INSERT dbo.Employee
  VALUES( 4,'Reagan','Frank',75000,2.9,'4/1/00','4/1/2000' )
INSERT dbo.Employee
  VALUES( 4,'Adams','Hank',34000,3.2,'9/1/98','9/1/1998' )
```

Assuming 5/1/2002 is the effective date of the raise, this query tests the sample data:

```
SELECT LastName, Salary,
  DateDiff(yy, DateHire, '5/1/2002') as YearsCo,
  DateDiff(mm, DatePosition, '5/1/2002') as MonthPosition,
  CASE
    WHEN Employee.PerformanceRating >= 2
      THEN Employee.PerformanceRating
    ELSE 0
  END as Performance,
  Dept.RaiseFactor AS 'Dept'
```

```
FROM dbo.Employee
JOIN dbo.Dept
  ON Employee.DeptID = Dept.DeptID
```

**Result:**

| LastName | Salary | YearsCo | MonthPosition | Performance | Dept |
|----------|--------|---------|---------------|-------------|------|
| Smith | 54000 | 5 | 13 | 2.00 | 1.20 |
| Nelson | 78000 | 14 | 28 | .00 | 1.20 |
| Ball | 45000 | 3 | 16 | 3.50 | .80 |
| Kelly | 85000 | 19 | 44 | 2.40 | .80 |
| Guelzow | 120000 | 7 | 11 | 4.00 | 2.50 |
| Anderson | 95000 | 3 | 56 | .00 | 2.50 |
| Reagan | 75000 | 2 | 25 | 2.90 | 1.00 |
| Adams | 34000 | 4 | 44 | 3.20 | 1.00 |

Based on the sample data, the following query tests the formula that calculates the raise:

```
SELECT LastName,
  (2 + (((DateDiff(yy, DateHire, '5/1/2002') * .1)
  + (DateDiff(mm, DatePosition, '5/1/2002') * .02)
  + (CASE
      WHEN Employee.PerformanceRating >= 2
        THEN Employee.PerformanceRating
      ELSE 0
    END * .5 ))
  * Dept.RaiseFactor))/100 as EmpRaise
FROM dbo.Employee
JOIN dbo.Dept
  ON Employee.DeptID = Dept.DeptID
```

**Result:**

| LastName | EmpRaise |
|----------|----------|
| Smith | .041120000 |
| Nelson | .043520000 |
| Ball | .038960000 |
| Kelly | .051840000 |
| Guelzow | .093000000 |
| Anderson | .055500000 |
| Reagan | .041500000 |
| Adams | .048800000 |

With the data in place and the formulas verified, the `update` command is ready to adjust the salaries:

```
UPDATE Employee SET Salary = Salary * (1 +
  (2 + (((DateDiff(yy, DateHire, '5/1/2002') * .1)
  + (DateDiff(mm, DatePosition, '5/1/2002') * .02)
  + (CASE
      WHEN Employee.PerformanceRating >= 2
        THEN Employee.PerformanceRating
      ELSE 0
    END * .5 ))
  * Dept.RaiseFactor))/100 )
```

```
    FROM dbo.Employee
JOIN dbo.Dept
   ON Employee.DeptID = Dept.DeptID
```

The next select statement views the fruits of the labor:

```
SELECT FirstName, LastName, Salary
    FROM Employee
```

Result:

```
FirstName    LastName                   Salary
-----------  ------------------------   -----------
Sam          Smith                      56220
Slim         Nelson                     81394
Sally        Ball                       46753
Jeff         Kelly                      89406
Dave         Guelzow                    131160
Missy        Anderson                   100272
Frank        Reagan                     78112
Hank         Adams                      35659
```

The final step of the exercise is to clean up the sample tables:

```
DROP TABLE dbo.Employee
DROP TABLE dbo.Dept
```

This sample code pulls together techniques from many of the previous chapters: creating and dropping tables, case expressions, joins, and date scalar functions, not to mention the inserts and updates from this chapter. The previous example is long because it demonstrates more than just the update statement. It also shows the typical process of developing a complex update, which includes:

1. *Checking the available data*—The first select joins employee and dept, and lists all the columns required for the formula.

2. *Testing the formula*—The second select is based on the initial select and assembles the formula from the required rows. From this data, a couple of rows can be hand-tested against the specs and the formula verified.

3. *Performing the update*—Once the formula is constructed and verified, the formula is edited into an update statement and executed.

The SQL update command *is* powerful. I have replaced terribly complex record sets and nested loops that were painfully slow and error-prone with update statements and creative joins that worked well, and seen execution times reduced from minutes to a few seconds. I cannot over-emphasize the importance of approaching the selection and updating of data in terms of datasets instead of data rows.

# Deleting Data

The delete command is dangerously simple. In its basic form it deletes all the rows from a table, and because the delete command is a row-based operation it doesn't require specifying any column names. The first from is optional, as are the second from and the where conditions. However, even though the where clause is optional, it is the primary subject of concern when you're using the delete command. Here's an abbreviated syntax for the delete command:

```
DELETE FROM] owner.Table
   [FROM data sources]
   [WHERE condition(s)]
```

Notice that everything is optional except the actual delete command and the table name. The following command would delete all data from the product table — no questions asked and no second chances:

```
DELETE
   FROM OBXKites.dbo.Product
```

SQL Server has no inherent "undo" command. Once a transaction is committed, that's it. That's why the where clause is so important when you're deleting.

Log Explorer by Lumigent is a transaction-log viewer that enables you to select and roll back transactions. Using Log Explorer is a possible workaround for an accidental delete. An evaluation copy of Log Explorer is on the book's CD.

By far the most common use of the delete command is to delete a single row. The primary key is usually the means of selecting the row:

```
USE OBXKites
DELETE FROM dbo.Product
   WHERE ProductID = 'DB8D8D60-76F4-46C3-90E6-A8648F63C0F0'
```

## Referencing Multiple Tables While Deleting

The update command uses the from clause to join the updated table with other tables for more flexible row selection. The delete command uses the exact same technique. What makes it look confusing is that first optional from. To improve readability and consistency, I recommend that you leave out the first from in your code.

For example, the following delete statement ignores the first from clause and uses the second from clause to join Product with ProductCategory so the where clause can filter the delete based on the ProductCategoryName. This query removed all videos from the Product table:

```
DELETE Product
   FROM dbo.Product
   JOIN ProductCategory
     ON Procduct.ProductCategoryID
       = ProductCategory.ProductCategoryID
   WHERE ProductcategoryName = 'Video'
```

As with the update command's from clause, the delete command's second from clause is no ANSI standard. If portability is important to your project, use a subquery to reference additional tables.

## Cascading Deletes

*Referential integrity* (RI) refers to the fact that no secondary row may point to a primary row unless that primary row does in fact exist. This means that attempting to delete a primary row will fail if a foreign-key value somewhere points to that primary row.

**Cross-Reference**    For more about referential integrity and when to use it, turn to Chapter 2, "Modeling the Logical Database Schema."

RI will block any delete operation that would violate it. The way around this is to first delete the secondary rows that point to the primary row, and then delete the primary row. This technique is called *cascading the delete* to the lower level. In large databases the cascade might bounce down several levels before working its way back up to the original row being deleted.

Implementing cascading deletes manually is a lot of work. Because foreign-key constraints are checked before triggers, cascading-delete triggers don't work with SQL Server Declared Referential Integrity (DRI) via foreign keys. Therefore, not only will triggers have to handle the cascading delete, but they will have to perform RI checks as well.

Fortunately, SQL Server 2000 offers cascading deletes as a function of the foreign key. Cascading deletes may be enabled via Enterprise Manager (as shown in Figure 10-2) or SQL code.

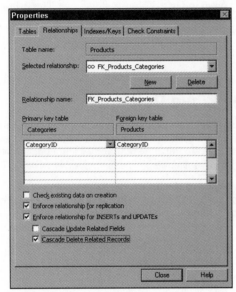

**Figure 10-2:** Setting foreign keys to cascade delete in Enterprise Manager.

The sample script that creates the Cape Hatteras Adventures version 2 database (CHA2_Create.sql) provides a good example of setting the cascade-delete option for referential integrity. In this case, if either the event or the guide is deleted, the rows in the event-guide many-to-many table are also deleted. The on delete cascade foreign-key option is what actually specifies the cascade action:

```
CREATE TABLE dbo.Event_mm_Guide (
  EventGuideID
    INT IDENTITY NOT NULL PRIMARY KEY NONCLUSTERED,
  EventID
    INT NOT NULL
```

```
   FOREIGN KEY REFERENCES dbo.Event ON DELETE CASCADE,
GuideID
   INT NOT NULL
   FOREIGN KEY REFERENCES dbo.Guide ON DELETE CASCADE,
LastName
   VARCHAR(50) NOT NULL,
)
ON [Primary]
```

As a caution, cascading deletes, or even referential integrity, are not for every relationship. It depends on the permanence of the secondary row. If deleting the primary row makes the secondary row moot or meaningless, then cascading the delete makes good sense. But if the secondary row is still a valid row after the primary row is deleted, referential integrity and cascading deletes would cause the database to break its representation of reality.

For a couple of examples of determining the usefulness of cascading delete from the Cape Hatteras Adventures database, if a tour is deleted, all scheduled events for that tour become meaningless, as are the many-to-many schedule tables between event and customer, and between event and guide.

On the other hand, a tour must have a base camp, so referential integrity is required on the Tour.BaseCampID foreign key. However, if a base camp is deleted, the tours originating from that base camp might still be valid (if they can be rescheduled to another base camp), so cascading a base-camp delete down to the tour is not a reasonable action. If RI is on and cascading deletes are off, a base camp with tours cannot be deleted until all tours for that base camp are either manually deleted or reassigned to other base camps.

## Alternatives to Physically Deleting Data

Many developers choose to completely avoid deleting data. Instead they build systems to remove the data from the user's view while retaining them for safekeeping. This can be done in several different ways:

✦ A logical-delete bit flag in the row may indicate that the row is deleted. This makes deleting or restoring a single row a straightforward matter of setting or clearing a bit. But because relational database involves multiple related tables, there's more work to it than that. All queries must check the logical-delete flag and filter out logically deleted rows. In addition, since the rows still physically exist in SQL Server, and the SQL Server referential-integrity system does not know about the logical-delete flag, custom referential integrity and cascading of logical deletes might also be required, depending on how far you want to take the logical-delete system. This method offers fast logical deletes but can slow down selects. Cascading logical deletes can become very complex, and restoring cascaded logical deletes can become a nightmare.

✦ Another alternative to physically deleting rows is to archive the deleted rows in a second table or database. This method is best implemented by a stored procedure that inserts the deleted rows into the archive location and then deletes them from the main production database.

This method offers several advantages. Data is physically removed from the database so there's no need to artificially modify select queries. Using partitioned views, or a federated database scheme makes archiving data easier by allowing queries to automatically gather data from multiple databases. Physically removing the data lets SQL Server referential integrity remain in effect. Also, the database is not burdened with unnecessary data. Retrieving archived data remains relatively straightforward. On the down side, using the archive method requires maintaining an archive location.

**Cross-Reference**

See Chapter 30, "Advanced Scalability," for more on partitioned views and federated databases. Chapter 31, "Analysis Services," contains some strategies for data warehousing archived data.

✦ The most complete alternative to deleting rows is using a full audit trail of all data modifications. An audit trail is not only useful for viewing a history of updates, but can be used for restoring deleted rows as well. Audit trails have their own cost in terms of complexity, performance, and storage space.

**Cross-Reference**

Chapter 16, "Advanced Server-Side Programming," explains how to build triggers that perform cascading deletes, manage custom referential integrity, build audit trails, archive data, and logically delete rows.

# Potential Data-Modification Obstacles

Even assuming that the logic is correct and that the data-modification command is in fact modifying the correct rows with the correct values, plenty can still go wrong. This section is a survey of several types of potential problems and how to avoid them.

As Table 10-2 illustrates, insert and update operations face more obstacles than delete operations because they are creating new data in the table that must pass multiple validation rules. The delete operation only removes data and is therefore only faced with a few possible obstacles.

### Table 10-2: Potential Data Modification Obstacles

| Potential Problem | Insert Operation | Update Operation | Delete Operation |
|---|---|---|---|
| Data Type/Length | X | X | |
| Primary Key | X | X | |
| Foreign Key | X | X | X |
| Unique Index | X | X | |
| Not Null and No Default | X | X | |
| Check Constraint | X | X | |
| Instead of Trigger | X | X | X |
| After Trigger | X | X | X |
| Non-Updatable Views | X | X | X |
| Views with check option | X | X | |
| Security | X | X | X |

## Data Type/Length Obstacles

Column data type/length may affect insert and update operations.

One the first checks the new data must pass is that of data type and data length. Often, a data type error is caused by missing or extra quotes. SQL Server is particular about implicit, or automatic, data-type conversion. Conversions that function automatically in other programming languages often fail in SQL Server, as shown in the following code sample:

```
USE OBXKites
INSERT Price (ProductID, Price, EffectiveDate)
   Values ('DB8D8D60-76F4-46C3-90E6-A8648F63C0F0',
             '15.00', 6/25/2002 )
```

```
Server: Msg 260, Level 16, State 1, Line 1
Disallowed implicit conversion from data type varchar
to data type money, table 'OBXKites.dbo.Price',
column 'Price'.
Use the CONVERT function to run this query.
```

The problem with the preceding code is the quotes around the new price value, which SQL Server doesn't automatically convert from string to numeric. If this is the problem, using the cast() or convert() function is the best means of handling the data

**Cross-Reference**
For more details about data types and tables refer to Chapter 5, "Implementing the Physical Database Schema." Data-type conversion and conversion scalar functions are discussed in Chapter 6, "Retrieving Data with Select."

Working with very large data objects such as ntext, text, or image columns can sometimes present difficulties. If the object is less than 8,000 bytes in size then you can handle it as standard data. However, larger data objects must often be retrieved or updated in smaller units by the calling API interface. ADO, for example uses a getchunk method to retrieve a portion of a BLOB (Binary Large Object).

## Primary Key Obstacles

Primary keys may affect insert and update operations.

Primary keys, by definition, must be unique. Attempting to insert a primary key that's already in use will cause an error.

Technically speaking, updating a primary key to a value already in use will also cause an error. However, if you are following good design practices the primary key is meaningless to humans, and there should be no reason ever to update a primary key.

Updating a primary key may also break referential integrity, causing the update to fail. In this case, however, it's not a primary-key constraint that's the obstacle, but the foreign-key constraint that references the primary key.

**Cross-Reference**
For more about the design of primary keys refer to Chapter 2, "Modeling the Logical Database Schema." For details on creating primary keys refer to Chapter 5, "Implementing the Physical Database Schema."

One particular issue related to inserting is the creation of primary-key values for the new rows. SQL Server provides two excellent means of generating primary keys: *identity columns* and *GUIDs*. Each method has its pros and cons, and its rules for safe handling.

Identity columns are SQL Server–generated incrementing integers. SQL Server generates them at the time of the insert and the SQL insert statement can't interfere with that process by supplying a value for the identity column.

The fact that identity columns refuse to accept data can be a serious issue if you're inserting existing data whose primary key is already referenced by secondary tables. In the Aesop's Fables sample database, for example, the primary keys are hard-coded into the insert/value statements in the populate scripts, much as the primary keys are already known during data conversions.

The solution is to use the identity_insert database option. When set on it temporarily turns off the identity column and permits the insertion of data into an identity column. This means that the insert has to explicitly provide the primary-key value. The identity_insert option may only be set on for one table at a time within a database. The following SQL batch uses the identity_insert when supplying the primary key:

```
USE CHA2

-- attempt to insert into an identity column
INSERT dbo.Guide (GuideID, FirstName, LastName)
  VALUES (10, 'Bill', 'Fletcher')
```

Result:

```
Server: Msg 544, Level 16, State 1, Line 1
Cannot insert explicit value for identity column in table
'Guide' when IDENTITY_INSERT is set to OFF.
```

The next step in the batch sets the identity_insert option and attempt some more inserts:

```
SET IDENTITY_INSERT Guide On

INSERT Guide (GuideID, FirstName, LastName)
  VALUES (10, 'Bill', 'Mays')

INSERT dbo.Guide (GuideID, FirstName, LastName)
  VALUES (7, 'Sue', 'Atlas')
```

To see what value the identity column is now assigning, the following code re-enables the identity column and inserts another row, and then selects the new data:

```
SET IDENTITY_INSERT Guide Off

INSERT Guide ( FirstName, LastName)
  VALUES ( 'Arnold', 'Bistier')

SELECT GuideID, FirstName, LastName
  FROM dbo.Guide
```

Result:

```
GuideID     FirstName     LastName
----------- ------------- -------------------------
1           Dan           Smith
2           Jeff          Davis
3           Tammie        Commer
4           Lauren        Jones
5           Greg          Wilson
10          Bill          Mays
7           Sue           Atlas
11          Arnold        Bistier
```

As this code demonstrated, manually inserting a GuideID of "10" set the identity column next value to "11."

Another potential problem when working with identity columns is in determining the value of the identity that was just created. Because the new identity value is created with SQL Server at the time of the insert, the code causing the insert is unaware of the identity value. The `insert` works fine, the problem occurs when the code inserts a row and then tries to display the row on a user-interface grid within an application, because the code is unaware of the new data's database assigned primary key.

SQL Server provides three methods of determining the identity value.

✦ `@@identity` — This venerable global variable returns the last identity value generated by SQL Server for any table, connection, or scope. If another insert takes place between the time of your insert and the time when you check `@@identity`, `@@identity` will return not your insert, but the last insert.

✦ `scope_identity ()` — New to SQL Server 2000, this system function returns the last generated identity value within the scope of the calling batch or procedure. I recommend using this method, as it is the safest way to determine the identity value you last generated.

✦ `ident_current (table)` — Also new to SQL Server 2000, the `ident_current ()` function returns the last identity value per table. While this option seems similar to `scope_identity()`, `ident_current()` returns the identity value for the given table regardless of inserts to any other tables that may have occurred. This prevents another insert, buried deep within a trigger, from affecting the identity value returned by the function.

Global unique identifiers (GUIDs) make excellent primary keys. With regard to the insertion of new rows, the major difference between identity columns and GUIDs is that GUIDs are generated by the SQL code or by a column default rather than automatically at the time of the insert. This means that the developer has more control over the GUID creation. If a value is inserted into a column with a default, it's no problem: The inserted value is placed into the new row. The default is only used when no value is provided by the `insert` statement. While GUIDs are a good choice for other reasons as well, the ease of working with a GUID default is certainly a good reason by itself.

**Cross-Reference**    For more about the design issues that pertain to primary keys, and for more about GUIDs versus identity columns, see Chapter 5, "Implementing the Physical Database Schema."

GUIDs are created by the `newid()` function. If the default of the primary key is set to `NewID()` a new GUID is generated for any new row. In addition, the `newid()` function may be declared within an `insert/values` list. The `newid()` function will even work as an expression in an `insert/select` that selects multiple rows. Within stored procedures or front-end code the function may be called and the GUID stored in a variable. The variable is then used in the `insert/values` statement and inserted into the new row. Any of these options will work well, and they may be combined within an application.

The advantage of predetermining the GUID in code and then sending it with the `insert/values` command is that the program then already knows the primary key of the new row and can continue working with it without having to figure out the primary key of the row it just inserted. The flexibility of the GUID is that if the situation warrants predetermining the GUID, that's great, while if there's no reason to predetermine the GUID, the default `newid ()` works just as well.

The following sample code demonstrates various methods of generating GUID primary keys during the addition of new rows to the ProductCategory table in the OBXKites database. The first query simply tests the newid() function:

```
USE OBXKites

Select NewID()
```

Result:

```
5CBB2800-5207-4323-A316-E963AACB6081
```

The next three queries insert GUID, each using a different method of generating the GUID:

```
--  GUID from Default (the columns default is NewID())
INSERT dbo.ProductCategory
  (ProductCategoryID, ProductCategoryName)
  VALUES (DEFAULT, 'From Default')

-- GUID from function
INSERT dbo.ProductCategory
    (ProductCategoryID, ProductCategoryName)
  VALUES (NewID(), 'From Function')

-- GUID in variable
DECLARE @NewGUID UniqueIdentifier
SET @NewGUID = NewID()

INSERT dbo.ProductCategory
    (ProductCategoryID, ProductCategoryName)
  VALUES (@NewGUID, 'From Variable')
```

To view the results of the previous three methods of inserting GUID, the following select statement is filtered to those rows that are like "from %":

```
SELECT ProductCategoryID, ProductCategoryName
  FROM dbo.ProductCategory
    WHERE ProductCategoryName LIKE 'From %'
```

Result:

```
ProductCategoryID                    ProductCategoryName
------------------------------------ ----------------------
25894DA7-B5BB-435D-9540-6B9207C6CF8F From Default
393414DC-8611-4460-8FD3-4657E4B49373 From Function
FF868338-DF9A-4B8D-89B6-9C28293CA25F From Variable
```

This insert statement uses the newid() function to insert multiple GUIDs:

```
INSERT dbo.ProductCategory
    (ProductCategoryID, ProductCategoryName)
  Select NewID(), LastName
    From CHA2.dbo.Guide
```

The following select statement retrieves the new GUIDs:

```
SELECT ProductCategoryID, ProductCategoryName
  FROM dbo.ProductCategory
```

Result:

```
ProductCategoryID                       ProductCategoryName
------------------------------------    --------------------
1B2BBE15-B415-43ED-BCA2-293050B7EFE4    Kite
23FC5D45-8B60-4800-A505-D2F556F863C9    Accessory
3889671A-F2CD-4B79-8DCF-19F4F4703693    Video
...
5471F896-A414-432B-A579-0880757ED097    Fletcher
428F29B3-111B-4ECE-B6EB-E0913A9D34DC    Atlas
E4B7D325-8122-48D7-A61B-A83E258D8729    Bistier
```

SQL Server provides the flexibility of two excellent candidates for primary key generation. Whether the database relies on identity columns or GUIDs may be based on other factors. Either way, there are multiple methods for inserting new rows. And you, as the SQL developer, or DBA, are in control.

## Foreign Key Obstacles

Foreign keys may affect `insert`, `update`, and `delete` operations.

A foreign key may cause block inserts, updates, and deletes. Inserting a new secondary table row with a foreign key value that doesn't match an existing primary key will cause the secondary row insert to fail.

In the following insert example, the `ProductCategoryID` supplied does not exist in the `ProductCategory` table. This causes the foreign-key constraint to block the `insert` operation, as the error message indicates:

```
-- Foreign Key: Insert Obstacle
INSERT Product (ProductID, Code,
    ProductCategoryID, ProductName)
  VALUES ('9562C1A5-4499-4626-BB33-E5E140ACD2AC',
    '999'
    'DB8D8D60-76F4-46C3-90E6-A8648F63C0F0',
    'Basic Box Kite 21"')


Server: Msg 547, Level 16, State 1, Line 1
INSERT statement conflicted with COLUMN FOREIGN KEY
constraint 'FK__Product__Product__7B905C75'.
The conflict occurred in database 'OBXKites',
table 'ProductCategory', column 'ProductCategoryID'.
The statement has been terminated.
```

Note that since every GUID is unique, the GUIDs you will use on your system will be different.

Foreign key constraints can also block updates to either the primary or secondary table. If the primary key is updated and a foreign key is pointed to that primary key, the update will fail.

In the following sample code the update is blocked because the secondary table update is trying to set the foreign key, `ProductCategoryID`, to a value that does not exist in the `ProductCategory` table:

```
-- Foreign Key: Secondary table Update Obstacle
UPDATE Product
  SET ProductCategoryID =
```

```
      'DB8D8D60-76F4-46C3-90E6-A8648F63C0F0'
  WHERE ProductID = '67804443-7E7C-4769-A41C-3DD3CD3621D9'

Server: Msg 547, Level 16, State 1, Line 1
UPDATE statement conflicted with COLUMN FOREIGN KEY
Constraint 'FK__Product__Product__7B905C75'.
The conflict occurred in database 'OBXKites',
table 'ProductCategory', column 'ProductCategoryID'.
The statement has been terminated.
```

Updating a primary key to a new value, if foreign keys are pointing to it, has the same effect as deleting a primary-table row with an existing secondary-table row referring to it. In both cases the error is caused not by the primary key but by the foreign key referencing the primary key.

In the following code the error is generated not by the `ProductCategory` table, even though it's the table being updated, but by the `Product` table. This is because the `Product` table has the foreign key reference constraint and the row that will be violated if the primary key value no longer exists:

```
-- Foreign Key: Primary table Update Obstacle
UPDATE ProductCategory
  SET ProductCategoryID =
    'DB8D8D60-76F4-46C3-90E6-A8648F63C0F0'
  WHERE ProductCategoryID =
    '1B2BBE15-B415-43ED-BCA2-293050B7EFE4'

Server: Msg 547, Level 16, State 1, Line 1
UPDATE statement conflicted with COLUMN REFERENCE constraint
'FK__Product__Product__7B905C75'. The conflict occurred
in database 'OBXKites', table 'Product',
column 'ProductCategoryID'.
The statement has been terminated.
```

**Cross-Reference**

For more about referential integrity in the design of foreign keys refer to Chapter 2, "Modeling the Logical Database Schema." For more about creating foreign keys refer to Chapter 5, "Implementing the Physical Database Schema."

## Unique Index Obstacles

Unique indexes may affect `insert` and `update` operations.

If a column has a unique index (even if it's not a key) attempting to insert a new value, or an update to a new value that's already in use, will fail.

Typically the entire transaction, including all the inserted or updated rows, will fail. However, there's an index option, `ignore dup key`, that will allow the transaction to succeed with only a warning, and just skip any duplicate rows.

**Cross-Reference**

For more about creating unique indexes refer to Chapter 5, "Implementing the Physical Database Schema."

## Null and Default Obstacles

Column nullability and defaults may affect insert and update operations.

An insert or update operation can send one of four possible values to a table column: data values, null, default, or nothing at all. The table column can be configured with a default value and nullability. Table 10-3 indicates the result of the operation, according to the column configuration and the new value to be inserted or updated. For example, if the column properties are set so that the column has a default and accept nulls (in the far-right column) and the SQL insert or update sends a null the result is an error.

### Table 10-3: Data Modifications, Defaults, and Nulls

| *Column Properties:* | | | | |
|---|---|---|---|---|
| *Column Default:* | no default<br>has default | no default | has default | |
| *Column Nullability:* | null | not null | null | not null |
| *SQL Sent:* | *Result:* | | | |
| data | data | data | data | data |
| null | null | error | null | error |
| default | null | error | default | default |
| nothing sent | null | most common error | default | default |

By far the most common error in the preceding table is submitting nothing when no default exists and nulls are not permitted.

For more about creating defaults and null constraints refer to Chapter 5, "Implementing the Physical Database Schema." For more information about dealing with nulls when retrieving data, see Chapter 6, "Retrieving Data with Select."

## Check Constraint Obstacles

Check constraints may affect insert and update operations.

Each table column may have multiple check constraints. These are fast Boolean operations that determine if the update will pass or fail.

The following check constraint permits Dr. Johnson's insert, but blocks Greg's insert (note that the check constraint is already applied to the database by the Create_CHA2.sql script):

```
USE CHA2
go
ALTER TABLE dbo.Guide ADD CONSTRAINT
  CK_Guide_Age21 CHECK (DateDiff(yy,DateOfBirth, DateHire)
    >= 21)
```

The following query inserts Dr. Johnsons' data. Since she is 26 years old, her row is accepted by the check constraint:

```
INSERT Guide(lastName, FirstName, Qualifications, DateOfBirth,
DateHire)
   VALUES ('Johnson', 'Mary',
                'E.R. Physician', '1/14/71', '6/1/97')
```

Greg, on the other hand, is only 19, so his insert is rejected by the check constraint:

```
INSERT Guide (lastName, FirstName,
    Qualifications, DateOfBirth, DateHire)
   VALUES ('Franklin', 'Greg',
     'Guide', '12/12/83', '1/1/2002')


Server: Msg 547, Level 16, State 1, Line 1
INSERT statement conflicted with TABLE CHECK constraint
'CK_Guide_Age21'.
The conflict occurred in database 'CHA2', table 'Guide'.
The statement has been terminated.
```

**Cross-Reference**    For more about creating check constraints, their benefits and limitations, refer to Chapter 5, "Implementing the Physical Database Schema."

## Instead of Trigger Obstacles

Instead of triggers may affect insert, update, and delete operations.

Triggers are special stored procedures that are attached to a table and that fire when certain data-modification operations hit that table. Two types of triggers exist: instead of and after. They differ both in their timing and in how they handle the data-modification operation.

An instead of trigger always causes the insert, update, or delete operation to be canceled. The SQL command submitted to SQL Server is discarded by the instead of trigger; the code within the instead of trigger is executed *instead of* the submitted SQL command, hence the name. The instead of trigger might be programmed to repeat the requested operation so that it looks like it went through, or it could do something else altogether.

The problem with the instead of trigger is that it reports back "one row affected" when in fact nothing is written to database. There is no error warning because the instead of trigger works properly; however, the operation doesn't go through.

In the following code sample, the InsteadOfDemo trigger causes the insert operation to disappear into thin air:

```
USE CHA2
go

CREATE TRIGGER InsteadOfDemo
ON Guide
INSTEAD OF INSERT
AS
  Print 'Instead of trigger demo'
Return
```

With the instead of trigger in place, the following query inserts a test row:

```
INSERT Guide(lastName, FirstName,
    Qualifications, DateOfBirth, DateHire)
  VALUES ('Jamison', 'Tom',
    'Biologist, Adventurer', '1/14/56', '9/1/99')
```

Result:

```
Instead of trigger demo
(1 row(s) affected)
```

The insert operation appears to have worked, but is the row in the table?

```
SELECT GuideID
  FROM Guide
  WHERE LastName = 'Jamison'
```

Result:

```
GuideID
-----------

(0 row(s) affected)
```

Building triggers is explained in detail in Chapter 15, "Implementing Triggers." The flow of data-modification transactions and the timing of triggers are also discussed in Chapter 11, "Transactional Integrity."

Note that the sample code for this chapter on the CD drops the InsteadOfDemo trigger before moving on.

## After Trigger Obstacles

After triggers may affect insert, update, and delete operations.

After triggers are often used for complex data validation. These triggers can roll back, or undo, the insert, update, or delete, if the code inside the trigger doesn't like the operation in question. The code can then do something else, or it can just fail the transaction. But if the trigger doesn't explicitly rollback the transaction, the data-modification operation will go through as originally intended. Unlike instead of triggers, after triggers normally report an error code if an operation is rolled back.

As the next chapter will discuss in greater detail, every DML command implicitly occurs within a transaction even if no transaction begin command exists. The after trigger takes place after the write but before the implicit commit, so the transaction is still open when the after trigger is fired. Therefore, a transaction rollback command in the trigger will roll back the command that fired the trigger.

This code sample creates the AfterDemo after trigger on the Guide table, which includes raiserror and rollback transaction commands:

```
USE CHA2

CREATE TRIGGER AfterDemo
ON Guide
AFTER INSERT, UPDATE
```

```
AS
  Print 'After Trigger Demo'
  -- logic in a real trigger would decide what to do here
  RAISERROR ('Sample Error', 16, 1 )
  ROLLBACK TRAN
Return
```

With the `after` trigger applied to the `Guide` table, the following insert will result:

```
INSERT Guide(lastName, FirstName,
    Qualifications, DateOfBirth, DateHire)
  VALUES ('Harrison', 'Nancy',
    'Pilot, Sky Diver, Hang Glider,
      Emergency Paramedic', '6/25/69', '7/14/2000')
```

Result:

```
After Trigger Demo
Server: Msg 50000, Level 16, State 1,
    Procedure AfterDemo, Line 7
Sample Error
```

A select searching for Nancy Harrison would find no such row because the after trigger rolled back the transaction.

**Cross-Reference**    For more information on `after` triggers, see Chapter 15, "Implementing Triggers." Additional trigger strategies are discussed in Chapter 16, "Advanced Server-Side Programming."

Note that the sample code on the book's CD for this chapter drops the `AfterDemo` trigger so the code in the remainder of the chapter will function.

## Non-Updateable View Obstacles

Non-updateable views may affect `insert`, `update`, and `delete` operations.

Several factors will cause a view to become non-updateable. The most common causes of non-updateable views are aggregate functions (including `distinct`), group bys, and joins. If the view includes other nested views, any nested view that is non-updateable will cause the final view to be non-updateable as well.

The view `vMedGuide`, created in the following sample code, is non-updateable because the `distinct` predicate eliminates duplicates making it impossible for SQL to be sure of which underlying row should be updated:

```
CREATE VIEW dbo.vMedGuide
AS
SELECT DISTINCT GuideID, LastName, Qualifications
  FROM dbo.Guide
  WHERE Qualifications LIKE '%Aid%'
  OR Qualifications LIKE '%medic%'
  OR Qualifications LIKE '%Physician%'
```

To test the updateability of the view, the next query attempts to perform an `update` command through the view:

```
UPDATE dbo.vMedGuide
  SET Qualifications = 'E.R. Physician, Diver'
  WHERE GuideID = 1
```

Result:

```
Server: Msg 4404, Level 16, State 1, Line 1
View or function 'dbo.vMedGuide' is not updatable
because the definition contains the DISTINCT clause.
```

**Cross-Reference** For more about creating views, and a more complete list of the causes of non-updateable views, refer to Chapter 9, "Creating Views."

A related issue to non-updateable views involves updating calculated columns. Just like non-updateable views, these will block updates to the column.

## Views With-Check-Option Obstacles

Views with check option may affect insert, update operations.

Views can cause two specific problems, both related to the with check option. A special situation called *disappearing rows* occurs when rows are returned from a view and then updated such that they no longer meet the where clause's requirements for the view. The rows are still in the database but they are no longer visible in the view.

**Cross-Reference** For more about disappearing rows, the with check option, and their implications for security, refer to Chapter 9, "Creating Views." SQL Server security roles are discussed in Chapter 27, "Securing Databases."

Adding the with check option to a view prohibits disappearing rows, but causes another problem. A view that includes the with check option will apply the where-clause condition to both data being retrieved through the view and data being inserted or updated through the view. If the data being inserted or updated will not be retrievable through the view after the insert or update of the operation, the with check option will cause the data-modification operation to fail.

The following code sample modifies the previous view to add the with check option and then attempts two updates. The first update passes the where clause requirements. The second update would remove the rows from the result set returned by the view, so it fails.

```
ALTER VIEW dbo.vMedGuide
AS
SELECT GuideID, LastName, Qualifications
  FROM dbo.Guide
  WHERE Qualifications LIKE '%Aid%'
  OR Qualifications LIKE '%medic%'
  OR Qualifications LIKE '%Physician%'
WITH CHECK OPTION
```

The following queries test the views with check option. The first one will pass because the qualifications includes "Physician," but the second query will fail:

```
UPDATE dbo.vMedGuide
  SET Qualifications = 'E.R. Physician, Diver'
  WHERE GuideID = 1

UPDATE dbo.vMedGuide
  SET Qualifications = 'Diver'
  WHERE GuideID = 1
```

```
Server: Msg 550, Level 16, State 1, Line 1
The attempted insert or update failed because the target
view either specifies WITH CHECK OPTION or spans a view
that specifies WITH CHECK OPTION and one or more rows
resulting from the operation did not qualify
under the CHECK OPTION constraint.
The statement has been terminated.
```

## Security Obstacles

Security may affect insert, update, and delete operations.

A number of security settings and roles will cause any operation to fail. Typically security is not an issue during development; however, for production databases, security is often paramount. Documenting the security settings and security roles will help you to solve data-modification problems caused by security.

For more about security and roles, refer to Chapter 27, "Securing Databases."

Best Practice

Every data-modification obstacle is easily within the SQL developer's or DBA's ability to surmount. Understanding SQL Server and documenting the database, as well as being familiar with the database schema, stored procedures, and triggers, will prevent most data-modification problems.

# Summary

Data retrieval and data modification are primary tasks of a database application. This chapter examined the insert, update, and delete DML commands and how they may be blocked by the database.

While this chapter detailed the syntax and use of the data-modification commands, the next chapter studies transactional theory and SQL Server architecture to see how SQL Server manages transactions and locks so that data-modification operations function properly.

✦    ✦    ✦

# Transactional Integrity

**E**very operation that involves data occurs within a transaction. The way in which a database handles transactions is as critical to the database industry as the aerodynamic curve of a wing is to the aircraft industry. This chapter, more than any other in the book, is about what makes SQL Server fly.

A gold heist can be a complicated task. But to illustrate transactions, let me tell you a tale about a ring of gold thieves, their plan, and the database transaction that might catch them.

The gold thief ring has cased the depository and they've learned that the gold is tracked by a computer database. To get the gold they're planning to unplug the server during a gold transfer and then steal the transferred gold. That way they figure that there won't be a computer trail to alert anyone to the fact that the gold is missing.

Next Thursday, one ton of gold bars is being moved from Vault A to Vault 12. The gold bar inventory system will record the move as subtracting gold from Vault A and then adding gold to Vault 12. The plan is to unplug the SQL Server after the subtraction but before the addition, making it look as if the ton of gold bars isn't even in the system. Will the thieves get away with the gold? That depends on how well the database developer understood transactional integrity. And, I suppose, on whether the database developer is in on the heist.

This chapter explains the database theory behind transactions, how SQL Server accomplishes transactional integrity, and how to get the best performance while maintaining data integrity.

## Transactional Basics

A *transaction* is a sequence of tasks that together constitute a logical unit of work. All the tasks must complete or fail as a single unit. In the gold heist example the inventory subtraction and addition must both be written to the disk, or neither will be written to the disk.

In SQL Server, every DML operation is a transaction whether it has a `begin transaction` or not. An `insert` command that inserts 25 rows is a logical unit of work. Each and every one of the 25 rows must be updated. An update to even a single row operates within a transaction so that the data, and all indexes, are updated or rolled back.

To wrap multiple commands within a single transaction, a little code is needed. Two markers — one at the *beginning* of the transaction, and the other at its completion, at which time the transaction is *committed* to disk — define the perimeter of a transaction. If the code detects an error the transaction can be *rolled back*, or undone. The following three commands appear simple, but a volume of sophistication is behind them:

✦ begin transaction

✦ commit transaction

✦ rollback transaction

The following example demonstrates a typical transaction. The sequence of work is wrapped inside a begin transaction and a commit transaction. Each task in the sequence is followed by basic error-handling code and aborts the transaction with a rollback transaction command if a problem arises. If the first task (the subtraction) executes fine, but the second task (the addition) fails, the rollback transaction will undo the first and second tasks. The transaction log will even roll back the transaction if the plug is pulled halfway through the transaction. This is how the gold bar–inventory system should handle the inventory move:

```
BEGIN TRANSACTION
  INSERT GoldInventory (InventoryID, Location, Quantity)
    VALUES (101, 'Vault A', -2000)
  IF @@error <> 0
    BEGIN
      ROLLBACK TRANSACTION
      RAISERROR('There was an error', 16, 1)
      RETURN
    END
  INSERT GoldInventory (InventoryID, Location, Quantity)
    VALUES (101, 'Vault 12', 2000)
  IF @@error <> 0
    BEGIN
      ROLLBACK TRANSACTION
      RAISERROR('There was an error', 16, 1)
      RETURN
    END
COMMIT TRANSACTION
```

**Cross-Reference**

Program flow control (if, begin, end, return) and error handling (@@error and raiserror) are explained in Chapter 12, "Programming with Transact SQL."

Transactions can be nested, although as soon as one transaction is rolled back, all pending transactions are rolled back as well. Attempting to commit or rollback a transaction if no pending transactions exist will cause an error.

While SQL Server requires an explicit begin transaction to initiate a transaction, this behavior can be modified so that every batch assumes a transaction. The following code alone will not update the Nickname column in the CHA2 database:

```
USE CHA2
SET Implicit_Transactions ON
```

```
UPDATE CUSTOMER
  SET Nickname  = 'Nicky'
  WHERE CustomerID = 10
```

Adding a `commit transaction` to the end of the batch commits the transaction and the update actually takes place:

```
COMMIT TRANSACTION
```

**Note**  Implicit transaction is the default behavior for Oracle, and the adjustment takes getting used to for Oracle developers moving up to SQL Server.

It is also possible to declare a *save point* within the sequence of tasks and then roll back to that save point only. However, I believe that this mixes program flow of control with transaction handling. If an error makes it necessary to redo a task within the transaction, it's cleaner to handle the error with standard error handling than to jury-rig the transaction handling.

# Transactional Integrity

*Transactional integrity* refers to the quality of a transaction as measured by its ACID properties. There are three types of problems that violate transactional integrity; dirty reads, non-repeatable reads, and phantom rows. Solving these three problems involves enforcing various levels of integrity or *isolation* between the transactions.

## The ACID Properties

The quality of a database product is measured by its transactions' adherence to the ACID properties. ACID is an acronym for four interdependent properties — atomicity, consistency, isolation, and durability. Much of the architecture of SQL Server is founded on these properties. Understanding the ACID properties of a transaction is a prerequisite for understanding SQL Server.

**Best Practice**  The nemesis of transactional integrity is concurrency — multiple users simultaneously attempting to retrieve and modify data. Isolation is less of an issue in small databases, but in a production database with thousands of users, concurrency competes with transactional integrity. You must carefully balance the two, or either data integrity or performance will suffer.

SQL Server's architecture meets all the transactional-integrity ACID properties, providing that you as the developer understand them and develop the database to take advantage of SQL Server's capabilities, and that the DBA implements a sound recovery plan. A synergy exists among SQL Server, the hardware, the database design, the code, the database-recovery plan, and the database-maintenance plan. When the database developer and DBA cooperate to properly implement all these components, the database performs well and transactional integrity is high.

### Atomicity

The transaction must be *atomic*, meaning all or nothing. At the end of the transaction either all of the transaction is successful, or all of the transaction fails. If a partial transaction is written to disk the atomic property is violated.

## Consistency

The transaction must preserve database *consistency*, which means that the database must begin in a state of consistency and return to a state of consistency once the transaction is complete. For the purposes of ACID, consistency means that every row and value must agree with the reality being modeling, and every constraint must be enforced. If the order rows are written to disk but the order detail rows are not written, the consistency between the `Order` and `OrderDetail` tables is violated.

## Isolation

Each transaction must be *isolated* or separated from the effects of other transactions. Regardless of what any other transaction is doing, a transaction must be able to continue with the exact same data sets it started with. Isolation is the fence between two transactions. A proof of isolation is the ability to replay a serialized set of transactions on the same original set of data and always receive the same end result.

For example, assume Joe is updating 100 rows. While Joe's transaction is under way, Sue deletes one of the rows Joe is working on. If the delete takes place, Joe's transaction is not sufficiently isolated from Sue's transaction. This property is less critical in a single-user database than in a multi-user database.

## Durability

The *durability* of a transaction refers to its permanence regardless of system failure. Once a transaction is committed it stays committed. The database product must be constructed so that even if the data drive melts, the database can be restored up to the last transaction that was committed a split second before the hard drive died.

# Transactional Faults

The isolation between transactions can be less than perfect in one of three ways: dirty reads, non-repeatable reads, and phantom rows. These transactional faults can potentially affect the integrity of the transactions.

## Dirty Reads

The most egregious fault is a transaction's work being visible to other transactions before the transaction even commits its changes. When a transaction can read another transaction's uncommitted updates, this is called a *dirty read*, illustrated in Figure 11-1.

To illustrate a dirty-read transactional fault, the following code represents a setup that uses two transactions (transaction one is on the left, and transaction two is on the right). The second transaction will see the first transaction's update before that update is committed.

```
BEGIN TRANSACTION
SET TRANSACTION ISOLATION LEVEL
  READ COMMITTED
USE CHA2

-- Transaction 1
USE CHA2
BEGIN TRANSACTION
  UPDATE Customer
    SET Nickname = 'Transaction Fault'
    WHERE CustomerID = 1
```

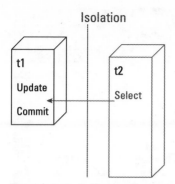

Isolation

**Figure 11-1:** A dirty read occurs when transaction two can read uncommitted changes made by transaction one.

In a separate Query Analyzer window, as shown in Figure 11-2, execute another transaction in its own connection window. This transaction will set its isolation level to permit dirty reads. (The isolation level must be set here if the dirty read is to be demonstrated. The isolation-level command will be explained further in the next section.)

```
-- Transaction 2
SET TRANSACTION ISOLATION LEVEL
   READ UNCOMMITTED
USE CHA2
SELECT Nickname
   FROM Customer
   WHERE CustomerID = 1
```

Result:

```
NickName
---------------------
Transaction Fault
```

Transaction one isn't done working with the dataset, but transaction two was able to read "Transaction Fault." That's a violation of transactional integrity.

To finish the task, the first window still needs to commit the transaction:

```
-- Transaction 1
COMMIT TRANSACTION
```

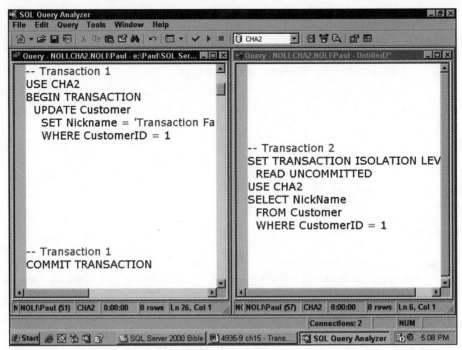

**Figure 11-2:** Opening two windows in Query Analyzer is the best way to experiment with two transactions.

## Non-Repeatable Reads

A *non-repeatable read* is similar to a dirty read, but a non-repeatable read occurs when a transaction can see the committed updates from another transaction (Figure 11-3). *True isolation* means that one transaction never affects another transaction. If the isolation is complete, then no data changes from outside the transaction should be seen by the transaction. Reading a row inside a transaction should produce the same results every time. If reading a row twice results in different values, that's a non-repeatable read type of transaction fault.

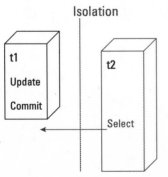

Isolation

**Figure 11-3:** When transaction one's committed changes are seen by transaction two, that's a *non-repeatable read* transaction fault.

The following sequence sets up two transactions. Transaction one updates the nickname and commits the changes. Transaction two is able to read the row and sees the values from transaction one's update. First, transaction two will check the initial value:

```
SET TRANSACTION ISOLATION LEVEL
    READ COMMITTED
BEGIN TRANSACTION
  USE CHA2
  SELECT NickName
    FROM Customer
    WHERE CustomerID = 1
```

Result:

```
Nickname
------------------------
Transaction Fault
```

```
-- Transaction 1
USE CHA2
BEGIN TRANSACTION
  UPDATE Customer
    SET Nickname = 'Non-Repeatable Read'
    WHERE CustomerID = 1
COMMIT TRANSACTION
```

With transaction one's update committed, transaction two re-selects the same row:

```
-- Transaction 2
USE CHA2
SELECT Nickname
  FROM Customer
  WHERE CustomerID = 1
```

Result:

```
Nickname
---------------------
Non-Repeatable Read
```

To complete the work, transaction two commits its changes:

```
COMMIT TRANSACTION
```

Sure enough, transaction two's read was not repeatable. The second select reflected transaction one's update.

## Phantom Rows

The least severe transactional-integrity fault is a *phantom row*. Like a non-repeatable read, a phantom row is when updates from another transaction affect not only the result set's data values, but causes the select to return a different set of rows, as shown in Figure 11-4.

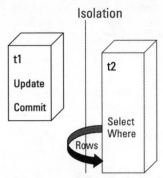

**Figure 11-4:** When the rows returned by a select are altered by another transaction, the phenomenon is called a phantom row.

In the following code, transaction one will update a nickname to 'Missy' while transaction two is selecting rows with that nickname value:

```
-- Transaction 2
BEGIN TRANSACTION
  USE CHA2
  SELECT CustomerID, LastName
    FROM Customer
    WHERE NickName = 'Missy'
```

Result:

```
CustomerID  LastName
----------  ----------------
2           Anderson
```

```
-- Transaction 1
USE CHA2
BEGIN TRANSACTION
  UPDATE Customer
    SET Nickname = 'Missy'
    WHERE CustomerID = 1
COMMIT TRANSACTION
```

If the isolation between the transactions is complete, transaction two's result set will contain the same row set as the previous select:

```
-- Transaction 2
  USE CHA2
  SELECT CustomerID, LastName
    FROM Customer
    WHERE Nickname = 'Missy'
```

Result:

```
CustomerID  LastName
----------  ----------------
1           Adams
2           Anderson
```

Adams is a phantom row because it appears for the first time in the second result set because of a change in the data based on another transaction's data modification.

The final line of code in this series closes transaction two's transaction:

```
COMMIT TRANSACTION
```

Of these transactional faults, dirty reads are the most dangerous, while non-repeatable reads are less so, and phantom rows are the least dangerous of all.

## Isolation Levels

Databases deal with the three transactional faults by establishing isolation between transactions. The level of isolation, or the height of the fence between transactions, can be adjusted to control which transactional faults are permitted. The ANSI SQ-92 committee has specified four isolation levels, listed in Table 11-1.

### Table 11-1: ANSI SQL-92 Isolation Levels

| Isolation Level | Dirty Read Seeing another transaction's non-committed changes | Non-Repeatable Read Seeing another transaction's committed changes | Phantom Row Seeing rows selected by where clause change as a result of another transaction |
|---|---|---|---|
| Read Uncommitted *(least restrictive)* | Possible | Possible | Possible |
| Read Committed *(SQL Server default; moderately restrictive)* | Prevented | Possible | Possible |
| Repeatable Read | Prevented | Prevented | Possible |
| *Serializable* (most restrictive) | Prevented | Prevented | Prevented |

SQL Server implements isolation levels with locks. Since locks affect performance, there's a trade-off between tight transaction isolation and performance. SQL Server's default isolation, read committed, is a balance appropriate for most OLTP projects.

You can set the isolation level within a connection or batch. Alternately, you can declare the isolation level for a single DML statement by using table-lock hints in the `from` clause.

### Level 1 — Read Uncommitted

The least restrictive isolation level is *read uncommitted*, which doesn't prevent any of the transactional faults. It's like having no fence at all because it provides no isolation between transactions. Setting the isolation level to read uncommitted is the same as setting SQL Server's locks to no locks. This mode is best for reporting and data-reading applications. Because this mode has just enough locks to prevent data corruption, but not enough to handle row contention, it's not very useful for databases whose data is updated regularly.

### Level 2 — Read Committed

*Read committed* prevents the worst transactional fault, but doesn't bog the system down with excessive lock contention. For this reason, it's the SQL Server default isolation level and an ideal choice for most OTLP projects.

### Level 3 — Repeatable Read

By preventing dirty reads and non-repeatable reads, the *repeatable read* isolation level provides an increase in transaction isolation without the extreme lock contention of serializable isolation.

### Level 4 — Serializable

This most restrictive isolation level prevents all transactional faults and passes the serialized-transaction test mentioned in the definition of isolation. This mode is useful for databases for which absolute transactional integrity is more important than performance. Banking, accounting, and high-contention sales databases, such as the stock market, typically use serialized isolation.

Using the serializable isolation level is the same as setting locks to hold locks, which holds even share locks for the length of the transaction. While this setting provides absolute transaction isolation, it can cause serious lock contention and performance delays.

# Transaction-Log Architecture

SQL Server's design meets the transactional-integrity ACID properties, largely because of its write-ahead transaction log. The write-ahead transaction log ensures the durability of every transaction.

## Transaction Log Sequence

Every data-modification operation goes through the same sequence, in which it writes first to the transaction log and then to the data file. The following sections describe the 12 steps in a transaction.

### Database Beginning State

Before the transaction begins, the database is in a consistent state. All indexes are complete and point to the correct row. The data meet all the enforced rules for data integrity. Every foreign key points to a valid primary key.

Some data pages are likely already cached in memory. Additional data pages or index pages are copied into memory as needed.

**1.** The database is in a consistent state.

## Data-Modification Command

The transaction is initiated by a submitted query, batch, or stored procedure, as shown in Figure 11-5.

**2.** The code issues a `begin transaction` command. Even if the DML command is a stand-alone command without a `begin transaction` and `commit transaction`, it is still handled as a transaction.

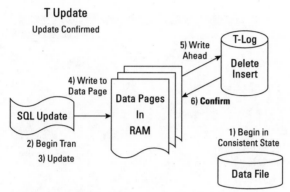

**Figure 11-5:**The SQL DML commands are performed in memory as part of a transaction.

**3.** The code issues a single DML `insert`, `update`, or `delete` command, or a series of them.

To give you an example of the transaction log in action, the following code initiates a transaction and then submits two update commands:

```
BEGIN TRANSACTION

UPDATE Product
  SET ProductDescription = 'Transaction Log Test A',
      DiscontinueDate = '12/31/2003'
  WHERE Code = '1001'

UPDATE Product
  SET ProductDescription = 'Transaction Log Test B',
      DiscontinueDate = '4/1/2003'
  WHERE Code = '1002'
```

**4.** The query-optimization plan is either generated or pulled from memory. Any required locks are applied and the data modifications, including index updates, page splits, and any other required system operation, are performed in memory.

## Transaction Log Recorded

The most important feature of the transaction log is that all data modifications are written to it and confirmed prior to being written to the data file, as shown in Figure 11-6.

5. The data modifications are written to the transaction log.

SQL Server 2000 does not include a viewer for the transaction log, so Lumigent's Log Explorer fills the void. The `begin transaction` log entry is a system entry that is not visible in the Lumigent Log Explorer unless the User Data Only option is unchecked and Begin XACT is enabled in the Log Filter.

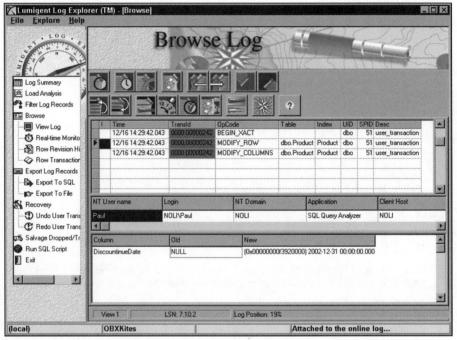

**Figure 11-6:** Using Lumigent's Log Explorer to view the transaction log, the data modifications are written to the log.

A 30-day trial version of Lumigent's Log Explorer version 3.0 is on the CD included with this book. I highly recommend loading it and observing the transaction log to better understand SQL Server and how to deal with transactional issues.

6. The transaction-log DML entries are confirmed. This ensures that the log entries are in fact written to the transaction log.

**Best Practice**

The write-ahead nature of the transaction log is what makes it critical that the transaction log be stored on a different disk subsystem from the data file. If they are stored separately and either disk subsystem fails, the database will still be intact and you will be able to recover it to the split second before the failure. But if they are on the same drive, a drive failure will require you to restore from the last backup.

## Transaction Commit

When the sequence of tasks is complete, the `commit transaction` closes the transaction. Even this task is written to the transaction log, as shown in Figure 11-7.

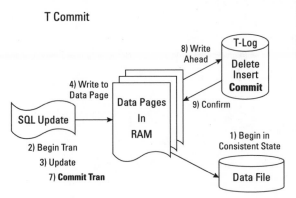

T Commit

**Figure 11-7:** The `commit transaction` **command** launches another `insert` into the transaction log.

7. The code closes the transaction:

```
COMMIT TRANSACTION
```

8. The `commit` entry is written to the transaction log (Figure 11-8).

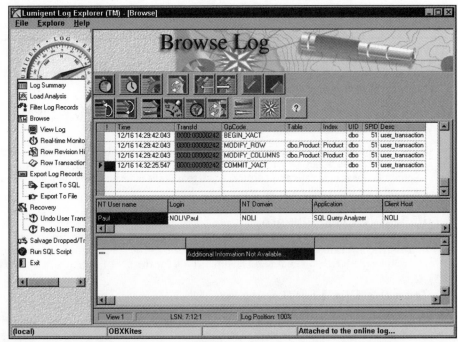

**Figure 11-8:** The `commit` entry is written to the transaction log, just as the data modifications were.

**9.** The transaction-log `commit` entry is confirmed.

## Data-File Update

With the transaction safely stored in the transaction log, the last disk operation writes the data modification to the data file, as shown in Figure 11-9.

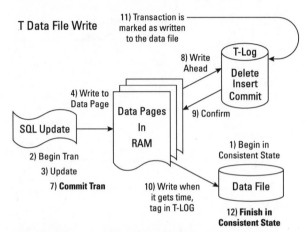

**Figure 11-9:** As one of the last steps, the data modification is written to the data file.

**10.** In the background, SQL Server writes the data modifications to the data file.

**11.** When SQL Server performs a checkpoint, it marks the oldest open transaction. All older, committed transaction and therefore confirmed in the transaction log. The `DBCC OpenTran` command reports the oldest open transaction.

## Transaction Complete

The sequence comes full circle and returns the database to a consistent state.

**12.** The database finishes in a consistent state.

In ancient Hebrew poetry, an *inclusion* is a line or phrase that begins a poem and is repeated at the close of the poem, providing a theme or wrapper for the poem. In the same way, the beginning consistent state and ending consistent state together provide a stable wrapper, or bookends, for the database transaction.

## Transaction-Log Rollback

If the transaction is rolled back, the DML operations are reversed in memory, and a transaction-abort entry is made in the log. Figure 11-10 shows the transaction-log entries made if a `rollback transaction` command is substituted for the `commit transaction` of Step 7.

# Transaction-Log Recovery

The primary benefit of a write-ahead transaction log is that it maintains the atomic transactional property in the case of system failure.

**Figure 11-10:** The rollback transaction command initiates DML commands to undo the transaction and closes the transaction with an xact abort entry in the log.

If SQL Server should cease functioning the transaction log is automatically examined once it recovers, as follows:

✦ If any entries are in the log as DML operations but are not committed, they are rolled back.

To test this feature you must be brave. Begin a transaction and unplug the server before issuing a `commit transaction`. The server must be physically turned off. Simply closing Query Analyzer won't do it; Query Analyzer will request permission to commit the pending transactions, and will roll back the transaction if permission isn't given. If SQL Server is shut down normally, it will wait for any pending tasks to complete before stopping. You have to turn off the server to see the transaction log recover from a failed transaction.

If you have followed the steps outlined previously, and you disable the system just before Step 7, the transaction-log entries will be identical to those shown in Figure 11-10. SQL Server will recover from the crash very nicely and roll back the unfinished transaction.

✦ If any entries are in the log as DML operations and committed but not marked as written to the data file, they are written to the data file. This feature is nearly impossible to demonstrate.

# Understanding SQL Server Locking

SQL Server implements the isolation property with locks that protect a transaction's rows from being affected by another transaction. SQL Server locks are not just a "page lock on" and "page lock off" scheme. These are serious locks. Before they can be controlled, they must be understood.

Within SQL Server, you can informally picture two processes: a query processor and a lock manager. The goal of the lock manager is to maintain transactional integrity as efficiently as possible by creating and dropping locks.

Every lock has the following three properties:

✦ *Granularity*—The size of the lock.

✦ *Mode*—The type of lock.

✦ *Duration*—The isolation mode of the lock.

Locks are not impossible to view, but some tricks will make viewing the current set of locks easier. Also, lock contention, or the compatibility of various locks to exist or block other locks, can adversely affect performance if it's not understood and controlled.

## Lock Granularity

A size of the data controlled by a lock can vary from only a row to the entire database, as shown in Table 11-2. Several combinations of locks, depending on the lock granularity, could satisfy a locking requirement.

### Table 11-2: Lock Granularity

| Lock Size | Description |
|---|---|
| Row Lock | Locks a single row. This is the smallest lock available. SQL Server does not lock columns. |
| Page Lock | Locks a page, or 8KB. One or more rows may exist on a single page. |
| Extent Lock | Locks eight pages, or 64KB. |
| Table Lock | Locks the entire table. |
| Database Lock | Locks the entire database. This lock is used primarily during schema changes. |
| Key Lock | Locks nodes on an index. |

The SQL Server lock manager tries to balance the size of the lock against the number of locks for performance. The struggle is between concurrency (smaller locks allow more transactions to access the data) and performance (fewer locks are faster). To achieve that balance, the lock manager dynamically swaps one set of locks for another set. For example:

1. Twenty-five row locks might be escalated to a single page lock.

2. Then, if 25 more rows are locked that extend over four other pages on the same extent, the page lock and 25 row locks might be escalated to an extent lock because more than 50 percent of the pages on the extent are affected.

3. If enough extents are affected, the entire set of locks might be escalated to a table lock.

Dynamic locking brings significant benefits for SQL Server developers:

✦ It automatically provides the best performance/concurrency balance without custom programming.

✦ The performance of the database is preserved as the database grows and the lock manager continually applies the appropriate lock granularity.

✦ Dynamic locking simplifies administration.

# Lock Mode

Locks not only have granularity, or size, but also a mode that determines their purpose. SQL Server has a rich set of lock modes (such as shared, update, exclusive). Failing to understand lock modes will almost guarantee that you will develop a poorly performing database.

## Lock Contention

The interaction and compatibility of the locks plays a vital role in SQL Server's transactional integrity and performance. Certain lock modes block other lock modes, as detailed in Table 11-3.

### Table 11-3: Lock Compatibility

| | T2 Requests: | | | | | |
| --- | --- | --- | --- | --- | --- | --- |
| T1 has: | IS | S | U | IX | SIX | X |
| Intent shared (IS) | Yes | Yes | Yes | Yes | Yes | Yes |
| Shared (S) | Yes | Yes | Yes | No | No | No |
| Update (U) | Yes | Yes | No | No | No | No |
| Intent exclusive (IX) | Yes | No | No | Yes | No | No |
| Shared with intent exclusive (SIX) | Yes | No | No | No | No | No |
| Exclusive (X) | No | No | No | No | No | No |

## Shared Lock (S)

By far the most common and most abused lock, a shared lock (listed as an "S" in SQL Server) is a simple "read lock." If a transaction gets a shared lock it's saying, "I'm looking at this data." Multiple transactions are typically allowed to view the same data, depending on the isolation mode.

**Best Practice**

Be careful with shared locks. I believe that misused share locks are a common cause of `update`-performance problems. Applications should grab the data in a way that doesn't hold the shared lock. This is one compelling reason to use stored procedures to retrieve data.

## Exclusive Lock (X)

An exclusive lock means that the transaction is performing a write to the data. As the name implies, an exclusive lock means that only one transaction may hold an exclusive lock at a time, and that no transactions may view the data during the exclusive lock.

## Update Lock (U)

An update lock can be confusing. It's not applied while a transaction is performing an update—that's an exclusive lock. Instead, the update lock means that the transaction is getting ready to perform an exclusive lock and is currently scanning the data to determine the row(s) it wants for that lock. Think of the update lock as a shared lock that's about to morph into an exclusive lock.

To help prevent deadlocks (explained later in this chapter), only one transaction may hold an update lock at a time.

## Intent Locks

An intent lock is a yellow flag or a warning lock that alerts other transactions to the fact that something more is going on. The primary purpose of an intent lock is to improve performance. Because an intent lock is used for all types of locks and for all lock granularities, SQL Server has many types of intent locks. The following is a sampling of the intent locks:

- ✦ Intent Shared Lock (IS)
- ✦ Shared with Intent Exclusive Lock (SIX)
- ✦ Intent Exclusive Lock (IX)

Intent locks serve to stake a claim for a shared or exclusive lock without actually being a shared or exclusive lock. In doing so they solve two performance problems, hierarchical locking and permanent lock block.

Without intent locks, if transaction one holds a shared lock on a row, and transaction two wants to grab an exclusive lock on the table, transaction two would need to check for table locks, extent locks, page locks, row locks, and key locks.

Instead, SQL Server uses intent locks to propagate a lock to higher levels of the data's hierarchical levels. So when transaction one gains a row lock, it also places an intent lock on the row's page and table.

The intent locks move the overhead from the checking transaction to the establishing transaction by allowing the transaction gaining the lock to place intent locks on the greater scope of its lock. That one-time write of three locks potentially saves hundreds of searches later as other transactions check for locks.

The intent locks also prevent a serious shared-lock contention problem — what I call "permanent lock block." As long as a transaction has a shared lock, another transaction can't gain an exclusive lock. What would happen if someone grabbed a shared lock every 5 seconds and held it for 10 seconds while a transaction was waiting for an exclusive lock? The update transaction could theoretically wait forever. However, once the transaction has an intent exclusive lock (IX), no other transaction can grab a shared lock. The intent exclusive lock isn't a full exclusive lock, but it lays claim to gaining an exclusive lock in the future.

### Schema Lock (Sch-M, Sch-S)

Schema locks protect the database schema. SQL Server will apply a schema stability (Sch-S) lock during any query to prevent Data Definition Language (DDL) commands.

A schema modification lock (Sch-M) is applied only when SQL Server is adjusting the physical schema. If SQL Server is in the middle of adding a column to a table, the schema lock will prevent any other transactions from viewing or modifying the data during the schema-modification operation.

## Lock Duration

The third lock property, lock duration, is determined by the isolation level of the transactions involved — the tighter the isolation, the longer the locks will be held. SQL Server implements all four previously described transaction-isolation levels. An absolute level of isolation (serialization) will create the strictest locks. At the other extreme, a low level of transaction isolation (read uncommitted) will effectively turn off locks, as detailed in Table 11-4.

### Table 11-4: Isolation Levels and Lock Duration

| Isolation Level | Share-Lock Duration | Exclusive-Lock Duration |
|---|---|---|
| Read Uncommitted | None. | Only long enough to prevent physical corruption; otherwise exclusive locks are neither applied nor honored. |
| Read Committed | Held while the transaction is reading the data. | Held until transaction commit. |
| Repeatable Read | Held until the transaction is committed. | Held until transaction commit. |
| Serializable | Held until transaction commit. | Held until transaction commit. The exclusive lock also uses a keylock (also called a range lock) to prevent inserts. |

## Viewing Locks

Without the ability to see the lock, the various types of locks and their durations may seem like pure theory. Fortunately, SQL Server is a relatively open environment, and it's easy to inspect the current locks.

With Enterprise Manager, the locks may be viewed in the current activity node under each server, as shown in Figure 11-11.

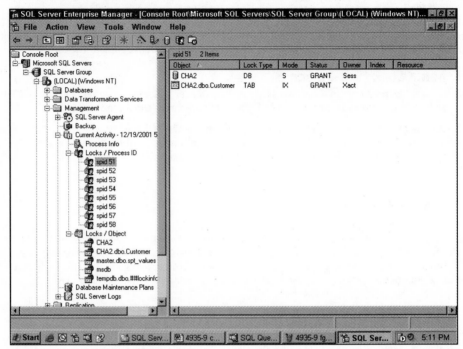

**Figure 11-11:** Enterprise Manager displays a wealth of information about the current locks.

The first node under current activity lists the processes currently running in SQL Server. Most processes are user connections, but some are system processes. The details available for each process include application, wait time, wait type, wait resource, CPU, physical I/O, memory usage, login time, last batch time, host, network library, network address, blocked by, and blocking.

The second node lists the locks by process and reports the object locked, lock type, lock mode, lock status, owner, index, and resource of each. The third node lists the same information, but by object rather than by process.

**Caution**    Locks are very fluid — they change with nearly every operation. The Enterprise Manager view of locks, however, is static. The information listed is only current as of the last refresh.

A system stored procedure, sp_lock, also lists the current locks. By default, Query Analyzer has Ctrl+2 set to sp_lock for ready use. Unfortunately, sp_lock reports cryptic raw data rather than useful information, as demonstrated in this sample execution of sp_lock:

```
sp_lock
```

Result:

```
spid dbid ObjId    IndId  Type Resource       Mode     Status
---- ---- -------- ------ ---- ------------- -------- ------
51   8    0        0      DB                 S        GRANT
51   8    85575343 1      PAG  3:22          IX       GRANT
51   1    85575343 0      TAB                IS       GRANT
51   8    85575343 0      TAB                IX       GRANT
51   8    85575343 1      KEY  (530050d8f078) X       GRANT
52   4    0        0      DB                 S        GRANT
53   4    0        0      DB                 S        GRANT
54   4    0        0      DB                 S        GRANT
55   4    0        0      DB                 S        GRANT
56   4    0        0      DB                 S        GRANT
60   8    0        0      DB                 S        GRANT
```

Because I like locks, I've written a stored procedure that grabs the information from sp_lock, looks up the database, user, and object information, and presents a view more to my liking. pGetLocks (in the /Utility directory on the book's CD) reports the loginname, spid, database, object, cmd, locksize, lockmode, blocked, and waittime.

```
EXEC pGetLocks
```

Result (abbreviated and formatted):

```
LoginName   spid db       Object  Cmd    LSize LMode Status
---------  ---- -------- ------- ------ ----- ----- ------
NOLI\Paul  60   OBXKites Contact SELECT TAB   IS    GRANT
```

Continued:

```
Blocked Waittime
------- --------
0       0
```

# Controlling SQL Server Locking

If you've written manual locking schemes in other database languages to overcome their locking deficiencies (as I have), you may feel as if you still need to control the locks. Let me assure you that the SQL Server lock manager can be trusted. Nevertheless, SQL Server exposes several methods of controlling locks, which are detailed in this section.

**Best Practice**

Don't apply lock hints or adjust the isolation level casually — trust the SQL Server lock manager to balance concurrency and transaction integrity. Only after you're positive that the database schema is well tuned and the code is polished should you consider tweaking the lock manager to solve a specific problem. When this is the case, setting select queries to no lock solves most problems.

## Setting the Isolation Level

The isolation level determines the duration of the share lock or exclusive lock for the connection. Setting the isolation level affects all queries and all tables for the duration of the connection, or until the isolation level is changed again. The following code sets a tighter-than-default isolation level and prevents non-repeatable reads:

```
SET TRANSACTION ISOLATION LEVEL REPEATABLE READ
```

The valid isolation levels are the following:

✦ read uncommitted

✦ read committed

✦ repeatable read

✦ serializable

The current isolation level may be verified with the database consistency checker (DBCC):

    DBCC USEROPTIONS

Results (abbreviated):

    Set Option          Value
    ------------------  ------------------
    isolation level     repeatable read

The isolation levels may also be set on a query and table level by means of locking hints.

## Using Locking Hints

*Locking hints* enable you to make minute adjustments in the locking strategy. While the isolation level affects the entire connection, locking hints are specific to one table within one query (Table 11-5). The with (locking hint) option is placed after the table in the from clause of the query. You can specify multiple locking hints by separating them with commas.

### Table 11-5: Locking Hints

| Locking Hint | Description |
|---|---|
| ReadUnCommitted | Isolation level. Doesn't apply or honor locks. Same as no lock. |
| ReadCommitted | Isolation level. Uses the default transaction-isolation level. |
| RepeatableRead | Isolation level. Holds share and exclusive locks until transaction commit. |
| Serializable | Isolation level. Applies the serializable transaction isolation–level durations to the table which holds the shared lock until the transaction is complete. |
| ReadPast | Skips locked rows instead of waiting. |
| RowLock | Forces row-level locks instead of page, extent, or table locks. |
| PagLock | Forces the use of page locks instead of a table lock. |
| TabLock | Automatically escalates row, page, or extent locks to the table-lock granularity. |
| NoLock | Doesn't apply or honor locks. Same as ReadUnCommitted. |
| TablockX | Forces an exclusive lock on the table. This prevents any other transaction from working with the table. |
| HoldLock | Holds the share lock until the commit transaction. (Same as Serializable.) |
| Updlock | Uses an update lock instead of a shared lock and holds the lock. This blocks any other writes to the data between the initial read and a write operation. |
| XLock | Holds an exclusive lock on the data until the transaction is committed. |

The following query uses a locking hint in the `from` clause of an `update` query to prevent the lock manager from escalating the granularity of the locks:

```
USE OBXKites
UPDATE Product
  FROM Product WITH (RowLock)
  SET ProductName = ProductName + ' Updated'
```

If a query includes subqueries, don't forget that each query's table references will generate locks and can be controlled by locking hint.

## Index-Level Locking Restrictions

Isolation levels and locking hints are applied from the connection and query perspective. The only way to control locks from the table perspective is to restrict the granularity of locks on a per-index basis. Using the `sp_indexoption` system stored procedure, rowlocks and/or page-locks may be disabled for a particular index, as follows:

```
sp_indexoption
  'indexname',
  AllowRowlocks or AllowPagelocks,
  1 or 0
```

This is useful for a couple of specific purposes. If a table frequently causes waiting because of page locks, setting `allowpagelocks` to `off` will force rowlocks. The decreased scope of the lock will improve concurrency. Also, if a table is seldom updated but frequently read, row- and page-level locks are inappropriate. Allowing only table locks is suitable during the majority of table accesses. For the infrequent update a table-exclusive lock is not a big issue.

`Sp_indexoption` is for fine-tuning the data schema; that's why it's on an index level. To restrict the locks on a table's primary key, use `sp_help` *tablename* to find the specific name for the primary-key index.

The following commands configure the `ProductCategory` table as an infrequently updated look-up table. First, `sp_help` will report the name of the primary key index:

```
sp_help ProductCategory
```

Result (abridged):

```
index                         index          index
name                          description    keys
----------------------------- -------------- ----------------
PK__ProductCategory__79A81403 nonclustered,  ProductCategoryID
                              unique,
                              primary key
                              located
                              on PRIMARY
```

Having identified the actual name of the primary key, the `sp_indexoption` system stored procedure can now set the index lock options:

```
EXEC sp_indexoption
  'ProductCategory.PK__ProductCategory__79A81403',
  'AllowRowlocks', FALSE
EXEC sp_indexoption
  'ProductCategory.PK__ProductCategory__79A81403',
  'AllowPagelocks', FALSE
```

## Controlling Lock Timeouts

If a transaction is waiting for a lock, it will continue to wait until the lock is available. By default no timeout exists — it can theoretically wait forever.

Fortunately, you can set the lock time using the `set lock_timeout` connection option. You can set the option to a number of milliseconds, or set it to infinity (the default) by setting it to `-1`. Setting the `lock_timeout` to 0 means that the transaction will instantly give up if any lock contention occurs at all. The application will be very fast, and very ineffective.

The following query sets the lock timeout to two seconds (2,000 milliseconds):

```
SET Lock_Timeout 2000
```

When a transaction does time out while waiting to gain a lock, a 1222 error is raised.

**Best Practice**

I do recommend that you set a lock timeout in the connection. The length of the wait you should specify depends on the typical performance of the database. I usually set a five-second timeout.

## Evaluating Database Concurrency Performance

It's easy to build a database that doesn't exhibit lock contention and concurrency issues when tested with a handful of users. The real test is when several hundred users are all updating orders.

**Best Practice**

Multi-user concurrency should be tested during the development process several times. To quote the MCSE exam guide, "...don't let the real test be your first test."

Concurrency testing requires a concerted effort. At one level, it can involve everyone available running the same front-end form concurrently. A VB program that constantly simulates a user viewing data and updating data is also useful. A good test is to run 20 instances of the script that constantly pounds the database and then let the test crew use the application. Performance monitor (covered in Chapter 28, "Advanced Performance") can watch the number of locks.

## Application Locks

SQL Server uses a very sophisticated locking scheme. Sometimes a process or a resource other than data requires locking. For example, a procedure might need to run that would be ill affected if another user started another instance of the same procedure.

Several years ago, I wrote a program that routed cables for nuclear power plant designs. After the geometry of the plant (what's where) was entered and tested, the design engineers entered the cable-source equipment, destination equipment, and type of cable to be used. Once several cables were entered, a procedure wormed each cable through the cable trays so that cables were as short as possible. The procedure also considered cable failsafe routes and separated incompatible cables. While I enjoyed writing that database, if multiple instances of the worm procedure ran simultaneously, each instance attempted to route the cables and the data became fouled. An application lock is the perfect solution to that type of problem.

Application locks open up the whole world of SQL Server locks for custom uses within applications. Instead of using data as a locked resource, application locks use any named user resource declared in the sp_GetAppLock stored procedure.

Application locks must be obtained within a transaction. The lock mode (Shared, Update, Exclusive, IntentExclusive, or IntentShared) may be declared. The return code indicates whether or not the procedure was successful in obtaining the lock, as follows:

✦ 0 — Lock was obtained normally.

✦ 1 — Lock was obtained after another procedure released it.

✦ -1 — Lock request failed (timeout).

✦ -2 — Lock request failed (canceled).

✦ -3 — Lock request failed (deadlock).

✦ -999 — Lock request failed (other error).

The sp_ReleaseAppLock stored procedure releases the lock. The following code shows how the application lock can be used in a batch or procedure:

```
DECLARE @ShareOK INT
EXEC @ShareOK = sp_GetAppLock
                @Resource = 'CableWorm',
                @LockMode = 'Exclusive'
IF @ShareOK < 0
   ...Error handling code

  ... code ...

EXEC sp_ReleaseAppLock @Resource = 'CableWorm'
Go
```

When the application locks are viewed using Enterprise Manager or sp_Lock the lock appears as an "APP"-type lock. The following is an abbreviated listing of sp_lock executed at the same time as the previous code:

```
Sp_Lock
```

Result:

```
spid  dbid  ObjId  IndId  Type  Resource        Mode  Status
----- ----- ------ ------ ----  --------------  ----- ------
57    8     0      0      APP   Cabl1f94c136    X     GRANT
```

A couple of minor differences from the way application locks are handled by SQL Server are:

✦ Deadlocks are not automatically detected.

✦ If a transaction gets a lock several times, it will have to release that lock the same number of times.

# Deadlocks

A deadlock is a special situation that occurs only when transactions with multiple tasks compete for the same data resource. For example:

✦ Transaction one has a lock on data A and needs to lock data B to complete its transaction.

and

✦ Transaction two has a lock on data B and needs to lock data A to complete its transaction.

Each transaction is stuck waiting for the other to release its lock, and neither can complete until the other does. Unless an outside force intercedes, or one of the transactions gives up and quits, this situation could last until the end of time.

In earlier days a deadlock was a serious problem. Fortunately, SQL Server handles deadlocks refreshingly well.

## Creating a Deadlock

It's easy to create a deadlock situation in SQL Server using two connections in Query Analyzer, as illustrated in Figure 11-12. Transaction one and transaction two will simply try to update the same rows but in the opposite order. Using a third window to run pGetLocks will help you monitor the locking situation.

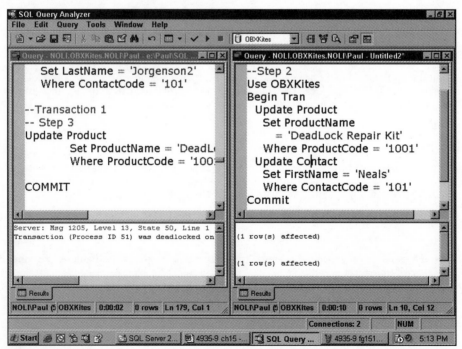

**Figure 11-12:** Creating a deadlock situation in Query Analyzer using two connections tiled vertically.

To execute the code, you'll need to do the following:

1. Create a second window in Query Analyzer.

2. Move the code in Step 2 to the second window.

3. In the first window, select the code in Step 1 and execute it by pressing F5.

4. In the second window, execute Step 2.

5. Back in the first window, execute Step 3.

6. After a short moment, SQL Server will detect the deadlock and automatically resolve it.

Here's the code:

```
-- Transaction 1
-- Step 1
USE OBXKites
BEGIN TRANSACTION
UPDATE Contact
  SET LastName = 'Jorgenson'
  WHERE ContactCode = '101'
```

Transaction one now has an exclusive lock on `ContactCode` "101." Transaction two will gain an exclusive lock on `ProductCode` "1001" and then also try to grab an exclusive lock on `ContactCode` "101," but transaction one already has it locked:

```
              -- Transaction 2
              -- Step 2
              USE OBXKites
              BEGIN TRANSACTION
                UPDATE Product
                  SET ProductName
                    = 'DeadLock Repair Kit'
                  WHERE ProductCode = '1001'
                UPDATE Contact
                  SET FirstName = 'Neals'
                  WHERE ContactCode = '101'
              COMMIT TRANSACTION
```

It's not a deadlock yet, because although transaction two is waiting for transaction one, transaction one is not waiting for transaction two. At this point, if transaction one finished its work and issued a `commit transaction`, the data resource would be freed; transaction two could get its lock on the contact row and be on its way as well.

The trouble begins when transaction one tries to update `ProductCode` "1001." It can't get an exclusive lock because transaction two already has an exclusive lock:

```
-- Transaction 1
-- Step 3
UPDATE Product
  SET ProductName
    = 'DeadLock Identification Tester'
  WHERE ProductCode = '1001'
COMMIT TRANSACTION
```

Transaction one returns the following friendly error message in about two seconds:

```
Server: Msg 1205, Level 13,
 State 50, Line 1
Transaction (Process ID 51) was
 deadlocked on lock resources with
 another process and has been chosen
 as the deadlock victim. Rerun the
 transaction.
```

Transaction two completes as if there's no problem. Result:

```
                    (1 row(s) affected)
                    (1 row(s) affected)
```

## Automatic Deadlock Detection

As the previous deadlock code demonstrated, SQL Server will automatically detect a deadlock situation by examining the blocking processes and rolling back the transaction that has performed the least amount of work. A process within SQL Server is constantly checking for cross-blocking locks. The deadlock-detection delay is typically instantaneous to two seconds. The longest I've waited for a deadlock to be detected is about five seconds.

**Caution**   SQL Server does not always detect more complex deadlocks. A *three-way deadlock* occurs when T1 is waiting for T2, which is waiting for T3, which is waiting for T1. Books Online claims that SQL Server will recursively search the blocking processes until it detects a cycle. However, in my experience, SQL Server only rarely detects a three-way deadlock because the blocking report typically lists only one process as the blocking process. These situations will wait forever if the lock timeout is set to the default (infinite), or time out waiting for the lock if the lock timeout time has been set.

## Handling Deadlocks

Once a deadlock occurs, the connection that's selected as the deadlock victim will need to re-perform the transaction again. Since the work will need to be redone, it's good that the transaction that has completed the least amount of work is the transaction that has to go back to the beginning and try again.

The error code 1205 will need to be trapped by the client application and the transaction should be re-executed. If all goes well, users will not be aware that a deadlock occurred.

Instead of letting SQL Server decide which transaction will be the "deadlock victim," a transaction can volunteer to serve as the deadlock victim. The following code inside a transaction will inform SQL Server that the transaction should be rolled back in case of a deadlock:

```
SET DEADLOCK_PRIORITY LOW
```

## Minimizing Deadlocks

Even though deadlocks can be detected, it's better to avoid them altogether. The following practices will help prevent deadlocks:

✦ Keep the transaction short and to the point. Any code that doesn't have to be in the transaction shouldn't be in the transaction.

✦ Never code a transaction to depend on user input.

✦ Try to write batches and procedures so that they obtain locks in the same order — for example, TableA, then TableB, then TableC. This way one procedure will wait for the next, and a deadlock will be avoided.

✦ Plan the physical scheme to keep data that might be selected simultaneously close on the data page by normalizing the schema and carefully selecting the clustered indexes. Reducing the spread of the locks will help prevent lock escalation. Smaller locks will help prevent lock contention.

✦ Don't increase the isolation level unless it's necessary. A stricter isolation level will increase the duration of the lock.

# Application Locking Design

Aside from SQL Server locks, another locking issue deserves to be addressed. How the front-end application holds locks and deals with multi-user contention is important to the user's experience and to the integrity of the data.

## Implementing Optimistic Locking

The two basic means of dealing with multi-user access are *optimistic locking* and *pessimistic locking*. The one you use determines the coding methods of the application.

Optimistic locking assumes that no one else will attempt to change the data while a user is working on the data in a form. Therefore, optimistic locking does not apply locks while a user is working with data in the front-end application. The disadvantage of optimistic locking is that it can result in lost updates.

The pessimistic (or "Murphy") method takes a different approach. If anything can go wrong it will. So while a user is working on some data, a pessimistic locking scheme locks those data.

While pessimistic locking may work in small workgroup applications on desktop databases, large client/server applications require higher levels of concurrency. If SQL Server locks are held while a user has data open in a VB or Access form, the application will be unreasonably slow.

The best method is to implement an optimistic locking scheme using minimal SQL Server locks as well as a method for preventing lost updates.

## Lost Updates

A lost update occurs when two users edit the same row, complete their edits, and save the data, and the second user's update overwrites the first user's update. For example:

1. Joe opens Product "1001," 21-inch box kite, in the Visual Basic front-end application. SQL Server applies a shared lock for a split second while retrieving the data for VB.

2. Sue also opens the Product "1001" using the front-end application.

3. Joe and Sue both make edits to the box-kite data. Joe rephrases the product description, and Sue fixes the product category.

4. Joe saves the row from VB to SQL Server. The update command replaces the old product description with Joe's new description.

5. Sue presses the "save and close" button and her data are sent to SQL Server in an `update` statement. The product category is now fixed, but the old description was in Sue's form, so Joe's new description was overwritten with the old description.

6. Joe discovers the error and complains to the IT vice president during the next round of golf about the unreliability of that new SQL Server–based database.

Because lost updates only occur when two users edit the same row at the same time, the problem might not occur for months. Nonetheless, it's a flaw in the transactional integrity of the database and it needs to be prevented.

## Minimizing Lost Updates

If the application is going to use an optimistic locking scheme, try to minimize the chance that a lost update can occur, as well as minimize the effects of a lost update, using the following methods:

✦ Normalize the database so that it has many long, narrow tables. With fewer columns in a row the chance of a lost update is reduced. For example, the OBXKites database has a separate table for prices. A user can work on product pricing and not interfere with another user working on other product data.

✦ If the `update` statement is being constructed by the front-end application, have it check the controls and send an update for only those columns that are actually changed by the user. This technique alone would prevent the lost update in the previous example of Joe and Sue's updates, and most lost updates in the real world. As an added benefit, it reduces client/server traffic and the workload on SQL Server.

✦ If an optimistic locking scheme is not preventing lost updates, the application is using a "he who writes last, writes best" scheme. Although lost updates may occur, a data-audit trail can minimize the effect by exposing updates to the same row within minutes, and tracking the data changes.

Cross-Reference

Building a data-audit trail is discussed in Chapter 16, "Advanced Server-Side Programming."

## Preventing Lost Updates

A stronger solution to the lost update problem than just minimizing the effect is to block lost updates using the `rowversion` method. The `rowversion` data type, previously known as a `timestamp` in earlier versions of SQL Server, automatically provides a new value every time the row is updated. By comparing the `rowversion` value retrieved during the row select and the `rowversion` value at the time of update, it's trivial for code to detect a lost update.

The `rowversion` method can be used in `select` and `update` statements by adding the `rowversion` value in the `where` clause of the `update` statement.

The following sequence demonstrates the `rowversion` technique using two user updates. Both users begin by opening the 21-inch box kite in the front-end application. Both `select` statements retrieve the `RowVersion` column and `ProductName`:

```
SELECT RowVersion, ProductName
  FROM Product
  WHERE ProductCode = '1001'
```

Result:

```
RowVersion          ProductName
------------------  -------------------------
0x0000000000000077  Basic Box Kite 21 inch
```

Both front-end applications can grab the data and populate the form. Joe edits the `ProductName` to "Joe's Update." When Joe is ready to update the database, the "save and close" button executes the following SQL statement.

```
UPDATE Product
  SET ProductName = 'Joe''s Update'
  WHERE ProductCode = '1001'
    AND RowVersion = 0x0000000000000077
```

Once SQL Server has processed Joe's update, it automatically updates the `RowVersion` value as well. Checking the row again, Joe sees that his edit took effect:

```
SELECT RowVersion, ProductName
  FROM Product
  WHERE ProductCode = '1001'
```

Result:

```
RowVersion          ProductName
------------------  -------------------------
0x00000000000000B9  Joe's Update
```

If the update procedure checks to see if any rows were affected, it can detect that Joe's edit was accepted:

```
SELECT @@ROWCOUNT
```

Result:

```
1
```

Although the `RowVersion` columns' value was changed, Sue's front-end application isn't aware of the new value. When Sue attempts to save her edit, the `update` statement won't find any rows meeting that criterion:

```
UPDATE Product
  SET ProductName = 'Sue''s Update'
  WHERE ProductCode = '1001'
    AND RowVersion = 0x0000000000000077
```

If the update procedure checks to see if any rows were affected, it can detect that Sue's edit was ignored:

```
SELECT @@ROWCOUNT
```

Result:

```
0
```

This method can also be incorporated into applications driven by stored procedures. The fetch or get stored procedure returns the `rowversion` along with the rest of the data for the row. When the VB application is ready to update and calls the update stored procedure, it includes the rowversion as one of the required parameters. The update stored procedure can then check the rowversion and raise an error if the two don't match. If the method is sophisticated, the stored procedure or the front-end application can check the audit trail to see whether or not the columns updated would cause a lost update or report back the last user in the error message.

## Summary

A transaction is a logical unit of work. Although SQL Server can work well automatically using the default locks, there are several means of manipulating and controlling the locks. To develop a serious SQL Server application, your understanding of the ACID database principles, SQL Server's transaction log, and locking will contribute to the quality, performance, and reliability of the database.

The next chapter adds programming structure to the DML commands that have been used so far, so that a series of commands can be controlled as a batch.

✦     ✦     ✦

# Programming with Transact-SQL

Standard SQL Data Manipulation Language (DML) commands only modify or return data. SQL DML lacks both the programming structure to develop procedures and algorithms, and the database-specific commands to control and tune the server. To compensate, each full-featured database product must complement the SQL standard with some proprietary SQL language extension.

Transact-SQL, better known as T-SQL, is Microsoft's implementation of SQL plus its collection of extensions to SQL. The purpose of T-SQL is to provide a set of procedural tools for the development of a transactional database.

T-SQL is often thought of as synonymous with stored procedures. In reality it's much more than that. It may be employed in several different ways within a SQL Server client/server application:

 ◆ T-SQL is used within expressions as part of DML commands (insert, update, and delete) submitted by the client process.

 ◆ T-SQL is used within blocks of code submitted to SQL Server from a client as a batch or script.

 ◆ T-SQL functions are used as expressions within check constraints.

 ◆ T-SQL code is used within batches of code that have been packaged within SQL Server as stored procedures, functions, or triggers.

Truth be told, this book has been covering T-SQL programming since Chapter 6, "Retrieving Data with Select." The DML commands are the heart of T-SQL. This chapter merely adds the programmatic elements required to develop server-side procedural code. The language features explained in this chapter are the foundation for developing stored procedures, user-defined functions, and triggers.

## Transact-SQL Fundamentals

T-SQL is designed to add structure to the handling of sets of data. Because of this, it does not provide several language features that Visual Basic and C need. If you do a lot of VB-style development, you'll find that T-SQL is in many ways the exact opposite of VB.

# T-SQL Batches

A *query* is a single SQL DML statement, and a *batch* is a collection of one or more T-SQL statements. The entire collection is sent to SQL Server from the front-end application as a single unit of code.

SQL Server parses the entire batch as a unit. Any syntax error will cause the entire batch to fail, meaning that none of the batch will be executed. However, the parsing does not check any object names or schemas because a schema may change by the time the statement is executed.

## Terminating a Batch

A SQL script file or a Query Analyzer window may contain multiple batches. If this is the case, a batch-separator keyword terminates each batch. By default, the batch-separator keyword is go. (Similar to how the Start button is used to shut down Windows.) The batch-separator keyword must be the only keyword in the line. Any other characters, even a comment, on the same line will neutralize the batch separator.

The batch separator is actually a function of the Query Analyzer, not SQL Server. It can be modified in the Query Analyzer options, but I wouldn't recommend creating a custom batch separator (at least not for your friends).

Terminating a batch will kill all local variables, temporary tables, and cursors created by that batch.

## Switching Databases

The current database is indicated in the Query Analyzer toolbar and can be changed there. In code the current database is selected with the use command. Use can be inserted within a batch to specify the database from that point on.

It's a good practice to explicitly use the correct database with the use command, rather than to assume that the user will select the correct database.

## DDL Commands

Certain T-SQL commands must be in their own batch, or must be separated from other commands. As a rule, data definition language commands (create, alter, and delete) should be in their own batch.

## Executing Batches

A batch can be executed in several ways:

✦ All the batches in a SQL script may be executed by means of opening the .sql file with Query Analyzer and pressing F5 or selecting Query ➪ Execute. I have altered my Windows file settings so that double-clicking a .SQL file opens Query Analyzer.

✦ Selected T-SQL statements may be executed within Query Analyzer by means of highlighting those commands and pressing F5 or selecting Query ➪ Execute.

✦ An application can submit a T-SQL batch using ADO or ODBC for execution.

✦ A SQL script may be executed by means of running the OSQL command-line application and passing the SQL script file as a parameter (as demonstrated in Figure 12-1). ISQL can be found in the C:\Program Files\Microsoft SQL Server\80\Tools\Binn directory. The basic syntax for executing isql is as follows:

```
osql - Iscript_filename -Ooutput_file_name -Uuser_name
  -Ppassword -Sservername
```

OSQL, which uses ODBC, replaces the older ISQL, which uses DB Library to communicate with SQL Server.

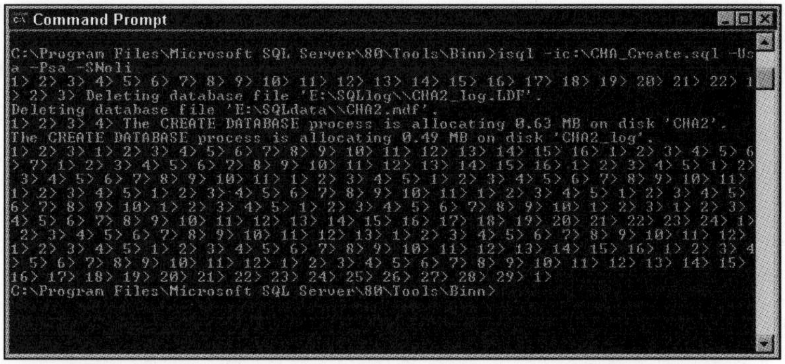

**Figure 12-1:** Executing the CHA_Create.sql script using OSQL in the command prompt.

## Executing a Stored Procedure

When calling a stored procedure within a SQL batch the `exec` command executes the stored procedure with a few special rules. In a sense, because line returns are meaningless to SQL Server, the `exec` command is serving to terminate the previous T-SQL command.

If the stored-procedure call is the first line of a batch (and if it's the only line then it's also the first line), the stored-procedure call doesn't require the `exec` command. However, including the `exec` command anyway won't cause any problems and prevents an error if the code is cut and pasted later.

The following two system-stored–procedure calls demonstrate the use of the `exec` command within a batch:

```
sp_help
EXEC sp_help
```

This section covered the batch aspects of `exec`. More about creative ways to use `exec` can be found in the "Dynamic SQL" section later in this chapter.

**Cross-Reference** SQL Server is configurable on three levels: the server level, the database level, and the connection, or batch, level. For more information about configuring the current connection, turn to Chapter 23, "Configuring SQL Server."

# T-SQL Formatting

Throughout this book, T-SQL code has been formatted for readability, which means that T-SQL formatting has been observed. This section specifies the details of formatting T-SQL code.

## Line Continuation

T-SQL commands, by their nature, tend to be long. Some of the queries in the last chapter, with multiple joins and subqueries, were over a page long. I like that T-SQL ignores spaces and end-of-line returns. This smart feature means that long lines can be continued without a special line-continuation character, which makes T-SQL code significantly more readable.

Other SQL implementations, Access for example, require a semicolon to terminate a SQL query. SQL Server will accept a semicolon, but does not require one.

## Comments

T-SQL accepts both ANSI-standard comments and C-style comments within the same batch.

The ANSI-standard comment begins with two hyphens and concludes with an end-of-line:

```
-- This is an ANSI-style comment
```

ANSI-style comments may be embedded within a single SQL command:

```
Select FirstName, LastName    -- selects the columns
  FROM Persons                -- the source table
  Where LastName Like 'Hal*'  -- the row restriction
```

Query Analyzer can apply or remove ANSI-style comments to all selected lines with the Edit ➪ Advanced ➪ Comment Out (Ctrl+Shift+C) and Edit ➪ Advanced ➪ Remove Comments (Ctrl+Shift+R) menu commands.

C language–style comments begin with /* and conclude with */. These comments are useful for commenting out a block of lines:

```
/*
Order table Insert Trigger
Paul Nielsen
ver 1.0 Sept 1, 1998
Logix: etc.
ver 1.1: Nov. 19, 1998
*/
```

The problem is that Query Analyzer will still read a go batch terminator within a C-style comment if it's the only word on the line, and that will terminate variables and cause other problems as well.

```
/*
go
*/
```

Result:

```
Server: Msg 113, Level 15, State 1, Line 1
Missing end comment mark '*/'.
Server: Msg 170, Level 15, State 1, Line 1
Line 1: Incorrect syntax near '*'.
```

This sure looks odd, but the go batch separator within the comment block terminates the first batch. Query Analyzer therefore submits this three-line script as two distinct batches. The first batch is only a begin-comment mark that is missing an end-comment mark. The second batch begins with an end-comment mark that is seen as a syntax error by SQL Server.

# Debugging Commands

Often the error won't occur at the exact word that is reported as the error. The word reported is simply how far SQL Server or the parser got before it detected the error. Usually the actual error is somewhere just before or after the reported error. Nevertheless, the error messages are generally close.

The Query Analyzer will display the error and the line number of the error within the batch. Double-clicking on the error message will place the cursor on the offending line.

SQL Server offers a few commands that aid in debugging T-SQL batches.

The `print` command sends a message without generating a result set. I find `print` messages useful progress notifications. With Query Analyzer in grid mode, execute the following batch:

```
Select 3
Print 6
```

The result is a record set displayed in the grid with a single row containing "3." The Messages tab displays the following result:

```
 (1 row(s) affected)
6
```

It is sometimes useful to slow down the code to check for locks or contention. The `waitfor` command can pause the code for a specified time. When the following batch executes, the output from the batch is displayed after a two-second pause:

```
Print 'Beginning'
waitfor delay '00:00:02'
Print 'Done'
```

Result:

```
Beginning
Done
```

# Variables

Every language requires variables to temporarily store values in memory. T-SQL variables are created with the `declare` command. The `declare` command is followed by the variable name and data type. The available data types are identical to those used to create tables with the addition of the table and the `SQLvariant` data types. Multiple comma-separated variables can be declared with a single `declare` command.

## Variable Default and Scope

The scope, or application and duration, of the variable is only the current batch. Newly declared variables default to `null` and must be initialized before they are included in an expression.

The following script creates two test variables and demonstrates their initial value and scope. The entire script is a single execution, even though it's technically two batches (separated by a `go`), so the results of the three `select` statements appear at the conclusion of the script.

```
DECLARE  @Test INT,
         @TestTwo NVARCHAR(25)
SELECT @Test, @TestTwo

SET @Test = 1
SET @TestTwo = 'a value'
```

```
SELECT @Test, @TestTwo
Go

SELECT @Test as BatchTwo, @TestTwo
```

**Result of the entire script:**

```
----------- -------------------------
NULL        NULL

(1 row(s) affected)


value
----------- -------------------------
1           a value

(1 row(s) affected)

Server: Msg 137, Level 15, State 2, Line 2
Must declare the variable '@Test'.
```

The first select returned two null values. After the variables have been initialized they properly return the sample values. When the batch concludes (due to the go terminator), so do the variables. Error message 137 is the result of the final select statement.

## Using the Set and Select Commands

Both the set command and the select command can assign the value of an expression to a variable. The main difference between the two is that a select can retrieve data from a table, subquery, or view and can include the other select clauses as well, while a set is limited to retrieving data from expressions. Both set and select can include functions.

Of course, a select statement may retrieve multiple columns. Each column may be assigned to a variable. If the select statement retrieves multiple rows, the values from the last row will be stored in the variables. No error will be reported.

The following SQL batch creates two variables and initializes one of them. The select statement will retrieve 32 rows, ordered by PersonID. The PersonID and the LastName of the last person returned by the select will be stored in the variables:

```
Declare @TempID INT,
        @TempLastName VARCHAR(25)
SET @TempID = 99
SELECT @TempID = PersonID,
    @TempLastName = LastName
  FROM Person
  ORDER BY PersonID
SELECT @TempID, @TempLastName
```

**Result:**

```
----------- -------------------------
32          Campbell
```

If no rows are returned from the select statement, the select does not affect the variables. In the following query, there is no person with a PersonID of 100, so the select statement does not affect the @TempID variable:

```
Declare @TempID INT,
         @TempLastName VARCHAR(25)
SET @TempID = 99
SELECT @TempID = PersonID,
    @TempLastName = LastName
  FROM Person
  WHERE PersonID = 100
  ORDER BY PersonID
SELECT @TempID, @TempLastName
```

The final select statement reports the value of @TempID, and indeed, it's still "99." The first select did not alter its value:

```
----------- -------------------------
99          NULL
```

## Conditional Select

Because the select statement includes a where clause, the following syntax works well, although those not familiar with it may be confused:

```
SELECT @Variable = expression WHERE BooleanExpression
```

The where clause functions as a conditional if statement. If the Boolean expression is true the select takes place. If not, the select is not performed, and the @variable is not altered in any way because the select command is not executed.

## Using Variables Within SQL Queries

One of my favorite features of T-SQL is that variables may be used with SQL queries without having to build any complex dynamic SQL strings to concatenate the variables into the code. Dynamic SQL still has its place, but the single value can simply be modified with a variable.

Anywhere an expression can be used within a SQL query, a variable may be used in its place. The following code demonstrates using a variable in a where clause:

```
USE OBXKites

DECLARE @ProductCode CHAR(10)
SET @ProductCode = '1001'

SELECT ProductName
  FROM Product
  WHERE Code = @ProductCode
```

Result:

```
Name
--------------------------------------------------
Basic Box Kite 21 inch
```

# Procedural Flow

At first glance it would appear that T-SQL is weak in procedural-flow options. While it's less rich than some other languages, it suffices. The data-handling Boolean extensions — such as exists, in, and case — offset the limitations of if and while.

## If

This is your grandfather's if. What's odd about the T-SQL if command is that it determines the execution of only the next single statement — one if, one command. Also, there's no then and no end if command to terminate the if block.

```
IF Condition
   Statement
```

In the following script, the if condition should return a false, preventing the next command from executing:

```
IF 1 = 0
   PRINT 'Line One'
PRINT 'Line Two'
```

Result:

```
Line Two
```

## Begin/End

An if command that can control only a single command is less than useful. However, a begin/end block can make multiple commands appear to the if command as the next single command:

```
IF Condition
   Begin
     Multiple lines
   End
```

I confess. Early one dreary morning a couple of years ago, I spent an hour trying to debug a stored procedure that always raised the same error no matter what I tried, only to realize that I had omitted the begin and end, causing the raiserror to execute regardless of the actual error condition. It's an easy mistake to make.

## If Exists()

While the if command may seem limited, the condition clause can include several powerful SQL features similar to a where clause, such as if exists() and if ...in().

The if exists() structure uses the presence of any rows returned from a SQL select statement as a condition. Because it looks for any row, the select statement should select all columns (*). This method is faster then checking an @@rowount >0 condition, because the total number of rows isn't required. As soon as a single row satisfies the if exists(), the query can move on.

The following example script uses the if exists() technique to process orders only if any open orders exist:

```
USE OBXKITES
IF EXISTS(SELECT * FROM [ORDER] WHERE Closed = 0)
```

```
BEGIN
  Print 'Process Orders'
END
```

Placing `select *` inside the `exists()` function is preferable to selecting the primary key for two reasons. One, the * might be faster because SQL Server is free to select the fastest index. Two, depending on the service pack level of SQL Server 2000, selecting the primary key will fail if the table is using a `GUID` as the primary key.

## If/Else

The optional `else` command defines code that is executed only when the `if` condition is false. Like `if`, `else` controls only the next single command or `begin`/`end` block.

```
IF Condition
  Single line or begin/end block of code
ELSE
  Single line or begin/end block of code
```

# While

The `while` command is used to loop through code while a condition is still true. Just like the `if` command, the `while` command will determine only the execution of the following single T-SQL command. To control a full block of commands the `begin`/`end` is used.

Some looping methods differ in the timing of the conditional test. The T-SQL `while` works in the following order:

1. The `while` command tests the condition. If the condition is true `while` executes the following command or block of code; if not it skips the following command or block of code, and moves on.

2. Once the following command or block of code is complete, flow of control is returned to the `while` command.

The following short script demonstrates using the `while` command to perform a loop:

```
Declare @Temp Int
Set @Temp = 0

While @Temp <3
  Begin
    Print 'tested condition' + Str(@Temp)
    Set @Temp = @Temp + 1
  End
```

Result:

```
tested condition        0
tested condition        1
tested condition        2
```

The `continue` and `break` commands enhance the `while` command for more complex loops. The `continue` immediately jumps back to the `while` command. The condition is tested as normal.

The break command immediately exits the loop and continues with the script as if the while condition were false. The following pseudo-code (not intended to actually run) demonstrates the break command:

```
CREATE PROCEDURE MyLife()
AS
WHILE Not @@Eyes2blurry = 1
  BEGIN
    EXEC Eat
    INSERT INTO Book(Words)
      FROM Brain(Words)
      WHERE Words
        IN('Make sense', 'Good Code', 'Best Practice')
    IF @StarTrekEnterprise_Status = 'On the tube'
      BREAK
  END
```

## Goto

Before you associate the T-SQL goto command with bad memories of 1970s-style spaghetti-BASIC, this goto command is limited to jumping to a label within the same batch or procedure and is rarely used for anything other than jumping to an error handler at the close of the batch or procedure.

The label is created by means of placing a colon after the label name:

```
LabelName:
```

The following code sample uses the goto command to branch to the errorhandler: label, bypassing the 'more code':

```
GOTO ErrorHandler
Print 'more code'
ErrorHandler:
Print 'Logging the error'
```

Result:

```
Logging the error
```

If you explore the Microsoft-developed system stored procedures you'll see a few development styles, most of which use goto and labels to create a structured procedure.

# Examining SQL Server with Code

One of the benefits of using SQL Server is the variety of interfaces with which to develop and administer the database. Enterprise Manager is great for graphically exploring a database; T-SQL code, while more complex, exposes even more detail within a programmer's environment.

## sp_help

Sp_help, and its 84 variations, return information regarding the server, the database, objects, connections, and more. The basic sp_help lists the available objects in the current database and the other variations provide detailed information about the various objects or settings.

Adding an object name as a parameter to `sp_help` returns further appropriate information about the object.

**Cross-Reference** Information on the schema is also available from the system tables and the information-schema views, as detailed in Chapter 3, "Installing and Configuring SQL Server."

## Global Variables

In most programming languages, a global variable is a variable with greater scope; not so in T-SQL. Global variables should be called system variables. They are read-only windows into the system status for the current connection and/or batch.

Global variables can't be created. There's a fixed set of 33 global variables, all beginning with two @ signs (listed in Table 12-1). The most commonly used global variables are @@Error, @@Identity, @@NestLevel, and @@ServerName.

### Table 12-1: Global Variables

| Global Variable | Returns | Scope |
|---|---|---|
| @@Connections | The total number of attempted connections since SQL Server started. | Server |
| @@CPU_Busy | The total amount of CPU time, in milliseconds, since SQL Server started. | Server |
| @@Cursor_Rows | The number of rows returned by the last cursor to be opened. | Connection |
| @@DateFirst | The day of the week currently set as the first day of the week; 1 represents Monday, 2 represents Tuesday, and so on. For example, if Sunday is the first day of the week @DateFirst returns a 7. | Connection |
| @@DBTS | Current database-wide timestamp value. | Database |
| @@Error | The error value for the last T-SQL statement executed. | Connection |
| @@Fetch_Status | The row status from the last cursor fetch command. | Connection |
| @@Identity | The last identity value generated for the current connection. | Connection |
| @@Idle | The total number of milliseconds SQL Server has been idle since it was started. | Server |
| @@IO_Busy | The total number of milliseconds SQL Server has been performing disk operations since it was started. | Server |
| @@LangID | The language ID used by the current connection. | Connection |
| @@Language | The language, by name, used by the current connection. | Connection |

*Continued*

## Table 12-1: (continued)

| Global Variable | Returns | Scope |
|---|---|---|
| @@Lock_TimeOut | The lock timeout setting for the current connection. | Connection |
| @@Max_Connections | The current maximum number of concurrent connections for SQL Server. | Server |
| @@Max_Precision | The decimal and numeric maximum precision setting. | Server |
| @@Nestlevel | The current number of nested stored procedures. | Connection |
| @@Options | A binary representation of all the current connection options. | Connection |
| @@Pack_Received | The total number of network communication packets received by SQL Server since it was started. | Server |
| @@Pack_Sent | The total number of network-communication packets sent by SQL Server since it was started. | Server |
| @@Packet_Errors | The total number of network communication–packets errors recognized by SQL Server since it was started. | Server |
| @@ProcID | The stored procedure identifier for the current stored procedure. This can be used with SysObjects to determine the name of the current stored procedure, as follows:<br><br>SELECT Name<br>  FROM SysObjects<br>   WHERE id = @@ProcID | Connection |
| @@RemServer | The name of the login server when running remote stored procedures. | Connection |
| @@RowCount | The number of rows returned by the last T-SQL statement. | Connection |
| @@ServerName | The name of the current server. | Server |
| @@ServiceName | SQL Server's Windows service name. | Server |
| @@SPID | The current connection's server-process identifier—the ID for the connection. | Connection |
| @@TextSize | The current maximum size of BLOB data (text, ntext, or image) | Connection |
| @@TimeTicks | The number of milliseconds per tick. | Server |
| @@Total_Errors | The total number of disk errors committed by SQL Server since it was started. | Server |

| Global Variable | Returns | Scope |
|---|---|---|
| @@Total_Read | The total number of disk reads by SQL Server since it was started. | Server |
| @@Total_Write | The total number of disk reads by SQL Server since it was started. | Server |
| @@TranCount | The number of active transactions for the current connection. | Connection |
| @@Version | The SQL Server edition, version, and service pack. | Server |

# Temporary Tables and Table Variables

Temporary tables and table variables play a different role from standard user tables. By their temporary nature, these objects are useful as a vehicle for passing data between objects or as a short-term scratch-pad table intended for very temporary work.

## Local Temporary Tables

A temporary table is created the same way as a standard user-defined table, except the temporary table must have a pound (hash sign) sign (#) preceding its name. Temporary tables are actually created on the disk in tempdb.

```
CREATE TABLE #ProductTemp (
ProductID INT PRIMARY KEY
)
```

A temporary table has a short life. When the batch or stored procedure that created it ends, the temporary table is deleted. If the table is created during an interactive session (such as a Query Analyzer window), it survives only until the end of that session. Of course, a temporary table can also be normally dropped within the batch.

The scope of a temporary table is also limited. Only the connection that created the local temporary table can see it. Even if a thousand users all create temporary tables with the same name, each user will only see his or her own temporary table. The temporary table is created in the tempdb with a unique name that combines the assigned table name and the connection identifier. Most objects can have names up to 128 characters in length, but temporary tables are limited to 116, so that the last 12 characters can make the name unique. To demonstrate the unique name, the following code creates a temporary table and then examines the name stored in sysobjects:

```
SELECT Name
   FROM TempDB.dbo.SysObjects
   WHERE Name Like '#Pro%'
```

Result (shortened to save space; the real value is 128 characters wide):

```
Name
-----------------------------------------------------------------
#ProductTemp_____00000000002D
```

Despite the long name in sysobjects, SQL queries still reference any temporary tables with the original name.

## Global Temporary Tables

Global temporary tables are similar to local temporary tables, but have a broader scope. All users can reference a global temporary table, and the life of the table extends until the last session accessing the table disconnects.

To create a global temporary table, begin the table name with two pound signs, (*##TableName*). The following code sample tests to see if the global temporary table exists, and creates one if it doesn't:

```
IF NOT EXISTS(
  SELECT * FROM Tempdb.dbo.Sysobjects
    WHERE Name = '##TempWork')
CREATE TABLE ##TempWork(
  PK INT,
  Col1 INT
)
```

When a temporary table is required, it's likely being used for a work in progress. Another alternative is to simply create a standard user table in `tempdb`. Every time the SQL Server is restarted it dumps and rebuilds `tempdb`, effectively clearing the alternative temporary worktable.

## Table Variables

Table variables are similar to temporary tables, but offer the benefit of existing only in memory. Table variables have the same scope and life as a variable. They are only seen by the batch, procedure, or function that creates them. They cease to exist when the batch, procedure, or function concludes. Table variables do have a few limitations:

✦ Table variables may not be created by means of the `select * into` or `insert into @tablename exec` table syntax.

✦ Table variables may not be created within functions.

✦ Table variables are limited in their allowable constraints: no foreign keys or check constraints are allowed. Primary keys, defaults, nulls, and unique constraints are OK.

✦ Table variables may not have any dependent objects, such as triggers or foreign keys.

Table variables are declared as variables rather than created with SQL DDL statements. When a table variable is being referenced with a SQL query, the table is used as a normal table but named as a variable. The following script must be executed as a single batch, or it will fail:

```
DECLARE @WorkTable TABLE (
  PK INT PRIMARY KEY,
  Col1 INT NOT NULL)

INSERT INTO @WorkTable (PK, Col1)
  VALUES ( 1, 101)

SELECT PK, Col1
  FROM @WorkTable
```

Result:

```
PK          Col1
----------- -----------
1           101
```

# Dynamic SQL

The term *dynamic SQL* has a couple conflicting definitions. Some say it describes any SQL query submitted by a client other than a stored procedure. It's more accurate to say that it describes any SQL DML statement assembled dynamically at runtime as a string and then submitted.

Dynamic SQL is very useful for doing the following:

✦ Assembling a custom where clause from multiple possible query criteria.

✦ Assembling a custom from clause that includes only the tables and joins required to meet the where conditions.

✦ Creating a dynamic order by clause sorting the data differently depending on the user request.

## Executing Dynamic SQL

The execute command, or exec for short, in effect creates a new instance of the batch as if the code executed were a called stored procedure. While the execute command is normally used to call a stored procedure, it can also be used to execute a T-SQL query or batch:

```
EXEC[UTE] ('T-SQL batch)
   WITH RECOMPILE
```

The with recompile option forces SQL Server to perform a fresh compile and not reuse any existing query-execution plans. If the T-SQL string and its parameters greatly change, the with recompile option will prevent a mismatched query-execution plan from performing poorly. But if the T-SQL string is a similar query, the needless recompile process will slow the execution. Most dynamic SQL procedures create extremely different SQL queries, so the with recompile option is generally appropriate.

For example, the following exec command executes a simple select statement:

```
USE Family
EXEC ('Select LastName from Person Where PersonID = 12')
```

Result:

```
LastName
---------------
Halloway
```

**Caution**

A problem with the execute command is that the SQL string is executed using the security context (login rights) of the user executing the stored procedure, rather than the user who created the stored procedure. This is in sharp contrast to the normal way that a stored procedure uses the security context of its owner if the ownership chain is unbroken. This fact alone can defeat the purpose of using dynamic SQL, depending on your security scheme.

## sp_excecuteSQL

A newer method of executing dynamic SQL is to use the sp_executeSQL system stored procedure. It offers greater compatibility with complex SQL queries than the straight execute command. In several situations I have found that the execute command would fail to execute the dynamic SQL, but that sp_executeSQL worked flawlessly.

```
EXEC Sp_ExecuteSQL
  'T-SQL query',
  Parameters Definition,
  Parameter, Parameter...
```

Concatenating strings is not allowed within 'T-SQL query', so parameters fill the need. The query and the definition must be Unicode strings.

Parameters provide optimization. If the T-SQL query has the same parameters for each execution, these parameters can be passed to sp_executeSQL so that the SQL query plan can be stored and future executions are optimized. The following example executes the same query from the Person table in the Family database, but this example uses parameters. (The N before the parameters is necessary because sp_executeSQL requires Unicode strings.)

```
EXEC sp_executeSQL
  N'Select LastName
      From Person
      Where PersonID = @PersonSelect',
  N'@PersonSelect INT',
  @PersonSelect = 12
```

Result:

```
LastName
---------------
Halloway
```

## Developing Dynamic SQL Code

Building a dynamic SQL string usually entails combining a select columns literal string with a more fluid from clause and where clause.

Once the SQL string is complete, the SQL statement is executed by means of the exec command. The following example builds both a custom from and where clause based on the user's requirements.

Within the batch, the NeedsAnd bit variable tracks the need for an and separator between where-clause conditions. If the product category is specified, the initial portion of the select statement includes the required joins to fetch the Product Category table. The where clause portion of the batch examines each possible user criterion. If the user has specified a criterion for that column, the column, with its criterion, is added to the @SQLWhere string.

Real-world dynamic SQL sometimes includes dozens of complex options. This example uses three possible columns for optional user criteria:

```
USE OBXKites

DECLARE
  @SQL NVARCHAR(1024),
  @SQLWhere NVARCHAR(1024),
  @NeedsAnd BIT,

  -- User Parameters
  @ProductName VARCHAR(50),
  @ProductCode VARCHAR(10),
  @ProductCategory VARCHAR(50)
```

```
-- Initialize Variables
SET @NeedsAnd = 0
SET @SQLWhere = ''

-- Simulate User's Requirements
SET @ProductName = NULL
SET @ProductCode = 1001
SET @ProductCategory = NULL


-- Assembly Dynamic SQL

-- Set up initial SQL Select
IF @ProductCategory IS NULL
  SET @SQL = 'Select ProductName from Product'
ELSE
  SET @SQL = 'Select ProductName
                from Product
                  Join ProductCategory
                    on Product.ProductCategoryID
                      = ProductCategory.ProductCategoryID'

-- Build the Dynamic Where Clause
IF @ProductName IS NOT NULL
  BEGIN
    SET @SQLWhere = 'ProductName = ' + @ProductName
    SET @NeedsAnd = 1
  END

 IF @ProductCode IS NOT NULL
  BEGIN
    IF @NeedsAnd = 1
      SET @SQLWhere = @SQLWhere + ' and '
    SET @SQLWhere = 'Code = ' + @ProductCode
    SET @NeedsAnd = 1
  END

IF @ProductCategory IS NOT NULL
  BEGIN
    IF @NeedsAnd = 1
      SET @SQLWhere = @SQLWhere + ' and '
    SET @SQLWhere = 'ProductCategory = ' + @ProductCategory
    SET @NeedsAnd = 1
  END

-- Assemble the select and the where portions of the dynamic SQL
IF @SQLWhere <> ''
  SET @SQL = @SQL + ' where ' + @SQLWhere

Print @SQL
EXEC sp_executeSQL @SQL
  WITH RECOMPILE
```

The results seen are both the printed text of the dynamic SQL and the data returned from the execution of the dynamic SQL statement:

```
Select Name from Product where Code = 1001

Name
----------------------------------------------------
Basic Box Kite 21 inch
```

**Cross-Reference**    The dynamic audit-trail method uses a complex dynamic SQL method in its stored procedure. The audit trail is covered in Chapter 16, "Advanced Server-Side Programming."

# Recursive Select Variables

A *recursive select variable* is a fascinating method that appends a variable to itself using a select statement and a subquery. I've traced this method back to B. P. Margolin, and applaud the creative use of the SQL select. This section demonstrates two real-world uses of recursive select variables, but because it's an unusual use of the select statement here it is in its basic form:

```
SELECT @variable = @variable + d.column
   FROM  (Derived Table) as d
```

Each row from the derived table is appended to the variable, changing the vertical column in the underlying table into a horizontal list. This makes some of the uses of a cursor obsolete. For example, cursors are traditionally required for denormalizing a list or creating a dynamic crosstab query, but a recursive select variable handles the job dramatically faster and with less code.

## Denormalizing a List

This type of data retrieval is quite common. Often a vertical list of values is better reported as a single comma delimited horizontal list than as a subreport or another subheading level several inches long. A short horizontal list is more readable and saves space.

The following example builds a list of event dates for the Outer Banks Lighthouses tour offered by Cape Hatteras Adventures in the sample database:

```
USE CHA2
DECLARE
  @EventDates VARCHAR(1024)
SET @EventDates = ''

SELECT @EventDates = @EventDates
  + CONVERT(VARCHAR(15), a.d,107 ) + ';  '
      FROM (select DateBegin as [d]
              from Event
                join Tour
                  on Event.TourID = Tour.TourID
          WHERE Tour.[Name] = 'Outer Banks Lighthouses') as a

SELECT Left(@EventDates, Len(@EventDates)-1)
  AS 'Outer Banks Lighthouses Events'
```

Result:

```
Outer Banks Lighthouses Events
------------------------------------------------------------
Feb 02, 2001;  Jun 06, 2001;  Jul 03, 2001;  Aug 17, 2001;
   Oct 03, 2001;  Nov 16, 2001
```

## Dynamic Crosstab Queries

Another complex database task is generating crosstabs. Chapter 7, "Merging Data Using Relational Algebra," discussed how to build crosstabs with fixed columns. Building a crosstab with dynamic columns requires more than just a well-written query, because the X values, or columns, are unknown before the query is executed. A dynamic crosstab, much like Microsoft Access's crosstab, has the benefits of flexibility and reduced maintenance.

There are several crosstab options, but very few dynamic-crosstab options. Traditionally cursors have been used to brute-force through the data, or to assemble the columns so that dynamic SQL can execute the dynamic crosstab query.

To set the goal of the following code sample, this first query is a copy of the case-style crosstab used in Chapter 7 for a fixed-column crosstab:

```
SELECT Y,
   SUM(Case X WHEN 'A' THEN Data ELSE 0 END) AS A,
   SUM(Case X WHEN 'B' THEN Data ELSE 0 END) AS B,
   SUM(Case X WHEN 'C' THEN Data ELSE 0 END) AS C,
   SUM(Case X WHEN 'D' THEN Data ELSE 0 END) AS D,
   SUM(Data) as Total
   FROM RawData
   GROUP BY Y
   ORDER BY Y
```

The job of the dynamic query code is to assemble the fixed-code crosstab query without specifying the X, or column, values. The subquery returns a list of X values. The recursive select variable appends the values, along with the other text required to build the dynamic crosstab query, to the @XColumns variable. The final set statement builds the completed dynamic-SQL string:

```
USE TempDB

DECLARE   @XColumns NVARCHAR(1024)
SET @XColumns = ''
SELECT @XColumns
   = @XColumns
     + ' SUM(Case X
           WHEN ''' + [a].[Column] + ''' THEN Data
           ELSE 0
           END) AS '
     + [a].[Column] + ','
   FROM
     (SELECT DISTINCT X as [Column]
       FROM RawData  ) as a
SET @XColumns = 'SELECT Y,' + @XColumns
   + ' SUM(Data) as Total FROM RawData GROUP BY Y ORDER BY Y'

EXEC sp_executesql @Xcolumns
```

Result:

```
Y    A    B   C   D   Total
---- ---- --- --- --- -----
X    6    2   3   0   11
Y    12   5   0   56  73
Z    7    8   9   10  34
```

**On the CD-ROM** If dynamic crosstabs are important to your project, you should consider Steve Dassin's freeware program, Relational Application Companion (RAC). It's a very impressive crosstab-generating stored procedure for SQL Server 2000. A trial copy is on the book's CD.

# Cursors

SQL is designed to handle sets of rows. However, some situations require that the code work with individual rows. For these cases, SQL provides cursors to step through the set of rows one row at a time.

Cursors are appropriate for very few situations:

✦ To step through a complex series of row-dependent processes.

That's a short list. I used to include dynamic crosstabs, denormalizing lists, and stepping through recursive relationships in my list of tasks that required cursors, but advanced queries and the recursive select variable technique solves those problems significantly faster than a cursor. I included them in this section anyway, as additional examples of real-world tasks that can be solved with cursors.

**Best Practice** To quote a genuine programming hero, Bill Vaughn, "Cursors are evil!" (VBits 97 Conference at The Dolphin, DisneyWorld, Orlando, Florida).

In my informal testing, row-based cursors are 50–70 *times* slower than set-based SQL selects. *Never* use a cursor unless it is absolutely required and you've proven after days of trying and posting messages to the SQL forums that the job can't be done with a set-based query. In all my SQL programming days I've resorted to using a cursor in a production database twice: once to traverse an object-class hierarchy, and once when allocating inventory during an MRPII process. And, today I think I could do both with set-based queries.

Procedural programmers tend to think in terms of rows and loops. Unlearning this style of programming and learning to solve problems using a set-based mindset is the biggest challenge to procedural programmers who become database developers.

A server-side T-SQL cursor is different from a client-side ADO cursor. The T-SQL cursor occurs inside the server before any data is ever sent to the client. Client-side cursors are used to scroll through the rows in a record set.

## Cursor Basics

A cursor establishes a result set from a select statement and then fetches a single row at a time. The five steps in the life of a cursor are:

1. **Declaring** the cursor establishes the select statement the cursor will pull data from. Declaring the cursor doesn't retrieve any data; it only sets up the select statement. This is the one time that declare doesn't require an ampersand:

```
DECLARE CursorName CURSOR CursorOptions
  FOR Select Statement
```

**2.** Opening the `cursor` retrieves the data and fills the `cursor`:

```
OPEN CursorName
```

**3.** Fetching moves to the next row and assigns the values from each column returned by the `cursor` into a local variable. The variables must have been previously declared.

```
FETCH CursorName INTO @Variable1, @Variable2
```

`Fetch` can optionally move to an absolute position in the result set, or move forward or backward *n* number of rows. However, I don't recommend doing that much work with a cursor.

Typically the batch will use a `while` loop to repeatedly fetch rows from the cursor until the `cursor` doesn't return any more rows. The top of the `cursor` loop examines the `@@Fetch_Status` global variable to tell if the `cursor` is done:

```
WHILE @@Fetch_Status = 0
```

**4.** Closing the `cursor` releases the data but retains the `select` statement. The `cursor` can be opened again at this point. (`Close` is the counterpart to `open`.)

```
Close CursorName
```

**5.** Deallocating the `cursor` releases the memory and removes the definitions of the cursor. (`Deallocate` is the counterpart to `create`.)

```
DEALLOCATE CursorName
```

The next few examples will also help illustrate how to create a `cursor`.

## Cursor Options

Cursors have a few additional features that extend their capability to manage data and update data. These features include dynamic cursors, scrollable cursors, the option to pass cursors as parameters, and the option to store cursors in variables. However, if you limit cursors to reading the data and the one legitimate purpose previously discussed, the additional options are of little value.

**Best Practice**

Cursors have too many options such as `scrollable` and `updateable`. SQL grew out of the old ISAM databases and cursors are like the gnarly old roots that won't go away. Many of the `cursor` options are left over from SQL implementations that required the database developer to build a `cursor` to perform work or return a data set. Ignore them.

The complexity of cursors deceives developers into thinking, "Cursors must be good. This looks just like an ADO record set. Look at all the cool options available to optimize the cursor."

For the sake of reducing locks and improving performance, I suggest using only read-only fast-forward cursors. If the data requires updating, do it with an `update` statement inside the procedure. If cursor options are required to perform the task, you're probably overlooking a better set-based approach.

## Cursor Scope

The scope of the `cursor` determines whether the cursor lives only in the batch in which it was created, or the scope of a `cursor` extends to any called procedures. The scope can be configured as the `cursor` is declared:

```
DECLARE CursorName CURSOR Local or Global
  FOR Select Statement
```

The default cursor scope is set at the database level with the cursor_default option:

```
ALTER DATABASE Family SET CURSOR_DEFAULT LOCAL
```

The current cursor scope is important to the execution of the procedure. To examine the current default setting use the database property's examine function:

```
SELECT  DATABASEPROPERTYEX('Family', 'IsLocalCursorsDefault')
```

Result:

```
1
```

## Working with Cursors

Two global variables are essential for working with a cursor. @@cursor_rows will return the number of rows in the cursor. If the cursor is populated asynchronously then @@cursor_rows will return a negative number.

The @@Fetch_Status global variable reports the state of the cursor after the last fetch command. This information is useful to control the flow of the cursor as it reaches the end of the result set. The possible @@Fetch_Status values indicate the following:

✦ 0 — The last fetch successfully retrieved a row.

✦ 1 — The last fetch reached the end of the result set.

✦ 2 — The last row fetched was not available; the row has been deleted.

Combining @@Fetch_Status with the while command builds a useful loop with which to move through the rows.

## Denormalizing a List with a Cursor

The first example of a cursor in action solves the Outer Banks Lighthouses tour date problem that was previously solved with the recursive select variable. The cursor locates all dates for the tours. The while loop repeatedly fetches the date and appends each fetched date to the @EventDates local variable. The @SemiColon bit local variable determines whether a semicolon separator is required between the dates. At the end of the batch, the select statement returns the denormalized list of dates.

```
USE CHA2
DECLARE
  @EventDates VARCHAR(1024),
  @EventDate DATETIME,
  @SemiColon BIT

SET @Semicolon = 0
SET @EventDates = ''

DECLARE cEvent CURSOR FAST_FORWARD
  FOR SELECT DateBegin
      FROM Event
        JOIN Tour
          ON Event.TourID = Tour.TourID
        WHERE Tour.[Name] = 'Outer Banks Lighthouses'
```

```
    OPEN cEvent
    FETCH cEvent INTO @EventDate   -- prime the cursor

    WHILE @@Fetch_Status = 0
      BEGIN
        IF @Semicolon = 1
          SET @EventDates
            = @EventDates + '; '
              + Convert(VARCHAR(15), @EventDate, 107 )
        ELSE
          BEGIN
            SET @EventDates
                = Convert(VARCHAR(15), @EventDate,107 )
            SET @SEMICOLON = 1
          END

          FETCH cEvent INTO @EventDate   -- fetch next
      END
    CLOSE cEvent
DEALLOCATE cEvent

SELECT @EventDates
```

Result:

```
----------------------------------------------------------
Feb 02, 2001; Jun 06, 2001; Jul 03, 2001; Aug 17, 2001;
  Oct 03, 2001; Nov 16, 2001
```

# Building a Dynamic-Crosstab Query with a Cursor

While using the recursive select variable is a much more elegant solution to the dynamic-crosstab problem than using a cursor, it's still an excellent example of building a cursor. This batch uses the same set of data as the fixed-column crosstab example in Chapter 7, "Merging Data Using Relational Algebra."

The batch creates a cursor that will step though each X-dimension value. As the cursor is fetching each X value, a set command assembles the dynamic SQL for the columns of the crosstab query. The final set command near the end concatenates the initial portion of the crosstab query (select Y) with the dynamic columns and the conclusion of the query. By assembling the dynamic SQL query code into a variable, the code can be inspected for debugging. The last line executes the dynamic string:

```
DECLARE
  @XColumns NVARCHAR(1024),
  @XColumn VARCHAR(50),
  @SemiColon BIT

SET @Semicolon = 0
SET @XColumns = ''

DECLARE ColNames CURSOR FAST_FORWARD
  FOR
  SELECT DISTINCT X as [Column]
    FROM RawData
    ORDER BY X
```

```
OPEN ColNames

FETCH ColNames INTO @XColumn
WHILE @@Fetch_Status = 0
  BEGIN
    SET @XColumns = @XColumns  +
      ', SUM(Case X WHEN ''' + @XColumn + '''
       THEN Data ELSE 0 END) AS ' + @XColumn
      FETCH ColNames INTO @XColumn  -- fetch next
  END
CLOSE ColNames
DEALLOCATE ColNames

SET @XColumns = 'SELECT Y' + @XColumns
  + ', SUM(Data) as Total FROM RawData GROUP BY Y ORDER BY Y'

EXEC sp_executesql @Xcolumns
```

Result:

```
Y    A     B    C    D    Total
----  ----  ---  ---  ---  -----
X    6     2    3    0    11
Y    12    5    0    56   73
Z    7     8    9    10   34
```

# Navigating a Tree with a Recursive Cursor

Another case in which a cursor is typically employed is navigating a *reflexive* relationship, sometimes called a *recursive* or *self-join* relationship, which creates a hierarchical tree structure. This type of structure is often used in human-resource organizational charts, genealogies, and bill-of-materials databases. It's also used to navigate the class hierarchy in an object-oriented database.

## Using a Standard Select Statement

Generating a result listing is difficult because the number of generations is dynamic, whereas a SQL select query requires a known set of tables. A select query can handle a fixed number of generations. But, when the number of generations isn't known, a pre-coded select statement can't handle the flexibility. As a sample, the following query returns the grandfather and two generations:

```
USE Family
SELECT
    Person.FirstName + ' ' + IsNull(Person.SrJr,'')
      as Grandfather,
    Gen1.FirstName  + ' ' +  IsNull(Gen1.SrJr,'') as Gen1,
    Gen2.FirstName  + ' ' +  IsNull(Gen2.SrJr,'') as Gen2
  FROM Person
    LEFT JOIN Person Gen1
      ON Person.PersonID = Gen1.FatherID
    LEFT JOIN Person Gen2
      ON Gen1.PersonID = Gen2.FatherID
  WHERE Person.PersonID = 2
```

Result:

```
Grandfather          Gen1                 Gen2
-----------------    -----------------    -----------------
James 1              James 2              Melanie
James 1              James 2              Corwin
James 1              James 2              Dara
James 1              James 2              James 3
```

Alternately, the query could report every parent and every child by joining two instances of the Person table. However, that still doesn't produce a useful tree.

## Using a Recursive Cursor

To produce a tree, the cursor examines each child and prints the child indented to the generation level. The cursor does this by selecting all the children of the current person (persons whose MotherID or FatherID matches the current person). Once the cursor is declared and opened each fetch will print the child and recursively call another instance of the procedure to see if the current person has any children. If so, the children will be examined — and so on, and so on.

For every person, the recursive routine is called to check for any children.

The recursive nature of the routine will cause it to run straight down the tree, finding each firstborn child ("5", "8", "15"), followed by finding the siblings of "15" ("16", "29"). The recursive routine then moves back up to the siblings of "8" and finds "10." "10"'s children are examined and the firstborn is found to be "19." The recursive routine is called for "19"'s children and "22" and "21" are returned. The recursive routine is called for "22" and "2" but no children are found.

**Cross-Reference** This example of a cursor creates a stored procedure so the cursor may be called recursively. Saving batches as stored procedures is covered in Chapter 13, "Developing Stored Procedures."

By default, the scope of a cursor extends to any called procedures. But the recursive tree problem requires that each called cursor fetch its own results. Setting the cursor option to local restricts the scope of the cursor and allows a recursive cursor. The option can be set in the cursor declaration or as a database option. The following example demonstrates both methods:

```
ALTER DATABASE Family SET CURSOR_DEFAULT LOCAL
SELECT DATABASEPROPERTYEX('Family', 'IsLocalCursorsDefault')
```

Return:

```
1
```

The following batch creates the ExamineChild procedure, which includes the cursor that tests for children of the current Person row. If children are detected, the stored procedure calls itself recursively:

```
CREATE PROCEDURE ExamineChild
  (@ParentID INT)
AS
SET Nocount On
DECLARE @ChildID INT,
  @Childname VARCHAR(25)
```

```
DECLARE cChild CURSOR LOCAL FAST_FORWARD
  FOR SELECT PersonID,
          Firstname + ' ' + LastName + ' ' + IsNull(SrJr,'')
          as PersonName
        FROM Person
        WHERE Person.FatherID = @ParentID
        OR Person.MotherID = @ParentID
        ORDER BY Person.DateOfBirth
  OPEN cChild
  FETCH cChild INTO @ChildID, @ChildName   -- prime the cursor
  WHILE @@Fetch_Status = 0
    BEGIN
      PRINT
        SPACE(@@NestLevel * 2) + '+ '
          + Cast(@ChildID as VARCHAR(4))
          + ' ' + @ChildName
      -- Recursively find the grandchildren
      EXEC ExamineChild @ChildID
        FETCH cChild INTO @ChildID, @ChildName
    END
  CLOSE cChild
DEALLOCATE cChild
```

The recursive cursor stored procedure is called passing to it `PersonID 2`, **James Halloway the First**. The cursor will locate all of his descendents:

```
EXEC ExamineChild 2
```

Result:

```
+ 5 James Halloway 2
  + 8 Melanie Campbell
    + 15 Shannon Ramsey
    + 16 Jennifer Ramsey
    + 29 Adam Campbell
  + 10 James Halloway 3
    + 19 James Halloway 4
      + 22 Chris Halloway
      + 21 James Halloway 5
    + 18 Abbie Halloway
    + 17 Allie Halloway
  + 9 Dara Halloway
    + 23 Joshua Halloway
    + 24 Laura Halloway
  + 7 Corwin Halloway
    + 14 Logan Halloway
```

Using a `cursor` is an adequate solution to the recursive tree problem when the data set is small, but it fails for large data sets for two reasons. First, SQL Server limits the stored procedures nesting level to 32 level deep, so for recursive trees with more than 32 levels (less any code used to call the recursive `cursor` code) will fail. The second concern is performance (which is generally the case with any `cursor` solution).

A recursive tree data set with five million rows organized into 12 tree levels will work, but it will have five million iterations of the cursor and the equivalent of five million single row select statements.

## Using a Set-Based Solution

Nearly all cursors can be replaced with creative set-based solutions. In this case, the set-based solution handles each level, or generation, in a single insert/select. The performance gains are dramatic.

The batch begins with a single person and stuffs that into the #FamilyTree temp table. Then, the batch steps though each generation and appends every person with a parent in the previous generation to the temp table using a multi-condition join.

For each person in the #FamilyTree temp table, the FamilyLine column contains the parent's FamilyLine data concatenated with the parent's PersonID. The FamilyLine column provides the data required to sort the tree.

When no new people are found, the while condition is no longer satisfied and the batch is complete. So, here's the set-based code that makes the cursor obsolete for solving recursive tree problems:

```
CREATE TABLE #FamilyTree (
  PersonID INT,
  Generation INT,
  FamilyLine VarChar(25) Default ''
  )

DECLARE
  @Generation INT,
  @FirstPerson INT

SET @Generation = 1
SET @FirstPerson = 2

-- prime the temp table with the top person(s) in the queue
INSERT #FamilyTree (PersonID, Generation, FamilyLine)
  SELECT @FirstPerson, @Generation, @FirstPerson

WHILE @@RowCount > 0
  BEGIN
    SET @Generation = @Generation + 1

    INSERT #FamilyTree (PersonID, Generation, FamilyLine)
      SELECT Person.PersonID,
             @Generation,
             #FamilyTree.FamilyLine
             + ' ' + Str(Person.PersonID,5)
        FROM Person
          JOIN #FamilyTree
            ON #FamilyTree.Generation = @Generation - 1
              AND
              (Person.MotherID = #FamilyTree.PersonID
                OR
               Person.FatherID = #FamilyTree.PersonID)

  END
```

With the #FamilyTree temp table populated, the following query examines the raw data:

```
SELECT PersonID, Generation, FamilyLine
  FROM #FamilyTree
  Order by FamilyLine
```

Result (abridged):

```
PersonID    Generation  FamilyLine
----------- ----------- -------------------------
2           1           2
5           2           2    5
7           3           2    5    7
14          4           2    5    7    14
...
22          5           2    5    10   19   22
```

Similar to the previous cursor solution, the next query uses the same space() function to format the result and it joins with the Person table so it can display the name:

```
SELECT SPACE(Generation * 2) + '+ '
          + Cast(#FamilyTree.PersonID as VARCHAR(4)) + ' '
          + FirstName + ' ' + LastName
          + IsNull(SrJr,'') AS FamilyTree
  FROM #FamilyTree
    JOIN Person
      ON #FamilyTree.PersonID = Person.PersonID
  ORDER BY FamilyLine
```

Result:

```
FamilyTree
------------------------------------------------------
+ 2 James Halloway 1
  + 5 James Halloway 2
    + 7 Corwin Halloway
      + 14 Logan Halloway
    + 8 Melanie Campbell
      + 15 Shannon Ramsey
      + 16 Jennifer Ramsey
      + 29 Adam Campbell
    + 9 Dara Halloway
      + 23 Joshua Halloway
      + 24 Laura Halloway
  + 10 James Halloway 3
    + 17 Allie Halloway
    + 18 Abbie Halloway
    + 19 James Halloway 4
      + 21 James Halloway 5
      + 22 Chris Halloway
```

In a dramatic contrast to the cursor based solution to the recursive tree problem, if the recursive tree was loaded with five million rows in 12 hierarchical levels, the set-based solution would perform 12 iterations and 12 optimizable queries.

While cursors may seem to be the standard computer science method of handling data, the previous examples have demonstrated that, for the majority of cases, a set-oriented solution will do the same job with greater performance and scalability.

# Error Handling

Of course, all robust programming languages provide some method for trapping, logging, and handling errors. In this area, T-SQL is a mixed bag. The error handling works well (aside from a few quirks), but some fatal errors cause the code to simply bomb out of T-SQL without giving you the opportunity to test for the error or handle it.

## Using @@Error

The @@Error global variable contains the error status for the previous T-SQL command in the code. 0 indicates success.

The difficulty is that @@Error is not like other languages that hold the last error in a variable until another error occurs. @@Error is updated for every command, so even testing its value updates it.

The following code sample attempts to update the primary key to a value already in use. This violates the marriage foreign-key constraint and generates an error. The two print commands demonstrate how @@Error is reset by every T-SQL command. The first print command displays the success or failure of the update. The second print command displays the success or failure of the first:

```
USE Family
UPDATE Person
  SET PersonID = 1
  Where PersonID = 2
Print @@Error
Print @@Error
```

Result:

```
Server: Msg 547, Level 16, State 1, Line 1
UPDATE statement conflicted with COLUMN REFERENCE constraint
  'FK__Marriage__Husband__7B905C75'. The conflict occurred in
  database 'Family', table 'Marriage', column 'HusbandID'.
  The statement has been terminated.
547
0
```

The solution to the last error status problem is to save the error status to a local variable. This method retains the error status so it may be properly tested and then handled. The following batch uses @err as a temporary error variable:

```
USE Family
DECLARE @err INT

UPDATE Person
  SET PersonID = 1
  Where PersonID = 2
SET @err = @@Error

IF @err <> 0
  Begin
    -- error handling code
    Print @err
  End
```

Result:

```
Server: Msg 547, Level 16, State 1, Line 1
UPDATE statement conflicted with COLUMN REFERENCE constraint
'FK__Marriage__Husband__7B905C75'. The conflict occurred in database
'Family', table 'Marriage', column 'HusbandID'.
The statement has been terminated.
547
```

## Using @@RowCount

Another way to determine if the query was a success is to check the number of rows affected. Even if no error was generated it's possible that the data didn't match and the operation failed. The @@RowCount global variable is useful for checking the effectiveness of the query.

The reset issue that affects @@Error also affects @@RowCount. However, there's no need to store the 0 value.

The following batch uses @@RowCount to check for rows updated. The failure results from the incorrect where clause condition. No row with PersonID = 100 exists. @@RowCount is used to detect the query failure.

```
USE FAMILY
UPDATE Person
  SET LastName = 'Johnson'
  WHERE PersonID = 100

IF @@RowCount = 0
  Begin
    -- error handling code
    Print 'no rows affected'
  End
```

Result:

```
no rows affected
```

## T-SQL Fatal Errors

If T-SQL encounters a fatal error the batch will immediately abort without giving you the opportunity to test @@Error, handle the error, or correct the situation.

Fatal errors are rare enough that they shouldn't pose much of a problem. Generally, if the code works once it should continue to work unless the schema is changed or SQL Server is reconfigured. The most common fatal errors are those caused by the following:

✦ Data-type incompatibilities

✦ Unavailable SQL Server resources

✦ Syntax errors

✦ Incompatible SQL Server advanced settings that are incompatible with certain tasks

✦ Missing objects or misspelled object names

Chapter 12 ✦ **Programming with Transact-SQL**    397

For a list of most of the fatal error messages, run the following query:

```
SELECT Error, Severity, Description
  FROM Master.dbo.SysMessages
  WHERE Severity >= 19
  ORDER BY Severity, Error
```

@@Error does a good job of handling typical day-to-day user errors, such as constraint-violation errors. Nevertheless, to be safe, the front-end application developers should also include error-handling code in their programs.

# Raiserror

To return custom error messages to the calling procedure or front-end application, use the raiserror command. Two forms for raiserror exist: a legacy simple form and the recommended complete form.

## The Simple Raiserror Form

The simple form, which dates from the Sybase days, passes only a hard-coded number and message. The severity level is always passed back as 16 — user error severe.

```
RAISERROR ErrorNumber, ErrorMessage
```

For example, this code passes back a simple error message:

```
RAISERROR 5551212  'Unable to update customer.'
```

Result:

```
Server: Msg 5551212, Level 16, State 1, Line 1
'Unable to update customer.'
```

## The Complete Raiserror Form

The improved form incorporates the following four new useful features into the raiserror command:

✦ Specifies the severity level

✦ Dynamically modifies the error message

✦ Uses server-wide stored messages

✦ May optionally log the error to the event log

The syntax for the Windows raiserror adds parameters for the severity level, state (seldom used), and message-string arguments:

```
RAISERROR (
  message or number, severity, state, optional arguments
  ) With Log
```

## Error Severity

Windows has established standard error-severity codes, listed in Table 12-2. The other severity codes are reserved for Microsoft use.

---

### Table 12-2: Available Severity Codes

| Severity Code | Description |
|---|---|
| 10 | Status message: Does not raise an error, but returns a message, such as a `print` statement. |
| 11–13 | No special meaning. |
| 14 | Informational message. |
| 15 | Warning message: Something may be wrong. |
| 16 | Critical error: The procedure failed. |

---

## Adding Variable Parameters to Messages

The error message can be a fixed-string message or the error number of a stored message. Either type can work with optional arguments.

The arguments are substituted for placeholders within the error message. While several types and options are possible, the placeholders I find useful are `%s` for a string and `%i` for a signed integer. The following example uses one string argument:

```
RAISERROR ('Unable to update %s.', 14, 1, 'Customer')
```

Result:

```
Server: Msg 50000, Level 14, State 1, Line 1
Unable to update Customer.
```

## Stored Messages

The Windows `raiserror` command can also pull a message from the `Master.dbo.SysMessages` table. Message numbers 1–50,000 are reserved for Microsoft. Higher message numbers are available for user-defined messages. The benefit of using stored messages is that any messages are forced to become consistent and numbered.

An issue with `SysMessages` stored messages is that the message-number scheme is server-wide. If two vendors or two databases use overlapping messages then no division exists between databases, and there's no solution beyond recoding all the error handling on one of the projects. The second issue is that when migrating a database to a new server, the messages must also be moved.

Messages can be added to the `SysMessages` table in two ways. As illustrated in Figure 12-2, Enterprise Manager has an interface for searching for, modifying, and managing system messages. You can get to the dialog box by selecting a server and then choosing All Tasks ➪ Manage SQL Server Messages from the right-click menu.

The `SysMessages` table includes columns for the `MessageId`, `Message`, `Severity` and whether the error should be logged. However, the severity of the `raiserror` command is used instead of the `Severity` from the `SysMessage` table, so `SysMessage.Severity` is moot.

To manage messages in code use the `sp_addmessage` system stored procedure:

```
EXEC sp_addmessage 50001, 16, 'Unable to update %s'
```

For database projects that may be deployed in multiple languages, the optional `@lang` parameter can be used to specify the language for the error message.

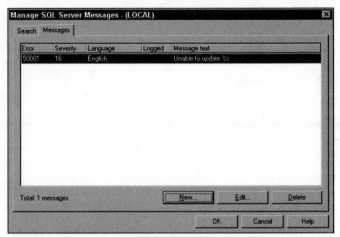

**Figure 12-2:** Enterprise Manager can be used to manage user-defined error messages.

If the message already exists, a `replace` parameter must be added to the system stored procedure call, as follows:

```
EXEC sp_addmessage 50001, 16,
   'Still unable to update %s', @Replace = 'Replace'
```

To move messages between servers do any one of the following:

✦ Use the Copy Database Wizard or DTS.

✦ Save the script that was originally used to load the messages.

✦ Use the following query to generate a script that adds the messages:

```
SELECT 'EXEC sp_addmessage, '
   + Cast(Error as VARCHAR(7))
   + ', ' + Cast(Severity as VARCHAR(2))
   + ', ''' + [Description] +  ''''
FROM Master.dbo.SysMessages
WHERE Error > 50000
```

Result:

```
------------------------------------------------------------

   EXEC sp_addmessage, 50001, 16, 'Still unable to update %s'
```

To drop a message use the `sp_dropmessage` system stored procedure with the error number:

```
EXEC sp_dropmessage 50001
```

## Logging the Error

Another advantage of using the Windows form of the `raiserror` command is that it can log the error to the Windows NT Application Event Log and the SQL Server event log. The downside to the Application Event Log is that it's stored on individual workstations. While they're great places to log front-end "unable to connect" errors, they're inconvenient places to store database errors.

There are two ways to specify that an event should be logged:

✦ If the stored message is created with the @with_log = 'with_log' option, or the "always log" checkbox is selected during the addition of a new message with Enterprise Manager, the error will be logged.

✦ From the raiserror command, the with log option causes the current error message to be logged.

The following raiserror command writes the error to the event log:

```
RAISERROR ('Unable to update %s.', 14, 1, 'Customer')
   WITH LOG
```

Result:

```
Server: Msg 50000, Level 14, State 1, Line 1
Unable to update Customer.
```

To view errors in the Application Event Log (Figure 12-3), select Control Panel ➪ Administrative Tools ➪ Event Viewer. The Event Viewer might also be available in a program menu.

## SQL Server Log

SQL Server also maintains a series of log files. Each time SQL Server starts, it creates a new log file. Six archived log files are retained for a total of seven log files; you can view them using Enterprise Manager by selecting a server ➪ Management ➪ SQL Server Logs, as shown in Figure 12-4.

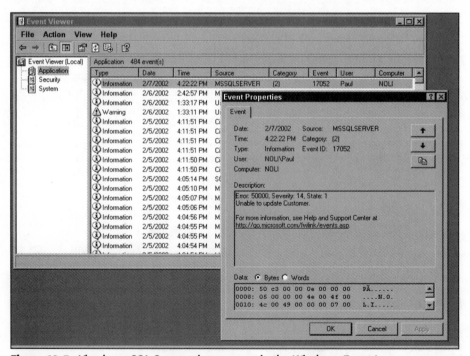

**Figure 12-3:** Viewing a SQL Server raiserror error in the Windows Event Log.

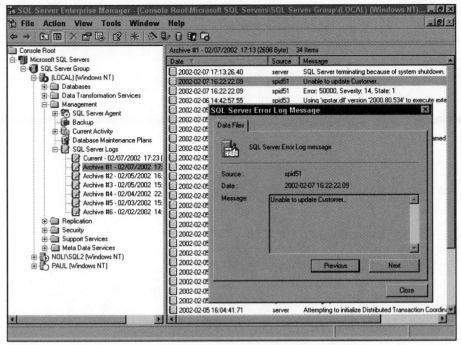

**Figure 12-4:** Viewing an error in the SQL log using Enterprise Manager.

## Error-Handling

When an error does occur, the typical way to handle it is to do the following:

1. If the batch is using logical transactions (`begin tran`/`commit tran`) then the error handler should roll back the transaction. I recommend rolling back the transaction as the first action so that any locks the transaction might be holding are released.

2. If the error is one that the stored procedure logic detects, and it's not a SQL Server error, raise the error message so the user, or front-end application, is informed. If it's an error that SQL Server detects then SQL Server will automatically raise the error.

3. Optionally, log the error to an error table.

4. Terminate the batch. If it's a stored procedure, user-defined function, or trigger, terminate it with a `return` command.

The following stored procedure from the OBX Kites sample database demonstrates handling errors. If a SQL Server error occurs while selecting the customer type or inserting the new contact, the error is stored in @err and the error-handler at the end of the procedure handles the error. If the procedure is called with an invalid customer type, that error is trapped and a custom error message is raised that includes the name of the customer type that wasn't found.

```
CREATE PROCEDURE pContact_AddNew(
  @ContactCode NVARCHAR(20),
  @LastName NVARCHAR(50),
  @FirstName NVARCHAR(50),
  @CompanyName NVARCHAR(50) = NULL,
```

```
  @Name NVARCHAR(50) = NULL
  )
AS
  SET NOCOUNT ON
  DECLARE
    @CustomerTypeID UNIQUEIDENTIFIER,
    @Err INT

  SELECT @CustomerTypeID = CustomerTypeID
   FROM dbo.CustomerType
     WHERE Name = @Name
   SET @Err = @@ERROR
   IF @Err <> 0 GOTO ErrorHandler

  IF @CustomerTypeID IS NULL
    SELECT @CustomerTypeID = CustomerTypeID
      FROM dbo.CustomerType
      WHERE [Default] = 1
  IF @CustomerTypeID IS NULL
    BEGIN
      RAISERROR
        ('Customer Type: ''%s'' not found', 15,1,@Name)
      RETURN -100
    END

  INSERT dbo.Contact (
     ContactCode,SoundexCode, LastName,
     FirstName, CompanyName, CustomerTypeID)
    VALUES (
     @ContactCode, SOUNDEX(@LastName), @LastName,
     @FirstName, @CompanyName, @CustomerTypeID)
   SET @Err = @@ERROR
   IF @Err <> 0 GOTO ErrorHandler

  RETURN 0

ErrorHandler:
  -- if using begin tran: ROLLBACK TRANSACTION
  -- optional: log error to error table
  RETURN -100
go
```

# Summary

T-SQL extends the SQL query with a set of procedural commands. While it's not the most advanced programming language, T-SQL gets the job done. T-SQL batch commands can be used in expressions or packaged as stored procedures, user-defined functions, or triggers.

The next three chapters discuss packaging T-SQL batches inside stored procedures, user-defined functions, and triggers.

✦        ✦        ✦

# Developing Stored Procedures

The primary purpose of client/server development is to move the processing as close to the data as possible. Moving data processing from a client application to the server reduces network traffic and improves both performance and data integrity.

One of the most popular methods of moving the processing closer to the data is developing stored procedures, sometimes called *procs*, or *sprocs*. Stored procedures aren't mysterious. All the features of T-SQL queries and batches are in full force. In the same way that a view is a SQL query saved under a view name, a stored procedure is a batch that has been stored with a name so it can be pre-compiled.

Within a client-server database project, code can be created in any of several places. One of the distinctive differences about the various places is how close to the data the code is executed. On the continuum between "close to the data" and "separate from the data," illustrated in Figure 13-1, stored procedures mix the benefits of server-side code with custom programmability.

As server-side code, stored procedures offer several benefits:

+ Stored procedures are compiled and are the fastest possible means of executing a batch or query.

+ Executing the processing at the server instead of the desktop greatly reduces network traffic.

+ Stored procedures offer modularity and are an easy means of deploying features and code changes. If the front-end application calls a stored procedure to perform some processing, modifying a stored procedure in a single location upgrades all users.

+ Stored procedures can be an important component in database security. If all user access goes through stored procedures, direct access to the tables can be denied and all access to the data can be controlled.

To write an efficient stored procedure, don't start with this chapter. A well-written stored procedure is based on a well-written batch (Chapter 12) consisting of well-written set-oriented SQL queries (Chapters 6 and 7). This chapter explains how to pull together the batch and wrap it as a stored procedure.

Processing Continuum

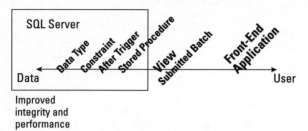

**Figure 13-1:** On the continuum of processing, the closer the processing is to the data, the better.

# Managing Stored Procedures

The actual management of stored procedures is simple compared to the logic within them. Once you know the basic facts and syntax, managing stored procedures should present no problems.

## Create, Alter, and Drop

Stored procedures are managed by means of the Data Definition Language (DDL) commands: create, alter, and drop.

Create must be the first command in a batch; the termination of the batch ends the creation of the stored procedure. The following example creates a simple stored procedure that retrieves data from the ProductCategory table in the OBXKites database:

```
USE OBXKites
go

CREATE PROCEDURE CategoryList
AS
SELECT ProductCategoryName, ProductCategoryDescription
  FROM dbo.ProductCategory
```

As this chapter progresses, more features will be added to the CategoryList example stored procedure.

Dropping a stored procedure removes it from the database. Altering a stored procedure replaces the entire existing stored procedure with new code. When modifying a stored procedure, altering it is preferable to dropping and recreating it, because the latter method removes any permissions.

## Returning a Record Set

If a stored procedure is a saved batch, then whatever a batch can do, a stored procedure can do. Just as a batch returns a record set from a SQL `select` query, a stored procedure will also return a record set from a query.

Referring back to the stored procedure that was created in the previous section, when the `CategoryList` stored procedure is executed, the query within the stored procedure returns all rows from the `productcategory` table:

```
EXEC CategoryList
```

Result:

```
ProductCategoryName    ProductCategoryDescription
--------------------   -----------------------------------
Accessory              kite flying accessories
Book                   Outer Banks books
Clothing               OBX t-shirts, hats, jackets
```

## Compiling Stored Procedures

Compiling a stored procedure is an automatic process. Stored procedures compile and are stored in memory the first time they are executed. If the server reboots, all the compiled stored procedures are lost. They are again compiled when they are called.

SQL Server uses the `Master.dbo.SysCacheObjects` table to track compiled objects. To view the compiled stored procedures, run the following query:

```
SELECT cast(C.sql as Char(35)) as StoredProcedure, cacheobjtype,
usecounts as Count
  FROM Master.dbo.SysCacheObjects C
  JOIN  Master.dbo.SysDatabases D
    ON C.dbid = C.dbid
  WHERE D.Name = DB_Name()
    AND ObjType = 'Proc'
  ORDER BY StoredProcedure
```

Result (abridged):

```
StoredProcedure                       cacheobjtype       Count
-----------------------------------   ----------------   ------
CategoryList                          Executable Plan    20
CategoryList                          Compiled Plan      1
fGetPrice                             Executable Plan    32
fGetPrice                             Compiled Plan      1
...
pContact_AddNew                       Executable Plan    21
pOrderPriority_AddNew                 Compiled Plan      1
pPrice_AddNew                         Executable Plan    122
```

The compiled stored procedure includes any query plans for SQL statements within the stored procedure. If the data distribution changes radically, or indexes are created or dropped, recompiling the stored procedure will result in improved performance. To manually force a recompile of a stored procedure, use the `sp_recompile` system stored procedure. It flags the stored procedure (or trigger) so that it will be compiled the next time it's executed.

```
EXEC sp_recompile CategoryList
```

Result:

```
Object 'CategoryList' was successfully marked
  for recompilation.
```

## Stored Procedure Encryption

When the stored procedure is created, the text of the stored procedure is saved in the `SysComments` table. The text is not stored for the execution of the stored procedures, but only so that it may be retrieved later if the stored procedure needs to be modified.

The `sp_helptext` system stored procedure will extract the original text of the stored procedure:

```
sp_helptext CategoryList
```

Result:

```
Text
-------------------------------------------
CREATE PROCEDURE  CategoryList
AS
SELECT *
  FROM dbo.ProductCategory
```

If the stored procedure is created with the `with encryption` option, the stored procedure text in `SysComments` is not directly readable. It's common practice for third-party vendors to encrypt their stored procedures. The following `alter` command stores the `CategoryList` procedure with `with encryption` and then attempts to read the code:

```
ALTER PROCEDURE CategoryList
WITH ENCRYPTION
AS
SELECT *
  FROM dbo.ProductCategory

sp_helptext CategoryList
```

Result:

```
The object comments have been encrypted.
```

The problem with this scheme is that the encryption does not require a key, so it's easily hacked. The `dSQLSRVD` freeware utility, shown in Figure 13-2 from dOMNAR, enables any user in the SysAdmin role to decrypt encrypted objects. `dSQLSRVD` is available at `http://www.geocities.com/d0mn4r/`.

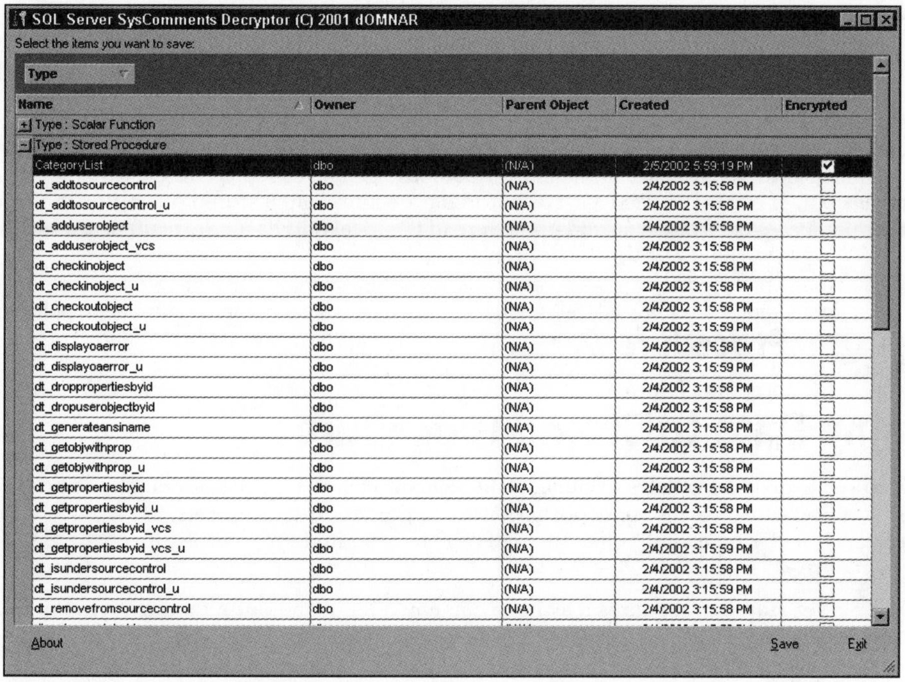

**Figure 13-2:** The dSQLSRVD utility by dOMNAR easily decrypts encrypted stored procedures, functions, and views.

Once dSQLSRVD has decrypted the object, it saves the script to a .sql file. The following script was created from the encrypted CategoryList stored procedure:

```
/*********************************************************/
/* File written by SQL Server SysComments Decryptor v1.1 */
/* Copyright (C) 2001 dOMNAR                            */
/*********************************************************/


USE OBXKites
go


------------------------------------------------------------
-- Type: Stored Procedure
-- Name: CategoryList
------------------------------------------------------------


CREATE PROCEDURE CategoryList
WITH ENCRYPTION
AS
SELECT *
  FROM dbo.ProductCategory
```

## System Stored Procedures

The basic SQL syntax includes only 10 commands: select, insert, update, delete, create, alter, drop, grant, revoke, and deny. Microsoft performs hundreds of tasks with system stored procedures stored in the master database. To make these procedures available to all databases, special rules govern the scope of system stored procedures. Any procedures beginning with sp_ that are in the master database can be executed from any database. If a name conflict exists between a system stored procedure and a stored procedure in the local user database, the system stored procedure in the local database is executed.

**Best Practice**

When creating stored procedures, use a consistent naming convention other than sp_ to name your stored procedures. Using sp_ can only cause name conflicts and confusion. I prefix the names of stored procedures with p, but even no prefix is better than sp_.

# Passing Data to Stored Procedures

A stored procedure is more useful if it can be manipulated by parameters. The CategoryList stored procedure created previously returns all the product categories, but a procedure that performs a task on an individual row will require a method for passing the row ID to the procedure.

SQL Server stored procedures may have numerous input and output parameters (up to 2,100 to be exact).

## Input Parameters

You can add input parameters that pass data to the stored procedure by listing the parameters after the procedure name in the create procedure command. Each parameter must begin with an @ sign, and becomes a local variable within the procedure. Like local variables, the parameters must be defined with valid data types. When the stored procedure is called the parameter must be included (unless the parameter has a default value).

The following code sample creates a stored procedure that returns a single product category. The @CategoryName parameter can accept a unicode character input upto 35 charaters in length. The value passed by means of the parameter is available within the stored procedure as the variable @CategoryName in the where clause:

```
USE OBXKites

go
CREATE PROCEDURE CategoryGet
  (@CategoryName NVARCHAR(35))
AS
SELECT ProductCategoryName, ProductCategoryDescription
  FROM dbo.ProductCategory
  WHERE ProductCategoryName = @CategoryName
```

In the following code sample, when executed, the string literal 'Kite' is passed to the stored procedure and substituted for the variable in the where clause:

```
EXEC CategoryGet 'Kite'
```

Result:

```
ProductCategoryName    ProductCategoryDescription
-------------------    ----------------------------------
Kite                   a variety of kites, from simple to
                       stunt, to Chinese, to novelty kites
```

If multiple paramenters are involved, the paramenter name can be specified or the parameters listed in order. If the two methods are mixed, then as soon as the parameter is provided by name all the following parameters must be as well.

The following three examples each demonstrate calling a stored procedure and passing the parameters by original position and by name:

```
EXEC StoredProcedure
  @Parameter1 = n,
  @Parameter2 = 'n'

EXEC StoredProcedure n, 'n'

EXEC StoredProcedure n, @Parameter2 = 'n'
```

## Parameter Defaults

You must supply every parameter when calling a stored procedure, unless that parameter has been created with a default value. You establish the default by appending an equals sign and the default to the parameter, as follows:

```
CREATE PROCEDURE StoredProcedure (
  @Variable DataType = DefaultValue
    )
```

The following code, extracted from the OBX Kites sample database, demonstrates a stored-procedure default. If a product category name is passed in this stored procedure, the stored procedure returns only the selected product category. However, if nothing is passed, the null default is used in the where clause to return all the product categories.

```
CREATE PROCEDURE pProductCategory_Fetch(
  @Search NVARCHAR(50) = NULL
)
-- If @Search = null then return all ProductCategories
-- If @Search is value then try to find by Name
AS
  SET NOCOUNT ON
  SELECT ProductCategoryName, ProductCategoryDescription
    FROM dbo.ProductCategory
    WHERE ProductCategoryName = @Search
      OR @Search IS NULL
  IF @@RowCount = 0
    RAISERROR(
      'Product Category ''%s'' Not Found.',14,1,@Search)
```

The first execution passes a product category:

```
EXEC pProductCategory_Fetch 'OBX'
```

Result:

```
ProductCategoryName     ProductCategoryDescription
--------------------    ------------------------------
OBX                     OBX stuff
```

When pProductCategory_Fetch executed without a parameter, the @Search parameter's
default of null allows every row to be seen as true within the where clause, as follows:

```
EXEC pProductCategory_Fetch
```

Result:

```
ProductCategoryName     ProductCategoryDescription
--------------------    ------------------------------
Accessory               kite flying accessories
Book                    Outer Banks books
Clothing                OBX t-shirts, hats, jackets
Kite                    a variety of kites, from simple to
                        stunt, to Chinese, to novelty kites
Material                Kite construction material
OBX                     OBX stuff
Toy                     Kids stuff
Video                   stunt kite contexts and lessons,
                        and Outer Banks videos
```

# Returning Data from Stored Procedures

SQL Server provides four means of returning data from a stored procedure. A batch can
return data via a select statement or a raiserror command. Stored procedures inherit
these from batches and add output variables and the return command.

## Output Parameters

Output parameters enable a stored procedure to return data to the calling client procedure.
The keyword output is required both when the procedure is created and when it is called.
Within the stored procedure the output parameter appears as a local variable. In the calling
procedure or batch, a variable must have been created to receive the output parameter.
When the stored procedure concludes, its current value is passed to the calling procedure's
local variable.

Although output parameters are typically used solely for output they are actually two-way
parameters.

Output parameters are useful for returning single units of data when a whole record set is not
required. For returning a single row of information, using output parameters is significantly
faster then preparing a record set.

The next code sample uses an output parameter to return the product name for a given
product code from the Product table in the OBX Kites sample database. To set up for the
output parameter:

1. The batch declares the local variable @ProdName to receive the output parameter.

2. The batch calls the stored procedure, using @Prod Name in the exec call to the stored
   procedure.

3. Within the stored procedure the @ProductName output parameter/local variable is created in the header of the stored procedure. The initial value is null.

   With everything in place, the process continues. The data path for the @ProductName output parameter is as follows:

4. The select statement inside the stored procedure sets @ProductName to Basic Box Kite 21 inch, the product name for the product code "1001."

5. The stored procedure finishes and execution is passed back to the calling batch. The value is transferred to the batch's local variable, @ProdName.

6. The calling batch uses the print command to send @ProdName to the user.

This is the stored procedure:

```
USE OBXKites
go
CREATE PROC GetProductName (
  @ProductCode CHAR(10),
  @ProductName VARCHAR(25) OUTPUT )
AS
SELECT @ProductName = ProductName
  FROM dbo.Product
  WHERE Code = @ProductCode
```

This is the calling batch:

```
USE OBXKITES
DECLARE @ProdName VARCHAR(25)
EXEC GetProductName '1001', @ProdName OUTPUT
PRINT @ProdName
```

Result:

```
Basic Box Kite 21 inch
```

Later in this chapter, in "The Complete Stored Procedure" section, is a more complex example taken from the OBX Kites sample database that uses an output parameter to pass the order number from the pOrder_AddNew stored procedure to the pOrder_AddItem stored procedure.

## Using the Return Command

A return command unconditionally terminates the procedure and returns a value to the calling batch or client. Technically, a return can be used with any batch, but it can only return a value from a stored procedure or a function.

A return value of 0 indicates success and is the default. Microsoft reserves -99 to -1 for SQL Server use. It's recommended that you use -100 or lower to pass back a failure status.

When calling a stored procedure, the exec command must use a local integer variable if the returned status value is to be captured:

```
EXEC @IntLocalVariable = StoredProcedureName
```

The following basic stored procedure returns a success or failure depending on the parameter:

```
CREATE PROC IsItOK (
  @OK VARCHAR(10) )
AS
IF @OK = 'OK'
  RETURN 0
ELSE
  RETURN -100
```

The calling batch:

```
DECLARE @ReturnCode INT
EXEC @ReturnCode = IsITOK 'OK'
PRINT @ReturnCode
EXEC @ReturnCode = IsItOK 'NotOK'
PRINT @ReturnCode
```

Return:

```
0
-100
```

# Path and Scope of Returning Data

Any stored procedure has four possible methods of returning data (`select`, `raiserror`, output parameters, and `return`). Deciding which method is right for a given stored procedure depends on the quantity and purpose of the data to be returned, and the scope of the scope of the method used to return the data. The return scope for the four methods is as follows:

✦ `return` and `output` parameters are both passed to local variables in the immediate calling procedure or batch within SQL Server.

✦ `raiserror` and a selected record set are both passed to the end-user client application. The immediate calling procedure or batch is completely unaware of the `raiserror` or selected record set.

If Query Analyzer executes a batch that calls stored procedure A, which then calls stored procedure B, stored procedure A will not see any `raiserrors` or record sets returned by procedure B, as shown in Figure 13-3.

If a stored procedure needs to work with a result set generated by a stored procedure it's calling, a temporary table can be used to pass the data. If the calling procedure creates the temporary table, the scope of the temporary table will make it available within any called procedures.

In Figure 13-3, procedure B can execute DML statements against any temporary table created in procedure A. When procedure B is complete, the data are ready for procedure A.

**Best Practice**

With every returned record set, SQL Server will by default also send a message stating the number of rows affected or returned. Not only is this a nuisance, but I have found in my informal testing that it can slow a query by up to 17 percent.

Therefore, by habit, begin every stored procedure with the following code:

```
AS
SET NoCount ON
```

There's more about configuring the connection in Chapter 23, "Configuring SQL Server."

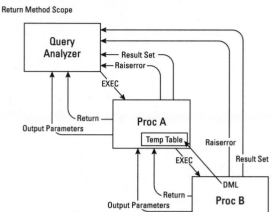

Return Method Scope

**Figure 13-3:** The path and scope of return methods differs among the four possible methods of returning data.

# Using Stored Procedures Within Queries

Stored procedures are typically executed with the exec command or submitted by the client application. However, a stored procedure can be used within the from portion of a query if the stored procedure is called from within an openquery() function.

Openquery() is a distributed query function that sends a pass-through query to an external data source for remote execution. When the openquery() function includes a stored procedure, it simply submits the stored procedure to the local server.

**Cross-Reference**  The openquery() function is explained in more detail in Chapter 18, "Working with Distributed Queries."

Since the result set of the stored procedure is returned via a function being used by a data source in the from clause of the select statement, a where clause can further reduce the output of the stored procedure.

While this technique enables the use of stored procedures within a select statement, it's not as optimized as the technique of passing any row restrictions to the stored procedure for processing within the stored procedure. The only benefit of using openquery() is that it enables a complex stored procedure to be called from within an ad hoc query.

For the purpose of the following code, assume that a linked server connection has been established to the local server with the name NOLI:

```
SELECT * FROM OpenQuery(
  NOLI
  'EXEC OBXKites.dbo.pProductCategory_Fetch')
  WHERE ProductCategoryDescription Like '%stuff%'
```

Result:

```
ProductCategoryName    ProductCategoryDescription
---------------------  ----------------------------------
OBX                    OBX stuff
Toy                    Kids stuff
```

**Best Practice**

If you need to call complex code within a select statement, using openquery() to call a stored procedure works, but it's a bit bizarre. A better method is to use a case expression or to create a user-defined function.

# Debugging Stored Procedures

Query Analyzer includes a stored-procedure debugger similar to the debugging environment found in Visual Studio. While it is limited to debugging saved stored procedures, and a procedure cannot be edited within the debugger, it does offer several useful features, including:

✦ The ability to watch local and global variables.

✦ The ability to watch the execution flow when working with a complex while loop or cursor.

✦ The ability to observe the call stack, which is very useful when you are debugging a complex set of nested stored procedures and triggers.

To use the debugger, follow these steps:

1. Open the Object Browser pane by either (1) clicking the object browser toolbar button, (2) pressing F8, or (3) selecting Tools ➪ Object Browser ➪ Show/Hide.

2. In the Object Browser, select the stored procedure to be debugged.

3. Right-click the stored procedure and select Debug from the bottom of the menu.

4. Enter any parameters into the Debug Procedure dialog box, as shown in Figure 13-4.

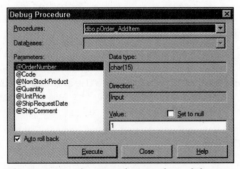

**Figure 13-4:** The stored-procedure debugger first gathers any required parameters.

To enter the parameters, select each individual parameter in the list and enter the value in the Value text box. A null may be passed to the parameter using the "Set to null" checkbox. Query Analyzer will retain the parameters for subsequent debugging runs of the stored procedure.

Because the debugger might be used repeatedly to test a procedure with the same parameter data, you can, by checking the "Auto roll back" checkbox, set the debugger to automatically roll back all the work done by the stored procedure during debugging.

Once the parameters are set, the debugger opens a new connection window for interactive debugging. The debugging window (Figure 13-5) adds a Debugging toolbar to the code pane as well as three new panes: the Local Variable pane, the Global Variable pane, and the Call Stack pane.

Most of the toolbar buttons are self-explanatory. However, go (F5), which executes the stored procedure, can also start the debugger if the "stepping through the procedure" toolbar button appears unavailable.

The whole point of the debugger is to execute the stored procedure one command at a time. This process of stepping through the code can be controlled using the toolbar buttons. When stepping through the procedure, the "Step into" button executes a single command and steps into any called procedures. "Stepping over" executes any called code without stepping through the called code. "Step to cursor" runs until the cursor fetches a new row.

The local variables are automatically listed in the Local Variable pane. The value can be manipulated in the pane. Additional valid global variables may be added to the global variable pane, but, of course, their values will be read-only.

The debugger actually runs sp_sdidebug, a system stored procedure that simulates the SQL Server T-SQL environment. If you don't have permission to execute sp_sdidebug, the debugger won't work.

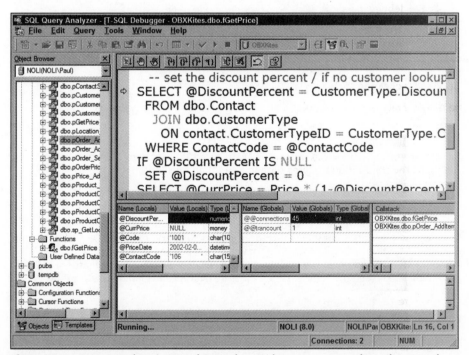

**Figure 13-5:** Query Analyzer's Stored Procedure Debugger can step through a stored procedure and expose the variables and execution flow.

# Executing Remote Stored Procedures

Two methods exist for calling a stored procedure located on another server: a four-part name reference and a distributed query. Both methods require that the remote server be a linked server. Stored procedures may only be called remotely; they may not be created remotely.

**Cross-Reference** Establishing security links to external data servers is covered in Chapter 18, "Working with Distributed Queries."

The remote stored procedure may be executed by means of the four-part name:

```
server.database.owner.procedurename
```

For example, the following code adds a new product category to the OBX Kites database on Noli's (my development server) second instance of SQL Server:

```
EXEC [Noli\SQL2].OBXKites.dbo.pProductCategory_AddNew
  'Food', 'Eatables'
```

Alternately, the `OpenQuery()` function can be used to call a remote stored procedure:

```
OpenQuery(linked server name, 'exec stored procedure')
```

The next code sample executes the `pCustomerType_Fetch` stored procedure in the default database for the user login being used to connect to Noli\SQL2. If the default database is incorrect, a three-part name can be used to point to the correct database.

```
SELECT CustomerTypeName, DiscountPercent, [Default]
  FROM OPENQUERY(
    [Noli\SQL2], 'OBXKites.dbo.pCustomerType_Fetch')
```

Result:

```
CustomerTypeName     DiscountPercent Default
-------------------- --------------- -------
Preferred            10              0
Retail               00              1
Wholesale            15              0
```

As with any other distributed query, the Distributed Transaction Coordinator service must be running if the transaction updates data in more than one server.

# The Complete Stored Procedure

This section presents a complete stored procedure scenario from the OBX Kites sample database. The three stored procedures, pGetPrice, pOrder_AddNew, and pOrder_AddItem, work together to add orders to the database. They demonstrate many features of T-SQL programming and stored procedures. Each of these headings explains the stored procedure and then lists the code.

**On the CD-ROM** The code for these three stored procedures and the batch files that call them can be found within the OBXKites_Create.sql and OBXKites_Populate.sql files.

# The pGetPrice Stored Procedure

The pGetPrice stored procedure demonstrates parameter defaults, output parameters, error handling, lock timeout, and deadlock handling. It accepts a product code, optional date, and optional customer-contact code. Using that information, it determines the correct price and returns that price as an output variable.

A contact may be assigned to a customer type, and each customer type may have a standing discount. If the customer's contact code was supplied, the first task of the stored procedure is to locate the discount. If no contact code was supplied, the discount percentage is set to zero.

The OBX Kites database uses a price table in which each product may have a different price each day. This method stores a history of prices and enables the store to enter price changes in advance. If pGetPrice is run with a null data parameter, the current date is used. In either case, the procedure must locate the most recent price. To do that it must determine the effective date of the price by finding the max price date that's less than or equal to the required date. Once the effective price date is determined, locating the correct price is easy. pGetPrice uses a subquery to determine the effective date.

Every SQL DML statement is followed by a general error check that passes control to an error handler. If the error is a lock timeout or deadlock, the error handler waits for .25 seconds and goes to the LockTimeOutRetry: label at the beginning of the procedure to try again to gain the lock and complete the procedure. If after five attempts the lock can't be gained, the error handler reports the error and bombs out of the procedure. Here's the actual code:

```
CREATE PROCEDURE pGetPrice(
  @Code CHAR(10),
  @PriceDate DATETIME = NULL,
  @ContactCode CHAR(15) = NULL,
  @CurrPrice MONEY OUTPUT
  )
AS
-- Will return the current price for the product
--   for today or any other date
-- The customer type determines the discount percentage
-- the output parameter, @CurrPrice, will contain
--   the effective price

-- example code for calling this sproc
-- Declare @Price money
-- EXEC GetPrice '1006', NULL, @Price OUTPUT
-- Select @Price

SET NOCOUNT ON
DECLARE
  @DiscountPercent NUMERIC (4,2),
  @Err INT,
  @ErrCounter INT

SET @ErrCounter = 0
SET @CurrPrice = NULL

LockTimeOutRetry:
```

```
IF @PriceDate IS NULL
  SET @PriceDate = GETDATE()
 -- set the discount percent
 -- if no customer lookup then it's zilch discount
SELECT @DiscountPercent = CustomerType.DiscountPercent
  FROM dbo.Contact
    JOIN dbo.CustomerType
      ON contact.CustomerTypeID = CustomerType.CustomerTypeID
    WHERE ContactCode = @ContactCode
SET @Err = @@ERROR
  IF @Err <> 0 GOTO ErrorHandler

IF @DiscountPercent IS NULL
  SET @DiscountPercent = 0

SELECT @CurrPrice = Price * (1-@DiscountPercent)
  FROM dbo.Price
    JOIN dbo.Product
      ON Price.ProductID = Product.ProductID
  WHERE Code = @Code
    AND EffectiveDate =
      (SELECT MAX(EffectiveDate)
        FROM dbo.Price
          JOIN dbo.Product
            ON Price.ProductID = Product.ProductID
        WHERE Code = @Code
          AND EffectiveDate <= @PriceDate)
  IF @CurrPrice IS NULL
    BEGIN
      RAISERROR(
      'Code: ''%s'' has no established price.',15,1, @Code)
      RETURN -100
    END

SET @Err = @@ERROR
  IF @Err <> 0 GOTO ErrorHandler
RETURN 0

ErrorHandler:
  IF (@Err = 1222 OR @Err = 1205) AND @ErrCounter = 5
    BEGIN
      RAISERROR (
        'Unable to Lock Data after five attempts.', 16,1)
      RETURN -100
    END
  IF @Err = 1222 OR @Err = 1205 -- Lock Timeout / Deadlock
    BEGIN
      WAITFOR DELAY '00:00:00.25'
      SET @ErrCounter = @ErrCounter + 1
      GOTO LockTimeOutRetry
    END
  -- else unknown error
  RAISERROR (@err, 16,1) WITH LOG
  RETURN -100
```

# The pOrder_AddNew Stored Procedure

An order consists of data in two tables, the [Order] table and the OrderDetail table. The [Order] table holds header information and the OrderDetail table contains the products on the order. Initiating an order involves collecting and validating the header information, generating an OrderNumber, and inserting a row in the [Order] table.

The pOrder_AddNew stored procedure accepts the customer-contact code, the employee code for the salesperson responsible for the sale, the location of the sale, and the date of the sale.

Sales are sometimes after the fact, so pOrder_AddNew can't assume the current date is the sales date. If the order date is the default (null), the insert statement uses the current date.

The customer code is also optional. If a customer-contact code is not provided, the default sets it to 0, which is then converted to a ContactID of null. The database schema accepts a null as the customer, recognizing that some sales are anonymous.

Every entry is in human-recognizable codes, but the database uses GUIDs for replication, and therefore the procedure looks up the GUID for the customer, location, and employee, validating the codes during the lookup.

When all the codes are validated, the procedure finds the current order number and increases it by one. The order is finally inserted within the same transaction in which the order number is gathered. This occurs within a serialized transaction to prevent duplicates. (Real-world applications typically have a more complex method of generating an invoice number or order number that handles generating order numbers at multiple sites.)

The procedure uses a similar error-handling scheme as pGetPrice. One notable difference is that the error-detection code within the transaction rolls back the transaction prior to jumping to the error handler.

The last act of the stored procedure is to return the order number as an output variable, permitting the calling batch to use the order number when adding items to the order. The following code creates the pOrder_AddNew stored procedure:

```
CREATE PROC pOrder_AddNew (
  @ContactCode CHAR(15) = 0,
     -- if default then non-tracked customer
  @EmployeeCode CHAR(15),
  @LocationCode CHAR(15),
  @OrderDate DATETIME = NULL,
  @OrderNumber INT OUTPUT
  )
AS
-- Logic:
-- If supplied, check CustomerID valid
  SET NOCOUNT ON
  DECLARE
    @ContactID UNIQUEIDENTIFIER,
    @OrderID UNIQUEIDENTIFIER,
    @LocationID UNIQUEIDENTIFIER,
    @EmployeeID UNIQUEIDENTIFIER,
    @Err INT,
    @ErrCounter INT

  SET @ErrCounter = 0
```

```
LockTimeOutRetry:

-- Set Customer ContactID
   IF @ContactCode = 0
    SET @ContactID = NULL
   ELSE
    BEGIN
      SELECT @ContactID = ContactID
        FROM dbo.Contact
          WHERE ContactCode = @ContactCode
      SET @Err = @@ERROR
        IF @Err <> 0 GOTO ErrorHandler
      IF @ContactID IS NULL
        BEGIN  -- a customer was submitted but not found
         RAISERROR(
           'CustomerCode: ''%s not found',15,1, @ContactCode)
         RETURN -100
        END
    END

-- Set LocationID
  SELECT @LocationID = LocationID
    FROM dbo.Location
    WHERE LocationCode = @LocationCode
  SET @Err = @@ERROR
    IF @Err <> 0 GOTO ErrorHandler
  IF @LocationID IS NULL
    BEGIN  -- Location not found
      RAISERROR(
        'LocationCode: ''%s'' not found',15,1, @LocationCode)
      RETURN -100
    END
  IF EXISTS(SELECT *
                   FROM dbo.Location
                   WHERE LocationID = @LocationID
                     AND IsRetail = 0)
    BEGIN  -- Location not found
      RAISERROR(
        'LocationCode: ''%s'' not retail',15,1, @LocationCode)
      RETURN -100
    END

-- Set EmployeeID
  SELECT @EmployeeID = ContactID
    FROM dbo.Contact
      WHERE ContactCode = @EmployeeCode
  SET @Err = @@ERROR
    IF @Err <> 0 GOTO ErrorHandler
  IF @EmployeeCode IS NULL
    BEGIN  -- Location not found
      RAISERROR(
        'EmployeeCode: ''%s'' not found',15,1, @EmployeeCode)
      RETURN -100
    END
```

```
-- OrderNumber
  SET @OrderID = NEWID()
  SET TRANSACTION ISOLATION LEVEL SERIALIZABLE
  BEGIN TRANSACTION
    SELECT @OrderNumber = Max(OrderNumber) + 1
      FROM [Order]
    SET @OrderNumber =  ISNULL(@OrderNumber, 1)
    SET @Err = @@ERROR
    IF @Err <> 0
      BEGIN
        ROLLBACK TRANSACTION
        GOTO ErrorHandler
      END
  -- All OK Perform the Insert
  INSERT dbo.[Order] (
      OrderID, ContactID, OrderNumber,
      EmployeeID, LocationID, OrderDate )
    VALUES (
      @OrderID, @ContactID,@OrderNumber,
      @EmployeeID, @LocationID, ISNULL(@OrderDate,GETDATE()))
  IF @Err <> 0
    BEGIN
      ROLLBACK TRANSACTION
      GOTO ErrorHandler
    END
  COMMIT TRANSACTION

RETURN -- @OrderNumber already set

ErrorHandler:
  IF (@Err = 1222 OR @Err = 1205) AND @ErrCounter = 5
    BEGIN
      RAISERROR ('Unable to Lock Data after five attempts.', 16,1)
      RETURN -100
    END
  IF @Err = 1222 OR @Err = 1205 -- Lock Timeout / Deadlock
    BEGIN
      WAITFOR DELAY '00:00:00.25'
      SET @ErrCounter = @ErrCounter + 1
      GOTO LockTimeOutRetry
    END
  -- else unknown error
  RAISERROR (@err, 16,1) WITH LOG
  RETURN -100
```

## The pOrder_AddItem Store Procedure

With the order inserted, the third procedure in the set adds items to the order. Sales and inventory have to be flexible, so this procedure has lots of defaults. The order number and the quantity are the only required parameters. The item is identified by either the product code or a description. The unit price can be either passed to the stored procedure or looked up with the pGetPrice procedure. Lastly, if the item is going to be shipped, a requested ship date and ship comment can be entered. If the ship information is null, the procedure assumes the item was delivered at the time of the sale.

As with the other stored procedures, pOrder_AddItem begins by validating every parameter and fetching the associated GUID to be inserted in the OrderDetail table.

The code that handles the unit price only calls pGetPrice if the unit-price parameter is not null. (The following chapter, Chapter 14, "Building User-Defined Functions," will develop an fGetPrice function.) For the purpose of comparison this procedure also illustrates retrieving the price using the function, but that part of the code is commented out. Here's the code:

```sql
CREATE PROCEDURE pOrder_AddItem(
  @OrderNumber CHAR(15),
  @Code CHAR(15) = 0, -- if default then non-stock Product
  @NonStockProduct NVARCHAR(256) = NULL,
  @Quantity NUMERIC(7,2),
  @UnitPrice MONEY = 0, -- If Default then lookup the Price
  @ShipRequestDate DATETIME = NULL, --default to Today
  @ShipComment NVARCHAR(256) = NULL -- optional
  )
AS

DECLARE
  @OrderID UNIQUEIDENTIFIER,
  @ProductID UNIQUEIDENTIFIER,
  @ContactCode CHAR(15),
  @PriceDate DATETIME,
  @Err INT,
  @ErrCounter INT

  SET @ErrCounter = 0

LockTimeOutRetry:

-- Fetch OrderID
  SELECT @OrderID = OrderID
    FROM dbo.[Order]
    WHERE OrderNumber = @OrderNumber
  SET @Err = @@ERROR
    IF @Err <> 0 GOTO ErrorHandler

-- Fetch ProductID
  SELECT @ProductID = ProductID
    FROM Product
    WHERE Code = @Code
  SET @Err = @@ERROR
    IF @Err <> 0 GOTO ErrorHandler

--- Fetch Contact Code / PriceDate
  SELECT @ContactCode = ContactCode, @PriceDate = OrderDate
    FROM dbo.[Order]
      LEFT JOIN Contact
        ON [Order].ContactID = Contact.ContactID
  SET @Err = @@ERROR
    IF @Err <> 0 GOTO ErrorHandler
```

```
-- Fetch UnitPrice
  IF @UnitPrice IS NULL
    EXEC pGetPrice
     @Code, @PriceDate, @ContactCode, @UnitPrice OUTPUT
     -- Alternate GetPrice function method
     -- SET @UnitPrice = dbo.fGetPrice (
     --                  @Code,@PriceDate, @ContactCode)
  SET @Err = @@ERROR
    IF @Err <> 0 GOTO ErrorHandler
  IF @UnitPrice IS NULL
    BEGIN
      RAISERROR(
        'Code: ''%s'' has no established price.',15,1, @Code)
      RETURN -1
    END

-- Set ShipRequestDate
  IF @ShipRequestDate IS NULL
    SET @ShipRequestDate = @PriceDate
-- Do the insert
  INSERT OrderDetail(
    OrderID, ProductID, NonStockProduct, Quantity,
    UnitPrice, ShipRequestDate, ShipComment)
  VALUES (
    @OrderID, @ProductID, @NonStockProduct, @Quantity,
    @UnitPrice, @ShipRequestDate, @ShipComment)
  SET @Err = @@ERROR
    IF @Err <> 0 GOTO ErrorHandler

RETURN 0

ErrorHandler:
  IF (@Err = 1222 OR @Err = 1205) AND @ErrCounter = 5
    BEGIN
      RAISERROR (
        'Unable to Lock Data after five attempts.', 16,1)
      RETURN -100
    END
  IF @Err = 1222 OR @Err = 1205 -- Lock Timeout / Deadlock
    BEGIN
      WAITFOR DELAY '00:00:00.25'
      SET @ErrCounter = @ErrCounter + 1
      GOTO LockTimeOutRetry
    END
  -- else unknown error
  RAISERROR (@err, 16,1) WITH LOG
  RETURN -100
```

## Adding an Order

So you can see the stored procedures in action, the following batch from OBXKites_Populate. sql illustrates creating two orders. This is the exact code that would be sent to SQL Server to by the front-end application to insert two orders.

The pOrder_AddNew stored procedure creates a new order row and returns the order number to the calling batch. The calling batch can then create order detail rows using the same order number by calling the pOrder_AddItem stored procedure. The batch's @OrderNumber local variable is used to capture the order number from pOrder_AddNew and pass it to each call of pOrder_AddItem.

The first order explicitly names the parameters. The second order is entered and provides the parameters by order.

```
DECLARE @OrderNumber INT

--Order 1
EXEC pOrder_AddNew
  @ContactCode = '101',
  @EmployeeCode = '120',
  @LocationCode = 'CH',
  @OrderDate=NULL,
  @OrderNumber = @OrderNumber output

EXEC pOrder_SetPriority @OrderNumber, '1'

EXEC pOrder_AddItem
  @OrderNumber = @OrderNumber,
  @Code = '1002',
  @NonStockProduct = NULL,
  @Quantity = 12,
  @UnitPrice = NULL,
  @ShipRequestDate = '11/15/01',
  @ShipComment = NULL

-- Order 2
EXEC pOrder_AddNew
  '101', '120', 'CH', NULL, @OrderNumber output
EXEC pOrder_AddItem
  @OrderNumber, '1002', NULL, 3, NULL, NULL, NULL
EXEC pOrder_AddItem
  @OrderNumber, '1003', NULL, 5, NULL, NULL, NULL
EXEC pOrder_AddItem
  @OrderNumber, '1004', NULL, 2, NULL, NULL, NULL
EXEC pOrder_AddItem
  @OrderNumber, '1044', NULL, 1, NULL, NULL, NULL
```

## Summary

Using stored procedures is a way to save and optimize batches. Stored procedures are compiled and stored in memory the first time they are executed. No method is faster at executing SQL commands, or more popular for moving the processing close to the data. Like a batch, a stored procedure can return a record set by simply executing a select command.

The next chapter covers user-defined functions, which combine the benefits of stored procedures with the benefits of views at the cost of portability.

✦    ✦    ✦

# Building User-Defined Functions

**S**QL Server 2000 introduces user-defined functions, which offer the benefits of both views and stored procedures at the cost of portability.

User-defined functions offer the benefits of views because they can be used within the `from` clause of a `select` statement or an expression, and they can be schema-bound. In addition, user-defined functions can accept parameters while views cannot.

User-defined functions offer the benefits of stored procedures because they are compiled and optimized in the same way.

The chief argument against developing with user-defined functions has to do with their portability. User-defined functions are not in the ANSI SQL 92 Standard and, while they are included in the ANSI SQL 99 Standard, they have by no means been adopted by the industry. As a result, any user-defined function will have to be rewritten as a view or stored procedure if the database must be ported to another database platform in the future. To complicate matters further, any client-side code that references a user-defined function within a `select` statement will have to be rewritten and likely redesigned as well.

**Best Practice**

If your IT shop is committed to Microsoft database technologies, user-defined functions offer several compelling benefits. However, if there's a chance that the database may be ported to a different database platform in the future, I recommend avoiding user-defined functions for portability reasons.

User-defined functions come in three distinct types:

✦ Scalar functions that return a single value.

✦ Updatable inline table functions similar to views.

✦ Multi-statement table functions that build a result set with code.

## Scalar Functions

A scalar function is one that returns a single specific value. The function can accept multiple parameters, perform a calculation, and then return a single value. These user-defined functions may be used within any expressions within SQL Server, even expressions within check constraints. The value is passed back through the function by means of a `return` command. The `return` command should be the last command in the user-defined function.

The scalar function must be *deterministic*, meaning that it must repeatedly return the same value for the same input parameters. For this reason, certain functions and global variables that return variable data — such as `@@connections`, `getdate()`, `rasd()`, `newid()`, and others — are not allowed within scalar functions.

User-defined scalar functions are not permitted to update the database, but they may work with a local temporary table. They cannot return BLOB data such as `text`, `ntext`, or `image` data-type variables, nor can they return table variables or `cursor` data types.

## Creating a Scalar Function

User-defined functions are created, altered, or dropped with the same DDL commands used for other objects, although the syntax is slightly different to allow for the returned value:

```
CREATE FUNCTION FunctionName (InputParameters)
RETURNS DataType
AS
BEGIN
  Code
  RETURN Expression
END
```

The input parameters include a data-type definition and may optionally include a default value similar to stored procedure parameters. Function parameters differ from stored procedure parameters in that even if the default is desired, the parameter is required to call the function. Parameters with defaults don't become optional parameters. To request the default when calling the function, pass the keyword `default` to the function.

The following user-defined scalar function performs a simple mathematical function. The second parameter includes a default value:

```
CREATE FUNCTION dbo.Multiply (@A INT, @B INT = 3)
RETURNS INT
AS
BEGIN
    RETURN @A * @B
End
go

SELECT dbo.Multiply (3,4)
SELECT dbo.Multiply (7, DEFAULT)
```

Result:

```
-----------
12
21
```

**Note**    Microsoft-developed system functions are stored in the master database and must be called with a prefix of two colons, as in `::fnFunctionName`.

For a more complex scalar user-defined function, the `pGetPrice` stored procedure from the OBX Kites sample database returns a single result via an output parameter. The `fGetPrice` stored procedure or function has to determine the correct price for any given date and for any customer discount. Because it returns a single value, it's a prime candidate for a scalar user-defined function.

The function uses the same internal code as the stored procedure, except that the @CurrPrice is passed back through the final return instead of an output variable. The function uses a default value of null for the contact code. Another difference between the two is that the stored-procedure version of fGetPrice can accept a null default for the data and assume the current date for the sale, whereas user-defined functions must be deterministic and don't allow getdate() within the function, meaning that the date must always be passed to the function. Here is the code for the fGetPrice user-defined scalar function:

```
CREATE FUNCTION fGetPrice (
  @Code CHAR(10),
  @PriceDate DATETIME,
  @ContactCode CHAR(15) = NULL)
RETURNS MONEY
As
BEGIN
  DECLARE @CurrPrice MONEY
   DECLARE @DiscountPercent NUMERIC (4,2)
     -- set the discount percent
     -- if no customer lookup then it's zilch discount
  SELECT @DiscountPercent = CustomerType.DiscountPercent
    FROM dbo.Contact
      JOIN dbo.CustomerType
        ON contact.CustomerTypeID =
            CustomerType.CustomerTypeID
    WHERE ContactCode = @ContactCode
  IF @DiscountPercent IS NULL
    SET @DiscountPercent = 0
  SELECT @CurrPrice = Price * (1-@DiscountPercent)
    FROM dbo.Price
      JOIN dbo.Product
        ON Price.ProductID = Product.ProductID
    WHERE Code = @Code
    AND EffectiveDate =
      (SELECT MAX(EffectiveDate)
          FROM dbo.Price
            JOIN dbo.Product
              ON Price.ProductID = Product.ProductID
          WHERE Code = @Code
            AND EffectiveDate <= @PriceDate)
    RETURN @CurrPrice
END
```

## Calling a Scalar Function

Scalar functions may be used anywhere within any expression that accepts a single value. User-defined scalar functions must always be called by means of at least a two-part name (owner.name). The following script demonstrates calling the fGetPrice() function within OBX Kites:

```
USE OBXKites
SELECT dbo.fGetPrice('1006',GetDate(),DEFAULT)
```

```
SELECT dbo.fGetPrice('1001','5/1/2001',NULL)
```

Result:

```
--------------------
125.9500
--------------------
14.9500
```

dbo.GenColUpdated is a user-defined scalar function used within the dynamic audit trail that is covered in Chapter 16, "Advanced Server-Side Programming." The user-defined scalar function, dbo.TitleCase, is created in Chapter 6, "Retrieving Data with Select."

## Creating Functions with Schema Binding

All three types of user-defined functions may be created with the significant benefit of schema binding. Views may be schema-bound, but this feature is not available for stored procedures. Schema binding prevents altering or dropping of any object the function depends upon. If a schema-bound function references TableA, columns may be added to TableA, but no existing columns can be altered or dropped and neither can the table itself.

To create a function with schema binding, add the option after returns and before as during the function creation, as shown here:

```
CREATE FUNCTION FunctionName (Input Parameters)
RETURNS DataType
WITH SCHEMA BINDING
AS
BEGIN
  Code
  RETURNS Expression
END
```

Schema binding not only alerts the developer that the change will affect an object, it prevents the change. To remove schema binding so that changes can be made, alter the function so that schema binding is no longer included.

Enterprise Manager's table designer removes schema binding without notification in order to make object changes.

# Inline Table-Valued Functions

The second type of user-defined function is very similar to a view. Both are wrapped for a stored select statement. An inline table-valued user-defined function retains the benefits of a view, and adds compilation and parameters. As with a view, if the select statement is updateable, the function will be updateable.

## Creating an In-Line Table-Valued Function

The inline table-valued user-defined function has no begin/end body. Instead, the select statement is returned as a table data type:

```
CREATE FUNCTION FunctionName (InputParameters)
RETURNS Table
AS
RETURN (Select Statement)
```

The following inline table-valued user-defined function is functionally the equivalent to the vEventList view created in Chapter 9, "Creating Views."

```
USE CHA2
go
CREATE FUNCTION fEventList ()
RETURNS Table
AS
RETURN(
SELECT dbo.CustomerType.Name AS Customer,
   dbo.Customer.LastName, dbo.Customer.FirstName,
   dbo.Customer.Nickname,
   dbo.Event_mm_Customer.ConfirmDate, dbo.Event.Code,
   dbo.Event.DateBegin, dbo.Tour.Name AS Tour,
   dbo.BaseCamp.Name, dbo.Event.Comment
FROM dbo.Tour
   INNER JOIN dbo.Event
      ON dbo.Tour.TourID = dbo.Event.TourID
   INNER JOIN dbo.Event_mm_Customer
      ON dbo.Event.EventID = dbo.Event_mm_Customer.EventID
   INNER JOIN dbo.Customer
      ON dbo.Event_mm_Customer.CustomerID
            = dbo.Customer.CustomerID
   LEFT OUTER JOIN dbo.CustomerType
      ON dbo.Customer.CustomerTypeID
            = dbo.CustomerType.CustomerTypeID
   INNER JOIN dbo.BaseCamp
      ON dbo.Tour.BaseCampID = dbo.BaseCamp.BaseCampID)
```

## Calling an Inline Table-Valued Function

To retrieve data through fEventList, call the function within the from portion of a select statement:

```
SELECT LastName, Code, DateBegin
   FROM dbo.fEventList()
```

Result:

```
LastName      Code        DateBegin
-----------   ----------  ----------------------------
Anderson      01-003      2001-03-16 00:00:00.000
Brown         01-003      2001-03-16 00:00:00.000
Frank         01-003      2001-03-16 00:00:00.000
```

As with stored procedures, a significant performance hit occurs the first time the function is called while the code is being compiled and stored in memory. The subsequent calls are fast.

In comparison to an inline table-valued user-defined function to other SQL Server objects, the performance of an inline function is similar to that of a stored procedure and about 5–10 percent faster than a view.

## Using Parameters

An advantage of inline table-valued functions over views is the function's ability to include parameters within the pre-compiled `select` statement. Views, on the other hand, do not include parameters, and restricting the result at runtime is typically done by means of adding a `where` clause to the `select` statement that calls the view.

The following examples compare adding a restriction to the view to using a function parameter. The following view returns the current price list for all products:

```
USE OBXKites
go

CREATE VIEW vPricelist
AS
SELECT Code, Price.Price
  FROM dbo.Price
    JOIN dbo.Product P
      ON Price.ProductID = P.ProductID
  WHERE EffectiveDate =
      (SELECT MAX(EffectiveDate)
        FROM dbo.Price
        WHERE ProductID = P.ProductID
          AND EffectiveDate <= GetDate())
```

To retrieve the current price for a single product, the calling `select` statement adds a `where` clause restriction when calling the view:

```
SELECT *
  FROM vPriceList
  WHERE Code = '1001'
```

Result:

```
Code             Price
---------------  ----------------------
1001             14.9500
```

SQL Server internally creates a new SQL statement from vPricelist and the calling `select` statement's `where`-clause restriction and then generates a query execution plan.

In contrast, a function allows the restriction to be passed as a parameter to the pre-compiled SQL `select` statement:

```
CREATE FUNCTION dbo.fPriceList (
  @Code CHAR(10) = Null, @PriceDate DateTime)
RETURNS Table
AS
RETURN(
SELECT Code, Price.Price
  FROM dbo.Price
    JOIN dbo.Product P
      ON Price.ProductID = P.ProductID
  WHERE EffectiveDate =
      (SELECT MAX(EffectiveDate)
        FROM dbo.Price
```

```
        WHERE ProductID = P.ProductID
          AND EffectiveDate <= @PriceDate)
    AND (Code = @Code
      OR @Code IS NULL)
  )
```

If the function is called with a default code, the price for the entered date is returned for all products:

```
SELECT * FROM dbo.fPriceList(DEFAULT, '2/20/2002')
```

Result:

```
Code             Price
---------------  ---------------------
1047             6.9500
1049             12.9500
...
```

If a product code is passed in the first input parameter, the pre-compiled `select` statement within the function returns the single product row:

```
SELECT * FROM dbo.fPriceList('1001', '2/20/2002')
```

Result:

```
Code             Price
---------------  ---------------------
1001             14.9500
```

# Multistatement Table-Valued Functions

The multistatement table-valued user-defined function combines the scalar function's ability to contain complex code with the inline table-valued function's ability to return a result set. This type of function creates a table variable and then populates it within code. The table is then passed back from the function so that it may be used within `select` statements.

The primary benefit of the multistatement table-valued user-defined function is that complex result sets may be generated within code and then easily used with a `select` statement. Because of this, these functions may be used in place of stored procedures that return result sets.

## Creating a Multistatement Table-Valued Function

The syntax to create the multistatement table-valued function is very similar to that of the scalar user-defined function:

```
CREATE FUNCTION FunctionName (InputParamenters)
RETURNS @TableName TABLE (Columns)
AS
BEGIN
  Code to populate table variable
  RETURN
END
```

The following example builds a multistatement table-valued user-defined function that returns a basic result set:

1. The function first creates a table variable called @Price within the create function header.

2. Within the body of the function, two insert statements populate the @Price table variable.

3. When the function completes execution, the @Price table variable is passed back as the output of the function.

The fPriceAvg function returns every price in the Price table and the average price for each product:

```
USE OBXKite
go

CREATE FUNCTION fPriceAvg()
RETURNS @Price TABLE
  (Code CHAR(10),
    EffectiveDate DATETIME,
    Price MONEY)
AS
  BEGIN
    INSERT @Price (Code, EffectiveDate, Price)
      SELECT Code, EffectiveDate, Price
        FROM Product
          JOIN Price
            ON Price.ProductID = Product.ProductID

    INSERT @Price (Code, EffectiveDate, Price)
      SELECT Code, Null, Avg(Price)
        FROM Product
          JOIN Price
            ON Price.ProductID = Product.ProductID
        GROUP BY Code
    RETURN
  END
```

## Calling the Function

To execute the function, refer to it within the from portion of a select statement. The following code retrieves the result from the fPriceAvg function:

```
SELECT *
  FROM dbo.fPriceAvg()
```

Result:

```
Code   EffectiveDate              Price
------ -------------------------  --------
1001   2001-05-01 00:00:00.000    14.9500
1001   2002-06-01 00:00:00.000    15.9500
1001   2002-07-20 00:00:00.000    17.9500
```

# Summary

User-defined functions expand the capabilities of SQL Server objects and open up a world of flexibility within expressions and the select statement, but at the steep price of non-portability.

Scalar user-defined functions return a single value and must be deterministic. Inline table-valued user-defined functions are very similar to views and return the results of a single select statement. Multistatement table-valued user-defined functions use code to populate a table variable, which is then returned.

T-SQL code can be packaged in stored procedures, user-defined functions, and triggers. The next chapter delves into triggers, specialized T-SQL procedures that fire in response to table-level events.

✦        ✦        ✦

# Implementing Triggers

CHAPTER

15

Triggers are special stored procedures attached to table events. They can't be directly executed; they fire only in response to an insert, update, or delete event on a table. In the same way that attaching code to a form or control event in Visual Basic or Access causes that code to execute on the form or control event, triggers fire on table events.

Users can't bypass a trigger, and unless the trigger sends a message to the client the end user is unaware of the trigger.

Developing triggers involves several SQL Server topics. Understanding transaction flow and locking, T-SQL, and stored procedures is a prerequisite for developing smooth triggers. Triggers contain a few unique elements, and require careful planning, but provide rock-solid execution of complex business rules and data validation.

Some DBAs oppose the use of triggers because they are proprietary in nature. If the database is ported to another platform, all triggers have to be rewritten. Triggers are also accused of hindering performance. In defense of triggers, if a rule is too complex for a constraint, a trigger is the only other acceptable location for it. A business rule implemented outside the server is not a rule; it's a suggestion. If a trigger is poorly written, it will have a significant negative effect on performance. However, a well-written trigger ensures data integrity and provides good performance.

## Trigger Basics

SQL Server triggers fire once per DML operation, not once per affected row. This is different from Oracle, which can fire a trigger once per operation, or once per row. While this may seem at first glance to be a limitation, being forced to develop set-based triggers actually helps ensure clean logic as well as fast performance.

Triggers may be created for the three table events that correspond to the three data-modification commands: insert, update, and delete.

SQL Server 2000 has two kinds of triggers: *instead of* triggers and *after* triggers. They differ in their purpose, timing, and effect, as detailed in Table 15-1.

### Table 15-1: Trigger Type Comparison

|  | *Instead of Trigger* | *After Trigger* |
| --- | --- | --- |
| DML statement | Automatically rolled back | Executed unless trigger rolls back the transaction |
| Timing | Before PK and FK constraints | After the transaction is complete, but before it's committed |
| Number possible per table event | One | Multiple |
| May be applied to views? | Yes | No |
| Nested? | Depends on server option | Depends on server option |
| Recursive? | No | Depends on database option |

## Transaction Flow

Developing triggers requires understanding the overall flow of the transaction; otherwise conflicts between constraints and triggers can cause designing and debugging nightmares.

Every transaction moves through the various checks and code in the following order:

1. `Identity insert` check.

2. Nullability constraint.

3. Data-type check.

4. `Instead of` trigger execution. If an `instead of` trigger exists, execution of the DML stops here. `Instead of` triggers are not recursive. Therefore, if the `insert` trigger executes a DML command that fires the same event (`insert`, `update` or `delete`), the `instead of` trigger will be ignored the second time around.

5. Primary-key constraint.

6. Check constraints.

7. Foreign-key constraint.

8. DML execution and update to the transaction log.

9. `After trigger` execution.

10. Commit transaction.

11. The data file is written.

Based on SQL Server's transaction flow, a few points concerning developing triggers are worth noting:

✦ An `after` trigger occurs after all constraints. Because of this it can't correct data, and therefore the data must pass any constraint checks, including foreign-key constraint checks.

✦ An `instead of` trigger can circumvent foreign-key problems, but not nullability, data type, or identity-column problems.

✦ An `after` trigger can assume that the data has passed all the other built-in data-integrity checks.

✦ The `after` trigger occurs before the DML transaction is committed so it can roll back the transaction if the data is unacceptable.

## Creating Triggers

Triggers are created and modified with the standard DDL commands, `create`, `alter`, and `drop`, as follows:

```
CREATE TRIGGER TriggerName ON TableName
AFTER Insert, Update Delete
AS
Trigger Code
```

Prior to SQL Server 2000, SQL Server only had after triggers. Because no distinction between `after` and `instead of` was necessary, the old syntax was to create the trigger `for insert`, `update`, or `delete`. So that the old after triggers will still work, after triggers can be created by means of using the keyword `for` in place of `after`.

Triggers may be created with encryption, just like stored procedures. However, the encryption is just as easily broken.

## After Triggers

A table may have several after triggers for each of the three table events. After triggers may only be applied to tables.

The traditional trigger is an after trigger that fires after the transaction is complete, but before the transaction is committed. After triggers are useful for the following:

✦ Complex data validation

✦ Enforcing complex business rules

✦ Recording data-audit trails

✦ Maintaining modified date columns

✦ Enforcing custom referential-integrity checks and cascading deletes

**Best Practice**

Use `after` triggers if the transaction will likely be accepted because the work is complete and waiting only for a transaction commit. For this reason after triggers are excellent for validating data or enforcing a complex rule.

When learning a new programming language, the first program written is traditionally a "hello world" application that does nothing more than compile the program and prove that it runs buy printing "hello world". The following `after` trigger simply prints `after trigger` when the trigger is executed:

```
CREATE TRIGGER TriggerOne ON Person
AFTER Insert
AS
PRINT 'In the After Trigger'
```

With the after trigger enforced, the following code will insert a sample row:

```
INSERT Person(PersonID, LastName, FirstName, Gender)
   VALUES (50, 'Ebob', 'Bill','M')
```

Result:

```
In the After Trigger

(1 row(s) affected)
```

The insert worked and the trigger printed its "hello world" message.

# Instead of Triggers

Instead of triggers execute "instead of" (as a substitute for) the submitted transaction, so that the submitted transaction does not occur. It's as if the presence of an instead of trigger is an automatic rollback on the submitted transaction.

As a substitution procedure, each table is limited to only one instead of trigger per table event. In addition, instead of triggers may be applied to views as well as tables.

Don't confuse instead of triggers with before triggers or before update events. They're not the same. A before trigger, if such a thing existed in SQL Server, would not interfere with the transaction unless code in the trigger executed a transaction rollback.

Instead of triggers are useful when it's known that the DML statement firing the trigger will always be rolled back and some other logic executed instead of the DML statement. For example:

✦ When the DML statement attempts to update a non-updatable view, the instead of trigger updates the underlying tables instead.

✦ When the DML statement attempts to directly update an inventory table, an instead of trigger updates the inventory transaction table instead.

✦ When the DML statement attempts to delete a row, an instead of trigger moves the row to an archive table instead.

The following code creates a test instead of trigger and then attempts to insert a row:

```
CREATE TRIGGER TriggerTwo ON Person
INSTEAD OF Insert
AS
PRINT 'In the Instead of Trigger'
go

INSERT Person(PersonID, LastName, FirstName, Gender)
   VALUES (51, 'Ebob', '','M')
```

Result:

```
In the Instead of Trigger

(1 row(s) affected)
```

The result includes the instead of trigger's "hello world" declaration and a report that one row was affected. However, selecting personID 51 will prove that no rows were in fact inserted:

```
SELECT LastName
  FROM Person
  WHERE PersonID = 51
```

Result:

```
LastName
---------------
(0 row(s) affected)
```

The `insert` statement worked as if one row had been affected, although the effect of the `insert` statement was blocked by the `instead of` trigger. The `print` command was executed instead of the rows being inserted. Also, the `after` trigger is still in effect, but its `print` message failed to print.

## Trigger Limitations

Owing to the nature of triggers (code attached to tables), they have a few limitations. The following SQL commands are not permitted within a trigger:

✦ `Create`, `alter`, or `drop` **database**

✦ `Reconfigure`

✦ `Restore` **database or log**

✦ `Disk resize`

✦ `Disk init`

## Disabling Triggers

A user's DML statement can never bypass a trigger, but a system administrator can temporarily disable it, which is better than dropping it and then re-creating it if the trigger gets in the way of a data-modification task.

To temporarily turn off a trigger, use the `alter table` DDL command with the `enable trigger` or `disable trigger` option:

```
ALTER TABLE TableName ENABLE or DISABLE TRIGGER TriggerName
```

For example, the following code disables the `instead of` trigger (`TriggerOne` on the `Person` table):

```
ALTER TABLE Person
   DISABLE TRIGGER TriggerOne
```

To view the enabled status of a trigger, use the `objectproperty()` function, passing to it the object ID of the trigger and the `ExecIsTriggerDisabled` option:

```
SELECT OBJECTPROPERTY(
   OBJECT_ID('TriggerOne'),'ExecIsTriggerDisabled')
```

## Listing Triggers

Since triggers tend to hide in the table structure, the following query lists all the triggers in the database. It also examines the `sysobjects` table for `tr` type objects and then joins the `Trigger` table row with the parent object row to report the table name. The query uses a correlated subquery to call the objectproperty() function for each row. The result of the correlated subquery is passed to a case expression so it can be converted to a string:

```
SELECT SubString(S2.Name,1,30) as [Table],
   SubString(S.Name, 1,30) as [Trigger],
   CASE (SELECT -- Correlated subquery
           OBJECTPROPERTY(OBJECT_ID(S.Name),
             'ExecIsTriggerDisabled'))
     WHEN 0 THEN 'Enabled'
     WHEN 1 THEN 'Disabled'
   END AS Status
   FROM Sysobjects S
     JOIN Sysobjects S2
       ON S.parent_obj = S2.ID
   WHERE S.Type = 'TR'
   ORDER BY [Table], [Trigger]
```

Result:

```
Table           Trigger               Status
--------------  --------------------  --------
Person          Person_Parents        Enabled
Person          TriggerOne            Disabled
Person          TriggerTwo            Enabled
```

## Triggers and Security

Only users who are members of the sysadmin fixed server role, or in the dbowner or ddldmin fixed database roles, or the table's owners, have permission to create, alter, drop, enable, or disable triggers.

Code within the trigger is executed assuming the security permissions of the owner of the trigger's table.

# Working with the Transaction

A DML insert, update, or delete statement causes a trigger to fire. It's important that the trigger have access to the changes being caused by the DML statement so it can test the changes or handle the transaction. SQL Server provides four ways for code within the trigger to determine the effects of the DML statement. The inserted and deleted images contain the before and after datasets, and the updated() and columns_updated() functions may be used to determine which columns were affected by the DML statement.

## Determining the Updated Columns

SQL Server provides two methods of detecting which columns are being updated. The update() function returns true for a single column if that column is affected by the DML transaction:

```
IF UPDATE(ColumnName)
```

An insert will affect all columns, and an update will report the column as affected if the DML statement addresses the column. The following example demonstrates the update() function:

```
ALTER TRIGGER TriggerOne ON Person
AFTER Insert, Update
AS
IF Update(LastName)
  PRINT 'You modified the LastName column'
ELSE
  PRINT 'The LastName column is untouched.'
```

With the trigger looking for changes to the LastName column, the following DML statement will test the trigger:

```
UPDATE Person
  SET LastName = 'Johnson'
  WHERE PersonID = 25
```

Result:

```
You modified the LastName column
```

This function is generally used to execute data checks only when needed. There's no reason to test the validity of Column A's data if Column A isn't updated by the DML statement. However, the update() function will report the column as updated according to the DML statement alone, not the actual data. So if the DML statement modifies the data from 'abc' to 'abc' the update() will still report it as updated.

The columns_updated() function returns a bitmapped varbinary data type representation of the columns updated. If the bit is true the column is updated. The result of columns_updated() can be compared with integer or binary data by means of any of the bitwise operators to determine if a given column is updated.

The documentation states that the columns are represented by bits going from left to right, which is not entirely accurate. The columns are represented by right-to-left bits within left-to-right bytes. A further complication is that the size of the varbinary data retuned by columns_updated() depends on the number of columns in the table.

The following function simulates the actual behavior of the columns_updated() function. Passing the column to be tested and the total number of columns in the table will return the column bitmask for that column.

```
CREATE FUNCTION dbo.GenColUpdated
  (@Col INT, @ColTotal INT)
RETURNS INT
AS
BEGIN
-- Copyright 2001 Paul Nielsen
-- This function simulates the Columns_Updated() behavior
DECLARE
  @ColByte INT,
  @ColTotalByte INT,
  @ColBit INT

  -- Calculate Byte Positions
  SET @ColTotalByte =    1 + ((@ColTotal-1) /8)
  SET @ColByte = 1 + ((@Col-1)/8)
  SET @ColBit = @col - ((@colByte-1) * 8)

  RETURN Power(2, @colbit + ((@ColTotalByte-@ColByte) * 8)-1)
END
```

This function is used within the dynamic audit-trial trigger/stored procedure by means of performing a bitwise and (&) between `columns_updated()` and `GenColUpdated()`. If the bitwise and is equal to `GenColUpdated()`, then the column in question is indeed updated:

```
Set @Col_Updated = Columns_Updated()
...
Set @ColUpdatedTemp =dbo.GenColUpdated(@ColCounter,@ColTotal)
If (@Col_Updated & @ColUpdatedTemp) = @ColUpdatedTemp
```

 **Cross-Reference**  The dynamic audit trail trigger code is explained in Chapter 16, "Advanced Server-Side Programming." The `DynamicAudit.sql` script, on the book's CD, applies the code to the Northwind database.

## Inserted and Deleted Logical Tables

SQL Server enables code within the trigger to access the effects of the transaction that caused the trigger to fire. The `Inserted` and `Deleted` logical tables are read-only images of the data. They can be considered views to the transaction log.

The `Deleted` table contains the rows before the effects of the DML statement and the `Inserted` table contains the rows after the effects of the DML statement, as shown in Table 15-2.

### Table 15-2: The Inserted and Deleted Tables

| DML Statement | Inserted Table | Deleted Table |
|---------------|----------------|---------------|
| Insert | Inserted rows | Empty |
| Update | Rows in the database after the update | Rows in the database before the update |
| Delete | Empty | Rows to be deleted |

The `Inserted` and `Deleted` tables have a very limited scope. They are visible only within the trigger. Stored procedures called by the trigger will not see the `Inserted` or `Deleted` tables.

If the table includes `text`, `ntext`, or `image` data-type columns, those columns may not be accessed in the `Inserted` or `Deleted` tables. Attempting to access them will cause an error.

The following example uses the `Inserted` table to report any new values for the `LastName` column:

```
ALTER TRIGGER TriggerOne ON Person
AFTER Insert, Update
AS
SET NoCount ON
IF Update(LastName)
  SELECT 'You modified the LastName column to '
    + Inserted.LastName
  FROM Inserted
```

With `TriggerOne` implemented on the `Person` table, the following update will modify a `LastName` value:

```
UPDATE Person
  SET LastName = 'Johnson'
  WHERE PersonID = 32
```

Result:

```
-----------------------------------------------------
You modified the LastName column to Johnson
 (1 row(s) affected)
```

## Developing Multi-Row Enabled Triggers

Many triggers I see in production are not written to handle the possibility of multiple-row inserts, updates, or deletes. They take a value from the Inserted or Deleted table and store it in a local variable for data validation or processing. This technique only checks the last row affected by the DML statement and is a serious data integrity flaw. I've also seen databases that use cursors to step though each affected row. This is the type of slow code that gives triggers a bad name.

**Best Practice**

Because SQL is a set-oriented environment, every trigger must be written to handle DML statements that affect multiple rows. The best way to deal with multiple rows is to work with the Inserted and Deleted tables with set-oriented operations.

A join between the Inserted table and the Deleted or underlying table will return a complete set of the rows affected by the DML statement. Table 15-3 lists the possible join combinations for creating multi-row enabled triggers.

### Table 15-3: Multi-Row Enabled FROM Clauses

| DML Type | FROM Clause |
|---|---|
| Insert | FROM Inserted |
| Update | FROM Inserted |
|  | JOIN Deleted |
|  | ON Inserted.PK = Deleted.PK |
| Insert, Update | FROM Inserted |
|  | LEFT OUTER JOIN Deleted |
|  | ON Inserted.PK = Deleted.PK |
| Delete | FROM Deleted |

The following trigger sample alters TriggerOne to look at the inserted and deleted tables:

```
ALTER TRIGGER TriggerOne ON Person
AFTER Insert, Update
AS
SELECT D.LastName + ' changed to ' + I.LastName
  FROM Inserted I
    JOIN Deleted D
      ON I.PersonID = D.PersonID
```

```
UPDATE Person
  SET LastName = 'Carter'
  WHERE LastName = 'Johnson'
```

Result:

```
-----------------------------------------
Johnson changed to Carter
Johnson changed to Carter
(2 row(s) affected)
```

The following after trigger, extracted from the Family sample database, enforces a rule that the FatherID must not only point to a valid person (that's covered by the foreign key), but that the person must be male:

```
CREATE TRIGGER Person_Parents
ON Person
AFTER INSERT, UPDATE
AS
IF UPDATE(FatherID)
  BEGIN
    -- Incorrect Father Gender
    IF EXISTS(
        SELECT *
          FROM Person
            JOIN Inserted
              ON Inserted.FatherID = Person.PersonID
          WHERE Person.Gender = 'F')
      BEGIN
        ROLLBACK
        RAISERROR('Incorrect Gender for Father',14,1)
        RETURN
      END
  END
```

# Multiple-Trigger Interaction

Without a clear plan, database that employs multiple triggers can quickly become disorganized and extremely difficult to troubleshoot.

## Trigger Organization

In SQL Server 6.5, each trigger event could have only one trigger and a trigger could apply only to one trigger event. The coding style that was required to develop such limited triggers lingers on. However, SQL Server 7 and SQL Server 2000 allow multiple after triggers per table event and a trigger can apply to more than one event. This enables more flexible development styles.

After developing databases that included several hundred triggers, I recommend organizing triggers not by table event, but by the trigger's task. For example:

✦ Data validation

✦ Complex business rules

✦ Audit trail

✦ Modified date

✦ Complex security

**Cross-Reference**  These tasks are covered in more detail in Chapter 16, "Advanced Server-Side Programming."

## Nested Triggers

Trigger nesting is whether or not a trigger that executes a DML statement will cause another trigger to fire. For example, if the Nested Triggers server option is enabled, and a trigger updates TableA, and TableA also has a trigger, then any triggers on TableA will also fire, as demonstrated in Figure 15-1.

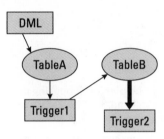

**Figure 15-1:** The Nested Triggers configuration option enables a DML statement within a trigger to fire additional triggers.

By default, the Nested Triggers option is enabled. The following configuration command is used to enable trigger nesting:

```
EXEC sp_configure 'Nested Triggers', 1
Reconfigure
```

If the database is developed with extensive server-side code, it's likely that a DML will fire a trigger, which will call a stored procedure, which will fire another trigger, and so on.

SQL Server triggers have a limit of 32 levels of recursion. For safety reasons it is useful to test the trigger-recursion level within the trigger. The Trigger_NestLevel() function returns the level of nesting. If the limit is reached SQL Server generates a fatal error.

## Recursive Triggers

A recursive trigger is a unique type of nested after trigger. If a trigger executes a DML statement that causes itself to fire, it's a recursive trigger, as shown in Figure 15-2. If the database recursive triggers option is off, the recursive iteration of the trigger won't fire.

A trigger is considered recursive only if it directly fires itself. If the trigger executes a stored procedure that then updates the trigger's table, that is an indirect recursive call and is not covered by the recursive-trigger database option.

Recursive triggers are enabled by means of the alter database command:

```
ALTER DATABASE DatabaseName SET RECURSIVE_TRIGGERS ON | OFF
```

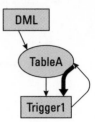

**Figure 15-2:** A recursive trigger is a self-referencing trigger — one that executes a DML statement that causes itself to be fired again.

An example of a useful recursive trigger is the `ModifiedDate` trigger. This trigger writes the current date and time to the modified column for any row that's updated. Using the OBX Kites sample database, the script first adds a `Created` and `Modified` column to the product table:

```
USE OBXKites

ALTER TABLE dbo.Product
  ADD
    Created DateTime Not Null DEFAULT GetDate(),
    Modified DateTime Not Null DEFAULT GetDate()
```

The trigger first prints the `TriggerNest()` level. This is very helpful for debugging nested or recursive triggers. The first `if` statement prevents the `Created` and `Modified` date from being directly updated by the user. If the trigger is fired by a user the nest level is 1.

The first time the trigger is executed the `update` is executed. Any subsequent executions of the trigger `return` because the trigger nest level is greater than 1. This prevents runaway recursion. Here's the trigger DDL code:

```
CREATE TRIGGER Products_ModifiedDate ON dbo.Product
FOR UPDATE
AS
SET NoCount ON

PRINT Trigger_NestLevel()

If Trigger_NestLevel() > 1
Return

If (Update(Created) or Update(Modified))
    AND Trigger_NestLevel() = 1
Begin
  Raiserror('Update failed.', 16, 1)
  Rollback
  Return
End

-- Update the Modified date
UPDATE Product
  SET Modified = getdate()
  FROM Product
    JOIN Inserted
      ON Product.ProductID = Inserted.ProductID
```

To test the trigger, the next `update` command will cause the trigger to `update` the `Modified` column. The select returns the `Created` and `Modified` date and time:

```
UPDATE PRODUCT
  SET [Name] = 'Modifed Trigger'
  WHERE Code = '1002'

SELECT Code, Created, Modified
  FROM Product
  WHERE Code = '1002'
```

Result:

```
Code    Created                   Modified
------  ------------------------  ------------------------
1002    2002-02-18 09:48:31.700   2002-02-18 15:19:34.350
```

**Note**     Recursive triggers are required for replicated databases.

## Instead of and After Triggers

If a table has both an `instead of` trigger and an `after` trigger for the same event, the following sequence is possible:

1. The DML statement initiates a transaction.

2. The `instead of` trigger fires in place of the DML.

3. If the `instead of` trigger executes DML against the same table event the process continues.

4. The `after` trigger fires.

## Multiple After Triggers

If the same table event has multiple `after` triggers they will all execute. The order of the triggers is less important than it may at first seem.

Every trigger has the opportunity to `rollback` the transaction. If the transaction is rolled back, all the work done by the initial transaction and all the triggers are rolled back.

Nevertheless, it is possible to designate an `after` trigger to fire `first` or `last` in the list of triggers. I recommend doing this only if one trigger is likely to roll back the transaction and, for performance reasons, you want that trigger to execute before other demanding triggers. Logically, however, the order of the triggers has no effect.

The `sp_settriggerorder` system stored procedure is used to assign the trigger order using the following syntax:

```
sp_settriggerorder
  @triggername = 'TriggerName',
  @order = 'first' or 'last' or 'none',
  @stmttype = 'INSERT' or 'UPDATE' or 'DELETE'
```

The effect of setting the trigger order is not cumulative. For example, setting `TriggerOne` to `first` and then setting `TriggerTwo` to `first` does not place `TriggerOne` in second place. In this case `TriggerOne` returns to being unordered.

## Summary

Triggers are a key feature in client/server databases. It's the trigger that enables the developer to create complex custom business rules that are strongly enforced at the database-engine level. SQL Server 2000 has two types of triggers, `instead of` triggers and `after` triggers.

The last four chapters have presented T-SQL programming and how to package the code within stored procedures, user-defined functions, and triggers. The next chapter draws on all of these chapters to present ideas for advanced server-side code.

✦　　✦　　✦

# Advanced Server-Side Programming

The U.S. Navy has a saying: "Not on *my* watch." It means that the individual sailor is accepting responsibility, without excuse, and that orders will be followed. The same attitude should apply to business rules. If a business rule isn't enforced 100 percent, it's not a rule — it's a suggestion.

As the logical schema is implemented, many business rules and entity relationships are implemented as constraints.

But some of the business rules may be too complex to implement as constraints. These rules may be implemented either in the front-end application, in a middle tier, or in the database server. Of these three possible locations, only the database server offers absolute compliance. There's no guarantee that future users will access the data solely through the current middle-tier object or front-end application.

Implementing business rules at the database-server level using T-SQL in triggers, stored procedures, and functions offers the same compelling benefits as constraints:

✦ The rules are absolute, and may not be ignored or bypassed by any DML request.

✦ The rules are as close to the data as possible, improving data-access speed and reducing network round trips.

Constraints, triggers, and stored procedures stand watch over the integrity of the data.

The past several chapters have discussed specific techniques for developing server-side code. A recurring theme in these chapters has been that processing should be moved as close to the data as possible. This chapter draws on all those techniques and suggests methods for developing databases that benefit from server-side code.

The methodology of the server-side–code database provides a stored procedure for every data-access requirement of the front-end application and implements all business rules in the server in either stored procedures or triggers. While this method is development-intensive, it provides several benefits:

✦ All access is through a consistent programmer interface.

✦ All database code is compiled and optimized.

✦ Security is improved.

✦ All actions, even reads, may be audited.

✦ Complex rules and processing are removed from the front-end application.

✦ Query errors are eliminated.

# Developing Application Stored Procedures

The database processing (`insert`, `update`, and `delete`) will take place on the server. Moving the application code to the server enables the code to be compiled on the server, and provides a consistent programmer method for performing database operations. Rather than handling some updates in ADO code, some in dynamic SQL generated in VB, and others in T-SQL batches, a database developed using the server-side–code methodology places all database operations in T-SQL code within stored procedures and triggers. Every database requirement from the front-end program is handled by means of calling a stored procedure.

Stored procedures must be written for the following:

✦ Inserting data

✦ Updating data

✦ Deleting data

✦ Fetching single rows and lists for every user-recognizable object

✦ Some stored procedures, such as an `AllocateProduct` stored procedure, may handle complex tasks that deal with multiple tables.

This section provides walks through stored procedures from the OBX Kites database, which demonstrate some of these tasks.

## The AddNew Stored Procedure

The *addnew* stored procedure handles inserting new rows into the database. The stored procedure's main tasks are to validate the data, convert any codes to foreign keys, and perform the `insert` operation. The addnew procedure might also handle lock-timeout issues. Here's the code for the sample stored procedure from the OBX Kites database:

```
CREATE PROCEDURE pProduct_AddNew(
  @ProductCategoryName NVARCHAR(50),
  @Code CHAR(10),
  @Name NVARCHAR(50),
  @ProductDescription NVARCHAR(100) = NULL
  )
AS
  SET NOCOUNT ON
  DECLARE
    @ProductCategoryID UNIQUEIDENTIFIER

  SELECT @ProductCategoryID = ProductCategoryID
    FROM dbo.ProductCategory
      WHERE ProductCategoryName = @ProductCategoryName
  IF @@Error <> 0 RETURN -100
```

```
IF @ProductCategoryID IS NULL
  BEGIN
    RAISERROR
     ('Product Category: ''%s'' not found',
        15,1,@ProductCategoryName)
    RETURN -100
  END

INSERT dbo.Product
  (ProductCategoryID, Code,
     ProductName, ProductDescription)
  VALUES (@ProductCategoryID, @Code, @Name,
     @ProductDescription )
IF @@Error <> 0 RETURN -100
RETURN 0
```

To test the procedure, the following command passes product code "999," thus inserting product code "999" in the Product table:

```
EXEC pProduct_AddNew
  @ProductCategoryName = 'OBX',
  @Code = '999',
  @Name = 'Test Kit',
  @ProductDescription
        = 'official kite testing kit for contests.'
```

To make sure the insert worked, the following select string returns product code "999":

```
SELECT ProductName, ProductCategoryName
  FROM dbo.Product
    JOIN ProductCategory
      ON Product.ProductCategoryID
         = ProductCategory. ProductCategoryID
  WHERE Code = '999'
```

Result:

```
Name              ProductCategoryName
---------------   ---------------------
Test Kit          OBX
```

## The Fetch Stored Procedure

The *fetch* stored procedure retrieves the data. A sophisticated fetch procedure can accept various parameters and respond with a single row, filtered rows, or all rows, depending on the requirement and the parameters, so multiple fetch procedures are not necessary for various scopes of data. The null default is used in the where clause to effectively nullify the criterion if the parameter is not supplied.

This stored procedure also handles lock-timeout and deadlock issues using the techniques covered in Chapter 11, "Transactional Integrity." The following sample fetch stored procedure retrieves product information for the OBX Kites database:

```
CREATE PROCEDURE pProduct_Fetch(
  @ProductCode CHAR(15) = NULL,
  @ProductCategory CHAR(15) = NULL )
AS
```

```
SET NoCount ON

SELECT Code, ProductName, ProductDescription, ActiveDate,
    DiscontinueDate, ProductCategoryName, [RowVersion] --,
--    Product.Created, Product.Modified
  FROM dbo.Product
    JOIN dbo.ProductCategory
      ON Product.ProductCategoryID
          = ProductCategory.ProductCategoryID
  WHERE ( Product.Code = @ProductCode
                OR @ProductCode IS NULL )
    AND ( ProductCategory.ProductCategoryName
          = @ProductCategory
                OR @ProductCategory IS NULL )
  IF @@Error <> 0 RETURN -100


RETURN
```

The following command executes the pProduct_Fetch stored procedure and retrieves data
for all the products when called without any parameters:

```
EXEC pProduct_Fetch
```

Result (columns and rows abridged):

```
Code  Name                            Modified
----- ------------------------------- -----------------------
1001  Basic Box Kite 21 inch          2002-02-18 09:48:31.700
1002  Dragon Flight                   2002-02-18 15:19:34.350
1003  Sky Dancer                      2002-02-18 09:48:31.700
...
```

With a @ProductCode parameter, the fetch stored procedure returns only the selected
product:

```
EXEC pProduct_Fetch
  @ProductCode = '1005'
```

Result (columns abridged):

```
Code  Name                            Modified
----- ------------------------------- -----------------------
1005  Eagle Wings                     2002-02-18 09:48:31.700
```

The second parameter causes the stored procedure to return all the products within a single
product category:

```
EXEC pProduct_Fetch
  @ProductCategory = 'Book'
```

Result (rows and columns abridged):

```
Code  Name                            Modified
----- ------------------------------- -----------------------
1036  Adventures in the OuterBanks    2002-02-25 17:13:15.430
1037  Wright Brothers Kite Designs    2002-02-25 17:13:15.430
1038  The Lighthouses of the OBX      2002-02-25 17:13:15.430
1039  Outer Banks Map                 2002-02-25 17:13:15.430
1040  Kiters Guide to the Outer Banks 2002-02-25 17:13:15.430
```

# The Update Stored Procedure

The *update* stored procedure accepts the primary method of identifying the row (in this case the product code) and the new data. Based on the new data, it performs a SQL DML update statement.

Updates are vulnerable to lost updates as discussed in Chapter 11, "Transactional Integrity." You can work around the lost update problem with timestamps or with minimal updates. Each technique is demonstrated in this section with a sample stored procedure.

The first example procedure handles lost updates by checking the rowversion timestamp column. Each time the row is updated, SQL Server automatically updates the rowversion value. If the rowversion is different, the row must have been updated by another transaction and the rowversion condition in the where clause prevents the update.

## Update with RowVersion

This version of the update procedure updates all the columns of the row, so all the parameters must be supplied even if that column is not being updated. The procedure assumes that the rowversion column was selected when the data was originally retrieved.

If the rowversion value differs from the one retrieved during the select, the update fails to take place. The procedure senses that using the @@rowcount global variable and reports the error to the calling object.

As a sample update procedure, here's the code for the pProduct_Update_RowVersion stored procedure from the OBX Kites database:

```
CREATE PROCEDURE pProduct_Update_RowVersion (
  @Code CHAR(15),
  @RowVersion Rowversion,
  @Name VARCHAR(50),
  @ProductDescription VARCHAR(50),
  @ActiveDate DateTime,
  @DiscontinueDate DateTime )
AS
SET NoCount ON

UPDATE dbo.Product
  SET
    ProductName = @Name,
    ProductDescription = @ProductDescription,
    ActiveDate = @ActiveDate,
    DiscontinueDate = @DiscontinueDate
  WHERE Code = @Code
    AND [RowVersion] = @RowVersion

  IF @@ROWCOUNT = 0
    BEGIN
    IF EXISTS ( SELECT * FROM Product WHERE Code = @Code)
      BEGIN
        RAISERROR ('Product failed to update because
            another transaction updated the row since your
            last read.', 16,1)
        RETURN -100
      END
    ELSE
```

```
        BEGIN
          RAISERROR ('Product failed to update because
            the row has been deleted', 16,1)
          RETURN -100
        END
      END
RETURN
```

To test the timestamp version of the `update` stored procedure, the `pProduct_Fetch` procedure will return the current timestamp for product code "1001":

```
EXEC pProduct_Fetch 1001
```

Result (columns abridged):

```
Code      Name                      RowVersion
--------  ----------------------    ------------------------
1001      Basic Box Kite 21 inch    0x0000000000000077
```

The `pProduct_Update_Rowversion` stored procedure must be called with the exact same `rowversion` value to perform the update:

```
EXEC pProduct_Update_Rowversion
  1001,
  0x0000000000000077,
  'updatetest',
  'new description',
  '1/1/2002',
  NULL
```

The procedure updates all the columns in the row and in the process the `rowversion` column is reset to a new value.

## Minimal-Update

The second version of the `update` stored procedure demonstrates the minimal-update method of minimizing lost updates. By updating only the specific column requiring update, you reduce the chance of overwriting another user's update significantly. The column-level `update` is like a surgical strike, hitting only where it's needed and reducing collateral damage.

The stored procedure does not use dynamic SQL to build a custom `update`, although that could easily be done. However, dynamic SQL executes using the security profile of the user and not the stored procedures, and it introduces a re-compile issue that causes performance to suffer. These problems may make using dynamic SQL within production stored procedures an unhealthy choice.

The minimal-update procedure simply performs a single-column `update` for each parameter provided to the stored procedure:

```
CREATE PROCEDURE pProduct_Update_Minimal (
  @Code CHAR(15),
  @Name VARCHAR(50) = NULL,
  @ProductDescription VARCHAR(50) = NULL,
  @ActiveDate DateTime = NULL,
  @DiscontinueDate DateTime = NULL )

AS
SET NoCount ON
```

```
IF EXISTS (SELECT * FROM dbo.Product WHERE Code = @Code)
  BEGIN
    BEGIN TRANSACTION
    IF @Name IS NOT NULL
      BEGIN
        UPDATE dbo.Product
          SET
            ProductName = @Name
          WHERE Code = @Code
        IF @@Error <> 0
          BEGIN
            ROLLBACK
            RETURN -100
          END
      END

    IF @ProductDescription IS NOT NULL
      BEGIN
        UPDATE dbo.Product
          SET
            ProductDescription = @ProductDescription
          WHERE Code = @Code
        IF @@Error <> 0
          BEGIN
            ROLLBACK
            RETURN -100
          END
      END

    IF @ActiveDate IS NOT NULL
      BEGIN
        UPDATE dbo.Product
          SET
            ActiveDate = @ActiveDate
          WHERE Code = @Code
        IF @@Error <> 0
          BEGIN
            ROLLBACK
            RETURN -100
          END
      END

    IF @DiscontinueDate IS NOT NULL
      BEGIN
        UPDATE dbo.Product
          SET
            DiscontinueDate = @DiscontinueDate
          WHERE Code = @Code
        IF @@Error <> 0
          BEGIN
            ROLLBACK
```

```
            RETURN -100
          END
       END
    COMMIT TRANSACTION
  END
ELSE
  BEGIN
    RAISERROR
      ('Product failed to update because the row has
          been deleted', 16,1)
    RETURN -100
  END
RETURN
```

When the minimal-update stored procedure is being called, only the columns requiring update are needed. The procedure first checks to see if the row exists; once that check is complete, the parameters that were passed to the procedure are updated in the table. In the following example, the product description for product code "1001" is updated:

```
EXEC pProduct_Update_Minimal
  @Code = '1001',
  @ProductDescription = 'a minimal update'
```

The pProduct_Fetch procedure can test the minimal-update procedure:

```
EXEC pProduct_Fetch 1001
```

Result (abridged):

```
Code      Name              ProductDescription
--------- ----------------- ------------------------
1001      updatetest 2      a minimal update
```

## The Delete Stored Procedure

The *delete* stored procedure executes the delete DML command. This procedure can be the most complex stored procedure, depending upon the level of data-archival and logical deletion implemented within the database (covered later in this chapter). This sample delete procedure taken from the OBX Kites database transforms the @ProductCode into a @ProductID, verifies that the product does in fact exist, and then deletes it.

```
CREATE PROCEDURE pProduct_Delete(
  @ProductCode INT
)
AS
  SET NOCOUNT ON
  DECLARE @ProductID UniqueIdentifier

  SELECT @ProductID = ProductID
    FROM Product
    WHERE Code = @ProductCode
  If @@RowCount = 0
    BEGIN
      RAISERROR
        ('Unable to delete Product Code %i
           - does not exist.', 16,1, @ProductCode)
```

```
        RETURN
      END
  ELSE
    DELETE dbo.Product
      WHERE ProductID = @ProductID
  RETURN
```

To test the pProduct_Delete store procedure, the following store procedure attempts to call a product. Since there is no product code "99," the error trapping raises the error:

```
EXEC pProduct_Delete 99
```

Result:

```
Unable to delete Product Code 99 - does not exist.
```

# Complex Business Rule Validation

The common answer to implementing data validation is check constraints; however, check constraints (sans user-defined functions) are limited to the current row.

Complex data validation deals with two concerns:

✦ Data validation that requires the access of data other than the current row, thus eliminating a check constraint as a possible means of implementing data validation.

✦ Data validation that must be dynamic, based on requirements that vary by installation, company, department, or some other data, or just varying over time. Data-validation routines that can pull the requirements from a configuration table enable the local administrator to alter the data requirements without physically changing the schema.

Complex data validation is best implemented within a trigger. Triggers are powerful, flexible, and 100 percent enforced. A user's DML statement cannot bypass a trigger.

The basic tactic when constructing a trigger to enforce complex data validation is to check for the existence of any data in the inserted table that does not meet the rule, and, if any is found, to roll back the transaction. It's important that the trigger test for invalid data. If the trigger tested for the existence of valid data and some rows of multi-row update were valid but some were not then the trigger would let the bad in with the good.

Alternately, if the existence of invalid data is simply too difficult to code, the trigger could compare the @@Rowcount of the transaction with the count() of valid data in the Inserted table. But checking for invalid data will typically be faster and easier.

As an example of a need for complex data validation, the following business rule is from the Cape Hatteras Adventures database: *any lead guide for a tour event must be qualified as a guide for that tour.*

Guides are assigned to the event in the Event_mm_Guide table, so the trigger will check data being inserted into the Event_mm_Guide table.

To check for data that violates the rule, a select statement joins the triggers' Inserted table with the event table to determine the TourID, and then joins with the Tour_mm_Guide table so the guide's qualifications can be checked. Notice that the Event_mm_Guide table is not required in the join; the Inserted table has the required data. The select is then restricted to any rows in which the guide is the lead guide, and in which either the qualification date has not yet occurred or the qualification has been revoked.

If this select statement returns any rows, the insert or update DML operation will be rolled back and an error raised to the client software. Here's the code:

```
CREATE TRIGGER LeadQualified ON Event_mm_Guide
AFTER INSERT, UPDATE
AS
SET NoCount ON
IF EXISTS(
  SELECT *
    FROM Inserted
      JOIN dbo.Event
        ON Inserted.EventID = Event.EventID
      LEFT JOIN dbo.Tour_mm_Guide
        ON Tour_mm_Guide.TourID = Event.TourID
        AND Inserted.GuideID = Tour_mm_Guide.GuideID
    WHERE
      Inserted.IsLead = 1
      AND
        (QualDate > Event.DateBegin
      OR
        RevokeDate IS NOT NULL
      OR
        QualDate IS NULL )
      )
  BEGIN
    RAISERROR('Lead Guide is not Qualified.',16,1)
    ROLLBACK TRANSACTION
  END
```

The follow two queries test the complex rule validation method by attempting to schedule a qualified guide and an unqualified guide. First, John Johnson is scheduled to lead a Gauley River Rafting trip:

```
INSERT Event_mm_Guide (EventID, GuideID, IsLead)
  VALUES (10, 1, 1)
```

Result:

```
Lead Guide is not Qualified.
```

When Ken Frank is scheduled for the class 5 rapids of the Gauley River, the trigger allows the insert:

```
INSERT Event_mm_Guide (EventID, GuideID, IsLead)
  VALUES (10, 2, 1)
```

Result:

```
(1 row(s) affected)
```

# Complex Referential Integrity

Implementing declarative referential integrity via foreign-key constraints is definitely the right way to implement referential integrity.

That said, it's useful to see the code for a standard referential-integrity trigger before building a complex referential-integrity trigger. The code for a basic referential-integrity trigger would perform a set difference query joining the secondary table's foreign key and the primary table's primary key to locate any foreign-key values in the `Inserted` table that don't have a match in the primary table. In this example, `TableB` has a foreign key that points to `TableA`. Note that this generic code doesn't apply to any specific database:

```
CREATE TRIGGER RICheck ON Tour
AFTER INSERT, UPDATE
AS
SET NoCount ON
IF Exists(SELECT *
            FROM Inserted
              LEFT OUTER JOIN BaseCamp
                ON Inserted.BaseCampID
                  = BaseCamp.BaseCampID
              WHERE BaseCamp.BaseCampID IS NULL)
  BEGIN
    RAISERROR
      ('Inappropriate Foreign Key: Tour.BaseCampID', 16, 1)
    ROLLBACK TRANSACTION
    RETURN
  END
```

The following code attempts to assign the "Amazon Trek" tour to `BaseCampID` 99. Since there is no base camp "99" the referential integrity trigger will block the update:

```
UPDATE Tour
  SET BaseCampID = 99
  WHERE TourID = 1
```

Indeed, the result is that the trigger raises an error:

```
Inappropriate Foreign Key: Tour.BaseCampID
```

However rare, some creative advanced physical-data schemas require referential integrity that can't be enforced by the standard foreign key constraint. These schemas tend to involve multiple-way relationships.

An example of complex referential integrity is from an MRP II system I worked on. The system could allocate a product to fill an order detail from either an inventory item or from a purchase-order detail. One of the designs we experimented with allowed the `Allocation` table to use two foreign keys. The first foreign key pointed to the `OrderDetail` row and handled the `Product` requirement. The second foreign key pointed to the fulfillment source, which could *either* be a `PurchaseOrderDetail` GUID or an `InventoryItem` GUID. Because the foreign-key column could relate to either the purchase order or an inventory item a standard foreign-key constraint would not do the job.

To implement the complex referential integrity, a trigger on the `Allocation` table checked for either a valid `PurchaseOrderDetailID` or a valid `InventoryItemID` using a set difference query that checked for any rows in the `Inserted` table with a `SourceID` that was in neither the `Inventory` table nor the `PurchaseOrderDetail` table:

```
CREATE TRIGGER AllocationCheck ON Allocation
AFTER INSERT, UPDATE
AS
SET NoCount ON
-- Check For invalid Inventory Item
IF Exists(SELECT *
```

```
            FROM Inserted I
                LEFT OUTER JOIN InventoryItem
                    ON I.SourceID = InventoryItem.InventoryItemID
                LEFT OUTER JOIN PurchaseOrderDetail
                    ON I.SourceID = PurchaseOrderDetail.PODID
                WHERE Inventory.InventoryID IS NULL
                    AND PurchaseOrderDetail.PODID IS NULL)
        BEGIN
          RAISERROR
            ('Invalid product allocation source', 16, 1)
          ROLLBACK TRANSACTION
          RETURN
        END
```

Alternately, having two foreign keys in the allocation table, one pointing to the inventory-item table and one pointing to the purchase-order–detail table, could also solve the same problem with a less creative approach. The twist is that one, and only one, of the two foreign keys must be null—similar to a logical exclusive or. A standard check constraint could handle that requirement:

```
ALTER TABLE Allocation
  ADD CONSTRAINT AllocationSourceExclusive CHECK
    (PurchaseOrderID IS NULL AND InventoryID IS NOT NULL)
      OR
    (PurchaseOrderID IS NOT NULL AND InventoryID IS NULL)
```

The choice between the two complex referential-integrity methods should be made based on the ease of selecting the correct information and the comfort level of the developers. Both methods would require extensive use of left outer joins and the coalesce() function when calculating product allocation.

# Row-Level Custom Security

SQL Server is excellent at vertical security (tables and columns) but it lacks the ability to dynamically check row-level security. Views, with check option, can provide a hard-coded form of row-level security, but basing a database on views used in this manner would create a performance and maintenance headache.

Enterprise databases often include data that is sensitive on a row level. Consider these four real-life business-security rules:

✦ Material data, inventory-cost data, and production scheduling are owned by a department and should not be available to those outside that department. However, the MRP system contains materials and inventory tracking for all locations and all departments in the entire company.

✦ HR data for each employee must be available to only the HR department and an employee's direct supervisors.

✦ A company-wide purchasing system permits only lumber buyers to purchase lumber, and hardware buyers to purchase hardware.

✦ Each bank branch should be able to read any customer's data file, but only edit those customers who frequent that branch.

A row-based security solution is to develop the database using server-side code. This is a good idea for the following reasons:

✦ A security table can contain the list of users and their departments, or branch read and write rights.

✦ A security procedure checks the user's rights against the data being requested and returns an approved or a denied.

✦ The fetch procedure checks the security procedure for permission to return the data.

✦ Triggers call the security procedure to check the user's right to perform the DML statement on the requested rows.

To demonstrate this design, the following topics implement row-level security to the OBX Kites database. Each employee in the Contact table can be granted read, write, or administer privileges for each location's inventory and sales data. With this row-based security scheme, security can be checked by means of a stored procedure, function, NT login, or trigger.

# The Security Table

The Security table serves as a many-to-many associative table (junction table) between the Contact and Location tables. The security levels determine the level of access:

0 or no row—No access

1—Read access

2—Write access

3—Admin access

Alternately, three bit columns could be used for read, write, and administer rights, but the privileges are cumulative, so an integer column seems appropriate.

## Creating the Table

The security table has two logical foreign keys. The foreign key to the location table is handled by a standard foreign key constraint; however, the reference to the contact table should only allow contacts who are flagged as employees, and therefore a trigger is used to enforce that complex referential-integrity requirement. The security assignment is meaningless without its contact or location, so both foreign keys are cascading deletes. A constraint is applied to the security-level column to restrict any entry to the valid security codes (0-3), and another constraint ensures that a contact may only have one security code per location.

```
USE OBXKites

CREATE TABLE dbo.Security (
  SecurityID UniqueIdentifier NOT NULL
    Primary Key NonClustered,
  ContactID UniqueIdentifier NOT NULL
    REFERENCES Contact ON DELETE CASCADE,
  LocationID UniqueIdentifier NOT NULL
    REFERENCES Location ON DELETE CASCADE,
  SecurityLevel INT NOT NULL DEFAULT 0
  )
```

The following three commands add the constraints to the security table:

```
CREATE TRIGGER ContactID_RI
ON dbo.Security
AFTER INSERT, UPDATE
AS
SET NoCount ON
IF EXISTS(SELECT *
            FROM Inserted
              LEFT OUTER JOIN dbo.Contact
                ON Inserted.ContactID = Contact.ContactID
              WHERE Contact.ContactID IS NULL
              OR Contact.IsEmployee = 0 )
  BEGIN
    RAISERROR
      ('Foreign Key Constraint: Security.ContactID', 16, 1)
    ROLLBACK TRANSACTION
    RETURN
  END

ALTER TABLE dbo.Security
  ADD CONSTRAINT ValidSecurityCode CHECK
    (SecurityLevel IN (0,1,2,3))

ALTER TABLE dbo.Security
  ADD CONSTRAINT ContactLocation UNIQUE
    (ContactID, LocationID)
```

**On the CD-ROM**

Because OBX Kites uses GUIDs for primary keys, it's easier to use stored procedures to enter data. The chapter script (ch16 - Advanced Server Side Code.sql) on the book's CD has stored procedures similar to those used previously in this chapter to enter data into the security table. The chapter script also includes sample data.

## Security Fetch

So that the Security table can be viewed, the first procedure created is pSecurity_Fetch. This procedure returns all the row-based security permissions or can be restricted to returning those permissions for a single user or a single location:

```
CREATE PROCEDURE pSecurity_Fetch(
  @LocationCode CHAR(15) = NULL,
  @ContactCode CHAR(15) = NULL )
AS
SET NoCount ON
SELECT Contact.ContactCode,
       Location.LocationCode,
       SecurityLevel
    FROM dbo.Security
      JOIN dbo.Contact
        ON Security.ContactID = Contact.ContactID
      JOIN dbo.Location
        ON Security.LocationID = Location.LocationID
          WHERE (Location.LocationCode = @LocationCode
```

```
                                 OR @LocationCode IS NULL)
                  AND (Contact.ContactCode = @ContactCode
                            OR @ContactCode IS NULL)
```

## Assigning Security

Row-based security permissions are set by means of adding or altering rows in the security table, which serves as a junction between contact and location. In keeping with the theme of server-side code, this stored procedure assigns a security level to the contact/location combination. There's nothing new about this procedure. It accepts a contact code and location code, converts the codes into GUID IDs, and then performs the `insert`:

```
CREATE PROCEDURE pSecurity_Assign(
  @ContactCode VARCHAR(15),
  @LocationCode VARCHAR(15),
  @SecurityLevel INT
  )
AS
  SET NOCOUNT ON
  DECLARE
    @ContactID UNIQUEIDENTIFIER,
    @LocationID UNIQUEIDENTIFIER

  -- Get ContactID
  SELECT @ContactID = ContactID
    FROM dbo.Contact
    WHERE ContactCode = @ContactCode
  IF @@ERROR <> 0 RETURN -100
  IF @ContactID IS NULL
    BEGIN
      RAISERROR
        ('Contact: ''%s'' not found', 15,1,@ContactCode)
      RETURN -100
    END

  -- Get LocationID
  SELECT @LocationID = LocationID
    FROM dbo.Location
    WHERE LocationCode = @LocationCode
  IF @@ERROR <> 0 RETURN -100
  IF @LocationID IS NULL
    BEGIN
      RAISERROR
        ('Location: ''%s'' not found', 15,1,@LocationCode)
      RETURN -100
    END

  -- Insert
  INSERT dbo.Security (ContactID,LocationID, SecurityLevel)
    VALUES (@ContactID, @LocationID, @SecurityLevel)
  IF @@ERROR <> 0 RETURN -100
  RETURN
```

With the pSecurity_Fetch and pSecurity_Assign stored procedures created, the following batch adds some test data. The first two queries return some valid data for the test:

```
SELECT ContactCode
  FROM Contact
  WHERE IsEmployee = 1
```

Result:

```
ContactCode
---------------
118
120
119
```

The next query returns valid locations:

```
SELECT LocationCode FROM Location
```

Result:

```
LocationCode
---------------
CH
Clt
E1C
JR
KH
W
```

Based on this data, the next four procedure calls assign security:

```
EXEC pSecurity_Assign
  @ContactCode = 118,
  @LocationCode = CH,
  @SecurityLevel = 3

EXEC pSecurity_Assign
  @ContactCode = 118,
  @LocationCode = Clt,
  @SecurityLevel = 2

EXEC pSecurity_Assign
  @ContactCode = 118,
  @LocationCode = Elc,
  @SecurityLevel = 1

EXEC pSecurity_Assign
  @ContactCode = 120,
  @LocationCode = W,
  @SecurityLevel = 2
```

The following two commands test the data inserts using the pSecurity_Ffetch procedure. The first test examines the security settings for the "W" location:

```
EXEC pSecurity_Fetch @LocationCode = 'W'
```

Result:

```
ContactCode      LocationCode     SecurityLevel
---------------  ---------------  -------------
120              W                3
```

The next batch examines the security setting for "Dave Boston" (Contact Code "118"):

```
EXEC pSecurity_Fetch @ContactCode = '118'
```

Result:

```
ContactCode      LocationCode     SecurityLevel
---------------  ---------------  -------------
118              Clt              2
118              CH               3
118              ElC              1
```

The row-based security schema includes several constraints. The following commands test those constraints using the stored procedures.

Testing the unique constraint:

```
EXEC pSecurity_Assign
  @ContactCode = 120,
  @LocationCode = W,
  @SecurityLevel = 2
```

Result:

```
Server: Msg 2627, Level 14, State 2,
  Procedure pSecurity_Assign, Line 35
Violation of UNIQUE KEY constraint 'ContactLocation'.
Cannot insert duplicate key in object 'Security'.
The statement has been terminated.
```

Testing the valid security-code check constraint:

```
EXEC pSecurity_Assign
  @ContactCode = 118,
  @LocationCode = W,
  @SecurityLevel = 5
```

Result:

```
Server: Msg 547, Level 16, State 1,
  Procedure pSecurity_Assign, Line 35
INSERT statement conflicted with COLUMN CHECK constraint
  'ValidSecurityCode'. The conflict occurred in database
  'OBXKites', table 'Security', column 'SecurityLevel'.
The statement has been terminated.
```

Testing the employees-only complex-business-rule trigger:

```
Select ContactCode FROM Contact WHERE IsEmployee = 0
EXEC pSecurity_Assign
  @ContactCode = 102,
  @LocationCode = W,
  @SecurityLevel = 3
```

Result:

```
Foreign Key Constraint: Security.ContactID
```

Testing the contact foreign-key constraint, which is first checked by the stored procedure:

```
EXEC pSecurity_Assign
  @ContactCode = 999,
  @LocationCode = W,
  @SecurityLevel = 3
```

Result:

```
Server: Msg 50000, Level 15, State 1, Procedure pSecurity_Assign, Line
19

Contact: '999' not found
```

Testing the location-code foreign-key constraint. It's also checked within the stored procedure:

```
EXEC pSecurity_Assign
  @ContactCode = 118,
  @LocationCode = RDBMS,
  @SecurityLevel = 3
```

Result:

```
Server: Msg 50000, Level 15, State 1, Procedure pSecurity_Assign, Line
30
Location: 'RDBMS' not found
```

## Handling Security-Level Updates

The pSecurity_Assign procedure used in the previous examples handles new security assignments, but fails to accept adjustments to an existing security setting.

The following alteration to the procedure checks to see if the security combination of contact and location is already in the security table, and then performs either the appropriate insert or update. Security permissions may be created or adjusted with the new version of the procedure and the same parameters. Here's the improved procedure:

```
ALTER PROCEDURE pSecurity_Assign(
  @ContactCode CHAR(15),
  @LocationCode CHAR(15),
  @SecurityLevel INT
  )
AS
  SET NOCOUNT ON
  DECLARE
    @ContactID UNIQUEIDENTIFIER,
    @LocationID UNIQUEIDENTIFIER
  -- Get ContactID
  SELECT @ContactID = ContactID
    FROM dbo.Contact
    WHERE ContactCode = @ContactCode
  IF @ContactID IS NULL
    BEGIN
      RAISERROR
        ('Contact: ''%s'' not found', 15,1,@ContactCode)
```

```
        RETURN -100
    END
-- Get LocationID
SELECT @LocationID = LocationID
  FROM dbo.Location
  WHERE LocationCode = @LocationCode
IF @LocationID IS NULL
  BEGIN
    RAISERROR
    ('Location: ''%s'' not found', 15,1,@LocationCode)
    RETURN -100
  END
-- IS Update or Insert?
IF EXISTS(SELECT *
            FROM dbo.Security
            WHERE ContactID = @ContactID
              AND LocationID = @LocationID)
-- Update
  BEGIN
    UPDATE dbo.Security
      SET SecurityLevel = @SecurityLevel
      WHERE ContactID = @ContactID
        AND LocationID = @LocationID
    IF @@ERROR <> 0 RETURN -100
  END

-- Insert
ELSE
  BEGIN
    INSERT dbo.Security
        (ContactID,LocationID, SecurityLevel)
        VALUES (@ContactID, @LocationID, @SecurityLevel)
    IF @@ERROR <> 0 RETURN -100
  END
RETURN
```

The following script tests the new procedure's ability to modify a security permission for a contact/location combination. The first command modifies contact 120's security for location W:

```
EXEC pSecurity_Assign
  @ContactCode = 120,
  @LocationCode = W,
  @SecurityLevel = 2

EXEC pSecurity_Fetch
  @ContactCode = 120
```

**Result:**

```
ContactCode     LocationCode    SecurityLevel
--------------  --------------- -------------

120             W               2
```

The following two commands issue a new security permission as well as edit an existing security permission. The third command fetches the security permissions for contact code "120":

```
EXEC pSecurity_Assign
  @ContactCode = 120,
  @LocationCode = CH,
  @SecurityLevel = 1

EXEC pSecurity_Assign
  @ContactCode = 120,
  @LocationCode = W,
  @SecurityLevel = 3

EXEC pSecurity_Fetch
  @ContactCode = 120
```

Result:

```
ContactCode      LocationCode     SecurityLevel
---------------  ---------------  -------------
120              W                3
120              CH               1
```

## The Security-Check Stored Procedure

The security-check stored procedure is central to the row-based security system. It's designed to return a true or false for a security request for a user, a location, and a requested security level.

The procedure selects the security level of the user for the given location and then compares that value with the value of the requested security level. If the user's permission level is sufficient, a 1 (indicating true) is returned; otherwise a 0 (for false) is returned:

```
CREATE PROCEDURE p_SecurityCheck (
  @ContactCode CHAR(15),
  @LocationCode CHAR(15),
  @SecurityLevel INT,
  @Approved BIT OUTPUT )
AS
SET NoCount ON

DECLARE @ActualLevel INT

SELECT @ActualLevel = SecurityLevel
  FROM dbo.Security
    JOIN dbo.Contact
      ON Security.ContactID = Contact.ContactID
    JOIN dbo.Location
      ON Security.LocationID = Location.LocationID
  WHERE ContactCode = @ContactCode
    AND LocationCode = @LocationCode

IF    @ActualLevel IS NULL
      OR
      @ActualLevel < @SecurityLevel
```

```
    OR
      @ActualLevel = 0
  SET @Approved = 0
ELSE
  SET @Approved = 1

RETURN 0
```

The following batch calls the p_SecurityCheck procedure and uses the @OK local variable to capture the output parameter. When testing this from the script on the CD, try several different values. Use the pSecurity_Fetch procedure to determine possible parameters. The following code checks to see if contact code 118 has administrative privileges at the Charlotte warehouse:

```
DECLARE @OK BIT
EXEC p_SecurityCheck
  @ContactCode = 118,
  @LocationCode = Clt,
  @SecurityLevel = 3,
  @Approved   = @OK OUTPUT
SELECT @OK
```

Result:

```
0
```

## The Security-Check Function

The security-check function includes the same logic as the pSecurity_Check stored procedure. The advantage of a function is that it can be used directly within an if command without a local variable being used to store the output parameter. The function uses the same three input parameters as the stored-procedure version and the same internal logic, but it returns the approved bit as the return of the function rather than as an output parameter. Here's the function's code:

```
CREATE FUNCTION dbo.fSecurityCheck (
  @ContactCode CHAR(15),
  @LocationCode CHAR(15),
  @SecurityLevel INT)
RETURNS BIT
BEGIN
DECLARE @ActualLevel INT,
  @Approved BIT

SELECT @ActualLevel = SecurityLevel
  FROM dbo.Security
    JOIN dbo.Contact
      ON Security.ContactID = Contact.ContactID
    JOIN dbo.Location
      ON Security.LocationID = Location.LocationID
  WHERE ContactCode = @ContactCode
    AND LocationCode = @LocationCode

IF @ActualLevel IS NULL
  OR @ActualLevel < @SecurityLevel
```

```
   OR @ActualLevel = 0
   SET @Approved = 0
ELSE
   SET @Approved = 1

RETURN @Approved
END
```

The next batch demonstrates how to call the function to test security within a stored procedure. If the function returns a 0, the user does not have sufficient security and the procedure terminates:

```
-- Check within a Procedure
IF dbo.fSecurityCheck( 118, 'Clt', 3) = 0
  BEGIN
    RAISERROR('Security Violation', 16,1)
    ROLLBACK TRANSACTION
    RETURN -100
  END
```

## Using the NT Login

Some applications are designed so that the user logs in with the application, and the row-based security code so far has assumed that the user name is supplied to the procedures. However, if the SQL Server instance is using NT authentication, the security routines can use that identification.

Rather than request the contact code as a parameter, the security procedure or function can automatically use suser_sname() the NT login to identify the current user. The login name (domain and user name) must be added to the Contact table. Alternately, a secondary table could be created to hold multiple logins per user. Some wide-area networks require users to log in with different domain names according to location, so a ContactLogin table is a good idea.

The following function is modified to check the user's security based on his or her NT login and a ContactLogin table. The first query demonstrates retrieving the login within T-SQL code:

```
SELECT suser_sname()
```

Result:

```
--------------
NOLI\Paul
```

The following code creates the secondary table to store the logins:

```
CREATE TABLE dbo.ContactLogin(
  ContactLogin UNIQUEIDENTIFIER
    PRIMARY KEY NONCLUSTERED DEFAULT NewId(),
  ContactID UniqueIdentifier NOT NULL
    REFERENCES dbo.Contact ON DELETE CASCADE,
  NTLogin VARCHAR(100) )
```

With the table in place, a simple insert will populate a single row using my login so the code can be tested:

```
INSERT CONTACTLOGIN (ContactID, NTLogin)
  SELECT ContactID, 'NOLI\Paul'
    FROM dbo.Contact
    WHERE ContactCode = 118
```

Check the data:

```
SELECT ContactCode, NTLogin
  FROM dbo.Contact
    JOIN ContactLogin
      ON Contact.ContactID = ContactLogin.ContactID
```

Result:

```
ContactCode      NTLogin
--------------   --------------
118              Paul/NOLI
```

The security-check function is modified to join the contactlogin table and to restrict the rows returned to those that match the NT login name. Since the contact code is no longer required, this select can skip the contact table and join the Security table directly with the ContactLogin table:

```
CREATE FUNCTION dbo.fSecurityCheckNT (
  @LocationCode CHAR(15),
  @SecurityLevel INT)
RETURNS BIT
BEGIN
DECLARE @ActualLevel INT,
  @Approved BIT

SELECT @ActualLevel = SecurityLevel
  FROM dbo.Security
    JOIN dbo.Location
      ON Security.LocationID = Location.LocationID
    JOIN dbo.ContactLogin
      ON Security.ContactID = ContactLogin.ContactID
  WHERE NTLogin = suser_sname()
    AND LocationCode = @LocationCode

IF @ActualLevel IS NULL
  OR @ActualLevel < @SecurityLevel
  OR @ActualLevel = 0
  SET @Approved = 0
ELSE
  SET @Approved = 1

RETURN @Approved
END
```

To test the new function, the following batch will repeat the security check performed in the last section, but this time the user will be captured from the NT login instead of being passed to the function:

```
IF dbo.fSecurityCheckNT('Clt', 3) = 0
  BEGIN
    RAISERROR('Security Violation', 16,1)
    ROLLBACK TRANSACTION
    RETURN -100
  END
```

The function did not return an error, so I'm allowed to complete the procedure.

## The Security-Check Trigger

The security-check stored procedure and function both work well when included within a stored procedure, such as the `fetch`, `addnew`, `update`, or `delete` procedures mentioned in the beginning of this chapter. But to implement row-based security in a database that allows access from views, ad hoc queries, or direct table DML statements, you must handle the row-based security with a trigger. The trigger can prevent updates, but will not be able to check data reads. If row-based security is a requirement for reads, all reads must go through a stored procedure.

The following trigger is similar to the security-check function. It differs in that the trigger must allow for multiple orders with potential multiple locations. The joins have to match up [Order] rows and their locations with the user's security level for each location. The join can go directly from the `ContactLogin` table to the `Security` table. Since this is an `insert` and `update` trigger, any security level below 2 for any order being written will be rejected and a security-violation error will be raised. The `rollback transaction` command will undo the original DML command that fired the trigger:

```
CREATE TRIGGER OrderSecurity ON [Order]
AFTER INSERT, UPDATE
AS
IF EXISTS (
SELECT *
  FROM dbo.Security
    JOIN dbo.ContactLogin
      ON Security.ContactID = ContactLogin.ContactID
    JOIN Inserted
      ON Inserted.LocationID = Security.LocationID
  WHERE NTLogin = suser_sname()
    AND SecurityLevel < 2 )
BEGIN
  RAISERROR('Security Violation', 16,1)
  ROLLBACK TRANSACTION
END
```

# Auditing Data Changes

Data auditing is added to a database to increase its data-integrity level. A full data-audit trail can answer many questions, such as by doing the following:

✦ Showing all data changes to a row since it was inserted.

✦ Showing all data changes made by a specific user last week.

✦ Showing all data changes from a certain workstation during lunch.

✦ Showing all data changes made from an application other than the standard front-end application.

Data-audit trails solve significant problems for DBAs as well as users. My consulting firm had developed a legal compliance/best-practices document-management system for a Fortune 100 company and its law firm was populating the database with regulatory laws. The law firm fell behind on its schedule and claimed that it was unable to enter data for two weeks because of software problems. When we provided a list of the 70,000+-column–level data changes made during those two weeks from the data-audit trail, the claim vanished.

I've seen published methods of auditing data that add a few columns to the table, or duplicate the table, to store the last change. Neither of these methods is worth doing. A partial audit, or a last-value audit, is of no real value. A data-audit trail must permanently record the data changes, or anyone who understands the system can just make another change and erase the original values.

**Note**    Lumigent's Log Explorer can be used to view the transaction log, and data can be selected on a table basis, making Log Explorer similar to a data-audit trail. However, the Log Explorer is limited to viewing only a single transaction log file at a time. Assembling a complete data-audit trail of every change to a certain row might require searching through hundreds or thousands of transaction log files. Log Explorer is excellent for debugging transactions, but I don't recommend it as a replacement for a trigger-based data-audit trail.

## The Audit Table

The Audit table's purpose is to provide a single location in which to record the data changes for the database. The following audit-trail table can store all non-BLOB changes to any table. The Operation column stores an I, U, or D, depending on the DML statement.

```
CREATE TABLE dbo.Audit (
  AuditID UNIQUEIDENTIFIER RowGUIDCol  NOT NULL
    CONSTRAINT DF_Audit_AuditID DEFAULT (NEWID())
    CONSTRAINT PK_Audit PRIMARY KEY NONCLUSTERED (AuditID),
  AuditDate DATETIME NOT NULL,
  SysUser VARCHAR(50) NOT NULL,
  Application VARCHAR(50) NOT NULL,
  TableName VARCHAR(50)NOT NULL,
  Operation CHAR(1) NOT NULL,
  PrimaryKey VARCHAR(50) NOT NULL,
  RowDescription VARCHAR(50) NULL,
  SecondaryRow    VARCHAR (50) NULL,
  [Column] VARCHAR(50) NOT NULL,
  OldValue VARCHAR(50) NULL,
  NewValue VARCHAR(50) NULL
  )
```

The PrimaryKey column stores the pointer to the row that was modified, and the RowDescription column records a readable description of the row. These two columns allow the audit trail to be joined with the original table or viewed directly. The PrimaryKey column is important because it can quickly find all changes to a single row regardless of how the description has changed over time.

## The Fixed Audit Trail Trigger

The brute-force method of auditing data uses a trigger on every table, which examines every column using the updated() function and writes any changes to the audit table.

The insert statement joins the Inserted and Deleted tables to correctly handle multiple-row inserts and updates. The join is a left outer join so that an insert operation, with only rows in the Inserted table, can still be recorded. The join is also restricted with a theta join condition so that when a multiple-row update only affects some of the rows for a given column, only those rows that are actually changed are recorded to the audit trail.

For an example of a fixed audit-trail trigger, the following code audits the `Product` table for the OBX Kites database:

```
CREATE TRIGGER Product_Audit
ON dbo.Product
AFTER Insert, Update
NOT FOR REPLICATION
AS

DECLARE @Operation CHAR(1)

IF EXISTS(SELECT * FROM Deleted)
  SET @Operation = 'U'
ELSE
  SET @Operation = 'I'

IF UPDATE(ProductCategoryID)
    INSERT dbo.Audit
      (AuditDate, SysUser, Application, TableName, Operation,
       PrimaryKey, RowDescription, SecondaryRow, [Column],
       OldValue, NewValue)
      SELECT GetDate(), suser_sname(), APP_NAME(), 'Product',
          @Operation, Inserted.ProductID, Inserted.Code,
          NULL, 'ProductCategoryID',
          OPC.ProductCategoryName, NPC.ProductCategoryName
        FROM Inserted
          LEFT OUTER JOIN Deleted
            ON Inserted.ProductID = Deleted.ProductID
            AND Inserted.ProductCategoryID
                <> Deleted.ProductCategoryID
          -- fetch ProductCategory Names
          LEFT OUTER JOIN dbo.ProductCategory OPC
            ON Deleted.ProductCategoryID
                = OPC.ProductCategoryID
          JOIN dbo.ProductCategory NPC
            ON Inserted.ProductCategoryID
                = NPC.ProductCategoryID

IF UPDATE(Code)
    INSERT dbo.Audit
      (AuditDate, SysUser, Application, TableName, Operation,
       PrimaryKey, RowDescription, SecondaryRow, [Column],
       OldValue, NewValue)
      SELECT GetDate(), suser_sname(), APP_NAME(),
          'Product', @Operation, Inserted.ProductID,
          Inserted.Code, NULL, 'Code',
          Deleted.Code, Inserted.Code
        FROM Inserted
          LEFT OUTER JOIN Deleted
            ON Inserted.ProductID = Deleted.ProductID
              AND Inserted.Code <> Deleted.Code

IF UPDATE(ProductName)
    INSERT dbo.Audit
```

```
         (AuditDate, SysUser, Application, TableName, Operation,
         PrimaryKey, RowDescription, SecondaryRow, [Column],
         OldValue, NewValue)
      SELECT GetDate(), suser_sname(), APP_NAME(),
            'Product', @Operation,
            Inserted.ProductID, Inserted.Code, NULL, 'Name',
            Deleted.ProductName, Inserted.ProductName
         FROM Inserted
            LEFT OUTER JOIN Deleted
               ON Inserted.ProductID = Deleted.ProductID
                  AND Inserted.ProductName <> Deleted.ProductName

IF UPDATE(ProductDescription)
   INSERT dbo.Audit
      (AuditDate, SysUser, Application, TableName, Operation,
      PrimaryKey, RowDescription, SecondaryRow, [Column],
      OldValue, NewValue)
      SELECT GetDate(), suser_sname(), APP_NAME(), 'Product',
            @Operation, Inserted.ProductID, Inserted.Code,
            NULL, 'ProductDescription',
            Deleted.ProductDescription,
            Inserted.ProductDescription
         FROM Inserted
            LEFT OUTER JOIN Deleted
               ON Inserted.ProductID = Deleted.ProductID
                  AND Inserted.ProductDescription
                     <> Deleted.ProductDescription

IF UPDATE(ActiveDate)
   INSERT dbo.Audit
      (AuditDate, SysUser, Application, TableName, Operation,
      PrimaryKey, RowDescription, SecondaryRow, [Column],
      OldValue, NewValue)
      SELECT GetDate(), suser_sname(), APP_NAME(), 'Product',
            @Operation, Inserted.ProductID, Inserted.Code,
            NULL, 'ActiveDate',
            Deleted.ActiveDate, Inserted.ActiveDate
         FROM Inserted
            LEFT OUTER JOIN Deleted
               ON Inserted.ProductID = Deleted.ProductID
                  AND Inserted.ActiveDate != Deleted.ActiveDate

IF UPDATE(DiscontinueDate)
   INSERT dbo.Audit
      (AuditDate, SysUser, Application, TableName, Operation,
      PrimaryKey, RowDescription, SecondaryRow, [Column],
      OldValue, NewValue)
      SELECT GetDate(), suser_sname(), APP_NAME(), 'Product',
            @Operation, Inserted.ProductID, Inserted.Code,
            NULL, 'DiscontinueDate',
            Deleted.DiscontinueDate, Inserted.DiscontinueDate
         FROM Inserted
            LEFT OUTER JOIN Deleted
```

```
          ON Inserted.ProductID = Deleted.ProductID
          AND Inserted.DiscontinueDate
            != Deleted.DiscontinueDate
```

With the fixed audit tail trigger installed, the following batch exercises it by inserting and updating product data using both DML statements and the previously created stored procedures. The first trigger test uses the pProduct_AddNew procedure:

```
EXEC pProduct_AddNew 'Kite', 200, 'The MonstaKite',
  'Man what a big Kite!'

SELECT TableName, RowDescription, [Column], NewValue
  FROM dbo.Audit
```

Result:

```
TableName RowDescription
                Column                      NewValue
--------- ----- -------------------- --------------------Product
200     ProductCategoryID        Kite
Product   200   Code                 200
Product   200   Name                 The MonstaKite
Product   200   ProductDescription   Man what a big Kite!
Product   200   ActiveDate           Mar  1 2002  1:35PM
Product   200   DiscontinueDate      NULL
```

The trigger is the right place to implement an audit trail because it will catch all the changes, even those made directly to the table with DML commands. This example is a non-stored procedure direct DML update. The audit trail can show the original value as well as the new value:

```
UPDATE dbo.Product
  SET ProductDescription = 'Biggie Sized'
  WHERE Code = 200
```

The following query pinpoints the data history of the product-description column for product 200:

```
SELECT AuditDate, OldValue,  NewValue
  FROM dbo.Audit
  WHERE TableName = 'Product'
    AND RowDescription = '200'
    AND [Column] = 'ProductDescription'
```

Result:

```
AuditDate                     OldValue          NewValue
----------------------------- ----------------- -------------
2002-03-01 13:35:17.093       NULL              Man what a
                                                big Kite!
2002-03-01 15:10:49.257       Man what a        Biggie Sized
                              big Kite!
```

# Rolling Back from the Audit Trail

If the audit system is complete, all the changes for a given row since its creation are easily listed for the user. From this list, the user can select a data modification and roll back that modification. Once an audit trail row is selected, rolling back the change is simply a matter of submitting an update statement based on the data in the audit trail.

The following code demonstrates rolling back a change from the audit table. The pAudit_RollBack stored procedure accepts an Audit table primary key and from that builds a dynamic SQL update DML command for the correct table, row, column, and rollback value.

```
CREATE PROCEDURE pAudit_RollBack (
  @AuditID UNIQUEIDENTIFIER)
AS
SET NoCount ON

DECLARE
  @SQLString NVARCHAR(4000),
  @TableName NVARCHAR(50),
  @PrimaryKey NVARCHAR(50),
  @Column NVARCHAR(50),
  @NewValue NVARCHAR(50)

SELECT
  @TableName = TableName,
  @PrimaryKey = PrimaryKey,
  @Column = [Column],
  @NewValue = OldValue
  FROM dbo.Audit
  WHERE AuditID = @AuditID

SET @SQLString =
  'UPDATE ' + @TableName
    + ' SET ' + @Column + ' = ''' + @NewValue +''''
    + ' WHERE ' + @TableName + 'ID = ''' + @PrimaryKey + ''''

EXEC sp_executeSQL @SQLString
Return
```

With the procedure in place, the following script simulates the logic needed to roll back an update. The original product description value for product 200 was "Man what a big Kite," and during testing of the fixed audit trail trigger it was changed to "Biggie Sized." The script finds the audit-trail row for that change and passes the GUID to pAudit_RollBack, which rolls back the previous change:

```
DECLARE @AuditRollBack UNIQUEIDENTIFIER

SELECT @AuditRollBack = AuditID
  FROM dbo.Audit
  WHERE TableName = 'Product'
    AND RowDescription = '200'
    AND OldValue = 'Man what a big Kite!'
```

```
EXEC pAudit_RollBack @AuditRollBack

SELECT ProductDescription
  FROM dbo.Product
  WHERE Code = 200
```

Result:

```
ProductDescription
-------------------------
Man what a big Kite!
```

This procedure undoes a single specific change. The procedure could be modified to roll back a row to a certain point in time by selecting the history of the row from the audit trail and then looping through each change in a descending order.

# Auditing Complications

Besides the additional development time, adding auditing can present several complications.

**Best Practice**

Develop the entire database and prove that the data scheme is correct prior to implementing a data-audit trail. Changes to the data schema are more complex once audit-trail triggers are in place.

## Auditing Related Data

The most significant complication involves auditing related data such as secondary rows. For example, a change to an OrderDetail row is actually a change to the order. A user will want to see the data history of the order and see all changes to any of the data related to the order. Therefore, a change to the OrderDetail table should be recorded as a change to the [Order] table, and the line number of the order detail item that was changed is recorded in the SecondaryRow column.

Recording foreign key changes is another difficult aspect of a full audit trail. A user does not want to see the new GUID or identity value for a foreign-key update. If the order-ship–method foreign key is changed from "Slow Boat" to "Speedy Express," the audit-trail trigger should look up the foreign key and record a readable value. In the Product_Audit sample fixed audit trail trigger, changes to the ProductCategoryID column write the product category name to the Audit table.

## Date Created and Date Modified

When you are using a full data-audit trail, the row's creation date and last-modified date can easily be derived from the audit table. In reality, if an application displays the created and modified date for a table in a large user-interface grid, I strongly recommend de-normalizing the row's created and modified dates and storing the columns directly in the audited table.

**Cross-Reference**

Chapter 15, "Implementing Triggers," includes a trigger that updates the created and modified columns while preventing problems with recursion.

## Auditing Select Statements

Data-audit triggers are limited to auditing insert, update, and delete DML statements. To audit data reads, implement the read audit in the fetch stored procedure. Use SQL Server security to limit access to the table so that all reads must go through a stored procedure or a function.

### Data Auditing and Security

Another concern for those creating a full data-audit history is the security of the data-audit trail. Anyone who has read rights to the audit table will be able to effectively see all the data from every audited table. If users will have the ability to see the data history for a given row, use a stored procedure to fetch the audit data so that security can be persevered.

### Data Auditing and Performance

A full data audit trail will add some level of overhead to the system. A single row insert to a 20-column–wide table will add 20 inserts to the audit table. To reduce the performance impact of the audit trail, do the following:

✦ Limit the indexes on the audit table.

✦ Locate the audit table on its own filegroup and disk subsystem. A separate filegroup will make backups easier as well.

✦ Using the fixed audit trigger, limit the auditing to those columns that require such a high level of data integrity.

## The Dynamic Audit-Trail Trigger and Procedure

Having spent several months writing fixed audit trail triggers for a project with hundreds of tables, I felt driven to develop a dynamic auditing system.

The dynamic audit trail is implemented with small triggers on every table. All the trigger does is copy the `Inserted` and `Deleted` tables to temporary tables and pass a few variables to a stored procedure where the real work is done. It examines the `Columns_Updated` binary value, determines the right value to use instead of nulls, and generates a dynamic SQL statement to write the audit trail.

That's the catch: to execute a dynamic SQL statement, `sp_execSQL` is required and it functions as nested T-SQL batch. The scope of the `Inserted` and `Deleted` tables is limited to the trigger—they aren't available to any called stored procedure or dynamic SQL statement. That's why the temporary tables are used to pass the changes to the stored procedure and then to the dynamic SQL. The temporary table's scope includes called stored procedures and execs, and that makes the dynamic audit trigger possible.

Every method has its trade-off. On the pro side, this trigger/stored procedure/dynamic SQL method is extremely easy to implement. It works with nearly any table. The limitations of this version of the dynamic audit trigger are:

✦ It uses a temporary table to pass the `Inserted` and `Deleted` tables to the stored procedure, so it isn't the fastest method possible. In addition, the temporary tables are created using a `select ... into` syntax which causes further performance and locking issues.

✦ The current dynamic audit trail doesn't automatically audit related data or secondary tables. Nor does it audit tables with composite primary keys.

✦ It doesn't audit any tables with BLOB columns (`image`, `text`, or `ntext`) because these can't be selected from the `Inserted` and `Deleted` tables.

Because of these limitations, use the dynamic audit trail method for tables that aren't updated frequently, during the early life stages of a database, or for databases that have acceptable performance when the dynamic audit trail is enabled. For high performance, it's better to employ the fixed audit trigger and brute-force through the columns. However, the fixed audit trigger involves significantly more code and maintenance.

With those disclaimers, here is the code for the dynamic audit trail:

```
/*
Dynamic Audit Trigger Table and Code
Paul Nielsen  www.IsNotNull.com
This sample script adds the dynamic audit trigger to
Northwind Customers and Products table.

Version 1.1 - Aug 6, 2001
*/

USE Northwind
-------------------------------------------------------------
-- Create the table to store the Audit Trail

IF Exists (SELECT * FROM sysobjects WHERE NAME = 'Audit')
  DROP TABLE Audit

Go
CREATE TABLE dbo.Audit (
  AuditID UNIQUEIDENTIFIER ROWGUIDCOL  NOT NULL
    CONSTRAINT DF_Audit_AuditID DEFAULT (NEWID())
    CONSTRAINT PK_Audit PRIMARY KEY NONCLUSTERED (AuditID),
  AuditDate DATETIME NOT NULL,
  SysUser VARCHAR(50) NOT NULL,
  Application VARCHAR(50) NOT NULL,
  TableName VARCHAR(50)NOT NULL,
  Operation CHAR(1) NOT NULL,
  PrimaryKey VARCHAR(50) NOT NULL,
--   RowDescription VARCHAR(50) NULL,
  SecondaryRow    VARCHAR(50) NULL,
  [Column] VARCHAR(50) NOT NULL,
  OldValue VARCHAR(50) NULL,
  NewValue VARCHAR(50) NULL
  )

GO

-------------------------------------------------------------
-- Create function to simulate the Columns_Updated() value

IF EXISTS (SELECT *
            FROM sysobjects
            WHERE NAME = 'GenColUpdated')
  DROP FUNCTION GenColUpdated
Go

CREATE FUNCTION dbo.GenColUpdated
  (@Col INT, @ColTotal INT)
RETURNS INT
AS
BEGIN
-- Copyright 2001 Paul Nielsen
-- This function simulates Columns_Updated()
```

```
DECLARE
  @ColByte INT,
  @ColTotalByte INT,
  @ColBit INT

  -- Calculate Byte Positions
  SET @ColTotalByte =    1 + ((@ColTotal-1) /8)
  SET @ColByte = 1 + ((@Col-1)/8)
  SET @ColBit = @col - ((@colByte-1) * 8)

  -- gen Columns_Updated() value for given column position
  RETURN
    POWER(2, @colbit + ((@ColTotalByte-@ColByte) * 8)-1)
END
go


------------------------------------------------------------
-- Create the Dynamic Audit Stored Procedures

IF EXISTS (SELECT * FROM SysObjects WHERE NAME = 'pAudit')
  DROP PROC pAudit
Go

CREATE PROCEDURE pAudit (
  @Col_Updated VARBINARY(1028),
  @TableName VARCHAR(100),
  @PrimaryKey SYSNAME)
AS
-- dynamic auto-audit trigger/stored procedure
-- Copyright 2001 Paul Nielsen
SET NoCount ON
DECLARE
  @ColTotal INT,
  @ColCounter INT,
  @ColUpdatedTemp INT,
  @ColName SYSNAME,
  @BlankString CHAR(1),
  @SQLStr NVARCHAR(1000),
  @ColNull NVARCHAR(50),
  @SysUser NVARCHAR(100),
  @ColumnDataType INT,
  @IsUpdate BIT,
  @tempError INT

 SET @SysUser = suser_sname()
 SET @BlankString = ''

-- Initialize Col variables
SELECT @ColCounter = 0
SELECT @ColTotal = Count(*)
  FROM SysColumns
    JOIN SysObjects
      ON SysColumns.id = SysObjects.id
  WHERE SysObjects.name = @TableName
```

```
-- Set IsUpdated Flag
IF EXISTS(SELECT * FROM #tempDel)
  SELECT @IsUpdate = 1
ELSE
  SELECT @IsUpdate = 0

-- Column Updates
WHILE ((SELECT @ColCounter) != @ColTotal)
  -- run through some columns
  BEGIN
    SELECT @ColCounter = @ColCounter + 1
    SET @ColUpdatedTemp
        = dbo.GenColUpdated(@ColCounter,@ColTotal)

  -- bitwise AND between updated bits
  -- and the selected column bit
  IF (@Col_Updated & @ColUpdatedTemp) = @ColUpdatedTemp
    BEGIN
      SET @ColNull = null
      SELECT
        @ColName = SysColumns.[name],
          -- get the column name & Data Type
        @ColumnDataType = SysColumns.xtype
      FROM SysColumns
        JOIN SysObjects
          ON SysColumns.id = SysObjects.id
        WHERE SysObjects.[NAME] = @TableName
          and SysColumns.ColID = @ColCounter
      IF @ColName NOT IN ('Created', 'Modified')
        BEGIN
          -- text columns
          IF  @ColumnDataType IN
              ( 175, 239, 99, 231, 35, 231, 98, 167 )
            SET @ColNull =  ''''''
          -- numeric + bit columns
          ELSE IF  @ColumnDataType IN
              (  106, 62, 56, 60, 108, 59, 52, 122, 104 )
            SET @ColNull = '0'
          -- date columns
          ELSE IF  @ColumnDataType IN ( 61, 58 )
            SET @ColNull =  '''1/1/1980'''
          -- uniqueidentifier columns
          ELSE IF  @ColumnDataType IN ( 36 )
            SET @ColNull =  ''''''

            IF @ColNull IS NOT NULL
              BEGIN
                IF @IsUpdate = 1
-- had to adjust indenting
SET @SQLStr =
  ' Insert Audit(TableName, PrimaryKey, SysUser, [Column],'
  +' AuditDate, Application, OldValue, NewValue,Operation)'
  +' Select '''+ @TableName + ''',
  #tempIn.['+ @PrimaryKey + '],
```

```
      ''' + @SysUser + ''', ' +
      '''' + @ColName + ''', GetDate(), App_Name(),' +
      ' IsNull(convert(nvarchar(100),
          #tempDel.[' + @ColName + ']),''<null>''), ' +
      ' IsNull(convert(nvarchar(100),
          #tempIn.[' + @ColName +    ']),''<null>''),''U''' +
      ' From #tempIn' +
      ' Join #tempDel' +
      ' On #tempIn.['+ @PrimaryKey + ']
          = #tempDel.['+ @PrimaryKey + ']' +
      ' AND isnull(#tempIn.' + @ColName +    ',' + @ColNull + ')
          != isnull(#tempDel.' + @ColName +    ',' + @ColNull + ')'
        + ' Where Not (#tempIn.[' + @ColName + '] Is Null
          and #tempDel.[' + @ColName + ']  Is Null)'

    ELSE -- Insert
      SET @SQLStr =
      ' Insert Audit(TableName, PrimaryKey, SysUser, [Column],'
      +' AuditDate, Application, OldValue, NewValue,Operation)'
      +' Select '''+ @TableName + ''',#tempIn.['+ @PrimaryKey
      + '], ''' + @SysUser + ''', ' +
      '''' + @ColName + ''', GetDate(), App_Name(),' +
      ' Null, ' +
      ' IsNull(convert(nvarchar(100),
      #tempIn.[' + @ColName +']),''<null>''),''I''' +
      ' From #tempIn' +
      ' Where Not (#tempIn.[' + @ColName + '] Is Null)'

    EXEC sp_executesql  @SQLStr
    SET @TempError = @@Error
    IF @TempError <> 0
      BEGIN
        -- turn rollback on only if you want a
        -- failure to record audit to cancel
        -- the data modification operation
        -- Rollback
        RAISERROR ('Audit Trail Error', 15, 1)
      END
END END END END RETURN
Go


------------------------------------------------------------
-- sample Table Triggers
-- this will need to be added to every table
-- and the Table and Primary Key settings

-- Products Trigger

IF EXISTS (SELECT *
            FROM sysobjects
            WHERE NAME = 'Products_Audit')
  DROP TRIGGER Products_Audit
Go
```

```
CREATE TRIGGER Products_Audit
ON dbo.Products
AFTER Insert, Update
NOT FOR REPLICATION
AS
-- Dynamic Audit Trail Code Begin
-- (c)2001 Paul Nielsen
DECLARE
  @Col_Updated VARBINARY(1028),
  @TableName VARCHAR(100),
  @PrimaryKey SYSNAME

SET NoCount ON

-- Set up the Audit data
-- set to the table name
SET @TableName = 'Products'
-- set to the column to identify the row
SET @PrimaryKey = 'ProductID'
SET @Col_Updated = Columns_Updated()
SELECT * INTO #TempIn FROM Inserted
SELECT * INTO #TempDel FROM Deleted

-- call the audit stored procedure
EXEC pAudit @Col_Updated, @TableName, @PrimaryKey

Go
-------------------------------------------------------------
-- Customer Trigger

IF EXISTS (SELECT *
            FROM SysObjects
            WHERE [NAME] = 'Customers_Audit')
  DROP TRIGGER Customers_Audit
Go

CREATE TRIGGER Customers_Audit
ON dbo.Customers
AFTER Insert, Update
NOT FOR REPLICATION
AS
-- Dynamic Audit Trail
-- (c)2001 Paul Nielsen
DECLARE
  @Col_Updated VARBINARY(1028),
  @TableName VARCHAR(100),
  @PrimaryKey SYSNAME
SET NoCount ON
SET @TableName = 'Customers'
SET @PrimaryKey = 'CustomerID'
SET @Col_Updated = Columns_Updated()
SELECT * INTO #TempIn FROM Inserted
SELECT * INTO #TempDel FROM Deleted
EXEC pAudit @Col_Updated, @TableName, @PrimaryKey
```

**On the CD-ROM** The sample script on the CD, `DynamicAudit.sql`, includes several test inserts and updates as well as example queries for retrieving data from the audit table and joining the audit table with the products table. As I continue to develop these utility procedures, new versions are posted on `www.IsNotNull.com`.

# Transaction-Aggregation Handling

Stored procedures are excellent for maintaining de-normalized aggregate data. A common example of this is an inventory system that records all transactions in an inventory-transaction table, calculates the inventory quantity on hand, and stores the calculated quantity in the inventory table for performance.

To protect the integrity of the inventory table, the following logic rules should typically be implemented with triggers:

✦ The inventory table should not be updateable by any process other than the inventory transaction table triggers. Any attempt to directly update the inventory table's quantity should be recorded as a manual adjustment in the inventory-transaction table.

✦ Inserts in the inventory-transaction table should write the current on-hand value to the inventory table.

✦ The inventory-transaction table should not allow updates.

The OBX Kites database includes a simplified inventory system. To demonstrate transaction aggregation handling, the following triggers implement the required rules.

The first script creates a sample valid inventory item for test purposes:

```
USE OBXKites

DECLARE
  @ProdID UniqueIdentifier,
  @LocationID UniqueIdentifier

SELECT @ProdID = ProductID
  FROM dbo.Product
  WHERE Code = 1001
SELECT @LocationID= LocationID
  FROM dbo.Location
  WHERE LocationCode = 'CH'

INSERT dbo.Inventory (ProductID, InventoryCode, LocationID)
  VALUES (@ProdID,'A1', @LocationID)

SELECT Product.Code, InventoryCode, QuantityOnHand
  FROM dbo.Inventory
    JOIN dbo.Product
      ON Inventory.ProductID = Product.ProductID
```

Result:

| Code | InventoryCode | QuantityOnHand |
| --- | --- | --- |
| 1001 | A1 | 0 |

## The Inventory-Transaction Trigger

The inventory-transaction trigger performs the aggregate function of maintaining the current quantity–on-hand value in the `Inventory` table. With each row inserted into the `InventoryTransaction` table, the trigger updates the `Inventory` table. The `join` between the `Inserted` image table and the `Inventory` table lets the trigger handle multiple-row inserts.

```
CREATE TRIGGER InvTrans_Aggregate
ON dbo.InventoryTransaction
AFTER Insert
AS

UPDATE dbo.Inventory
  SET QuantityOnHand
    = Inventory.QuantityOnHand + Inserted.Value
  FROM dbo.Inventory
    JOIN Inserted
      ON Inventory.InventoryID = Inserted.InventoryID

Return
```

The next batch tests the `InvTrans_Aggregate` trigger by inserting a transaction and observing the inventory transaction and the inventory tables:

```
INSERT InventoryTransaction (InventoryID, Value)
  SELECT InventoryID, 5
    FROM dbo.Inventory
    WHERE InventoryCode = 'A1'

INSERT InventoryTransaction (InventoryID, Value)
  SELECT InventoryID, -3
    FROM dbo.Inventory
    WHERE InventoryCode = 'A1'

INSERT InventoryTransaction (InventoryID, Value)
  SELECT InventoryID, 7
    FROM dbo.Inventory
    WHERE InventoryCode = 'A1'
```

The following query views the data within the `InventoryTransaction` table:

```
SELECT InventoryCode, Value
  FROM dbo.InventoryTransaction
    JOIN dbo.Inventory
      ON Inventory.InventoryID
        = Inventorytransaction.InventoryID
```

Result:

```
InventoryCode    Value
---------------  ------
A1               5
A1               -3
A1               7
```

The `InvTrans_Aggregate` trigger should have maintained a correct quantity on-hand value through the inserts to the `InventoryTransaction` table. Indeed, the next query proves the trigger functioned correctly:

```
SELECT Product.Code, InventoryCode, QuantityOnHand
  FROM dbo.Inventory
    JOIN dbo.Product
      ON Inventory.ProductID = Product.ProductID
```

Result:

```
Code              InventoryCode    QuantityOnHand
---------------   ---------------  ---------------
1001              A1               9
```

## The Inventory Trigger

The quantity values in the Inventory table should never be directly manipulated. Every quantity adjust must go through the `InventoryTransaction` table. However, some users will want to make manual adjustments to the Inventory table. The gentlest solution to the problem is to use server-side code to perform the correct operations regardless of the user's method. Therefore, the inventory trigger has to redirect direct updates intended for the `Inventory` table to the `InventoryTransaction` table, while permitting the `InvTrans_Aggregate` trigger to update the `Inventory` table.

As a best practice the trigger must accept multiple-row updates. The goal then is to undo the original DML `update` command while keeping enough of the data to write the change as an `insert` to the `InventoryTransaction` table.

Rolling back the DML `update` won't work because that would obliterate the data within the `Inserted` and `Deleted` images, as well as any inserts to a temporary table created within the trigger. Neither can the values be stored in local variables because a single variable couldn't handle a multiple-row update.

The solution is to undo the original DML `update` command by writing the pre-update values from the `Deleted` table back into the `Inventory` table. Then the difference between the `Deleted` table `QuantityOnHand` and the `Inserted` table `QuantityOnHand` can be written to the `InventoryTransaction` table as a manual adjustment.

The trigger logic is only executed if the `QuantityOnHand` column is updated and the trigger is being called by a user's DML statement. If the `Inventory` table's `QuantityOnHand` column is being updated by the `InvTrans_Aggregate` trigger, the `NestLevel()` will be higher than 1. Here's the `Inventory` table side of the `Inventory - InventoryTransaction` table trigger solution:

```
CREATE TRIGGER Inventory_Aggregate
ON Inventory
AFTER UPDATE
AS
-- Redirect direct updates
If Trigger_NestLevel() = 1 AND Update(QuantityOnHand)
  BEGIN
    UPDATE Inventory
      SET QuantityOnHand = Deleted.QuantityOnHand
      FROM Deleted
        JOIN dbo.Inventory
          ON Inventory.InventoryID = Deleted.InventoryID
```

```
INSERT InventoryTransaction
  (Value, InventoryID)
  SELECT
    Inserted.QuantityOnHand - Inventory.QuantityOnHand,
    Inventory.InventoryID
      FROM dbo.Inventory
        JOIN Inserted
          ON Inventory.InventoryID = Inserted.InventoryID
END
```

To demonstrate the trigger, the following update attempts to change the quantity on hand from "9" to "10." The new Inventory_Aggregate trigger traps the update and resets the quantity on hand back to "9." But it also writes a transaction of "+1" to the InventoryTransaction table. (If the transaction table had transaction type and comment columns, the transaction would be recorded as a manual adjustment by User X.) The inventory transaction table's InvTrans_Aggregate trigger sees the insert and properly adjusts the Inventory.QuantityOnHand to "10":

```
-- Trigger Test
Update dbo.Inventory
  SET QuantityOnHand = 10
  Where InventoryCode = 'A1'
```

Having performed the manual adjustment, the following query examines the InventoryTransaction table:

```
SELECT InventoryCode, Value
  FROM dbo.InventoryTransaction
    JOIN dbo.Inventory
      ON Inventory.InventoryID
        = Inventorytransaction.InventoryID
```

Sure enough, the manual adjustment of 1 has been written to the InventoryTransaction table:

```
InventoryCode    Value
---------------  ----------------------------------
A1               5
A1               -3
A1               7
A1               1
```

As the adjustment was being inserted into the InventoryTransaction table, the InvTrans_Aggregate trigger posted the transaction to the Inventory table. The following query double checks the QuantityOnHand for inventory item "A1":

```
SELECT Product.Code, InventoryCode, QuantityOnHand
  FROM dbo.Inventory
    JOIN dbo.Product
      ON Inventory.ProductID = Product.ProductID
```

Result:

```
Code             InventoryCode    QuantityOnHand
---------------  ---------------  --------------
1001             A1               10
```

# Logically Deleting Data

To further increase data integrity, many database developers prohibit the physical deletion of data. Instead, they enable the logical deletion of data. The most common method is to use a delete flag bit column. When the user deletes a row in the front-end application, a trigger actually marks the row as deleted by setting the delete flag to true. A logical delete flag can be implemented in several ways:

✦ The front-end application can set the delete flag to true.

✦ The delete stored procedure can set the delete flag to true.

✦ An instead of trigger can trap the delete DML command and set the delete flag instead of physically deleting the row.

**Note**    A logical delete flag is not as advanced as it seems. dbase III used a delete flag to mark rows as deleted until the file compress command purged the deleted rows.

The ability to logically delete data is a cool high-end feature that is desirable in mature databases. I would caution you, however, to let logical deletions be among the last features you implement because doing so can be very time-consuming and can open a huge can of worms. Here, my goal is to demonstrate a single-table logical delete system, and also to explain the problems with logically deleted data and suggest some strategies to work around those problems.

## Logical Delete Triggers

An instead of trigger implements the logical delete system at the table level and ensures that it's always enforced. The trigger has two goals: converting physical deletes into logical deletes, and enabling some method of physically deleting the row.

This trigger allows the sa user to physically delete any row, so there is some method of physically purging the database. An instead of trigger will not recursively fire, so the delete DML command within the trigger will execute. The first command alters the Product table and adds the IsDeleted bit flag:

```
ALTER TABLE Product
  ADD IsDeleted BIT NOT NULL DEFAULT 0

CREATE Trigger Product_LogicalDelete
On dbo.Product
INSTEAD OF Delete
AS

IF (suser_sname() = 'sa')
  BEGIN
    PRINT 'physical delete'
    DELETE FROM dbo.Product
      FROM dbo.Product
        JOIN Deleted
          ON Product.ProductID = Deleted.ProductID
  END
ELSE
  BEGIN
    PRINT 'logical delete'
```

```
UPDATE Product
  SET IsDeleted = 1
  FROM dbo.Product
    JOIN Deleted
      ON Product.ProductID = Deleted.ProductID
END
```

To test the logical delete trigger, the next query deletes from the Product table while I'm logged in as Noli\Paul:

```
DELETE Product
  WHERE Code = '1053'
```

Result:

```
logical delete
```

To following select views the logical deleted flag:

```
SELECT Code, IsDeleted
  FROM dbo.Product
    WHERE Code = 1053
```

Result:

```
Code            IsDeleted
--------------- ---------
1053            1
```

Having reconnected as the sa user, I again issued the same delete command:

```
DELETE dbo.Product
  WHERE Code = '1053'
```

Result:

```
physical delete

(1 row(s) affected)


(1 row(s) affected)
```

The first (1row(s) affected) result is the DML delete statement. Even though it was intercepted by the Instead Of trigger and the initial delete was ignored, it is still reported as an affected row. The second (1row(s) affected) result is the delete statement within the Product_LogicalDelete trigger. This delete was effective and physically deleted the row.

## Undeleting a Logically Deleted Row

Prior to being physically deleted by the sa user, the row can easily be undeleted by means of updating the IsDeleted column back to false. If the row-based custom security method described earlier in this chapter is implemented, an after update trigger could test that the user has administrative privileges to the row to update the IsDeleted column to 0.

# Filtering out Logically Deleted Rows

An issue with a logical delete system is that every `select` statement must consider the `IsDeleted` flag, otherwise deleted data may erroneously affect the result. The best way to ensure that the front-end application retrieves only current and correct data is to use stored procedures for fetching data.

The problem is that when the user issues an ad hoc query there's no guarantee that he or she is aware of the `IsDeleted` flag or that every query is correct. A solution is to create views or, better still, table-valued user-defined functions for data retrieval, and to limit the users to those views or functions using SQL Server security.

# Cascading Logical Deletes

This is where logically deleting data becomes a potential nightmare. If a primary row is physically deleted, the secondary rows that have no meaning without the primary row should also be deleted. Should logical deletes cascade as well?

If an order is logically deleted, the associated order-detail rows must be logically deleted either in the write or in every future read. Both methods have problems.

## Cascading During the Read

If an order is logically deleted, its order-detail rows must be excluded from any calculations that are considering open order details. One possible method is to join the order table and include `order.isdeleted` in the `where` clause. This can become very complex as logical deletes cascade through multiple levels. From my experience, implementing cascading logical deletes in the read end of the process can kill performance as the number of tables, joins, and `where` conditions multiply exponentially to cover all the logical `delete` combinations.

## Cascading During the Write

If the secondary rows are logically deleted during the primary table's logical `delete` operation, the advantage is that the secondary rows are already marked for deletion, so the read operation won't have to check the primary table for logically deleted rows. The problem is determining whether the logically deleted secondary row has been logically deleted itself, or because its primary row was logically deleted.

It's possible to use two flags, one for the row logical `delete`, and one for a cascade logical `delete`. In keeping with the saying that today's solution is tomorrow's problem, even this causes headaches. Assume an order is logically deleted, and the logical `delete` is cascaded to the order-detail table. One of the order-detail rows pointed to a product that has been logically deleted. When the order is undeleted and the order-detail rows are undeleted, the order-detail row that was logically deleted because of the product logical `delete` should stay logically deleted.

There are two possible solutions. The first solution is to add a logical cascade `delete` flag for each foreign key relationship for a table. This makes the code less than generic and potentially very messy, so I don't like this solution.

The second solution is to use a single logical `delete` cascade flag, but to build a very comprehensive undelete system that examines every primary-table relationship before undeleting a row. While this method entails the most work, it's the best solution.

### Logical Deletes and Referential Integrity

Implementing a complete logical delete method also creates a potential referential-integrity problem. It would violate referential integrity to refer to a row that has been logically deleted. However, SQL Server's declarative referential integrity does not consider whether the row is logically deleted, only if it's physically in the table.

A database with a logical delete system therefore requires a complex referential-integrity trigger that not only determines whether the primary key value exists in the primary table, but also checks the row's IsDeleted bit flag.

## Degrees of Inactivity

A system that incorporates logical deletions often also includes some other measure of row inactivity such as an active flag or a retired flag. These flags enable the user to mark a row as less significant without deleting the data. For example, an R&D lab is most concerned with the current formulae or material revisions, so its researchers don't want to wade through the thousands of obsolete formula revisions. However, they don't want to delete the data either. Marking a formula inactive serves to hide it, but the user can still select the inactive data if desired.

# Archiving Data

Old data is often no longer required for day-to-day activities, and can be safely archived or moved to a separate database location. The easiest way to archive data yet keep it easily available to the user is to move it to a separate table with an identical structure within the same database or within another database.

Archiving data is a good alternative to logically deleting it. The issues of referential integrity and cascading logical deletes are no longer problems if logically deleted data is moved to an archive.

A stored procedure can easily perform the move by inserting the data into the archive table and deleting it form the current table:

```
CREATE PROCEDURE pProduct_Archive (
  @Code CHAR(15) )
AS
SET NoCount ON

BEGIN TRANSACTION

INSERT Product_Archive
  SELECT *
    FROM dbo.Product
    WHERE Code = @Code
IF @@ERROR <> 0
  BEGIN
    ROLLBACK TRANSACTION
    RETURN
  END
```

```
DELETE dbo.Product
  WHERE Code = @Code
IF @@ERROR <> 0
  BEGIN
    ROLLBACK TRANSACTION
  END

COMMIT TRANSACTION
RETURN
```

The stored procedure will likely have to move more than just one table's rows. For example, archiving an order involves both the [Order] table and the OrderDdetail table.

**Cross-Reference** Partitioned views, discussed in Chapter 30, "Advanced Scalability," are an excellent means of retrieving a combination of both current and archived data.

## Summary

Complex business rules and processing are best implemented as server-side code. Only when the rule is implemented in the server is it 100 percent enforced. A rule implemented outside the server isn't a rule, it's a suggestion. Server-side code is excellent for insert, update, delete, and fetch procedures, complex business rules, complex referential integrity, data-audit trails, and logical deletions.

This chapter concludes Part II of the book, "Developing SQL Server Databases." From here, Part III, "Data Connectivity," discusses connecting with data outside SQL Server, from the sophisticated Data Transformation Services to the building of distributed queries with code.

✦     ✦     ✦

# Data Connectivity

◆   ◆   ◆   ◆

If a tree falls in the forest and no one hears it, the tree may as well be a null.

The same is true of the data. If it's not delivered on time to those who need it, then the database has failed. It's not the existence of the data that matters but the delivery.

Part III is about thinking outside the box, and delivering the data to the rest of the world using more connectivity options than ever before.

◆   ◆   ◆   ◆

# Transferring Databases

Transferring data may be a mundane task, but SQL Server databases are often developed on one server and deployed on other servers. Without a reliable and efficient method of moving database schemas and whole databases, the project won't get very far.

SQL Server enables multiple means of moving databases. As a database developer or DBA, you should have basic skills in the following topics, three of which are covered in this chapter:

✦ Copy Database Wizard

✦ SQL scripts

✦ Detach/attach

✦ Backup/restore (covered in Chapter 26, "Recovery Planning")

The keys to deciding the best way to move a database are knowing how much of it needs to be moved, and knowing whether or not the servers are directly connected by a fast network. Table 17-1 lists the copy requirements and the various methods of moving a database.

### Table 17-1: Database Transfer Methods

| Requirement | Copy Database Wizard | SQL Scripts | Detaching Attaching | Backup Restore |
|---|---|---|---|---|
| Requires Exclusive Access to the Database | Yes | No | Yes | No |
| Copies Between Disconnected Servers | No | Yes | Yes | Yes |
| Copies Database Schema | Yes | Yes | Yes | Yes |
| Copies Data | Yes | No | Yes | Yes |
| Copies Security | Server logins, database users, security roles, and permissions | Depends on the script | Database users, security roles, and permissions | Database users, security roles, and permissions |
| Copies Jobs/ User-Defined Error Messages | Yes | Depends on the script | No | No |

## Copy Database Wizard

The Copy Database Wizard actually generates a Data Transformation Service package that can copy or move one or more databases from one server to another. If the database is being moved to a server on the same network server, this is the premiere method. The Copy Database Wizard offers the most flexibility and capability. The only limitation is that it requires exclusive access to the database.

On pages 1 and 2 of the Copy Database Wizard, the wizard begins by gathering the name of the source and destination servers and the required security information to log into the server.

On page 3 the wizard displays the default locations for the database files on the destination server. You can also modify the locations here if needed. The wizard will move all the objects and data.

On page 4 (Figure 17-1) you can optionally direct the wizard to move the following:

✦ All logins, or only those that have access to the database.

✦ All or selected non-system stored procedures in the Master database that are used by the database.

✦ All or selected SQL Agent jobs (automated and optionally scheduled tasks).

✦ All or selected user-defined error messages (used by the raiserror T-SQL command).

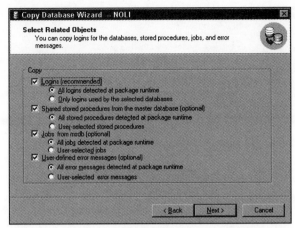

**Figure 17-1:** The Copy Database Wizard can move server-related information as it moves the database.

Depending on the options selected, the wizard may offer pages to select the Master database non-system stored procedures, the SQL Server Agent jobs, and the user-defined error messages.

The Schedule the DTS Package page, shown in Figure 17-2, directs the wizard to either run the package once upon completion of the wizard, run it once later, or set it up on a regular schedule. Optionally, the DTS package's name can be changed to something other than `CDW_sourceserver_destinationserver`.

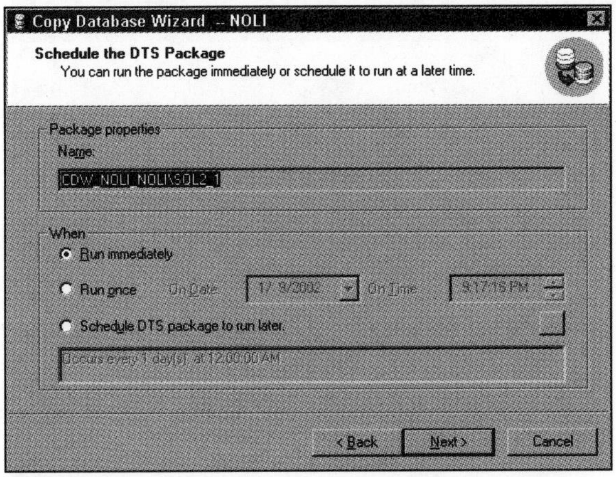

**Figure 17-2:** The Copy Database Wizard can run the DTS package once now, once later, or on a schedule.

When finished, the wizard generates and runs a DTS package (Figure 17-3) and saves it on the destination server.

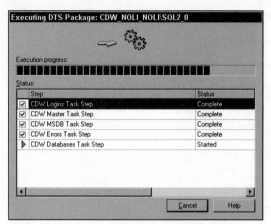

**Figure 17-3:** When the Copy Database Wizard executes the DTS package, it displays its progress as it works its way through the steps.

You may open the generated DTS package, shown in Figure 17-4, by opening the Local Packages node under Data Transformation Services in the console tree, and then double-clicking on the package. If the name was not edited in the wizard's schedule page, then the name should be CDW followed by the two server names and an integer. The creation date is also listed.

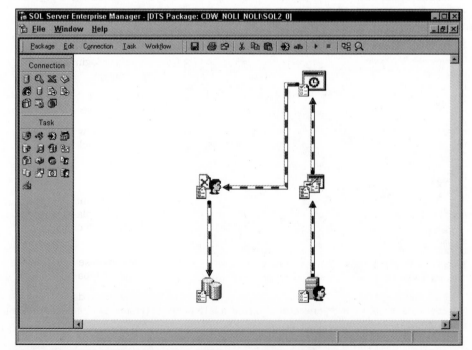

**Figure 17-4:** The DTS package is a workflow sequence of five tasks.

Each of the five tasks, if double-clicked, will open a dialog to gather information about how that task should run. The blue lines between the tasks are workflow connections that launch the next task only after the previous task is complete.

You may run the DTS package by clicking the Run tool in the toolbar or by pressing F5.

**Cross-Reference** For more details on creating and executing DTS packages, refer to Chapter 19, "Migrating Data with DTS."

# Working with SQL Script

Of the four methods of moving a database, running a SQL Script, or batch, is the only method that creates a new database. Perhaps it's false logic, but the idea of starting with a fresh installation at a client site, without any residue from test data, is a reassuring thought.

Scripts are smaller than databases. They often fit on a floppy, and they can be edited with Notepad. As an example, the sample databases for this book are distributed by means of scripts.

Scripts are useful for distributing the following:

✦ Database schema (databases, tables, views, stored procedures, functions, and so on)

✦ Security roles

✦ Database jobs

✦ Limited sample data or priming data

Though it's possible, I wouldn't recommend creating a script to move the following:

✦ *Data* — A script can insert rows, but this is a difficult method of moving data.

✦ *Server logins* — A script can easily create server logins, but server logins tend to be domain-specific, so this option is only useful within a single domain.

✦ *Server Jobs* — Server specific jobs generally require specific tweaking. While a script may be useful to copy jobs, they will likely require editing prior to execution.

Scripts may also be used to implement a change to a database. The easiest way to modify a client database is to write a script. The change script can be tested on a backup of the database.

Scripts may be generated in several ways:

✦ The database can be developed initially in Query Analyzer using a hand-written DDL script. Chapter 5, "Implementing the Physical Database Schema," explains how to create such a script. Also, the sample databases on the book's CD are all created using a DDL script. This is my preferred method.

✦ Enterprise Manager can generate a script to create the entire database or a change script for schema changes made with the Table Designer or the Database Diagrammer.

✦ Most third-party database-design tools generate scripts to create the database or apply changes.

Focusing in on generating scripts with Enterprise Manager, to open the Enterprise Manager script generator, select the database in the console tree, right-click, and select All Tasks ⇨ Generate SQL Script.

In Enterprise Manager's Generate SQL Scripts tool, use the General tab (Figure 17-5) to select the objects to be included in the script.

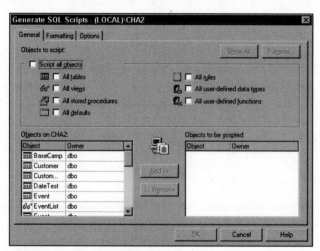

**Figure 17-5:** Enterprise Manager can generate scripts for any object in the database.

The Formatting tab (Figure 17-6) is ill named. Only one option offered here is truly a formatting option. Most of the options direct the SQL Script Generator as to which additional object to script. The "Generate the DROP <object> command for each object" option generates a DROP command for each object before that object is created. The "Generate scripts for all dependent objects" option includes any dependent object that was omitted in the previous tab.

The Options tab (Figure 17-7) includes additional database features that might be included in the script, such as security, users, login, roles, indexes, triggers, and keys. I recommend including all of the table options.

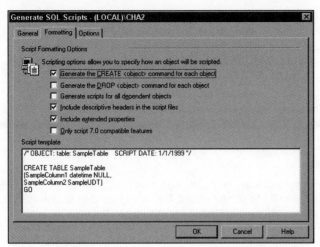

**Figure 17-6:** The critical options in the Formatting tab are the "Generate the DROP <object> command for each object" and the "Generate scripts for all dependent objects" options.

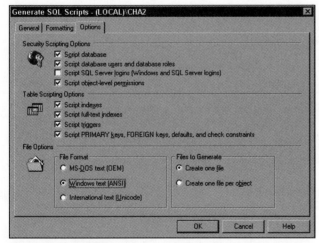

**Figure 17-7:** Additional items may be added to the script by means of the Options tabs.

# Detaching and Attaching

Though it is often overlooked, one of the easiest ways to move a database from one computer to another is to detach the database, copy the files, and attach the database to SQL Server on the destination computer.

For developers who frequently move databases between notebooks and servers, this is the recommended method. Detaching a database effectively deletes the database from SQL Server's awareness, but leaves the files intact. The database must have no current connections and not be replicated if it is to be detached. Only members of the SysAdmins Fixed Server Role (see Chapter 27, "Securing Databases," for more details on the security roles) may detach and attach databases.

Detaching and attaching the database will carry with it any database users, security roles, and permissions, but it will not replicate server logins. These will need to be resolved manually on the destination server. It's best to coordinate security with the network administration folks and leverage their security groups. If the source and destination servers have access to the same network security groups, this will alleviate the security login issues for most installations.

Using Enterprise Manager, right-click the database to be copied and select All Tasks ➪ Detach Database. The Detach Database dialog box is shown in Figure 17-8.

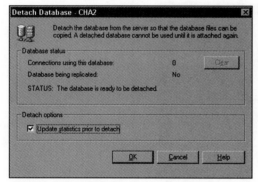

**Figure 17-8:** The Detach Database feature removes the database from SQL Server's list of databases and frees the files for copying.

Once the file is detached, it will disappear from the list of databases in Enterprise Manager. The files may be copied or moved like regular files.

To reattach the database file, select Databases in the Enterprise Manger console tree and All Tasks ➪ Attach Database from the action menu or the right-click menu. The Attach Database dialog box (Figure 17-9) simply offers a place to select the file and verify the file locations and names.

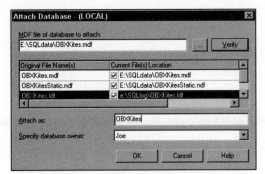

**Figure 17-9:** The database may be reattached by means of Enterprise Manager's Attach Database tool.

In code the database is detached by means of running the sp_detach_db system stored procedure. The first parameter is the database to be detached. A second optional parameter simply turns off automatic updating of the index statistics. The following command detaches the OBX Kites sample database:

```
sp_detach_db 'OBXKites'
```

If you wish to reattach a database with code, the counterpart to sp_detach_db is the sp_attach_db system stored procedure. Attaching a database requires specifying the files' locations as well as the database name, as follows:

```
EXEC sp_attach_db @dbname = 'OBXKites',
   @filename1 = 'e:\SQLData\OBXKites.mdf',
   @filename2 = 'f:\SQLData\OBXKitesStatic.ndf',
   @filename3 = 'g:\SQLLOG\OBXKites.ldf'
```

# Summary

When you need to move a database, don't back it up; there are better ways to move it. Choose the right transfer method based on the network proximity of the servers and the objects and/or data to be moved.

Part III of this book, "Data Connectivity," addresses the multiple means of moving data or connecting to data outside of SQL Server. The next chapter moves outside the realm of the single database to distributed data, covering retrieving and modifying data in other SQL Server databases, other SQL Server instances, and even other data formats, including Access and Excel.

✦ ✦ ✦

# Working with Distributed Queries

**D**ata is seldom in one place. In today's distributed world, most new projects enhance or at least connect to existing data. That's not a problem. SQL Server can read and write data to most other data sources. Heterogeneous joins can even merge SQL Server data with an Excel spreadsheet.

SQL Server offers several methods of accessing data external to the current database. From simply referencing another local database to executing pass-through queries that engage another client/server database, SQL Server can handle it.

Chapter 11, "Transactional Integrity," explored the ACID properties of a database and transactions. SQL Server uses the Distributed Transaction Coordinator to escalate a transaction to a two-phase commit, meaning that data modifications that affect multiple SQL servers still have atomicity.

The code listings in this chapter are also in the ch18.sql script file. In addition, the Cape Hatteras Adventures conversion script (CHA2_Convert.sql) uses distributed queries exclusively to convert the data from Access and Excel to SQL Server.

In this chapter, I refer to the two data sources as local and external. Other descriptions of distributed queries might refer to the same two servers as local and remote, or sending and receiving.

## Distributed Query Concepts

*Linking* to an external data source is nothing more than configuring the name of the linked server, along with the necessary location and login information, so that SQL Server can access data on the linked server.

Linking is a one-way configuration, as illustrated in Figure 18-1. If Server A links to Server B, it means that Server A knows how to access and log into Server B. As far as Server B is concerned, Server A is just another user.

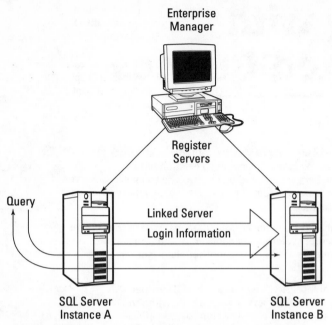

**Figure 18-1:** A linked server is a one-way direct connection and is not dependent on Enterprise Manager's registering the servers. In this diagram, SQL Server Instance A sees SQL Server Instance B as a linked server so A can access B's data.

If linking a server is a new concept to you it could easily be confused with registering a server in Enterprise Manager. As illustrated in Figure 18-1, Enterprise Manager is only communicating with the servers as a client application. Linking the servers enables SQL Server Instance A to communicate directly with SQL Server instance B.

Links can be established in Enterprise Manager or with T-SQL code. The latter has the advantage of repeatability in case a hasty rebuild is necessary, although building the links in code requires more steps.

A linked server can be a SQL server or any other data source with either an OLE DB provider or ODBC drivers. Distributed queries can select data and modify (insert, update, delete) it, according to the features of the OLE DB provider or ODBC driver.

SQL Server queries can reference external data by referring to the pre-configured linked server or specifying the link in the query code.

In a sense, linking to an external data source only moves declaring the link from the query code to a server administration task. Because queries can refer to the named link without concern for the location or security particulars of the link, queries that use linked servers are more portable and easier to maintain than queries that declare the external data source in the query code. If the database is moved to a new server, once the database administrator creates the appropriate links, the queries will work without modification.

In the case of a distributed query, SQL Server is the client process receiving the results from the external data source. Distributed queries can either pull the data into SQL Server for processing, or pass the query to the external data source for processing.

 **Cross-Reference** There's more than one way to distribute data. You might want to consider replication (Chapter 20, "Replicating Databases"), using a federated database (Chapter 30, "Advanced Scalability"), or setting up a standby server as a reporting server (Chapter 29, "Advanced Availability").

## Accessing a Local SQL Server Database

When you access a second database on a single server, the same SQL Server engine processes the data. So although the data is outside the local database, the query's not actually a distributed query.

A SQL Server query may access another database on the same server by referring to the table using the database name:

```
Server.Database.Owner.ObjectName
```

Because the database is on the same server, the server name is optional. Typically the tables are owned by the database owner (dbo). If that's the case, then dbo can be assumed:

```
USE CHA2
SELECT LastName, FirstName
  FROM OBXKites.dbo.Contact
```

The previous query is the functional equivalent of this one:

```
SELECT LastName, FirstName
  FROM OBXKites..Contact
```

Result (abbreviated):

```
LastName      FirstName
------------  ------------
Adams         Terri
Andrews       Ed
...
```

## Linking to External Data Sources

SQL Server is also capable of establishing a link to any other data source that is ODBC- or OLE-DB-compatible. The link can be created using Enterprise Manager or T-SQL code.

### Linking with Enterprise Manager

A link to another SQL server can be established by means of Enterprise Manager or code. Within Enterprise Manager, linked servers are listed under the security node, which makes sense because a link is really defining how to log onto another server. Right-click the security node under the server and select New Linked Server to open the Linked Server Properties form (Figure 18-2).

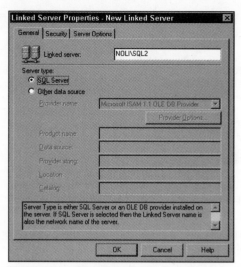

**Figure 18-2:** The General tab of Enterprise Manager's Linked Server Properties form is used to name the link and specify the data-source type.

Linking to non–SQL Server data sources is covered later in this chapter.

## Selecting the Server

In the General tab of the Linked Server Properties form, enter the name of the external SQL server in the Linked server field, and click the SQL Server button in the Server Type section. To link to a named instance of SQL Server, enter the instance name as ***server\instance*** without square brackets. In Figure 18-2, the linked server is Noli\SQL2.

SQL Server 2000 can link to any other SQL Server 2000 instance, or a SQL Server 7 server, but SQL Server 2000 won't link to a SQL Server 6.5 server without going through an OBDC driver.

## Configuring the Logins

The whole point of linked servers is to enable local users to run queries that access data from other data sources. If the external data source is SQL Server, it will require some type of user authentication, which is accomplished via mapping logins, and, for those local users whose logins are not mapped, via setting the default behavior.

The login map will either pass the user along without translating the login name if the impersonate option is checked, or translate any user's login to a remote login and password if the impersonate option is not checked. Of course, on the external server, the login must be a valid login and must have been granted security rights for the link to be effective.

The default connection options for a user not mapped are as follows:

✦ *Connection: Not be made.* Restricts the ability to run distributed queries to those users in the user mapping list. If a user not on the user mapping list attempts to run a distributed query he or she will receive the following error:

```
Server: Msg 7416, Level 16, State 1, Line 1
Access to the remote server is denied
  because no login-mapping exists.
```

✦ *Connection: Be made without using a security context.* This option is for non–SQL Server external-data sources and is not useful for SQL Server. SQL Server will attempt to connect as the user SQL without a password. If a user not on the user mapping list attempts to run a distributed query he or she will receive the following error:

```
Server: Msg 18456, Level 14, State 1, Line 1
Login failed for user 'SQL'.
```

This is the default for Enterprise Manager.

✦ *Connection: Be made using the login's current security context.* When the local SQL server connects to the external SQL Server, it can delegate security, meaning that the local SQL Server will connect to the external SQL Server using the local user's login. Using this method is similar to listing the user and selecting the impersonate option except that this uses security delegation, and to pass the security context, the login must be the exact same account, not just the same login and password.

The user's rights and roles for the distributed query will be those assigned at the external SQL Server.

To use security deligation every server must run Windows 2000,and both Kerberos and Active Directory must be enabled.

This is the default when creating the link usign T-SQL code.

**Best Practice**

For most SQL Server–to–SQL Server distributed queries, the local login's security context is the best linked-server security option because it preserves the user's identity and conforms to the SQL Server security plan. If the infrastructure doesn't support Kerberos and Active Directory, then map the users.

✦ *Connection: Be made using this security context.* The final option simply assigns every non-mapped local user to a hard-coded external SQL Server login. While this may be the simplest method, it also allows every local user the same access to the external SQL Server. Using this option should violate any responsible security plan. It would certainly exclude the external SQL Server from achieving C2-level security certification.

## Configuring the Options

The third tab, Server Options, in the Linked Server Properties form presents the following options, which control how SQL Server expects to receive data from the external SQL Server:

✦ *Collation Compatibility*—Set this option to true if the two servers are using the same collation (character set and sort order).

✦ *Data Access*—If this option is set to false, this option disables distributed queries to the external server.

✦ *RPC*—If this option is set to true, remote-procedure calls may be made to the external server.

✦ *RPC Out*—If this option is set to true, remote-procedure calls may be made from the external server.

✦ *Use Remote Collation* — If this option is set to `true`, distributed queries will use the collation of the external SQL Server rather than that of the local server.

✦ *Collation Name* — Specifies a collation for distributed queries. This option cannot be chosen if collation compatibility is set.

✦ *Connection Timeout* — The connection timeout in milliseconds.

✦ *Query Timeout* — The distributed query timeout in milliseconds.

Once the link is properly established, a table listing will likely be available in the table node under the linked server. The tables listed will be those of the login's default database. If the default database is the master, and Enterprise Manager is configured in the local server registration to hide system objects, no tables should appear.

Deleting a linked server in Enterprise Manager will also delete all security-login mappings.

## Linking with T-SQL

Enterprise Manager handles the connection and the login information in a single form. However, if you choose to establish a linked server with T-SQL code, the server connection and the login information are handled by separate commands.

### Establishing the Link

To establish the server link with code, use the `sp_addlinkedserver` system stored procedure. If the link is being made to another SQL Server, and the name of the other SQL Server instance is acceptable as the name for the link, then only two parameters are required: the linked server name and the server product. The following command creates a link to the `SQL2` instance on my test server (`Noli`):

```
EXEC sp_addlinkedserver
  @server = 'Noli\SQL2',
  @srvproduct = 'SQL Server'
```

To link to another SQL Server instance using a linked server name other than the SQL Server instance name, two parameters are added. The provider parameter must specify `SQLOLEDB`, and the `@datasrc` (data source) parameter passes the actual SQL Server instance name of the linked server. The `@srvproduct` (server product) parameter is left blank. The `@server` parameter will be the name the linked server will be known by. The example links to the `SQL2` instance on `Noli`, but the linked server will be referred to as `Yonder` in queries:

```
EXEC sp_addlinkedserver
  @server = 'Yonder',
  @datasrc = 'Noli\SQL2',
  @srvproduct = '',
  @provider='SQLOLEDB'
```

The `sp_linkedservers` system stored procedure also provides basic information about the current linked servers:

```
EXEC sp_linkedservers
```

Result (abridged):

```
SRV_NAME      SRV_PROVIDERNAME    SRV_PRODUCT      V_DATASOURCE
----------    ------------------  -------------    -------------
NOLI          SQLOLEDB            SQL Server
NOLI\SQL2     SQLOLEDB            SQL Server       NOLI\SQL2
Yonder        SQLOLEDB                             NOLI\SQL2
...
```

To drop an existing linked server, which only severs the link and does not affect the external server, use the `sp_dropserver` system stored procedure:

```
EXEC sp_DropServer @server = 'Yonder'
```

If any login mappings exist for the linked server, they too will be dropped.

## Distributed Security and Logins

In Enterprise Manager the security question was broken down into two parts, login mapping and what to do with non-mapped logins. T-SQL uses the `sp_addlinkedsrvlogin` system stored procedure to handle both parts, as follows:

```
sp_addlinkedsrvlogin
  @rmtsrvname = 'rmtsrvname',
  @useself = 'useself', (default True)
  @locallogin = 'locallogin', (default Null)
  @rmtuser = 'rmtuser', (default Null)
  @rmtpassword = 'rmtpassword' (default Null)
```

If the linked server was added using T-SQL instead of Enterprise Manager, then the security option for non-mapped logins is already configured to use the login's current security context.

If the `@locallogin` is `null`, the setting applies to all non-mapped users. The useself option is the same as impersonate.

The following stored procedure call enables the `Noli\Paul` login to access the Noli\SQL2 server as the `sa` user with the password `secret`:

```
sp_addlinkedsrvlogin
  @rmtsrvname = 'NOLI\SQL2',
  @useself = 'false',
  @locallogin = 'NOLI\Paul',
  @rmtuser = 'sa',
  @rmtpassword = 'secret'
```

The next example sets all non-mapped users to connect using their own security context (the recommended option). The local user is `null` so this linked server login applies to all non-mapped users. The `@useself` option is not specified, so the default setting, `true`, will apply, causing the users to use the local security context.

```
EXEC sp_addlinkedsrvlogin
  @rmtsrvname = 'NOLI\SQL2'
```

The third example will prevent all non-mapped users from executing distributed queries. The second parameter, @useself, is set to false, and the mapping user login and password are left as null:

```
EXEC sp_addlinkedsrvlogin 'NOLI\SQL2', 'false'
```

To list the current mapped logins for a linked server, a variation of sp_help (of course) provides the information:

```
sp_helplinkedsrvlogin
```

Result:

```
Linked server   Local Login    Is Self Mapping    Remote Login
--------------  -------------  ------------------  --------------
NOLI            NULL           1                   NULL
Noli\SQL2       NULL           1                   NULL
Noli\SQL2       NOLI\Paul      0                   sa
```

To drop a linked server login, use the sp_droplinkedsrvlogin system stored procedure:

```
sp_droplinkedsrvlogin
  @rmtsrvname = 'rmtsrvname', (no default)
  @locallogin = 'locallogin'  (no default)
```

The following code example will remove the Noli\Paul login that's mapped to NOLI\SQL2:

```
EXEC sp_droplinkedsrvlogin
  @rmtsrvname = 'NOLI\SQL2',
  @locallogin = 'NOLI\Paul'
```

To remove the non-mapped user's default mapping, run the same procedure, but specify a null local login, as follows:

```
EXEC sp_droplinkedsrvlogin 'NOLI\SQL2', NULL
```

## Linked Server Options

The linked server options shown in the Server Options tab of the Linked Server Properties form may be set in code using the sp_serveroption system stored procedure. The procedure must be called once for each option setting:

```
sp_serveroption
  @server = 'server',
  @optname = 'option_name',
  @optvalue = 'option_value'
```

The options are the same as those in the form, with the addition of lazy schema validation, which disables the checking of the table schema for distributed queries. You may want to use lazy schema validation when you're sure of the schema but want to reduce network overhead.

The linked servers' options are reported by the sp_helpserver system stored procedure. This rendition of sp_help returns the server logical name and physical location, as well as the options:

```
EXEC sp_helpserver
```

Result (abridged—the actual listing also includes the linked server's ID, collation_name, connect_timeout, and query_timeout):

```
name             network_name   status
---------------- -------------- --------------------------
[Noli\SQL2]      [Noli\SQL2]    rpc,rpc out,data access,
                                use remote collation
CHA1_Customers   NULL           data access,
                                use remote collation
CHA1_Schedule    NULL           data access,
                                use remote collation
NOLI             NOLI           rpc,rpc out,
                                use remote collation
Yonder           NULL           rpc,rpc out,
                                use remote collation
```

An optional sp_helpserver parameter, @show_topology = 't', causes sp_helpserver to display the topological relationship between the local server and the external server.

## Linking with Non-SQL Server Data Sources

If the external data source isn't SQL Server, SQL Server can likely still access the data. It depends on the availability and the features of the ODBC drivers or OLE DB providers. SQL Server uses OLE DB for external data, and several OLE DB providers are included with SQL Server. If for some reason OLE DB isn't available for the external data source, use the "Microsoft OLE DB Provider for ODBC Drivers" provider. Nearly every data-source type has an ODBC driver.

To set up the linked server, either with code or via Enterprise Manager, data source (or location) and possibly a provider string to supply additional information are required, in addition to the name of the linked server, the provider name, and the product name, to establish the link. Some common data-source settings are listed in Table 18-1.

### Table 18-1: Common Other Data Source Settings

| Link To: | Provider Name | Product Name | Data Source | Provider String |
|----------|---------------|--------------|-------------|-----------------|
| Access | MS Jet 4.0 OLE DB | Access 2000 | Database File Location | null |
| Excel | MS Jet 4.0 OLE DB | Excel | Spreadsheet File Location | Excel 5.0 |
| Oracle | MS OLE Provider for Oracle | Oracle | Oracle System Identifier | null |

As two examples of linking to non–SQL Server data sources, the Cape Hatteras Adventures sample database uses distributed queries to pull data from both Access and Excel. The sample database models a typical small business that is currently using Access and Excel to store its customer list and schedule.

### Linking to Excel

The code samples used in this section are taken directly from the CHA2_Convert.sql script, which moves the data from the old version 1 (Access and Excel) to version 2 (SQL Server). The Cape Hatteras Adventures folks have been keeping their tour schedule in Excel, as shown in Figure 18-3.

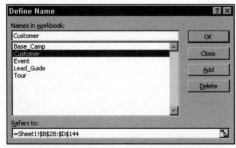

Figure 18-3 (full spreadsheet screenshot):

Microsoft Excel - CHA1_Schedule

File Edit View Insert Format Tools Data Window Help

B6    =  01-001

| | A | B | C | D | E | F | G |
|---|---|---|---|---|---|---|---|
| 2 | | Cape Hatteras Adventures | | | | | |
| 3 | | *Schedule* | | | | | |
| 4 | | | | | | | |
| 5 | | EventCode | Date | Tour | Base Camp | Lead Guide | |
| 6 | | 01-001 | 02-Feb-01 | Outer Banks Lighthouses | Cape Hatteras | Sam Wilson | |
| 7 | | 01-002 | 09-May-01 | Bahamas Dive | FreePort | Ken Frank | |
| 8 | | 01-003 | 16-Mar-01 | Amazon Trek | Ft Lauderdale | Joe Johnson | |
| 9 | | 01-004 | 06-Jun-01 | Outer Banks Lighthouses | Cape Hatteras | Sam Wilson | |
| 10 | | 01-005 | 25-Jun-01 | Appalachian Trail | Ashville NC | Sam Wilson | |
| 11 | | 01-006 | 03-Jul-01 | Bahamas Dive | FreePort | Ken Frank | |
| 12 | | 01-007 | 03-Jul-01 | Outer Banks Lighthouses | Cape Hatteras | Sam Wilson | |
| 13 | | 01-008 | 14-Jul-01 | Appalachian Trail | Ashville NC | Sam Wilson | |
| 14 | | 01-009 | 12-Aug-01 | Bahamas Dive | FreePort | Ken Frank | |
| 15 | | 01-010 | 14-Aug-01 | Appalachian Trail | Ashville NC | Sam Wilson | |
| 16 | | 01-011 | 17-Aug-01 | Outer Banks Lighthouses | Cape Hatteras | Sam Wilson | |
| 17 | | 01-012 | 14-Sep-01 | Gauley River Rafting | West Virginia | Ken Frank | |
| 18 | | 01-013 | 15-Sep-01 | Gauley River Rafting | West Virginia | Ken Frank | |
| 19 | | 01-014 | 03-Oct-01 | Outer Banks Lighthouses | Cape Hatteras | Sam Wilson | |
| 20 | | 01-015 | 05-Nov-01 | Amazon Trek | Ft Lauderdale | Joe Johnson | |
| 21 | | 01-016 | 16-Nov-01 | Outer Banks Lighthouses | Cape Hatteras | Sam Wilson | |
| 22 | | | | | | | |
| 23 | | | | | | | |
| 24 | | | | | | | |
| 25 | | | | | | | |

Sheet1 / Sheet2 / Sheet3 /

Ready                                                                    NUM

**Figure 18-3:** Prior to the conversion to SQL Server, the Cape Hatteras Adventures company had been managing its tour schedule in the CHA1_Schedule.xls spreadsheet.

Within Excel, each spreadsheet page and named range appears as a table when accessed from an external data provider. Within Excel, the named ranges are set up by means of the Insert ➪ Name ➪ Define menu command. The Excel Define Name dialog box is used to create new named ranges and edit the existing named ranges. The CHA1_Schedule spreadsheet has five named ranges (as shown in Figure 18-4), which overlap much like SQL Server views. Each of the five named ranges appears as a table when SQL Server links to the spreadsheet. SQL Server can select, insert, update, and delete rows just as if this table were a SQL Server table.

Define Name dialog box:

Names in workbook:
Customer

Base_Camp
Customer
Event
Lead_Guide
Tour

[OK] [Close] [Add] [Delete]

Refers to:
=Sheet1!$B$28:$D$144

**Figure 18-4:** Tables are defined within the Excel spreadsheet as named ranges. The CHA1_Schedule spreadsheet has five named ranges.

The following code sample sets up the Excel spreadsheet as a linked server:

```
Execute sp_addlinkedserver
  @server = 'CHA1_Schedule',
  @srvproduct = 'Excel',
  @provider = 'Microsoft.Jet.OLEDB.4.0',
  @datasrc = 'C:\SQLServerBible\CHA1_Schedule.xls',
  @provstr = 'Excel 5.0'
```

Once the linked server to Excel is established the named ranges appear as tables in Enterprise Manager, as shown in Figure 18-5.

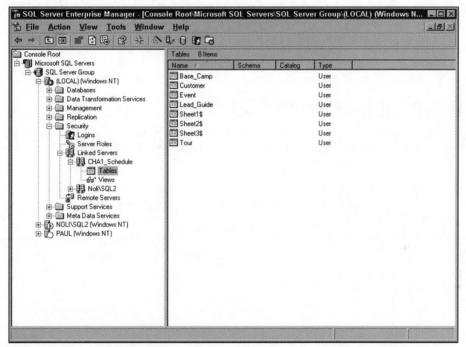

**Figure 18-5:** The Excel spreadsheet pages and named ranges appear as tables under the linked server in Enterprise Manager.

**Note**  Excel spreadsheets are not multi-user spreadsheets. SQL Server can't perform a distributed query that accesses an Excel spreadsheet while that spreadsheet is open in Excel.

## Linking to MS Access

Not surprisingly, SQL Server links easily to MS Access databases. SQL Server uses the OLE DB Jet provider to connect to Jet and request data from the MS Access .mdb file.

Since Access is a database, there's no trick to preparing it for linking, as there is with Excel. Each Access table will appear as a table under the linked-server node in Enterprise Manager.

The Cape Hatteras Adventures customer/prospect list was stored in Access prior to upsizing the database to SQL Server. The following code from the CHA2_Convert.sql script links to the CHA1_Customers.mdb Access database so SQL Server can retrieve the data and populate the SQL Server tables:

```
EXEC sp_addlinkedserver
  'CHA1_Customers',
  'Access 2000',
  'Microsoft.Jet.OLEDB.4.0',
  'C:\SQLServerBible\CHA1_Customers.mdb'
```

If you are having difficult with a distributed query, one of the first places I check is the security context. Excel expects that connections do not establish a security context so the non-mapped user login should be set to no security context:

```
EXEC sp_addlinkedsrvlogin
  @rmtsrvname = 'CHA1_Schedule',
  @useself    = 'false'
```

# Developing Distributed Queries

Once the link to the external data source is established, SQL Server can reference the external data within queries. Table 18-2 shows the four basic syntax methods that are available, which differ in query-processing location and setup method.

### Table 18-2: Distributed Query Method Matrix

| Link Setup | Query-Execution Location | |
| --- | --- | --- |
| | *Local SQL Server* | *External Data Source (Pass-Through)* |
| Linked Server | Four-part name | Four-part name |
| | | OpenQuery() |
| Ad Hoc Link Declared in the Query | OpenDataSource() | OpenRowSet() |

## Distributed Queries and Enterprise Manager

Enterprise Manager doesn't supply a graphic method of initiating a distributed query. There's no way to drag a linked server or remote table into the Query Designer. However, the distributed query can be entered manually in the SQL pane (as shown in Figure 18-6) and then executed as a query.

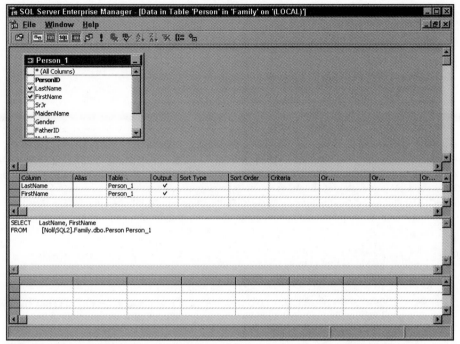

**Figure 18-6:** A distributed query may be executed from Enterprise Manager if the distributed query source is manually entered in the SQL pane ([Noli\SQL2].Family. dbo.Person).

## Distributed Views

Views are saved SQL select statements. While I don't recommend building a client/server application based on views, they are useful for ad hoc queries. Because most users (and even developers) are unfamiliar with the various methods of performing distributed queries, wrapping a distributed query inside a view might be a good idea.

## Local-Distributed Queries

A local-distributed query sounds like an oxymoron, but it's a query that pulls the external data into SQL Server and then processes the query at the local SQL Server. Because the processing occurs at the local SQL Server, local-distributed queries use T-SQL syntax and are sometimes called T-SQL distributed queries.

### Using the Four-Part Name

If the data is in another SQL Server a complete four-part name is required. The four-part name may be used in any select or data-modification query. On my writing computer is a second instance of SQL Server called [Noli\SQL2]. The object's owner name is required if the query accesses an external SQL Server.

The following query retrieves the Person table from the SQL2 instance:

```
SELECT LastName, FirstName
  FROM [NOLI\SQL2].Family.dbo.person
```

Result:

```
LastName          FirstName
---------------   ---------------
Halloway          Kelly
Halloway          James
```

When performing an insert, update, or delete command as a distributed query, either the four-part name, or a distributed query function, must be substituted for the table name. For example, the following SQL code, extracted from the CHA2_Convert.sql script that populates the CHA2 sample database, uses the four-part name as the source for an insert command. The query retrieves base camps from the Excel spreadsheet and inserts them into SQL Server.

```
INSERT BaseCamp(Name)
  SELECT DISTINCT [Base Camp]
    FROM CHA1_Schedule...[Base_Camp]
    WHERE [Base Camp] IS NOT NULL
```

**Note**  If you've already executed CHA2_Convert.sql and populated your copy of CHA2, then you may want to re-execute CHA2_Create.sql so you'll start with an empty database.

As another example of using the four-part name for a distributed query, the following code updates the family database on the second SQL Server instance:

```
UPDATE [Noli\SQL2].Family.dbo.Person
  SET LastName = 'Wilson'
  WHERE PersonID = 1
```

## OpenDataSource()

Using the OpenDataSource() function is functionally the same as using a four-part name to access a linked server, except that the OpenDataSource() function defines the link within the function instead of referencing a pre-defined linked server. While defining the link in code bypasses the linked server requirement, if the link location changes the change will effect every query that uses OpenDataSource(). And OpenDataSource() won't accept a variables as parameters.

The OpenDataSource() function is substituted for a server in the four-part name and may be used within any DML statement.

The syntax for the OpenDataSource() function seems simple enough:

```
OPENDATASOURCE ( provider_name, init_string )
```

However, there's more to it than the first appearance betrays. The init string is a semicolon-delimited string containing several parameters (the exact parameters used depending on the external data source). The potential parameters within the init string include data source, location, extended properties, connection timeout, user ID, password, and catalog. The init string must define the entire external data-source connection, and the security context, within a function. No quotes are required around the parameters within the `init` string. The common error committed in building `OpenDataSource()` distributed queries is mixing the commas and semicolons.

If `OpenDataSource()` is connecting to another SQL Server using Windows, authentication delegation via Kerberos security is required.

A relatively straightforward example of the `OpenDataSource()` function is as a means of accessing a table within another SQL Server instance:

```
SELECT FirstName, Gender
  FROM OPENDATASOURCE(
        'SQLOLEDB',
        'Data Source=NOLI\SQL2;User ID=Joe;Password=j'
        ).Family.dbo.Person
```

Result:

```
FirstName        Gender
---------------  ------
Adam             M
Alexia           F
```

The following example of a distributed query that uses `OpenDataSource()` references the Cape Hatteras Adventures sample database. Since an Access location contains only one database and the tables don't require the owner to specify the table, the database and owner are omitted from the four-part name.

```
SELECT ContactFirstName, ContactLastName
  FROM OPENDATASOURCE(
     'Microsoft.Jet.OLEDB.4.0',
     'Data Source =
        C:\SQLServerBible\CHA1_Customers.mdb'
      )...Customers
```

Result:

```
ContactFirstName      ContactLastName
--------------------  ---------------------
Neal                  Garrison
Melissa               Anderson
Gary                  Quill
```

As an example of `OpenDataSource()` used in an update query, the following query example will update any rows inside the `CHA1_Schedule.xls` Excel 2000 spreadsheet. A named range was previously defined as `Tours '=Sheet1!$E$5:$E$24'`, which now appears to the SQL query as a table within the data source. Rather than update an individual spreadsheet cell, this query performs a `update` operation that affects every row in which the tour column is equal to "Gauley River Rafting" and updates the `Base Camp` column to the value "Ashville."

The distributed SQL Server query will use OLE DB to call the Jet engine, which will open the Excel spreadsheet. The `OpenDataSource()` function supplies only the server name in a four-part name; as with Access, the database and owner values are omitted.

```
UPDATE OpenDataSource(
    'Microsoft.Jet.OLEDB.4.0',
    'Data Source=C:\SQLServerBible\CHA1_Schedule.xls;
    User ID=Admin;Password=;Extended properties=Excel 5.0'
    )...Tour
SET [Base Camp] = 'Ashville'
WHERE Tour = 'Gauley River Rafting'
```

Figure 18-7 illustrates the query-execution plan for the distributed update query, beginning at the left with a Remote Scan that returns all 19 rows from the Excel named range. The data is then processed within SQL Server. The details of the Remote Update logical operation reveal that the distributed update query actually only updated two rows.

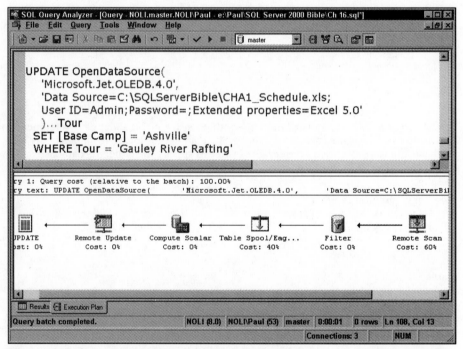

**Figure 18-7:** The query-execution plan for the distributed query using OpenDataSource().

To complete the example, the following query reads from the same Excel spreadsheet and verifies that the update took place. Again the OpenDataSource() function is only pointing the distributed query to an external server.

```
SELECT *
    FROM OpenDataSource(
    'Microsoft.Jet.OLEDB.4.0',
    'Data Source=C:\SQLServerBible\CHA1_Schedule.xls;
    User ID=Admin;Password=;Extended properties=Excel 5.0'
    )...Tour
WHERE Tour = 'Gauley River Rafting'
```

Result:

```
Base Camp         Tour
---------------   ------------------------
Ashville          Gauley River Rafting
Ashville          Gauley River Rafting
```

# Pass-Through Distributed Queries

A pass-through query executes a query at the external data source and returns the result to SQL Server. The primary reason for using a pass-through query is to reduce the amount of data being passed from the server (the external data source) and the client (SQL Server). Rather than pull a million rows into SQL Server so that it can use 25 of them, it may be better to select those 25 rows from the external data source.

Be aware that the pass-through query will use the query syntax of the external data source. If the external data source is Oracle or Access, PL/SQL or Access SQL must be used in the pass-through query.

In the case of a pass-through query that modifies data, the remote data type determines whether the update is performed locally or remotely:

✦ When another SQL Server is being updated, the remote SQL Server will perform the update.

✦ When non–SQL Server data is being updated, the data providers determine where the update will be performed. Often, the pass-through query merely selects the correct rows remotely. The selected rows are returned to SQL Server, modified inside SQL Server, and then returned to the remote data source for the update.

Two forms of local distributed queries exist, one for linked servers and one for external data sources defined in the query, and two forms of explicitly declaring pass-through distributed queries exist as well. OpenQuery() uses an established linked server, and OpenRowSet() declares the link within the query.

## Using the Four-Part Name

If the distributed query is accessing another SQL Server, the four-part name becomes a hybrid distributed query method. Depending on the from clause and the where clause, SQL Server will attempt to pass as much of the query as possible to the external SQL Server to improve performance.

When building complex distributed query using the four-part name it's difficult to predict how much of the query SQL Server will pass-through. I've seen SQL Server take a single query and depending on the where clause, the whole query was passed through, each table became a separate pass-through query, or only one table was pass-through.

**Best Practice**

Of the four distributed-query methods, the best two use the four-part name and the OpenQuery() function, respectively. Both offer the administrative benefit of pre-defined links, making the query more robust if the server configuration changes.

The decision between the four-part name and OpenQuery() will depend on the amount of data, the selection of data, and the performance of the server. I would recommend that you test both methods and compare the query execution plans to determine the one that works best in your situation with your data. If both are similar, then use the four-part name to enable SQL Server to automatically optimize the distributed query.

## OpenQuery()

For pass-through queries, the OpenQuery() function leverages a linked server, so it's the easiest to develop. It also handles changes in server configuration without changing the code.

The OpenQuery() function is used within the SQL DML statement as a table. The function accepts only two parameters, the name of the linked server and the pass-through query. The next query uses OpenQuery() to retrieve data from the CHA1_Schedule Excel spreadsheet:

```
SELECT *
  FROM OPENQUERY(CHA1_Schedule,
    'SELECT * FROM Tour WHERE Tour = "Gauley River Rafting"')
```

Result:

```
Tour                         Base Camp
---------------------------- ----------------------------
Gauley River Rafting         Ashville
Gauley River Rafting         Ashville
```

As demonstrated in Figure 18-8, the OpenQuery() pass-through query requires almost no processing by SQL Server. The Remote Scan returns exactly two rows to SQL Server. The where clause is executed by the Jet engine as it reads from the Excel spreadsheet.

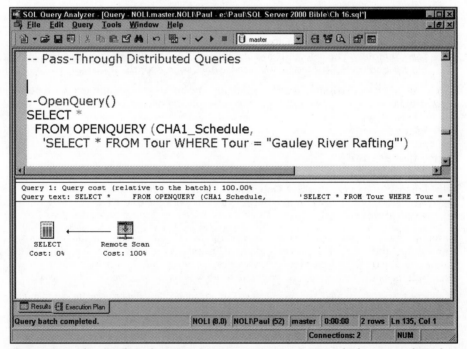

**Figure 18-8:** The distributed query using OpenQuery() returns only the rows selected by the where clause.

In the next example, the `OpenQuery()` requests from Jet engine that it extract only the two rows requiring the update. The actual `update` operation is performed in SQL Server, and the result written back to the external dataset. In effect, the pass-through query is only performing the `select` portion of the `update` command:

```
UPDATE OPENQUERY(CHA1_Schedule,
  'SELECT * FROM Tour WHERE Tour = "Gauley River Rafting"')
  SET [Base Camp] = 'Ashville'
  WHERE Tour = 'Gauley River Rafting'
```

### OpenRowSet()

The `OpenRowSet()` function is the pass-through counterpart to the `OpenDataSet()` function. Both require the remote data source to be fully specified in the distributed query. `OpenRowSet()` adds a parameter to specify the pass-through query.

```
SELECT ContactFirstName, ContactLastName
  FROM OPENROWSET ('Microsoft.Jet.OLEDB.4.0',
  'C:\SQLServerBible\CHA1_Customers.mdb'; 'Admin';'',
  'SELECT * FROM Customers WHERE CustomerID = 1')
```

Result:

```
ContactFirstName    ContactLastName
------------------- ----------------------
Tom                 Mercer
```

To perform an update using the `OpenRowSet()` function, use the function in place of the table being modified. The following code sample modifies the customer's last name in an Access database. The `where` clause of the `update` command is handled by the pass-through portion of the `OpenRowSet()` function:

```
UPDATE OPENROWSET ('Microsoft.Jet.OLEDB.4.0',
  'C:\SQLServerBible\CHA1_Customers.mdb'; 'Admin';'',
  'SELECT * FROM Customers WHERE CustomerID = 1')
  SET ContactLastName = 'Wilson'
```

## Distributed Transactions

Transactions are key to data integrity. If the logical unit of work includes modifying data outside the local SQL server, a standard transaction is unable to handle the atomicity of the transaction. If a failure should occur in the middle of the transaction, a mechanism must be in place to roll back the partial work, or else a partial transaction will be recorded and the database will be left in an inconsistent state.

**Cross-Reference**

Chapter 11, "Transactional Integrity," explores how SQL Server performs transactions and the underlying ACID properties of the database.

SQL Server uses the Distributed Transaction Coordinator (DTC) to handle multiple server transactions, commits, and rollbacks. The DTC service uses a two-phase commit scheme for multiple server transactions. The two-phase commit ensures that every server is available and handling the transaction by performing the following steps:

1. Each server is sent a "prepare to commit" message.

2. Each server performs the first phase of the commit, ensuring that it is capable of committing the transaction.

3. Each server replies when it has finished preparing for the commit.

4. Only after every participating server has responded positively to the "prepare to commit" message is the actual commit message sent to each server.

If the logical unit of work only involves reading from the external SQL server, the DTC is not required. Only when remote updates are occurring is a transaction considered a distributed transaction.

## Distributed Transaction Coordinator

The Distributed Transaction Coordinator is a separate service from SQL Server. DTC is started or stopped with the SQL Server Service Manager.

Only one instance of DTC runs per server regardless of how many SQL Server instances may be installed or running on that server. The actual service name is msdtc.exe and it consumes only about 2.5MB of memory.

DTC must be running when a distributed transaction is initiated or the transaction will fail.

## Developing Distributed Transactions

Distributed transactions are similar to local transactions with a few extensions to the syntax:

```
SET xact_abort on
BEGIN DISTRIBUTED TRANSACTION
```

In case of error, the xact_abort connection option will cause the current transaction, rather than only the current T-SQL statement, to be rolled back. The xact_abort on option is required for any distributed transactions accessing a remote SQL server and for most other OLE DB connections as well.

The begin distributed transaction command, which determines whether the DTC service is available, is not strictly required. If a transaction is initiated with only begin tran, the transaction is escalated to a distributed transaction and DTC is checked as soon as a distributed query is executed. It's considered a better practice to use begin distributed transaction so that DTC is checked at the beginning of the transaction. When DTC is not running, an 8501 error is raised automatically:

```
Server: Msg 8501, Level 16, State 3, Line 7
MSDTC on server 'NOLI' is unavailable.
```

The following example demonstrates a distributed transaction between the local SQL Server and the second instance:

```
USE Family
SET xact_abort on
BEGIN DISTRIBUTED TRANSACTION
```

```
UPDATE Person
  SET LastName = 'Johnson2'
  WHERE PersonID = 10

UPDATE [Noli\SQL2].Family.dbo.Person
  SET LastName = 'Johnson2'
  WHERE PersonID = 10

COMMIT TRANSACTION
```

Rolling back a nested SQL Server local transaction rolls back all pending transactions. However, DTC uses true nested transactions, and rolling back a DTC transaction will roll back only the current transaction.

## Monitoring Distributed Transactions

As a separate service, Distributed Transaction Coordinator activity can be viewed from within the Windows operating system by means of opening Control Panel ⇨ Administrative Tools ⇨ Component Services. Component Services provides both a list of current pending distributed transactions (Figure 18-9) and an overview of DTC statistics (Figure 18-10).

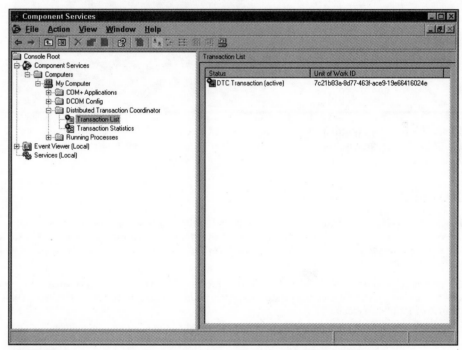

**Figure 18-9:** Component Services includes a list of current DTC transactions.

If a distributed transaction is having difficulty, it will likely be aborted. However, if the transaction is marked "In Doubt," forcibly committing, aborting, or forgetting the transaction using the right-click menu in Component Services may resolve the transaction.

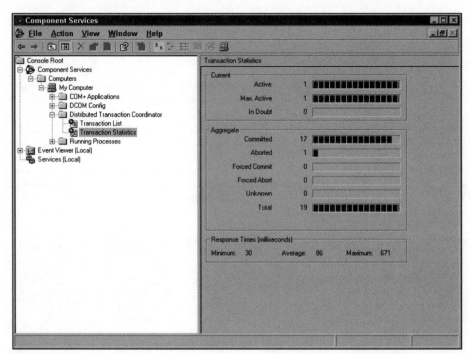

**Figure 18-10:** The current and accumulated count of distributed transactions as viewed in Component Services. The statistics begin at 0 when DTC is restarted.

# Summary

Large database applications data tend to involve multiple platforms and locations. SQL Server's ability to leverage OLE DB and ODBC to perform distributed queries is a key factor in the success of many database projects, and knowing how to build distributed queries well is a necessary component in the DBA's skill set.

Beyond moving data directly with distributed queries, SQL Server includes an amazing tool designed specifically for complex data migration tasks. The next chapter introduces Data Transformation Services (DTS).

✦　　✦　　✦

# Migrating Data with DTS

**D**ata Transformation Services, affectionately called DTS, is a database developer's dream. It can move data from anywhere to anywhere and clean up the data in the process. While technically there's nothing that DTS does that some creative T-SQL and distributed queries can't do, comparing DTS to a distributed query script is like comparing Sarah Hughes' Salt Lake City Olympic–gold-medal figure-skating presentation to a junior-league hockey game. If any other company owned DTS it would be the flagship product instead of a feature tacked onto another product.

DTS is usually used to move data into SQL Server, although it can easily move data between nearly any data sources. DTS could be used to migrate data from dBASE to FoxPro.

In a nutshell, DTS is a graphical means of connecting to various data sources and defining how to move data. With a graphic diagram or a short script, the data can be manipulated, tested, or transformed during the move. DTS also includes most of the administrative tasks required by scheduled data migrations, including FTP, e-mail, and logging. All of these features make DTS an ideal tool for the following tasks:

- ✦ Data conversion and migration tasks
- ✦ Merging data from dissimilar data sources
- ✦ Data warehouse Extract Transform Load (ETL) tasks
- ✦ Data schema upgrades and conversions
- ✦ Scheduled data collections from other data sources

As evidence of its versatility, the SQL Server team leverages DTS in the SQL Server wizards. The Copy Database Wizard and the import/export wizards actually create and execute DTS packages. One way to get a jumpstart in DTS is to run one of these wizards and then explore the DTS package it creates.

Although it's incorporated with SQL Server, Data Transformation Services is complex and broad enough to be considered a separate tool. Because of this, the developing and programming DTS packages topic could easily consume several hundred pages if it were to dig deeply into DTS. But the purpose of this chapter is to present a survey of DTS and explain the commonly used tasks.

**Note**    The Web site `http://www.sqldts.com/` is dedicated to Data Transformation Services tips and solutions. I recommend it as a resource.

# The DTS Designer

DTS solutions are constructed as self-contained DTS packages built within Enterprise Manger. A DTS connection can connect to any database, so a DTS package belongs to the server, not to any particular database.

To create a new DTS package or open an existing one, open the Data Transformation Services node in Enterprise Manager. The Local Packages node lists the available DTS packages. Use the Action menu or right-click menu to create a new DTS package.

DTS packages are developed by means of a separate DTS Designer window, shown in Figure 19-1, which includes the Connection and Task dockable toolbars. (To re-dock a floating toolbar, use the right-click menu on the toolbar's toolbar.)

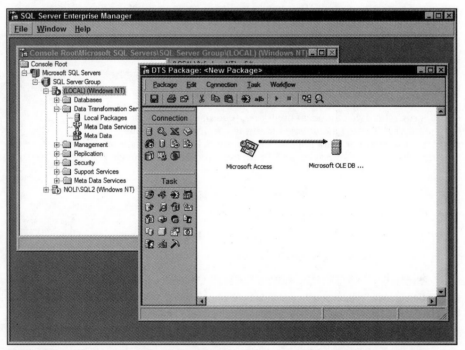

**Figure 19-1:** The Data Transformation Services Designer within Enterprise Manager.

The Connection toolbar lists the available connection objects including SQL Server, Access, Excel, dBase 5, HTML, Paradox 5, text files, and the Microsoft ODBC driver for Oracle. In addition, two connection types are available. The Microsoft Data Link and Other Connection objects can be used for other installable drivers, including XML. The connections are also available from the Connection menu.

The Task toolbar and the Task menu, include 19 key data-conversion tasks. The two most common tasks are Transform Data and Execute SQL.

A complete DTS package will likely have a few dozen connections and tasks, and DTS will execute multiple tasks simultaneously when executing the package. This could be a problem if some of the data must be transformed before other data. A primary table and secondary table present an example of this kind of problem. The primary data must be loaded before the secondary table's data or the secondary table's foreign key will block the `insert`.

To solve this problem, the workflow and the order of precedence (including the next task based on the completion, success, or failure of the previous task) may be specified.

# DTS Package Properties

The DTS Package Properties dialog is opened within the DTS workspace by means of the Package ➪ Properties menu command or the associated toolbar command. The DTS Package Properties dialog box (Figure 19-2) presents the package name and version information, including the creation date, and offers three editable options.

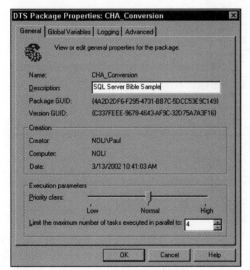

**Figure 19-2:** The DTS Package Properties dialog box sets several behaviors for the package.

The General tab in the DTS Package Properties dialog may also be used to set the Windows execution priority for the package and the maximum number of parallel tasks. I do not typically adjust these values.

DTS global variables are created in the Global Variables tab. The Logging tab sets up activity logs and error handling for the DTS package. The Advanced tab includes metadata options such as enabling lineage columns and setting metadata object-scanning options. Transaction integrity is also set in the Advanced tab.

# Connecting to Data

The first step in developing a DTS package is creating a connection to either the data source and the data destination. To add a connection to a package, click on the connection type in the Connection toolbar or drag the connection type from the Connection toolbar to the workspace. The Connection dialog box will ask for the appropriate location and authentication information required to establish the data connection.

Most DTS packages will connect to SQL Server. Using the SQL Server Connection Properties dialog box (Figure 19-3) is similar to creating a linked server or registering a server in Enterprise Manager.

DTS connection security can be quite complicated. It depends on where the package is executed. If the package runs as a job, it uses the authentication of the SQL Server Agent. If a user executes the package manually from a workstation, it uses the authentication of the user (assuming the connection properties are using NT authentication).

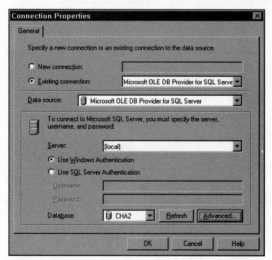

**Figure 19-3:** The SQL Server Connection Properties dialog box establishes the server, database, and authentication context for the connection.

Once the connection is created, DTS can access the data with the security restrictions of the login used in the connection.

**On the CD-ROM** The Cape Hatteras Adventures data was stored in Access and Excel prior to being moved to SQL Server. The CHA_Conversion DTS package connects to the Access CHA_Customer.mdb files and the CHA_Schadule.xls file. (The DTS package assumes the files are in the C:\SQLServerBible directory.) The data is then transformed into the CHA2 SQL Server database.

Note: The DTS Open Package command is in the right-mouse menu under Data Transformation Services.

With DTS connections, the locations and user login are hard-coded into the connection object. As DTS packages are moved from one server to another, the connections will often break. If you use (local) as the server name for SQL Server, a package that is moved from one server to another will still connect to the (local) server.

**Note** Connection user IDs and logins can be a problem with DTS packages that are moved to different servers. One solution is to use the Dynamic Properties Task to modify the connection properties at runtime.

# Transformations

The real work is done with transformation tasks, which move data from one data connection to another. Transformations are powerful; they can merge and twist data, perform lookups and replace data, or even run scripts to perform complex transformations.

Adding the Transform Data Task to the workspace from either the Task menu or the toolbar creates a transformation-task object, which appears as a gray line from the source connection to the destination connection. Creating a Transform Data Task requires two clicks — one for the source connection and one for the destination connection. If a source connection is already selected, only the destination connection is required. The result is a transformation line from the source connection to the destination connection, as shown in Figure 19-4. Two connections would have multiple transformations if several data sets are moved between the connections.

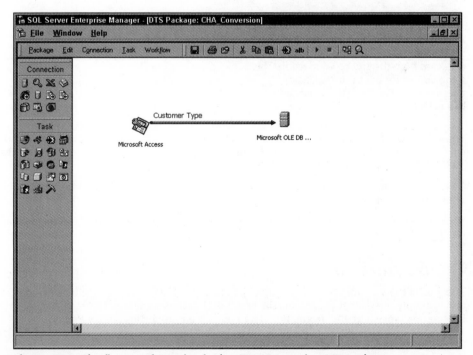

**Figure 19-4:** The first transformation in the CHA_Conversion DTS package.

The Transformation Task Properties dialog is opened by means of double-clicking the transformation-task line. The five tabs are in the same order as the process of setting up a transformation.

## The Source

The Source tab (Figure 19-5) defines the data to be extracted from the source connection.

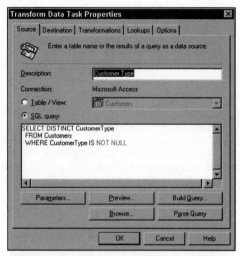

**Figure 19-5:** The Transform Task Properties'
Source tab determines how the data is
extracted from the source connection. This
is the source for the Customer Type
transformation in the CHA_Conversion
DTS package.

The source can be a single table or view in the source connection, or an ad hoc query typed into the Properties dialog. For testing purposes, the query can be executed and the results displayed by means of the Browse button.

Often, a key factor in the success of a DTS data migration project is the ability to carefully select the clean data. Building the source query is a good opportunity to filter out bad data.

The Build Query button opens a variation of the Query Designer in which to visually assemble the SQL query.

## The Destination

The goal of the transformation is to move data into the destination connection. The destination is simply the table that receives the result of the transformation. Figure 19-6 shows the Destination tab, where the destination data connection properties are configured.

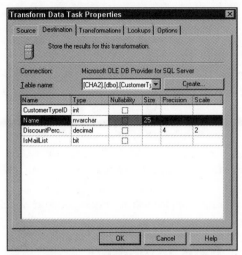

**Figure 19-6:** The Destination tab sets the table to receive the transformed data and displays the schema of the destination table.

## The Transformation

Once the source and destination are defined, the Transformations tab (Figure 19-7) may be used to match or link the columns from the data source to the destination. This transformation accepts a distinct list of customers from the CHA_Customers Access database and inserts the list into the Customer table in CHA2 SQL Server database. The transformations align the columns between the source and destination. The CustomerType transformation uses an ActiveX script and a lookup to convert from the CustomerType name to the CustomerTypeID.

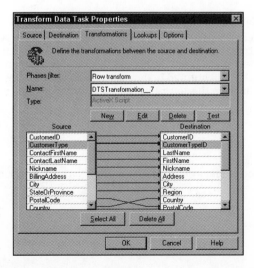

**Figure 19-7:** The Transformations tab sends data from a source column to a destination column.

To transform a column, click and drag the column from the source-column list to the destination-column list as shown in Figure 19-7. (The click-and-drag is a little buggy; you have to click the actual text of the column name, not the space to the right of the name.) A column transformation can be one of the following:

✦ *Copy column* is the most common type of transformation. Multiple columns may be moved in a single transformation, so moving nine columns doesn't necessarily require nine transformations.

✦ *DateTime string, Lowercase string, middle of string, trim string,* and *uppercase string* are all similar to a copy column transformation, but each adds some type of data conversion.

✦ *Read file* and *write file* imports or exports data, respectively, to a file specified within the source column.

✦ *ActiveX script* executes an ActiveX script for complex transformations that can include logic or data lookups.

# Lookups and ActiveX Script Transformations

Simply moving data from one table to another is a straightforward task. Often, however, the data must be modified in the transformation. A transformation can call a lookup from a script and replace a value from the source dataset with a value from the lookup. A common example is migrating data from a flat-file schema to a relational schema and converting a value to a foreign key.

The CHA_Conversion DTS package includes several transformations that include lookups and ActiveX scripts. The customer's customer type is stored as the name of the customer type in the Access database, but is stored as a foreign key integer value in the SQL Server schema. The transformation has to convert the CustomerTypeName into the correct integer.

## The Lookup

The initial step in the process is to define a lookup for the transformation using the Lookups tab, as shown in Figure 19-8.

The Query Builder button (the ellipsis on the right side of the lookup grid) opens a variation of the Query Designer, which is used to define a valid query from any connection. The query needs to accept a value from the source list and return the value that will be inserted in the destination. The input parameter is handled by a ? placeholder, and the returned column in the select statement is the value that will be substituted in the destination. In the following example, the customer-type name is read in from the source list and is replaced by the CustomerTypeID returned by the query:

```
SELECT CustomerTypeID
  FROM CustomerType
 WHERE (Name = ?)
```

The Cache value in the Lookup tab sets the number of query results DTS can cache during execution to improve performance.

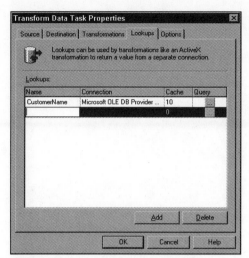

**Figure 19-8:** The Transform Data Task Properties' Lookups tab determines how the source data is compared to lookup data and transformed to a relating value.

## The ActiveX Script

One of the transformation types is the ActiveX transformation. This type can use either VBA or Java ActiveX scripts to test and manipulate the data as it's read by DTS. The script's logic can decide what data is inserted into the destination dataset or even whether the row is passed on to the destination.

The script is actually built within the ActiveX Script Transformation Properties page, as shown in Figure 19-9.

In the `CHA_Converison` sample DTS package the `CustomerType` transformation script is executed for every row from the source. The destination is populated from the `DTSLookups` function. The function calls the `CustomerName` lookup query and passes the `CustomerType` source column to the lookup. The return from the lookup is then sent to the `CustomerTypeID` column in the `DTSDestination`.

```
'*******************************************************
'  Visual Basic Transformation Script
'*******************************************************
'  Copy each source column to the destination column
Function Main()
   DTSDestination("CustomerTypeID") =
     DTSLookups("CustomerName")
     .Execute(DTSSource("CustomerType"))
  Main = DTSTransformStat_OK
End Function
```

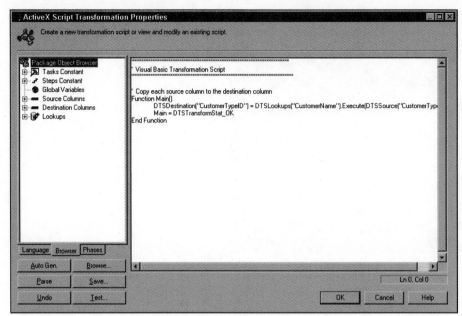

**Figure 19-9:** The Transform Task's script is created on the ActiveX Script Transformation Properties page, which is opened by means of double-clicking the transformation line.

This script scratches the surface of the possibilities of VBA scripting within DTS. Using scripts, DTS transformations can perform complex data scrubbing, error checking, and data validation.

## Transformation Options

For each individual transformation, the Options tab (Figure 19-10) determines how DTS handles errors. If a row is not accepted by the destination, DTS can log the row to the exception file. The format and details of the data written to the file may be customized with the file-type and format options.

The Data Movement portion of the Options tab determines how many errors may occur before the transformation task fails. The bottom third of the Options tab sets insert options for the destination connection.

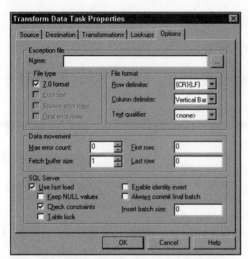

**Figure 19-10:** The Transform Data Task Properties' Option tab determines how file formats, data exceptions, and SQL Server connection configurations are handled.

# Other DTS Tasks

Without question, the transformation task is the meat and potatoes of DTS, but the additional DTS tasks give DTS an advantage over T-SQL distributed-query batches.

## SQL Server Transfer Tasks

Several DTS tasks serve SQL Server as means of transferring SQL Server objects and databases from one server to another. The Copy Database Wizard creates a DTS package that uses these tasks:

✦ Transfer Error Messages

✦ Transfer Master Stored Procedures

✦ Transfer Jobs

✦ Transfer Logins

✦ Transfer Databases

✦ Copy SQL Server Objects

## Messaging Tasks

So that DTS can notify DBAs of any issues or error, the following two messaging tasks may be added to a DTS package:

✦ *Message Queue* — If message queuing is installed on the server, this task can leverage that service.

✦ *Send Mail* — Standard e-mail using MAPI is sent by means of this task. This task is different from the SQL Agent Mail, which can only send mail to defined operators.

## Data Transfer Tasks

DTS is often used to move data among various locations. To do this it uses the following tasks:

✦ *FTP* — The FTP task establishes the FTP connection as would any other FTP tool (Figure 19-11). The Files tab is used to set up a list of files to upload or download. This task is extremely useful for managing data transfers over the Internet. If DTS handles the FTP transfer, then DTS can respond to the transfer's completed, successful, or failure status. If the FTP transfer fails, DTS can log the problem and even generate an e-mail.

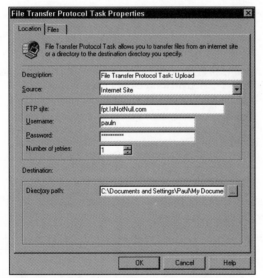

**Figure 19-11:** The FTP Task is extremely useful for sharing data files over the Internet.

✦ *Bulk Insert* — The Bulk Insert Task simply executes bulk copy — SQL Server's built-in means of rapidly receiving data from a text file. The location of the source text file and the file-formatting options are set in the Task Properties dialog.

## DTS Processing Tasks

DTS is often used to automate batch process within a database environment. To facilitate that, DTS include several tasks that are geared toward executing processes:

✦ *Execute SQL* — The Execute SQL task returns to the familiar Transact-SQL environment and submits a T-SQL batch to SQL Server (Figure 19-12). I find the Execute SQL task useful for purging data at the beginning of a repeatable data conversion and performing SQL queries on the data after it's moved into SQL Server.

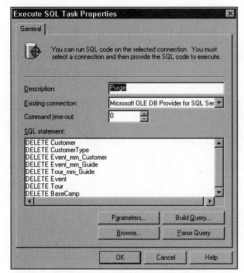

**Figure 19-12:** The Execute SQL Task Properties dialog box.

✦ *Execute Package* — This task launches another DTS package.

✦ *Execute Process* — This task executes another external Windows program.

✦ *Data Driven Query* — Similar to the standard transformation task, this variation can reference additional queries from the script.

✦ *Dynamic Properties* — With this task DTS global variables may be dynamically set at runtime from an .ini file, query result, or other variable by means of the Dynamic Properties Task.

## Data Warehousing Tasks

✦ *Analysis Services Processing Task* — Analysis Services cubes can be processed by this task. It allows DTS to serve as an Extract-Transform-Load (ETL) component of a complete decision support service (DSS) solution by importing the data and then signaling Data Analysis Services to update the cubes. Very cool.

✦ *Data Mining Prediction* — If a data-mining model is predefined in Data Analysis Services, this task can reference that model and create a data-mining prediction result.

# Workflow Precedence

Rare is the DTS package that uses only a few tasks. Most DTS packages involve a complex maze of a few dozen tasks. The order of execution becomes critical in preventing errors.

DTS precedence includes the following options to control workflow:

✦ On Completion (blue)

✦ On Success (green)

✦ On Failure (red)

To establish a workflow order, select the first and second task and then choose the workflow type in the workflow menu. To include a transformation task in the workflow choose the source connection of the transformation. Figure 19-13 shows an On Completion workflow connector between the Purge task and the Access data source connection object.

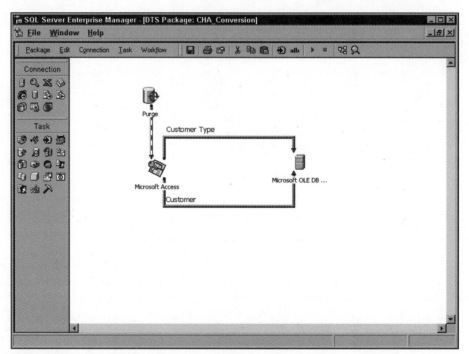

**Figure 19-13:** The Workflow Connector determines that the Execute SQL task must complete before the transformation tasks from Access can begin.

Workflow can also be established by means of the Workflow Properties command in the task's right-click menu.

# Executing the DTS Package

Microsoft is generous in the variety of methods that immediately execute and schedule the execution of DTS packages. To execute a DTS package, use any of the following methods:

✦ During development and testing, highlight the task and select Execute Step from the right-click menu to execute specific tasks.

✦ Within the DTS package workspace, click on the green Run button in the toolbar, or select the Package ⇨ Execute menu command.

✦ From the Enterprise Manager Console, select the package in the local DTS package list and choose Execute Package from the Action menu or the right-click menu.

✦ From within a DTS package, add an Execute Package task to the package. Global variables may be passed between the outer and the called package.

✦ From a Windows command prompt, use the dtsrun or dtsrunui command. The /? parameter will display all the possible parameters. If no parameters are provided, a dialog will appear to execute the DTS package.

✦ From within a T-SQL batch or stored procedure, use the xp_cmdshell system stored procedure to execute the dtsrun command-line utility to launch a DTS package.

DTS packages may be scheduled by means of any of the following methods:

✦ In the Enterprise Manager Console, selecting the package to schedule, and using the Schedule Package command in the Action menu or the right-click menu. The standard SQL Server scheduling dialog will appear to set up the schedule. It will create a SQL Server Agent job that executes the package using dtsrun.

✦ Using the dtsrunui command to schedule the DTS package to run as a reoccurring SQL Agent job.

✦ Manually creating a SQL Server Agent job using the dtsrun command.

# Saving and Moving DTS Packages

The simple Package ⇨ Save menu command saves the package to the local server using the SQL Server format. Packages stored using the SQL Server format are listed in the Local Packages node under Data Transformation Services node in the Enterprise Manager console tree.

The Package ⇨ Save As command offers several other formats and options, as shown in Figure 19-14.

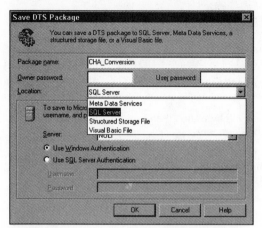

**Figure 19-14:** The Save DTS Package dialog, opened from the Package ➪ Save As menu command, may be used to specify the location to store the DTS package to.

A DTS package may be saved in one of four formats:

✦ *SQL Server* — This method saves the package to the `sysdtspackages` table in the MSDB database inside any registered SQL Server. If the servers are registered, this is the easiest way to move a DTS package to another server. To move a package to a server that isn't registered, use the Structured Storage File option.

✦ *Meta Data Services* — This advanced method enables tracking of the data that has been changed using DTS.

✦ *Structured Storage File* — This method enables a file to be copied to another SQL Server and then opened on another server. Be careful about SQL Server versions and service packs. There's no guarantee that DTS packages saved to a Structured Storage File can be retrieved by SQL Server 2000 instances with different service-pack levels.

To open a package that's been saved using the Structured Storage File format, use the DTS Open Package command in the right-click menu under Data Transformation Services node in the Enterprise Manager console tree.

✦ *Visual Basic File* — This option actually generates a VB script to perform the same tasks as the SQL Server DTS package.

If the package has been saved using the Package ➪ Save As command, the Package ➪ Save command uses same format and location choices as the last Save As command.

# Deltas and Versions

A nice feature of Data Transformation Services is the way it handles changes to DTS packages. Each save is stored as a new version in a continuous list of versions.

The saved versions of any package may be viewed within Enterprise Manager by means of selecting the DTS package from the list of local packages and selecting Action ⇨ Versions or right-click menu ⇨ Versions. The DTS Package Versions dialog, shown in Figure 19-15, displays the version date and description.

**Figure 19-15:** The DTS Package Versions dialog lists all the saved versions of the package for editing or deleting.

Using the DTS Package Versions dialog you can purge or open previous versions for editing. To revert to a previous version as the current version, open the previous version for editing and use the Package ⇨ Save As menu command to save the package using a new name.

# Summary

I'm glad that Microsoft includes Data Transformation Services within SQL Server 2000. I regularly use it as a data-connectivity tool in my database projects. Any database developer, using any database product, would be wise to consider using DTS for data-migration projects.

The next chapter continues the data connectivity theme by introducing database replication, which keeps the data in multiple locations in sync.

✦　　✦　　✦

# Replicating Databases

**R**eplication is basically the automatic migration of data from one server to another. Replication can perform many tasks:

✦ Pushing data one way to remote locations.

✦ Synchronizing mobile users.

✦ Updating a server reserved for queries and reports.

✦ Sharing data between servers in various parts of the world.

✦ Synchronizing a sales server and a production server.

Database replication has a mixed reputation. While some developers are successful with replication, others find it a nightmare. In my experience, replication works well when SQL Server 2000 is running on a clean server. However, when the replication configuration or database schema is repeatedly altered, then replication becomes less stable.

Replicating data merely means duplicating changes from one database to another. While SQL Server includes the stored procedures and interfaces to perform replication among multiple servers, this is not the only way to replicate data. Dave Catherman, a database developer, has developed a send-and-forward method of replication that uses e-mail to perform merge replication. I suspect that future replication methods will use XML. However, unless you can justify recreating the wheel, I suggest trying SQL Server's built-in replication first.

You can move data from one server to another in several ways other than SQL Server Replication:

✦ With the Bulk Copy utility (bcp)

✦ With the Data Transformation Services (DTS)

✦ By backing up and restoring a database

✦ With the Database Copy Wizard

✦ With distributed transactions using two-phase commit within custom-written stored procedures

Each will accomplish replication to various degrees and with more or fewer features. Depending on the frequency of the synchronization and how much data needs be transferred, any one of these techniques may be a simpler alternative to SQL Server replication. SQL Server's replication is a good choice when you want flexibility in which data is being copied and synchronization is a regularly scheduled process as opposed to an occasional export/import scenario.

# Replication Concepts

SQL Server replication operates according to a publishing metaphor and includes three agents—a distributor, a publisher, and a subscriber:

1. **Distributor:** To establish a publishing industry the first requirement is an established method of distributing the publication.

2. **Publication:** With a distribution method in place, the publisher can place content within the publication.

3. **Subscriber:** When the distributor and the publisher make the publication available, subscribers can subscribe to the publication.

In keeping with the publishing metaphor, three SQL Server servers cooperate to replicate data: the publisher, the distributor, and the subscriber server.

**Best Practice**

A single server can serve as both the publisher and the distributor and even as the subscriber. An excellent configuration for experimenting with replication is a server with multiple SQL Server instances. However, when performance is an issue, a dedicated distributor server is the best plan.

The publisher server organizes multiple articles (an article is a data source; a single table, view, function, or stored procedure) into a publication. The distributor server manages the replication process. The publisher can initiate the subscription and push data to the subscriber server, or the subscriber can set up the subscription and pull the subscription from the publisher.

# Transactional Consistency

The measure of transactional consistency is the degree of synchronization between two replicated servers. As the lag time between synchronizations increases, transactional consistency decreases. If the data is identical on both servers most of the time, transactional consistency is said to be high. A replication system that passes changes every two weeks by e-mail has low transactional consistency.

There is no perfect level of transactional consistency. The ideal level of transactional consistency depends on the client requirements balanced with both the monetary cost and the performance cost of performing the synchronization.

# Replication Types

SQL Server offers three basic types of data replication with a few variations:

✦ *Snapshot*—A one-way replication. Taking a snapshot is effectively the same as pushing a complete backup to the remote server.

✦ *Transactional*—Each transaction is synchronized between the servers. Using transactional data replication is conceptually somewhat similar to applying transaction-log backups to a snapshot.

✦ *Merge*—The data changes in each server are tracked and blended together, allowing changes to be made on any server participating in the merge replication.

Table 20-1 compares the multiple methods of synchronizing databases and the relative latency (delay between synchronization) and transactional consistency (synchronization of the data) each provides.

### Table 20-1: Data Sharing Methods

| Shared Data Method | Description | Transactional Consistency | Subscriber Independence |
|---|---|---|---|
| **Snapshot Replication** | The published data is moved from the publisher to the subscriber and overwrites any data on the subscriber. This replication method is similar to a scheduled backup and restore, but it provides the ability to limit the scope of the published data. | Typically low, depending on the synchronization schedule, which is commonly infrequent because of the need to replace all the data on the subscriber each time, which limits the frequency of synchronization. | High, because synchronization is infrequent so subscribers can operate even if the publisher is unavailable. |
| **Merge Replication** | Data changes from both the publisher and the subscriber are periodically synchronized. Any data conflicts are handled with rules and a conflict manager. | Typically low, depending on the synchronization schedule, but because only the changes to the data need to be transmitted each time (rather than all the data), synchronization may occur more often than with snapshot replication. However, a risk of data conflicts does exist with this method. | Highest, because changes can be made on the publisher or any subscriber at any time without a distributed transaction and the changes merged together in the future. |
| **Snapshot Replication with Immediate Updating Subscribers** | Similar to snapshot replication, except that a subscriber may update its local copy as well as the copy on the publisher through a distributed transaction. | Medium, depending on the synchronization schedule, but local changes are immediately reflected on the subscriber making the change. Other subscribers' changes are not seen until the next synchronization. | Medium, depending on the frequency of updates. Retrieval operations are highly independent, but updates require publisher availability for a distributed transaction. |

*Continued*

**Table 20-1** *(continued)*

| Shared Data Method | Description | Transactional Consistency | Subscriber Independence |
|---|---|---|---|
| *Transactional Replication* | Transactions are sent from the publisher to the subscriber. This is not a distributed two-phase commit transaction. The transaction is completed on the publisher and is then routed to the subscriber. | Medium; data may be synchronized more frequently or even immediately depending on the speed and availability of the network connection between the publisher and the subscriber. | Low, because the frequency of synchronization is typically high and this type of replication is generally used inside a good network environment. |
| *Transactional Replication with Immediate Updating Subscribers* | Similar to transactional replication, but subscribers can make immediate changes to their local copies through distributed transactions. Other subscribers see these changes on the next synchronization. | High; data is synchronized almost immediately as long as the servers are connected, but only between the publisher and the subscriber making the change. | Lowest; servers have virtually no independence because of the frequency of transactional posting and need for a distributed transaction to make any changes. |

# Configuring Replication

Using wizards is the simplest way to implement replication. Developers and DBAs generally avoid wizards because they have limited features, but implementing replication without wizards requires numerous calls to arcane stored procedures and is a tedious and painful process prone to user errors.

## Creating a Publisher and Distributor

The initial configuration step is to run the Configure Publishing and Distribution Wizard. The wizard is located in the list of wizards opened from Tools ➪ Wizards menu or the Wizards button on the toolbar.

Key decisions while running the wizard include:

✦ Whether the publisher will also serve as its own distributor, or whether to configure a separate (pre-setup) distribution server.

✦ Which folder will be used to store snapshot files.

✦ What the name of the distribution database will be (if you choose Advanced Options).

✦ If non-default settings are chosen, then you will have to configure multiple publishing servers, configure individual databases for transaction or merge replication, and configure servers as potential subscribers.

✦ You must also make sure to configure the startup account for your server in order to use a domain account and not the local system account. Otherwise, replication between different servers will fail. If the startup account is not changed, you will be warned when you run the wizard. The same holds true for the SQL Server Agent startup account. In addition, you must make sure that the SQL Server Agent is set to automatically start up on reboot.

Running the wizard is fairly simple and will not produce many surprises. If SQL Server Agent is not configured to start up automatically already, the wizard will ask if you want to configure it this way. Next you are prompted for the directory in which the snapshot files will be stored (Figure 20-1). Create a directory on the distributor and share this folder with a simple name — no spaces and short, so a simple Universal Naming Convention (UNC) name can be used to reference the path instead of relying on the default administrative share to C$.

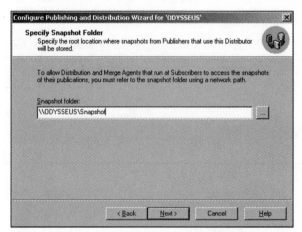

**Figure 20-1:** The snapshot folder using UNC pathname to a shared folder.

If you choose to customize the settings, specify the name and location of the distribution database. Generally it's a good idea to keep the name *distribution;* however, it's OK to specifically locate the database on a drive of your choosing. The distribution database is marked as a system database and will be hidden from Enterprise Manager's view if the registration for that server is configured to hide system databases and tables. It is also possible to enable other publishers to use this server as a distributor, enable merge and transactional replication, and enable subscribers at this time, or these choices can be deferred until later.

Once finished, the wizard will create the distribution database (if this server is the distributor) and enable the publishers and subscribers specified to use this server, and also enable whatever replication agents are necessary for the types of replication specified.

If this sever is the distributor, then you will be notified that because this server is acting as a distributor, the Replication Monitor will be added to the Enterprise Manager tree view. The first time the Replication Monitor is clicked it will inform you that it can be set to automatically refresh. You may select a refresh rate or choose manual refreshes if you wish. These settings can be changed later by right-clicking the Replication Monitor and choosing Refresh Rate and Settings.

## Creating a Publication

Once a distributor is set up for your server, you can make publications. A publication is defined as a collection of articles, where an article is an item to be published. An article in SQL Server can be a table, a view, a user-defined function, or even a stored procedure. Typically tables are published, but views can also be published although there are many pitfalls involved in doing so and unless you are well experienced with replication it is best to avoid this. Publishing stored procedures is useful for transactional replication to reduce the network traffic associated with keeping the subscribers in synch. Publishing stored procedures eliminates the need to log each individual change the procedure makes; instead the server logs that the procedure was called and the identical procedure is called on the subscriber, thereby yielding the same data changes on the subscriber.

To create a publication you can manually type out a series of stored procedure calls or run the Create Publication Wizard (Figure 20-2). Launch the wizard to see a list of all the user databases on the server; expand the branches to see the existing publications in each database. It is possible to modify an existing publication, create a new push subscription for it, remove it, or create a script to recreate it or create a new publication.

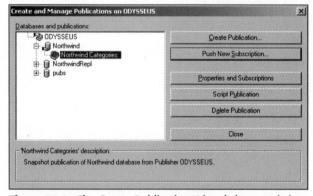

**Figure 20-2:** The Create Publication Wizard shows existing publications and enables the creation of new ones.

Follow the wizard steps and decide whether you want to see the advanced options. Advanced options include *immediate updating subscribers* or *queued updates*. Follow the wizard steps and choose the database for the publication. If there already are publications in that database, use one of them as a template for the new publication, or create the publication from scratch. The next question asks what type of replication you want — snapshot, transactional, or merge. Remember that if you want snapshot or transactional with immediate updating subscribers, you must first choose show advanced options.

Once the wizard is running it presents the following pages:

1. **Subscriber Type page.** The data in the distribution database is saved in different formats according to the checkboxes you select. If only other SQL Servers will be subscribers then the publishing server can save the data in the more efficient internal format, but if heterogeneous servers such as Jet or Oracle are used, the publishing SQL Server must save the data in the less efficient ASCII format.

2. **Articles Published page.** The next page is used to choose which tables, views, user-defined functions, and stored procedures to be published. Several articles (objects) may be combined in a single publication or each article can be an individual publication. The advantage of placing several articles in one publication is that they are all managed on a single schedule. It is possible, however, to have different articles published on different schedules or even to mix snapshot, merge, and transactional replication to serve different business needs. Figure 20-3 shows the dialog box used to select the articles. By default it only lists tables unless you select the checkboxes to show views and stored procedures as well. The Article Defaults button in the lower left-hand corner of this box enables you to specify table properties as well as how conflicts will occur if an article already exists on a subscriber and how indexes, triggers, collations, extended properties, and referential integrity will be carried over to the subscriber.

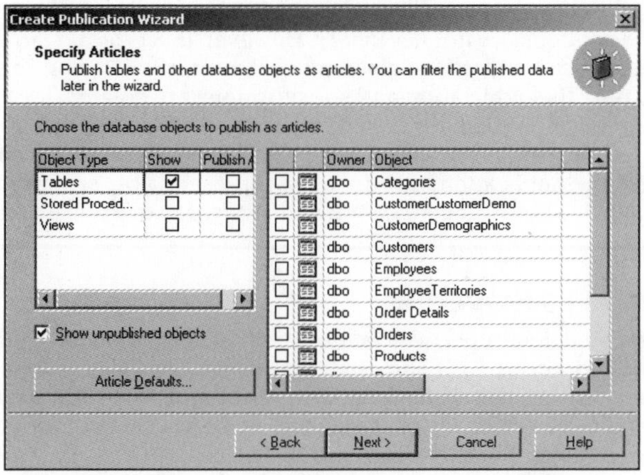

**Figure 20-3:** The Specify Articles dialog of the Create Publication Wizard.

If any problems related to publishing any of the selected articles come up, the next page will enumerate them and suggest ways to resolve them. For example, replicating a table with identity columns can be handled in different ways, depending on whether the subscribers will allow updates or not. The wizard will suggest ways to handle this situation before you enable replication on the article. Then you will be prompted for a name and description of the article.

The last page of the wizard enables you to further customize the publication. If you choose to customize the settings you can create vertical and horizontal partitions, allow for anonymous subscriptions, and/or change the frequency with which the snapshots are refreshed.

## Partitions

Partitions enable you to publish only part of the data from a table. A vertical partition enables you to filter out columns you do not want to publish, and a horizontal partition enables you to filter out rows you do not want to publish. Typically one does not replicate sensitive columns or unnecessary columns. For example, if publishing a list of products, you presumably want to publish only active products. So, create a horizontal partition to filter out inactive products, and hide the column for status altogether because it would be redundant to have a column in which every value is the same in the result set.

Horizontal partitioning can be either *static* or *dynamic*. Static filters make the same set of data available to all subscribers based on some multiple criteria, typically a status column or date. Dynamic filtering enables each subscriber to receive different data based on criteria specific to each server. For example, subscribers in different geographical regions might be set to receive different data. This is set by means of having the subscriber server pass some information back to the publisher. This information is used in the where-clause criteria to determine which rows are passed back to the subscriber. This feature is only available with merge replication.

## Anonymous Subscriptions

Anonymous subscriptions simplify the administrative workload by not requiring that each subscriber server be registered with the publisher. If you have a small number of known subscribers, anonymous subscriptions are not necessary. However, in a typical merge-replication scenario there may be dozens or hundreds of disconnected subscribers using computers that may not be known at the time the publication and subscriptions are created. If each subscriber had to be manually registered before it could receive a publication the situation would be an administrative nightmare. Although anonymous subscriptions can enable an unknown server to receive the publication, this does not represent a big security hole. The subscribers still need to make a network connection and authenticate using either SQL or Windows authentication.

## Modifying a Publication's Properties

Once the publication is created, its properties can be modified by right-clicking on the publication name and choosing Properties. This shows all the options you selected during the creation of the publication as well as a few additional options not available through the wizard. One such useful option is Generate SQL Script, which will write a SQL script to recreate the publication without your having to run the wizard again. This is useful for creating the publication on a test server and then implementing it on a production server, or to create the same publication on multiple servers. Another benefit is to use this item to see all the work you would have had to do if not for the wizard.

The replication information is stored in several system tables in the database that contains the publication. These tables include SysPublications, SysArticles, SysArticleUpdates, and SysSubscriptions, among others. Some replication information is also stored in the distribution database, and the MSDB database contains the jobs that refresh the snapshots and push subscriptions. Once the replication is started it sets up a whole chain of interrelated threads and therefore it's difficult to change the structures of tables, detach databases, or perform other radical operations. Keep in mind all the places both user data and replication configuration data are stored, so you can plan your backup strategy accordingly. It is always a good idea to save a copy of the replication scripts independently of the database backups, just as it is a good idea to keep the scripts you would need to recreate the database.

Because of the tangle that replication creates, modifying tables involved in replication can also get tricky. It is best to plan ahead and not make modifications to tables once replication is in place. One option is to remove the replication on these tables altogether, and then to make the modifications and recreate the replication anew. But if you have a lot of replications in place, this could prove cumbersome. Limited support exists for adding and removing columns to a table involved in replication, but it generally works without a problem.

**Note** SQL Server 2000 supports replicating added and dropped columns through the stored procedures `sp_repladdcolumn` and `sp_repldropcolumn`. Use these stored procedures instead of the usual `alter table add column` command.

# Replication Data

Once the publication is set up, SQL Server is ready to replicate data. The subscribing server can pull the replication or the publisher can push the replication.

## Subscribing to the Publication

Once a publication exists, it's ready for subscribers. The two types of subscriptions are *push* and *pull*.

A push subscription is one in which the publisher determines when to send the updates to the subscribers; a pull subscription is one in which each subscriber determines its own synchronization schedule. Push subscriptions are generally used for centralized administration in systems in which a constant, reliable network connection exists among all the servers. This is typically the type of subscription used in a transactional replication.

Pull subscriptions are more appropriate in networks that have a lot of subscribers, some of whom may not always be available for synchronization at a given time. This kind of subscription is also generally used for merge replication, in which each subscriber is an independent user and synchronizes with the publisher at its own convenience.

Both push and pull subscriptions can be scheduled as jobs or done on demand. The jobs for push subscriptions are stored in the MSDB database of the publisher, and the jobs for pull subscriptions are stored in the MSDB databases of the subscribers.

When a publication is first made, the server does not need to create a snapshot until there are subscribers. When the first subscriber subscribes to the publication, the snapshot agent will create a new snapshot of the publication and then apply it to the subscriber. Thereafter, the snapshots will be updated according to the schedule defined for refreshing them.

**Best Practice** Creating the snapshot is not without its cost. Just like any other read process, the Snapshot Agent must acquire share locks on the articles being read for snapshotting. This can block other update operations resulting in serious performance issues. For this reason it is usually best to prepare the snapshots at a non–peak-usage time. Avoid creating the initial snapshot on a production server when a lot of transactions are occurring. Instead, do all your work on a development server, test it out, and then generate the scripts for the replication and apply them on the production server as a scheduled job in the middle of the night.

# Pushing a Subscription

To create a push subscription on the publisher server, either choose from the wizard's menu or right-click a publication and select Push New Subscription from the menu. Either option will launch the Push Subscription Wizard, which presents the following pages:

1. **Select Subscribers page.** Decide which subscribers you want to push the subscription to. You may select more than one by clicking on each new server name while pressing the Ctrl key. You may select all the servers in a group by picking the group name. The next screen prompts you for the name of the database on the subscriber that will receive the publication.

2. **Subscription Frequency page.** Choose how frequently the subscription is refreshed. *Continuously* means that synchronization occurs immediately after a change is made on the publisher. A moment of latency occurs between the time when the change is committed on the publisher and the time when it is propagated to the subscribers. This type of refreshing is not to be confused with a distributed transaction in which the change is made simultaneously to both servers. So continuously does not mean *simultaneously* or *immediately*, but rather *very quickly*. The other option is to synchronize on a timed schedule. This involves scheduling a job with the SQL Server Agent just as you would schedule a backup job.

3. **Snapshot Agent option.** If the subscribers do not already have a database schema defined that matches the publication, then you must let the Snapshot Agent create the tables for you on the subscriber. It is usually a good idea to let the agent create the initial schema for you so no mismatches occur in the structures; but if you have a mature database, or you need to deploy an application that will later be brought into a replication subscription, then you may want to manually create the schema and skip this step when you actually create the subscription.

**Note**    The system stored procedures `sp_publication_validation` and `sp_article_validation` can test the publication and data integrity. These are very sensitive to the data schema and the way that replication is configured.

When the wizard is done, it has created the subscription. If you checked the option to create the initial snapshot, it will have done that, but not yet applied it to the subscribers. It is the job of the distribution agent to apply the snapshots to the subscribers. To force the initial subscription, go to the Publications branch either in the *publisher* database or under the Replication branch below Management. Choose the publication and the Details panel on the right will show the subscriptions for it. Right-click the subscription and choose Start Synchronizing. This will kick off the distribution agent and populate the subscriber with the initial snapshot. If this fails, it could be because the initial snapshot has not yet been created or has not finished yet. You may need to manually launch the Snapshot Agent or try synchronizing again. If synchronization still fails, delete the subscription and recreate it, or delete the publication and recreate it, and try it all again. Sometimes it is just a simple matter of the synchronization timing being off and recreating the subscription can make it work.

**Note**    No menu item enables you to script the creation of push subscriptions. Instead, when you generate a script for the creation of the publication, the push subscriptions are included at the bottom of the script. Therefore, if you add new subscriptions, just rescript the publication to get the new push subscriptions.

# Pulling a Subscription

A pull subscription is much the same as a push subscription except that it is accomplished on the subscriber server instead of the publisher. You can create a new pull subscription either from the wizards menu or by right-clicking the database and choosing New ➪ Pull Subscriptions. Both will launch the Pull Subscription Wizard. The steps are pretty much the same as those of the Push Subscription Wizard. The information is saved in the subscriber database under a branch called Pull Subscriptions. It is also saved on the publisher and can be seen by means of looking at the publications branch. All the subscriptions, both push and pull, are visible in the details panel on the right.

Pull subscriptions can be scripted separately, unlike push subscriptions. This can be done by right-clicking the subscription at the subscriber server and choosing Generate SQL Script. If you examine one of the scripts, you will notice that some code is to be run on the publisher and some is to be run on the subscriber. Although the subscriber is the server that controls when the actual synchronization occurs, a record of the subscription is kept in the publisher. The following sample from Generate SQL script illustrates this:

```
-- Adding the snapshot pull subscription: PUBLISHER:Northwind:Northwind
Categories

/**** Begin: Script to be run at Subscriber: SUBSCRIBER ****/
use [NorthwindRepl]
GO

exec sp_addpullsubscription @publisher = N'Publisher', @publisher_db =
N'Northwind', @publication = N'Northwind Categories', ...

exec sp_addpullsubscription_agent @publisher = N'Publisher',
@publisher_db = N'Northwind', @publication = N'Northwind Categories',
...
GO

/***** End: Script to be run at Subscriber: SUBSCRIBER *****/

/***** Begin: Script to be run at Publisher: PUBLISHER *****/
use [Northwind]
GO

exec sp_addsubscription @publication = N'Northwind Categories',
@subscriber = N'PUBLISHER', @destination_db = N'NorthwindRepl', ...
GO
/****** End: Script to be run at Publisher: PUBLISHER ******/
```

# Removing Replication

Removing replication manually is nearly impossible. To remove replication from a server, run the Disable Publishing and Distribution Wizard. If this fails to work, try to delete all publications first, and then try running the wizard again. If *this* fails, you may need to rebuild the server and restore your backups of the system and user databases. For this reason it is a good idea to make backups of all your databases, including the system databases, before you first implement replication.

# Replicating to an Access Database

Other databases, such as Access and Oracle, may be subscribers to a SQL Server database. You may use either push or pull subscriptions for these heterogeneous subscribers as well. The following sections will show you how to make a Jet database a subscriber to a SQL Server publication.

## Pushing a Subscription

In order to replicate to an Access Database with a push subscription, you must define the Jet database as a linked server, and run a configuration dialog in Enterprise Manager. You can set up the linked server first, or you can do it from within the dialog box. On the menu, choose Tools ⇨ Replication ⇨ Configuring Publishing, Subscribers, and Distribution. Then create a new subscriber on the Subscribers tab and select Microsoft Jet 4.0 database (Microsoft Access). Choose a name for the linked server and point to the file path of the Jet .mdb file; if there is any security on it, provide the user name and password. (If no security exists just use "admin" as the login and a blank password.) This will create the linked server and enable it as a subscriber. Now that the linked Jet database is enabled as a subscriber, you can create a push subscription to it, just as you would to any registered server.

## Pulling a Subscription

Pulling a subscription to an Access database, or any heterogeneous database is a little trickier than pushing push subscription, but push subscriptions are the more typical type for these databases because of the disconnected nature of an Access application. You need to use the Microsoft Replication ActiveX controls. These are a set of programmable COM (Component Object Model)-based controls that you include in the front-end program that manages the Jet database. (Using these controls is a minor programming effort that is not worth exploring here as it has more to do with programming Access and Visual Basic than it does with replication itself.)

**Note**    The replication controls are available in Access by means of opening a form, clicking the More Controls icon on the toolbar, and scrolling down until you see the Microsoft SQL Replication tools. They are available in Visual Basic by means of adding the controls to the toolbar and dropping them onto a form.

## Access Replication Issues

You need to keep a few issues in mind when replicating to a Jet database. Microsoft Jet 4.0 does not support case-sensitive sort orders, so make sure you do not try to subscribe to a publication created on a case-sensitive SQL Server. In order for the Microsoft ActiveX replication controls to work you must enable anonymous subscriptions. You cannot replicate both transactional and merge publications from the same publication database to a Jet subscriber.

Although it is not very difficult to allow Jet subscribers it is probably best to replace Jet altogether and use the SQL Server MSDE instead.

# Merge Replication Conflict Management

Merge replication is a versatile technique that offers you a great deal of independence while still enabling you to share data among many computers. It even enables the subscribers to make changes to their local copies of the data and upload those changes back to the publisher; the other replication types are all one-way from the publisher to the subscriber.

All this flexibility is not without its costs, however. In order for merge replication to work, you must modify the structure of the tables that will be merge-replicated to include a globally unique identifier (GUID) data-type column. A GUID is a 16-byte hexadecimal number that looks like this: 80F77599-025B-4D97-87B4-30AFD8BDE4FB. A GUID can be generated over and over by each computer on Earth and the same number will never be recreated twice. It is a guaranteed unique value for a row in the table. When you implement merge replication using the wizards, the wizards will automatically modify the published tables to add the GUID column.

Another cost of merge replication is the possibility of data conflicts. With the other replication types the changes are only made on the publisher and then eventually synchronized to the subscribers. The only differences that can occur among the sets of data are caused by the timeliness with which the changes make it to the subscribers. With merge replication, the subscribers can locally change the data on their copies of the database. Also, the publisher may be making changes to the data. Because anyone can change his or her local copy of the data, the possibility does exist of two people changing the same record to different values. This inconsistency is known as a *data conflict*.

When conflicts are detected during the synchronization process, something has to happen to resolve the conflict. After the synchronization, the data on the publisher and subscriber should be the same, so one of the changes has to be rejected in favor of the other. A conflict-resolution logic determines which change is accepted. Various techniques can be used to handle the conflict. One method is to assign different priorities to different servers; in the event of a data conflict, the server with the highest priority wins. Another method is to allow whichever change occurred first to win. It is also possible to configure whether a conflict is tracked at the record or field level. If none of these techniques is acceptable, custom resolution logic may be written and compiled to a DLL.

No matter which technique is used to resolve the conflict, one change will be a winner and the other a loser. The winner is propagated to the publisher and all the subscribers. The loser is kept in a history table so that a manual Q&A process can be used to override the automatic conflict resolution and implement the loser or an altogether different value.

## Creating and Resolving Conflicts

Now take a look at how conflicts are handled by means of creating a merge publication on the Employees table. Remember that this will modify the structure of the table by adding a column called rowguid that is a uniqueidentifier data type. Once the first subscription is initialized you can change values in rows in both the publisher and subscriber copies. Depending on how you set up the publication, a conflict may occur if any change is made to a row by either server, even if the row is in different columns, or if a different change is made to the same column. The second option is the default, but you can edit the publication properties to log a conflict if any change is made to the same row. To do this, right-click a publication and choose Properties. In the lower right-hand corner of the Articles tab of the Properties dialog box, find the Article Defaults button. Choose to modify the table articles, and at the bottom of the General tab you are presented with an option that can be used to determine whether there is a conflict (Figure 20-4).

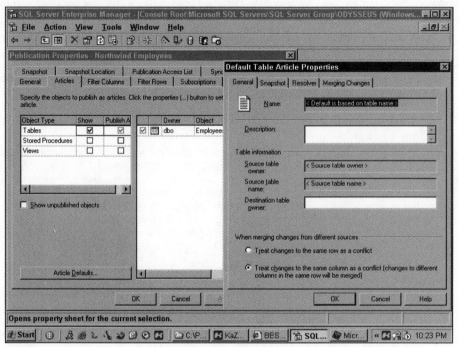

**Figure 20-4:** Use the Publication Properties dialog box to determine when a conflict occurs.

After you make some changes to both the publisher and the subscriber that will result in a conflict, and you synchronize the publication, you will see the last status of the synchronization displayed on the Details panel of the subscriptions for the publication. It will look something like the following:

```
Merged 2 data changes (0 inserts, 2 updates, 0 deletes, 1 resolved
conflicts).
```

The conflicts can now be viewed and manually resolved. If you right-click the subscription and choose the View Conflicts option, a dialog will appear, but it will not show any of the actual conflicts. This is a bug in Enterprise Manager. The proper way to view conflicts is to go to the publisher level, and then to right-click and choose View Conflicts. The same dialog will appear, but this time it will show the actual conflicts. The first screen will show each article and the number of conflicts in parentheses. Click the View button and you will be presented with each conflict, one record at a time (Figure 20-5).

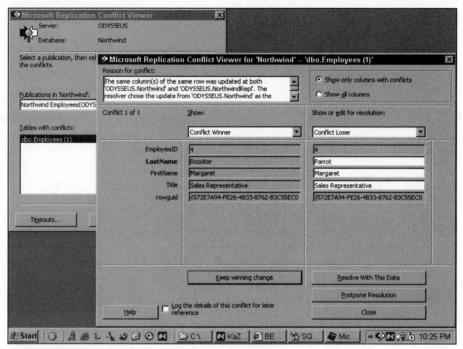

**Figure 20-5:** Resolving conflicts from merge replication.

You will be able to see the values of each conflict's winner and loser and decide how you want to resolve the conflict. You can leave the values as they were automatically resolved, select the loser to become the winner, modify the record with entirely different values, or postpone any resolution and keep the conflict in the list for later resolution. If you make any changes they will occur at the publisher and be propagated to the subscribers during the next synchronization.

You can also write custom interfaces to manually resolve conflicts by using the Microsoft Replication ActiveX controls on a Visual Basic or Access form, so that someone other than a DBA using Enterprise Manager can handle conflict resolution.

# Summary

Replication is a complex and powerful feature of SQL Server, and to describe it could easily take a book all by itself. Using the wizards and dialogs that Microsoft has written into the Enterprise Manager greatly simplifies the process of configuring and deploying replication.

✦　　✦　　✦

# ADO and ADO.NET

So far, this book has concentrated on the Database Management System (DBMS) and associated databases. Since building and maintaining the database is the main work that a database administrator will do, it's important to know how to create tables and stored procedures. However, a database is of little use if someone can't access the data. To create a connection between a client and the DBMS, you need technology such as ActiveX Data Objects (ADO). In fact, in Visual Studio .NET you also have a second choice in the form of ADO.NET. Both technologies serve the same purpose—they enable the developer to create a connection between the client and the DBMS.

Microsoft has created a plethora of database technologies over the years. In fact, so many of them exist that I doubt many developers have used them all. All of these technologies have had three things in common. First, they have made creating a connection between the client and the DBMS easier. Second, they have provided greater flexibility and improved features. Finally, each addition has repaired problems in areas such as support for referential integrity.

This chapter covers both ADO and ADO.NET. The first new bit of information to learn is that the two technologies are not mutually exclusive—both should have a place in your toolkit. Next you need to know how these two technologies differ so that you can make good development decisions. During the course of learning this information, you'll also learn how the technologies work.

Along with ADO and ADO.NET, this chapter provides information on the Visual Studio environment and how it supports the developer and the database administrator. Previous versions of Visual Studio were a tad difficult to use—some would say they were nearly impossible to use. This version comes with a new feature called Server Explorer that's going to make life a lot easier for everyone. You'll find that you don't have to leave your desk constantly to perform some task on the server. Once you know about these Visual Studio .NET features, you'll use them to perform two essential tasks: working with stored procedures from within the Visual Studio .NET environment and using automation to build a simple client application.

## An Overview of ADO

ADO first appeared as a companion to Visual Basic 6. It's a high-level wrapper around the functionality provided by Object Linking and Embedding for Databases (OLE-DB). While Visual C++ users pondered the low-level details of OLE-DB, Visual Basic users were quickly creating applications with ADO. ADO and OLE-DB both offer trade-offs for developers that will be described in the sections that follow.

Part of working with a connection technology is gaining an understanding of the various elements used to create it. For this chapter, we'll take a quick look at the one essential element of both ADO and OLE-DB, the objects that you use when working with them. We'll also discuss the data types and providers that ADO supports. Finally, we'll discuss how developers use ADO in a variety of programming efforts, including scripting. You may find that scripts offer a lightweight means of creating the connection between client and DBMS in some situations.

## ADO and OLE-DB

As previously mentioned, OLE-DB is a low-level technology used mainly by Visual C++ developers who value its flexibility and speed. ADO is a higher-level wrapper around OLE-DB that helps a developer create code more quickly, with fewer errors, and with some level of automation.

For both ADO and OLE-DB programmers, the main reason to use OLE-DB is that it provides a set of interfaces for data access. You can query, create, and destroy an OLE-DB object just as you would any other COM object. Each of the interfaces constitutes a specific unit or area of expertise for database management. For example, OLE-DB provides a record-set object that manages the set of records obtained from the DBMS.

OLE-DB also relies on events, just as any COM object would. These events tell you when an update of a table is required to show new entries made by other users or when the table you've requested is ready for viewing. You'll also see events used to signal various database errors and other activities that require polling immediately.

It's essential to understand the basis for describing OLE-DB as a connection between client and DBMS. Because ADO relies on OLE-DB for low-level access, the technology used to create an OLE-DB connection also affects ADO. Microsoft designed OLE-DB as an upgrade to ODBC. We won't discuss the whole history of Microsoft connection technology because that could require another book. However, Open Database Connectivity (ODBC) is an important connection technology because it affected Microsoft's decisions in creating OLE-DB.

ODBC is an extremely reliable technology that provides connections to many different DBMSes. The fact is that many people still use ODBC because they think of it as easier to use than OLE-DB or ADO and they don't want to lose the connectivity they currently enjoy with ODBC. Note that this view is so pervasive that Microsoft finally created ODBC.NET for those developers who refused to make the change. So how does OLE-DB differ from ODBC? Table 21-1 shows the major differences between the two products.

The most problematic feature of ODBC is that the administrator must configure the connection for it on each machine. ODBC relies on special connectivity information managed with the ODBC Data Source Administrator. OLE-DB (and therefore ADO) relies on data that's persisted as part of the application. The administrator doesn't have to perform any special configuration with these technologies, which makes the application easier to install on the system. This emphasizes the point I made at the beginning of the chapter that each new version of Microsoft DBMS connectivity technology seeks to create faster connections with fewer problems and less chance for error.

## Table 21-1: OLE-DB Versus ODBC Technology Comparison

| Element | OLE-DB | ODBC | Description |
|---|---|---|---|
| Access type | Component | Direct | OLE-DB provides interfaces that interact with the data; user access to the data is through components designed to interact with OLE-DB. |
| Data-access specialization | Any tabular data | SQL | Microsoft designed ODBC to use SQL as the basis for data transactions. In some cases, this means that the programmer has to make concessions to force the data to fit into the SQL standard. |
| Driver-access method | Component | Native | As mentioned earlier, all access to an OLE-DB provider is through COM interfaces by means of components of various types. ODBC normally requires direct programming of some type and relies heavily on the level of SQL compatibility enforced by the database vendor. |
| Programming model | COM | C/C++ | OLE-DB relies on COM to provide the programmer with access to the provider. This means that OLE-DB is language-independent, while ODBC is language-specific. |
| Technology standard | COM | SQL | OLE-DB adheres to Microsoft's COM standard, which means that it's much more vendor- and platform-specific than the SQL technology standard used by ODBC. |

# The ADO Object Model

Now that you've gotten a handle on OLE-DB, where does ADO fit in? ADO represents a way to provide database access through the combination of databound ActiveX controls and five specialty classes. You can divide the classes into two functional areas: *data provider* and *dataset*. Each of these classes provides part of the connection to the database, and Microsoft designed each class to provide some level of automation for the developer.

✦ *Data provider*—Contains the classes that create the connection, issue commands, handle the data reader, and provide data-adapter support. The connection provides the conduit for database communications. The command enables the client to request information from the database server. It also enables the client to perform updates and other tasks. The data reader is a one-way, read-only, disconnected method of viewing data. The data adapter provides the real-time connection support normally associated with live data connections. We'll discuss the data provider in more detail in the "Understanding Data Providers" section.

✦ *Dataset*—The representation of information within the database. It contains two collections: `DataTableCollection` and `DataRelationCollection`. The `DataTable Collection` contains the columns and rows of the table, along with any constraints imposed on that information. The `DataRelationCollection` contains the relational information used to create the dataset.

ADO isn't just a wrapper over OLE-DB. It provides real value to the developer and has several advantages over previous database-access methods. The following list describes those advantages for you.

✦ Independently created objects — You no longer have to thread your way through a hierarchy of objects. This feature enables you to create only the objects you need, thus reducing memory requirements and increasing application speed.

✦ *Batch updating* — Instead of sending one change to the server, you can collect them in local memory and send all of them at once. Using this feature improves application performance (because the data provider can perform the update in the background) and reduces network load.

✦ *Stored procedures* — These procedures reside on the server as part of the database manager. You'll use them to perform specific tasks on the dataset. ADO uses stored procedures with in/out parameters and return values.

✦ *Multiple cursor types* — Essentially, cursors point to the data you're currently working with. You can use both client-side and server-side cursors.

✦ *Returned row limits* — You only get the amount of data you actually need to meet a user request.

✦ *Multiple record-set objects* — Helps you to work with multiple record sets returned by stored procedures or batch processing.

✦ *Free threaded objects* — This feature enhances Web-server performance by enabling the server to perform multiple tasks.

Two databinding models are used for ActiveX controls. The first, simple databinding, provides the means for an ActiveX control like a textbox to display a single field of a single record. The second, complex databinding, enables an ActiveX control like a grid to display multiple fields and records at the same time. Complex databinding also requires the ActiveX control to manage which records and fields the control will display. Visual Studio comes with several ActiveX controls that support ADO, including these controls:

✦ DataGrid

✦ DataCombo

✦ DataList

✦ Hierarchical Flex Grid

✦ Date and Time Picker

Like OLE-DB, Microsoft based ADO on COM. ADO provides a dual interface: a program ID of ADODB for local operations and a program ID of ADOR for remote operations. The ADO library itself is free-threaded, even though the registry shows it as using the apartment-threaded model. The thread safety of ADO depends on the OLE-DB provider that you use. In other words, if you're using Microsoft's ODBC OLE-DB provider you won't have any problems. If you're using a third-party OLE-DB provider, you'll want to check the vendor documentation before assuming that ADO is thread-safe (a requirement for using ADO over an Internet or intranet connection).

You'll use seven different objects to work with ADO. Table 21-2 lists these objects and describes how you'll use them. Most of these object types are replicated in the other technologies that Microsoft has introduced, although the level of ADO-object functionality is much greater than that offered by previous technologies.

### Table 21-2: ADO-Object Overview

| Object | Description |
|--------|-------------|
| Command | A command object performs a task using a connection or record-set object. Even though you can execute commands as part of the connection or record-set object, the command object is much more flexible and enables you to define output parameters. |
| Connection | A connection object defines the connection with the OLE-DB provider. You can use this object to perform tasks like beginning, committing, and rolling back transactions. There are also methods for opening or closing the connection and for executing commands. |
| Error | ADO creates an error object as part of the connection object. The error object provides additional information about errors raised by the OLE-DB provider. A single error object can contain information about more than one error. Each object is associated with a specific event, such as committing a transaction. |
| Field | A field object contains a single column of data contained in a record-set object. In other words, a field can be thought of as a single column in a table; it contains one type of data for all the records associated with a record set. |
| Parameter | The parameter object defines a single parameter for a command object. A parameter modifies the result of a stored procedure or query. Parameter objects can provide input, output, or both. |
| Property | Some OLE-DB providers will need to extend the standard ADO object. Property objects represent one way to do this. A property object contains attribute, name, type, and value information. |
| Record set | The record set contains the result of a query, and a cursor for choosing individual elements within the returned table. C# gives you the option of creating both a connection and a record set using a single record-set object, or of using an existing connection object to support multiple record-set objects. |

## Understanding Data Providers

Remember that a data provider manages the connection between the client and the DBMS using a number of objects. Of course, this means that a data provider requires a source of information and has to define the specifics for creating that connection. Generally, a provider is database-specific or provides a means for configuring a specific database. Figure 21-1 shows a typical list of database providers. As you can see, some of the providers on the list are quite specific.

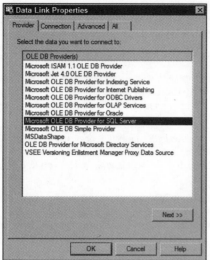

**Figure 21-1:** A typical list of database providers

The source of an OLE-DB object is a provider. Consequently, the ADO also relies on data providers as a source of data. The .NET Framework includes only a few of the OLE-DB providers found in the unmanaged version of the product. More will likely arrive as vendors upgrade their database products. The nice thing about OLE-DB is that the same provider works with any Visual Studio product: Visual C++, Visual Basic, or C#.

Generally, for SQL Server developers, it's better to use the SQL Server–specific provider. Even though other, general-purpose providers will work, Microsoft has optimized the SQL Server provider for use with SQL Server. You can easily measure the performance difference between using the SQL Server driver and using a general-purpose driver.

## Data Types

When you work exclusively within SQL Server, the problem with data types amounts to choosing the right type for a given data-storage need. However, when you begin to move the data from the DBMS through a data provider to a client, several layers of transition occur. For some DBMSes this is an extreme problem because the general providers supplied with OLE-DB don't support many special data types. The problem of data typing is another reason to the use the SQL Server–specific data providers when working with ADO.

When you want to use data found in a SQL Server table in your client application, the provider must map the data from a type that SQL Server understands to a type that the client application will understand. Fortunately for SQL Server developers, the mapping is relatively straightforward. Table 21-3 shows how the SQL Server provider maps data types. As you can see, not every SQL Server data type has a precise ADO data-type equivalent. The biggest problem occurs when ADO uses the same data type to represent two or three SQL Server data types and you want the subtle differences to appear in your application.

## Table 21-3: SQL Sever Data Mapping

| SQL Server Data Type | ADO Data Type | Notes |
|---|---|---|
| bigint | adBigInt | The `bigint` data-type value ranges from $-2^63$ (-9,223,372,036,854,775,807) through $2^63-1$ (9,223,372,036,854,775,807). This value is only available for SQL Server 2000, but the OLE-DB provider will still try to send it to SQL Server 7.0 and older systems, and data loss will result. Use the adBigInt type only when necessary and then with caution. |
| binary | adBinary | ADO uses the same data-type equivalence for both `binary` and `timestamp`. |
| bit | adBoolean | While this data transfer always works, conceptual differences exist between the two. For example, a bit can have values of 1, 0, or NULL, while an adBoolean always has either a true or false value. |
| char | adChar | ADO uses the same data-type equivalence for `char`, `varchar`, and `text` data types. |
| datetime | adDBTimeStamp | |
| decimal | adNumeric | ADO uses the same data-type equivalence for both `decimal` and `numeric` data types. |
| float | adDouble | |
| image | adVarbinary | This data type can be so large that it won't fit in memory. The lack of memory can cause provider errors and you might see only a partial retrieval. When this happens, the developer must write a custom routine to retrieve the data in pieces. ADO uses the same data-type equivalence for `image`, `tinyint`, and `varbinary`. |
| int | adInteger | |
| money | adCurrency | ADO uses the same data-type equivalence for `money` and `smallmoney`. |
| nchar | adWChar | ADO uses the same data-type equivalence for `nchar`, `ntext`, `nvarchar`, and `sysname`. |
| ntext | adWChar | This data type can be so large that it won't fit in memory. The lack of memory can cause provider errors and you might see only a partial retrieval. When this happens, the developer must write a custom routine to retrieve the data in pieces. ADO uses the same data-type equivalence for `nchar`, `ntext`, `nvarchar`, and `sysname`. |
| numeric | adNumeric | ADO uses the same data-type equivalence for both `decimal` and `numeric` data types. |

*Continued*

**Table 21-3:** *(continued)*

| SQL Server Data Type | ADO Data Type | Notes |
|---|---|---|
| nvarchar | adWChar | ADO uses the same data-type equivalence for nchar, ntext, nvarchar, and sysname. |
| real | adSingle | |
| smalldatetime | adTimeStamp | |
| smallint | adSmallInt | |
| smallmoney | adCurrency | ADO uses the same data-type equivalence for money and smallmoney. |
| sql_variant | adVariant | This data type can contain any of a number of small data types such as smallint, float, and char. It can't contain larger data types such as text, ntext, and image. The adVariant type maps to the OLE-DB DBTYPE_VARIANT data type and is only usable with SQL Server 2000. Be careful when using this data type because it can produce unpredictable results. Even though OLE-DB provides complete support for it, ADO doesn't. |
| sysname | adWChar | ADO uses the same data-type equivalence for nchar, ntext, nvarchar, and sysname. |
| text | adChar | This data type can be so large that it won't fit in memory. The lack of memory can cause provider errors and you might see only a partial retrieval. When this happens, the developer must write a custom routine to retrieve the data in pieces. ADO uses the same data-type equivalence for char, varchar, and text data types. |
| timestamp | adBinary | ADO uses the same data-type equivalence for both binary and timestamp. |
| tinyint | adVarbinary | ADO uses the same data-type equivalence for image, tinyint, and varbinary. |
| uniqueidentifier | adGUID | The data provider supports a string GUID, not a true GUID. This means that if you need an actual GUID, you'll have to convert it by hand into a GUID data structure. |
| varbinary | adVarbinary | ADO uses the same data-type equivalence for image, tinyint, and varbinary. |
| varchar | adChar | ADO uses the same data-type equivalence for char, varchar, and text data types. |

Table 21-3 only touches on the most significant problems that come up in the process of mapping data between the data provider and SQL Server. You also have to consider data-conversion errors. According to Microsoft, all non-direct data translations are subject to data loss. For example, neither the provider nor SQL Server will complain if you convert an 8-byte number into a 4-byte, but data loss may occur. In addition, you can't convert some types to other types. For example, it's impossible to convert an `adBinary` data type into an `adSmallInt` data type. In this situation, the development environment would complain.

## ADO and Scripting

ADO often appears in scripts of various types. Because ADO relies on COM technology, any scripting language capable of creating an object can probably use ADO to retrieve data from a database. Using scripts to perform small tasks makes sense because you can easily modify them if necessary and they're quick to write.

Of course, scripting languages don't provide the same interactive environment that you'll find in a full programming languages such as C# or Visual Basic. That is, unless you're using the script within a Web page (in which case, Visual Studio provides the required support). Consequently, you'll want to restrict your use of scripts to small tasks such as calling on a stored procedure to perform some task automatically or to retrieve the result of a data query to display on screen.

Microsoft makes a point of demonstrating the flexibility of ADO with a number of languages including Java. You can see several examples of ADO in use with scripting languages in the Visual Studio help file. Two of the more interesting technical articles are "Implementing ADO with Various Development Languages" (`ms-help://MS.VSCC/MS.MSDNVS/dnado/html/msdn_adorosest.htm`) and "Microsoft ADO and SQL Server Developer's Guide" (`ms-help://MS.VSCC/MS.MSDNVS/dnsqlsg/html/msdn_adosql.htm`).

# An Overview of ADO.NET

This section discusses ADO.NET. Many developers labor under the misconception that ADO.NET is simply the upgrade to ADO. In part, this misconception stems from the early marketing that Microsoft provided for ADO+, which is actually a different product from ADO or ADO.NET. The "Understanding ADO and ADO.NET Differences" section later in this chapter fills you in on some of the details about how ADO evolved into ADO+ and, finally, into ADO.NET. For now, consider ADO.NET a technology that is based on ADO, but that is useful for an entirely different class of applications.

The following sections describe ADO.NET from an ADO perspective. In other words, we'll build on the information you already know to create a picture of what ADO.NET is like. You'll find for the most part that ADO.NET is a managed version of ADO designed to create applications in disconnected environments such as the Internet.

## The ADO.NET Object Model

The ADO.NET object model is very different from the object model used by ADO because the emphasis of ADO.NET is on the Internet and Web-based applications. Microsoft made certain design considerations when creating the ADO.NET object model, most of which make sense, but some of which cause developer concerns. For example, ADO.NET doesn't provide a full implementation of server-side cursors. The developer has full access only to client-side cursors, which means that some data manipulations are less efficient.

You can divide the ADO.NET object model into two components: the DataSet and the data provider. The DataSet is a special object that contains one or more tables. The data provider is actually composed of the Connection, Command, DataReader, and DataAdapter objects. Each of these objects also has capabilities not found in ADO. For example, a DataAdapter can actually handle more than one connection and one set of rules. As with many managed objects, you'll use enumerators to access the various objects within these main objects in your application. Table 21-4 provides an overview of the ADO.NET data objects.

### Table 21-4: ADO.NET Object Overview

| Object | Description |
| --- | --- |
| Command | Defines an action to perform on the DBMS, such as adding, deleting, or updating a record. You won't normally need to create a Command object with ADO.NET unless you need to perform a special task. The DataAdapter includes the command objects required to query, delete, insert, and edit records. |
| Connection | Creates the physical connection between the DBMS and the DataAdapter. This object is the embodiment of the data provider. The Connection object also includes logic that optimizes the use of connections within the distributed-application environment. |
| DataAdapter | Translates the raw data from the DBMS into a form the DataSet can accept. The DataAdapter performs all queries, translates data from one format to another, and even performs table mapping. One DataAdapter can manage one database relation. The result set can have any level of complexity, but it must be a single result set. The DataAdapter is also responsible to issuing requests for new connections and terminating connections after it obtains the data. |
| DataReader | Provides a live connection to the database. However, it only provides a means of reading the database. In addition, the DataReader cursor works only in the forward direction. This is the object to use if you need to perform a fast retrieval of a local table and don't need to perform any updates. The DataReader blocks the DataAdapter and associated Connection objects, so it's important to close the DataReader immediately after using it. |
| DataSet | Contains a local copy of the data retrieved by one or more DataAdapters. The DataSet uses a local copy of the data, so the connection to the database isn't live. A user makes all changes to the local copy of the database, and then the application requests an update. (Updates can occur in batch mode or a single record at a time.) The DataSet maintains information about both the original and current state of each modified row. If the original row data matches the data on the database, the DataAdapter makes the requested update. If not, the DataAdapter returns an error, which the application must handle. |

It's important to note that ADO.NET doesn't have a single object that's named Command or DataAdapter. It actually supports several objects that perform these tasks, and you need to select the object that works best for your application. When working with SQL Server, that means using the objects that Microsoft has optimized for SQL Server use, such as SqlCommand or SqlDataAdapter. When you work with DBMS from other vendors, you'll need to use the generic OleDbCommand or OleDbDataAdapter.

**Note** Variations of these objects also exist for ODBC and XML. However, all these objects provide output to the same DataSet object. The connection and data adapter perform the conversions required to create a single DataSet-object representation.

## Managed Providers

The managed-database providers for ADO.NET incorporate a certain level of intelligence not found in the ADO version of the same providers. For example, the providers make better use of database connections. The providers also create and break connections as necessary to ensure optimal use of server and client resources. You can easily break the differences between an unmanaged and a managed provider into four areas:

✦ *Object Access Technique* — An unmanaged provider will use a COM progID to access the required objects. When working with a managed provider, the application relies on a command class. The command class still has to access the COM progID, but the command class hides the details of the access from the developer, which makes development faster and less error-prone.

✦ *Data Result Handling* — The unmanaged provider relies on the `Rowset` or `Recordset` object provided by ADO to present the data to the application. The managed equivalent is the DataSet or DataReader class. We've already discussed the many differences between these two implementations in "The ADO.NET Object Model" section.

✦ *Data Updates* — The fact that the unmanaged environment uses a live connection means that resources are in constant use and that the user must have a connection to the database. In addition, the developer spends plenty of time creating the commands by hand. The managed environment uses connections only as needed to actually transfer data, so resource usage is more efficient and the user doesn't need a connection at all times. As you'll see later in the chapter, the managed environment also provides a wealth of automation techniques.

✦ *Data-Transfer Format* — The unmanaged environment uses binary data transfer. The managed-data provider relies on XML for data transfer.

The differences in data-transfer method between the managed and unmanaged data providers require close examination. The XML data-transfer format used by a managed provider is better suited to the Internet because it enables data transfer through firewalls that normally block binary data transfers. However, XML is a bulkier data-transfer method and isn't very secure. Consequently, the unmanaged data provider used by ADO is actually more efficient and more secure than the one used by ADO.NET. As mentioned several times in the chapter, it pays to use ADO for local database needs and ADO.NET for distributed applications.

## Data Types

ADO.NET relies on managed data types to represent data on screen. What this really means is that Microsoft has added yet another translation layer to the mix. All of the data restrictions, oddities, and problems that we discussed in the ADO section also apply to ADO.NET. Consequently, you need to consider the same problems, such as data loss and compatibility problems, during development.

Fortunately, the managed environment provides good marshaling for data types used in database management. Using ADO.NET does introduce a small performance penalty, but so far, no one has reported any additional data-translation problems being introduced by the managed environment.

# Understanding ADO and ADO.NET Differences

ADO.NET has had a rough childhood in some respects. It began as ADO+, the new and improved form of ADO, but Microsoft quickly changed the name when it became obvious that ADO.NET was going to become something different. (For a detailed view of the ADO+ concept, see the Visual Studio .NET help article entitled, "Introducing ADO+: Data Access Services for the Microsoft .NET Framework" at `ms-help://MS.VSCC/MS.MSDNVS/dnmag00/html/adoplusnet.htm`.) In fact, ADO and ADO.NET are very different technologies, despite the similarities in their names. Of course, this begs the question of why Microsoft used the term at all if the technologies are so different. The answer lies in the few similarities between them.

Both ADO and ADO.NET are high-level database-access technologies. This means that to accomplish any given task you do less work with either of them than with a low-level technology such as OLE-DB, but also that you lose some flexibility and control. In addition, both of these technologies rely on OLE-DB as the low-level technology that performs most of the behind-the-scenes work. The final point of similarity between these two technologies is that they rely on similar access techniques, such as the use of cursors and an in-memory data representation. This feature is hardly surprising, considering that both technologies come from the same company.

You learned earlier in the chapter that the basic in-memory representation for ADO is the Recordset object. This object contains a single table that can come from a query, individual table, stored procedure, or any other source of a single table of information. In some respects, this representation is limited because you can only work with one set of information per Recordset object. However, nothing prevents you from creating more than one Recordset object, so in reality, the limit is more one of perception than anything else. In fact, some developers state that using recordsets makes their code more readable than the ADO.NET alternative would.

The ADO.NET alternative is to use a DataSet object. This is the same object that OLE-DB uses under .NET. A DataSet can contain multiple tables, which means that you don't need exotic queries to gain access to precisely the information you need. The DataTable objects within the DataSet can have relations, just as they would within the database. The result is that you can create complex database setups within your application. Of course, this scenario operates under the assumption that you have so much data that you require such a complex setup for a single application. Some companies do have that much data, which is why this approach is so valuable.

The simple single-table Recordset object used by ADO enables ADO to use simple commands to move between records. The Recordset objects relies on the `Move()`, `MoveFirst()`, `MovePrevious()`, `MoveNext()`, and `MoveLast()` functions to do all the work required to move from one record to another. In addition, you can easily determine the EOF and BOF conditions using the associated Recordset property values. This means that moving to the beginning or end of a table is easy and you can always determine your current position within the table. The record pointer associated with all of this movement is called a cursor. ADO supports cursors that reside on both the server and the client, which means that an application can track the current record position wherever it makes sense within a LAN application environment.

ADO.NET makes use of collections within the dataset. Actually, there are groups of collections, and collections within collections. The advantage of the collection technique is that you can examine records using a `foreach` statement — the same technique you'd use to enumerate any other collection. Using collections also makes it easier to transfer data to display elements such as the DataGrid object. (Although the Recordset object is actually easier to use with detail forms.) The use of collections means that it's easier to read a DataSet object from end to end than it is to address an individual record or to move backward within the collection. For example, let's say you want to address a single record field within the dataset: You'd probably require code similar to this:

```
MyString = MyData.Tables[0].Rows[0].ItemArray.GetValue(1).ToString();
```

The equivalent code for ADO is simpler and easier to understand. Here's an example:

```
MyString = DBRecordset.get_Collect("Name").ToString()
```

As you can see, a Recordset object does have an advantage in requiring less code to access an individual value because the technology doesn't bury it in multiple layers. In addition, notice that you can access the field by name when using a Recordset object — the DataSet object offers you an integer value that you must derive from the field's position within the data result. Still, using ADO.NET offers significant advantages, as you'll see in the sections that follow.

This brings us to the DataReader object, which uses a read-only, forward-only cursor. The main purpose of the DataReader object is to enable disconnected mode operation for applications. A user can download data from the company database while using an Internet (or other) connection. The data is then available for viewing offline (but not for modification, because the connection to the database is lost).

While both ADO and ADO.NET rely on OLE-DB as their connectivity technology, they both use different techniques to accomplish their goals. Both database technologies do rely on a connection. However, ADO provides few options regarding the way data updates occur once the connection is established. As a contrast, with ADO.NET you can either create the individual update elements of the DataAdapter object or rely on automation. The use of individual update elements and automation provides you with a lot of flexibility in performing updates.

The final point for consideration is the issue of connectivity. ADO does provide remote-connectivity features, but like all other COM-based technologies, it uses DCOM as the basis for data exchange across a remote network. This means that the connection-port number changes often and that the data itself is in binary form. The benefit of this approach is that few crackers have the knowledge required to peer at your data (assuming they can unscramble it after they locate it). The disadvantage is Web-server firewall support — vendors design most firewalls to keep ports closed and to restrict binary data.

ADO.NET gets around the firewall problems by using XML to transfer the data using HyperText Transport Protocol (HTTP) or some other appropriate data transfer technology. The point is that the data is in pure ASCII and relies on a single port for data transfers. Unfortunately, many people criticize XML as being a security risk and vendors have done little to make it more secure. Any attempt to encrypt the data would open the Pandora's box of binary data transfer again, making the use of XML dubious. In short, XML is a good solution, but not a perfect solution, to the problem of remote connectivity.

# Using Server Explorer

Server Explorer is a part of the Visual Studio IDE that replaces many of the tools that you used to get as extras on the Visual Studio disk. It also creates new tools for exploring your network in ways that you might not have thought possible in the past. In fact, the term Server Explorer is a bit of a misnomer because Server Explorer provides access to any resource on any machine to which you have access. In fact, when you begin using Server Explorer, the connection points to your local machine, not to a server on the network.

This ability to explore all the accessible machines on the network makes the Visual Studio .NET IDE more useful than any previous IDE you might have used. The capacity to explore and use resources without leaving the IDE makes application development a lot easier. This section provides an in-depth view of this essential tool.

## An Overview of the Server Explorer Hierarchy

You might not notice Server Explorer the first time you open Visual Studio. Server Explorer shares the same area of your IDE as the Toolbox. Click the upper icon and you'll see Server Explorer; click the lower icon and the Toolbox appears. Figure 21-2 shows a typical example of the Server Explorer with connections to two machines. Because I have administrator privileges on both machines, all of the resources of both machines are at my disposal.

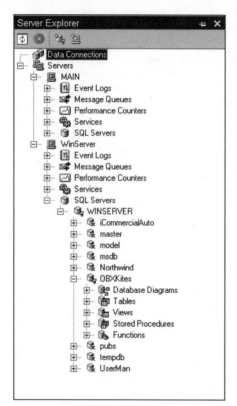

**Figure 21-2:** Server Explorer not only gives you the grand view of your network to start, but enables you to drill down as needed.

Notice that I opened the SQL Server connection to the server, WinServer. If you get the idea that you won't need to use the server-side tools much anymore, you're correct. You can perform most (but not all) tasks right from Server Explorer. If you need a new database, or to reconfigure a table or create a query, Server Explorer does it all.

The following sections contain two examples that will acquaint you with Server Explorer. No, they aren't SQL Server–specific — we'll explore SQL Server specific examples later in the chapter. For now, all we want to do is show you some of the tasks you can perform with Server Explorer that might be helpful for your client-side programming. For example, creating an Event Log entry when an error occurs could be helpful, even for someone who normally works only with SQL Server. Likewise, because it's important to monitor the performance of your application, knowing how to access the performance counters is essential.

You'll find that using Server Explorer will make working with objects found in the display trivial. This is in contrast to the many operating systems that require odd coding techniques to access many features (especially the event log and performance counters) in previous versions of Visual Studio. As you'll see, Server Explorer provides a drag-and-drop method with which to work with just about any object it can access (and there's little that it can't access).

## Working with the Event Log

One of the features that developers appreciate about Server Explorer is that it helps you categorize information. You drill down to the information you need, but ignore everything else. For example, when you open the Application Event Log you need to connect to the remote server, locate the log, and then search through the list of messages for the particular message you need. Server Explorer categorizes event messages by type, so all you see is the message you want.

If you want to build a quick application to monitor certain types of messages only, all you need to do is drag the requisite folder to a form and add some quick code to monitor it. Here's a short example of how you could use this feature in an application:

```
private void btnCreateEvent_Click(object sender, System.EventArgs e)
{
    // Create an event entry.
    ApplicationEvents.WriteEntry("This is a test message",
                                 EventLogEntryType.Information,
                                 1001,
                                 1);
}

private void ApplicationEvents_EntryWritten(object sender,
    System.Diagnostics.EntryWrittenEventArgs e)
{
    // Respond to the entry written event.
    MessageBox.Show("The Application Generated an Event!" +
                    "\r\nType:\t\t" +
                    e.Entry.EntryType.ToString() +
                    "\r\nCategory:\t" +
                    e.Entry.Category.ToString() +
                    "\r\nEvent ID:\t\t" +
                    e.Entry.EventID.ToString() +
                    "\r\nSource:\t\t" +
                    e.Entry.Source.ToString() +
                    "\r\nMessage:\t\t" +
                    e.Entry.Message.ToString() +
                    "\r\nTime Created:\t" +
                    e.Entry.TimeGenerated.ToString(),
                    "Application Event",
                    MessageBoxButtons.OK,
                    MessageBoxIcon.Information);
}
```

**Cross-Reference**     The above code sample is included on the book's CD.

The btnCreateEvent_Click() method writes an event to the event log. The private void ApplicationEvents_EntryWritten() monitors the event log and displays a message when it sees the event entry posted by the btnCreateEvent_Click() method. You could place such code in just about any application you create. The application will continuously monitor the event log in the background and let you know if something happens. This particular feature is even good for debugging because many server-side controls only log errors in the event logs.

The Event Log entry you create by dragging the Event Log from the Server Explorer will have a default configuration. The EnableRaisingEvents property will enable your application to detect changes to the log and notify you. However, this feature only works on the local machine. If you want to monitor events on a remote machine, your application will have to perform some form of polling or use a remote component that connects to your local application.

## Working with Performance Counters

While event logs are an essential part of the Windows experience, monitoring them isn't so important that you'd want to spend a lot of time doing it. However, one slightly more difficult type of monitoring involves the performance counters. Working with performance counters has been notoriously difficult in the past. Server Explorer makes it almost too simple to monitor all the performance counters on your machine. Again, all you need to do is drag the counter of interest from Server Explorer to the application form. This next example uses a DataSet to store the intermediate values and a DataGrid to show the values. (See, we even got a little database coding in this example.) A Timer is the means of obtaining constant data updates. The following code shows how to create a performance-counter monitor (note that it doesn't include the report setup, which you can view in the source code):

```
private void DataTimer_Elapsed(object sender,
System.Timers.ElapsedEventArgs e)
{
    DataTable    CounterTable;
    DataRow      NewRow;

    // Create the data table object.
    CounterTable = CounterData.Tables["UserProcessorTime"];

    // Create a new row for the data table.
    NewRow = CounterTable.NewRow();

    // Obtain the current performance counter value.
    NewRow["Total Percent User Time"] =
        UserProcessorTime.NextValue();

    // Store the value in the data table.
    CounterTable.Rows.Add(NewRow);

    // Verify the size of the data table and remove
    // a record if necessary.
    if (CounterTable.Rows.Count >=
        CounterDataView.VisibleRowCount)
            CounterTable.Rows.RemoveAt(0);
}

private void btnStopCounter_Click(object sender, System.EventArgs e)
{
```

```
      // Start and stop the timer as needed.  Change the
      // caption to show the current timer state.
      if (btnStopCounter.Text == "Stop Counter")
      {
          DataTimer.Stop();
          btnStopCounter.Text = "Start Counter";
      }
      else
      {
          DataTimer.Start();
          btnStopCounter.Text = "Stop Counter";
      }
  }

  private void txtTimerInterval_TextChanged(object sender,
  System.EventArgs e)
  {
      try
      {
          // Verify the timer change value has a number in it.
          if (Int64.Parse(txtTimerInterval.Text) == 0)
              // If not, reset the value.
              txtTimerInterval.Text = DataTimer.Interval.ToString();
          else
              // If so, use the new value.
              DataTimer.Interval = Int64.Parse(txtTimerInterval.Text);
      }
      catch
      {
          // Catch invalid values.
          MessageBox.Show("Type Only Numeric Values!",
              "Input Error",
              MessageBoxButtons.OK,
              MessageBoxIcon.Error);
          txtTimerInterval.Text = DataTimer.Interval.ToString();
      }
  }
```

**Cross-Reference**  The above code sample is included on the book's CD.

Notice that most of the code in this part of the example relates to the presentation of data. For example, the txtTimerInterval_TextChanged() method modifies the display speed of the application, while the btnStopCounter_Click() method enables and disables the timer. Disabling the DataTimer has the effect of stopping the display so you can see the current data value along with the value history.

The DataTimer_Elapsed() method contains the code that updates the display at the interval specified by DataTimer.Interval. CounterTable contains the entire data table used for the example. The NewRow() method of this object creates a new row represented by NewRow. The Item property, Total Percent User Time, is a particular column within the table and we'll use it with the current processed value for the UserProcessorTime performance counter using the NextValue() method. The final step is to add the new row to the data table using the Add() method. Figure 21-3 shows an example of the output from this application.

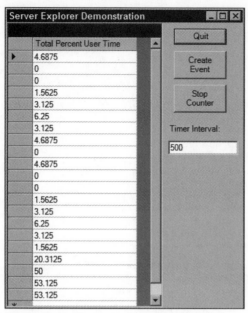

**Figure 21-3:** The Server Explorer example shows how easy it is to use performance counters in C#.

One of the interesting things about this example is that this view isn't available through the System Monitor component of the Performance console. The Report View of the utility shows the current counter value, but doesn't provide any history. The Graph View and Histogram View might prove less than accurate for developer needs. So this report view with history fulfills a developer need. It enables you to capture precise counter values over a period of time in a way that helps you look for data patterns. The fact that the table automatically sizes itself ensures that you won't end up with too much data in the table. Of course, you can always change the method used to delete excess records to meet specific needs.

It's interesting to note that Visual Studio installs a number of .NET Common Language Runtime (CLR) specific performance counters for you. For example, you have access to memory, network, and data-related counters with which to adjust the performance of your application. A special Interop object contains counters that measure the impact of external calls on application performance. Not only do these counters help you work on performance issues, but you can also use them to locate bugs or enable an application to tune itself. For example, you could monitor memory usage and get rid of nonessential features when application memory is low. In addition, a special Exceptions object contains counters that help you monitor application exceptions, including those that your application handles without any other visible signs.

## Accessing SQL Server

Server Explorer provides the means for accessing SQL Server. You can't access some features, but many of them are accessible. For example, Figure 21-2 shows the WinServer entry. If you want to create a new database on WinServer, you can follow a simple process to do so (see the "Working with SQL Server Databases" section later in this chapter for details).

Sever Explorer is even good at performing mundane tasks. Let's say that you want to check the data in the `Contact` table in the OBX Kites database. You can drill down to the table using the hierarchical features of Server Explorer. Right-click the `Contact` table and you'll see a list of actions you can perform, like the list shown in Figure 21-4.

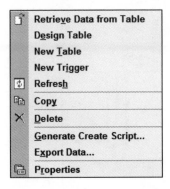

**Figure 21-4:** Server Explorer helps you interact with every component in SQL Server — at least from a developer perspective.

As you can see, you can do everything from designing the table to generating the scripts required to create it. To see what the table contains, you'd select the Retrieve Data from Table option. Visual Studio will query the DBMS and obtain the raw content from the `Contact` table. Figure 21-5 shows some sample output as seen in design area of Visual Studio .NET (that's right, we still haven't left the IDE). Notice that the tabbed view keeps multiple application elements within easy access, yet keeps screen clutter to a minimum.

| ContactID | ContactCode | SoundexCode | LastName | FirstName | CompanyName | CustomerTypeID | Cus |
|-----------|-------------|-------------|----------|-----------|-------------|----------------|-----|
| {9587AD14-6382-4 | 102 | A352 | Adams | Terri | <NULL> | {DA245D5E-38CC-4 | <N |
| {8CE5111F-9A45-4 | 117 | A536 | Andrews | Ed | <NULL> | {E1E3B1A7-9F9A-4 | <N |
| {F42CCCA0-0D73-4 | 118 | B235 | Boston | Dave | <NULL> | {E1E3B1A7-9F9A-4 | <N |
| {85A61F16-2F05-4 | 105 | D360 | Dowdry | Quin | <NULL> | {DA245D5E-38CC-4 | <N |
| {305A2B5F-F27B-4 | 120 | E640 | Earl | Betty | <NULL> | {E1E3B1A7-9F9A-4 | <N |
| {5E8B1B5D-DBAB-4 | 104 | F652 | Franklin | Rondey | <NULL> | {DA245D5E-38CC-4 | <N |
| {1A53EFF3-18CD-4 | 106 | G653 | Grant | Peter | Southern Beach | {D426F7DB-3059-4 | <N |
| {43EC0493-40EF-4 | 108 | H520 | Hanks | Nickolas | Norfolk Kite Flight | {D426F7DB-3059-4 | <N |
| {FBB6DEB5-0C36-4 | 119 | H625 | Harrison | Charlie | <NULL> | {E1E3B1A7-9F9A-4 | <N |
| {0E8B209F-67E2-4 | 109 | J520 | James | Mike | Boston Kites | {D426F7DB-3059-4 | <N |
| {4B22248A-C0F3-4 | 116 | J525 | Jamison | Frank | <NULL> | {E1E3B1A7-9F9A-4 | <N |
| {E0C6DD83-FC3E-4 | 110 | K530 | Kennedy | Lisa | Wright Brothers Me | {D426F7DB-3059-4 | <N |
| {73E8966F-391C-4 | 113 | L360 | Laudry | Irene | <NULL> | {E1E3B1A7-9F9A-4 | <N |
| {F4976E7E-B678-4 | 115 | M460 | Miller | Ginger | <NULL> | {E1E3B1A7-9F9A-4 | <N |
| {24217EE8-F6A3-4 | 114 | N425 | Nelson | Harry | <NULL> | {E1E3B1A7-9F9A-4 | <N |
| {13AA030B-513E-4 | 112 | Q520 | Quincy | Jennifer | <NULL> | {E1E3B1A7-9F9A-4 | <N |
| {7B586B8B-D8AC-4 | 103 | R250 | Reagan | Steve | <NULL> | {DA245D5E-38CC-4 | <N |
| {5CF273A5-BCA9-4 | 101 | S530 | Smith | Ulisius | <NULL> | {DA245D5E-38CC-4 | <N |
| {EBF732AA-0007-4 | 107 | S530 | Smith | Oscar | Cape Hatteras Gen | {D426F7DB-3059-4 | <N |
| {4888D855-697F-4 | 111 | W452 | Williams | Kid | <NULL> | {E1E3B1A7-9F9A-4 | <N |
| {2FDFC416-5E22-4 | 121 | Z520 | Zing | Chei | <NULL> | {E1E3B1A7-9F9A-4 | <N |

**Figure 21-5:** You can explore the content of any table or the output of any stored procedure right within the Visual Studio .NET IDE.

The feature we appreciate most is the ability to create diagrams right within the Visual Studio .NET IDE. Figure 21-6 shows a database diagram that we created in about half a minute using the Server Explorer. To create this diagram, all we did was right-click the Database Diagrams entry and select New Diagram from the context menu. When the Add Table dialog box appeared we selected all the tables in the list and clicked OK. It took Visual Studio .NET just a few seconds to generate the diagram, because the server was on a LAN (even Internet connections don't take long).

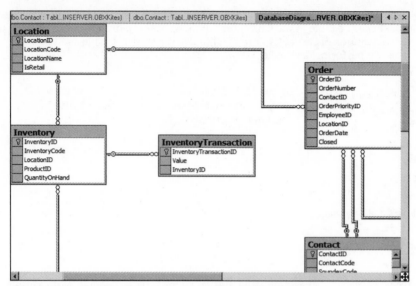

**Figure 21-6:** Creating diagrams is easy using Server Explorer.

The one issue that most developers will experience problems with is that Server Explorer keeps the connection open, even after you close the hierarchical structure. It's essential that you right-click the database you're using and then select Close Connection from the context menu. Otherwise, the database connection will remain open until you reboot the client machine (or until SQL Server times out from inactivity). Microsoft assumes that if you have access to this tool, you'll also have the knowledge required to perform some tasks by hand. Even so, some developers are bound to forget to close their connections and run out of resources on the local machine.

## Working with SQL Server Databases

One of the advantages of using Server Explorer is that you don't need to run to the server to perform most development-related tasks. Normally you'd use the tools provided with SQL Server to create and manage your database. In some situations you'll still need those tools because they provide essential abilities that the Visual Studio .NET IDE can't provide, such as the need to run local scripts to perform updates. However, in many cases, you can at least begin the design process and perform some testing without ever leaving the IDE.

The following steps show how to create a simple database using the Server Explorer. We won't use this database anywhere else in the book—it's simply here for demonstration purposes. However, this procedure does show that you can create a database using Server Explorer of any complexity or size. The difference for the developer is in working constantly within the IDE, rather than moving between tools or machines. Using a single tool, especially for design, translates into higher efficiency and means you can develop an application faster and with less effort.

1. Open Server Explorer, locate the server with SQL Server installed on it, open the SQL Servers folder, and open the SQL Server instance of interest. In most cases, you'll only see one. My server is named WinServer—your server will probably have a different name.

2. Right-click the SQL Server instance and choose New Database from the context menu. You'll see a Create Database dialog box.

3. Type a name in the New Database Name field. The example uses SimpleData as the database name.

4. Choose between Windows NT integrated security and SQL Server authentication. The example uses SQL Server authentication with the default user name and appropriate password.

5. Click OK and SQL Server will create a new database for you (which will appear in the Visual Studio .NET IDE). Now it's time to create a table for the database.

6. Right-click Tables and choose New Table from the context menu. You'll see a blank table form similar to the one shown in Figure 21-7. (Note that we've already filled this table out, so it's ready for use.)

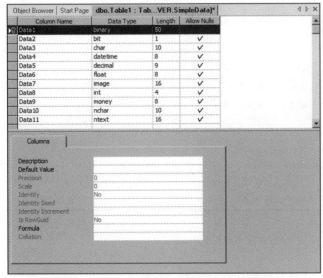

**Figure 21-7:** This form shows the table structure for a simple table.

7. Fill in the required table entries. Of course, every table requires the use of one or more columns as a primary key.

8. Highlight the Data1 column. (You can Ctrl-click any number of columns for the primary key, but we'll use just one in this case.) Right-click the highlighted field and choose Set Primary key from the context menu. Our table still lacks indexes, so that's what we'll set in the next step.

9. Right-click any column entry and choose Indexes/Keys from the context menu. You'll see the Indexes/Keys tab of the Property Pages dialog box (shown in Figure 21-8). Notice that this dialog box also helps you configure the table-specific data, relationships, and constraints for this table. You should also notice that the Indexes/Keys tab contains an entry for the primary key. Just as when you work within SQL Server Enterprise Manager, Visual Studio .NET will create required entries automatically.

10. Click New and then type a name for the index in the Index Name field. The example uses MyIndex. Select several of the columns and choose a sort order for each of them. Add any special properties for the index, and then click Close.

**11.** Save the table and close it. The example uses a table name of SimpleTable.

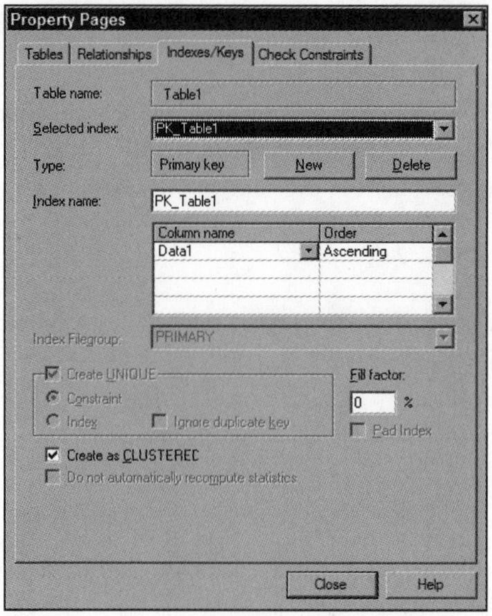

**Figure 21-8:** The Property Pages dialog helps you consider the table for use.

This is obviously the short tour of working with Server Explorer to create a database. You'll also need to add other entries to a complete database. The point is that we were able to create the database without exiting the Server Explorer even once. You can create a complete database application using Server Explorer.

# Working with Stored Procedures

A great deal of the material in this book has focused on working with stored procedures, so the point of this section is not to show you yet more ways to create the perfect stored procedure for your server; what it does show you is how to work with stored procedures from within Server Explorer and ultimately from a Visual Studio application. It's theoretically possible to create a Visual Studio application that relies exclusively on stored procedures, which means using only two of the objects we discussed in detail at the beginning of this chapter (Connection and Command). With this in mind, the following sections are your guide to stored-procedure use in the Visual Studio .NET IDE.

## Accessing Stored Procedures with Server Explorer

First you need to know how to access a stored procedure. The stored procedures are (naturally) located in the Stored Procedures folder for the database of interest. Figure 21-9 shows a typical example of a stored-procedure listing for the OBX Kites database. Notice that the stored-procedure display shows the inputs and outputs for the stored procedure. Select any of these objects and you'll see the properties associated with them, including type and source information.

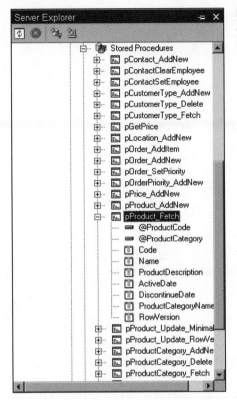

**Figure 21-9:** The stored procedure tells you about the stored procedure, including its inputs and outputs.

You can choose to work with the stored procedure directly within Server Explorer in some cases. If the stored procedure requires input to run, Server Explorer will display a Run Stored Procedure dialog box that asks for the required parameters. Enter the data as you'd expect an application to do, and then click OK. The Visual Studio IDE will display any results in the Output window. You won't see error results in most cases, unless the stored procedure is set up to provide them.

Editing a stored procedure is easy. All you need to do is right-click the stored procedure and choose Edit Stored Procedure from the context menu. The Visual Studio IDE highlights the various stored-procedure areas, as shown in Figure 21-10. When you save the stored procedure, it will also change on the server.

Server Explorer also offers options that enable you to step into (or debug) a stored procedure using the Visual Studio .NET IDE. The debugger works similar to a standard application. You can set break points, check the content of variables, and use the Command window to perform other types of checks. The Debug window provides the normal level of output. However, you can only see what happens on the local machine. The debugger won't tell you what happens on SQL Server, except as inputs and outputs.

Finally, you can perform the same standard tasks with stored procedures that you can with every other SQL Server element. For example, Server Explorer provides a way to create new stored procedures. You can also create scripts from the stored procedures and make local copies of them.

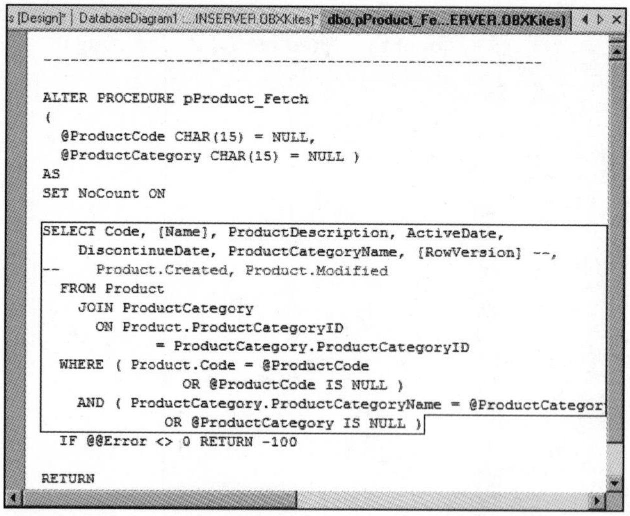

```
------------------------------------------------
ALTER PROCEDURE pProduct_Fetch
  (
    @ProductCode CHAR(15) = NULL,
    @ProductCategory CHAR(15) = NULL )
AS
SET NoCount ON

SELECT Code, [Name], ProductDescription, ActiveDate,
    DiscontinueDate, ProductCategoryName, [RowVersion] --,
--    Product.Created, Product.Modified
  FROM Product
    JOIN ProductCategory
      ON Product.ProductCategoryID
          = ProductCategory.ProductCategoryID
  WHERE ( Product.Code = @ProductCode
              OR @ProductCode IS NULL )
    AND ( ProductCategory.ProductCategoryName = @ProductCategor
            OR @ProductCategory IS NULL )
  IF @@Error <> 0 RETURN -100

RETURN
```

**Figure 21-10:** Editing a stored procedure is easy using Server Explorer.

## Adding Stored Procedures to Visual Studio Projects

Earlier in the chapter I mentioned that using stored procedures in a Visual Studio .NET project is as easy as dragging and dropping. It's time to check out that claim and see if it actually works as advertised. The following steps will get you started.

1. Create a new Visual Studio .NET project. The example is written in C#, but you can also use Visual Basic. The one language that won't work is Visual C++, because it lacks form-designer support.

2. Locate the pProductFetch stored procedure in the OBXKites database and drag it to the Visual Studio .NET form. Drag the folder containing this stored procedure to the form. You have to place the folder on the form before you can drop it. Visual Studio. NET will create a Connection and a Command object for you.

3. Rename the objects if you like — the example uses OBXKitesConnect for the Connection object and pProductFetch for the Command object.

4. Add DataSet, DataGrid, and Run command buttons to the project. The DataSet will hold the information from the database, the DataGrid will display it on screen, and the Run command will initial the process. Figure 21-11 shows what you should end up with at this point.

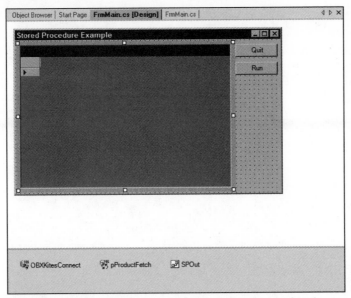

**Figure 21-11:** The sample program will display the results of a stored procedure on screen.

The example application will need some way of interacting with the stored procedure, so you'll need to create a series of objects to store intermediate data results. One of these objects is a DataReader, which is the one-way data object described earlier in the chapter. Here's what the code looks like for this example:

```
private void btnRun_Click(object sender, System.EventArgs e)
{
    SqlDataReader  Output;  // The results of the query.
    DataColumn     Column;  // A single data column.
    DataRow        Row;     // A single data row.
    DataTable      Table;   // The addition to the DataSet.

    // Open a connection to the database and execute the
    // stored procedure.
    OBXKitesConnect.Open();
    Output = pProductFetch.ExecuteReader();

    // Create a DataTable to store the information.
    Table = new DataTable("pProductFetch Output");

    // Create the columns found within the DataReader.
    for (int Counter = 0;
        Counter < Output.FieldCount;
        Counter++)
    {
        Column = new DataColumn(Output.GetName(Counter),
                            Output.GetFieldType(Counter));
        Table.Columns.Add(Column);
    }
```

```
// Read the data one row at a time.
while (Output.Read())
{
    // Create a new row in the DataTable.
    Row = Table.NewRow();

    // Read the data from the DataReader into the DataTable.
    for (int Counter = 0;
         Counter < Output.FieldCount;
         Counter++)

        // Fill the row with data
        Row[Counter] = Output.GetValue(Counter);

    // Add the data to the table.
    Table.Rows.Add(Row);
}

// Add the table to the DataSet and then display it in the
// DataGrid.
SPOut.Tables.Add(Table);
SPDisplay.DataMember = "pProductFetch Output";
SPDisplay.CaptionText = "pProductFetch Output";
SPDisplay.Refresh();

// Close the connection now that we have the data.
Output.Close();
pProductFetch.Connection.Close();
OBXKitesConnect.Close();
}
```

 **Cross-Reference** The previous code sample is included on the book's CD.

The code begins by opening a connection to the database and executing the stored procedure. The output of the ExecuteReader() is a DataReader object. This object requires a live connection to the database, so the code can't close the connection until the code has finished creating the DataSet.

Before the code can create a DataSet, it must create a DataTable to place within the DataSet. Remember that a DataSet can hold multiple DataTables. The new DataTable requires some column headers. The best way to provide them is create a new DataColumn for each column in the result set and add it to the DataTable using the Columns.Add() method.

Once the code has some columns in place, it can begin scanning the DataReader for data. The Read() method reads one entry at a time from the result set. If there are no entries to read, the Read() method returns false. The code also has to add a new row to the DataTable using the NewRow() method. The output of this call is a DataRow object. The code fills each column of the DataRow with data and then adds the modified DataRow to the DataTable using the Rows.Add() method.

At this point, you have built a basic table. The code adds the DataTable to the DataSet using the Tables.Add() method. However, performing this step doesn't necessarily display the data on the DataGrid, even though the two objects are linked through the DataSource property. The code updates the DataGrid's DataMember property so it points to the new DataTable contained within the DataSet. It then modifies the caption for the grid and tells the DataGrid to update its content using the Refresh() method. The final act you need to perform is to close the connection. Figure 21-12 shows the output from the example.

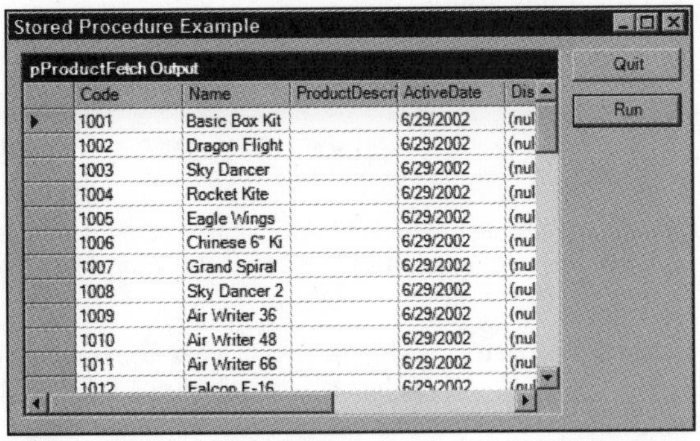

**Figure 21-12:** The example application displays the output of a stored procedure.

## Passing Parameters to the Stored Procedure

The previous example is nice if you want to display everything that a stored procedure can provide. However, what do you do if you want to limit the output of the stored procedure by passing parameters to it? Actually, it's easier than you think, because you've already done all the hard work. The following code shows all you need to add to filter the output shown in Figure 21.12:

```
// See if we have any input for the stored procedure.
if (txtProdCode.Text.Length != 0)
    pProductFetch.Parameters["@ProductCode"].Value =
        txtProdCode.Text;
```

As you can see, all you need to do is access the Parameters enumeration that Visual Studio .NET automatically sets up. The txtProdCode.Text property contains the code that the application should provide from the database.

# Creating a Basic Application

There are a number of ways to drag-and-drop your way to a client application in Visual Studio .NET. For example, you can simply drag and drop the tables you want to use onto the form. The IDE will automatically create the required connection for you. The problem with this method is that it limits you to using the commands that Microsoft thinks you should use, rather than the stored procedures you've worked so hard to construct.

Another technique is to drag the components from the Data tab of the Toolbox onto the form. The easiest method is to drag and drop a DataAdapter, so that's the technique we use in this case. Dragging the DataAdapter to the form opens a wizard that leads you through the process of configuring your system. The following sections show how to create a connection and then use it to display information in a grid view.

## Creating the DataAdapter

The procedure in this section provides you with some insights into the various ways that you can create a DataAdapter. The DataAdapter is the centerpiece of application communication with the database, just as the DataSet is the main storage medium. The following steps concentrate on the DataAdapter portion of the application.

1. Create a new Visual Studio .NET application. As before, you can use either C# or Visual Basic.

2. Open the Toolbox and click the Data tab. Drag a SqlDataAdapter object to the form. You'll see the Data Adapter Configuration Wizard dialog box. Click Next.

3. The Data Adapter Configuration Wizard will ask which connection you want to use or if you want to create a new one. No connection is established for this example, so you need to create a new one.

4. Click New Connection. The Data Link Properties dialog box that we discussed earlier in the chapter (see Figure 21-11) will appear. You'll probably want to check the Provider tab to ensure that the Microsoft OLE DB Provider for SQL Server option is selected.

5. Click the Connection tab. Fill out the name of your server and the security information. Select the OBX Kites option from the list of databases.

6. Click Test Connection to verify that the connection works. (If you don't perform this step, you won't know if the connection is causing problems should an error occur later. Many developers don't make this simple check and end up spending hours trying to figure out why their application won't work.) Click OK.

7. You should see the Data Adapter Configuration Wizard dialog box again. Click Next. The Data Adapter Configuration Wizard will ask you to select a query type, as shown in Figure 21-13. Notice that you can choose to use an existing stored procedure, create a new stored procedure, or use the default of SQL statements. If you choose the Use SQL statements option, the Data Adapter Configuration Wizard will configure the data adapter with four default commands based on the data relation you set up. You can build a query using the Visual Studio Query Builder. The process involves selecting tables, drawing relationships between them, and then selecting the columns you want to use. Let's assume you want to use the stored procedures again for the product information.

8. Select the "Use existing stored procedures" option, and then click Next. You'll see a Bind Commands to Existing Stored Procedures dialog box, similar to the one shown in Figure 21-14. This dialog box points out that you still need to provide the four commands required to create a DataAdapter — at least, you need to if you want full functionality. In this case, all the example will do is show the results of a query, perform updates, and insert new records. There won't be an option to delete anything.

9. Select the stored procedures shown in Figure 21-14 and click Next.

10. You'll see a Data Adapter Configuration Wizard results dialog box. This dialog box tells you which features the DataAdapter has implemented. It also tells you if there were any implementation errors that you'll need to correct later. Click Finish. The DataAdapter is ready to use.

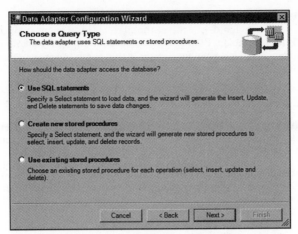

**Figure 21-13:** The Data Adapter Configuration Wizard can build a data adapter using stored procedures or a query that you create graphically.

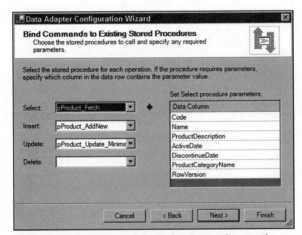

**Figure 21-14:** A DataAdapter always needs stored procedures to perform at least one of the four tasks, and it's usually good to include all four.

## Creating a Grid View

At this point, you have communication with the DBMS and a specific database controlled by the DBMS. You still can't display any information, or do anything else with the data for that matter. What you have, at this point, is akin to a telephone cable with no telephone connected to it. The communication's there, but you can't use it. The following steps show you how to implement the "telephone" portion of the communication:

1. Right click sqlDataAdapter1 and choose Generate Dataset from the context menu. You could generate the DataSet by hand, but the automated method saves a lot of time and effort. You'll see a Generate Dataset dialog box. No DataSet objects exist, so your only choice is to create a new one. However, you can use this same process to recreate an existing DataSet should the need arise.

2. Accept the default DataSet name by clicking OK. The Generate Dataset Wizard will create a DataSet named dataSet11.

3. Add a DataGrid to the form. Configure the DataSource property for dataSet11 and the DataMember property for pProduct_Fetch. These options should be available in the dropdown list box.

The example is just about ready to run. Have you noticed that you haven't typed any code yet? Well, now you need to type. The example requires that you add a single line of code to the Form1 constructor, as shown here:

```
public Form1()
{
    //
    // Required for Windows Form Designer support
    //
    InitializeComponent();

    // Fill the dataset with data.
    sqlDataAdapter1.Fill(dataSet11);
}
```

At this point you're probably wondering what the catch is, because database applications normally require a lot of code. This example will perform updates, display the records in the database, and add new records. It won't delete records because you didn't provide a stored procedure to perform that task. The connections you've established are all that you'll need for a simple client.

## Summary

ADO and ADO.NET provide connectivity between the client application and the DBMS. They're the most recent connectivity options in a long line of technologies developed by Microsoft. Using ADO and ADO.NET helps you build robust clients. Of course, the Visual Studio .NET IDE provides a wealth of other tools for building client applications, such as Server Explorer.

This section of the book helps you understand connectivity techniques. The information in this chapter has demonstrated one type of connection between the client and the DBMS. The next chapter continues the discussion of connectivity by looking at the issues surrounding SQL Server and XML.

✦      ✦      ✦

# XML and Web Publishing

The Internet is moving from being a vehicle primarily for e-mail and data presentation into a phase of high-performance data connectivity. HTML, as a common mark-up language, describes how data should be presented, but eXtensible Markup Language, or XML, goes deeper than HTML and describes the content of the document.

Mark-up languages began in 1969 when Charles F. Goldfarb, Ed Mosher, and Ray Lorie developed Generalized Markup Language (GML) for IBM, to standardize documents for publication. In 1974, Charles Goldfarb published Standard Generalized Markup Language (SGML), which became "the International Standard (ISO 8879) language for structured data and document representation" (HTTP://www.sgmlsource.com). Basically, SGML defines the rules for creating mark-up languages. As a presentation mark-up language that follows the SGML rules, HTML formats the look of data for Web browsers. XML is a subset of SGML that essentially uses '60s technology to create a new mark-up language that describes a set of data. In 1998, the World Wide Web Consortium (HTTP://www.W3C.org) published version 1.0 of the official XML specs.

By itself, XML does nothing; it's only a file format. There is no such thing as an XML application—only applications that read or generate XML documents. However, the wide acceptance of XML makes it an excellent format for transporting data between dissimilar systems, especially over the Internet. The prosaic comma-delimited text file usually identifies the fields in the first line, and, more often than not, the data does not follow the format rule, making comma-delimited files frustrating. As a welcome relief, XML explicitly tags every individual piece of data, reducing the errors caused by varying or incomplete data schemas.

XML uses a hierarchical data structure: each XML element may contain a nested XML element. For example, a customer element that describes a single customer might contain a few order elements, which could contain order-detail elements. Every XML document uses this top-down hierarchal method to contain data. This makes XML very powerful for sharing data sets, but prevents XML from being a replacement for a relational-database system.

While the SQL Server–specific code is in the chapter code script as usual, this chapter also refers to several XML document and validation files located on the CD in the `C:\SQLServerBible\Sample Databases\CapeHatterasAdventures` directory. All the XML samples are pulled from the Cape Hatteras Adventures sample database.

In the sample XML document `CHA2_Events.xml`, data extracted from the Cape Hatteras Adventures sample database is painstakingly identified using XML tags. This allows the data to be self-describing and represented in a format that is identical to its representation within the database.

```xml
<?xml version="1.0" encoding="UTF-8"?>
<Tours>
  <Tour Name="Amazon Trek">
    <Event Code="01-003" DateBegin="2001-03-16T00:00:00"/>
    <Event Code="01-015" DateBegin="2001-11-05T00:00:00"/>
  </Tour>
  <Tour Name="Appalachian Trail">
    <Event Code="01-005" DateBegin="2001-06-25T00:00:00"/>
    <Event Code="01-008" DateBegin="2001-07-14T00:00:00"/>
    <Event Code="01-010" DateBegin="2001-08-14T00:00:00"/>
  </Tour>
  <Tour Name="Bahamas Dive">
    <Event Code="01-002" DateBegin="2001-05-09T00:00:00"/>
    <Event Code="01-006" DateBegin="2001-07-03T00:00:00"/>
    <Event Code="01-009" DateBegin="2001-08-12T00:00:00"/>
  </Tour>
  <Tour Name="Gauley River Rafting">
    <Event Code="01-012" DateBegin="2001-09-14T00:00:00"/>
    <Event Code="01-013" DateBegin="2001-09-15T00:00:00"/>
  </Tour>
  <Tour Name="Outer Banks Lighthouses">
    <Event Code="01-001" DateBegin="2001-02-02T00:00:00"/>
    <Event Code="01-004" DateBegin="2001-06-06T00:00:00"/>
    <Event Code="01-007" DateBegin="2001-07-03T00:00:00"/>
    <Event Code="01-011" DateBegin="2001-08-17T00:00:00"/>
    <Event Code="01-014" DateBegin="2001-10-03T00:00:00"/>
    <Event Code="01-016" DateBegin="2001-11-16T00:00:00"/>
  </Tour>
</Tours>
```

SQL Server 2000 has first-generation XML capabilities to publish to the Web and work with XML data. XML and .NET Web services easily fill a couple more books. The purpose of this chapter is to provide an understanding of how XML fits into the database world, as well as the commonly used features of XML as used by SQL Server.

# XML and EDI

XML is the best means of moving data among various dissimilar databases and programs. As such, it is replacing the expensive Electronic Data Interchange (EDI) systems of the '80s and '90s and is the new B2B data-exchange standard. The issue with XML is that both companies sharing data must agree on the XML schema or data-descriptor tags. Most industries have already established XML standards.

The Commercial XML standard (`HTTP://www.cXML.org`) has taken the lead as the universal transactional B2B XML standard. cXML is a set of XML Document Type Definitions (DTDs) that define the structure of XML mark-up languages for handling common B2B transactions such as catalogs, product suppliers, punch outs (instances of interactive procurement over the Internet), master agreements, purchase orders, order confirmations, ship notices, and invoices.

Other XML standards include:

✦ XMLLife — For insurance companies

✦ Channel Definition Format (CDF) — For pushing media over the Web

✦ Open Financial eXchange (OFX) — For the stock market and financial industry

✦ Mathematical Markup Language (MathML) — For describing equations

✦ Chemical Markup Language (CML) — For chemical formulas and products

In addition, several server software packages are already on the market that convert one XML schema to another for data sharing, including Microsoft BizTalk.

# Working with XML

Like an HTML document, an XML document is just a text document with tags — often a very long document with an abundance of tags. While XML documents can be viewed and created using Notepad, XML is not intended for human consumption. Most developers who work with XML use a parser to decode the XML within an application and an XML viewer to peruse the XML document.

## XML Parsing

To work with XML data from within custom application programs, you'll want to use a pre-written parser. A parser will decode the XML document and handle the complexities of XML. Several vendors offer XML parsers; Microsoft's parser, XML Core Services V4.0 (formerly known as MSXML), is one of the more complete parsers available and is a free download from:

```
HTTP://msdn.microsoft.com/downloads/default.asp?
  url=/downloads/topic.asp?
  url=/MSDN-FILES/028/000/013/topic.xml
```

Within a custom application, code can access the XML Core Services objects to inspect and create XML documents. The Document Object Model (DOM) is the standard API for XML documents. Simple API for XML (SAX) is an alternative to DOM. Microsoft Core Services includes:

✦ An XML parser

✦ An XSL style-sheet processor

✦ Support for DOM

## XML Viewing

A number of tools can aid in the viewing and creation of raw XML documents. I highly recommend XML Spy, shown in Figure 22-1, because it's a full suite of XML tools in a slick integrated development environment (IDE) that includes many views and features. It can graphically create or display XMLs, XSLs, DTDs, and XML Schemas, and can validate XML documents.

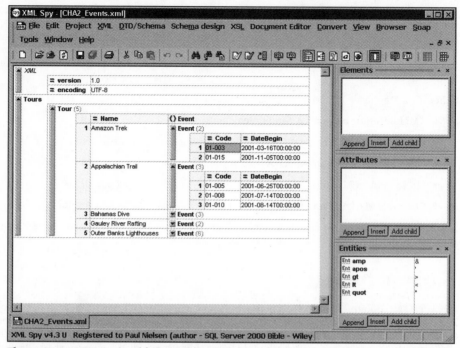

**Figure 22-1:** XML Spy's grid view makes it easy to visualize the elements and attributes of the sample CHA_Event.xml document.

**On the CD-ROM**

XML Spy is the best tool for working with XML documents. A 30-day trial version of XML Spy is on the CD included with this book. XML Spy includes several example documents.

An XML document can be opened and viewed within Internet Explorer. IE 5 includes a default XML style sheet (Figure 22-2) for browsing the XML data.

## XML Publishing

Because XML describes the content of the data, various style sheets can locate data within the XML document and format it for various devices. A single XML document might be viewed using any of the following:

✦ *Computer browsers using XSL*—XML style sheets that merge XML data into an HTML document

✦ *Cell phones or other wireless devices using Wireless Markup Language (WML)*—The following link provides details on the Wireless Application Protocol specifications:

```
www.wapforum.org/what/technical.htm
```

✦ *Acrobat Reader – XML:FOP* —IBM's Formatting Objects to PDF tool can use XML and XSL to produce PDF files.

```
HTTP://www-106.ibm.com/developerworks/education
  /transforming-xml/xmltopdf/
```

```
HTTP://www.wapforum.org/what/technical.htm
```

A major component of Microsoft's .Net initiative is Web services, which reply to queries with XML data. Combining Web services with XSL is an excellent way to publish dynamic data on the Web.

## XML Validation

A key benefit of XML is its ability to validate data using Data Type Documents or XML Schema documents. These additional documents describe the data structure so the receiving application can compare the data to the expected structure. The validation information can be stored inside the XML document, or the XML document can point to the validation document.

You can use the validation and publishing features of XML to develop powerful Web-based applications.

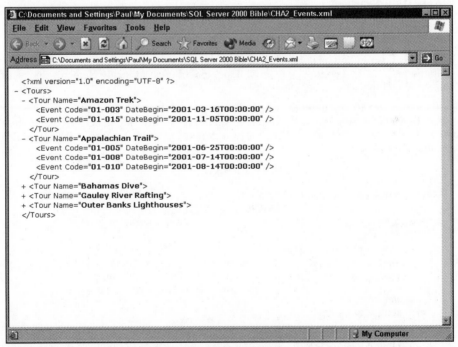

**Figure 22-2:** IE 5 provides a cool collapsible-list feature, which is not a standard XML view but is actually the default XSL style sheet within IE 5.

# Inside an XML Document

An XML document consists of two sections: the Declaration section, which contains information for the XML parser, and the Root-Element section, which contains the data.

As a database developer, you won't spend your days writing XML documents by hand; instead a tool or SQL Server will generate the documents.

## Declaration Section

The Declaration section is an optional prologue to the document and contains Processing Instructions (PI). Typically, the Declaration section specifies instructions, such as the following, for the parser:

```
<?procname procatt="attribvalue" ?>
```

The most common instruction identifies the document as an XML document using the reserved PI, XML:

```
<?xml version="1.0" encoding="UTF-8"?>
```

Other instructions can specify the DTD file for data validation, or the XSL file for translation into an HTML document.

## Root Element

Each data object in XML is defined as an element. The root element is the overarching object container. All the data contained in an XML document must fit inside elements and attributes contained within a single root element.

In this sense an XML document is no different from an HTML document that uses the <HTML> tag as its root element. The XML root name should be a word that describes the content of the XML document, such as <Orders>, <Customers>, or, as in the case of the sample XML document, <Events>.

```
<?xml version="1.0" encoding="UTF-8"?>
<Tours>
  <Tour Name="Amazon Trek">
    <Event Code="01-003" DateBegin="2001-03-16T00:00:00"/>
    <Event Code="01-015" DateBegin="2001-11-05T00:00:00"/>
  </Tour>
  <Tour Name="Appalachian Trail">
    <Event Code="01-005" DateBegin="2001-06-25T00:00:00"/>
    <Event Code="01-008" DateBegin="2001-07-14T00:00:00"/>
    <Event Code="01-010" DateBegin="2001-08-14T00:00:00"/>
  </Tour>
  <Tour Name="Bahamas Dive">
    <Event Code="01-002" DateBegin="2001-05-09T00:00:00"/>
    <Event Code="01-006" DateBegin="2001-07-03T00:00:00"/>
    <Event Code="01-009" DateBegin="2001-08-12T00:00:00"/>
  </Tour>
  <Tour Name="Gauley River Rafting">
```

```
      <Event Code="01-012" DateBegin="2001-09-14T00:00:00"/>
      <Event Code="01-013" DateBegin="2001-09-15T00:00:00"/>
   </Tour>
   <Tour Name="Outer Banks Lighthouses">
      <Event Code="01-001" DateBegin="2001-02-02T00:00:00"/>
      <Event Code="01-004" DateBegin="2001-06-06T00:00:00"/>
      <Event Code="01-007" DateBegin="2001-07-03T00:00:00"/>
      <Event Code="01-011" DateBegin="2001-08-17T00:00:00"/>
      <Event Code="01-014" DateBegin="2001-10-03T00:00:00"/>
      <Event Code="01-016" DateBegin="2001-11-16T00:00:00"/>
   </Tour>

</Tours>
```

The element concludes with a closing tag, `</Events>`, as seen in the example above.

## Elements

XML is loose in its usage of elements and attributes. An element is generally an item similar to a tuple or row. However, a column can also be represented within XML as an element. Element names cannot contain spaces, must be unique, and are case-sensitive.

Elements can contain the following:

+ Other nested elements to represent secondary table information or columns

+ Attributes, which are similar to database columns

+ Text data

The `element` tag is repeated for each instance of the element. For example, the `CHA2_Events.xml` sample XML document has a series of `Tour` elements beginning with the `<Tour>` tag and closing with the `</Tour>` tag. The first `Tour` element is this:

```
<Tour Name="Amazon Trek">
```

The tag denotes a Tour. In this case, the element has an attribute, `Name`, with a value of `"Amazon Trek"`.

If an element contains nested elements, it will close with a closing tag:

```
<Tour Name="Amazon Trek">
   Other elements
</Tour>
```

If the element does not contain any additional elements, it can be self-closed with a slash at the conclusion of the element:

```
<Event Code="01-003" DateBegin="2001-03-16T00:00:00"/>
```

Data that a database developer would consider an attribute is often expressed within an XML document as a valid nested element:

```
<Tour>
   <Name="Amazon Trek">
</Tour>
```

An element may also contain stand-alone text referred to as *PCData* (parsable character data):

```
<Thing "This is a PCData text within an element">
</Thing>
```

Although elements and attributes seem interchangeable, elements can be repeated while attributes cannot. While Java Web developers might consider an element a valid location for a column data, database developers have been describing data for a few decades now, and know better.

## Attributes

Database tables have columns and XML documents can have attributes to further describe the element. Attribute names must be unique and contain no spaces. The attribute value is enclosed in single or double quotes. Each attribute may only be applied to an element once. In the following case, name is an attribute describing the tour element:

```
<Tour Name="Amazon Trek">
```

**Note**    XML lacks an explicit `null` value. An attribute can be an empty string, but `null`s cannot be passed with XML without an explicit `Column-Null` attribute being specified and the attribute being set to 1 to indicate a `null`.

## Namespaces

XML can share data between dissimilar systems, and data names are not always unique. For example the term *stock* has a different meaning in the financial, stock-car racing, firearms, and lumber industries. XML uses a namespace to differentiate between similar terms by providing a unique name qualifier. The namespace is a shortcut that refers to a unique string. While any unique string can differentiate namespaces, the standard practice is to use the string to point to the URL location of the Data Type Document for the data associated with the namespace.

In the following example, the `tr` namespace refers to a unique URL string:

```
<?xml version="1.0" encoding="UTF-8"?>
<Tours xmlns:tr="HTTP://www.CHA2.com/tr.dtd">
  <tr:Tour Name="Amazon Trek">
</Tours>
```

## Well-Formed XML Documents

XML is very strict concerning formatting and syntax, much stricter than HTML or SQL. HTML browsers have become very liberal in their allowance for poorly formed HTML tags (`<p>` without `</p>`, tags improperly nested, tags with the wrong case, and so forth). The following are the five rules for a well-formed XML document:

1. Each XML document must have one root element.

2. Element or attribute names must not include any spaces.

3. All elements must be correctly nested and terminated:

```
<x> <y> </y> </x>
```

**4.** All tags are case-sensitive.

**5.** All attribute values must be in quotes.

XMLSpy's yellow checkmark tool tests the current XML document for adherence to the well-formed rules.

# XML Text

XML is primarily a text document and as such it has a few well-defined rules concerning text, substituting special characters, and comments.

## PCData

Parsable Character Data, or PCData, is any text that the parser will see as it reads the document. Elements must be PCData.

## CData

CData (Character Data) is text that the parser will ignore. CData is defined with brackets and the term `CDATA`. The following text is invalid because of the ampersand in the text. Using CData, the parser bypasses the text:

```
<Couple><![CDATA[Paul & Melissa]]</ Couple >
```

## Entities

An entity is a predefined shortcut, or placeholder, for a symbol that would otherwise cause a syntax error. For example, angle brackets (< >) are illegal because they are used to create tags. The standard entities are listed in Table 22-1:

### Table 22-1: Standard Entities

| Entity | Meaning |
|--------|---------|
| &lt; | < |
| &gt; | > |
| &amp; | & |
| &quot; | " |
| &apos; | ' |

The invalid XML element shown previously can be legally written with an entity:

```
<Couple "Paul &amp; Melissa" />
```

## Comments

XML comments are the same as HTML comments, except that XML comments can't include extra hyphens:

```
<!-- Comment  -->
```

# Document Type Definitions (DTDs)

An advantage of XML over SQL record sets is that an XML document can include data validation and schema information.

A Document Type Definition is a set of rules that defines the structure of an SGML document. Each SGML document may use only one DTD file. (HTML uses a DTD document that's built into the browser.) XML documents can use custom DTDs. The DTD may be in a separate file or included within the XML document. If the DTD is in a separate file, multiple XML documents can share the same DTD.

An XML document must pass two tests. The first test is whether it's a well-formed XML document that adheres to the five rules. In XML terms, a valid document is one that is well formed and has passed a second data-validation test using its DTD. XML Spy's green check tool performs a validation check.

## DTD Structure

The DTD defines the root, elements, repetition of elements, and PCData within the elements. DTD syntax keywords start with a bang (exclamation point) and are uppercase.

**Best Practice**

I recommend developing DTD for your XML documents as a method of improving data validity. XML Schemas are more powerful than DTDs, but they aren't accepted by as many parsers. For now, DTDs are the standard.

### Elements

The following DTD example (CHA2_Events.DTD) defines the elements within the sample XML document:

```
<?xml version="1.0" encoding="UTF-8"?>
<!ELEMENT Event EMPTY>
<!ATTLIST Event
   Code CDATA #REQUIRED
   DateBegin CDATA #REQUIRED
>
<!ELEMENT Tour (Event+)>
<!ATTLIST Tour
   Name CDATA #REQUIRED
>
<!ELEMENT Tours (Tour+)>
```

**Note**

XMLSpy can automatically generate DTDs from existing XML documents and can even create database tables from DTDs.

The <!ELEMENT tag defines an element and specifies any nested elements within the element. For example, the <!ELEMENT Tour (Event+)> tag indicates that the Tour element contains an Event element.

### Nested Elements

Any nested elements are added to elements in a DTD by being listed within parentheses following the element. The nested element's cardinality (which XML refers to as *repetition*) is defined by the occurrence indicators, as listed in Table 22-2. The occurrence indicator is added to the nested element as a suffix.

### Table 22-2: Nested Element Occurrence Indicators

| Indicator | Element Repetition | Element Required |
|---|---|---|
| None (Default) | One | Required |
| + | One to many | Required |
| ? | Zero to one | Optional |
| * | Zero to many | Optional |

In the sample DTD file, the + in the root-element definition indicates that the Events root element must include one to many Event elements:

```
<!ELEMENT Tours (Tour+)>
```

In the following DTD sample line, a Customer element may include any number of order elements, must include at least one address element, and must include exactly one account element:

```
<!ELEMENT Customer (Order*, Address+, Account)>
```

Each element definition includes the definition of the next level of nested elements. If the Order element includes OrderDetail elements, the OrderDetail element must be defined within the Order element, not the Customer element.

Listing the nested elements within parentheses also defines the order of the nested elements. So in the case of the previous Customer element, the subelements must be in the following order: Order elements (if any), Address elements, and Account elements.

Nested elements, which may be substituted, are separated by pipe symbols (|) rather than commas. The following example indicates that the MainElement must contain one element1 and one or more of either element2 or element3:

```
MainElement(element1, (element2 | element3)+ )
```

In addition to listing specific elements, ANY allows any defined keyword in any order and EMPTY allows elements with no data.

## General Entities

In addition to the special character entities such as (&quot;), general entities may be defined in the DTD and then used in the XML document. A general entity is similar to a constant in a procedural programming language. Parameter entities may be nested. The following line creates a companyname entity:

```
<!ENTITY COMPANYNAME "OBX Kites Company">
```

Within the XML document, the general entity will be replaced by the value when the data is read. For example,

```
Company - &COMPANYNAME;
```

becomes

```
Company - OBX Kites Company
```

General entities are useful for building generic XML documents with values that change depending on the DTD document used.

## Parameter Entities

A DTD parameter entity (defined with a %) is used to insert an external DTD document similar to a #include compiler command in procedural languages. The parameter entity must be defined before it's used.

The following example demonstrates including the tour element as a parameter entity. The tour.dtd file is inserted into the event.dtd document:

```
Tour.dtd file:
<!ELEMENT Tour (Event+)>
<!ATTLIST Tour
    Name CDATA #REQUIRED
>

Event.dtd file:
<?xml version="1.0" encoding="UTF-8"?>
<!ENTITY % TOUR SYSTEM "tour.dtd">
<!ELEMENT Event EMPTY>
<!ATTLIST Event
    Code CDATA #REQUIRED
    DateBegin CDATA #REQUIRED
>
%Tour;
<!ELEMENT Tours (Tour+)>
```

## Defining Attributes

Within a DTD, an element's attributes may be defined with the ATTLIST keyword. In the sample DTD document shown previously, the Code and DateBegin attributes of the Event element are defined in the following tag:

```
<!ATTLIST Event
    Code CDATA #REQUIRED
    DateBegin CDATA #REQUIRED
>
```

XML DTDs don't provide for full-featured data-typing or constraints as database developers would think of constraints. But they can configure the required status of an attribute using the following keywords:

✦ #REQUIRED — An attribute value must be present in the XML document.

✦ #IMPLIED — If the attribute value is missing in the XML document, the application will supply the value.

✦ #FIXED — The DTD's attribute value will be passed as data regardless of the value in the XML document. (The parser should produce an error if the DTD's fixed value is changed in the XML document, but many parsers don't check this.)

Unlike elements, DTDs, XSD (XML Schema Document) don't establish an attribute order.

## ID Attributes

The ID attribute option defines a unique constraint on the data within the XML document. ID is limited by the fact that it cannot accept numeric data, so it's useful only for unique names or codes that include mixed character data.

The following example forces the tour names to be unique:

```
<!ATTLIST Tour
    Name CDATA ID #REQUIRED
>
```

## IDREF Attributes

An IDREF attribute option is a loose foreign-key reference within the XML document. An attribute defined as an IDREF must have data that refers to data that's been validated by an ID attribute—any ID attribute. Since by the very nature of XML documents (elements nested with elements) most one-to-many relationships are handled, IDREF attributes are useful for reflexive relationships.

# Referencing the DTD

A DTD is only useful when an XML document references it for validation. An XML document may either include the DTD definition itself within the XML document or reference an external DTD document. The advantage of an external DTD is that it becomes a single point of reference for multiple XML documents.

Internal DTDs are useful for working with a changing schema, such as during development or testing. Each version of an XML document contains its own validation information.

## Referencing an External DTD

When the DTD is an external document, it's referenced within the declaration section of an XML document. The location of the DTD document is often an HTTP URL (although if you installed the book's CD the Tours DTD document is located under the SQLServerBible directory). The CHA2_Events_DTDexternal.xml file includes a reference to an external DTD:

```
<!DOCTYPE Tours SYSTEM
  "C:\SQLServerBible\Sample Databases\CapeHatterasAdventures\
  CHA2_Tours.dtd">
```

## Referencing an Internal DTD

To include the DTD validation information inside the XML document, the entire DTD definition is inserted within a DOCTYPE tag and square brackets:

```
<?xml version="1.0" encoding="UTF-8"?>
<!DOCTYPE Tours [
    DTD definition goes here
]>
<Tours>
  <Tour Name="Amazon Trek">
    <Event Code="01-003" DateBegin="2001-03-16T00:00:00"/>
...
```

The CHA2_Events_DTDinternal.xml file includes an internal DTD definition.

# XML Schema — XSDs

To database professionals the term *schema* refers to the logical or physical design of the data. Within the Web-oriented XML community, a schema is a specific type of XML validation.

XML Schema Document, or XSD, is an elegant means of performing XML document validation. XML itself is used to define the XML elements. While Data Type Definition documents are the accepted means of XML validation, the newer XML Schema is more powerful and is used within .Net.

✦ XSDs are themselves XML documents. As such, the familiar XML syntax may be created and edited using standard XML tools. XSDs must be well-formed XML documents.

✦ From a database viewpoint, an important factor is that XSDs include data typing, something that's lacking in DTDs.

✦ XSD can include namespace definitions.

XSD was approved as a recommendation by W3C on May 2, 2001, and at the end of 2002 was starting to be used. Be sure to check HTTP://www.w3c.org for updates to the XSDs.

On the CD-ROM

Altnova's XML Spy will work with XSDs. An XSD within XML Spy is referred to as a W3C schema in the Generate DTD/Schema dialog.

The following is the XSD definition for the previous sample XML document, which contains event data from the CHA2 database generated by XML Spy (CHA2_Events.XSD). In the declaration section of the XML document the XMLSchema namespace is referenced. Each XML element and attribute (in bold) is defined within with the XSD element structure:

```
<?xml version="1.0" encoding="UTF-8"?>
<!--W3C Schema generated by
      XML Spy v4.3 U (HTTP://www.xmlspy.com)-->
<xs:schema xmlns:xs
      ="HTTP://www.w3.org/2001/XMLSchema"
      elementFormDefault="qualified">
  <xs:element name="Event">
    <xs:complexType>
      <xs:attribute name="Code"
          type="xs:string" use="required"/>
      <xs:attribute name="DateBegin"
          type="xs:dateTime" use="required"/>
    </xs:complexType>
  </xs:element>
  <xs:element name="Tour">
    <xs:complexType>
      <xs:sequence>
        <xs:element ref="Event" maxOccurs="unbounded"/>
      </xs:sequence>
      <xs:attribute name="Name"
          type="xs:string" use="required"/>
    </xs:complexType>
```

```
    </xs:element>
    <xs:element name="Tours">
      <xs:complexType>
        <xs:sequence>
          <xs:element ref="Tour" maxOccurs="unbounded"/>
        </xs:sequence>
      </xs:complexType>
    </xs:element>
  </xs:schema>
```

XML Schemas are generally much longer than the equivalent DTD definitions. While DTDs are relatively simple, XML Schemas can be very complex.

An XSD document is an XML document that describes an XML document, so an XML element is defined by an xsd:element (xsd is the XSD namespace). XML Schema includes two types of XML elements, *simple* and *complex*. A simple element only includes text (PCData), no subelements or attributes. The XML Item element is defined in XSD as a simple element:

```
XML: <Item> Big Kite</Item>
XSD: <xsd:element name="Item" type="xsd:string">
```

Complex elements can contain subelements and attributes and mixed content (PCData and other elements). The previous sample XSD document includes complex elements.

# XSD Elements

Elements and attributes defined within the root element are considered global elements and may be referenced later in the XSD document. This adds consistency and reusability to elements within XSD documents. An element, once defined, may be referenced by means of the following syntax:

```
<xsd:element ref="Event"/>
```

## Element Cardinality

XSD includes a flexible method of defining the occurrences of a subelement using the MinOccurs and MaxOccurs element options. The default is 1; setting the MaxOccurs to unbounded permits a true one-to-many relationship:

```
<xsd:element name="Event"
    minOcurrs = "0"
    maxOccurs = "unbounded"
```

## Element Grouping

XSD has three methods of ordering subelements:

✦ <xsd:sequence> — The XML elements may be in the sequenced order.

✦ <xsd:all> — The XML elements may be used once, in any order.

✦ <xsd:choice> — Any one of the elements may be in the XML document.

The grouping tags (sequence, all, or choice) are wrapped around the subelements.

## XSD Attributes

XML Schemas define attributes within an attribute XSD element called `xsd:attribute`. For example, within the sample XSD schema, the `name` attribute is defined by a subelement under the `tour` element:

```
<xs:attribute name="Name"
     type="xs:string" use="required"/>
```

The `use` option may be used to define the attribute as `required` or `optional` (default).

## XSD Data Types and Validation

This is the area where XSDs show significant improvement over DTDs. The W3C XML Schema defines over 40 data types, most of which map well with SQL Server.

Beyond the base data types, derived type, much like a user-defined type, may be added by means of using the `simpletype` data type and building data facets to describe the data validation. An XSD facet is a data-validation constraint, similar to a check constraint, that can perform one of several data checks.

## Referencing an XSD Schema

An XSD Schema document may be referenced within the root element of an XML document. The following code in the `CHA2_Tours_XSD.xml` document references the `CHA2_Tours.xsd` document (abridged):

```
<?xml version="1.0" encoding="UTF-8"?>
<Tours xmlns:xsi="HTTP://www.w3.org/2001/XMLSchema-instance"
   xsi:noNamespaceSchemaLocation="C:\SQLServerBible\
     Sample Databases\CapeHatterasAdventures\CHA2_Event.xsd">
<Tour Name="Amazon Trek">
   <Event Code="01-003" DateBegin="2001-03-16T00:00:00"/>
...
```

XML Spy can automatically generate the XSD and reference it within the XML document.

**Best Practice**

You don't need to decide between DTD and XSD for validation — use both. Because DTDs are more established, I recommend always using DTDs and optionally sending an XSD schema for those data partners who may opt to use it.

# XML and SQL Server

SQL Server 2000 enables you to create and read XML data from within a `select` statement.

## Creating XML with SQL Server 2000

SQL Server 2000 can produce XML documents directly from queries. The `for XML` optional `select` suffix directs SQL Server to format the query-data result as an XML document rather than as a standard SQL result set.

**Note** The XML output appears as a single-column result. By default, the Query Analyzer `maximum size per column` is set too low to view the XML result set. It may be changed to its maximum setting of 8192 in the Results tab of the Options dialog opened from Tools ⇨ Options.

The `For XML` suffix generates the XML data, but not the declaration section or the `root` element. The application will need to wrap the data from SQL Server correctly to create a result set that qualifies as a well-formed XML document.

### For XML Raw

The `For XML` suffix has three modes: `raw`, `auto`, and an `elements` option. The `For XML Raw` mode simply dumps the result-set rows to an XML document without generating any hierarchical structure. Each SQL row becomes an XML `row` element:

```
SELECT Tour.Name, Event.Code, Event.DateBegin
  FROM Tour
  JOIN Event
    ON Tour.TourID = Event.TourID
  FOR XML RAW
```

Result (abridged):

```
<row Name="Amazon Trek" Code="01-003"
  DateBegin="2001-03-16T00:00:00"/>
<row Name="Amazon Trek" Code="01-015"
  DateBegin="2001-11-05T00:00:00"/>
<row Name="Appalachian Trail" Code="01-005"
  DateBegin="2001-06-25T00:00:00"/>
<row Name="Appalachian Trail" Code="01-008"
  DateBegin="2001-07-14T00:00:00"/>
<row Name="Appalachian Trail" Code="01-010"
  DateBegin="2001-08-14T00:00:00"/>
  ...
```

### For XML Auto

The `auto` mode determines any hierarchies within the data structure and generates a much more useable XML document. The previous sample XML document at the beginning of this chapter was produced with the following query:

```
SELECT Tour.Name, Event.Code, Event.DateBegin
  FROM Tour
  JOIN Event
    ON Tour.TourID = Event.TourID
  FOR XML AUTO
```

The `elements` option causes the `for XML auto` mode to generate elements instead of attributes. The following variation of the sample XML document uses the `elements` option to generate elements exclusively:

```
SELECT Tour.Name, Event.Code, Event.DateBegin
  FROM Tour
  JOIN Event
    ON Tour.TourID = Event.TourID
  FOR XML AUTO, ELEMENTS
```

Results (abridged):

```
<Tour>
  <Name>Amazon Trek</Name>
  <Event>
    <Code>01-003</Code>
    <DateBegin>2001-03-16T00:00:00</DateBegin>
  </Event>
  <Event>
    <Code>01-015</Code>
    <DateBegin>2001-11-05T00:00:00</DateBegin>
  </Event>
</Tour>
<Tour>
  <Name>Appalachian Trail</Name>
  <Event>
    <Code>01-005</Code>
    <DateBegin>2001-06-25T00:00:00</DateBegin>
  </Event>
  <Event>
    <Code>01-008</Code>
    <DateBegin>2001-07-14T00:00:00</DateBegin>
  </Event>
  <Event>
    <Code>01-010</Code>
    <DateBegin>2001-08-14T00:00:00</DateBegin>
  </Event>
</Tour>
...
```

# Reading XML into SQL Server

Applications read XML using a parser that in turn exposes the XML data within the Document Object Mode, or DOM. This W3C-established standard is an object-oriented representation of an XML document. The XML document, and each element, attribute, and text within the document, becomes a DOM object. DOM is very powerful and may be used within object-oriented code to create, read, or modify an XML document.

SQL Server uses the Microsoft XML parser and DOM to read an XML document in a two-stage process:

1. The sp_xml_preparedocument stored procedure reads the XML document using the MSXML parser and creates the DOM objects internal to SQL Server. The DOM object is identified by an integer returned by the stored procedure.

2. OpenXML is used as a data source within an SQL DML statement. OpenXML identifies the DOM object using the integer returned from sp_xml_preparedocument.

The following code sample first sets the sample XML data into the @XML SQL Server local variable. SQL Server then reads data into SQL using the previous two stages, as follows:

1. When the sp_xml_preparedocument store procedure is executed, the DOM is created. The DOM ID is received as an output parameter from the stored procedure and stored in the @iDOM variable.

2. The `Select` statement refers to the `OpenXML` system function as a data source. It accepts three parameters:

   - The integer ID of the internal DOM object, which was stored in the `@iDOM` variable.

   - The `rowpattern` of the XML document, which `OpenXML` used to identify the element structure of the XML data. In this case the `rowpattern` is `'/Tours/Tour/Event'`.

   - The XML configuration flag, which determines how the elements and attributes are interpreted by `OpenXML` according to Table 22-3.

3. The `OpenXML`'s `With` option forces a column matching for the result set passed back from `OpenXML`. A column is defined by its XML name, data type, and optional XML element location.

### Table 22-3: OpenXML Configuration Flags

| Flag Value | Setting | Description |
|---|---|---|
| 0 | Default | Defaults to attribute-centric |
| 1 | Attribute-centric | `OpenXML` looks for attributes |
| 2 | Element-centric | `OpenXML` looks for elements |
| 8 | Combined | `Open XML` looks for attributes and then looks for elements |

The batch closes with the `sp_removedocument` system stored procedure, which releases the DOM from memory:

```
DECLARE
  @iDOM int,
  @XML VarChar(8000)

Set @XML = '
<?xml version="1.0" encoding="UTF-8"?>
<Tours>
  <Tour Name="Amazon Trek">
    <Event Code="01-003" DateBegin="2001-03-16T00:00:00"/>
    <Event Code="01-015" DateBegin="2001-11-05T00:00:00"/>
  </Tour>
  <Tour Name="Appalachian Trail">
    <Event Code="01-005" DateBegin="2001-06-25T00:00:00"/>
    <Event Code="01-008" DateBegin="2001-07-14T00:00:00"/>
    <Event Code="01-010" DateBegin="2001-08-14T00:00:00"/>
  </Tour>
  <Tour Name="Bahamas Dive">
    <Event Code="01-002" DateBegin="2001-05-09T00:00:00"/>
    <Event Code="01-006" DateBegin="2001-07-03T00:00:00"/>
    <Event Code="01-009" DateBegin="2001-08-12T00:00:00"/>
  </Tour>
  <Tour Name="Gauley River Rafting">
```

```
        <Event Code="01-012" DateBegin="2001-09-14T00:00:00"/>
        <Event Code="01-013" DateBegin="2001-09-15T00:00:00"/>
      </Tour>
      <Tour Name="Outer Banks Lighthouses">
        <Event Code="01-001" DateBegin="2001-02-02T00:00:00"/>
        <Event Code="01-004" DateBegin="2001-06-06T00:00:00"/>
        <Event Code="01-007" DateBegin="2001-07-03T00:00:00"/>
        <Event Code="01-011" DateBegin="2001-08-17T00:00:00"/>
        <Event Code="01-014" DateBegin="2001-10-03T00:00:00"/>
        <Event Code="01-016" DateBegin="2001-11-16T00:00:00"/>
      </Tour>
</Tours>'

-- Generate the internal DOM
EXEC sp_xml_preparedocument @iDOM OUTPUT, @XML

-- OPENXML provider.
SELECT *
  FROM OPENXML (@iDOM, '/Tours/Tour/Event',8)
        WITH ([Name] VARCHAR(25) '../@Name',
              Code VARCHAR(10),
              DateBegin DATETIME
             )
EXEC sp_xml_removedocument @iDOM
```

Result (abridged):

```
Name                Code      DateBegin
----------------    --------  -------------------------
Amazon Trek         01-003    2001-03-16 00:00:00.000
Amazon Trek         01-015    2001-11-05 00:00:00.000
Appalachian Trail   01-005    2001-06-25 00:00:00.000
Appalachian Trail   01-008    2001-07-14 00:00:00.000
...
```

# Transforming XML with XSL

One of the most powerful aspects of XML is the ability to present XML data in different formats defined by XML style sheets or XSL. Typically, the style sheet will wrap HTML around the XML to present a Web page. When an XML document that references an XSL style sheet is opened within a browser, the XSL style sheet becomes a framework HTML page, which is populated from the XML document's data.

Not all XML parsers perform XSL parsing; fortunately, the MSXML parser includes an XSL parser. The processor that performs the XSL transformation is referred to as the XSLT processor.

XSL is not limited to transforming the XML into desktop-computer HTML code. It can transform the data to WML for wireless browsers, to XHTML, or even to another XML definition for B2B transformations.

# XSL Style Sheets

The style sheet itself is a W3C standard. The style sheet is external to the XML document and referenced within the XML document. It must be a well-formed XML document.

The following XSL style sheet, CHA2_Events.XSL, formats the sample XML document we have been using thus far, to present a table of events for each tour run by the Cape Hatteras Adventure Company. The style sheet doesn't include any cool graphics or fancy styling so that the focus can be on how the XML data is integrated within the XSL style sheet. However, any good-looking HTML page can be built with XSL style sheets.

The declaration section identifies the style sheet as an XSL document, and references two namespaces. Within xsl:template match ="/", which identifies the root of the style sheet that contains the HTML framework, notice the familiar <html> and <body> tags. The <xsl:apply-templates select="Tours"/> tag is where the Tours template is inserted within the HTML framework.

Within the <xsl:template match="Tours"> tag, the XML tour element is read and the for-each element is used much like a loop to iterate through the XML data. The XML's attribute or text data is referenced with the value-of command:

```
<xsl:stylesheet version="1.0"
  xmlns:xsl="HTTP://www.w3.org/1999/XSL/Transform"
  xmlns:fo="HTTP://www.w3.org/1999/XSL/Format">

<xsl:template match="/">
  <html>
    <body>
      Cape Hatteras Adventures <br> </br>
      Event Schedule
      <hr></hr>
      <xsl:apply-templates select="Tours"/>
    </body>
  </html>
</xsl:template>

<xsl:template match="Tours">
  <xsl:for-each select= "Tour">
    <xsl:sort select="Name"/>
    <b><xsl:value-of select="@Name"/> </b><br></br>
    <table border="1">
      <xsl:for-each select= "Event">
      <xsl:sort select="DateBegin "/>
        <tr>
          <td><xsl:value-of select="@Code"/></td>
          <td><xsl:value-of select="@DateBegin"/></td>
        </tr>
      </xsl:for-each>
    </table>
  </xsl:for-each>
</xsl:template>

</xsl:stylesheet>
```

The declaration section of the sample XML document is altered to include a reference to the new style sheet (CHA2_Events_XSL.xml):

```
<?xml-stylesheet type="text/xsl" href="CHA_Tours.xsl"?>
```

The XSL style sheet can also ensure the sort order of the data by use of the `xsl:sort` tag:

```
<xsl:sort select="Name"/>
```

When the XML document is viewed with a browser the result is a basic Web page, as shown in Figure 22-3.

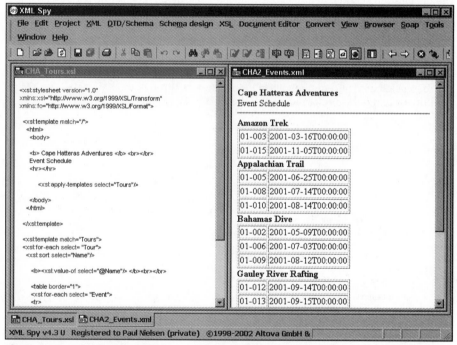

**Figure 22-3:** Viewing the XML data with the XSL style sheet applied reads the XML data into an HTML page. While this page isn't very fancy, XSL style sheets can produce any HTML code.

## Transforming XML to XML

XSL is simply a means of restyling XML into another format. While it's typically used to transform XML data into an HTML page, with some creative work XSL can transform an XML document into a different XML document, which is very useful to Web developers performing B2B XML transformations.

Combining this technique with XPath queries can "`select`" a subset of data from one XML document into another XML document. The element and attribute structure may also be changed in the transformation. During the creation of the XSL style sheet the `<xsl:element>` and `<xsl:attribute>` tags are used to create the new elements and attributes.

**Note** More information on XML transformation and XPath can be found in the *"XML Bible, Second Edition"* (John Wiley & Sons Inc.).

# XPATH

XPath is a feature of XML and adds result restriction and aggregation capabilities to XML while navigating through the XML hierarchy to access any node (element, attribute, or piece of text) within the XML document. The XPath code may be added to the XSL style sheet or to other XML queries to filter the data. The most applicable use of XPath for SQL Server is in templates. (While XPath is stable, its more powerful cousin, XQuery, is still evolving.)

XPath must first identify the node. Identifying a node is very similar to the column name within a SQL `select` statement's `where` clause. For example, to navigate to the `event` element under the `tour` element use the following structure:

    /Tours/Tour/Event

The previous example uses absolute location. The node location may also be selected by means of relative location, so that a portion of the XSL that's working with child data may select a parent node for the filtering process.

To navigate down the hierarchical XML tree to an attribute, use the @ sign, as follows:

    /Tours/Tour/@Name

Once the correct node is identified, XPath has several filtering features to select the correct data. For the execution of a `where` = filter the criteria are specified after the node in square brackets. The file, `CHA2_Events_XPath.xsl`, includes the following XPath code:

    /Tours/Tour/@Name ['Gauley River Rafting']

# SQLXML

Microsoft SQLXML installs as a layer between IIS and SQL Server and allows queries to be submitted to SQL Server from a browser. This is done with virtual directories in IIS.

## Virtual Directories

To set up HTTP queries, run the program Configure SQL XML Support in IIS. Right-click the default Web site and select New ➪ Virtual Directory. Figure 22-4 shows the dialog box that will appear.

The General tab of the dialog box will prompt you for a virtual-directory name and local path. Choose a name for the virtual directory that will appear after the server name in the HTTP request. Also, you need to have it point to a physical directory that will not really contain anything, but that needs to exist in order for the configuration to work. Choose a simple name like SQL or the name of the database against which the queries will run.

On the Security tab, enter the login ID the queries will be run as. The best approach is to create an account for the queries to run under. You can specify either a SQL or Windows login for this. Another approach is to require the browser to pass a client's Windows authentication if the session is taking place within an intranet; alternately, you can send a text login ID and password that would typically be stored in a database or configuration file. It is somewhat dangerous to pass clear-text login ID's and passwords and this is not a recommended practice.

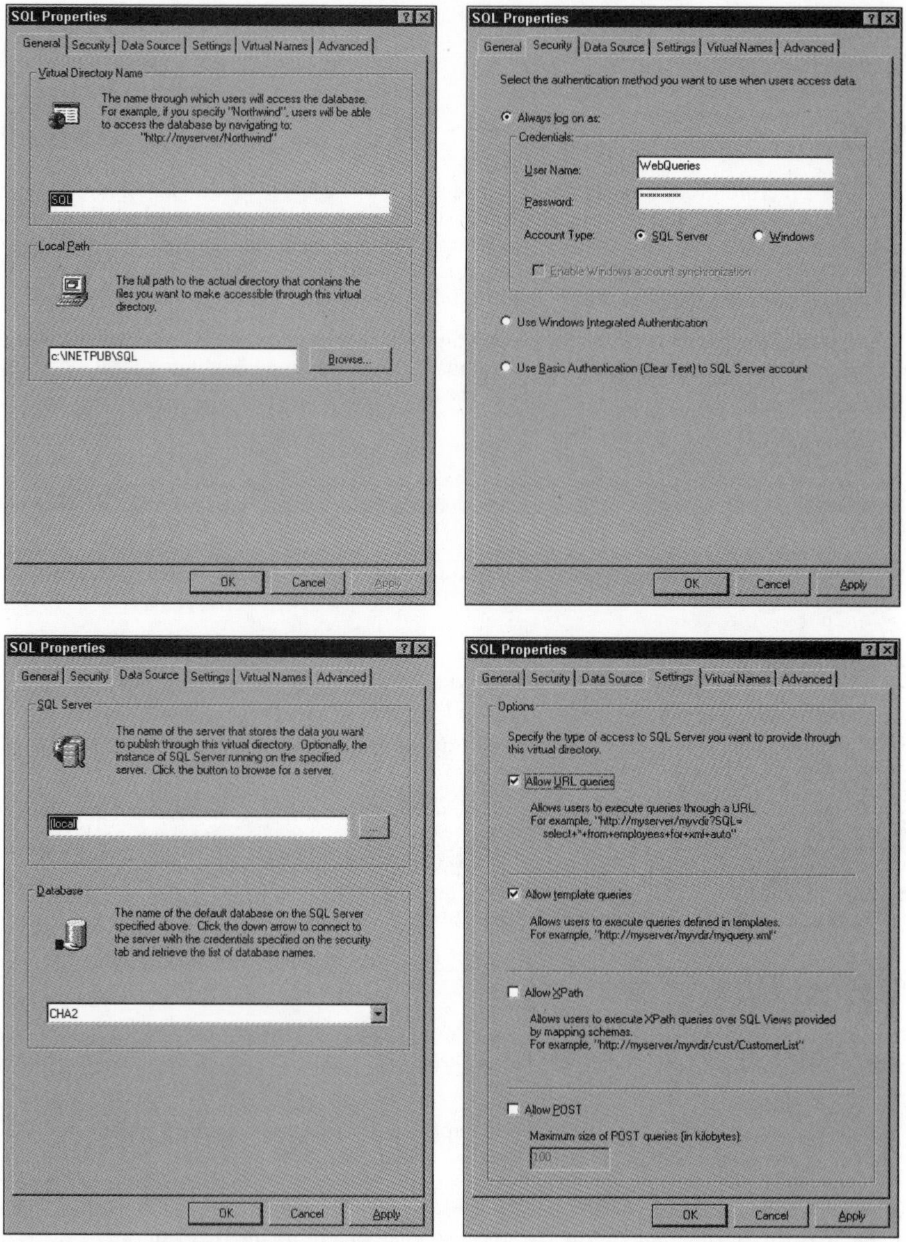

**Figure 22-4:** Configuring Virtual Directories in IIS to run HTTP queries in SQL Server

The Data Source tab is used to specify the server name and default directory for the queries. The Settings tab is where you enable the features you want to support. Allowing URL queries enables people to execute ad hoc queries against the SQL Server. Allowing template queries enables clients to only execute queries that have been previously saved into a template file. URL queries can be dangerous if you open up too much access to the account the queries run under, whereas template queries limit the clients to only those queries that have been pre-programmed.

Allowing XPath queries requires an XDR schema file to be created for each query that maps the columns to XML attributes. The URL query can then execute the SQL statement and use the XPath language to drill down into a particular node.

## HTTP Queries

If the virtual directory is enabled and allows HTTP queries, a browser pointed to the correct server can issue a query in the address line of the browser using the for xml syntax:

```
HTTP://server/virtualdirectory?sql=SELECT QUERY&
    Root=RootName
```

The select query cannot include any spaces, so substitute a + for any spaces. Also, the select...for xml command does not generate a well-formed XML document because it lacks an XML declaration section and root node. The second parameter, root, supplies the name of the root node. For example, the following HTTP query retrieves a list of tours and start dates into an XML document with a root named Tours:

```
HTTP://localhost/sql?sql=SELECT+Tour.Name,+Event.Code,+Event.DateBegin+
FROM+Tour+JOIN+Event+ON+Tour.TourID+=+Event.TourID+FOR+XML+AUTO,+ELEMEN
TS&root=Tours
```

The result of the HTTP query is shown in Figure 22-5.

Note that you may type the query with spaces, or with plus signs instead of spaces. However, if you use spaces, the Web server will convert each one to %20, which makes the URL difficult to read. The better way to handle this and make the URL more readable is to save the whole query in a stored procedure:

```
CREATE PROCEDURE GetTourBeginDates AS
SELECT Tour.Name, Event.Code, Event.DateBegin
FROM Tour JOIN Event ON Tour.TourID = Event.TourID
FOR XML AUTO, ELEMENTS
```

Then simply use the stored-procedure name in the HTTP query:

```
HTTP://localhost/sql?sql=GetTourBeginDates&root=root
```

The results will be identical but it will be much easier to manage and view the URL.

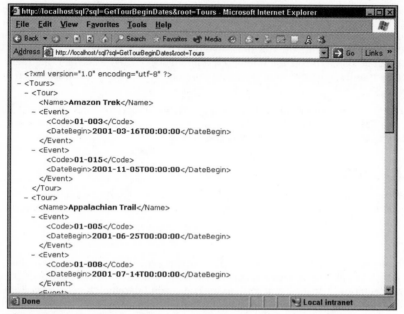

**Figure 22-5:** Viewing the XML data, with the XSL style sheet applied, reads the HTTP queries.

## Template Queries

Template queries enable you to assert a little more control over what queries can be run over an HTTP request, as well as over how the output will look. First you need to configure the virtual directory to allow template queries. Then create a Virtual Name as a template type and a directory to contain the template files. Once that is done, you need to create a template file and save it in the directory specified in the Virtual Name configuration. You can then run queries using the following format:

```
HTTP://server/virtualdirectory/virtualname/filename.xml
```

The XML template file is a fully formed XML document, but where you want the contents of a query substituted into the document, place the SQL statement between the tags `<sql:query>` and `</sql:query>`. Configure a virtual name called Temp with a type of template that points to a directory called `\temp` (see Figure 22-6). Make sure you create a subdirectory under the physical directory that the virtual directory points to.

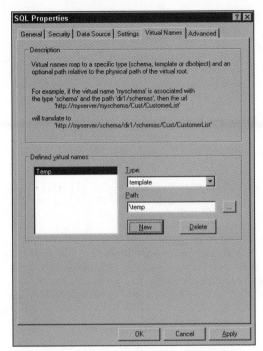

**Figure 22-6:** Allow template queries via the Virtual Names tab.

Once the virtual name exists, create a document called `Tours.xml` and save it in the path `C:\INETPUB\SQL\Temp\Tours.XML`.

```
<?xml version ='1.0' encoding='UTF-8'?>
  <root xmlns:sql="urn:schemas-microsoft-com:xml-sql">
    <sql:query>
        SELECT Tour.Name, Event.Code,
  Event.DateBegin
        FROM Tour
        JOIN Event ON Tour.TourID = Event.TourID
        FOR XML AUTO, ELEMENTS
    </sql:query>
  </root>
```

To execute this template query all you need to do is run the following:

```
HTTP://localhost/sql/Temp/Tours.xml
```

Running this will yield the same result as running the URL query, but it has been set up in advance so it does not open the door to potentially dangerous ad hoc queries. It also simplifies the URL for queries that are run frequently.

# Publishing Data on the Web

Apart from generating XML, SQL Server has the ability to generate HTML directly from a stored procedure.

The Web Assistant is a wizard in Enterprise Manager that can be used to generate calls to stored procedures that will generate HTML documents from a query. The documents it creates are called *static HTML files*, because a query is run at a given time and it generates a result set that is converted into HTML and saved as a file. The file itself is returned to the client. This method is different from a dynamic HTML page, which is generated through a script file such as ASP, ColdFusion, or JSP. With a dynamic page, a query is run against the database for each call to the Web page and a new HTML document is generated in memory for each client request. Both dynamic and static pages have advantages and disadvantages. For data that does not change much, such as a phone list or monthly-summary data, a static page is better because it eliminates the need for excessive calls to the SQL Server. For data that changes more frequently, such as an order-status or user-feedback page, the capabilities of a dynamic page are more appropriate.

The wizard is relatively easy to use, and you have only a few things to decide on when running it. You can allow the wizard to do basic formatting for you, or you can build a template file using any HTML-authoring tool. The template file enables you to make a page that fits seamlessly into the overall look and feel of the Web site. All that is necessary to make the template file work is the inclusion of a few special tags in the HTML files. If you want to dump the result set of a query into the HTML document as a simple HTML table, just use the tag `<%insert_data_here%>` where you want the table to appear. To have a little more control over the look of the output, use `<%begindetail%>` and `<%enddetail%>` tags, and between them type HTML code that you want repeated for each row of output. Use the tag `<%insert_data_here%>` for each column of the result set to control where they appear in the HTML code.

The other key decision to make is how frequently the Web page will be regenerated. Regeneration can be scheduled as a regular task, or it can occur each time the data changes. Regeneration is no different from any other scheduled job, it simply runs the stored procedure `sp_runwebtask`. To make the Web page refresh each time any data changes, you can create triggers on the table that is to be monitored for changes. Then, whenever there is an `insert`, `update`, or `delete` to that table, it will fire the trigger that runs the same `sp_runwebtask` stored procedure that you would use to recreate the page on a schedule. The advantage of triggers is that the pages are recreated immediately after the change is committed. The disadvantage is that if numerous changes are necessary, the trigger may fire after each change, causing the page to be recreated numerous times leading to serious performance drag.

Using the Web assistant does all the hard work of assembling a call to a stored procedure with a lot of parameters. Here is a sample of the `sp_makewebtask` procedure to create a simple Web page:

```
EXECUTE sp_makewebtask
  @outputfile = N'C:\SQLServerBible\Sample Databases
      \CapeHatterasAdventures\CHA_Events.htm',
  @query=N'SELECT Tour.Name, Event.Code, Event.DateBegin
          FROM Tour
            JOIN Event
              ON Tour.TourID = Event.TourID',
  @fixedfont=0,
  @HTMLheader=3,
  @webpagetitle=N'Cape Hatteras Adventures',
  @resultstitle=N'Tour Dates',
  @URL=N'HTTP://www.SQLServerBible.com',
  @reftext=N'www.SQLServerBible.com',
  @dbname=N'CHA2',
  @whentype=1,
  @procname=N'CHA2 Web Page',
  @codepage=65001,@charset=N'utf-8'
```

Running the stored procedure `sp_runwebtask @procname = N'CHA2 Web Page'` against the CHA database generates an HTML page (`CHA_Events.htm`) as seen below in Figure 22-7.

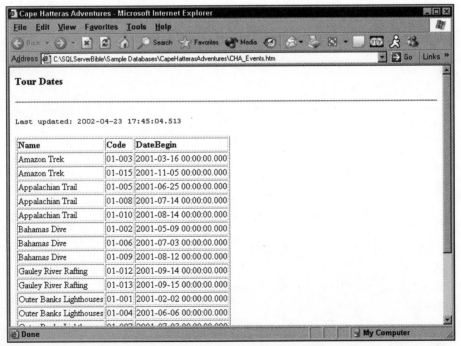

**Figure 22-7:** The Web assistant generates an HTML page of data with our query results.

## Summary

This chapter has briefly highlighted how SQL Server can serve data to the Web. We have explored the use of DTDs to validate XML data as well as how to properly implement them. We then touched on the use of style sheets to format XML data for presentation within a Web browser.

This chapter demonstrates the power SQL Server introduces with the use of XML. Unfortunately, due to space limitations, the chapter just scratches the surface of the vast use of XML. To learn more about XML, I highly suggest picking up the *XML Bible* (John Wiley & Sons, Inc.).

✦    ✦    ✦

# Administering SQL Server

◆ ◆ ◆ ◆

◆ ◆ ◆ ◆

The project isn't done when the production database goes live. A successful database requires preventive maintenance (tune-ups) and corrective maintenance (diligent recovery planning).

Databases are often developed without a thought to security, but security is also a day-to-day issue, or the database is obsolete.

Part IV is about keeping the box running smooth, day after day.

# Configuring SQL Server

S QL Server has a plethora of configuration options. The difficulty in mastering them lies in the fact that they are spread across three levels:

+ Server-level options generally configure how the server works with hardware and determines the database defaults.

+ Database-level options determine the behavior of the database and set the connection-level defaults.

+ Connection-level options determine the current behaviors within the connection or current procedure.

Several of the configuration options overlap or simply set the default for the level immediately below. This chapter pulls these three configuration levels into a single unified understanding of how they relate and affect each other.

## Setting the Options

Whether you choose to adjust the properties from Enterprise Manager's graphical tool or from code is completely up to you, but not every property is available from both Enterprise Manager and Query Analyzer. While Enterprise Manager has the advantages of being easy to use and walks you through easy to understand dialogs that prompt for the possible options in a pick and choose format, it lacks the repeatability of a T-SQL script run in Query Analyzer.

### Configuring the Server

The server-level configuration options control server wide settings, such as how SQL Server interacts with hardware, how it multi-threads within Windows, and whether triggers are permitted to fire other triggers. When configuring the server, keep in mind the goals of configuration — consistency and performance.

Graphically, many of the server options may be configured within the Server Property page, which can be open by right-clicking a server in the console tree.

The General tab in Enterprise Manager's SQL Server Properties (Configure) dialog box (Figure 23-1) reports the versions and environment of the server.

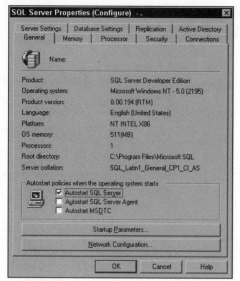

**Figure 23-1:** Enterprise Manager's Server Properties — the General tab

The same information is available to code. For example, the version may be identified with the @@Version global variable:

```
Select @@Version
-----------------------
Microsoft SQL Server  2000 - 8.00.532 (Intel X86)
    Oct  5 2001 20:31:34
    Copyright (c) 1988-2000 Microsoft Corporation
    Developer Edition on Windows NT 5.0 (Build 2195: Service Pack 2)
```

Many of the configuration properties do not take effect until SQL Server is restarted. For this reason, the Server Settings tab in the SQL Server Properties (Configure) dialog box may display either the configured values or the current running values, depending on the radio button selected at the bottom of the dialog box.

Within code, many of the server properties are set by means of the sp_configure system stored procedure. When executed without any parameters, this procedure reports the current settings, as in the following code (word-wrap adjusted to fit on page):

```
EXEC sp_configure
```

Result:

```
name            minimum      maximum       config_value run_value
--------------  -----------  -----------   ------------ ---------
affinity mask   -2147483648  2147483647    3            0
allow updates   0            1             0            0
awe enabled     0            1             0            0
c2 audit mode   0            1             0            0
cost threshold for parallelism
                0            32767         5            5
cursor threshold
```

```
                        -1        2147483647   -1             -1
default full-text language
                        0         2147483647   1033           1033
default language
                        0         9999         0              0
fill factor (%)0        100          0              0
index create memory (KB)
                        704       2147483647   0              0
lightweight pooling
                        0         1            1              1
locks         5000      2147483647   0              0
max degree of parallelism
                        0         32           0              0
max server memory (MB)
                        4         2147483647   128            128
max text repl size (B)
                        0         2147483647   65536          65536
max worker threads
                        32        32767        251            251
media retention
                        0         365          0              0
min memory per query (KB)
                        512       2147483647   1024           1024
min server memory (MB)
                        0         2147483647   16             16
nested triggers
                        0         1            1              1
network packet size (B)
                        512       65536        4096           4096
open objects   0        2147483647   0              0
priority boost 0        1            0              0
query governor cost limit
                        0         2147483647   0              0
query wait (s) -1       2147483647   -1             -1
recovery interval (min)
                        0         32767        0              0
remote access  0        1            1              1
remote login timeout (s)
                        0         2147483647   20             20
remote proc trans
                        0         1            0              0
remote query timeout (s)
                        0         2147483647   600            600
scan for startup procs
                        0         1            0              0
set working set size
                        0         1            1              1
show advanced options
                        0         1            1              1
two digit year cutoff
                        1753      9999         2049           2049
user connections
                        0         32767        0              0
user options   0        32767        0              0
```

The extended stored procedure, xp_msver, reports additional server and environment properties:

```
EXEC xp_msver
```

Result:

```
Index  Name                   Internal_Value Character_Value
------ --------------------   ----------     ------------------------
1      ProductName            NULL           Microsoft SQL Server
2      ProductVersion         524288         8.00.532
3      Language               1033           English (United States)
4      Platform               NULL           NT INTEL X86
5      Comments               NULL           NT INTEL X86
6      CompanyName            NULL           Microsoft Corporation
7      FileDescription        NULL           SQL Server Windows NT
8      FileVersion            NULL           2000.080.0532.00
9      InternalName           NULL           SQLSERVR
10     LegalCopyright         NULL           (c) 1988-2001 Microsoft
                                             Corp. All rights
                                             reserved.
11     LegalTrademarks        NULL           Microsoft(r) is a
                                             registered trademark of
                                             Microsoft Corporation.
                                             Windows(TM) is a
                                             trademark of Microsoft
                                             Corporation
12     OriginalFilename       NULL           SQLSERVR.EXE
13     PrivateBuild           NULL           NULL
14     SpecialBuild           34865152       NULL
15     WindowsVersion         143851525      5.0 (2195)
16     ProcessorCount         1              1
17     ProcessorActiveMask    1              00000001
18     ProcessorType          586            PROCESSOR_INTEL_PENTIUM
19     PhysicalMemory         192            192 (200855552)
20     Product ID             NULL           NULL
```

The ServerProperty system function is yet another means of determining information about the server. The advantage is that a function may be used as an expression within a select statement. The following use of the ServerProperty function to return the SQL Server instance edition:

```
SELECT ServerProperty('Edition')
```

Result:

```
Developer Edition
```

## Configuring the Database

The database-level options configure the current database's behavior regarding ANSI compatibility and recovery.

Most database options can be set in Enterprise Manager within the Database Properties page, which may be found by means of right-clicking a database in the console tree. The Options tab is shown in Figure 23-2.

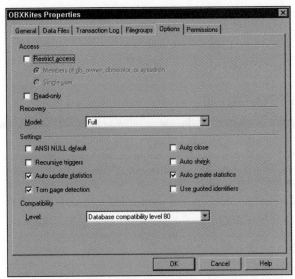

**Figure 23-2:** The Enterprise Manager's database properties Option tab can be used to configure the most common database properties.

The database configuration options can be set using code and the sp_dboption system stored procedure. When executed without any parameters, this procedure lists the available database settings:

```
EXEC sp_dboption
```

Result:

```
Settable database options:
----------------------------------
ANSI null default
ANSI nulls
ANSI padding
ANSI warnings
arithabort
auto create statistics
auto update statistics
autoclose
autoshrink
concat null yields null
cursor close on commit
dbo use only
default to local cursor
merge publish
numeric roundabort
offline
published
quoted identifier
read only
recursive triggers
```

```
select into/bulkcopy
single user
subscribed
torn page detection
trunc. log on chkpt.
```

## Configuring the Connection

Many of the connection-level options configure ANSI compatibility or specific connection-performance options.

Connection-level options are very limited in scope. If the option is set within an interactive session, the setting is in force until it's changed or the session ends. If the option is set within a stored procedure, the setting persists only for the life of that stored procedure.

The connection-level options are typically configured by means of the set command. The following code configures how SQL Server handle nulls within this current session:

```
Set Ansi_nulls Off
```

Result:

```
The command(s) completed successfully.
```

Connection properties can also be checked by means of the SessionProperty function:

```
Select SessionProperty ('ANSI_NULLS')
```

Result:

```
0
```

Query Analyzer sets several connection options when it makes a connection to the server. The connection defaults are found in the Tools ➪ Options menu under the Connection Properties tab. The current connection-level options are set by means of the Query ➪ Current Connection Properties menu command, as shown in Figure 23-3.

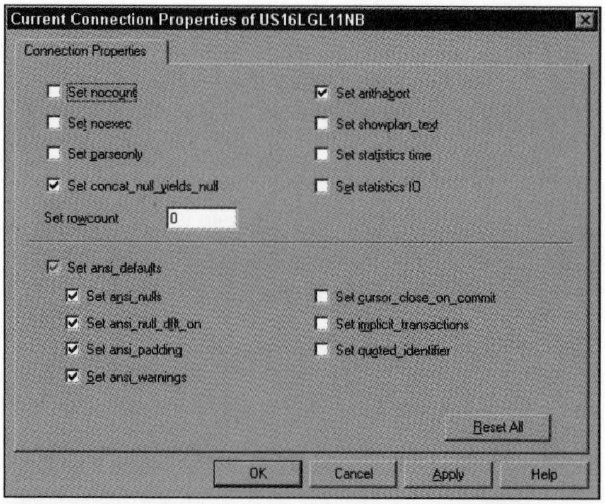

**Figure 23-3:** Query Analyzer's Current Connection Properties dialog can be used to view or set the connection-level options for the current session.

# Configuration Options

Because so many similar configuration options are controlled by different commands and at different levels (server, database, connection), this section organizes the configuration options by topic rather than command or level.

## Start/Stop-Configuration Properties

The start-up configuration properties control how SQL Server and the processes are launched and are listed in Table 23-1.

### Table 23-1: Start/Stop-Configuration Properties

| Property | Level* | Graphic Control | Code Option |
|----------|--------|-----------------|-------------|
| AutoStart SQL Server | S | SQL Manager | - |
| AutoStart SQL Server Agent | S | Enterprise Manager | - |
| AutoStart MS DTC | S | Enterprise Manager | - |
| Show Advanced Options | S | - | show advanced options |
| Scan for startup procs | S | - | scan for startup procs |
| Start-up Parameters | S | Em | - |
| AutoClose | D | Em | alter database autoclose |

\* The configuration level refers to Server, Database, or Connection.

In Enterprise Manager's Server Properties, the General tab controls the start-up of three of the SQL Server processes. SQL Server Service Manager can also set these processes, as well as MS Search and Analysis Services, to autostart.

### Start-up Parameters

The start-up parameters are similar to the parameters that are passed to a program when it is started from the DOS command line. Besides the standard master database–location parameters, the two parameters that are most useful are:

-m   Starts SQL Server in single-user mode and is required to restore or rebuild a lost master database. While the database is in single user mode, avoid Enterprise Manager.

-x   Disables tracking of CPU and cache-hit statistics for maximum performance.

Additional start-up parameters are:

-d   Used to include the full path of the Master file.

-e   Used to include the full path of the Error file.

-c   Starts SQL Server so that it is not running as a Windows service.

-f   Used to start up with a minimal configuration.

| | |
|---|---|
| -g | Specifies virtual memory (in MB) available to SQL Server for extended stored procedures. |
| -n | Disables logging to the Windows application log. |
| /Ttrace# | Enables trace-specific flags by trace flag number. |

### Start-up Stored Procedure

Two additional server properties are not exposed on Enterprise Manager's Server Property page but are available from code. SQL Server can be configured to scan for a start-up stored procedure every time the SQL Server starts — similar to how Microsoft DOS operating systems scan for the autoexec.bat file when they boot up. There's no fixed name for a start-up procedure, and there may be multiple start-up procedures. To create a start-up stored procedure, run the sp_procoption to mark a start-up stored procedure. So you can further control the start-up procedure, the server property scan for startup procs turns the startup procs feature on or off:

```
EXEC sp_configure 'scan for startup procs', 1
RECONFIGURE
```

## Memory-Configuration Properties

SQL Server can either dynamically request memory from the operating system or consume a fixed amount of memory. These settings can be configured by means of the SQL Server Properties Memory tab, shown in Figure 23-4, or from code by means of the sp_configure stored procedure.

The memory-configuration properties, listed in Table 23-2, control how SQL Server uses and allocates memory.

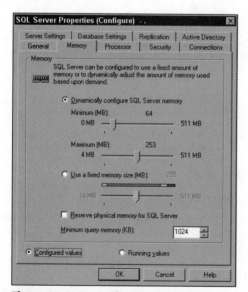

**Figure 23-4:** Enterprise Manager's SQL Server Properties — the Memory tab

## Table 23-2: Memory-Configuration Properties

| Property | Level* | Graphic Control | Code Option |
|---|---|---|---|
| Dynamic Memory Minimum | S | Enterprise Manager | min server memory |
| Dynamic Memory Maximum | S | Enterprise Manager | max server memory |
| Fixed Memory Size | S | Enterprise Manager | min server memory and max server memory |
| Reserve Physical Memory for SQL Server | S | Enterprise Manager | set working set size |
| Minimum Query Memory | S | Enterprise Manager | min memory per query |
| AWE Enabled | S | - | AWE Enabled |
| Index Create Memory | S | - | index create memory |
| Locks | S | - | locks |
| Max Text Repl Size | S | - | max text repl size |
| Open Objects | S | - | open objects |

\* The configuration level refers to Server, Database, or Connection.

## Dynamic Memory

If SQL Server is set to dynamic memory then SQL Server's memory footprint can grow or be reduced as needed within the minimum and maximum constraints based on the physical memory available and the workload. SQL Server will try to maintain its requirement and 4 to 10MB extra memory. Its goal is to have enough memory available while avoiding Windows having to swap pages from memory to the virtual-memory support file (pagefile.sys).

The minimum-memory property prohibits SQL Server from reducing memory below a certain point and hurting performance, but it doesn't set the initial memory footprint. The minimum simply means that once SQL Server has reached that point, it will not reduce memory below it.

The maximum-memory setting prevents SQL Server from growing to the point where it contends with the operating system, or other applications, for memory. If the maximum is set too low performance will suffer.

Microsoft Search Engine, used by SQL Server for full-text searches, is also memory-intensive. If you are doing a significant amount of full-text searching, be sure to leave plenty of memory available for Search Engine. The official formula from Microsoft is: Total virtual memory - (SQL Server maximum virtual memory + virtual memory requirements of other services) ≥ 1.5 times the physical memory. For example, for a server that has 192MB physical memory, allowing 96MB for SQL Server and 64MB for Search Engine, the total virtual memory must be greater than 288MB (physical memory times 1.5) plus 160MB (SQL Server and MS Search planning memory), for a total of 448MB required virtual memory. Since the server has 192MB of physical memory, the virtual-memory support file must be at least 252MB to meet the requirements set by the formula. So the more physical memory in the server, the larger the swap file required.

Personally, I run SQL Server configured for dynamic memory with the minimum set to 16MB and the maximum set to the computer's total RAM less 128MB. This reserves a minimum amount of memory for SQL Server and permits SQL Server to grow as it sees fit, but still reserves 128MB for Windows and prevents SQL Server from contending with Windows for memory when running several very huge queries. Depending on your configuration, you may want to leave more for the operating system.

Multiple SQL Server instances do not cooperate when requiring memory. In servers with multiple instances, it's highly possible for two busy instances to contend for memory and for one to become memory-starved. Reducing the maximum-memory property for each instance can prevent this from happening.

From T-SQL code, the minimum- and maximum-memory properties are set by means of the sp_configure system stored procedure. It's an advanced option, so it can only be changed if the show advanced options property is on:

```
EXEC sp_configure 'show advanced options', 1

EXEC sp_configure 'min server memory', 16
```

Result:

```
Configuration option 'min server memory (MB)'
   changed from 0 to 16.
Run the RECONFIGURE statement to install.
```

The following code sets the max-memory configuration:

```
EXEC sp_configure 'max server memory', 128
```

Result:

```
Configuration option 'max server memory (MB)'
   changed from 128 to 128.
Run the RECONFIGURE statement to install.
```

To automatically calculate the maximum memory based on the available physical memory, the following stored procedure examines the result set of xp_msver to determine the physical memory and then executes sp_configure:

```
CREATE PROC pSetMaxMemory (
   @Safe INT = 64 )
AS
  CREATE TABLE #PhysicalMemory (
    [Index] INT,
    [Name] VARCHAR(50),
    [Internal_Value] INT,
    [Character_Value] VARCHAR(50) )
  DECLARE @Memory INT
  INSERT #PhysicalMemory
    EXEC xp_msver 'PhysicalMemory'
  SELECT @Memory =
    (Select Internal_Value FROM #PhysicalMemory) - @safe
  EXEC sp_configure 'max server memory', @Memory
  RECONFIGURE

go
```

```
EXEC pSetMaxMemory  -- sets max memory to physical - 64Mb
EXEC pSetMaxMemory 32 --  sets max memory to physical - 32Mb
```

## Reconfigure

After a configuration setting is changed with `sp_configure`, the `reconfigure` command causes the changes to take effect. Some configuration changes only take effect after SQL Server is restarted.

```
RECONFIGURE
```

```
The command(s) completed successfully.
```

Instead of dynamically consuming memory, SQL Server may be configured to immediately request a fixed amount of memory from the operating system. To set a fixed amount of memory from code, set the minimum- and maximum-memory properties to the same value.

While calculating memory cost, polling the environment, and requesting memory may seem as if they would require overhead, I do not believe you would see any performance gains from switching from dynamic to fixed memory. The primary purpose of using fixed memory is to configure a dedicated SQL Server computer to prevent page-swapping by combining the fixed-memory setting with the next option presented in this chapter.

Regardless of the amount of memory SQL Server is allocated by Windows, the Windows Memory Manager may opt to swap some of the SQL Server pages to the swap file if SQL Server is idle. If SQL Server memory is set to a fixed size, swapping can be prevented by means of setting `Reserve Physical Memory for SQL Server` to true.

The SQL Server `Reserve Physical Memory` property may be set in code by means of the `set working set size` option along with the `sp_configure` system stored procedure:

```
EXEC sp_configure 'set working set size', 1
RECONFIGURE
```

SQL Server must restart for the `Reserve Physical Memory` property change to take effect.

At times, the SQL Server team amazes me with the level of detailed control it passes to DBAs. SQL Server will allocate the required memory for each query as needed. The `min memory per query` option sets the minimum threshold for the memory (KB) used by each query. While increasing this property to a value higher than the default 1MB may provide slightly better performance for some queries, I see no reason to override SQL Server automatic memory control and risk causing a memory shortage. The following code increases the minimum query memory to 2MB:

```
EXEC sp_configure 'min memory per query', 2048
RECONFIGURE
```

Six additional memory-related properties that are unavailable from Enterprise Manager can be configured from code.

## Query Wait

If the memory is unavailable to execute a large query, SQL Server will wait for the estimated amount of time necessary to execute the query times 25 and then time out. During this time the query will hold any locks and an undetectable deadlock may occur. If you are seeing this type of behavior, you can hard-code the query lack-of-memory timeout to a certain number of seconds using the following code:

```
EXEC sp_configure 'query wait', 20
RECONFIGURE
```

The previous code specifies that every query will either start execution within 20 seconds or time out.

## AWE Memory

SQL Server is normally restricted to the standard 3-GB physical-memory limit. However, SQL Server Enterprise Edition, when running on Windows 2000 Data Center, can use up to 64GB of physical memory by configuring SQL Server to address the Address Windowing Extensions (AWE) API. The AWE-enabled property turns on AWE memory addressing within SQL Server:

```
EXEC sp_configure 'AWE Enabled', 20
RECONFIGURE
```

## Index Memory

The amount of memory SQL Server uses to perform sorts when creating an index is generally self-configuring. However, you can control it by using sp_configure to hard-code a certain memory footprint (KB) for index creation. For example, the following code fixes the memory used to create an index to 8MB:

```
EXEC sp_configure ' index create memory', 8096
RECONFIGURE
```

## Lock Memory

Excessive locks can bring a SQL Server to its knees both in terms of waiting for locks and in terms of the memory consumed by the locks (96 bytes per lock). By default, SQL Server will begin with 2 percent of its memory reserved for locks and then dynamically allocate memory up to 40 percent of SQL Server's maximum available memory. That should be sufficient. If you are getting errors indicating there isn't enough memory for locks, don't just increase the lock property. There's a problem in the code. The following example disables the dynamic lock-memory allocation and allocates memory for 16,767 locks, consuming a little over 1.5MB of memory:

```
EXEC sp_configure 'locks', 16767
RECONFIGURE
```

## Max Open Objects

SQL Server prefers to dynamically control its memory, including the pool used to track the current open objects (tables, views, rules, stored procedures, defaults, and triggers). Each object takes only one allocation unit, even if it is referenced numerous times. SQL Server reuses memory space in the object pool, but if SQL Server is complaining that it is exceeded the number of open objects, the property can be manually configured. The following code sets the maximum number of open objects to 16,767:

```
EXEC sp_configure 'open objects', 16767
RECONFIGURE
```

## Processor-Configuration Properties

You can use the processor-configuration properties (listed in Table 23-3) to control how SQL Server makes use of symmetrical multi-processor computers for SQL Server.

### Table 23-3: Processor-Configuration Properties

| Property | Level* | Graphic Control | Code Option |
| --- | --- | --- | --- |
| SMP Processors Used | S | Enterprise Manager | affinity mask |
| Maximum Worker Threads | S | Enterprise Manager | max worker threads |
| Boost SQL Server Priority on Windows | S | Enterprise Manager | priority boost |
| Use Windows NT Fibers | S | Enterprise Manager | lightweight pooling |
| Number of processors for parallel execution of queries | S | Enterprise Manager | max degree of parallelism |
| Minimum query plan Threshold for parallel execution | S | Enterprise Manager | cost threshold for parallelism |
| Query wait | S | - | query wait |

\* The configuration level refers to Server, Database, or Connection.

The Processor tab of the SQL Server Properties page (Figure 23-5), determines how SQL Server will make use of symmetrical multi-processor computers. Most of these options are moot in a single-processor server.

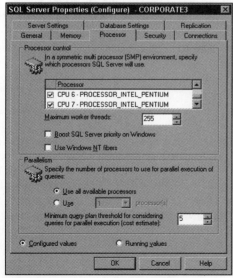

**Figure 23-5:** Enterprise Manager's SQL Server Properties — the Processor tab

## Affinity Mask

In a multi-CPU server the operating system can move processes to CPUs as the load requires. The SQL Server processor affinity, or the relationship between a task and a CPU, can be configured on a per-CPU basis. By enabling the affinity between SQL Server and a CPU you make that CPU available to SQL Server, but it is not dedicated to SQL Server. So while a CPU can't be forced to run SQL Server, it can be segmented from SQL Server.

Because of the overhead involved in switching processes, Windows performance benefits if it can run on one CPU without SQL Server. If the server has eight CPUs or more, I might recommend disabling a single CPU to free Windows processes from competing with SQL Server.

In Enterprise Manager, CPU affinity is configured by means of the checkboxes in the Processor tab, as shown in Figure 23-5.

In code, the individual CPUs are enabled by means of setting the `affinity mask` bits using `sp_configure`. Since 3 is 00000011 in base 2, the following code enables processors 0 and 1 in an SMP server:

```
EXEC sp_configure 'affinity mask', 3
RECONFIGURE
```

## Max Worker Threads

SQL Server is a multi-threaded application, meaning that it can execute on multiple processors concurrently for increased performance. The threads are designed as follows:

✦ A thread for each network connection.

✦ A thread to handle database checkpoints.

✦ Multiple threads to handle user requests. When SQL Server is handling a small number of connections, a single thread is assigned to each connection. However, as the number of connections grows, a pool of threads handles the connections more efficiently.

Depending on the number of connections and the percentage of time those connections are active (versus idle), making the number of worker threads less than the number of connections can force connection pooling, conserve memory, and improve performance.

From code, the maximum number of worker threads is set by means of the `sp_configure` stored procedure and the `max worker threads` option:

```
EXEC sp_configure 'max worker threads', 64
RECONFIGURE
```

## Priority Boost

Different processes in Windows operate at different priorities levels, ranging from 0 to 31. The highest priorities are executed first and are reserved for the operating-system processes. Typically Windows scheduling priority level settings for applications are 4 (low), 7 (normal), 13 (high), and 24 (real-time). By default, SQL Server installs with a Windows scheduling priority level of 7.

For single CPU servers, or systems running SQL Server along with other foreground applications, a Windows scheduling priority level of 7 is desired. Boosting the priority in this situation may cause less than smooth operations. However, for dedicated SQL Server multi-CPU servers, the higher Windows scheduling priority level of 13 is recommended. In code, to set the Windows scheduling priority level to 13, the `priority boost` option is set to 1:

```
EXEC sp_configure 'priority boost', 1
RECONFIGURE
```

## Lightweight Pooling

Another useful option for servers with symmetrical multi-processing helps reduce the overhead of frequently switching processes among the CPUs. Enabling the NT fiber threads option creates fewer process threads, but those threads are associated with additional fibers, or lightweight threads, that stay associated with their thread. The smaller number of threads helps reduce process-switching and improve performance. In Enterprise Manager, this option is referred to as `Use Windows NT fibers`. In code the configuration option is `lightweight pooling`:

```
EXEC sp_configure 'lightweight pooling', 1
RECONFIGURE
```

## Parallelism

The Enterprise Edition of SQL Server (and the Developer and Evaluation Editions because they are the same edition with different licensing) will execute complex queries using several processors in parallel instead of serially. That's great for the user running the massive query that aggregates every row in a 20GB database, but what about the other users who are now waiting while one user ties up all the processors? The solution is to limit the number of processors used in a single parallel query and to set the cost threshold (in estimated seconds) required before SQL Server will consider the query a candidate for parallel execution.

Additional overhead is involved in generating a parallel query-execution plan, synchronizing the parallel query, and terminating the query, so longer queries benefit the most from parallelism. However, parallel queries are amazingly fast. To see if a query is using parallelism, view the query-execution plan in Query Analyzer. A symbol shows the merger of different parallel query–execution threads.

My recommendation is to enable half of the available processors (remember the affinity mask) minus one for parallel-query execution. So if the server has eight processors, and seven are available for SQL Server, set SQL Server to use three processors for parallelism. Since parallel queries can greatly boost performance, depending on your CPU demand, you may want to try actually lowering the cost threshold slightly so more queries will benefit from parallelism.

In code, query parallelism is set by means of the `max degree of parallelism` and `cost threshold for parallelism` options. Setting `max degree of parallelism` to 0 enables all available processors for parallelism.

```
EXEC sp_configure 'max degree of parallelism', 1
EXEC sp_configure 'cost threshold for parallelism', 1
RECONFIGURE
```

**Best Practice**

While these server-tuning options can affect performance, performance begins with the database schema, queries, and indexes. No amount of server tuning can overcome poor design and development.

## Security-Configuration Properties

The security-configuration properties (Table 23-4) are used to control the security features of SQL Server.

### Table 23-4: Security-Configuration Properties

| Property | Level* | Graphic Control | Code Option |
|---|---|---|---|
| Security Authentication Mode | S | Enterprise Manager | - |
| Security Audit Level | S | Enterprise Manager | - |
| StartUp SQL Server Security Account | S | Enterprise Manager | - |
| C2 Audit Mode | S | - | C2 audit mode |

\* The configuration level refers to Server, Database, or Connection.

The same security-configuration options established during the installation are again presented in the Security tab of the Server Properties page (Figure 23-6), so the configuration may be adjusted after installation. The authentication model and the SQL Server Windows accounts are exactly the same as in the installation.

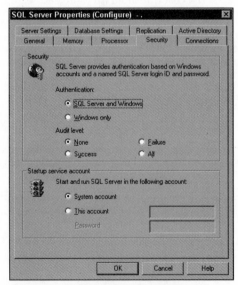

**Figure 23-6:** Enterprise Manager's SQL Server Properties — the Security tab

### Security-Audit Level

The additional option configures the level of user-login auditing performed by SQL Server. Based on this setting, SQL Server will record every successful or failed user login attempt to either the Windows application log or the SQL Server log.

### C2 Security

When configuring SQL Server for C2 level security, enabling C2 Audit Mode property ensures that SQL Server will refuse to continue if it is unable to write to the security-audit log. The property can be set with the following code and may not be set from within Enterprise Manager:

```
EXEC sp_configure 'C2 audit mode', 1
RECONFIGURE
```

**Cross-Reference**　For more about locking down SQL Server's security, refer to Chapter 27, "Securing Databases."

## Connection-Configuration Properties

The connection-configuration properties (Table 23-5) are used to set connection options in SQL Server.

### Table 23-5: Connection-Configuration Properties

| Property | Level* | Graphic Control | Code Option |
|----------|--------|-----------------|-------------|
| Max Concurrent User Connections | S | Enterprise Manager | user connections |
| Default Connections Options | S | Enterprise Manager | several user options |
| Permit Remote Server Connections | S | Enterprise Manager | remote access |
| Remote Query Timeout | S | Enterprise Manager | remote query timeout |
| Enforce DTC | S | Enterprise Manager | remote proc trans |
| Network Packet Size | S | - | network packet size |
| Remote Login Timeout | S | - | remote login timeout |

\* The configuration level refers to Server, Database, or Connection.

The Connections tab (Figure 23-7), sets connection-level properties including defaults, number of connections permitted, and timeout settings.

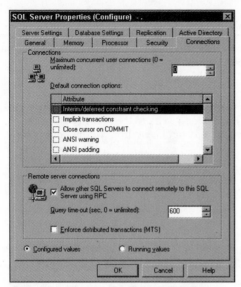

**Figure 23-7:** Enterprise Manager's SQL
Server Properties — the Connections tab

## Maximum Concurrent User Connections

The Maximum concurrent user connections option should probably not be set to the number of users, because applications often open several connections to SQL Server. For example, ODBC- and ADO-based applications will open a connection for every connection object in code — possibly as many as one for every form, list box, and/or combo box. Access tends to open at least two connections.

The purpose of this option is to limit the number of connections in a memory-starved server because each connection consumes 40KB. For most servers the default of 0, or unlimited connections, is appropriate.

The maximum number of user connections may be set within code by means of the user connections option:

```
EXEC sp_configure 'user connections', 0
RECONFIGURE
```

To determine the current setting in code, examine the value in the @@maxconnections global variable:

```
SELECT @@MAX_CONNECTIONS
```

## Remote Access

The remote-server's connection properties are used for distributed queries — referencing data from one SQL Server in another. By default, this feature is enabled. To disallow distributed queries from calling the server, disable the checkbox, or set the remote access option to 0:

```
EXEC sp_configure 'remote access', 0
RECONFIGURE
```

### Remote Query Timeout

The `remote query timeout` option sets the number of seconds SQL Server will wait on a remote query before assuming it failed and generating a timeout error. The default value of 10 minutes seems sufficient for executing a remote query:

```
EXEC sp_configure 'remote query timeout', 600
RECONFIGURE
```

### Enforce DTC

When updating multiple servers within a transaction (logical unit of work), SQL Server can enforce dual-phase commits using the Distributed Transaction Coordinator.

From code, the `Enforce DTC` property is enabled by means of setting the `remote proc trans` option to 1:

```
EXEC sp_configure 'remote proc trans', 1
RECONFIGURE
```

 **Cross-Reference**  Transactions are explained in Chapter 11, "Transactional Integrity."

### Network-Packet Size and Timeout

Two connection-related properties are available only through code. The network-packet size may be changed from its default of 4KB by means of the `network packet size` option. The following code sets the network-packet size to 2KB:

```
exec sp_configure 'network packet size', 2048
RECONFIGURE
```

Very rarely should the network-packet size need reconfiguring. Consider this property a fine-tuning tool and use it only if the data being passed tends to greatly exceed the default size, such as large text or image data.

The `remote login timeout` property is also unavailable from Enterprise Manager. This property sets the maximum wait time to log into a remote data source. The default of 20 can be changed to 30 with the following code:

```
EXEC sp_configure 'remote login timeout', 30
RECONFIGURE
```

### Max Large-Data-Replication Size

Although you can't configure it in Enterprise Manager, you can use the following code to configure the maximum size of the text and image data that may be sent via replication:

```
EXEC sp_configure 'max text repl size', 16767
RECONFIGURE
```

## Server-Configuration Properties

The server-configuration properties (Table 23-6) enable you to set server-wide performance and display properties in SQL Server.

The Server Settings tab of the Enterprise Manager's Server Properties page (Figure 23-8) is best left with the default values.

### Table 23-6: Server-Configuration Properties

| Property | Level* | Graphic Control | Code Option |
|---|---|---|---|
| Default Language for Server Messages | S | Enterprise Manager | default language |
| Allow Changes to System Tables | S | Enterprise Manager | allow updates |
| Query Cost Governor | S | Enterprise Manager | query governor cost limit |
| Two-digit Year Interpreter | S | Enterprise Manager | two-digit year cutoff |
| Default Full-text Language | S | - | default full-text language |

* The configuration level refers to Server, Database, or Connection.

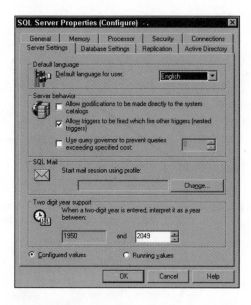

**Figure 23-8:** Enterprise Manager's SQL Server Properties — the Server Settings tab

## Default Message Language

The default language for server user messages can be set in Enterprise Manager as well as in code:

```
EXEC sp_configure 'default language', 0
RECONFIGURE
```

## Full-Text Search Default Language

The default language for full-text searches can only be set from within code:

```
EXEC sp_configure 'default full-text language', 'English'
RECONFIGURE
```

## Allow Changes to System Tables

The "Allow modifications to be made to the system catalogs" server-behavior option enables direct modifications to system tables; it should be avoided. I can think of no system-table value that should be directly manipulated, although any change is best made through Microsoft's system stored procedures, or through standard SQL `alter` commands. The `sp_configure` version of this option is `allow updates`.

### Query Governor Cost Limit

In the same way that a small gas-engine governor controls the top speed of the engine, the query governor limits the maximum number of queries SQL Server will perform according to the estimated query cost. If the user submits a query that exceeds the limit set by the query governor, SQL Server will not execute the query.

The following code sets the max-query plan to 10 seconds for the entire server:

```
EXEC sp_configure 'query governor cost limit', 10
RECONFIGURE
```

But in code, the query governor can be changed for the current connection. The following code disables the governor within the scope of the current connection/batch:

```
SET QUERY_GOVERNOR_COST_LIMIT  0
```

Personally, I don't use the query governor to limit user-query execution. However, if you have a smoothly-running database with all application queries running in under a second, and users are now submitting poorly written ad hoc queries that consume unreasonable resources, using the query governor might be a good way to prevent those queries from executing.

### Two-Digit-Year Cutoff

The two–digit-year support helps handle Y2K problems by converting a two-digit year to a four-digit year based on the values supplied. If the two-digit year falls after the first value (default 1959), it is interpreted as being in the twentieth century. If it falls before the second value (default 2049), it is interpreted as being in the twenty-first century. So, 01/01/69 remains 01/01/1969, and 01/01/14 is interpreted as 01/01/2014. The following example sets the two-digit-year cutoff to 41:

```
EXEC sp_configure 'two digit year cutoff', 2041
RECONFIGURE
```

## Index-Configuration Properties

The index statistics and fill-factor options (Table 23-7) establish the defaults for new indexes in SQL Server.

### Table 23-7: Index-Configuration Properties

| Property | Level* | Graphic Control | Code Option |
|---|---|---|---|
| Auto Create Statistics | D | Enterprise Manager | `auto_create_statistics` |
| Auto Update Statistics | D | Enterprise Manager | `auto_update_statistics` |
| Index Fill Factor | S | Enterprise Manager | `fill factor` |

* The configuration level refers to Server, Database, or Connection.

These options do not alter any existing indexes; they only set the defaults for new indexes.

**Cross-Reference**

The details of index creation are discussed in Chapter 5, "Implementing the Physical Database Schema." Index management is covered in Chapter 24, "Maintaining the Database." And techniques for tuning indexes are explained in Chapter 28, "Advanced Performance."

## Configuring Database Auto Options

Four database-configuration options determine the automatic behaviors of SQL Server databases (Table 23-8). In Enterprise Manager they are all set in the Options tab of the Database Properties page.

### Table 23-8: Index-Configuration Properties

| Property | Level* | Graphic Control | Code Option |
|----------|--------|-----------------|-------------|
| Auto Close | D | Enterprise Manager | `auto_close` |
| Auto Shrink | D | Enterprise Manager | `auto_shrink` |
| Auto Create Statistics | D | Enterprise Manager | `auto _create_statistics` |
| Auto Update Statistics | D | Enterprise Manager | `auto _ update _ statistics` |

\* The configuration level refers to Server, Database, or Connection.

### Auto Close

Auto close directs SQL Server to release all database resources (cached data pages, compiled stored procedures, saved query execution plans) when all users exit and all processes are complete. This frees memory for other databases. While this option will improve performance slightly for other databases, reloading the database will take longer, as will recompiling the procedures and recalculating the query-execution plans, once the database is again opened by a user.

Personal Edition and Desktop Edition install this option enabled as the default. All other editions set `auto_close` off as the default.

If the database is used regularly, do not enable auto close. If the database is used very occasionally, then auto close might be appropriate to save memory.

**Caution**

Many front-end client applications repeatedly open and close a connection to SQL Server. Setting auto close on in this type of environment is a sure way to kill SQL Server performance.

To set auto close in code:

```
ALTER DATABASE database SET AUTO_CLOSE ON | OFF
```

### Auto Shrink

If the database has more than 25 percent free space, this option causes SQL Server to perform a shrink database operation. This option also causes the transaction log to shrink after it's backed up.

Performing a file shrink is a costly operation because several pages must be moved within the file. This option also regularly checks the status of the data pages to determine whether they can be shrunk.

The default setting is on for Desktop and Personal edition; off for Standard and Enterprise.

Cross-Reference

Shrinking the data and transaction log files is discussed in detail in Chapter 26, "Recovery Planning."

To set the auto shrink option in code, do the following:

```
ALTER DATABASE database SET AUTO_SHRINK ON | OFF
```

### Auto Create Statistics

Data-distribution statistics are a key means of query execution plans. This option directs SQL Server to automatically create statistics for any columns for which statistics could be useful.

To set auto create statistics in code, do the following:

```
ALTER DATABASE database SET AUTO_CREATE_STATISTICS ON | OFF
```

### Auto Update Statistics

Out-of-date data-distribution statistics may cause more harm than good. This option keeps the statistics automatically updated. The default for this option is set to on.

To set the auto update statistics option in code, do the following:

```
ALTER DATABASE database SET AUTO_UPDATE_STATISTICS ON | OFF
```

Cross-Reference

Query and index tuning rely heavily on data-distribution statistics. The strategies involving statistics are explained in Chapter 28, "Advanced Performance."

## Cursor-Configuration Properties

The cursor-configuration properties (Table 23-9) are used to control cursor behavior in SQL Server.

### Table 23-9: Cursor-Configuration Properties

| Property | Level* | Graphic Control | Code Option |
|---|---|---|---|
| Cursor Threshold | S | - | cursor threshold |
| Cursor Close on Commit | SDC | - | cursor_close_on_commit |
| Cursor Default | D | - | cursor default |

\* The configuration level refers to Server, Database, or Connection.

### Cursor Threshold

The `cursor threshold` property sets the number of rows in a cursor set before the cursor keysets are generated asynchronously. Synchronous keysets are faster than other cursor types, but they consume more memory. Every cursor keyset will be generated asynchronously if the `cursor threshold` property is set to 0.

The default of `-1` causes all keysets to be generated synchronously, which is OK for smaller keysets. For larger cursor keysets this may be a problem. When you are working with cursors, the following code will permit synchronous cursor keysets for cursors of up to 10,000 rows:

To set the cursor threshold in code, do the following:

```
EXEC sp_configure 'cursor threshold', 5000
RECONFIGURE WITH OVERRIDE
```

### Cursor Close on Commit

This property will close an open cursor after a transaction is committed when set to `on`. If it is set to `off`, cursors will remain open across transactions until a `close cursor` statement is issued.

To set cursor close on commit in code, do the following:

```
SET CURSOR_CLOSE_ON_COMMIT ON
```

### Cursor Default

This property will make each cursor local to the object that declared it when set to `local`. When it is set to `global`, the scope of the cursor can be extended outside the object that created it.

To set cursor default in code, do the following:

```
ALTER DATABASE database SET CURSOR_DEFAULT LOCAL
```

## SQL ANSI–Configuration Properties

The SQL ANSI–configuration properties (Table 23-10) are used to set ANSI behavior in SQL Server.

The connection default properties (there are several) affect the environment of batches executed within a connection. Most of the connection properties change SQL Server behavior so that it complies with the ANSI standard. Because so few SQL Server installations modify these properties, it's much safer to modify them in code at the beginning of a batch if the code depends on a non-Microsoft behavior than to set them at the server or database level.

For example, T-SQL requires a `begin transaction` to start a logical unit of work. Oracle assumes a `begin transaction` is at the beginning of every batch. If you prefer to work with implicit (non-stated) transactions, you're safer if you set the implicit transaction connection property at the beginning of your batch then if you set it in the server defaults. The server default will affect every batch and may break Microsoft-standard T-SQL code. For these reasons, I recommend leaving the connection properties at the default values and setting them in code, if needed.

The SQL ANSI-configuration settings are set by means of the `alter database` command. For backwards compatibility, the `sp_dboption` is also available.

### Table 23-10: SQL ANSI–Configuration Properties

| Property | Level* | Graphic Control | Code Option |
|---|---|---|---|
| ANSI Defaults | C | - | `ansi defaults` |
| ANSI Null Behavior | SDC | Enterprise Manager | `ansi_null_Default` |
| ANSI Nulls | SDC | Enterprise Manager | `ansi_nulls` |
| ANSI Padding | SC | - | `ansi_padding` |
| ANSI Warnings | SDC | - | `ansi_warnings` |
| Arithmetic Abort | SC | - | `arithabort` |
| Arithmetic Ignore | SC | - | `arithignore` |
| Numeric Round Abort | D | - | `numeric_roundabort` |
| Null Concatenation | DC | - | `concat_null_yields_null` |
| Use Quoted Identifier | D | - | `quoted_identifier` |
| ANSI SQL 92 Compatibility Flag | C | - | `fips_flagger` |

\* The configuration level refers to Server, Database, or Connection.

## ANSI Null Default

The `ansi_null_default` setting controls the database's default nullability. This default setting is used when a `null` or `not_null` is not explicitly specified when creating a table.

To set the database `ansi_null_default` in code, do the following:

```
ALTER DATABASE database SET ANSI_NULL_DEFAULT ON | OFF
```

## ANSI NULLs

The `ansi_nulls` database setting is used to determine comparison evaluations. When the setting is set to `on` any comparison to a null value will evaluate to null. When the setting is set to `off`, then the comparison of two `null` values will evaluate to `true`.

To set ANSI nulls in code, do the following:

```
ALTER DATABASE database SET ANSI_NULLS ON | OFF
```

## ANSI Padding

The `ansi_padding` database setting affects only newly created columns. When this setting is set to `on`, data stored in variable data types will retain any padded zeros to the left of variable binary numbers, and any padded spaces to the right or left of variable-length characters. When it is set to `off`, all leading and trailing blanks and zeros are trimmed.

To set ANSI padding in code, do the following:

```
ALTER DATABASE database SET ANSI_PADDING ON | OFF
```

## ANSI Warnings

The `ansi_warnings` database setting is used to handle ANSI errors and warnings. When this setting is `off`, all errors, such as null values in aggregate functions and divide-by-zero errors, are suppressed. When the setting is `on`, then the warnings and errors will be raised.

To set ANSI warnings in code, do the following:

```
ALTER DATABASE database SET ANSI_WARNINGS ON | OFF
```

## Arithmetic Abort

The `arithabort` database setting, when set to `on`, will abort the data process if an arithmetic error occurs, such as data overflow or divide-by-zero. If the setting is set to `off`, only a warning message is passed if an arithmetic error occurs, and the data process is able to proceed.

To set arithmetic abort in code, do the following:

```
ALTER DATABASE database SET ARITHABORT ON | OFF
```

## Numeric Round Abort

The `numeric_roundabort` database setting is used to control the behavior of numeric decimal-precision-rounding errors in process. If the setting is set to `on`, the process will abort if the numeric-decimal precision is lost in an expression value. When it is set to `off`, the process will proceed without error, and the result will be rounded down to the precision of the object the number is being stored in.

To set numeric round abort in code, do the following:

```
ALTER DATABASE database SET NUMERIC_ROUNDABORT ON | OFF
```

## Concatination Null Yields Null

The `concat_null_yields_null` database setting is used to control the behavior of the resultant when concatenating a string with a `null`. If the setting is set to `on`, any string concatenated with a `null` will result in a `null`. If it is set to `off`, any string concatenated with a `null` will result in the original string, ignoring the `null`.

To set numeric round abort in code, do the following:

```
ALTER DATABASE database SET CONCAT_NULL_YIELDS_NULL ON | OFF
```

## Use Quoted Identifier

The `quoted_identifier` database setting enables you to refer to an identifier, such as a column name, by enclosing it within double quotes. When this database setting is set to `on`, identifiers can be delimited by double quotation marks. When it is set to `off`, identifiers cannot be placed in quotation marks and must not be keywords.

```
ALTER DATABASE database SET QUOTED_IDENTIFIER ON | OFF
```

The default is off. This option must be on to create or modify indexed views or indexes on calculated columns.

## Trigger Configuration Properties

The trigger configuration properties (Table 23-11) are used to control trigger behavior in SQL Server.

### Table 23-11: Trigger Configuration Properties

| Property | Level* | Graphic Control | Code Option |
|---|---|---|---|
| Allow Nested Triggers | S | Enterprise Manager | nested triggers |
| Recursive Triggers | D | Enterprise Manager | recursive triggers |

* The configuration level refers to Server, Database, or Connection.

Trigger behavior can be set at both the server and database levels.

### Nested Triggers

Triggers can be nested by means of being called in a recursive hierarchy up to a maximum of 32 levels. This is a server-level configuration setting.

To set nested triggers in code, do the following:

```
EXEC sp_configure 'nested triggers', 1
RECONFIGURE
```

### Recursive Triggers

A trigger is a small stored procedure that is executed upon an insert, update, or delete operation on a table. If the code in the trigger again inserts, updates, or deletes the same table, the trigger causes itself to be executed again. This recursive behavior is enabled or disabled by the recursive trigger database option.

**Cross-Reference**

Nested triggers, a server property, and recursive triggers (a database property) are often confused with each other. Refer to Chapter 15, "Implementing Triggers," for the complete explanation, including explanations of how triggers can call other triggers and how this server property controls trigger behavior.

The default is off. Nested triggers, a related option, is a server option. To set the option in T-SQL code, do the following:

```
ALTER DATABASE database SET RECURSIVE_TRIGGERS ON | OFF
```

## Database-State-Configuration Properties

The database state configuration properties (Table 23-12) are available in SQL Server. These configurations are mostly used when a DBA is performing maintenance on the database.

### Table 23-12: Database-State-Configuration Properties

| Property | Level* | Graphic Control | Code Option |
|---|---|---|---|
| Database Off-Line | D | - | offline |
| Read-Only | D | Enterprise Manager | read_only |
| Restricted Access — Members of db_owner, dbcreator, or sysadmin | D | Enterprise Manager | restricted_user |
| Restricted Access — Single user | D | Enterprise Manager | single_user |
| Restricted User — Disabled | D | Enterprise Manager | multi_user |
| Compatibility Level | D | Enterprise Manager | compatibility |

\* The configuration level refers to Server, Database, or Connection.

The state of the database can also be set by means of the `alter database` command. The `sp_dboption` is also available for backward compatibility.

### Database-Access Level

The database-access-configuration options are used to set the state of the database. When the database is offline, no access to the database is allowed.

To set a database to an `offline` state in code, do the following:

```
ALTER DATABASE database SET OFFLINE
```

The `read_only` database-state settings are used to allow only selects from the database. `read_only` cannot take effect if any users are in the database. To reset the database to a normal read-and-write state the `read_write` database setting is used.

To set a database to a `read_only` state in code, do the following:

```
ALTER DATABASE database SET READ_ONLY
```

The database restricted access database state settings are also available. The three restricted access levels are `single_user`, `restricted_user`, and `multi_user` states. These settings control which users are allowed to access the database. The `single_user` setting is best used when you are doing database maintenance. The `restricted_user` setting only allows access to the database to those users in the `db_owner`, `dbcreator`, and `sysadmin` roles. The `multi_user` setting is used to set the database in the normal operating state.

To set the database restricted access state in code, do the following:

```
ALTER DATABASE database SET SINGLE_USER
```

## Compatability Level

In SQL Server, the database-compatibility level can be set from 60 (SQL Server version 6.0) to 80 (SQL Server 2000). Setting the database-compatibility level to a level lower than 80 may be necessary if you are upgrading the database engine and still need to maintain the behavior of an earlier version of SQL Server.

To set compatibility level in code, do the following:

```
EXEC sp_dbcmptlevel database, 80
```

# Recovery-Configuration Properties

The recovery-configuration properties (Table 23-13) are used to set recovery options in SQL Server.

**Table 23-13: Recovery-Configuration Properties**

| Property | Level* | Graphic Control | Code Option |
|---|---|---|---|
| Recovery Model | D | Enterprise Manager | alter database recovery |
| Torn Page Detection | D | Enterprise Manager | alter database torn_page_detection |
| Backup Timeout | S | - | - |
| Media Retention | S | - | media retention |
| Recovery Interval | S | - | recovery interval |

\* The configuration level refers to Server, Database, or Connection.

The recovery options determine how SQL Server handles transactions and the transaction log, and how the transaction log is backed up.

## Recovery Model

SQL Server 2000 uses a recovery model to configure several settings that work together to control how the transaction log behaves regarding file growth and recovery possibilities. The three recovery model options are:

✦ *Simple* — The transaction log contains only transactions that are not yet written to the data file. This option provides no up-to-the-minute recovery.

✦ *Bulk-Logged* — The transaction log contains all DML operations, but bulk insert operations are only marked and not logged.

✦ *Full* — The transaction log contains all changes to the data file. This option provides the greatest recovery potential.

 **Cross-Reference** Chapter 26, "Recovery Planning," focuses on recovery planning and operations in detail.

The recovery option can be set in code by means of the set recovery option.

### Torn-Page Detection

Even though SQL Server works with 8KB data pages, the operating system I/O writes in 512-byte sectors. So it's possible that a failure might occur in the middle of a data-page write, causing some of the 512-byte sectors to be written and some not written.

In keeping with the ACID properties of the database, the torn-page detection option instructs SQL Server to toggle a bit on each 512-byte sector with each write operation. If all the sectors were updated, all the torn-page detection bits should be identical. If, upon recovery, any of the bits are different, SQL Server can detect the torn-page condition and mark the database as suspect.

Some argue that this option is not necessary if the server has battery backup and the disk subsystem has battery backup on the cache, but I still use it.

**Cross-Reference**  The additional minor recovery options (back-up timeout, media retention, and recovery interval) are all discussed in Chapter 26, "Recovery Planning."

## Summary

Configuration options are important for compatibility, performance tuning, and controlling the connection. The configuration options are set at the server, database, and connection level. Most of the options can be set by means of Enterprise Manager's Database Properties page; nearly all can be configured with code.

Continuing with SQL Server–administration tasks, the next chapter focuses on maintaining the databases with database-consistency checks.

✦    ✦    ✦

# Maintaining the Database

The Database Consistency Checker (DBCC) commands are at the heart of database maintenance, even since the earliest versions of SQL Server. However, thanks to Microsoft's zero-maintenance initiative, SQL Server 2000 is now easier to maintain than ever before. Not only are many of the traditional database maintenance duties no longer required, but the Database Maintenance Plan Wizard can set up a custom set of SQL Server Agent jobs that execute an excellent database maintenance plan.

## DBCC Commands

Microsoft SQL Server's primary command for database maintenance is the Database Consistency Checker (DBCC) command and its 34 options.

The first DBCC command to become familiar with is the `DBCC help` command, which returns the syntax with all the options for any DBCC command:

```
DBCC Help ('CheckDB')
```

Result:

```
CheckDB [('database_name'
  [, NOINDEX | REPAIR])]
  [WITH NO_INFOMSGS[, ALL_ERRORMSGS]
  [, PHYSICAL_ONLY]
  [, ESTIMATEONLY][, TABLOCK]]
DBCC execution completed. If DBCC printed
  error messages,contact your system
  administrator.
```

All DBCC commands report their activity or errors found, and then conclude with the standard execution-completed statement, including the puzzling request to report any error to the system administrator. You are the database pro. If you're running DBCC, you're the best person to handle it.

## Database Integrity

DBCC CheckDB performs several consistency checks on the internal physical structure of the database. It's critical for the health of the database that the physical structure is correct. DBCC CheckDB checks things like index pointers, data-page offsets, the linking between data pages and index pages, and the structural content of the data and index pages. If a hardware hiccup has left a data page half-written, DBCC CheckDB is the best means of detecting the problem:

```
DBCC CheckDB ('OBXKites')
```

Result (abridged):

```
DBCC results for 'OBXKites'.
DBCC results for 'sysobjects'.
There are 114 rows in 2 pages for object 'sysobjects'.
DBCC results for 'sysindexes'.
There are 77 rows in 3 pages for object 'sysindexes'.
...
DBCC results for 'ProductCategory'.
There are 8 rows in 1 pages for object 'ProductCategory'.
DBCC results for 'Product'.
There are 55 rows in 1 pages for object 'Product'.
CHECKDB found 0 allocation errors
    and 0 consistency errors in database 'OBXKites'.
DBCC execution completed. If DBCC printed error messages,
    contact your system administrator.
```

Two options simply determine which messages are reported without altering the functionality of the integrity check: all_errormsgs and no_infomsgs. The estimate_only option returns the estimated size of the tempdb required by CheckDB.

If the database is large, the noindex option can be used to skip checking the integrity of all user-table non-clustered indexes. For additional time savings, the Physical_Only option performs only the most critical checks on the physical structure of the pages. Use these options only if time prevents a complete CheckDB, or the indexes are about to be rebuilt.

### Repairing the Database

If an error is found, DBCC can attempt to repair it. This is a separate operation from the normal integrity checks because the database must be placed in single-user mode with sp_dboption command before a DBCC CheckDB can be executed with the Repair_Rebuild option.

```
EXEC sp_dboption OBXKites, 'Single_user', 'True'
DBCC CheckDB ('OBXKites', Repair_Rebuild)
```

DBCC offers three repair modes, each performing a more radical surgery on the internal structure than the last:

✦ Repair_Fast — The simplest repair mode repairs non-clustered index keys and does not touch the data pages.

✦ Repair_Rebuild — The mid-level repair method performs a complete check and rebuild of all non-clustered indexes and index pointers. Again, this method doesn't write to any data pages.

✦ Repair_Allow_Data_Loss — The most severe option performs all the index repairs and also rebuilds the data-page allocations and pointers, and removes any corruption found in the data pages. Because it updates the data-page structure, some data loss is possible.

**Best Practice**

Run a DBCC CheckDB every day and after any hardware malfunction. If an error is detected, run the Repair_Rebuild repair mode to attempt to repair the database before using the Repair_allow_data_loss option to perform a full data-page repair.

## Multi-User Concerns

Improved with SQL 2000, DBCC CheckDB can now be executed while users are in the database, and it will multithread using all CPUs. However, CheckDB is very processor and disk intensive and is best to run while the database has the fewest users.

DBCC CheckDB will normally use schema locks while it is checking the database if DBCC is run while users are in the database. The TabLock option reduces the lock granularity to only a table-shared lock. DBCC CheckDB will run less efficiently, but the database concurrency will be higher, thus allowing users to perform their work:

```
DBCC CheckDB ('OBXKites') With TabLock
```

## Object-Level Validation

DBCC CheckDB performs a host of database structural-integrity checks. It's possible to run these checks individually. As an advantage, each of these commands provides more detailed information about its specific database object. For that reason, it's best to run DBCC CheckDB for the daily database-maintenance plan and use these object specific versions for debugging.

If the database requires repair, always use the full CheckDB over one of the lesser versions.

✦ DBCC CheckAlloc ('*database*') — A subset of CheckDB that checks the physical structure of the database. The report is very detailed, listing the extent count (64KB or eight data pages) and data-page usage of every table and index in the database.

✦ DBCC CheckFileGroup ('*filegroup*') — Similar to a CheckDB but for a specific filegroup only.

✦ DBCC CheckTable ('*table*') — Performs multiple parallel checks on the table.

✦ DBCC CleanTable ('*database*', *table*') — Reclaims space from a varchar, nvarchar, text, or ntext column that was dropped from the table. This option actually updates the database and is not included in CheckDB unless the maximum-repair option is being used. Therefore CleanTable might be a useful option to include in the daily maintenance plan if the database experiences regular text updates.

## Data Integrity

Above the physical-structure layer of the database is the data layer, which can be verified by the following DBCC options. These three data-integrity DBCC commands are not automatically executed by the DBCC CheckDB command. They should be executed independently.

✦ DBCC CheckCatalog (*'database'*) checks the integrity of the system tables within a database, ensuring referential integrity among tables, views, columns and data types. While it will report any errors, under normal conditions no detailed report is returned. DBCC CheckCatalog won't repair any errors. If an error is found, we recommend rebuilding the table or database from a script and moving any data that is still recoverable from the old table to the new table. If no errors are found, nothing of interest is reported.

✦ DBCC CheckConstraints (*'table'*,*'constraint'*) examines the integrity of a specific constraint, or all the constraints for a table. It essentially generates and executes a query to verify each constraint, and reports any errors found. As with the CheckCatalog, if no issues are detected, nothing is reported.

✦ DBCC CheckIdent ('table') verifies the consistency of the current identity-column value and the identity column for a specific table. If a problem exists, the next value for the identity column is updated to correct any error. If the identity column is broken, the new identity value will violate a primary key or unique constraint and new rows cannot be added to the table.

The code below demonstrates the usage of the DBCC CheckIdent command:

```
Use CHA2
DBCC CheckIdent ('Customer')
```

Result:

```
Checking identity information:
  current identity value '127', current column value '127'.
DBCC execution completed. If DBCC printed error messages,
  contact your system administrator.
```

# Index Maintenance

Indexes provide the performance bridge between the data and SQL queries. Because of data inserts and updates, indexes fragment, the data-distribution statistics become out of date, and the fill factor of the pages can be less than optimal. Index maintenance is required to combat these three results of normal wear and tear and to prevent performance reduction.

 Chapter 5, "Implementing the Physical Database Schema," contains information on index creation. Chapter 28, "Advanced Performance," covers index design and tuning.

## Database Fragmentation

As data is inserted into the data pages and index pages, the pages fill to 100 percent. At that point SQL Server performs a page split, creating two new pages with about 50 percent page density each. While this solves the individual page problem, the internal database structure can become fragmented.

To demonstrate the DBCC commands that affect fragmented tables and indexes, a table large enough to become fragmented is required. The following script builds a suitable table and a non-clustered index. The clustered primary key is a GUID, so row insertions will occur throughout the table, generating plenty of good fragmentation.

```
USE Tempdb

CREATE TABLE Frag (
  FragID UNIQUEIDENTIFIER
    PRIMARY KEY CLUSTERED DEFAULT NewID(),
  Col1 INT,
  Col2 CHAR(200),
  Created DATETIME DEFAULT GetDate(),
  Modified DATETIME DEFAULT GetDate()
  )

CREATE NONCLUSTERED INDEX ix_col
  ON Frag (Col1)
```

The following stored procedure will add one hundred thousand rows each time it's executed:

```
CREATE PROC Add100K
as
set nocount on
DECLARE @X INT
SET @X = 0
  WHILE @X < 100000
    BEGIN
      INSERT Frag (Col1,Col2)
        VALUES (@X, 'sample data')
      SET @X = @X + 1
    END
go
```

The following batch calls Add100K several times and populates the Frag table:

```
EXEC Add10K
EXEC Add10K
EXEC Add10K
EXEC Add10K
EXEC Add10K
```

DBCC ShowContig (*table, index*) reports the fragmentation details and the density for a given table or index. With half a million rows, the Frag table is very fragmented and most pages are slightly more than half full, as the following command shows:

```
DBCC ShowContig (frag) WITH ALL_INDEXES
```

In the following result, Index 1 is the clustered primary-key index, so it's also reporting the data-page fragmentation. Index 2 is the non-clustered index.

```
DBCC SHOWCONTIG scanning 'Frag' table...
Table: 'Frag' (1977058079); index ID: 1, database ID: 2
TABLE level scan performed.
```

```
- Pages Scanned................................: 22015
- Extents Scanned.............................: 2769
- Extent Switches.............................: 22008
- Avg. Pages per Extent.......................: 8.0
- Scan Density [Best Count:Actual Count].......: 12.50%
                                               [2752:22009]
- Logical Scan Fragmentation ..................: 49.73%
- Extent Scan Fragmentation ...................: 12.53%
- Avg. Bytes Free per Page....................: 2531.6
- Avg. Page Density (full)....................: 68.72%

DBCC SHOWCONTIG scanning 'Frag' table...
Table: 'Frag' (1977058079); index ID: 2, database ID: 2
LEAF level scan performed.
- Pages Scanned................................: 2757
- Extents Scanned.............................: 348
- Extent Switches.............................: 2725
- Avg. Pages per Extent.......................: 7.9
- Scan Density [Best Count:Actual Count].......: 12.66%
                                               [345:2726]
- Logical Scan Fragmentation ..................: 47.99%
- Extent Scan Fragmentation ...................: 99.71%
- Avg. Bytes Free per Page....................: 3380.7
- Avg. Page Density (full)....................: 58.23%
```

DBCC IndexDefrag defragments the index pages of both clustered and non-clustered indexes. It will organize the nodes for faster performance, compact the index, and reestablish the fill factor for an index.

```
DBCC IndexDefrag (DatabaseName, TableName, IndexName)
```

Performing the DBCC IndexDefrag operation is similar to rebuilding an index, with the distinct advantage that defragmenting an index is performed in a series of small transactions that do not block users from performing inserts and updates.

The next two commands defrag both indexes:

```
DBCC IndexDefrag ('Tempdb', 'Frag', 'PK_Frag')
```

Result:

```
Pages Scanned Pages Moved Pages Removed
------------- ----------- -------------
22009         18374       3633
```

```
DBCC IndexDefrag ('Tempdb', 'Frag', 'ix_col')
```

Result:

```
Pages Scanned Pages Moved Pages Removed
------------- ----------- -------------
2753          1700        1052
```

A `DBCC ShowContig` command examines the index structure after the defragmenting of the index. Both the logical-fragmentation and page-density problems created by the insertion of half a million rows are resolved:

```
DBCC ShowContig (frag) WITH ALL_INDEXES
```

Result:

```
DBCC SHOWCONTIG scanning 'Frag' table...
Table: 'Frag' (1977058079); index ID: 1, database ID: 2
TABLE level scan performed.
- Pages Scanned...............................: 18382
- Extents Scanned............................: 2307
- Extent Switches............................: 2316
- Avg. Pages per Extent......................: 8.0
- Scan Density [Best Count:Actual Count]......: 99.18% [2298:2317]
- Logical Scan Fragmentation ..................: 0.03%
- Extent Scan Fragmentation ..................: 13.87%
- Avg. Bytes Free per Page...................: 1431.9
- Avg. Page Density (full)...................: 82.31%

DBCC SHOWCONTIG scanning 'Frag' table...
Table: 'Frag' (1977058079); index ID: 2, database ID: 2
LEAF level scan performed.
- Pages Scanned...............................: 1705
- Extents Scanned............................: 216
- Extent Switches............................: 221
- Avg. Pages per Extent......................: 7.9
- Scan Density [Best Count:Actual Count]......: 96.40% [214:222]
- Logical Scan Fragmentation ..................: 0.29%
- Extent Scan Fragmentation ..................: 99.54%
- Avg. Bytes Free per Page...................: 471.4
- Avg. Page Density (full)...................: 94.18%
```

## Index Statistics

The usefulness of an index is based on the data distribution within that index. For example, if 60 percent of the customers are in New York City, selecting all customers in NYC will likely be faster with a table scan than with an index seek. But to find the single customer from Delavan, Wisconsin, the query definitely needs the help of an index. The query optimizer depends on the index statistics to determine the usefulness of the index for a particular query.

The statistics appear as indexes in some listings with names beginning with `_WA_Sys` or `heed_`.

`DBCC Show_Statistics` reports the last date the statistics were updated and the basic information about the index statistics, including the usefulness of the index. A low density indicates that the index is very selective. A high density indicates that a given index node points to several table rows and may be less useful than a low-density index.

The following code demonstrates the `Update Statistics` command:

```
use cha2
exec sp_help customer
Update Statistics Customer
```

The procedures `sp_createstats` and `sp_updatestats` will create and update statistics on all tables in a database, respectively.

### Index Density

Index density refers to the percentage of the index pages that contains data. If the index density is low, SQL Server has to read more pages from the disk to retrieve the index data. The index's fill factor refers to the percentage of the index page that contains data when the index is created or defragmented, but the index density will slowly alter during inserts, updates, and deletes.

The DBCC DbReIndex command will completely rebuild the index. Using this command is essentially the equivalent of dropping and creating the index with the added benefit of allowing the user to set the fill factor as the index is recreated. In contrast, the DBCC IndexDefrag will repair the fragmentation to the index's fill factor but will not adjust the target fill factor.

The next command recreates the indexes on the Frag table and sets the fill factor to 98 percent:

```
DBCC DBReIndex ('Tempdb.dbo.Frag','',98)
```

**Cross-Reference**

Index density can affect performance. Chapter 28, "Advanced Performance," includes more information on planning the best index fill factor.

## Database File Size

SQL Server 7 moved beyond SQL Server 6.5's method of allocated space in fixed-size files called *devices*. Since SQL Server 7, data and transaction logs can automatically grow as required. File size is still an area of database-maintenance concern. Without some intervention or monitoring, the data files could grow too large. The following commands and DBCC options deal with monitoring and controlling file sizes.

### Monitoring Database File Sizes

Three factors of file size should be monitored: the size of the database files and their maximum growth size, the amount of free space within the files, and the amount of free space on the disk drives.

The current and maximum file sizes are stored within the sysfiles system table:

```
Select name, size, maxsize from sysfiles
```

To detect the percentage of the file that is actually being used, use the sp_spaceused system stored procedure. The DBCC Updateusage command ensures that the index-usage information is accurate:

```
DBCC Updateusage ('tempdb')
sp_spaceused
```

Result:

| database_name | database_size | unallocated space |
| --- | --- | --- |
| OBXKites | 3.00 MB | 0.92 MB |

| reserved | data | index_size | unused |
| --- | --- | --- | --- |
| 1104 KB | 376 KB | 584 KB | 144 KB |

To determine the size and the percentage of free space within the transaction log, use the
`DBCC SQLPerf (LogSpace)` command:

```
DBCC SQLPerf (LogSpace)
```

Result (abridged):

```
Database Name   Log Size (MB)   Log Space Used (%)    Status
--------------  --------------  --------------------  --------
master          3.3671875       33.207657             0
tempdb          0.7421875       59.473682             0
model           0.4921875       63.194443             0
...
OOD             0.484375        72.278229             0
MS              0.7421875       37.302631             0

DBCC execution completed.
  If DBCC printed error messages,
  contact your system administrator.
```

To monitor the amount of free space on the server's disk drives, use the `xp_fixeddrives`
procedure:

```
Xp_fixeddrives
```

Result:

```
Disk:
---
c:
```

**Cross-Reference** For more information about configuring the data and transaction log files for autogrowth and setting the maximum file sizes, refer to Chapter 5, "Implementing the Physical Database Schema."

## Shrinking the Database

Unless the database is configured to automatically shrink in the background, the file space
that is freed by deleting unused objects and rows will not be returned to the disk operating
system. Instead, the files will remain at the largest size the data file may have grown to. If data
is regularly added and removed, constantly shrinking and growing the database would be a
wasteful exercise. However, if disk space is at a premium, a large amount of data has been
removed from the database, and the database is not configured to automatically shrink, the
following commands may be used to manually shrink the database. The database can be
shrunk while transactions are working in the database.

`DBCC ShrinkDatabase` can reduce the size of the database files by performing two basic steps:

1. Packing data to the front of the file, leaving the empty space at the end of the file.

2. Removing the empty space at the end of the file, reducing the size of the file.

These two steps can be controlled with the following options:

✦ The `notruncate` option causes `DBCC ShrinkDatabase` to perform only Step 1, packing
the database file but leaving the file size the same.

✦ The `truncateonly` option eliminates the empty space at the end of the file, but does
not first pack the file.

✦ The target file size can be set by specifying the desired percent of free space after the file is shrunk. Because autogrowth can be an expensive operation, leaving some free space is a useful strategy. If the desired free space percentage is larger than the current amount of free space, this option will not increase the size of the file.

The following command shrinks OBX Kites and leaves 10 percent free space:

```
DBCC ShrinkDatabase ('OBXKites', 10)
```

DBCC ShrinkDatabase affects all the files for a database, while the DBCC ShrinkFile command shrinks individual files.

The database can be configured to automatically shrink the files. See Chapter 23, "Configuring SQL Server," for more information.

### Shrinking the Transaction Log

When the database is shrunk, the transaction log is also shrunk. The notruncate and truncateonly options have no effect on the transaction log. If multiple log files exist, SQL Server shrinks them as if they were one large contiguous file.

A common problem is a transaction log that grows and refuses to shrink. The most likely cause is an old open transaction. The transaction log is constructed of virtual logs partitions. The success or failure of shrinking the transaction log depends on the aging of transactions within the virtual logs and log checkpoints. SQL Server can only shrink the transaction log by removing data older than the oldest transaction within the structure of the virtual logs.

To verify that an old transaction has a hold on the transaction log, use the DBCC OpenTran command:

```
BEGIN TRAN
UPDATE Product
  SET ProductDescription = 'OpenTran'
  WHERE Code = '1002'

DBCC OpenTran ('OBXKites')
```

Result:

```
Transaction information for database 'OBXKites'.

Oldest active transaction:
    SPID (server process ID) : 58
    UID (user ID) : 1
    Name          : user_transaction
    LSN           : (33:77:2)
    Start time    : May 18 2002  5:39:51:440PM
DBCC execution completed. If DBCC printed error messages,
  contact your system administrator.
```

Based on this information, the errant transaction can be tracked down and the SPID (user connection) can be killed. Enterprise Manager's Current Activity node can provide more information about the SPID's activity. A more drastic option is to stop and restart the server and then shrink the database.

The recovery model and transaction log backups both affect how the transaction log grows and automatically shrinks. For more information on these critical issues refer to Chapter 26, "Recovery Planning."

## Miscellaneous DBCC Commands

The remaining seven DBCC commands are used in troubleshooting during testing of stored procedures and triggers.

✦ `DBCC DropCleanBuffers` — Cleans the memory of any buffered data so that it doesn't affect query performance during testing.

✦ `DBCC Inputbuffer (SPID)` — Returns the last statement executed by a client, as identified by the client's SPID. This command can only be executed by members of the sysadmin server group, for obvious security reasons.

✦ `DBCC Outputbuffer (SPID)` — Returns the results of the last statement executed by a client. Like the `DBCC InputBuffer` command, this command can only be executed by members of the sysadmin group.

✦ `DBCC PinTable (DatabaseID, ObjectID)` — Tags a table so that once it is in memory it will not be flushed from memory. We advise against pinning a table; it's far better to let SQL Server cache pages in memory as they are needed.

✦ `DBCC UnPinTable (DatabaseID, ObjectID)` — Removes a table from the pin list.

✦ `DBCC ProcCache` — Reports some basic statistics about the procedure cache as queries and procedures are compiled and stored in memory.

✦ `DBCC ConcurrencyViolation` — The Desktop and Personal editions of SQL Server are limited to five concurrent users. This command checks how many times that limitation was hit.

# Managing Database Maintenance

SQL Server provides a host of database maintenance commands. Fortunately, it also provides the DBA with ways to schedule maintenance tasks.

## Planning Database Maintenance

An ideal database maintenance plan includes the following functions in the following order:

✦ *Consistency checks* — `DBCC CheckDB` and `DBCC CleanTable(table)` for tables that experience heavy text updates, `DBCC CheckCatalog`, `DBCC CheckConstraints`, and `DBCC CheckIdent` for database structure integrity.

✦ *Updating the index statistics*

✦ *Defragmenting the database*

✦ *Rebuilding the indexes*

✦ *Backups* — A strategic backup plan includes a mix of full, differential, and transaction log backups of the system databases and all significant user databases.

✦ *Checking the file sizes and free disk space*

These maintenance tasks can be automated in SQL Server Agent jobs.

# Database Maintenance Plan Wizard

The Database Maintenance Plan Wizard, built into Enterprise Manager, helps automate a basic maintenance plan and can perform all the required maintenance tasks. Launch the Wizard by highlighting a database and then selecting the Action ⇨ All Tasks ⇨ Maintenance Plan menu item.

Once a maintenance plan is created it can be adjusted and different databases can be assigned to it by means of the Management ⇨ Databases Maintenance Plans node in Enterprise Manager's console tree.

The maintenance plans work by passing parameters to an external executable program, which then runs the job. This means that the maintenance plan can't be manually tweaked.

## The Select Databases Screen

Under the Select Databases screen (Figure 24-1), database maintenance can be set up for all databases in SQL Server, for only the system databases, for only the user databases, or for a combination of databases selected by the user.

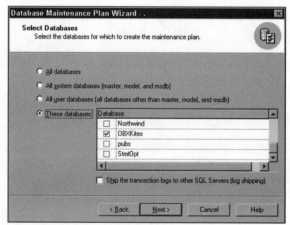

**Figure 24-1:** Database Maintenance Plan Wizard — the Select Databases screen.

## The Update Data Optimization Information Screen

The Update Data Optimization Information screen (Figure 24-2) enables the user to choose the level of indexing for the tables in the Database Maintenance Plan. Behind the scenes, DBCC DbReIndex, Update Statistics, and DBCC ShrinkDatabase are being executed on the tables in each database in the Database Maintenance Plan.

## The Database Integrity Check Screen

The Database Integrity Check screen (Figure 24-3) shows the levels of database integrity checks to choose from. Behind the scenes, DBCC CheckDb is executed.

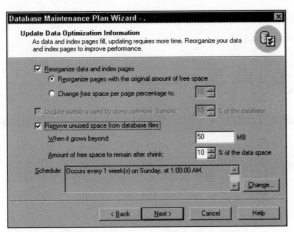

**Figure 24-2:** Database Maintenance Plan Wizard — the Update Data Optimization Information screen.

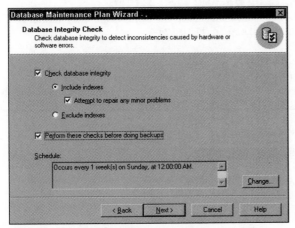

**Figure 24-3:** Database Maintenance Plan Wizard — the Database Integrity Check screen.

## The Specify the Database Backup Plan Screen

Under the Specify the Database Backup Plan screen (Figure 24-4), database backups are automated. The Database Maintenance Plan has the nice feature of saving the backup files to different directories for each database. It will also remove old backup files to help conserve disk space.

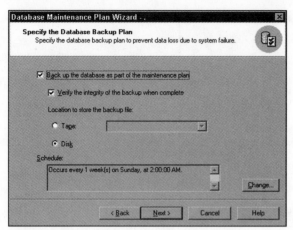

**Figure 24-4:** Database Maintenance Plan Wizard —
the Specify the Database Backup Plan screen.

## The Specify the Transaction Log Backup Plan Screen

On the Specify the Transaction Log Backup Plan screen the options are very similar to those
on the Specify the Database Backup Plan screen (Figure 24-4).

## The Reports to Generate Screen

The Reports to Generate screen (Figure 24-5) is an added benefit of the Database
Maintenance Plan. This final screen in the Database Maintenance Plan Wizard enables the cre-
ation of a report that summarizes the database maintenance activities in the Database
Maintenance Plan. The reports can be saved in a specific directory and/or e-mailed.

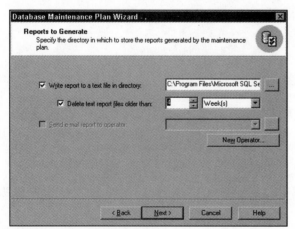

**Figure 24-5:** Database Maintenance Plan Wizard —
the Reports to Generate screen.

## Command-Line Maintenance

Database maintenance is normally performed within Query Analyzer or Enterprise Manager, or automated with SQL Server Agent. However, maintenance can be performed from the DOS command prompt by means of SQLMaint. This utility has numerous options that can perform backups, update statistics, and run DBCC. Specific information on SQLMaint can be found in SQL Server 2000 Books On-line.

SQLMaint may be useful in some situations, when using non–SQL Server schedulers or integrating the database maintenance plan with system utilities, such as third-party backups. Nevertheless, we recommend that you stay with SQL Server Agent over SQLMaint unless there's a compelling reason to abandon SQL Server's internal scheduler.

## Monitoring Database Maintenance

It's not enough to simply schedule the tasks; they must be monitored as well. In larger installations with dozens of SQL Servers spread around the globe, just monitoring the health of SQL Server and the databases becomes a full-time job. Table 24-1 provides a sample DBA daily checklist that can be a starting point for developing a database monitoring plan.

### Table 24-1: DBA Daily Checklist

| Item | S | M | T | W | T | F |
|------|---|---|---|---|---|---|
| System Databases Backup | | | | | | |
| Production User Databases Backup | | | | | | |
| SQL Agent, SQL Main, & DTC running | | | | | | |
| Database Size, Growth, Disk Free Space | | | | | | |
| Batch Jobs Execute OK | | | | | | |
| DBCC Jobs Execute OK | | | | | | |
| SQL Log Errors | | | | | | |
| Replication Log Agent Running | | | | | | |
| Replication Distribution Cleanup Job Execute OK | | | | | | |
| SQL Server Last Reboot | | | | | | |

Depending on the complexity and the number of servers, the DBA daily checklist can be maintained manually with an Excel spreadsheet or tracked in a SQL Server table.

# Summary

This chapter covered database maintenance in detail. SQL Server has a rich set of commands and utilities that can be used to monitor the health of, and to perform maintenance on, SQL Server. The Database Maintenance Plan is also available to streamline database maintenance. All installations of SQL Server should also include a database maintenance schedule to assist the DBA in keeping track of maintenance performed.

The next chapter explains how to use SQL Agent, which may be used to schedule jobs and create custom maintenance jobs.

✦    ✦    ✦

# Automating Database Maintenance with SQL Server Agent

T he automation of database maintenance is crucial to ensuring that a database is regularly monitored, maintained, and optimized. Monitoring consists of monitoring database size to identify issues before they generate mayhem; maintenance includes frequent backups; and optimization involves tweaking the index configuration for optimal performance. Automation ensures that these activities do not consume too much of your time, so you can focus on more pressing issues (such as improving your golf game, perhaps).

Ideally, you want SQL Server to monitor itself and alert you when it encounters a critical condition. And luckily for you, Microsoft grants this specific wish, since SQL Server 2000 includes a powerful component that can send alerts when specific critical conditions occur. Better still, this same component also enables you to schedule routine maintenance tasks either on a one-time basis or on a recurring basis. When scheduling a recurring task, specify how frequently the task should be executed, such as once a month or, say, on the first Saturday of every month. SQL Server Agent is the service responsible for processing alerts and running scheduled jobs.

## Setting up SQL Server Agent

Setting up SQL Server Agent is straightforward, as long as you avoid two pitfalls: The first is rather elementary, the second a bit more subtle. We'll cover the easy one first. Since SQL Server Agent is a Windows service, you want to make sure that the service is restarted if anybody reboots the server. This is an elementary step, but it is occasionally overlooked (and then, after someone restarts the server, none of the scheduled jobs run and, perhaps even worse, critical alerts go undetected).

The SQL Server Agent service is named SQLServerAgent if the default SQL Server instance in installed on the server. If more than one SQL Server instance is installed on the server, a SQL Server Agent service will exist for each instance, named SQLServerAgent$instancename (where instancename is the name of the SQL Server instance serviced).

As with any service, the SQL Server Agent start-up mode can be changed through the Services applet in the Control Panel. However, an easier way to accomplish the same goal is to use the SQL Server Service Manager whose icon is in the notification area of the taskbar (that's the area at the right of the taskbar, where the time is typically displayed). Double-click this icon to open the SQL Server Service Manager dialog box, shown in Figure 25-1.

**Figure 25-1:** The SQL Server Service Manager dialog box lets you easily change the start-up mode of the SQL Server Agent service.

Here are the steps to follow to ensure that the start-up mode of the SQL Server Agent service is set to automatic.

1. Open the SQL Server Service Manager dialog box by double-clicking its icon in notification area in the taskbar.

2. Make sure the correct server is selected.

3. Choose the SQL Server Agent service from the Services list box.

4. If the checkbox at the bottom of the dialog (labeled "Auto-start service when OS starts") is unchecked, check it to set the start-up mode to automatic.

It is a good idea to take one extra step to ensure that SQL Server Agent (and SQL Server for that matter) is always running. Here's how to accomplish this:

1. Start the SQL Server Enterprise Manager (its default location is Start ➪ Programs ➪ Microsoft SQL Server ➪ Enterprise Manager).

2. Expand the folders until you find the server you are configuring. If you are working on the actual server you are configuring, the path is Console Root/Microsoft SQL Server/ SQL Server Group/(local) (Windows NT).

3. Expand to see the folder below the server. One of these folders is entitled Management. Expand this folder to see the items under it.

4. One of the items under the Management folder is entitled SQL Server Agent. Right-click this item and select Properties, which opens a dialog box similar to the one shown in Figure 25-2.

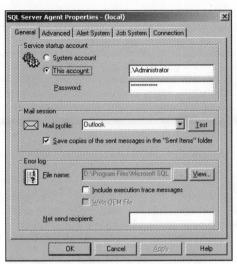

**Figure 25-2:** The General tab on the SQL Server Agent Properties dialog box enables you to configure how the service runs.

5. Click the Advanced tab. The Properties dialog now looks similar to the one shown in Figure 25-3. Under the Restart services group, make sure that both checkboxes have been clicked on. This will ensure that SQL Server and SQL Server Agent restart when they unexpectedly stop.

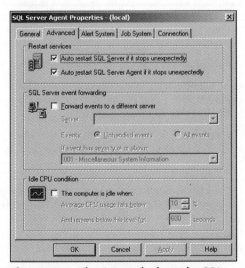

**Figure 25-3:** The Avanced tab on the SQL Server Agent Properties dialog helps you ensure that SQL Server and SQL Server Agent are running at all times.

The second pitfall to be aware of when setting up SQL Server Agent has to do with security. You have to determine which account will be used to run this service. By default, the SQL Server Agent service runs under the security context of the system account. Since the system account has access to only local resources, you must use a domain account if you want to access network resources in any of the scheduled jobs. You may, for example, want to back up a database to a different server. Typically, you will also need a domain account to enable SQL Server to send e-mail and pager notifications (the steps you need to follow to do this are outlined later in this section). You must also use a domain account for replication to work. You typically configure SQL Server Agent to use a Windows domain account that is a member of the sysadmin role so that you have the necessary permission to run jobs or send notifications.

Here are the steps to follow to change the account used to run the SQL Server Agent service:

1. Bring up the SQL Server Agent properties dialog box.

2. If needed, click the General tab. As shown in Figure 25-2 above, you will see a group called "Service startup account." Click the "This account" radio button and two text boxes will become enabled in which you can type the user name and password, respectively, for the Windows domain account that will be used for running the service.

3. If the account specified does not have the appropriate permissions for making connections to SQL Server, click the Connection tab and select "SQL Server Authentication." Then specify the SQL Server login account and password used to access the database.

The final step is to set up the SQL Server Agent Mail profile so that the service can send e-mail and pager notifications when alerts occur. This requires setting up and configuring a mail service and letting SQL Server Agent know how to access the mail service. The easiest mail service to use for this purpose is Exchange Server. If you are using Microsoft Exchange as the mail service, here are the steps you must follow.

1. Set up an Exchange mailbox for SQL Server Agent Mail on the Exchange server (normally this is a different server from the database server). Configure this mailbox for the domain account used to run the SQL Server Agent Mail service. Make sure to pick a descriptive name for the profile, identifying it as the SQL Server Agent profile. This will help prevent accidental deletion of this important profile.

2. Install MAPI-compliant mail-client software such as Outlook on the database server.

3. Set up a Mail profile for SQL Server Agent using the Mail utility on the Control Panel on the database server. This mail profile should point to the Mail Exchange server and the Exchange mailbox you set up in the first step of this procedure.

Now all that is left to do is to tell SQL Server Agent which Mail profile to use when sending e-mail. This is done in the SQL Server Agent Properties dialog, as follows:

1. Click the General tab.

2. In the Mail Session group, select the Mail Profile you have set up for this purpose. You can test whether mail has been properly configured by clicking the Test button.

## Understanding Alerts, Operators, and Jobs

An alert defines a specific action that will be carried out when a certain condition is met. Such a condition can be set up for a variety of performance counters, including number of connections, database file size, and number of deadlocks per second. A condition can also be tied to an error number or degree of error severity. When acting upon an alert condition, SQL Server Agent can notify one or more operators, run a job, or both.

Operators are the people responsible for handling critical conditions on the database server. As pointed out in the previous section, one of the neat things SQL Server Agent does is send messages to operators to report job status or make them aware of server conditions. Operators can be set up to receive messages via e-mail, pager, or Net Send. You can specify at which times an operator is available to receive messages via pager (9:00 a.m. to 5:00 p.m., Monday to Friday, for example). You can also suspend notification for a specified operator, such as when he or she is taking time off.

A job is a database task or group of database tasks. Examples of typical jobs are backing up a database, reorganizing the indexes, or executing a Data Transformation Services (DTS) package. SQL Server Agent jobs are also used behind the scenes to implement and schedule a maintenance plan using the Maintenance Plan Wizard in SQL Server Enterprise Manager.

# Managing Operators

Just like you need to create logins for the users that will be accessing a SQL Server database, you need to create operators in SQL Server to be able to send alert to these support people. Creating operators in SQL Server is straightforward. Here's how it works.

1. Start the SQL Server Enterprise Manager and find the Management folder below the server you are configuring.

2. One of the items under Management is entitled SQL Server Agent. Right-click this item and select New ➪ Operator from the context menu. (Alternatively, you may also expand the SQL Server Agent item and right-click Operators to bring up a pop-up menu containing the New Operator option.) This brings up the dialog box similar to the one shown in Figure 25-4.

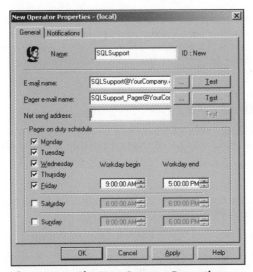

**Figure 25-4:** The New Operator Properties dialog box enables you to specify when an operator is available to receive pager notifications.

3. In the General tab of the New Operator dialog box, fill in the name of the operator as well as his or her e-mail address, pager e-mail address, and/or Net Send address, depending on how you want the notification to be sent. If you fill out a pager address you can specify when the operator is available to be paged. If an e-mail address is ambiguous you should specify a fully qualified e-mail address in square brackets, such as [SMTP:SQLSupport@YourCompany.com]. Alternatively, you can click the button with the ellipsis (. . .) to browse the address book on the database server.

4. If all your alerts have already been defined (you will learn how to define them in the next section, "Managing Alerts"), you can click the Notifications tab and select the notification method for each alert.

5. If an operator is unavailable to respond to notification, you can temporarily disable this operator by clearing the checkbox labeled "Operator is available to receive notifications" just under the Alert list on the Notifications tab. If you do this, make sure that another operator will be notified. Rather than disabling an operator, change the e-mail, pager, and Net Send addresses until the operator becomes available again.

# Managing Alerts

A number of default alerts are predefined when you install SQL Server. Another set of alerts are predefined when you install replication. Nine alerts are predefined in a default SQL Server installation. Two of these alerts are triggered by a full log file in either the msdb or tempdb database and the seven other alerts are triggered by errors of severity 19–25, respectively. All these alerts have names that start with "Demo:" and are enabled for use. However, no operators are configured to receive the notifications. Because errors of severity 19–25 are fatal errors, you should edit the properties of these alerts and configure them properly on each production server.

The names of the seven alerts created when you set up database replication start with "Replication:." These alerts include one for each status (success, failure, and retry) of the replication agent, one for each status (validation success, validation failure, and re-initialization) of a subscription, and one for when an expired subscription is dropped. By default these alerts are disabled and have no operators assigned to them.

## Creating User-Defined Errors

If you are deploying custom-written applications that use SQL Server as their data store, the application programmers may define their own set of errors. Here is how this is done:

1. Start SQL Server Enterprise Manager.

2. Expand the folders until you find the server you are configuring. If you are working on the actual server you are configuring, the path is Console Root/Microsoft SQL Server/ SQL Server Group/(local) (Windows NT). Select the server.

3. In the menu bar, select Action ➪ All Task ➪ Manage SQL Server Messages.

4. In the dialog box that appears, click the Messages tab and then click New. This brings up the New SQL Server Message dialog box (Figure 25-5).

5. Select an appropriate error number, severity level, message description, and language. You can also specify whether the error gets written to the Windows event log. By default, SQL Server error messages with a severity level of 19 or higher are logged in the Windows event log.

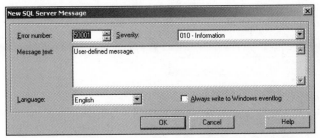

**Figure 25-5:** SQL Server enables application programmers to define their own error messages.

A programmer can also use the sp_addmessage system stored procedure to add a user-defined message. These user-defined messages can be triggered in code by means of the raiserror Transact-SQL facility.

As far as alerts are concerned, user-defined and native SQL Server messages are handled uniformly. Specify the error number or severity level, and when an error is raised that matches the alert condition, SQL Server Agent will initiate the specified response. The following section covers how to set up these kinds of alerts.

## Creating an Alert

You can create two kinds of alerts. The first is triggered by an error number or by an error of a specified severity. The second is triggered by a SQL Server performance counter. Here is how to set up both kinds of alerts:

1. Start SQL Server Enterprise Manager.

2. Expand the folders until you find the server you are configuring.

3. Expand to see the folder below the server. One of these folders is entitled Management. Expand to see the items under this folder.

4. One of the items under Management is entitled SQL Server Agent. Right-click this item and select New ⇨ > Alert. (Alternatively, you can expand the SQL Server Agent item and right-click Alerts to select New Alert.) This opens the New Alert Properties dialog box, similar to the one shown in Figure 25-6.

5. The Type list box enables you to specify which kind of alert you want to create: either a SQL Server event alert (triggered by an error number or level of severity) or a SQL Server performance-condition test. Figure 25-7 shows the changes to make to the New Alert Properties dialog box to create a SQL Server performance-condition test. A checkbox next to the Type list box enables you to enable or disable the alert.

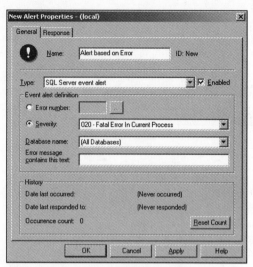

**Figure 25-6:** Error conditions is one of the two events that can trigger an alert.

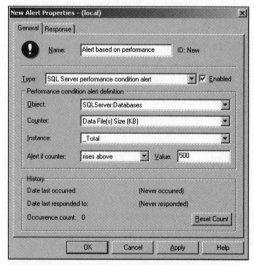

**Figure 25-7:** Performance conditions is one of the two events that can trigger an alert.

6. What to do in this step depends on the choice you made in previous step.

   1. If you are creating a SQL Server event alert, select the severity or error number you want to monitor. When specifying an error number, you can use the button with ellipsis to search for an error. If specifying severity, you typically focus on the critical errors, which by default have a severity of 19 or higher. You can either monitor all databases on the server or monitor a specific database. Finally, you

can also restrict alerts to messages containing a specific text string by specifying the filter text in the text box entitled "Error Message Contains This Text."

   **2.** If you are creating a SQL Server performance-condition test alert, select the object and counter you want to monitor. Then set the threshold for that counter. You can specify that the alert occur when the counter falls below, equals, or rises above the specified value. For some counters, you can specify the instance the counter is to be applied to. For example, you can monitor the data-file size for either all databases on the server or just one specific database.

**7.** In the Response tab, you can specify one or more operators to be notified, or which job to run, or both. You will learn how to set up jobs in the next section, "Managing Jobs." Of course, the New Operator button brings up the New Operator dialog box discussed in the previous section, "Managing Operators." Typically, you choose to send the error text in an e-mail or a Net Send, but not when you are paging an operator. Three checkboxes below the list of operators to be notified let you control when the error text is sent.

**8.** Finally, for recurring alerts, you can specify the delay between responses in minutes and seconds. This is especially important for SQL Server performance-condition alerts, because these conditions tend to exist for a long time and you do not want to flood the operators with multiple alerts for the same condition.

Another way of setting up an alert is through the Alert Wizard. You may access this wizard by starting SQL Server Enterprise Manager and selecting Tools ➪ Wizards on the menu bar. This brings up the Select Wizard dialog box, shown in Figure 25-8. Expand the Management section and select the Create Alert Wizard. Clicking OK will start this wizard. When you run this wizard, you will have to make similar choices as the one outlined in the procedure described previously in this section.

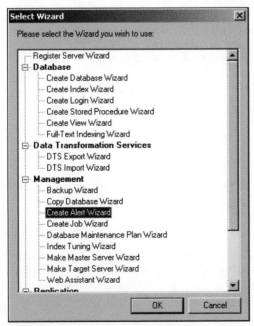

**Figure 25-8:** The Alert Wizard walks you through the creation of an Alert.

# Managing Jobs

A job is defined as a series of steps with a specific work flow. You can, for example, specify that Step 1 will execute Step 2 if it succeeds, but will execute Step 3 if it fails. Steps come in two basic types. The first type involves replication. The second can execute Transact-SQL script, ActiveX script (Visual Basic script or JScript), or any operating-system command. The latter are the most frequently used. After each step, you can specify the next action if the step succeeds and the next action if the step fails. Your choices are:

✦ Go to the next step

✦ Go to Step *x*, where *x* is the number of any step defined in the job

✦ Quit the job, reporting success

✦ Quit the job, reporting failure

You can also set the number of times you want a step to be attempted in case of failure. You can associate one or more schedules with a job. This enables you to automatically run a job at a specified time. A schedule can specify that a job runs once at a specific time or on a recurring basis. You can also schedule a job to run whenever SQL Server Agent starts or whenever the CPU becomes idle. In the Advanced tab of the SQL Server Agent Properties dialog (Figure 25-2), you can specify when you consider the CPU to be idle. This involves selecting the level of average CPU usage that the CPU must fall below for a specified time in seconds.

Finally, you can also set notifications for completion, success, or failure of a job.

Some wizards create jobs behind the scenes when you use them. Wizards that do so include the Maintenance Plan Wizard, the Backup Wizard, the DTS Import Wizard, and the DTS Export Wizard.

As with alerts, you can create a new job either with a wizard or using the New Job dialog box. Here are the steps to follow when using the New Job dialog box. (You will be confronted with similar choices when using the wizard.) Creating a job involves five distinct steps:

✦ Creating a job definition

✦ Setting each step to execute

✦ Setting the next action for each step

✦ Configuring a job schedule

✦ Handling completion-, success-, and failure-notification messages

We'll walk you through each of these steps. But first, an optional step is covered: creating a job category.

## Creating a job category

As you will see in the next section, when defining a job, you can assign a category to it. This enables you to group similar jobs together. Here are the steps you can use to manage job categories:

1. Start SQL Server Enterprise Manager and find the Management folder below the server you are configuring.

2. Expand the Management folder and click Jobs.

3. In the menu bar, select Action ⇨ All Tasks ⇨ Manage Job Categories. This brings up the Job Categories dialog box, shown in Figure 25-9.

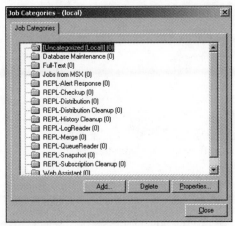

**Figure 25-9:** The Job Categories dialog box enables you to maintain the job categories used when you define a new job.

4. You can create a new job category by clicking the Add... button. This brings up the New Category properties dialog. Type in a descriptive name for the category.

5. You can then add jobs to this category by clicking the Show All Jobs checkbox and selecting the corresponding checkbox in the Member column of the job list.

## Creating a Job Definition

The main component of a job definition is the unique name that will be used to refer to the job. You use this unique name, for example, to specify which job to run when an alert is triggered. Here's how you create a job definition:

1. Start SQL Server Enterprise Manager and find the Management folder below the server you are configuring.

2. Expand the Management folder to see the items below it.

3. One of the items under Management is entitled SQL Server Agent. Right-click this item and select New ⇨ Job. (Alternatively, you can also expand the SQL Server Agent item and right-click Jobs to select New Job.) This brings up a New Job Properties dialog box similar to the one shown in Figure 25-10.

4. In the General tab, give the job a unique name (up to 128 characters), select an appropriate category and owner for the job, and type a short description (up to 512 characters) of the job. Only administrators can change the owner of an existing job. Only predefined logins can be used as the owner. If you do not find the login you want to use, exit the job definition by clicking the Cancel button and create a login for the account you want to use. To do this, expand the Security item a few items below the Management item in Enterprise Manager, right-click on Logins, and then select "New Login."

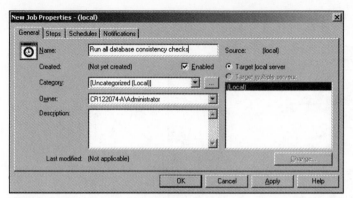

**Figure 25-10:** You can categorize and assign an owner to a new job in the New Job Properties dialog box.

5. If job scheduling across multiple servers is configured, select which server acts as the target server (the server on which the job runs). To run on the server on which you are working, select Target Local Server. To run on multiple servers, select Target Multiple Servers and specify the servers on which the job will run.

6. Click Apply to create the job definition. You are now ready for the next steps, as explained in the following sections.

## Setting up the Job Steps

After you have created a job definition, you may want to define what steps need to be performed during the job. You do this by clicking the Steps tab (Figure 25-11) in the New Job Properties dialog box. The usages of the buttons on this screen are as follows:

✦ *New* creates a new step.

✦ *Insert* inserts a step before the currently highlighted step.

✦ *Edit* modifies the currently highlighted step.

✦ *Delete* deletes the currently highlighted step.

✦ *Move Step Up* moves the currently highlighted step up one in the list.

✦ *Move Step Down* moves the currently highlighted step down one in the list.

✦ *Start Step* enables you to choose which step is executed first. This first step is indicated by a green flag.

When you create a new step, you are presented with the New Job Step dialog box (Figure 25-12). All steps require a unique name (up to 128 characters). For the three most common types of steps (Transact-SQL Script, ActiveX script, and operating-system commands), you simply type in the command box the code you want executed. You may also click the Open button to load the code from a file. The Parse button enables you to check the syntax of the command.

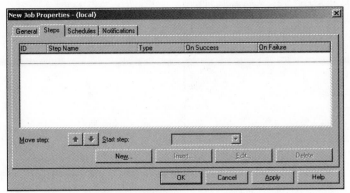

**Figure 25-11:** A job may consist of one or more steps, which are created in the Steps tab.

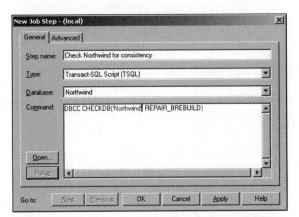

**Figure 25-12:** A step can execute any Transact-SQL code.

After you have entered the code that should run for the step, you can click the Advanced tab in the New Job Step dialog box (Figure 25-13) and determine what happens after the step executes. You can also specify how many times the step is attempted in case of initial failure, as well as the delay in minutes between the attempts.

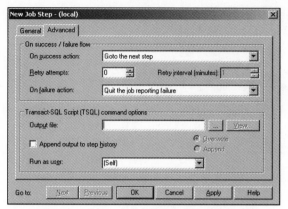

**Figure 25-13:** You can control what happens after a step executes.

## Configuring a Job Schedule

After you have entered the steps for a given job, you need to specify when the job is to be executed. You do this in the Schedule tab of the Job Properties dialog box. Clicking on the New Schedule button on this tab brings up the New Job Schedule dialog shown in Figure 25-14.

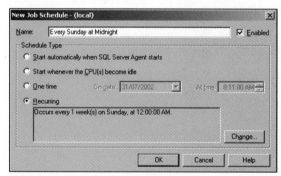

**Figure 25-14:** Jobs can be scheduled on a one-time basis or on a recurring basis.

For many maintenance tasks, you want to create a recurring job. If you don't like the default (every week on Sunday at 12:00:00 a.m.), you can click the Change button to define how frequently the task is to be repeated. As you can see from Figure 25-15, you have plenty of flexibility in scheduling a recurring job.

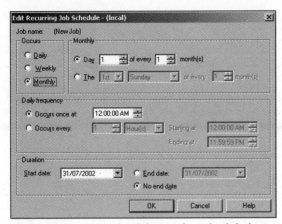

**Figure 25-15:** Recurring jobs can be scheduled on a daily, weekly, or monthly basis.

## Handling Completion-, Success-, and Failure-Notification Messages

Finally, click the Notifications tab of the New Job Properties dialog box (Figure 25-16) to specify the type of notification to be used when the job completes, fails, or succeeds. You can send a message to an operator (via e-mail, pager, or Net Send message), log the related event, automatically delete the step, or do any two or all three.

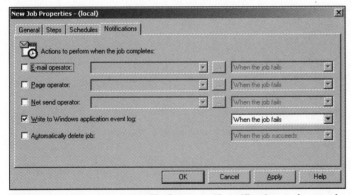

**Figure 25-16:** You can specify the type of notification to be used when the job completes, fails, or succeeds.

# Summary

SQL Server Agent is a powerful ally that will ensure you never forget to perform a crucial maintenance task, and that will alert you when something critical requires your attention. The former goal is achieved through recurring jobs, the latter through alerts.

In this chapter you learned how to set up SQL Server Agent. You learned what alerts, operators, and jobs are, and the steps required to manage them. In short, you should now be fully equipped to use all features of SQL Server Agent to automate crucial maintenance tasks.

✦    ✦    ✦

# Recovery Planning

*"When times are perilous, a wise fellow keeps his powder dry."*

— American Revolution saying

Obviously, we live in an imperfect world and bad things do happen to good people. Since you're bothering to read this chapter, I'll be honest and agree that doing backups isn't very exciting. In some jobs excitement means trouble, and this is one of them. To a good DBA, being prepared for the worst means having a sound recovery plan that's been tested more than once.

Consistent with the flexibility found in other areas of SQL Server, there are multiple ways to perform a backup, each suited to a different purpose. SQL Server 2000 introduces recovery models, which help organize the backup options and simplify database administration.

This chapter discusses the concepts that support the recovery effort, which entail both backup and restoration. It seems foolish to study backup without also learning about how restoration completes the recovery.

**Cross-Reference**  Recovery planning is not an isolated topic. Transactional integrity (Chapter 11) is deeply involved in the theory behind a sound recovery plan. Once the recovery strategy is determined, it's often implemented within a maintenance plan (Chapter 24). Aside from the backup and restoration, it is the constant availability of log shipping and failover servers (Chapter 28).

While backups tend to be boring, restores tend to occur while folks are excited. For this reason, it makes sense to be more familiar with restoration than with backup.

## Recovery Concepts

The concept of database recovery is based on the D in the transactional-integrity ACID properties — transaction *durability*. Durability means that a transaction, once committed, must be persistent. Regardless of hardware failure, the transaction must still exist in the database.

SQL Server accomplishes transactional durability with a write-ahead transaction log. Every transaction is written to the transaction log prior to being written to the data file. This provides a few benefits to the recovery plan:

✦ The transaction log ensures that every transaction can be recovered up to the very last moment before the server stopped.

✦ The transaction log permits backups while transactions are being processed.

✦ The transaction log reduces the impact of a hardware failure because the transaction log and the data file may be placed on different disk subsystems.

The strategy of a recovery plan should be based on the organization's tolerance level, or *pain level*, for lost transactions. Recovery-plan tactics involve choosing among the various backup options, generating a backup schedule, and off-site storage.

SQL Server backup and recovery are very flexible: You have three recovery models to choose from. The transaction log can be configured, based on your recovery needs, according to one of the following recovery models:

✦ *Simple* — No transaction-log backups

✦ *Bulk-logged* — Bulk-logged operations are not logged

✦ *Full* — All transactions are logged

And five backup options:

✦ *Full* — Complete backup of all data

✦ *Differential* — Backup of all data pages modified since the last full backup

✦ *Transaction log* — Backup of all transactions in the log

✦ *File or filegroup* — Backup of all the data in the file or filegroup

✦ *File differential* — Backup of all data pages modified since the last file or filegroup backup.

**Note**     Backing up the database may not be the only critical backup you have to perform. If the database-security scheme relies on Windows authentication, backing up the Windows users is important as well. The point is that the SQL Server recovery plan must fit into a larger IT recovery plan.

SQL Server backups are very flexible and can handle any backup-to-file ratio. A single backup instance can be spread across several backup files, creating a *backup set*. Conversely, a single backup set can contain multiple backup instances.

Restoration always begins with a full backup. Differential and transaction log backups then restore the transaction that occurred after the full backup.

# Recovery Models

The recovery model configures SQL Server database settings to accomplish the type of recovery required for the database, as detailed in Table 26-1. The key differences among the recovery models involve how the transaction log behaves and which data is logged.

## Table 26-1: SQL Server Recovery Models

| Recovery Model | Description | Transaction Atomicity | Transaction Durability | Bulk-Copy Operations |
|---|---|---|---|---|
| **Simple** | Transaction log is continuously truncated on checkpoints | Yes | No, can restore only to the last full or differential backup | Not logged — high performance |
| **Bulk-Logged** | Select-into and bulk-insert operations are not logged as ransactions | Yes | Maybe, can restore only to the last full or differential backup, or to the last transaction-log backup if no bulk-copy operations have been performed | Only marked — high performance |
| **Full** | All transactions are logged and stored until transaction-log backup | Yes | Yes, can restore up to the point of recovery | Slower than simple or bulk-logged |

While the durability of the transaction is configurable, the transaction log is still used as a write-ahead transaction log to ensure that each transaction is atomic. In case of system failure, the transaction log is used by SQL Server to roll back any uncommitted transactions as well as to complete any committed transactions.

## Simple Recovery Model

The simple recovery model is suitable for databases that require that each transaction be atomic, but not necessarily that it be durable. The simple recovery model directs SQL Server to truncate, or empty, the transaction log on checkpoints. The transaction log will keep a transaction until it's confirmed in the data file, but after that point the space may be reused by another transaction in a round-robin style.

Since the transaction log is only a temporary log, there are no transaction-log backups. This recovery model has the benefit of keeping the transaction log small at the cost of potentially losing all transactions since the last full or differential backup. Choosing the simple recovery model is the equivalent of setting the `truncate log on checkpoint` database option to `true` in SQL Server 7.0 or newer.

A recovery plan based on a simple recovery model might perform full backups once a week and differential backups every weeknight, as shown in Figure 26-1. The full backup copies the entire database, and the differential backup copies all the changes that have been made since the last full backup.

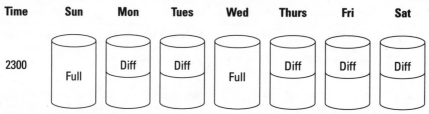

**Figure 26-1:** A typical recovery plan using the simple recovery model includes only full and differential backups.

When restoring from a simple recovery plan:

1. Restore the most recent full backup.

2. Restore the most recent (optional) single differential backup.

# The Full Recovery Model

The full recovery model offers the most robust recovery plan. Under this model all transactions, including bulk-logged operations, are fully logged in the transaction log. Even system functions such as index creation are fully logged. The primary benefit of this model is that every committed transaction in the database can be restored right up to the point when failure occurred.

**Best Practice**

For production databases, we recommend the full recovery model. While it will run on a single drive system, the transaction log should be located on a fault-tolerant disk subsystem separate from the data files to ensure a high level of transactional durability.

The trade-off for this high level of transactional integrity is a certain amount of performance:

✦ Bulk-logged and select-into operations will be slower. If the database doesn't import data using these methods, this is a moot point.

✦ The transaction log will be mammoth. If copious drive space is available, this, too, is a moot point.

✦ Backing up and restoring the transaction log will take longer than with the other recovery models. However, in a crisis, restoring all the data will likely be more important than quickly restoring partial data.

The full recovery model can use all five types of database backups. A typical backup schedule is illustrated in Figure 26-2.

A full-recovery backup plan will typically do a full database backup twice a week, and differential backups every other night. The transaction log is backed up throughout the day, from as little as two times to as often as every 15 minutes.

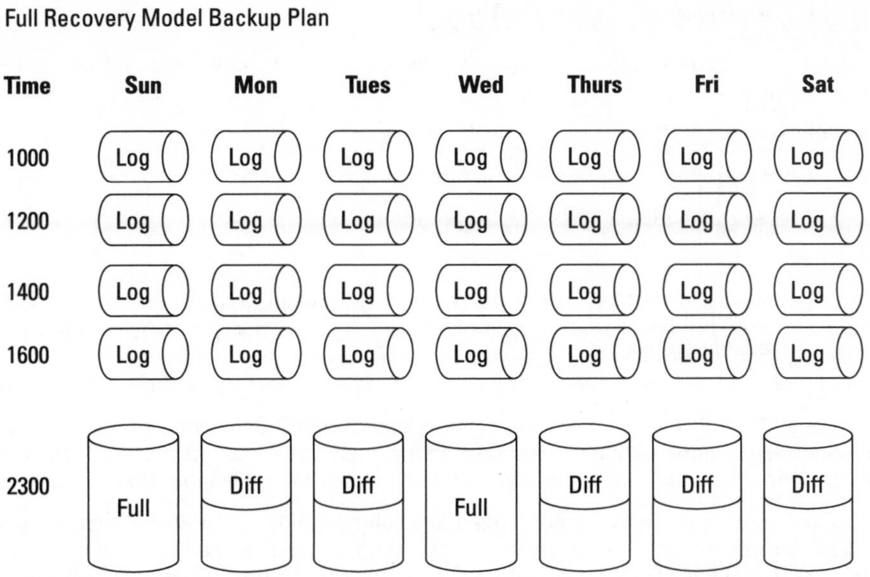

Full Recovery Model Backup Plan

**Figure 26-2:** A typical recovery plan using the full recovery model, using full, differential, and transaction-log backups.

When restoring from the full-recovery model, do the following:

1. Back up the current transaction log.

> **Note**
>
> If the disk subsystem containing the transaction log is lost, the database is marked suspect by SQL Server and it is not possible to back up the current transaction log. In this case the best recovery is to restore to the last transaction-log backup. Other reasons for a database being marked suspect would be that the database file itself has been removed or renamed, or the database is currently off-line.

2. Restore the most recent full backup.

3. Restore the most recent single differential backup, if one has been made since the last full backup.

4. Restore, in sequence, all the transaction-log backups made since the time of the last full or differential backup. If the last backup was a full backup then restoring it is sufficient. If the last backup was a differential backup, you will need to restore the most recent full backup before restoring the most recent differential.

The Enterprise Manager restore form (discussed in the section "Performing the Restore with Enterprise Manager," later in this chapter) automatically helps you choose the correct set of backups, so it's not as difficult as it sounds.

# Bulk-Logged Recovery Model

The bulk-logged recovery model is similar to the full recovery model, except that the following operations are not logged:

- ✦ Bulk inserts (BCP)
- ✦ `Select * into table` DML commands
- ✦ `Writetext` and `updatetext` BLOB operations
- ✦ `Create index` and create indexed views

Because this recovery model does not log these operations they run very fast. The transaction log only marks that the operations took place and tracks the extents (a group of eight data pages) that are affected by the bulk-logged operation. When the transaction log is backed up, the extents are copied to the transaction log in place of the bulk-logged marker.

The trade-off for bulk-logged operation performance is that the bulk-logged operation is not treated as a transaction. While the transaction log itself stays small, copying all affected extents to the transaction-log backup can make the log-backup file more than mammoth.

Since bulk-logged operations are not logged, if a failure should occur after the bulk-logged operation but before the transaction log is backed up, the bulk-logged operation is lost and the restore must be made from the last transaction log. Therefore, if the database is using the bulk-logged recovery model, every bulk-logged operation should be immediately followed by a transaction-log backup.

This model is useful only if the database sees a great number of bulk-logged operations, and if it's important to increase their performance. If the database is performing adequately during bulk-logged operations in the full recovery model, bypass the bulk-logged recovery model.

Note that the simple recovery model also does not log bulk-copy operations.

Using this setting is essentially the same as setting the `Select Into/Bulkcopy` database option to true.

# Setting the Recovery Model

The model system database's recovery model is applied to any newly created database. The full recovery model is the default for the Standard and Enterprise Editions. The Personal and Desktop editions use the simple recovery model as their default. But you can change the default by setting the recovery model for the model system database.

Using Enterprise Manager, you can easily set the recovery model on the Options tab of the Database Properties dialog box. Select the database and right-click to get to the Database Properties dialog.

In code, the recovery model is set by means of the `alter database` DDL command:

```
ALTER DATABASE DatabaseName SET Recovery Option
```

The valid options are `Full`, `Bulk_Logged`, and `Simple`. The following code sets the CHA2 sample database to the full recovery model:

```
ALTER DATABASE CHA2 SET Recovery Full
```

We recommend explicitly setting the recovery model in the code that creates the database.

The current recovery model can be determined from code by means of the database-property examine function:

```
SELECT DatabasePropertyEx('CHA2', 'Recovery')
```

Result:

```
FULL
```

## Modifying Recovery Models

While a database is typically set to a single recovery model, there's nothing to prevent you from switching between recovery models during operation to optimize performance and suit the specific needs of the moment.

It's perfectly valid to run during the day with the full recovery model for transaction durability, and then to switch to bulk-logged during data imports in the evening.

During recovery it's the full, differential, and transaction-log backups that count. The recovery operation doesn't care how they were made.

Because the simple recovery model does not permanently log the transactions, care must be taken in switching to or from the simple recovery model:

✦ If you are switching to simple, the transaction log should be backed up prior to the switch.

✦ If you are switching from simple, a full database backup should be performed immediately following the switch.

# Backing up the Database

The actual process of performing a backup presents as many options as the underlying concepts present.

## Backup Destination

A backup may copy the data to any one of two possible destinations:

✦ *Disk subsystem* — A backup can be performed either to a local disk (preferably not the same disk subsystem as the database files), or to another server's disk drive by means of the Universal Naming Convention (UNC). The SQL Server account must have write privileges to the remote drive in order to save the backup file

**Best Practice**

We prefer backing up to a disk file on another server and then copying the backup flies to tape using the organization's preferred IT backup method. This method is the fastest for SQL Server, and it enables the IT shop to continue using a familiar single-tape backup-software technique. If this creates a network bottleneck, use a dedicated network connection or backbone between the SQL Server and the file server.

✦ *Tape* — SQL Server can back up directly to most tape-backup devices.

**Note**    Several companies offer third-party backup for SQL Server that uses named pipes. While you may find third-party backup useful, we encourage you to become familiar with SQL Server's built-in recovery methods before making the decision to use it.

A disk- or tape-backup file is not limited to a single backup event. The file may contain multiple backups and multiple types of backups.

Two other issues to keep in mind when considering backup media are the *media retention* or *rotation*, and the off-site media-storage location.

A common technique is to rotate a set of five tapes for the weekly backups and another set of six tapes for the remaining daily backups. The weekly tapes would be labeled Sunday1, Sunday2, and so on, and the daily tapes would be labeled Monday, Tuesday, Wednesday, Thursday, Friday, and Saturday.

A palindrome is a word, phrase, or number that's the same backward or forward, such as "kayak," or "drab as a fool, aloof as a bard." Some numbers when reversed and added to itself will create a palindrome; for example, 236 + 632 = 868. Palindromes have a rich history: In ancient Greece they inscribed, "Nipson anomemata me monan opsin," meaning, "wash the sin as well as the face," on fountains.

Palindromes also represent a great method for rotating backup tapes. Using four tapes labeled A through D, a backup rotation might be ABCDCBA ABCDCBA....

Alternately, the palindrome method can be implemented so that each letter represents a larger interval, such as A for daily, B for weekly, C for monthly, and D for quarterly.

Rotating backup tapes off site is an important aspect of recovery planning. Ideally, a contract should support an off-site recovery site complete with server and workstations.

## Performing Backup with Enterprise Manager

The first backup must be a full database backup to begin the backup cycles.

A database backup can be performed from multiple locations in Enterprise Manager, as follows:

✦ Select the database to be backed up. From the right-click menu or Action menu select All Tasks ➪ Backup Database to open the SQL Server Backup form.

✦ From the Tools menu select Backup Database to open the SQL Server Backup form.

✦ Select Databases in the console tree, right-click on it, and select Backup Database to open the SQL Server Backup form.

✦ Select the database to be backed up. In the Wizards menu of the Taskpad select Backup a Database to launch the Backup Wizard.

✦ In the toolbar, click the wizards tool. Expand the Management wizards node. Select the Backup Wizard.

The SQL Server Backup form, shown in Figure 26-3, is the primary means of backing up databases within Enterprise Manager. The Backup Wizard simply asks the same questions, but with fewer questions per page.

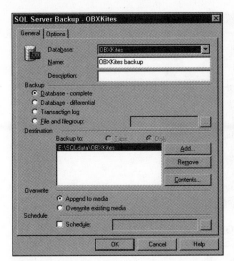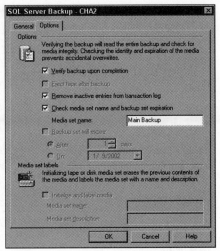

**Figure 26-3:** The SQL Server Backup form is the most common means of manually backing up a database.

The following is a list of the fields within the SQL Server Backup window as well as a description of each:

✦ *Database* — The database to be backed up. By default this is the current database in Enterprise Manager.

✦ *Name* — The required name of the backup.

✦ *Description* — Optional additional information about the backup.

✦ *Backup* — The type of backup: full, differential, transaction-log, file or filegroup. If the database is set to the simple recovery model, transaction-log will not be available.

✦ *Destination* — Sets the destination tape file or disk file. If the current destination is incorrect, delete it and add the correct destination

✦ *Contents* — Displays the backups already in the selected destinations.

✦ *Append to media* or *Overwrite existing media* — Determines if the current backup will be added to the backup file or if the backup media should be initialized and a new series of backups placed in them.

✦ *Schedule* — Launches a scheduler to create a SQL job that will run the configured backup according to the schedule, as shown in Figure 26-4

✦ *Verify backup upon completion* — Despite the name, this option does not compare the data in the backup with the data in the database, nor does it verify the integrity of the backup. It simply checks that the backup sets are complete, and that the file is readable. Nevertheless, we always use this option.

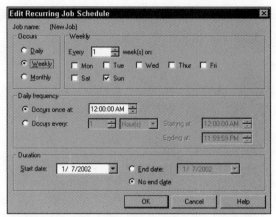

**Figure 26-4:** The scheduler creates a SQL Server Agent job that will perform backups on a regular schedule.

✦ *Eject tape after backup*—Directs the tape to eject, which helps prevent other backups from overwriting the backup file.

✦ *Remove inactive entries from the log*—This is the Enterprise Manager equivalent of truncating the transaction log. Once the transaction log has been successfully backed up it's common to remove transactions that were backed up so the log doesn't need to increase in size.

✦ *Check media set name and backup set expiration*—Tests the backup media to ensure that they're the correct media.

✦ *Backup set will expire*—Sets an expiration date for the backup. This establishes a protective waiting period for the backup, to prevent it from being overwritten before the date specified.

✦ *Initialize and labels*—Directs SLQ Server to initialize and label the tape.

## Backing up the Database with Code

The Backup command offers a few more options than Enterprise Manager, and using the backup command directly is useful for assembling SQL Server Agent jobs by hand rather than with the scheduler or the Maintenance Plan Builder.

Without all the options and frills, the most basic backup command is as follows:

```
BACKUP DATABASE Databasename
   TO DISK = 'file location'
   WITH
     NAME = 'backup name'
```

The following command backs up the CHA2 database to a disk file and names the backup CHA2Backup:

```
BACKUP DATABASE CHA2
  TO DISK = 'e:\Cha2Backup.bak'
  WITH
    NAME = 'CHA2Backup'
```

Result:

```
Processed 200 pages for database 'CHA2',
  file 'CHA2' on file 1.
Processed 1 pages for database 'CHA2',
  file 'CHA2_log' on file 1.
BACKUP DATABASE successfully processed 201 pages
  in 0.316 seconds (5.191 MB/sec).
```

The backup command has a few important options that deserve to mentioned first:

✦ Tape (Backup To:) — To back up to tape instead of disk, use the to tape option and specify the tape-drive location:

```
TAPE = '\\.\TAPE0'
```

✦ Differential — Causes the backup command to perform a differential backup instead of a full database backup. The following command performs a differential backup:

```
BACKUP DATABASE CHA2
  TO DISK = 'e:\Cha2Backup.bak'
  WITH
    DIFFERENTIAL,
    NAME = 'CHA2Backup'
```

✦ To back up a file or filegroup, list it after the database name. This technique can help organize backups. For example, for backup purposes the OBX Kites sample database is designed to place static tables in one filegroup and active tables in the primary filegroup.

✦ Password — If the backup is being made to a unsecured tape, a password is highly recommended. This password is for the specific backup instance.

The backup command has numerous additional options:

✦ Description — Identical to the Description field within Enterprise Manager.

✦ ExpireDate: Identical to Enterprise Manager; prevents the backup from being overwritten before the expiration date.

✦ RetainDays — The number of days, as an integer, before SQL Server will overwrite the backup.

✦ Stats = % — Tells SQL Server to report the progress of the backup in the percentage increment specified; the default increment is 10 percent.

✦ BlockSize — Sets the block size of the backup. For disk backups it's not needed; for tape drives it is probably not needed, but available to solve problems if required for compatibility. For disk backups the default Windows block size is used automatically, which is typically 4096 bytes on a drive over 2GB in size. If a backup to disk will later be copied to a CD/RW, try a block size of 2048.

✦ MediaName—Specifies the name of the media volume. This option serves as a safety check: If the backup is being added to the media, the name must match.

✦ MediaDescription—Writes an optional media description.

✦ MediaPassword—Creates an optional media password that applies to the entire medium (disk file or tape). The first time the medium is created the password can be set. If the password is specified when the medium is created, it must be specified every subsequent time the backup medium is accessed to add another backup or to restore.

✦ Init/NoInit—Initializes the tape or disk file, thus overwriting all existing backup sets in the medium. SQL Server will prevent initialization if any of the backups in the medium have not expired or still have the number of retaining days. NoInit is the default.

✦ NoSkip/Skip—This option "skips" the backup-name and -date checking that normally prevents overwriting backups. Noskip is the default.

The last options apply only when backing up to tape:

✦ NoFormat/Format — Will format the tape (not disk drive!) prior to the backup. Format automatically includes skip and init.

✦ Rewind/NoRewind — Directs SQL Server to rewind the tape. The default is to rewind.

✦ UnLoad/Load— Automatically rewinds and unloads the tape. This is the default until the user session specifies load.

✦ Restart— If a multi-tape backup fails in the middle of the backup (a tape breaks for example). The restart option will continue the backup sequence in midstream without having to go back to the first tape. The restart option can save time, but be sure to run a restore verifyonly (see next topic) after the backup to be sure.

## Verifying the Backup with Code

Enterprise Manager's backup includes an option to verify the backup, and the T-SQL Backup command does not. Enterprise Manager actually calls the T-SQL restore verifyonly command after the backup to perform the verification:

```
RESTORE VERIFYONLY
    FROM DISK =  'e:\Cha2Backup.bak'
```

Result:

```
The backup set is valid.
```

The verification has a few options, such as *Eject tape after backup*. Most of these verification options are for tapes and are self-explanatory.

# Working with the Transaction Log

Sometimes it seems that the transaction log has a life of its own. The space within the file seems to grow and shrink without rhyme or reason. If you've felt this way, you're not alone. This section should shed some light on why the transaction log behaves as it does.

# Inside the Transaction Log

The transaction log contains all the transactions for a database. Both transactions that have been written if the server crashes the transaction log are used to recover by rolling back uncommitted partial transactions, and by completing any transactions that were committed but not written to the data file.

Virtually, the log can be imagined as a sequential list of transactions sorted by date and time. Physically, however, SQL Server writes to different parts of the physical log file in virtual blocks without a specific order. Some parts might be in use, making other parts available. So the log reuses itself in a loose round-robin fashion.

## The Active and Inactive Divide

The transactions in the transaction log can be divided into two groups (Figure 26-5):

> ✦ *Active transactions* are uncommitted and not yet written to the data file.

> ✦ *Inactive transactions* are all those transactions before the earliest active transaction.

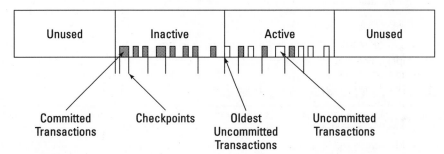

**Figure 26-5:** The inactive transactions are all those prior to the oldest active transaction.

Because transactions have varying durations, and are committed at different times, it's very likely that committed transactions are in the active portion of the log. The active portion does not merely contain all uncommitted transactions, but all transactions since the start of the oldest uncommitted transaction. One very old uncommitted transaction can make the active portion appear unusually large.

## Transaction Checkpoints

Understanding how SQL Server uses checkpoints in the transaction log is important to understanding how the transaction log is backed up and emptied. Checkpoints calculate the amount of work that must be done to recover the database.

A checkpoint automatically occurs under any of the following conditions:

✦ When an `alter database` command changes a database option

✦ When the server is shut down

✦ When the number of log entries exceeds the estimated amount of work required by the server's `recovery interval` configuration option.

✦ If the database is in the simple recovery model or log-truncate mode, when the transaction log becomes 70 percent full

Checkpoints may be manually initiated with a `checkpoint` command. Checkpoints perform the following activities:

✦ Marks the checkpoint spot in the transaction log

✦ Writes a checkpoint-log record, including:

• The oldest active transaction

• The oldest replication transaction that has not been replicated

• A list of all active transactions

• Information about the minimum work required to roll back the database

✦ Writes to disk all dirty data pages and log pages

So basically, a checkpoint gets everything up to date as best it can and then records the current state of the dividing line between active and inactive in the log.

## Backing up the Transaction Log

Performing a transaction log backup is very similar to performing a full or differential backup, with a few notable differences.

The T-SQL command is as follows:

```
BACKUP LOG CHA2
  TO DISK = 'e:\Cha2Backup.bak'
  WITH
    NAME = 'CHA2Backup'
```

Result:

```
Processed 1 pages for database 'CHA2',
  file 'CHA2_log' on file 9.
BACKUP LOG successfully processed 1 pages
  in 0.060 seconds (0.042 MB/sec).
```

The same media options apply to the transaction log backup that apply to the database backup; in addition, two options are transaction-log specific. The `no_truncate` option is for backing up the transaction log during a recovery operation and the `norecovery/standby` option is for running a standby server. Both are covered in more detail later in this chapter in the "Recovering with T-SQL Code" section.

The transaction log may not be backed up if any of the following conditions exist:

✦ The database is using a simple recovery model

✦ The database is using a bulk-logged recovery model, a bulk-logged operation has been executed, and the database files are damaged

✦ Database files have been added or removed.

In any of these cases, perform a full database backup instead.

## Truncating the Log

Updates and deletes might not increase the size of a data file, but to the transaction log every transaction of any type is simply more data. Left to its own devices, the transaction log will continue to grow with every data modification.

The solution is to back up the inactive portion of the transaction log and then remove it. By default, backing up the transaction log will also truncate the log, as shown in Figure 26-3.

If, for example, the disk is full, the transaction log might need to be truncated without the database being backed up. There's no way to just truncate the log without performing a backup. But with T-SQL, the transaction log can be truncated by means of the `Backup...NoLog` or `Backup...TruncateOnly` (the two are synonymous):

```
BACKUP LOG CHA2
  WITH TRUNCATE_ONLY
```

 **Caution**    If the transaction log is manually truncated and then backed up, there will be a gap in the transaction-log sequence. Any transaction-log pickups after the gap will not be restored. A full backup is recommended to restart the backup sequencing.

## The Transaction Log and Simple Recovery Model

When the database is using a simple recovery model, the transaction log ensures that each committed transaction is written to the data file, and that's it. When the transaction log is 70 percent full, SQL Server will perform a checkpoint and then truncate the log. So the free space of the transaction-log will fluctuate, but the minimum is the size of the active portion of the transaction log.

# Recovery Operations

There are any number of reasons to restore a database, including:

✦ A disk subsystem has failed.

✦ A sleepy programmer forgot a where clause in a SQL update statement and updated everyone's salary to minimum wage.

✦ The server melted into a pool of silicon and disk platters.

✦ A large import worked, but with yesterday's data.

The best reason to restore a database is to practice the backup/restore cycle, and to prove that the recovery plan works. Without confidence in the recovery, there's little point in doing backups.

## Detecting the Problem

If a problem with a database file does exist, Enterprise Manager will mark the database as suspect, as shown in Figure 26-6.

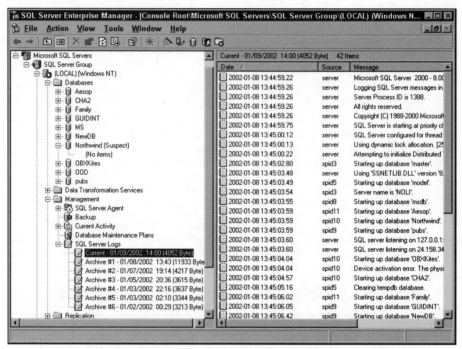

**Figure 26-6:** The Northwind database file is damaged (we deleted it). Enterprise Manager shows the database as suspect and without any objects. Further down the console tree are the SQL Server logs.

To further investigate a problem, check the SQL Server log. In Enterprise Manager, the log can be viewed under Management ➪ SQL Server Logs. SQL Server writes errors and events to an errorlog file in the \error directory under the MSSQL directory. SQL Server creates a new file every time the server is started. The six previous versions of the file are saved in the same directory. Some errors may also be written to the Windows Application Event Log.

## Recovery Sequences

The two most important concepts about recovering a database are:

✦ A recovery operation always begins by restoring a full backup and then restores any additional differential or transactional backups. The restore never copies only yesterday's work. It restores the entire database up to a certain point.

✦ There's a difference between restore and recover. A *restore* copies the data back into the database and leaves the transactions open. *Recovery* is the process of handling the transactions left open in the transaction log. If a database-recovery operation requires that four files be restored, only the last file is restored `with recovery`.

Only logins who are members of the `SysAdmins` fixed server role can restore a database that doesn't currently exist. `SysAdmins` and `db_owners` can restore databases that do currently exist.

The actual recovery effort depends on the type of damage and the previous recovery plans. Table 26-2 is a comparative listing of recovery operations.

**Table 26-2: Recovery Sequences**

| Recovery Model | Damaged Database File | Damaged Transaction Log |
|---|---|---|
| Simple | 1) Restart server.<br>2) Restore full backup.<br>3) Restore latest differential backup (if needed). | Restart the server. A new 1MB transaction log will be automatically created. |
| Full or Bulk-Logged | 1) Back up current transaction log with `no_truncate` option*.<br>2) Restore full backup.<br>3) Restore latest differential backup (if needed).<br>4) Restore all the transaction-log backups since the last differential or full backup. All committed transactions will be recovered. | 1) Restore full backup.<br>2) Restore latest differential backup (if needed).<br>3) Restore all the transaction-log backups since the last differential or full backup.<br><br>Transactions made since the last backup will be lost. |

If the database is using the bulk-logged recovery model and a bulk-insert operation occurred since the last transaction-log backup, the backup will fail. Transactions that occurred after the transaction-log backup will not be recoverable.

## Performing the Restore with Enterprise Manager

As with the backup command, there are numerous ways to launch the restore form within Enterprise Manager:

✦ Select the database to be backed up. From the right-click or Action menu select All Tasks ➪ Backup Restore to open the SQL Server Restore database form.

✦ Select Tools ➪ Restore Database to open the SQL Server Restore database form.

✦ Select Databases in the console tree, right-click, and select Restore Database from the context menu.

The Restore database form, shown in Figure 26-7, does a great job of intelligently navigating the potential chaos of the backup sequences, and it always offers only legal restore options.

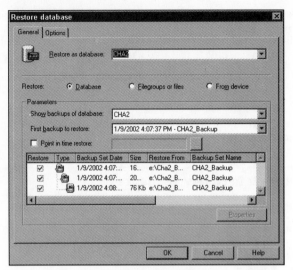

**Figure 26-7:** Only the correct sequences of restoring from multiple backup files is possible from Enterprise Manager's Restore database form.

The selection you make at the top of the form is the name of the database after the restore.

The Restore database form can restore database backups, file backups, or backups from a device (i.e., a tape drive). The restore wizard will present a hierarchical tree of backups, while the filegroups or file restore lists the files and must be manually restored in the correct order.

The "Show backups of database" option is used to select the first backup in the database-backup sequence to restore. Based on the sequence selected, the grid displays a hierarchical tree of the possible backup sequences:

✦ Full database backups are represented by gold hard-drive symbols at the highest level of the tree.

✦ Differential backups are represented by blue hard-drive symbols at the second level of the tree.

✦ Transaction-log backups are represented by notebook symbols at the lowest level of the tree.

Depending on the full and differential backups selected, only certain differential and transaction-log backups may be chosen.

The advantage is that the sequence of one full backup, the second differential backup, and the following 15 transaction-log backups can be correctly sequenced by means of selecting the final transaction log to be restored. Restoring the 17 backup files is performed with a single click of the OK button.

If one of the backup files being restored is a transaction log the "Point in time restore" option becomes available, because only a transaction log has the ability to restore only some of the transactions.

The point-in-time restore will restore all transactions committed before the time selected.

The Options tab of the Restore database dialog box (Figure 26-8) offers you a couple of significant options.

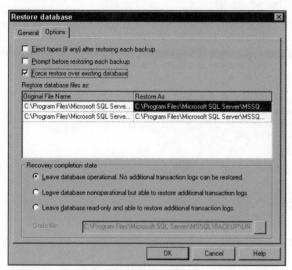

**Figure 26-8:** The Options tab of the Restore database dialog box enables you to restore the files to a different disk location.

The "Force restore over existing database" option disables a safety check that prevents Database A backup from being restored as Database B and accidentally overwriting an existing Database B. The safety check doesn't prohibit Database A backup being restored over Database A, so in most cases this option is moot. For the one time the database names are chosen incorrectly, the default for "Force restore over existing databases" ignores the safety check and allows the mistake. We don't like it either. We turn it off.

Because it is very possible that the database is being restored to a different file location than the original backup, the Option tab includes a way to assign new file locations.

The "Recovery completion state" option enables you to ship the log to a warm standby server. For a normal restore, the option should be left operational.

If only certain files or filegroups are being restored, the "Restore: File or file groups" option enables you to select the files or filegroup you wish to restore.

If the backup history, stored in msdb, is not available—because the server is being rebuilt or the database is being restored to a different server—then the Restore: From Device option can be used to manually select the specific backup disk file and backup instance within the file.

# Restoring with T-SQL Code

Database backup is a regularly scheduled occurrence, so if SQL Server's built-in maintenance plan wizard isn't to your liking, it makes sense to write some repeatable code to perform backups and set up your own SQL Server Agent jobs.

But unless the backup plan is only a full backup, it's impossible to know how many differential backups or transaction-log backups need to be restored. And because each backup file requires a separate `restore` command, it's impossible to script the recovery effort beforehand without writing lots of code to examine the msdb tables and determine the restore sequence properly.

The `restore` command will restore from a full, differential, or transaction-log backup:

```
RESTORE DATABASE (or LOG) DatabaseName
  Optional-File or Filegroup PARTIAL
  FROM BackUpDevice
  WITH
    FILE = FileNumber,
    PASSWORD = Password,
    NORECOVERY or RECOVERY or STANDBY = UnDoFileName,
    REPLACE,
    STOPAT datetime,
    STOPATMARK = 'markname'
    STOPBEFOREMARK = 'markname'
```

To restore a full or differential backup use the `restore database` command; otherwise use the `restore log` for a transaction log. To restore a specific file or filegroup add its name after the database name. If the file or filegroup is the only data being restored add the `partial` option.

A backup set often contains several backup instances. For example, a backup set might consist of the following:

  1 — Full backup

  2 — Differential backup

  3, 4, 5, 6 — Transaction-log backups

  7 — Differential backup

  8, 9 — Transaction-log backups

The `with file` option specifies the backup to restore. If it's left out of the command the first backup instance is restored.

The `recovery/norecovery` option is vital to the restore command. Every time a SQL Server starts it automatically checks the transaction log, rolling back any uncommitted transactions and completing any committed transactions. This process is called *recovery*, and it's a part of the ACID properties of the database.

So if the restore has the `norecovery` option SQL Server restores the log without handling any transactions. On the other hand, `recovery` instructs SQL Server to handle the transactions. In the sequence of the recovery operation, all the restores must have the `norecovery` option enabled, except for the last restore, which must have the `recovery` option enabled.

Deciding between `recovery` and `norecovery` is one of the complications involved in trying to write a script to handle any possible future recovery operation.

If the recovery operation includes a transaction-log restore, the recovery can stop before the end of the transaction log. The options, `stopat` and `stopatmark`, will leave the end of the transaction log unrestored. The `stopat` accepts a time, and the `stopatmark` restores only to a transaction that was created with a named mark. The `stopbeforemark` option restores everything up to the beginning of the marked transaction.

**Cross-Reference**  Chapter 15, "Implementing Triggers," details SQL Server transactions and how to create marked transactions.

The following script demonstrates a restore sequence that includes a full backup and two transaction-log backups:

```
-- BackUp and recovery example

CREATE DATABASE Plan2Recover
```

**Result:**

```
The CREATE DATABASE process
  is allocating 0.63 MB on disk 'Plan2Recover'.
The CREATE DATABASE process
  is allocating 0.49 MB on disk 'Plan2Recover_log'.
```

**Continue:**

```
USE Plan2Recover

CREATE TABLE T1 (
  PK INT Identity PRIMARY KEY,
  Name VARCHAR(15)
  )
Go
INSERT T1 VALUES ('Full')
go
BACKUP DATABASE Plan2Recover
  TO DISK = 'e:\P2R.bak'
  WITH
    NAME = 'P2R_Full',
    INIT
```

**Result:**

```
Processed 80 pages for database 'Plan2Recover',
  file 'Plan2Recover' on file 1.
Processed 1 pages for database 'Plan2Recover',
  file 'Plan2Recover_log' on file 1.
BACKUP DATABASE successfully processed 81 pages
  in 0.254 seconds (2.590 MB/sec).
```

Continue:

```
INSERT T1 VALUES ('Log 1')
go
BACKUP Log Plan2Recover
  TO DISK = 'e:\P2R.bak'
  WITH
    NAME = 'P2R_Log'
```

Result:

```
Processed 1 pages for database 'Plan2Recover',
  file 'Plan2Recover_log' on file 2.
BACKUP LOG successfully processed 1 pages
  in 0.083 seconds (0.055 MB/sec).
```

Continue:

```
INSERT T1 VALUES ('Log 2')
go
BACKUP Log Plan2Recover
  TO DISK = 'e:\P2R.bak'
  WITH
    NAME = 'P2R_Log'
```

Result:

```
Processed 1 pages for database 'Plan2Recover',
  file 'Plan2Recover_log' on file 3.
BACKUP LOG successfully processed 1 pages
  in 0.057 seconds (0.008 MB/sec).
```

Continue:

```
SELECT * FROM T1
```

Result:

```
PK          Name
----------- ---------------
1           Full
2           Log 1
3           Log 2
```

At this point the server is hit with a direct bolt of lightning and all drives are fried, with the exception of the backup files. The following recovery operation goes through the full backup and the two transaction-log backups. Notice the norecovery and recovery options:

```
-- NOW PERFORM THE RESTORE
Use Master
RESTORE DATABASE Plan2Recover
  FROM DISK = 'e:\P2R.bak'
  With FILE = 1, NORECOVERY
```

Result:

```
Processed 80 pages for database 'Plan2Recover',
```

```
    file 'Plan2Recover' on file 1.
Processed 1 pages for database 'Plan2Recover',
    file 'Plan2Recover_log' on file 1.
RESTORE DATABASE successfully processed 81 pages
    in 0.089 seconds (7.392 MB/sec).
```

Continue:

```
RESTORE LOG Plan2Recover
  FROM DISK = 'e:\P2R.bak'
  With FILE = 2, NORECOVERY
```

Result:

```
Processed 1 pages for database 'Plan2Recover',
    file 'Plan2Recover_log' on file 2.
RESTORE LOG successfully processed 1 pages
    in 0.009 seconds (0.512 MB/sec).
```

Continue:

```
RESTORE LOG Plan2Recover
  FROM DISK = 'e:\P2R.bak'
  With FILE = 3, RECOVERY
```

Result:

```
Processed 1 pages for database 'Plan2Recover',
    file 'Plan2Recover_log' on file 3.
RESTORE LOG successfully processed 1 pages
    in 0.044 seconds (0.011 MB/sec).
```

To test the recovery operation:

```
USE Plan2Recover
Select * from T1
```

Result:

```
PK           Name
-----------  ----------------
1            Full
2            Log 1
3            Log 2
```

As this script shows, it is possible to recover using T-SQL. But in this case Enterprise Manager beats code as the best way to accomplish the task.

# System Databases Recovery

So far, this chapter has dealt only with user databases. But the system databases are important to the recovery operation as well. The master database contains key database and security information, and the MSDB database holds the schedules and jobs for SQL Server, as well as the backup history. A complete recovery plan must include the system databases.

**Note**   System databases are visible in Enterprise Manager only if the "Show system databases and system objects" option is enabled in the server-registration properties.

# Master System Database

The master database, by default, uses the simple recovery model. Using only full backups for the master database is OK; it's not a transactional database.

## Backing up the Master Database

The master database is backed up in the same manner as user databases.

Be sure to back up the master database when:

✦ Create or delete databases

✦ Modify security by adding logins or changing roles

✦ Modify any server or database-configuration options

Since the MSDB database holds a record of all backups, back up the master database and then the MSDB.

## Recovering the Master Database

If the master database is corrupted or damaged SQL Server won't start. Attempting to start SQL Server with the Service Manager will have no effect. Attempting to connect to the instance with Enterprise Manager will invoke a report that the server does not exist or that access is denied.

To simulate this occurrence, delete the master database. It's located in the data directory of the following instance:

```
C:\Program Files\Microsoft SQL Server\MSSQL\Data\master.mdf
```

The first step to recovery is to install a fresh master database so that the server will at least start. From there, the actual master database can be restored. To install a fresh master database, double-click the rebuildm.exe utility found in the following directory:

```
C:\Program Files\Microsoft SQL Server\80\Tools\Binn
```

The rebuild master utility, shown in Figure 26-9, requires three entries:

✦ The name of the server to be recovered.

✦ The location of the original master database from the initial installation, which will likely be x86\data directory of the initial CD if the SQL Server is SP2. (In earlier versions, the initial data directory may need to be copied to a hard drive or a network drive because of a bug.)

✦ The server collation.

The rebuild process will re-create all four system databases, plus Northwind and Pubs, and then configure the server. The entire process will take several minutes, or even longer if the server has been upgraded to a service pack.

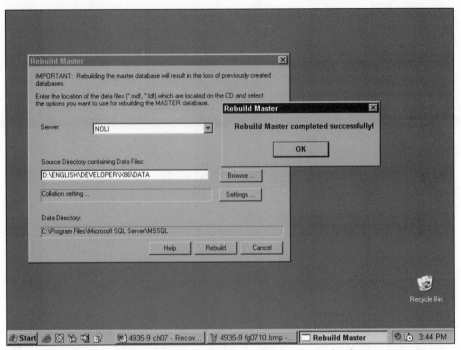

**Figure 26-9:** The rebuildm.exe utility will create a fresh master database so SQL Server can be started.

Step two of the recovery process is to start the server using Service Manager or Enterprise Manager.

Depending on your security configuration, it's highly likely that Enterprise Manager doesn't have permission to connect to the server. Rebuilding the master database lost all the logins except sa, and reset the sa password to blank. To adjust Enterprise Manager's connection setting so it connects as sa with a blank password, edit the SQL Server registration properties. Don't be concerned about the blank password; the real master database will soon be restored.

Once the server is again running, it will appear as if the user databases are gone because the rebuilt master database doesn't include any information about the user databases.

Step three is to put the server in single-user mode so the master may be restored. In Enterprise Manager, do the following:

1. Select the server.

2. Select properties in the right-click menu to open the Server Properties form.

3. Click the Startup Parameters button, shown in Figure 26-10.

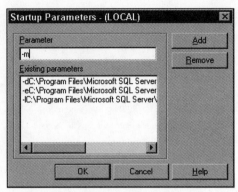

**Figure 26-10:** The server must be put in single-user mode (-m) for the master database to be restored.

4. Enter **-m** in the Parameter text box and press the Add button.

5. Press OK to close the Startup Parameters dialog box and close the server Properties form.

6. Close Enterprise Manager.

**Caution**    While the SQL Server instance is in single-user mode, avoid using Enterprise Manager. It's possible to get the instance locked into a mode that will not accept any future connections.

7. Stop and restart the SQL Server instance using SQL Server Manager.

The fourth step in recovering a lost master database is to perform the actual restore. Because SQL Server is now in single-user mode, this step must be performed within Query Analyzer. Attempting to restore the master database within Enterprise Manager can cause serious difficulties. From Query Analyzer execute the restore, as follows:

```
RESTORE DATABASE master
  FROM
  DISK = 'systembackup'
  WITH FILE = 1
```

Result:

```
The master database has been successfully restored.
  Shutting down SQL Server.
SQL Server is terminating this process.
```

Close Query Analyzer and restart the SQL Server instance using SQL Service Manager.

The final step in restoring the master database is to return the SQL Server instance to multi-user mode buy removing the `-m` startup parameter you inserted in Step three. Use Enterprise Manager's Server Properties form to modify the startup parameters.

Close Enterprise Manager and stop and restart the SQL Server instance using SQL Server Manager.

# MSDB System Database

Like the master database, the msdb database by default uses the simple recovery model.

Because the msdb database contains information regarding the SQL Server Agent jobs and schedules, as well as the backup history, it should be backed up whenever you:

✦ Perform backups

✦ Save DTS packages

✦ Create new SQL Server Agent jobs

✦ Configure SQL Server Agent mail or operators

✦ Configure replication

✦ Schedule tasks

The msdb database is backed up in the same way that a user database backs up.

To restore the msdb database you do not need to put the server in single-user mode, as you do with the master database. However, it's still not a normal restore, because without a current msdb, Enterprise Manager is not aware of the backup history. Therefore, the msdb backup can't be chosen as a backup database but must be selected as a backup device, as shown in Figure 26-11.

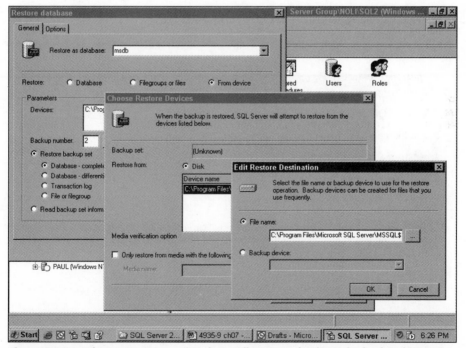

**Figure 26-11:** When you are restoring the msdb system database the backup history is not available, so the restore must select the backup directly from the backup file as a backup device.

The Contents button can be used to check the disk device for specific backups. If several backup instances are in the backup device the Contents dialog box (Figure 26-12) can be used to select the correct backup. It then fills in the file number in the restore form.

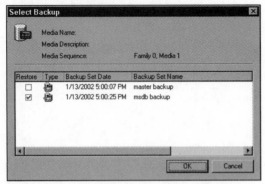

**Figure 26-12:** The backup file might contain several backup instances. The Contents dialog box is used to select the correct file number within the disk device.

# Performing a Complete Recovery

If the server has completely failed and all the backups must be restored onto a new server, this is the process to follow:

1. Build the Windows server and restore the domain logins to support Windows authentication.

2. Install SQL Server and any service-pack upgrades.

3. Put SQL Server in single-user mode and restore the master database.

4. Restore the msdb database.

5. If the model database was modified, restore it.

6. Restore the user databases.

**Best Practice**

Performing a flawless recovery is a "bet your career" skill. I recommend taking the time to work through a complete recovery of the production data to a backup server. The confidence it will build will serve you well as a SQL Server DBA.

# Summary

The recovery cycle begins with the backup of the databases. The ability to survive hardware failure or human error is crucial to the ACID properties of a database. Without the transaction's durability, the database can't be fully trusted. Because of this, recovery planning and the transaction log provide durability to committed transactions.

The recovery cycle transfers data from the past to the present. The next chapter moves on from this theme and explains how to secure the database.

✦     ✦     ✦

# Securing Databases

It's common practice to develop the database and then worry about security. While there's no point in applying security while the database design is in flux, the project benefits when you develop and implement the security plan sooner rather than later.

Security, like every other aspect of the database project, must be carefully designed, implemented, and tested. Security may affect the execution of some procedures and must be taken into account when the project code is being developed.

A simple security plan with a few roles and the IT users as sysadmins may suffice for a small organization. Larger organizations — the military, banks, or research organizations — will require a more complex security plan that's designed as carefully as the logical database schema.

If security is tightly implemented with full security audits performed by SQL Profiler, the SQL Server installation can be certified at C2-level security. Fortunately, SQL Server's security model is well thought-out and, if fully understood, both logical and flexible. While the tactics of securing a database are creating users and roles, and then assigning permissions; the strategy is identifying the rights and responsibilities of data access and then enforcing the plan.

## Security Concepts

The SQL Server security model is large and complex. In some ways it's more complex than the Windows security model. Because the security concepts are tightly intertwined, the best way to begin is to walk through an overview of the model.

SQL Server security is based on the concepts of users, roles, objects, and permissions. Users are assigned to roles, both of which may be granted permission to objects, as illustrated in Figure 27-1. Each object has an owner, and ownership also affects the permissions.

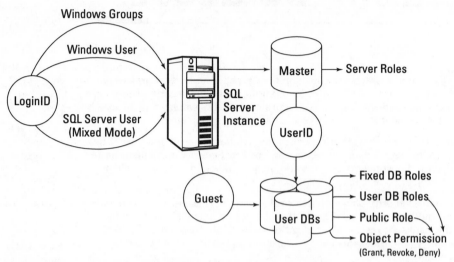

**Figure 27-1:** An overview of the SQL Server security model shows how users are first authenticated to the server, followed by the databases, and finally the objects within the databases. The circles represent how the user is identified.

## Server-Level Security

A user may be initially identified to SQL Server via one of three methods:

✦ Windows user login

✦ Membership in a Windows user group

✦ SQL Server–specific login (if the server uses mixed-mode security)

At the server level the user is known by his or her LoginID, which is either his or her SQL Server login, or his or her Windows domain and user name.

Once the user is known to the server and identified, the user has whatever server-level administrative rights have been granted via fixed server roles. If the user belongs to the sysadmin role he or she has full access to every server function, database, and object in the server.

A user can be granted access to a database, and his or her network login ID can be mapped to a database-specific user ID in the process. If the user doesn't have access to a database he or she can gain access as the guest user with some configuration changes within the database server.

## Database-Level Security

At the database level, the user may be granted certain administrative-level permissions by belonging to fixed database roles.

The user still can't access the data. He or she must be granted permission to the database objects (tables, stored procedures, views, functions). User-defined roles are custom roles that serve as groups. The role may be granted permission to a database object, and users may be assigned to a database user-defined role. All users are automatically members of the public standard database role.

Object permissions are assigned by means of grant, revoke, and deny. A deny permission overrides a grant permission, which overrides a revoke permission. A user may have multiple permission paths to an object (individually, through a standard database role, and through the public role). If any of these paths is denied the user is blocked from accessing the object. Otherwise, if any of the paths is granted permission, the user can access the object.

Object permission is very detailed and a specific permission exists for every action that can be performed (select, insert, update, run, and so on) for every object. Certain database fixed roles also affect object access, such as the ability to read or write to the database.

It's very possible for a user to be recognized by SQL Server and not have access to any database. It's also possible for a user to be defined within a database but not recognized by the server. Moving a database and its permissions to another server, but not moving the logins, will cause such orphaned users.

## Object Ownership

The final aspect of this overview of SQL Server's security model involves object ownership. Every object has an owner. The owner is automatically granted permission to the object, but this permission can be overridden by a deny in a role. The owner can be a specific database user, or the user, dbo.

Ownership becomes critical when permission is being granted to a user to run a stored procedure when the user doesn't have permission to the underlying tables. If the ownership chain from the tables to the stored procedure is consistent, the user can access the stored procedure and the stored procedure can access the tables as its owner. But if the ownership chain is broken, meaning that there's a different owner somewhere between the stored procedure and the table, the user must have rights to the stored procedure, the underlying tables, and every other object in between.

Most of the management of security can be performed in Enterprise Manager. With code, security is managed by means of the grant, revoke, and deny Data-Control Language (DCL) commands, and 53 system stored procedures.

# Windows Security

Because SQL Server exists within a Windows environment, one aspect of the security strategy must be securing the Windows server.

## Windows Security

SQL Server databases frequently support Web sites, so Internet Information Server (IIS) security and firewalls must be considered within the security plan.

Windows security is an entire topic in itself, and outside the scope of this book. If, as a DBA, you are not well supported by qualified network staff, we suggest that you make the effort to become proficient in Windows Server technologies, especially security (which is why you must pass the Windows server exam to receive MCDBA certification).

The Microsoft Personal Security Advisor will run a check on the Windows installation and report any security holes. You can find the Personal Security Advisor at the following URL:

```
http://www.microsoft.com/technet/mpsa/start.asp
```

## SQL Server Login

Don't confuse users access to SQL Server with SQL Server's Windows accounts. The two logins are completely different.

SQL Server users don't need access to the database directories or data files on a Windows level because the SQL Server process, not the user, will perform the actual file access. However, the SQL Server process needs permission to access the files, so it needs a Windows account. Two types are available:

✦ *Local admin account*—SQL Server can use the local admin account of the operating system for permission to the machine. This option is adequate for single-server installations but fails to provide the network security required for distributed processing.

✦ *Domain user account* (recommended)—SQL Server can use a Windows user account created specifically for it. The SQL Server user account can be granted administrator rights for the server and can access the network through the server to talk to other servers.

Cross-Reference

The SQL Server accounts were initially configured when the server was installed. Installation is discussed in Chapter 3, "Installing and Configuring SQL Server."

# Server Security

SQL Server uses a two-phase security-authentication scheme. The user is first authenticated to the server. Once the user is "in" the server, access can be granted to the individual databases.

SQL Server stores all login information within the master database.

## SQL Server Authentication Mode

When SQL Server was installed, one of the decisions made was which of the following authentication methods was used:

✦ *Windows authentication mode*—Windows authentication only.

✦ *Mixed mode*—Both Windows authentication and SQL Server user authentication.

This option can be changed after installation in Enterprise Manager, in the Security tab of the SQL Server Properties dialog box, as shown in Figure 27-2.

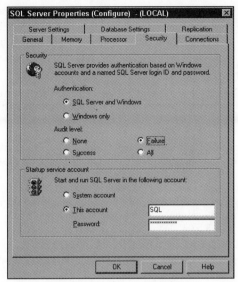

**Figure 27-2:** Server-level security is managed in the Security tab of the SQL Server Properties dialog box.

From code, the authentication mode can be checked by means of the `xp_loginconfig` system stored procedure, as follows:

```
EXEC xp_loginconfig 'login mode'
```

Results:

```
name                             config_value
-------------------------------  ----------------------------
login mode                       Mixed
```

Notice that the system stored procedure to report the authentication mode is an extended stored procedure. That's because the authentication mode is stored in the registry in the following entry:

```
HKEY_LOCAL_MACHINE\SOFTWARE\Microsoft\
   MicrosoftSQLServer\<instance_name>\MSSQLServer\LoginMode
```

A value of `LoginMode` is 0 is for Windows authentication and 1 for mixed mode.

The only ways to set the authentication mode are to use either Enterprise Manager or RegEdit.

## Windows Authentication

Windows authentication is superior to mixed mode because the user does not need to learn yet another password and because it leverages the security design of the network.

The use of Windows authentication means that users must exist as Windows users to be recognized by SQL Server. The Windows SID (Security Identifier) is passed from Windows to SQL Server.

Windows authentication is very robust in that it will authenticate not only Windows users, but also users within Windows user groups.

When a Windows group is accepted as a SQL Server login, any Windows user who is a member of the group can be authenticated by SQL Server. Access, roles, and permissions can be assigned for the Windows group; they will apply to any Windows user in the group.

**Best Practice**

If the Windows users are already organized into groups by function and security level, using those groups as SQL Server users provides consistency and reduces administrative overhead.

SQL Server also knows the actual Windows user name, so the application can gather audit information at the user level as well as at the group level.

## Managing Windows Users and Groups with Enterprise Manager

Windows users are created and managed in various places in the different Windows versions. In Windows XP classic view, users can be managed from Control Panel ➪ Administrative Tools ➪ Computer Management, as shown in Figure 27-3. The Windows XP category view offers fewer user management features.

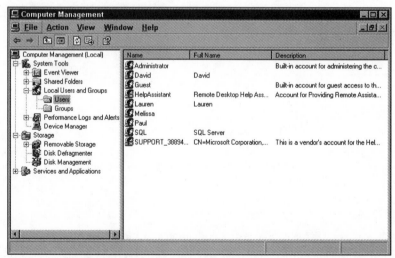

**Figure 27-3:** Windows users are managed and assigned to Windows groups by means of the Computer Management tool.

Once the users exist in the Windows user list or the Windows domain, SQL Server can recognize them. Follow these steps to add Windows users to SQL Server with Enterprise Manager (you must have `sysadmin` rights to add users):

1. Open the security node under the server.

2. Select Logins.

**3.** Right-click the Login node, or right-click in the right pane, and select New Login.

**4.** In the General tab of the SQL Server Login Properties dialog (Figure 27-4), click the builder button (...) to the right of the new user name.

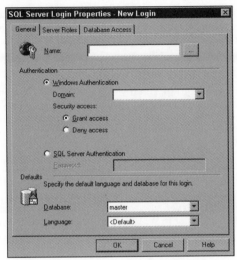

**Figure 27-4:** The General tab of the SQL Server Login Properties dialog is used to create and edit user logins at the server level.

**5.** A dialog box will appear that displays all the Windows users and groups (Figure 27-5). Select the Windows user or group, click Add, and then click OK.

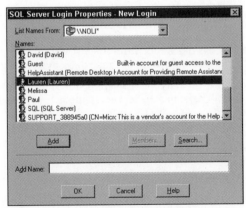

**Figure 27-5:** SQL Server will list all the Windows users and groups, making it easy to add Windows-authentication users.

The user may be assigned a default database and language at the bottom of the SQL Server Login Properties dialog. Unfortunately, assigning a default database does not grant access to that database. The user may be granted access to databases in the Database Access tab. (Database access is discussed in the next section.)

**Note**     There is a Create Login Wizard under the database grouping of wizards. However, it requires the domain and user name to be typed rather than selected from a list, and it provides no additional functionality. It's easier to add the Windows user security node than the wizard.

## Managing Windows Users and Groups with Code

To use T-SQL code to add a Windows user or group, run the `sp_grantlogin` system stored procedure. Be sure to use the full Windows user name, including the domain name, as follows:

```
EXEC sp_grantlogin 'Noli\Paul'
```

Result:

```
Granted login access to 'Noli\Paul'.
```

### Removing a Windows Login

To drop a Windows user or group from SQL Server, use the `sp_revokelogin` system stored procedure. The Windows user or group will exist in Windows; it just won't be recognized by SQL Server.

```
EXEC sp_revokelogin 'Noli\Paul'
```

Result:

```
Revoked login access from 'Noli\Paul'.
```

### Denying a Windows Login

Using the paradigm of `grant`, `revoke`, and `deny`, a user may be blocked for access using `sp_denylogin`. This can prevent a user or group from accessing SQL Server even if he or she could otherwise gain entry from another method.

For example, say the Accounting group is granted normal login access, while the Probation group is denied access. Joe is a member of both the Accounting group and the Probation group. The Probation group's denied access blocks Joe from the SQL Server even though he is granted access as a member of the Accounting group, because deny overrides grant.

To deny a Windows user or group, use the `sp_denylogin` system stored procedure. If the user or group being denied access doesn't exist in SQL Server, `sp_denylogin` adds and then denies him, her, or it:

```
EXEC sp_denylogin 'Noli\Paul'
```

Result:

```
Denied login access to 'Noli\Paul'.
```

To restore the login after denying access, you must first grant access with the `sp_grantlogin` system stored procedure.

## Orphaned Windows Users

If a Windows user is added to SQL Server and then removed from the Windows domain, the user still exists in SQL Server but is considered *orphaned*. Being an orphaned user means even though the user has access to the SQL Server, they may not necessarily have access to the network and thus no access to the SQL Server box itself.

The sp_validatelogins system stored procedure will locate all orphaned users and return their Windows NT security identifiers and login names. For the following code example, Joe was created as a Windows user and granted a Windows authentication login, and was then removed from Windows:

```
EXEC sp_validatelogins
```

Result (formatted):

```
SID                                              NT Login
------------------------------------------------ ----------
0x010500000000000515000000FCE31531A9314340BE043E32F1030000
                                                 Noli\Joe
```

This is not a security hole. Without a Windows login with a matching SID, the user can't log into SQL Server.

To resolve the orphaned user:

1. If the user owns any objects, transfer the ownership to another user or to the database owner using sp_changeobjectowner, or drop the objects (covered in the next section).

2. Remove the user from any database access using sp_revokedbaccess.

3. Revoke the user's server access using sp_revokelogin.

## Security Delegation

In an enterprise network with multiple servers and IIS, logins can become a problem because a user may be logging into one server that is accessing another server. This problem arises because each server must have a trust relationship with the others. For internal company servers, this may not be a problem, but when one of those servers sits in a DMZ on the Internet you may not want to establish that trust since it presents a security hole.

Security delegation is a Windows 2000 feature that uses Kerberos to pass security information among trusted servers.

For example, a user can access IIS, which can access a SQL Server, and the SQL Server will see the user as the user name even though the connection came from IIS.

A few conditions must be met in order for Kerberos to work:

✦ All servers must be running Windows 2000 running Active Directory in the same domain or within the same trust tree.

✦ The "Account is sensitive and cannot be delegated" option must not be selected for the user account.

✦ The "Account is trusted for delegation" option must be selected for the SQL Server service account.

✦ The "Computer is trusted for delegation" option must be selected for the server running SQL Server.

✦ SQL Server must have Service Principal Name (SPN), created by `setspn.exe`, available in the Windows 2000 Resource Kit.

Security delegation is difficult to set up and may require the assistance of your network-domain administrator. However, the ability to recognize users going through IIS is a powerful security feature.

## SQL Server Logins

The optional SQL Server logins are useful when Windows authentication is inappropriate or unavailable. It's provided for backward compatibility and for legacy applications that are hard-coded to a SQL Server login.

**Best Practice**

Implementing SQL Server logins (mixed mode) will automatically create an `sa` user, who will be a member of the `sysadmin` fixed server role and have all rights to the server. An `sa` user without a password is very common and the first attack every hacker tries when detecting a SQL Server. Therefore, the best practice is disabling the `sa` user and assigning different users, or roles, to the `sysadmin` fixed server role instead.

To manage SQL Server users in Enterprise Manager use the same steps as before, but enter the name instead of choosing a Windows user or group.

In T-SQL code, use the `sp_addlogin` system stored procedure. Because this requires setting up a user rather than just selecting one that already exists, it's much more complex than adding a `sp_grantlogin`. Only the login name is required:

```
sp_addlogin 'login', 'password', 'defaultdatabase',
    'defaultlanguage', 'sid', 'encryption_option'
```

For example, the following code adds Joe as a SQL Server user and sets his default database to the OBX Kite Store sample database:

```
EXEC sp_addlogin 'Joe', 'myoldpassword', 'OBXKites'
```

Result:

```
New login created.
```

The encryption option (`skip_encryption`) directs SQL Server to store the password without any encryption in the `sysxlogins` system table. SQL Server expects the password to be encrypted so the password won't work. Avoid this option.

The server user ID, or SID, is an 85-bit binary value that SQL Server uses to identify the user. If the user is being set up on two servers as the same user, the SID will need to be specified for the second server. The system stored procedure `sp_helplogins` will report the user's fSID:

```
EXEC sp_help_logins
```

Result (abridged):

```
LoginName SID                                 DefDBName
--------- ----------------------------------- ---------
Joe       0x6CC6F5C9C52D1E4E8916DE0C544D103F  OBXKites
```

### Setting the Default Database

The default database can be set from code by means of the sp_defaultdb system stored procedure:

```
EXEC sp_defaultdb 'Paul', 'OBXKites'
```

Result:

```
Default database changed.
```

### Updating a Password

The password can be modified by means of the sp_password system stored procedure:

```
EXEC sp_password 'myoldpassword', 'mynewpassword', 'Joe'
```

Result:

```
Password changed.
```

If the password was empty, use the keyword NULL instead of empty quotes (' ').

### Removing a Login

To remove a SQL Server login use the sp_droplogin system stored procedure:

```
EXEC sp_droplogin 'Joe'
```

Result:

```
Login dropped.
```

Removing a login will also remove all the login security settings.

## Server Roles

SQL Server includes only fixed, predefined server roles. Primarily these roles grant permission to perform certain server-related administrative tasks. A user may belong to multiple roles.

These following roles are best used to delegate certain server administrative tasks:

✦ *System administrators* (sysadmin) can perform any activity in the SQL Server installation, regardless of any other permission setting. The sysadmin role even overrides denied permissions on an object.

SQL Server automatically creates a user, 'BUILTINS/Administrators', which includes all Windows users in the Windows Admins group, and assigns that group to the SQL Server sysadmin role. The BUILTINS/Administrators user can be deleted or modified if desired.

If the SQL Server is configured for mixed-mode security it also creates an sa user and assigns that user to the SQL Server sysadmin role. The sa user is there for backward compatibility.

**Best Practice**

Disable or rename the sa user, or at least assign it a password, but don't use it as a developer and DBA sign on. Also, delete the BUILTINS/Administrators user. Instead, use Windows authentication and assign the DBAs and database developers to the sysadmin role.

✦ A user must reconnect for the full capabilities of the sysadmin role to take effect.

✦ *Bulk-insert administrators* can perform bulk-insert operations.

✦ *Database creators* can create and alter databases.

✦ *Process administrators* can kill a running SQL Server process.

✦ *Security administrators* can manage the logins for the server.

✦ *Server administrators* can configure the serverwide settings, including setting up full-text searches and shutting down the server.

✦ *Setup administrators* can configure linked servers, extended stored procedures, and the startup stored procedure.

✦ *Disk administrators* is a SQL Server 6.5 legacy role that can manage SQL Server 6.5–style disk files.

The server roles are set in Enterprise Manager in the Server Roles tab of the SQL Server Login Properties dialog (Figure 27-6). The Properties button opens a dialog box that describes the selected role and lists the specific commands or stored procedures to which the role grants permission.

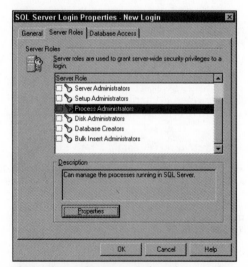

**Figure 27-6:** The Server Roles tab is used to assign server-administrative rights to users. The Properties button details the exact permissions granted by the server role.

In code, a user is assigned to a server role by means of a system stored procedure:

```
sp_addsrvrolemember
  [ @loginame = ] 'login',
  [ @rolename = ] 'role'
```

For example, the following code adds the login Noli\Lauren to the sysadmin role:

```
EXEC sp_addsrvrolemember  'Noli\Lauren', 'sysadmin'
```

Result:

```
'Noli\Lauren' added to role 'sysadmin'.
```

The counterpart of sp_addsrvrolemember, sp_dropsrvrolemember, removes a login from a server fixed role:

```
EXEC sp_dropsrvrolemember  'Noli\Lauren', 'sysadmin'
```

Result:

```
'Noli\Lauren' dropped from role 'sysadmin'.
```

# Database Security

Once a user has gained access to the server, access may be granted to the individual user databases. Database security is potentially complex.

Users are initially granted access to databases by means of adding the database to the user, or adding the user to the database.

## Guest Logins

Any user who wishes to access a database, but has not been declared a user within the database, will automatically be granted the user privileges of the guest database user if the guest user account exists.

The guest user is not automatically created when a database is created. It must be specifically added in code or as a database user. The guest login does not need to be predefined as a server login.

```
EXEC sp_adduser 'Guest'
```

**Caution**    Be very careful with the guest login. While it may be useful to enable a user to access the database without setting him or her up, the permissions granted to the guest user apply to everyone without access to the database.

The guest user must be removed from a database if guests are no longer welcome.

## Granting Access to the Database

Many security settings involve multiple objects such as users and databases or roles and object permissions. These settings can be made either from the user listing or database, or from the role or object permission.

To grant access to a database using Enterprise Manager, use either the user listing Server Login Properties, or the users listing under the database.

## Granting Access Using the Server Properties

In Enterprise Manager, the Server ➪ Security ➪ Logins node lists every user. Any user may be granted access to a database by right-clicking on the user and selecting Properties. The SQL Server Login Properties dialog is the same dialog we used to add users and groups previously in this chapter. The Database Access tab (Figure 27-7) lists all the system and user databases.

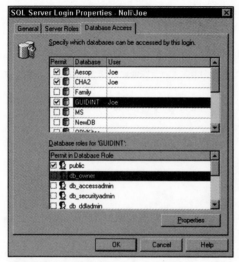

**Figure 27-7:** The SQL Server Login Properties dialog can add any database to the list of databases a user may access.

Using the SQL Server Login Properties dialog, select the databases the user should be able to access. If the user will be known by a database user name that is different from his or her server login name, enter the user name in the right-hand (User) column. The user-name cell will accept an entry only after the database is selected.

## Granting Access Using the Database User List

To start from the database side of the access:

1. Select the database in the Enterprise Manager console tree and open the node.

2. Select the Users node and right-click the node or in the right-hand pane.

3. Select New Database User.

4. In the Database User Properties dialog box (Figure 27-8), select the user to be added in the Login Name combo box. The dropdown list will display only users who do not currently have access to the database.

5. If the user will be known within the database by a user name that is different from the server login, enter the name in the "User name" text box.

6. Click OK.

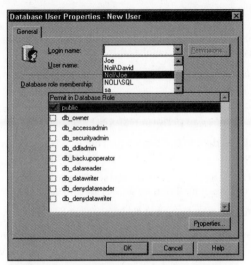

**Figure 27-8:** The Database User Properties dialog box can be used to add a new user to the database or to manage the current users.

### Granting Access Using T-SQL Code

Of course, a stored procedure exists to grant database access to a user: sp_grantdbaccess. The stored procedure must be issued from within the database to which the user is to be granted access. The first parameter is the server login and the second is the optional database user name:

```
USE Family
EXEC sp_grantdbaccess 'Noli\Lauren', 'LRN'
```

Result:

```
Granted database access to 'Noli\Lauren'.
```

Lauren now appears in the list of database users as 'LRN'.

To remove Lauren's database access, the system stored procedure sp_revokedbaccess requires her database user name, not her server login name:

```
USE Family
EXEC sp_revokedbaccess 'LRN'
```

Result:

```
User has been dropped from current database.
```

## Fixed Database Roles

SQL Server includes a few standard, or fixed, database roles. Like the server fixed roles, these primarily organize administrative tasks. A user may belong to multiple roles. The fixed database roles include:

✦ db_owner is a special role that has all permissions in the database. This role includes all the capabilities of the other roles. It is different from the dbo user role (see the section on database owner). This is not the database-level equivalent of the server sysadmin role; an object-level deny will override membership in this role.

✦ db_accessadmins can authorize a user to access the database, but not to manage database-level security.

✦ db_backupoperators can perform backups, checkpoints, and dbcc commands, but not restores (only server sysadmins can perform restores).

✦ db_datareaders can read all the data in the database. This role is the equivalent of a grant on all objects and it can be overridden by a deny permission.

✦ db_datawriters can write to all the data in the database. This role is the equivalent of a grant on all objects, and it can be overridden by a deny permission.

✦ db_ddladmins can issue DDL commands (create, alter, drop).

✦ db_denydatareaders can read from any table in the database. This deny will override any object-level grant.

✦ db_denydatawriters blocks from modifying data in any table in the database. This deny will override any object-level grant.

✦ db_securityadmins can manage database-level security—roles and permissions.

## Assigning Fixed Database Roles with Enterprise Manager

The fixed database roles can be assigned with Enterprise Manager by means of either of the following two procedures:

✦ Adding the role to the user in the user's Database User Properties dialog—either as the user is being created (Figure 27-8), or after the user exists (Figure 27-9).

**Figure 27-9:** The Database User Properties dialog lists the roles. Checking a role assigns the role to the user.

✦ Adding the user to the role in the Database Role Properties dialog. Select Roles under the database in the console tree, select a role, right-click, and select Properties to open the Database Role Properties dialog box (Figure 27-10).

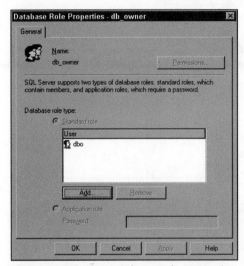

**Figure 27-10:** The Database Role Properties dialog lists all the users assigned to the current role. Users can be added or removed from the role by means of the Add and Remove buttons.

### Assigning Fixed Database Roles with T-SQL

From code, you can add a user to a fixed database role with the sp_addrole system stored procedure.

## Statement Permissions

Permission to execute specific statements may be granted, revoked, or denied in the Permissions tab of the Family Properties dialog (Figure 27-11). The statements that can be restricted are:

✦ Create Table

✦ Create View

✦ Create Sp

✦ Create Default

✦ Create Rule

✦ Create Function

✦ Backup DB

✦ Backup Log

In the Permissions tab a green check indicates that permission is granted, a red *x* indicates that permission is denied, and an empty checkbox revokes the permission.

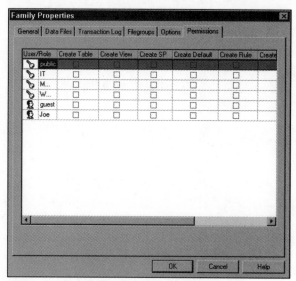

**Figure 27-11:** The Permissions tab of the Family Properties dialog is used to grant permission to execute specific commands within the database.

Unless you have a compelling reason to manage the permissions on an individual-statement level, it's easier to manage the database administrative tasks using the fixed database roles.

The `grant`, `revoke`, and `deny` commands are detailed in the next section.

## Application Roles

An application role is a database-specific role that's intended to allow an application to gain access regardless of the user. For example, if a specific Visual Basic program is used to search the `Customer` table, and it doesn't handle user identification, the VB program can access SQL Server using a hard-coded application role. Anyone using the application gains access to the database.

**Caution**    Because using an application role forfeits the identity of the user, we strongly advise against using application roles.

# Object Security

If the user has access to the database, permission to the individual database objects may be granted. Permission may be granted either directly to the user, or to a standard role and the user assigned to the role. Users may be assigned to multiple roles, so multiple security paths from a user to an object may exist.

# Object Permissions

Object permissions are assigned with the SQL DCL commands, grant, revoke, and deny. These commands have a hierarchy. A deny overrides a grant, and a grant overrides a revoke. Another way to think of the DCL commands is that any grant will grant permission unless the user is denied permission somewhere.

Several specific types of permissions exist:

✦ *Select* — The right to select data. Select permission can be applied to specific columns.

✦ *Insert* — The right to insert data.

✦ *Update* — The right to modify existing data. Update rights requires select rights as well. Update permission can be set on specific columns.

✦ *Delete* — The right to delete existing data.

✦ *DRI* (References) — The right to create foreign keys with DRI.

✦ *Execute* — The right to execute stored procedures or user-defined functions.

Object-level permission is applied with the three basic DCL commands, grant, deny, and revoke. Whether security is being managed from Enterprise Manager or from code, it's important to understand these three commands.

Granting object permission interacts with the server and database roles. Here's the overall hierarchy of roles and grants, with 1 overriding 2, and so on:

1. The sysadmin **server role**

2. Deny object permission

   or the db_denydatareader **database role**

   or the db_denydatawriter **database role**

3. Grant object permission

   or object ownership

   or the db_datareader **database role**

   or the db_datewriter **database role**

4. Revoke object permission

**Best Practice**

An easy way to test security is to configure the server for mixed mode and create a SQL Server Login test user. Using Query Analyzer, it's easy to create additional connections as different users — much easier than it is to change the server registration and log into Enterprise Manager as someone else.

If your environment prohibits mixed-mode security, the easiest way to check security is to right-click Enterprise Manager or Query Analyzer and use the Run As command to run then using a different user. But this entails creating dummy users on in the Windows domain.

## Granting Object Permissions with Code

Setting an object permission is the only security command that can be executed without a system stored procedure being called.

```
GRANT Permission, Permission
  ON Object
  TO User/role, User/role
  WITH GRANT OPTION
```

The permissions may be all, select, insert, delete, references, update, or execute. The role or user name refers to the database user name, any user-defined public role, or the public role. For example, the following code grants select permission to Joe for the Person table:

```
GRANT Select ON Person TO Joe
```

The next example grants all permissions to the public role for the Marriage table:

```
GRANT All ON Marriage TO Public
```

Multiple users or roles, and multiple permissions, may be listed in the command. The following code grants select and update permission to the guest user and to LRN:

```
GRANT Select, Update ON Person to Guest, LRN
```

The with grant option grants the ability to grant permission for the object. For example, the following command grants Joe the permission to select from the Person table and grant select permission to others:

```
GRANT Select ON Person TO Joe WITH GRANT OPTION
```

The with grant option may only be used when you are managing security with code. Enterprise Manager has no feature with which to access the with grant option.

## Revoking and Denying Object Permission with Code

Revoking and denying object permissions uses essentially the same syntax as granting permission. The following statement revokes select permissions from Joe on the Marriage table:

```
REVOKE All ON Marriage TO Public
```

If the permission was granted with grant option, then the permission must be revoked or denied with the cascade option so that the with grant option will be removed. The following command denies select permission from Joe permission on the Person table:

```
DENY Select ON Person TO Joe CASCADE
```

# Standard Database Roles

Standard database roles, sometimes called user-defined roles, can be created by any user in the server sysadmin, database db_owner, or database security admin role. These roles are similar to those in user groups in Windows. Permissions, and other role memberships, can be assigned to a standard database role, and users can then be assigned to the role.

**Best Practice**

The cleanest SQL Server security plan is to assign object permissions and fixed roles to standard database roles, and then to assign users to the roles.

## The Public Role

The public role is a fixed role but it can have object permissions like a standard role. Every user is automatically a member of the public role and cannot be removed, so the public role serves as a baseline or minimum permission level.

**Caution**  Use caution when applying permissions to the public role because it will affect everyone except members of the sysadmin role. Granting access will affect everyone; more importantly, denying access will block all users except the members of the sysadmins role, even object owners, from accessing data.

## Managing Roles with Code

Creating standard roles with code involves using the sp_addrole system stored procedure. The name can be up to 128 characters and cannot include a backslash, be null, or be an empty string. By default the roles will be owned by the dbo user. However, you can assign the role an owner by adding a second parameter. The following code creates the manager role:

```
EXEC sp_addrole 'Manager'
```

Result:

```
New role added.
```

The counterpart of creating a role is removing it. A role may not be dropped if any users are currently assigned to it. The sp_droprole system stored procedure will remove the role from the database:

```
EXEC sp_droprole 'Manager'
```

Result:

```
Role dropped.
```

Once a role has been created, users may be assigned to the role by means of the sp_addrolemember system stored procedure. The following code sample assigns Joe to the manager role:

```
EXEC sp_addrolemember 'Manager', Joe
```

Result:

```
'Joe' added to role 'Manager'.
```

Unsurprisingly, the system stored procedure sp_droprolemember removes a user from an assigned role. This code frees Joe from the drudgery of management:

```
EXEC sp_dropRoleMember 'Manager', Joe
```

Result:

```
'Joe' dropped from role 'Manager'.
```

## Hierarchical Role Structures

If the security structure is complex, a powerful permission-organization technique is to design a hierarchical structure of standard database roles. For example:

✦ The worker role may have limited access.

✦ The manager role may have all worker rights plus additional rights to look up tables.

✦ The administrator role may have all manager rights plus the right to perform other database-administration tasks.

To accomplish this type of design, do the following:

1. Create the worker role and set its permissions.

2. Create the manager role and set its permissions. Add the manager role as a user to the worker role.

3. Create the admin role. Add the admin role as a user to the manager role.

The advantage of this type of security organization is that a change in the lower level affects all upper levels, and as a result administration is required in one location rather than dozens.

## Object Security and Enterprise Manager

Object permissions, because they involve users, roles, and objects, can be set from numerous places within Enterprise Manager (Figure 27-12). It's almost a maze.

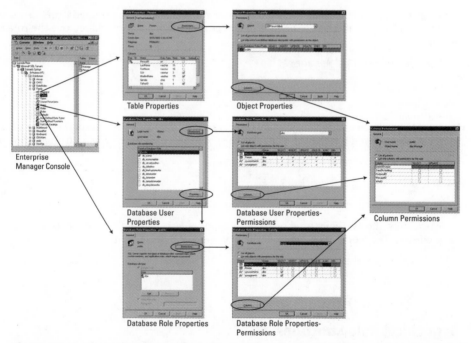

**Figure 27-12:** These thumbnails show the workflow involved in setting object permissions from a list of objects, users, or roles. Each of these forms is shown full-sized within this section.

## From the Object List

To modify an object's permissions:

1. From an object list (tables, views, stored procedures, or user-defined functions) in Enterprise Manager, double-click an object or select Properties from the right-click menu to open the Properties dialog for that object type.

2. Click the Permissions button to open the Object Properties dialog (Figure 27-13).

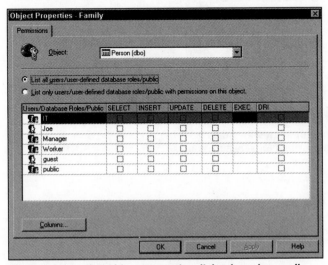

**Figure 27-13:** The Object Properties dialog box shows all users and roles, and can be used to modify their permissions.

As with setting statement permissions in the Database Properties Security tab, clicking the permissions box will cycle through the grant, revoke, and deny, as follows:

✦ A green check indicates permission is granted.

✦ A red *x* indicates that permission is denied.

✦ An empty box indicates a revoked permission.

The object list at the top of the dialog lists all the objects in the database. This list can be used to quickly switch to other objects without backing out of the form to the console and selecting a different object.

The Columns button at the bottom opens the Column Permissions dialog (Figure 27-14). Select the user and then click the button to set the columns permission for that user. Only select and update permissions can be set at the column level, because inserts and deletes affect the entire row.

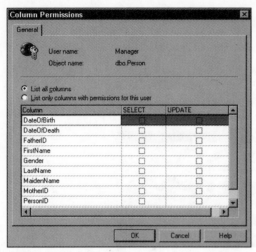

**Figure 27-14:** The Column Permissions dialog enables you to set permissions for selecting and updating individual columns.

## From the User List

From the list of database users in Enterprise Manager, select a user and double-click, or select Properties from the right-click menu. The Database User Properties dialog (Figure 27-15) is used to assign users to roles.

**Figure 27-15:** The Database User Properties dialog box.

Clicking the Properties button will open the properties of the selected role.

Clicking the Permissions button will open the Permissions tab of the Database User Properties dialog (Figure 27-16). This dialog is similar to the Permissions tab of the Database Object Properties dialog.

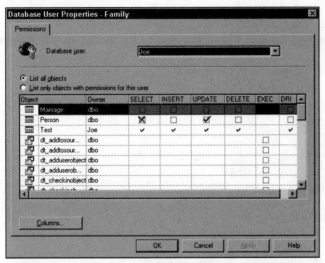

**Figure 27-16:** The Permissions tab of the Database User Properties dialog box is used to set individual permissions for the user.

Unfortunately, the list of objects appears to be unsorted, or only partially sorted, and the grid headers don't re-sort the list of objects. This dialog also desperately needs a select all function, and other features such as those in Access' permissions forms.

## From the Role List

The third way to control object permission is from the database role. To open the Database Role Properties dialog (Figure 27-17), double-click a role in the list of roles, or select Properties from the right-click menu. The Database Role Properties dialog can be used to assign users or other roles to the role, and to remove them from the role.

The Permissions button opens the permissions dialog box for the role (Figure 27-18). The form operates like the other permission forms, except that it's organized from the role's perspective.

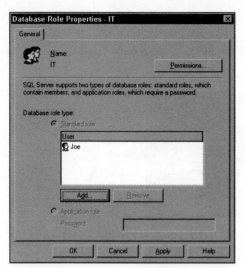

**Figure 27-17:** The Database Role Properties dialog box lists the users currently assigned to the role, and can be used to manage the role as well.

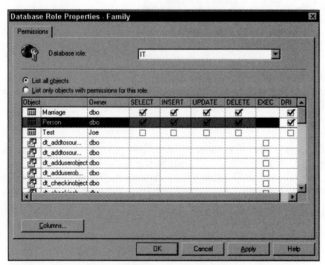

**Figure 27-18:** The Database Role Properties dialog box is used to set object permissions for the role.

# Object Ownership

Object ownership is an important yet easily misunderstood topic for SQL Server developers and DBAs.

Every object must have an owner. Whoever created the object owns it, with the notable exception of members of the `sysadmins` fixed server role. Enterprise Manager lists the object owner before the object name.

The full name of any object is the name of the owner and the name of the object. For example, in the family database, the `Person` table's full name is `dbo.Person`, not `Person`. It's possible, therefore, for Sue to create a `Person` table, and its name would be `sue.Person`.

The owner's individual permissions are permanently granted on their own objects. However, if the owner is assigned to a role that is denied permission to the object, or to the `db_denyreader` or `db_denywriter` roles, he or she will be blocked from his or her own object. Object ownership does not override a deny permission.

Object owners also have the right to manage the permissions of the objects they own.

## dbo

Any user in the `sysadmin` fixed server role is also mapped to a special system user, `dbo`. If the user creates a new object the object is owned by `dbo` rather than by the user. The `dbo` user has full permission in the database.

## Ownership Chains

In SQL Server databases users often access data by going through one or several objects. Ownership chains apply to views, stored procedures, and user-defined functions. For example:

✦ A Visual Basic program might call a stored procedure that then selects data from a table.

✦ A report might select from a view, which then selects from a table.

✦ A complex stored procedure might call several other stored procedures.

In these cases, the user must have permission to execute the stored procedure or select from the view. Whether the user also needs permission to select from the underlying tables depends on the ownership chain from the object the user called to the underlying tables.

If the ownership chain is unbroken from the stored procedure to the underlying tables, the stored procedure can execute using the permission of its owner, as shown in Figure 27-20. The user only needs permission to execute the stored procedure. The stored procedure can use its owner's permission to access the underlying tables. The user doesn't require permission to the underlying tables.

In the example shown in Figure 27-19, all the objects are owned by `dbo`. Since they have the same owner, the ownership chain is unbroken. Joe needs only to execute permission for the stored procedure `dbo.A`. The rest of the access takes place using `dbo`'s permissions rather than Joe's. In fact, since the lower-level objects are owned by the same owner, SQL Server does not even bother to check the permissions of the owner of these objects.

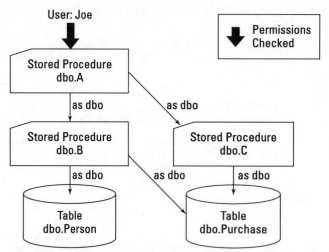

Figure 27-19: An unbroken ownership chain means that the called stored procedure can execute using the permissions of its owner instead of the permissions of the user who called the stored procedure.

Ownership chains are great for developing tight security where the users execute stored procedures but aren't granted direct permission to any tables.

If the ownership chain is broken (Figure 27-20), meaning that there's a different owner between an object and the next lower object, SQL Server checks the user's permission for every object accessed.

In the example,

✦ The ownership chain from dbo.A to dbo.B to dbo.Person is unbroken, so dbo.A can call dbo.B and access dbo.Person as dbo.

✦ The ownership chain from dbo.A to Sue.C to Joe.Purchase is broken because different owners are present. So dbo.A calls Sue.C using Joe's permissions, and Sue.C accesses Joe.Purchase using Joe's permissions.

✦ The ownership chain from dbo.A through dbo.B to Joe.Person is also broken. So dbo.A calls dbo.B using dbo's permissions, but dbo.B must access Joe.Purchase using Joe's permissions.

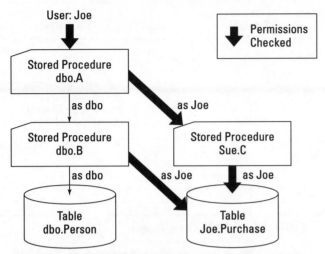

**Figure 27-20:** Two of the three ownership chains are broken. A broken ownership chain means that the user must have permission to every object accessed.

## Assigning Ownership

Since ownership chains are so important, SQL Server includes a method of modifying the ownership of an object. Unfortunately, you cannot change an object's ownership using Enterprise Manager. But with code, the `sp_changeobjectowner` system stored procedure reassigns the ownership:

```
sp_changeobjectowner object, newowner
```

For example, the following code makes Joe the owner of the `Person` table:

```
EXEC sp_changeobjectowner Person, Joe
```

Result:

```
Caution: Changing any part of an object name
could break scripts and stored procedures.
```

# A Sample Security Model Example

For a few examples of permissions using the OBX Kites database, Table 27-1 lists the permission settings of the standard database roles. Table 27-2 lists a few of the users and their roles.

### Table 27-1: OBX Kites Roles

| Hierarchical Standard Role | Primary Filegroup Role Structures | Static Filegroup Tables | Tables | Other Permissions |
|---|---|---|---|---|
| IT | sysadmin server role | - | - | - |
| Clerk | - | - | - | Execute permissions several stored procedures that read from and update required day-to-day tables |
| Admin | db_owner database fixed role | - | - | - |
| Public | - | Select permissions | - | - |

### Table 27-2: OBX Kites Users

| User | Database Standard Roles |
|---|---|
| Sammy | Admin |
| Joe | |
| LRN | IT |
| Clerk Windows group (Betty, Tom, Martha, and Mary) | Clerk |

From this security model, the following users can perform the following tasks:

✦ Betty, as a member of the Clerk role, can execute the VB application that executes stored procedures to retrieve and update data. Betty can run select queries as a member of the Public role.

✦ LRN, as the IT DBA, can perform any task in the database as a member of the sysadmin server role.

✦ Joe can run select queries as a member of the public role.

✦ As a member of the Admin role, Sammy can execute all stored procedures. He can also manually modify any table using queries. As a member of the admin role that includes the db_owner role, Joe can perform any database administrative task and select or modify data in any table.

✦ Joe can perform backups, but only LRN can restore from the backups.

## C2-Level Security

Organizations that require proof of their database security can investigate and implement C2-level security.

The Department of Defense Trusted Computer System Evaluation Criteria (TCSEC) evaluates computer and database security. The security scale ranges from A (very rare) meaning *verified design*, to D, meaning *minimal protection*. The C2-level security rating, meaning *controlled-access protection*, is required for classified data, IRS data, and most government contracts.

Essentially, C2-level security requires the following:

✦ A unique `loginID` for each user, protected from capture or eavesdropping. The user must be required to log in prior to accessing the database.

✦ A method of auditing every attempt by any user or process to access or modify any data.

✦ The default access to any object is no access.

✦ Access is granted at the discretion of the owner, or by the owner.

✦ Users are responsible for their data access and modifications.

✦ Data in memory is protected from unauthorized access.

For SQL Server's certification, Science Applications International Corp. of San Diego performed the tests as a third-party testing facility for the National Security Agency and the National Institute of Standards and Technology, which jointly run the government's security-certification program. The test took 14 months to complete and was funded by Microsoft.

The 47-page *SQL 2000 C2 Admin and User Guide* may be downloaded from: `http://www.microsoft.com/Downloads/Release.asp?ReleaseID=25503`.

Implementing C2-level security on SQL Server requires the following:

✦ SQL Server 2000 must be running on Windows NT 4 Service Pack 6a.

✦ Merge replication, snapshot replication, federated databases, and distributed databases are not allowed.

✦ Full auditing must be implemented using SQL Profiler.

✦ The C2 security option must be enabled, which shuts down SQL Server if the audit file is not functioning.

✦ Other restrictions on the location and size of the audit file exist.

## Views and Security

A popular, but controversial, method of designing security is to create a view that projects only certain columns, or that restricts the rows with a `where` clause and a `with check option`, and then grants permission to the view to allow users limited access to data. Some IT shops require that all access go through such a view. This technique is even assumed in the Microsoft certification tests.

**Cross-Reference**

Chapter 9, "Creating Views," explains how to create a view and to use the `with check option`.

Those opposed to using views for a point of security have several good reasons:

✦ Views are not compiled or optimized.

✦ Column-level security can be applied with standard SQL Server security.

✦ Using views for row-level security means that the `with check option` must be manually created with each view. As the number of row-level categories grows, the system requires manual maintenance.

## Summary

In this decade of cyber crime, security is more important than ever. While it's possible to set all the users to `sysadmin` and ignore security, with a little effort SQL Server security is functional and flexible enough to meet the needs presented by a variety of situations.

This chapter concludes Part IV of the book, which dealt with administering SQL Server. Part V dives into the more advanced operations of SQL Server.

✦　　✦　　✦

# Advanced Issues

**O**ne of the most enjoyable projects of my career was spending a couple years reworking and tuning an insurance document database search engine. When I first saw the project the queries were running as long as 20 minutes. At the end of the tuning the search time was consistently less than one second. There's nothing magical about it, just good solid design combined with optimization and scalability techniques.

Part V is about taking the box to the next level — adding those high-end features that differentiate a workgroup database from a polished mature database.

# Advanced Performance

T he all-encompassing goal of the computer industry is speed. However, too many benchmarks are based solely on response time as a measure of performance. True database performance is a composite of several factors:

- ✦ Accuracy (transactional integrity and data integrity)
- ✦ Availability
- ✦ Response time

If one of these goals is lacking the database is performing poorly, regardless of speed.

Of these performance goals, accuracy is paramount. Click and Clack, the NPR *Car Talk* brothers, say that the most important parts of a car are the wheels and the brakes: If the wheels fall off or the brakes fail, that's a real problem. Those two parts must perform; everything else is gravy. Database accuracy can be thought of in much the same way. If the query returns inaccurate results, response time is immaterial.

Another optimization myth is that performance can be added to a database after the development is complete. While databases can be tuned, the greatest impact on performance is made by the database design and development from day one. Often, what's called *performance tuning* is actually redevelopment of poorly designed portions of the database.

This chapter builds on the best practices from all the previous chapters and pulls together a strategy for measuring and maximizing database performance.

**Cross-Reference** Chapter 29, "Advanced Availability," discusses advanced availability designs, while Chapter 30, "Advanced Scalability," deals with techniques for managing very large databases.

# The Optimization Cycle

Typically, the most important concerns for the first version of a database project are the ship date, accuracy, and basic functionality. In what seems to be endless cycles of development, areas of the database or code are reworked and optimized in subsequent revisions.

Optimizing a database doesn't happen overnight, it takes a lot of time and patience monitoring the database and making changes when necessary. Here are some optimization best practices to keep in mind:

✦ As an organization, value good database design and well-written code.

✦ Put as much effort as possible into the database schema. All optimization depends on the schema.

✦ Focus the optimization effort on the most frequently run code, rather than just the slowest code.

✦ Optimize the database before upgrading the hardware. Bad code on a fast server is still bad code.

✦ Keep a list of possible optimization ideas, even if you don't have time to implement them now.

✦ New features compete with optimization for resources; therefore, a release that maintains the current functionality while improving performance is a good idea.

✦ Optimization is a discovery process and difficult to predict. Avoid making promises concerning performance gains or delivery dates.

✦ Consider indexes fluid components that are easily changed and tuned.

✦ Compatibility testing may require a server identical to one used in production, but develop and test on an old, slow server that won't mask performance issues.

✦ Focus on fixing the worst-performing aspect of the application.

✦ Spend some time using the application as a user. Go work for the department that uses the application for a week. It will provide valuable insights.

✦ Always leave some development time (25 percent?) for scenario testing.

✦ Consider any optimization project not only an investment in the software, but an investment in the knowledge base of the organization. If consultants are hired to perform some magic optimization tricks, the IT-development staff will be less confident and less likely to develop subsequent high-performing database projects. If consultants are employed, be sure to schedule plenty of time for knowledge transfer.

# Measuring Accuracy

The process of testing for accuracy involves a series of predictions and explanations. While testing an application or database with 10 rows is a standard joke in IT circles, using a testing scenario is the only valid method of proving the accuracy of an application.

A scenario test measures the accuracy of the database by comparing the answers to queries with the predicted results. A complex query that runs against 27 million rows is difficult to test; a scenario, however, is a carefully crafted set of data that represents all possible data combinations, but is small enough (5 to 50 rows per table) that the correct answer to any query is easily predicted. The scenario should be implemented in a script that creates the database and inserts the sample data, much like the sample database scripts on the book's CD.

The scenario test is any database's most significant test. If the database has not passed a careful scenario test, do not deliver or accept a database into production.

**Best Practice**

# Measuring Response Time

Performance may seem subjective, but it is possible to eliminate the variables and objectively measure the database performance. The purpose of the testing is to prove the capabilities of the database, expose any weaknesses, and objectively measure the performance loss or gain of any optimization efforts.

## Script Testing

A comprehensive response-time performance test consists of running a script against the database. The script should execute a series of queries or stored procedure calls that exercise the entire database. The balance of selects versus update queries, and the distribution of tables affected, should be representative of those of the actual front-end application and the batch processes.

The `OBXKites` sample database contains a benchmark file, `OBXKites_Benchmark.sql`, which executes a timed series of stored procedure calls and queries. The total time is reported at the end of the script.

Numerous factors can affect response-time performance. To objectively determine which factor accounted for which change in performance, it's important to alter only one factor per test, and to measure the response time using a consistent method. Each run of the performance test should begin with the same data, and the server used for testing should be free of other processes, connections, or users.

The performance of the test script can be calculated by means of saving the start time to a variable and subtracting it from the end time. Once the method of performing the test and measuring the result is decided and documented, a baseline test establishes the initial "as is" performance level.

## Load Testing

A load test evaluates the scalability of the database by measuring its response time at both half of the estimated load and the full estimated load.

### Data-Load Testing

To SQL Server, any database under 1GB in size can be considered minuscule and will perform well. The database schema and queries can only be load-tested when the data exceeds the memory capacity of the server by several times.

Index behavior is different when SQL Server has the luxury of loading all the required data pages and index pages into memory. If all the pages are in memory logical reads are the only significant factor. Because physical disk reads are not an issue, performance of the clustered index is less significant.

If you have access to several gigabytes of actual data, then that's the best data for the load test. If you don't, a large quantity of sample data can be generated using cross joins, a utility such as dbgen (included with the Microsoft SQL Server 2000 Resource Kit), DataSim (also included with the Resource Kit), or another third-party tool.

The graphical front end for dbgen is less than reliable, and it does not work well with GUID primary keys generated with a default value of newid(). However, dbgen works well with the command-line interface. In the following example, the data-generation commands for each column are contained in the example2.txt text file:

```
C:\Program Files\dbgenwin>dbgencom
    -Dguidint -Tsmexample -N1000 -iexample2.txt /Usa /Psa
Starting generation and copy
1000 of 1000 rows copied
1000 rows out of 1000 copied.
Done.
```

Although dbgen is less than intuitive, it's fast, and with a little effort and some time spent reading the help html files it's a useful utility.

DataSim examines the current data and generates similar $x$ number of rows for $x$ days of activity. The data is created as a SQL script with insert statements, so the same data can be reinserted at a later time.

### User-Load Testing

A database that's tested with only a single user, or just a few users, isn't fully tested. Locking contention, which is only exposed when the database tested with a large number of users, can cause serious performance problems.

To test the multi-user-load script, either run a continuous loop script from multiple connections using random parameters, or use a utility like dbhammer (which can be found in the SQL Server resource kit) to simulate a heavy user load. The closer the user load is to the number and type of queries generated by the actual active users, the better the test. (Keep in mind that not all current users are actually submitting queries at any given second.)

While the user load is running, execute the test script a few times and measure its performance at various user-load levels.

### Clean Testing

SQL Server is optimized to intelligently cache data in memory, and this will affect subsequent tests. Memory can be flushed by means of stopping and restarting the server, or with the DBCC DropCleanBuffers and DBCC FreeProcCache commands.

# Monitoring SQL Server

Tuning the server and database depends on solid and detailed information. Fortunately, SQL Server includes several tools for monitoring the activities and performance of the server.

Performance Monitor provides a performance overview of the database. While it can show detailed server information, it doesn't track the code-level details that SQL Profiler does.

Performance Monitor can help determine if the server needs a hardware upgrade, if transactions are waiting for locks, or if user activity has increased by a certain percentage. SQL Profiler can track down procedures that are holding the locks, the queries that are running slow, or the batches that are causing deadlocks.

## Performance Monitor

Performance Monitor, known as PerfMon, is familiar to anyone with experience with Windows administration. Performance Monitor is a separate MMC (Microsoft Management Console) application that can be launched from the SQL Server menu under the Start menu. Some servers have it installed in the Administrative Tools menu, and it's also found at Control Panel ➪ Administrative Tools ➪ Performance. If you have trouble finding it, the actual file (perfmon.exe or perfmon.mmc) is located in the c:\windows\system32 directory.

A performance trace consists of multiple performance counters, which are displayed graphically or logged to a file. The performance counters are added to the PerfMon trace one at a time with the plus-symbol button in the toolbar. A performance counter can watch the local server or a remote server, so it isn't necessary to run PerfMon at the SQL Server machine.

The counters can be watched as a timed line graph, a histogram bar graph, or a real-time report.

SQL Server, Analysis Services, and the Distributed Transaction Coordinator each add several additional SQL Server–oriented objects and counters to monitor key SQL Server or Window details in real time, as shown in Figure 28-1.

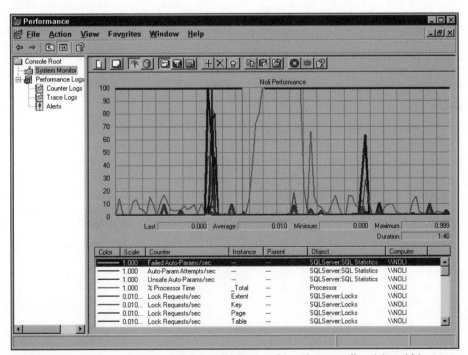

**Figure 28-1:** Performance Monitor is useful for watching the overall activity within SQL Server.

Typically, PerfMon is used to determine if the hardware is supporting the load. However, it can also be used to zero in on specific SQL Server problems. PerfMon can easily seem overwhelming because of the sheer number of possible counters that can be viewed; the most useful counters are listed in Table 28-1.

### Table 28-1: Key Performance-Monitor Counters

| Object | Counter | Description | Usefulness |
|--------|---------|-------------|------------|
| SQLServer: Buffer Manager | Buffer-cache hit ratio | The percentage of reads found already cached in memory. | SQL Server typically does an excellent job of pre-fetching the data into memory. If the ratio is below 95 percent, more memory will improve performance. |
| Processor | Percentage of processor time | The total percentage of processor activity. | If CPUs are regularly more than 60 percent active, additional CPUs or a faster server will increase performance. |
| SQLServer: SQL Statistics | Batch requests per second | SQL batch activity. | A good indicator of user activity. |
| Physical Disk | Average disk-queue length | The number of both reads and writes waiting on the disk; an indication of disk throughput; affected by the number of disk spindles on multi-disk RAID configurations. According to Microsoft, the disk-queue length should be less than the number of disk spindles plus two. (Check the scale when applying.) | Disk throughput is a key hardware-performance factor. Splitting the database across multiple disk subsystems will improve performance. |
| SQLServer: SQL Statistics | Failed auto-params per second | The number of queries that SQL Server could not cache the query execution plan in memory; an indication of poorly written queries (check the scale when applying). | Locating and correcting the queries will improve performance. |

| Object | Counter | Description | Usefulness |
|--------|---------|-------------|------------|
| SQLServer: Locks | Average wait time (in milliseconds), and lock waits and lock timeouts per second | A cause of serious performance problems; lock waits, the length of the wait, and the number of lock timeouts are all good indicators of the level of locking contention within a database. | If locking issues are detected, the indexing structure and transaction code should be examined. |
| SQLServer: User Connections | User connections | The number of current connections. | Indicates potential database activity. |
| SQLServer: Databases | Transactions per second | The number of current transactions within a database. | A good indicator of database activity. |

Using the properties dialog, available from the right-click menu, you can adjust the scale of the graph, the scale of each counter, and the presentation of each counter.

In addition to showing you the performance counters in real time, PerfMon can also log counters to a file or generate alerts using the other advanced options in the console tree.

# SQL Profiler

One of our favorite tools, SQL Profiler, watches the connection to a server and records the activity by tracking a copious number of items. The filters can be set to record all the activity, or they can focus on a specific problem. The activity can be watched on the SQL Profiler trace window, shown in Figure 28-2, or recorded to a file or table for further analysis.

When a new trace is created with the New Trace toolbar button or File ➪ New ➪ Trace, a connection is created to a SQL Server and the Trace Properties dialog box (Figure 28-3) is presented. The Trace Properties dialog box defines the events and data columns to be recorded, as well as the filter. If the trace is running the properties may be viewed, but not changed.

A trace configuration can be saved as a template to make creating new traces easier.

## Profiler-Trace Events

The Events tab determines the actions within SQL Server that the Profiler records. Like Performance Monitor, the Profiler can trace numerous key SQL Server events. The default events are useful for tracking user activity. Other events are useful for SQL detective work—looking for a specific problem.

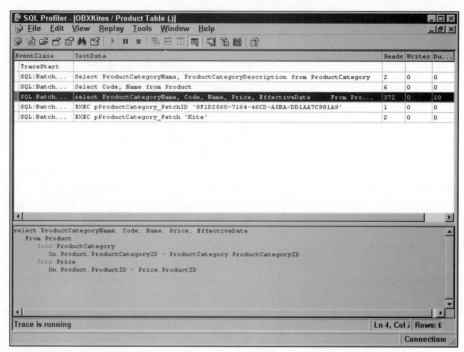

**Figure 28-2:** This SQL Profiler is set to record any SQL statement that references the product table in OBX Kites. Selecting a trace event in the trace window displays the details of the event in the bottom pane.

**Figure 28-3:** The Trace Properties dialog can define a new trace or alter the parameters of a stopped trace. The Events tab enables you to select the events tracked by the Profiler.

**Note**    The Profiler's SQL Batch Completed event is based on an entire batch (separated by a batch terminator), not a single SQL statement. So the profiler will capture one event's worth of data for even a long batch. Use the SQL Statement Complete even to capture single DML statement events.

If the trace is to be replayed certain events must be captured. For example, the SQL Batch Start event can be replayed, but SQL Batch Complete cannot.

## Profiler-Trace Data Columns

Depending on the events, different data becomes relevant to the trace. The Data Columns tab (Figure 28-4) defines the data columns and the `group by` within the trace output. As columns are added and removed, the event class and SPID columns become mandatory.

To add a column to the `group by`, select `group by` in the right-hand column before clicking the Add button. Columns can also be escalated to group status by means of the Up button. Any `group by` columns become the first columns in the trace window, and as new events are added to the trace window those events are automatically added within their group.

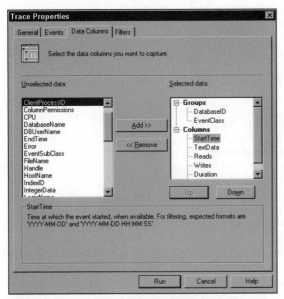

**Figure 28-4:** The Data Columns tab of the Trace Properties dialog box determines the data grouping and columns available in the trace output.

The data available for each column depends on the event, and often it isn't clear what you should expect. For example, the object name seems that it might display the object being locked, or the object being addressed for the Profiler filter. However, the object column seems to be populated only by some system objects for some events. The database name column seems to be populated only by security audit events.

The query batch being executed is found in the `text data` column.

## Data-Trace Filters

Profiler can capture so much information that it can fill a drive with data. Fortunately, the Profiler Trace Filter (Figure 28-5) can narrow the scope of your search to the data of interest.

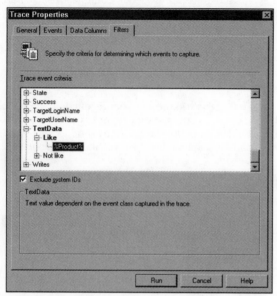

**Figure 28-5:** The Filters tab of the Trace Properties dialog box serves as a where clause for the trace, restricting the trace to certain events only.

The filter uses a combination of `equal` and `like` operators, depending on the data types captured. The frustrating aspect of the filter is that it only works against collected data, and the data collected for some columns may not be what was expected. For example, if you want to filter the trace to only those batches that reference a specific table or column, filtering by the object name won't work. But defining a `like` filter using wildcards on the `text data` column will cause the Profiler to select only those batches that include that table name.

Another popular Profiler trace filter is to filter for events with a duration greater than or equal to a specified time, to select all the longer-running batches.

The "Exclude system IDs" checkbox sets the filter to select only user objects.

## Using the Profiler Trace

Once the trace is captured it can be browsed through the Profiler trace window, although a more useful option is to configure the trace to save results to a database table. The data can then be analyzed and manipulated as in any other SQL table.

SQL Profiler has the ability to replay traces. However, the restrictions on the replay option are such that it's unlikely to be useful for most databases.

Additionally, the entire trace file can be submitted as a workload to the Query Tuning Wizard so that the Query Tuning Wizard can tune for multiple queries.

### Tracing in the Background

SQL Profiler is generally used interactively, and for smaller databases this is more than sufficient. However, larger databases or longer traces can easily generate hundreds of thousands of trace entries or more, which can cause problems at the workstation running the trace. However, it's possible to generate a script that executes an extended stored procedure to launch the profile trace, logging the trace details directly to a table without using the graphic interface.

To create a background trace, first define the trace using SQL Profiler as a normal trace. Once the events, data columns, and filters are configured, use the File ➪ Script Trace menu option to generate a script. The script will create a trace configuration in the registry so that the trace can be executed by means of the xp_trace extended stored procedure.

# Developing Well-Performing Databases

Database optimization begins in the initial planning stages; performance can't be easily added once the database development is complete. As the development of an ill-designed database progresses, the cost of correcting it increases dramatically. A constraint that would take five minutes to carefully implement in the initial stages could take weeks to correct after the database has been in use for a few years.

The big difference between a slow database and one that runs smoothly isn't subtle server tuning, hardware, or query-optimizer hints. In our experience, the following five factors determine that a database will perform well. If one of these factors is missing, the database will be slow:

- ✦ A data-driven normalized physical database schema design
- ✦ A complete and balanced indexing strategy
- ✦ Code that uses set-based queries and avoids procedural (row-by-row) grinding of the data
- ✦ Excellent use of database constraints and triggers to enforce rules
- ✦ Tables, indexes, and code designed to avoid locking contention

**Best Practice**

The best practice is to optimize the database and then upgrade the hardware. It's far better to improve performance by optimizing the design and the code than it is to buy new hardware. I believe that using hardware upgrades alone to improve performance will actually hinder performance in the long term, because management will feel that it has made an investment in optimization and will be less likely to focus on the real problems. In addition, the hardware solution may mask the true problems for a while. It's a question of bandages versus treatment.

# Database Design and Performance

The foundation of the application is the design of the database. Even the type of queries used depends in part on the style of the database design. Databases that use composite primary keys require multiple join conditions. Databases that aren't properly normalized require additional code to maintain data integrity, or require code to move the data from work table to work table — grinding the database to death. Databases without comprehensive constraints require extra code to validate the data either during data entry, while data is moved from work table to work table, or as part of the reporting queries.

A high-performance database schema will meet the following design ideals:

✦ Normalize the database to third normal form, but then be careful to implement a physical design that uses high-performance single-column keys.

✦ Don't over-normalize or over-complicate the database. Keep working until a simple and elegant design is found.

✦ Avoid database designs that shuttle data from table to table in a transactional manner.

✦ Use a data-driven database-design style rather than designs with any hard-coded values.

✦ If the code is building several temporary tables or extra work tables, that's an indication that the database design isn't sufficient.

✦ Design the database schema with queries in mind. We've seen databases that were perfectly normalized logical databases designed by DBAs who never wrote queries. It isn't pretty.

✦ When necessary, be bold and duplicate data from the OLTP tables into denormalized read-only tables for faster database reads.

# Constraints and Triggers

If performance includes data integrity, the quality and execution performance of the data rules are also vital to the database. The following list contains key points to consider during the implementation of Rules and Triggers:

✦ Rules should be implemented at the database level so that they are fast and always enforced.

✦ Implement database rules and business rules as database constraints, and then use triggers for rules that are too complex for database constraints.

✦ Triggers must handle multiple-row operations, and they should do this using set-oriented DML statements instead of cursors. Since the trigger fires for every `insert`, `update`, or `delete` operation, no pains should be spared to optimize the code.

# Query Design and Performance

The methods used to retrieve data significantly affect performance. The `select` statement is the heart of SQL and, as demonstrated in Chapters 6 and 7, an incredible amount of work can be performed by a single SQL DML statement. The greatest optimizations we've performed, or seen on a database, have involved replacing row-based procedures with set-based SQL code. The single worst thing anyone can do to a database is to write a cursor when it's not absolutely required.

With the goal of avoiding cursors or loops like the plague, and focusing on set-based queries to perform the database work, consider the following:

✦ Always specify the owner of the table, so the query-execution plan can be cached.

✦ Never use views within code, but only to support ad hoc user queries.

✦ Use subqueries to break down large complex queries into smaller logical units.

Comparing row-iterative procedural-style code to set-based queries using procedural-style code is like moving from New York to Los Angeles by transporting one item at a time in a Volkswagen, while using set-based queries is like loading the entire household into a FedEx overnight express jet. Sure, driving the script code 15 mph over the speed limit will cut a few hours off each round trip, but it's still buggy code.

## Query Optimization

SQL is a declarative language, meaning that the SQL query describes the question and SQL Server decides how to execute the query.

SQL Server's Query Optimizer examines several possible methods of solving each portion of the query, such as `where` conditions, joins, and functions. Considering the estimated cost of each logical cost of each operation, as well as the available indexes, hardware limitation, and data statistics, the query optimizer calculates the fastest possible query-execution plan.

This means that much of the optimization is being performed by SQL Server, not the query.

Optimizing queries is largely a matter of providing the right indexes so the query optimizer can perform fast index seeks instead of slow table scans. For some queries, altering the structure of the query can affect performance, but for the majority of queries, writing the query three different ways will return three identical query-execution plans.

**Best Practice**

We've seen some complex queries benefit from parts of the query being broken into subqueries, but sometimes when we're sure that altering a huge three-page query into subqueries will yield better performance, SQL Server generates the exact same query plan despite the time spent rewriting the query. When in doubt, develop the query three ways and see which yields the best performance.

## Query-Execution Plans

Another of our favorite parts of SQL Server is the Query Analyzer's display of the query-execution plan. You can view the estimated query plan by clicking the query plan toolbar button, and after a query is run you can view the actual plan if the Query ⇨ Show Execution Plan option is selected.

The logical operations are the same in both the estimated and actual query plans. Besides not waiting for the query to execute, the estimated-query execution plan uses the statistics to estimate the number of rows involved in each logical operation, while the actual execution plan reports actual data.

The query plan is read from right to left, as shown in Figure 28-6. Each logical operation is presented as an icon. But the display isn't just a static display. Here are a few of the operations you can perform while in the Query Execution plan window:

✦ Mousing over the logical operation causes a dialog box to appear containing detailed information about the logical operation, including the logical cost and the portion of the query handled by the operation.

✦ Mousing over a connector line presents detailed information about how much data is being moved by that connector.

✦ Right-clicking the execution plan opens a menu offering access to sizing options, index management, and the Statistics Manager.

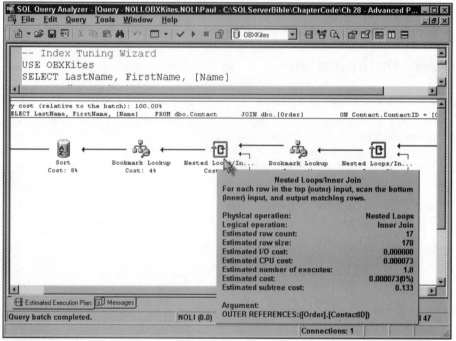

**Figure 28-6:** Query Execution Plans show the logical operations SQL Server uses to solve the query.

The estimated query plan uses the statistics to estimate the number of rows involved in each logical operation.

## Index Seeks and Nested Loops

When the indexes are available, the fastest way for SQL Server to fetch a row is for it to perform an index seek that quickly navigates the b-tree index from the root node, through the intermediate node, to the leaf node, and finally to the row.

Once the correct row is identified, if all the required columns are found in the index the seek is done. If additional columns are needed, SQL Server will likely use a bookmark operation to fetch the remaining data columns from the data page.

A key benefit of index seeks is that the where clause or join condition is applied directly at the table level instead of a filter operation being added later in the query-execution plan. Index seeks also provide the best data for a join operation, so the join can be performed by a fast nested-loop join instead of a slower hash join.

## Index Scans

When an index is available, but the data column being sought isn't in the correct ordinal position of the index, SQL Server may opt to use an index scan. While an index scan is better than a table scan, it's much slower than an index seek. Index scans indicate that the columns in the index aren't in the best order. An index scan will still return the correct rows, however, enabling SQL Server to perform fast joins and avoid filters.

## Table Scans and Hashes

Depending on the table size, a table scan can be very expensive. Several situations will cause a table scan, including:

✦ If no index is available, the query optimizer has no choice but to scan every row of the table.

✦ If SQL Server decides that the index isn't useful because of the data statistics or the small size of the table, the query optimizer will use a table scan.

**Best Practice**

If you see table scans accessing any table containing over 100 rows, the indexes for that table are drastically inadequate and should be reevaluated.

## Filters and Sorts

In some situations SQL Server retrieves all the data from a table and then uses filter operations to select the correct rows and sort operations to perform the order by. Filters and sorts are slow operations and indicate a lack of useful indexes.

## Optimizable SARGs

A key concept to the usability of the query optimization is by use of the where condition. If SQL Server can optimize the where condition using an index, the condition is referred to as a *search argument* or SARG. But not every condition is a "sargable" search argument. For instance:

✦ Multiple conditions that are ANDed together are SARGs, but ORed conditions are not SARGs.

✦ Negative search conditions (<>, !>, !<, Not Exists, Not In, Not Like) are not optimizable. It's easy to prove that a row exists, but to prove it doesn't exist requires examining every row.

✦ Conditions that begin with wildcards don't use indexes. An index can quickly locate Smith, but must scan every row to find any rows with ith anywhere in the string.

✦ Conditions with expressions are not SQL Server compliant so these expressions will be broken down with the use of algebra to aide with the procurement of valid input data.

✦ If the where clause includes a function, such as a string function, a table scan is required so every row can be tested with the function applied to the data.

**On the CD-ROM**

SQL Expert by Lecco is an amazing tool that takes any SQL DML statement and generates alternative SQL languages to make the same query—hundreds of variations are possible. Each variation is then submitted to SQL Server and the estimated execution plans are collected. The result is a list of every possible way to submit a query, sorted by the logical cost.

## Measuring Query Performance

SQL Server provides several query-performance indicators beside Query Analyzer's graphic query-execution plan. The statistics io connection option reports I/O (Input/Output) activity for each table in the query, including scans and reads:

```
SET statistics io ON
USE OBXKites
SELECT LastName + ' ' + FirstName as Customer, Product.[Name],
Product.code
  FROM dbo.Contact
    JOIN dbo.[Order]
      ON Contact.ContactID = [Order].ContactID
    JOIN dbo.OrderDetail
      ON [Order].OrderID = OrderDetail.OrderID
    JOIN dbo.Product
      ON OrderDetail.ProductID = Product.ProductID
  WHERE Product.Code = '1002'
  ORDER BY LastName, FirstName
```

Result (excluding data):

```
Table 'Contact'. Scan count 13, logical reads 26,
  physical reads 0, read-ahead reads 0.
Table 'Order'. Scan count 13, logical reads 26,
  physical reads 0, read-ahead reads 0.
Table 'Product'. Scan count 33, logical reads 66,
  physical reads 0, read-ahead reads 0.
Table 'OrderDetail'. Scan count 1, logical reads 1,
  physical reads 0, read-ahead reads 0.
```

The statistics time option reports CPU and overall execution time for the query, as well as for other system processes that may have run as a result of the query, such as compilation and storage of the query:

```
Set statistics time on
SELECT LastName + ' ' + FirstName as Customer
  FROM dbo.Contact
  ORDER BY LastName, FirstName
Set statistics time off
```

Result (excluding data):

```
SQL Server parse and compile time:
  CPU time = 0 ms, elapsed time = 2 ms.
```

```
SQL Server Execution Times:
   CPU time = 0 ms,  elapsed time = 1 ms.
```

A slight overhead is involved in reporting the statistics, so be sure to turn them off when you're finished.

The `showplan_all` connection option reports the query-execution plan in text, with lots of detail. While this option is not as pretty as the graphic query-execution plan, the text can be printed or captured for further text analysis.

```
Set showplan_all on
go
SELECT LastName
  FROM dbo.Contact
go
Set showplan_all off
```

Result (abridged, there are 17 more columns of detailed information):

```
StmtText
-------------------------------------------------
SELECT LastName
  FROM dbo.Contact
  |--Table Scan(OBJECT:([OBXKites].[dbo].[Contact
```

## Reusing Query Execution Plans

As the time statistics demonstrated, the query-parse and -compile time can be expensive. Stored query plans are therefore critical to the continued performance of the database. If the query qualifies, the first time it is executed SQL Server attempts to save the query plan in the procedure cache.

In order to be saved a query must have parameters and qualified table names. Fortunately, SQL Server 2000 will autoparameterize the query, replacing literals and constants in the query with parameters, thus allowing the query to be saved.

A more restrictive condition is that all table references must the qualified with a two-part name for the query plans to be saved.

You can look at the query-plan cache to verify that the query is in fact cached. The procedure cache can be large. While it's not recommended in a production environment, clearing the cache will make checking for a specific query easier:

```
DBCC FREEPROCCACHE
```

To examine the procedure cache, use the `syscacheobjects` table:

```
SELECT cast(C.sql as Char(35)) as StoredProcedure,
    cacheobjtype,  usecounts as Count
  FROM Master.dbo.syscacheobjects C
  JOIN  Master.dbo.sysdatabases D
    ON C.dbid = C.dbid
  WHERE D.Name = DB_Name()
    AND ObjType = 'Adhoc'
  ORDER BY StoredProcedure
```

Result (abridged):

```
cacheobjtype          Count          StoredProcedure
----------------      -----------    ------------------------------
Compiled Plan         1              INSERT [Lumigent_Profiler]([Pre
Executable Plan       1              SELECT LastName + ' ' + FirstNa
Compiled Plan         1              SELECT LastName + ' ' + FirstNa
Compiled Plan         1              UPDATE msdb.dbo.sysjobschedules
```

Performance depends on a combination of the query, the indexes, and the data. A saved query plan is useful only as long as the data statistics, indexes, and parameters are consistent. When the table or index structure changes, the data statistics are updated, or a significant amount of data is updated, SQL Server marks the query as unusable and generates a new query plan the next time it's executed.

To efficiently save memory, query plans are also aged out of the cache, with the most complex queries taking the longest time to be removed.

# A Balanced Index Strategy

Indexes play a vital role in database performance. Unfortunately, the topic of indexing is obscured by more misinformation than any other area of database development.

## Indexing Basics

Understanding SQL Server's basic types of indexes is critical to working with indexes. SQL Server uses clustered and nonclustered indexes, either of which may be created as a stand-alone index or the primary-key index.

### Clustered Indexes

A clustered index merges the data page with the leaf node of the index so that the data is in the same order as the index, as illustrated in Figure 28-7. A good example of a clustered index is a phone book. The phone book is indexed in the same order as the data. A table can only be in one physical sort order.

### Nonclustered Indexes

Nonclustered indexes are b-tree indexes that go from the root node through intermediate nodes to the leaf node, and that then point to the data row. A table can have up to 249 nonclustered indexes. An index in the back of a book is a nonclustered index: The index entries are sorted, but they only point to pages in the book.

If a clustered index is present the nonclustered leaf nodes point to the clustered index and the clustered index's columns function as if they were appended to the nonclustered index. For example, if a table has a clustered index on Column 1, a nonclustered index on Columns 3 and 4 is actually an index on Columns 3, 4, and 1.

### Primary Keys

A primary key can be initially defined as a clustered or nonclustered index. However, for the index type to be changed the primary-key constraint must be dropped and recreated — a painful task if numerous foreign keys are present or if the table is replicated.

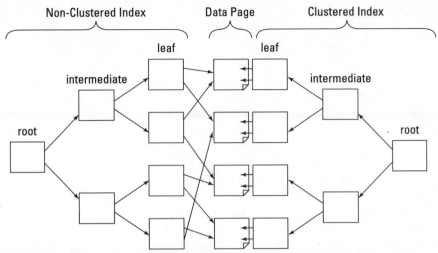

**Figure 28-7:** The clustered index merges the index page with the data page, while a nonclustered index points to the data page.

## Indexing and Database Size

One reason that there's so much misinformation regarding indexing is that index behavior is affected by database size. If the entire database can fit into memory, the question of how the database is indexed is much less critical than in the case of a database that's several times larger than the server memory, in which case data must be swapped in as needed.

The idea that primary keys should use a clustered index is based on the fact that a clustered index saves one logical read in moving from the index to the data page. However, the clustered index's ability to group similar rows on the same database for range selection of data becomes important when the data pages must be read from the disk.

## OLTP Indexing versus OLAP Indexing

Indexing affects both read and write performance. While read performance is dramatically improved by indexing, the improvement comes at a cost. The cost of inserting a single row into a few indexes is usually not an issue and is usually well worth the benefit to those reading from those indexes. However, adding numerous indexes to a transactional-processing database (OLTP or Online Transaction Processing) will have some affect when you are writing to multiple rows.

Because indexes benefit reads and degrade writes, they cause contention between the indexing needs of daily transactional data-entry indexing and reporting or online analysis processing (OLAP) indexing. One way to resolve this contention is to use two databases, one dedicated to transactions and the other to reporting. The indexes for each database are tuned to its specific needs, and the databases are kept in sync by a periodic DTS transfer of data or transactional replication. If the synchronization is sufficient, the front-end application can write to the transactional database and use the reporting database to populate grids and combo boxes, further reducing the need for indexes in the transactional database.

## The Base Indexes

Even before tuning, the locations of a few indexes are easy to determine. These base indexes are the first step in building a solid set of indexes. Here are a few things to keep in mind when building these base indexes:

1. Create every primary key as a nonclustered index. Primary keys are typically used for single-row retrieval and the *one* side of one-to-many joins, so a nonclustered index is the best choice.

2. Create a clustered index for every table. For primary tables, cluster the most common `order by` columns. Do not cluster the primary key. For secondary tables, create a clustered index for the most important foreign key.

3. Create nonclustered indexes for the columns of every foreign key, except for the foreign key that was indexed in Step 2.

4. Create a single-column index for every column referenced in a `where` clause or an `order by`.

While this indexing plan is far from perfect, it provides an initial compromise between no indexes and tuned indexes, and a baseline performance measure to compare the index tuning against.

## Index Tuning

Index tuning is part science and part art. You might consider several tactics when tuning the indexes. For every tactic the goal is the same — to reduce the number of physical data-page reads required per query.

**Best Practice**

While some indexes are obvious (such as foreign keys and common `where`-clause criteria), the best indexing strategy analyzes how queries are accessing the data and develops indexes as a performance bridge between the data and the queries.

### Using the Clustered Index

The clustered index is merged with the data page, so it saves one logical step by skipping the index leaf node; however, the true purpose of the clustered index is to speed physical reads from the disk. The clustered index can be the most critical index, and the most complex to determine.

Every table is in some physical order on the disk. If no clustered index exists, the data is simply arranged in the order of entry and the clustered index has been wasted.

As a rule, selecting a range of entries is faster with a clustered index than with a nonclustered. Using the phone book example, retrieving a list of all the Nielsens in a city is as easy as finding the Nielsen page and tearing that page from the book.

If a nonclustered index is used to select all the Nielsens from a book on Viking and Danish history, the nonclustered index in the back of the book will quickly find the Nielsens, but retrieving the data will require turning to several individual pages spread throughout the book.

The same is true within SQL Server. Because a clustered index arranges data in the order of the index, retrieving several rows of data with a similar clustered value requires significantly fewer data-page reads than the same retrieval would with a nonclustered index.

If the entire database fits in memory, data reads may not be a problem. But if SQL Server is fetching data from the disk, a significant performance difference exists between reading 2 data pages and reading 100 data pages.

Since the primary benefit of a clustered index is that it clusters, or groups, similar data and speeds the retrieval of ranges of data, clustered indexes are excellent for foreign keys on the *many* side of one-to-many relationships, such as the `orderid` column in an order-detail table. When an order is selected, all the related order-detail rows are already grouped into a single data page.

Primary tables can use a clustered index to group data according to the most frequently used range selection, such as an account number or region. Depending on how the front-end application is written, it may be beneficial to cluster by the columns used for the most common sort order for the data-view grid.

## Composite Index

An index created using multiple columns is considered a *composite* index. The key to building useful composite indexes is using the most useful order.

Referring again to the common phone book, finding *Doe, John* is easy because the first and second columns of the index are used in the search. On the other hand, searching for *John* using the index can be done, but every name must be examined to find every John.

The same logic applies to SQL Server's composite indexes. If an index includes three columns, the possible uses are Column 1, Columns 1 and 2, or Columns 1, 2, and 3. However, searching for Column 3 will not make the best use of an index. While a query can use an index scan, reading through every index entry, it can not seek the data, swiftly navigating the b-tree to the correct index value.

When planning composite indexes, consider that if the table has a clustered index that every nonclustered index is a composite index using the clustered-index columns.

## Covering Indexes

An excellent use of a composite index is eliminating data page reads by including all the required columns in the composite index. The composite index then covers the entire select. The data is fetched directly from the index without reading any data pages. This technique is very fast; the trick is designing a few covering indexes that serve multiple queries.

Building a covering index that includes both foreign keys of many-to-many junction tables, enables SQL Server to join from one primary table, through the junction table, and to the other primary table without reading the data pages of the junction table.

## Index Selectivity

Another aspect of indexing is the selectivity of the index. An index that is very selective has more index values and selects fewer data rows per index value. A primary key or unique index has the highest possible selectivity.

An index with only a few values spread across a large table is less selective. Indexes that are less selective may not even be useful as indexes. A column with three values spread throughout the table is a poor candidate for an index. A bit column has low selectivity and may not even be indexed.

SQL Server uses its internal index statistics to track the selectivity of an index. DBCC Show_Statistics reports the last date the statistics were updated and the basic information about the index statistics, including the usefulness of the index. A low density indicates that the index is very selective. A high density indicates that a given index node points to several table rows and that the index may be less useful.

```
Use CHA2
DBCC Show_Statistics (Customer, IxCustomerName)
```

Result (formatted and abridged; the full listing includes details for every value in the index):

```
Statistics for INDEX 'IxCustomerName'.
                      Rows                    Average
Updated    Rows    Sampled   Steps   Density  key length
---------  -----   --------  ------  -------- -----------
May 1,02   42      42        33      0.0      11.547619

All density     Average Length   Columns



--------------  ---------------  ---------------------------
3.0303031E-2    6.6904764        LastName
2.3809524E-2    11.547619        LastName, FirstName

DBCC execution completed. If DBCC printed error messages,
contact your system administrator.
```

## Index Fill Factor and Padding

As data is written to each data and index page, it must be inserted into an existing page unless the data is being added to the end of the index. The amount of empty space available for inserts is set by the index's fill factor. A setting of 1 or 100 will leave space for two rows; any other setting will determine what percentage of the page will be filled with data.

The fill factor affects performance. If the fill factor is set too low, more pages are required to contain the data. More pages means more physical data-page reads per query; both read and write performance will suffer.

If the page is full and a row is inserted, the page is split into two pages, each 50 percent full. The page-split process is costly, so page splits should be avoided. Setting the fill factor too high will cause page splits and write performance will suffer.

The best fill factor is based on the percentage of data changes expected between index rebuilds on a table-by-table basis. If a table with 100,000 rows sees 4,000 new rows and another 6,000 updates to an indexed column, the table sees about 10 percent writes. The fill factor is then calculated based on the activity plus some margin (5 percent?). Using this method, the fill factor would be set to 85 percent.

**Cross-Reference**

The index's fill factor will slowly become useless as the pages fill and split. The maintenance plan must include periodic reindexing to reset the fill factor. Chapter 24, Maintaining the Database," includes information on how to maintain indexes.

The fill factor for a clustered index will affect the data page. For a nonclustered index the fill factor affects the leaf node of the index, but not any intermediate nodes. To propagate the fill factor to the intermediate index nodes, set the pad index option to `true`.

If all the table activity is going through stored procedures, the rows affected by each operation can be logged to a table. A query can then easily calculate the table's activity between scheduled reindexing operations, and automatically set the fill factor to a level optimized for that table.

## Redundant-Index Analysis

Sometimes, tuning table indexes requires a careful analysis of the existing indexes to identify existing duplicate or inefficient indexes. Now we'll look at a scenario that works by cleaning a set of indexes within the `OBXKites.dbo.Product` table.

Table 28-2 is an example of a poorly planned set of indexes. Each index's columns are indicated by its position in the index. For example, index `Ix1` is a composite index consisting of the `OrderID` and `OrderDetailID` columns.

### Table 28-2: Redundant Indexes

| Column | Pk (cl) | Ix1 | Ix2 | Ix3 | Ix4 | Ix5 | Ix6 | Ix7 |
|---|---|---|---|---|---|---|---|---|
| OrderDetailID | 1 | 2 | (2) | 3 | (4) | (3) | (3) | (4) |
| OrderID | | 1 | | 2 | | 2 | 2 | 1 |
| ProductID | | | 1 | 1 | 3 | | | 2 |
| NonStockProduct | | | | | | | | |
| Quantity | | | | | | | | 3 |
| UnitPrice | | | | | | | | |
| ExtendedPrice | | | | | | | | |
| ShipRequestDate | | | | | 2 | | 1 | |
| ShipDate | | | | | 1 | 1 | | |
| ShipComment | | | | | | | | |

This set of indexes contains several duplicate indexes and indexes that include needless columns as well as other problems. Clustering the primary key fails to make the best use of the clustered index because it isn't used for the selection of a range of records.

Table 28-3 shows how the redundant indexes can be cleaned up:

✦ The clustered index is moved to Ix1. The order-detail rows are physically grouped by the order, and the clustered index serves as a covering index for an order/order-detail/product join.

✦ Indexes Ix2, Ix3, Ix4, and Ix7 are eliminated as duplicate indexes.

✦ Ix5 serves as a fast index for ordering by or selecting by the ship date.

✦ Ix6 is a covering index for queries that plan shipments.

### Table 28-3: Clean Indexes

| Column | Pk | Ix1 *(cl)* | Ix2 | ix3 | ix4 | ix5 | ix6 | ix7 |
|---|---|---|---|---|---|---|---|---|
| OrderDetailID | 1 | | | | | | | |
| OrderID | | 1 | | | | (2) | (4) | |
| ProductID | | 2 | | | | (3) | (5) | |
| NonStockProduct | | | | | | | | |
| Quantity | | | | | | | 2 | |
| UnitPrice | | | | | | | | |
| ExtendedPrice | | | | | | | | |
| ShipRequestDate | | | | | | | 1 | |
| ShipDate | | | | | | 1 | 3 | |
| ShipComment | | | | | | | | |

**Best Practice**

When cleaning indexes, be sure to check the query code for any index hints. If the index is dropped, a query that references it will fail.

## Using the Index Tuning Wizard

While indexes can be manually set, the process of matching data with queries to determine a set of useful indexes can be a very complex task. The SQL Server team has created the Index Tuning Wizard to automate it. Although it's not perfect, the Index Tuning Wizard can help identify holes in the indexing strategy.

The Index Tuning Wizard can be launched from SQL Profiler or Query Analyzer, and it can evaluate possible indexes for an entire Profiler workload or for the Query Analyzer selection. Be sure to check the validity of the workload's queries: A single query with an error will cause the Index Tuning Wizard to fail. If you exit the wizard you will have to reset every option when you run it again.

The Index Tuning Wizard walks you through several dialogs:

1. In the first page of the index, the server and database are selected, as shown in Figure 28-8. The wizard can optionally drop indexes that do not contribute to the creation of the query. Indexed views can be added by the wizard. The first page of the wizard also enables you to select the Tuning Mode, with the following three options:

   - Fast — A quick check of indexes. This option won't recommend clustered indexes or indexed views, or drop existing indexes.

   - Medium — The default; recommends clustered indexes and indexed views, and can drop existing indexes.

   - Thorough — Performs the most exhaustive analysis of the workload. This option is useful for generating a set of indexes that serves a large workload containing numerous queries.

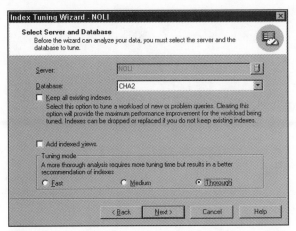

**Figure 28-8:** The Index Tuning Wizard can keep existing indexes and offers three levels of analysis.

**Best Practice**

Unless the wizard is analyzing a comprehensive workload, do not allow it to drop existing indexes. Doing so will negatively affect queries that are not in the set of analyzed queries.

2. Page two of the wizard allows you to select a set of queries for analysis:

- A workload file looks to a file for a set of queries from a SQL Profiler trace (.trc) or a SQL script (.sql).

- A captured workload stored in a SQL Profiler trace table.

- The current Query Analyzer selection.

The advanced options set the Index Tuning Wizard's properties, such as the number of queries it will examine, the maximum disk size, and the recommended width of composite indexes. If the wizard is tuning the indexes for a large workload, the advanced options will need to be increased.

3. The wizard's third page selects the tables that the wizard may adjust. In addition to simply selecting a table, the number of rows in a table affects the usefulness of an index. Manually adjust the projected number of rows to create indexes that will be more useful for the actual projected size of the database.

4. The recommendation of the Index Tuning Wizard is a list of the indexes. Indexes to be added have that new-index sparkle (Figure 28-9); indexes the wizard wants to drop have an *x* over them.

Click the Analysis button to receive several detailed explanations of how the wizard determined its index-change recommendations. Each individual analysis report can be saved to a text file.

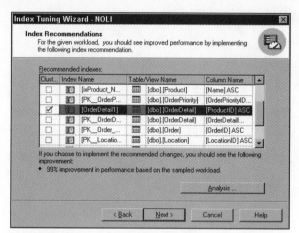

**Figure 28-9:** In this example, the Index Tuning Wizard recommends adding a clustered index and predicts a 99 percent performance improvement.

5. The last page of the wizard offers to apply the changes now or at a specified time. A better option is to generate a script so the indexes can be applied more than once.

**Best Practice**

Manually create a base set of indexes and the clustered index. Add indexes for the most critical queries. Then use the Index Tuning Wizard to validate and refine the indexing strategy. If the wizard wants to add an index, try to figure out why. An understanding of the data, the queries, and the indexing is too important for the database developer simply to let the Index Tuning Wizard do all the work.

# Locking and Performance

When a database is experiencing locking contention, it can be a serious problem. Depending on the time spent waiting for the lock to be released, the lock-timeout setting, and how the application handles the timeout, transactions might be waiting for locks without the user's awareness. To identify locking problems, track the lock waits per second Performance Monitor counter, or a `lock:cancel` or `lock:timeout` event in SQL Profiler.

The clustered order affects locking by grouping rows on the same page. This can cause a hot spot if the transactions are escalating from row locks to table locks and the locks are being held.

To reduce the severity of a locking problem, do the following:

✦ Check the transaction-isolation level and make sure it's not any higher than required.

✦ Make sure transactions begin and commit quickly. Redesign any transaction that includes a cursor.

✦ If two procedures are deadlocking, make sure they lock the resource in the same order.

✦ Make sure client applications are fetching the data and releasing any locks immediately.

✦ Examine the clustered index and fix any hot spots.

✦ Make sure any `select` statement that can be written with a (`nolocks`) hint uses the hint.

✦ Consider forcing page locks with the (`rowlock`) hint to prevent the locks from escalating.

# Summary

Performance is the aggregate of accuracy, availability, and speed. The best way to test accuracy is with a scenario test. The primary cause of database speed is set-based queries that access well-designed indexes. Avoid using code that iterates through the data row-by-row because it is the slowest possible method. The Performance Analyzer provides an overview of performance issues while the SQL Profiler gathers information about specific problems. Indexes bridge queries to data and are a fluid means of tuning performance. After the base indexes are manually built, the Index Tuning wizard can assist with index tuning.

The next chapter continues the discussion of performance with strategies to improve database availability.

✦     ✦     ✦

# Advanced Availability

The *availability* of a database refers to the overall reliability of the system. A database that's highly available is one that never goes down. For some databases, being down for an hour is not a problem; for others, 30 seconds of downtime is a catastrophe. It all depends on the organization's requirements.

A plan for maintaining availability is planned and executed at three distinct cascading levels:

1. Keeping the primary database available

2. Providing a near-instant substitute, or secondary, database

3. Recovering from a lost database

Several methods of increasing availability are unrelated to SQL Server proper. The quality and redundancy of the hardware, the quality of the electrical power, preventive maintenance of the machines and replacement of the hard drives, the security of the server room — all of these contribute to the availability of the primary database. The first line of availability defense is quality hardware.

 **Cross-Reference** Chapter 3, "Installing and Configuring SQL Server," covers selecting hardware and various RAID disk subsystems.

If a database is lost because of hardware failure, the third level of availability is executed and the database must be recovered according to the methods detailed in Chapter 26, "Recovery Planning." Even in the best of circumstances, recovering a database requires several minutes to an hour, and a more likely scenario is a half-day to build up a server and recover the data. Moreover, some data might be lost, depending on the recovery plan.

Advanced availability, the ability to handle a failure and switch to another server, is the layer between quality hardware and a last-resort recovery operation, and is often the difference between several hours of downtime and a few seconds.

**Best Practice**

Before implementing the middle layer of advanced availability, be sure the first layer is covered and the recovery planning is complete. Money spent on log shipping, if the primary computer's drives provide no redundancy, is wasted money.

SQL Server provides two options for advanced availability: log shipping and failover clustering.

**Cross-Reference**

Some IT shops have implemented transactional replication to keep a backup server in sync with the primary server. The advantage of this method is that each transaction is individually moved to the backup server, but at a performance cost. Replication is covered in Chapter 20, "Replicating Databases."

# Warm-Standby Availability

Log shipping involves periodically restoring a transaction log backup from the primary server to a warm-standby server, making that server ready to recover at a moment's notice. In case of a failure the recovery server and the most recent transaction-log backups are ready to go. Because of this, log shipping can be implemented without any exotic hardware and is significantly cheaper and simpler than a failover-cluster recovery plan. However, log shipping has a few drawbacks:

✦ When the primary server fails, any transactions made since the last time the log was shipped to the warm-standby server will be lost. For this reason, log shipping is usually set to occur every few minutes.

✦ The switch is not transparent. Some code must be executed at the warm-standby server, and any front-end-application connections must connect to the warm standby server and then continue. Sample code is provided later in this chapter.

✦ A DTS job must be created and periodically run to move user logins from the primary server to the warm-standby server.

✦ Once the primary server is repaired, returning to the original configuration requires manual DBA work.

If these issues are acceptable, log shipping to a warm-standby server is an excellent safeguard against downtime.

Keeping a warm-standby server populated with the correct backups can be tricky if things get out of order. The Enterprise Edition of SQL Server includes a wizard to set up the backup, copy the backup, and the process necessary to restore the backup. Alternately, the same process can be programmed with scripts and scheduled as a normal SQL Server Agent job.

The primary server and the warm-standby server should ideally be in different locations so that a disaster in one location will not affect the other. Also, log shipping can place a large demand on a network every few minutes. If the two servers can be connected with a private high-speed network, log shipping can take place without affecting other network users and the bandwidth they require. This private network connection would ideally be a SONET (Synchronous Optical Network) ring, which would provide the high bandwidth requirements imposed by very large databases, as well as adding redundancy to the connection.

# Log Shipping with Enterprise Edition

The high-end edition of SQL Server includes a Log Shipping Wizard (integrated into the Database Maintenance Plan Wizard) that creates a maintenance plan to back up, copy, and restore the transaction log from the primary server to the warm-standby server every few minutes.

## The Servers

Log shipping involves three SQL Servers: a primary server, a warm-standby server, and a monitor server.

✦ The *primary server* is the main server to which clients normally connect. This server should be a high-quality server with redundant disk drives.

✦ The *warm-standby server* is the backup server. If the source server fails, it becomes the primary server. This server should be capable of meeting the minimum performance requirements during a short-term crisis. Typically the performance capabilities of the warm-standby server are less than half that of the primary or source server, although the disk-drive capacity must be sufficient to hold the same amount of data.

✦ The *monitor server* polls both the primary server and the warm-standby server, generating an alert if the two are out of sync.

SQL Server 2000 allows multiple instances of a SQL Server to run on a single physical server, so while it would be foolish to locate the source and destination servers on the same physical server, it's possible for testing and learning about log shipping.

The monitor server can be an instance on the destination server, but locating the monitor server on the source server would be a self-defeating plan. If the source server physically failed, the monitor server would also fail and the destination server would not receive a signal to go live. If the monitor server is co-located on the destination server, no performance impact occurs during normal operation and minimal impact occurs during warm-standby operation.

Each primary-server database can have only one log-shipping plan, and each plan can ship only one database. However, a plan may ship to multiple destination servers.

## Configuring Log Shipping with Enterprise Manager

To assist in the configuration of log shipping, SQL Server provides a Log Shipping Wizard, located inside the Database Maintenance Wizard. The Database Maintenance Wizard is in the list of wizards available from the Wizard button in the Enterprise Manager toolbar. The wizard includes several steps:

1. The first page of the Database Maintenance Wizard presents a list of local databases that will use the maintenance plan. If only one eligible database is selected, a checkbox enables you to select the Log Shipping Wizard. Be sure to check the box or the log shipping pages or the wizard will not be available.

2. Skip past the data-optimization, database-integrity, backup-plan, backup–disk directory, and transaction-log backup disk–directory pages.

**Best Practice**

Keep the log-shipping maintenance plan separate from the standard database-maintenance plan. This will make scheduling and tracking the two plans easier and reduce problems later.

3. In the Transaction Log Share page, enter the network share that will be used to hold the transaction-log backups. The share location must be available to the warm-standby server. It will receive the backup files by copying them from this share.

4. Press the Add button to add a warm-standby server. The log-shipping destination page is used to specify the warm-standby server. Multiple warm-standby servers can be configured with the wizard.

5. Configure the warm-standby server in the Add Destination Database dialog box as seen here in Figure 29-1. The key portions of the dialog are the "Server Name," "Database name," "For data," and "For log" fields.

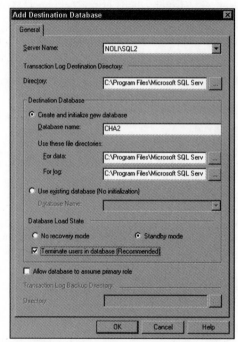

**Figure 29-1:** The warm-standby server, database, and log-shipping options are set in the Add Destination Database dialog box.

The Database Load State determines if the transaction log is restored with no recovery mode or with standby mode. The No recovery option leaves the database in a non-operational state. Enterprise Manager will show the database as "loading." Standby mode means that the transaction log is prepared enough for the database to be read but not modified. The section, "Configuring a Read-Only Standby Query Server," later in this chapter also discusses standby mode.

**Best Practice**

It's important to select the "Terminate users in database" option, especially if the warm standby server is in standby mode. If a user is in the standby database, the transaction-log restore will fail and the log shipping will get out of sync.

6. Log shipping is easier to implement if the wizard initially creates the database on the warm-standby server. This helps to ensure that the process starts in sync. The Initialize Destination Database page configures the wizard to use an existing backup or to make its own. We recommend letting the wizard create a backup.

7. The scheduling options shown in Figure 29-2 include:

- *Backup schedule* — The frequency of the transaction-log backup on the primary server. This schedule is created with the incredibly flexible SQL Server Agent scheduler.

- *Copy/load frequency* — How often the wizard's code will move the backup file to the warm-standby server.

- *Load delay* — A set delay between the transaction-log backup and restore, which acts as a safety buffer between the primary server and the warm-standby server.

- *File retention period* — How long to keep old transaction logs on the disk for archival purposes.

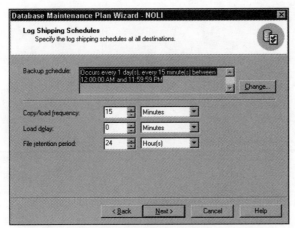

**Figure 29-2:** The log-shipping backup and handling schedule is created in the Log Shipping Wizard.

8. The alert threshold determines how far the warm-standby server can fall behind the primary server's live data before it issues an alert. The backup threshold ensures the primary server is performing its backups, and the out-of-sync threshold is in place to keep a watchful eye on the warm standby's restore process.

9. The final log-shipping portion of the Database Maintenance Plan Wizard identifies the monitor server. It should either be a third server or the warm-standby server, but definitely not the primary server.

10. In the summary page, be sure to name the maintenance plan.

To remove database-maintenance-plan log shipping, open the Maintenance Plan properties and remove Log Shipping using the Log Shipping tab.

## Monitoring Log Shipping

Once log shipping is running, a new node is available under the management node in the Enterprise Manager console tree, under the SQL Server configured as the monitor. The Log Shipping Monitor node lists all log-shipping pairs being monitored by that SQL Server, as shown in Figure 29-3.

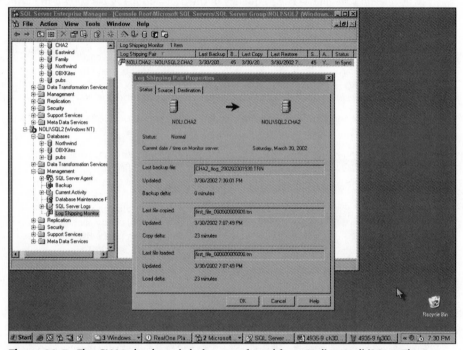

**Figure 29-3:** The CHA2 database is being transferred from Noli to Noli/SQL2. The Log Shipping Properties window displays the status of and information about the last log shipment.

For each log shipment listed, the Action menu (and context menu) include access to the following:

- ✦ A complete list of all backups
- ✦ A complete list of all transaction-log copies and loads
- ✦ The log-shipping pair properties, including the source server, destination server, and status (the details can be edited here as well)

## Switching Roles

The log-shipping method is heavily based on several system stored procedures and system tables. As the log-shipping environment changes, the roles may need to be changed. The roles of the servers can be swapped by means of the following system stored procedures. With these procedures the primary server becomes the warm-standby server, and the warm-standby server becomes the primary server:

- `sp_change_primary_role` — Run on the current primary server to remove the server from its log-shipping role.

- `sp_change_secondary_role` — Run on the current warm-standby server to upgrade it to the primary server.

- `sp_change_monitor_role` — Run on the monitor server to reconfigure it to monitor the new primary — warm-standby servers.

- `sp_resolve_logins` — Run on the new primary server to ensure that the logins are correct.

Each of these stored procedures has several parameters that must be carefully set. Ideally, they should be pre-configured and tested in a stored procedure so that change will be easy during a stressful time.

# Log Shipping with SQL Server Agent

A warm-standby server is still possible without the Enterprise Edition of SQL Server, because log shipping is really nothing more than backing up the transaction log, copying it to the warm-standby server, and restoring it with no recovery. With a little work, a SQL Server Agent job can be configured to perform these three tasks in sequence every five minutes.

**Best Practice**

The wizard does an excellent job of configuring a maintenance plan to perform and monitor the log shipping. But if you're willing to figure out the code necessary for shipping the log, you can bypass the Enterprise Edition and save the difference in cost between the Standard Edition and the Enterprise Edition. On a quad CPU server, that's $60,000.

As with the Enterprise Edition Log Shipping Wizard, a shared directory on the primary server serves as a common area for passing backup files.

## The Initialize Stored Procedures

The first step is to move a current copy of the primary database to the warm-standby server. The following stored procedures on the primary server and the warm-standby server cooperate to perform the backup to network share and restore the data to the warm-standby server.

The first stored procedure must be created locally on the warm-standby server. The stored procedure on the primary server will call this stored procedure to restore the database. The move option specifies the location on the warm-standby server for the files:

```
CREATE PROCEDURE LogShipInitializeReceive
AS
SET NoCount ON
RESTORE DATABASE CHA2
  FROM DISK = '\\Noli\LogShipping\CHA2Initilze.bak'
  WITH
    FILE = 1,
    NORECOVERY,
    MOVE 'CHA2' TO 'c:\SQL2\CHA2.mdf',
    MOVE 'CHA2_log' TO 'c:\SQL2\CHA2.ldf'
```

With the warm-standby server's stored procedure ready to receive the backup, the LogShipInitialze stored procedure can be created and run on the primary server. The LogShipInitializeReceive stored procedure is called from the primary server by means of the four-part name:

```
CREATE PROCEDURE LogShipInitialze
AS
SET NoCount ON
Print 'Backing up Primary Server'
BACKUP DATABASE CHA2
  TO DISK = 'c:\LogShipping\CHA2Initilze.bak'
  WITH
    NAME = 'CHA2Initilze',
    INIT
PRINT '----- '
Print 'Restoring Warm Standby Server'
EXEC [NOLI\SQL2].Master.dbo.LogShipInitializeReceive
```

To initialize the log shipping, execute the stored procedure on the primary server:

```
EXEC LogShipInitialze
```

Result:

```
Backing up Primary Server
Processed 160 pages for database 'CHA2',
  file 'CHA2' on file 1.
Processed 1 pages for database 'CHA2',
  file 'CHA2_log' on file 1.
BACKUP DATABASE successfully
  processed 161 pages in 0.433 seconds (3.029 MB/sec).
-----
Restoring Warm Standby Server
RESTORE DATABASE successfully
  processed 161 pages in 0.714 seconds (1.837 MB/sec).
Processed 1 pages for database 'CHA2',
  file 'CHA2_log' on file 1.
Processed 160 pages for database 'CHA2',
  file 'CHA2' on file 1.
```

At this point, the bulk of the data has been moved and the database on the warm-standby server is ready to receive subsequent transaction-log backups. The database is currently in a "loading" state and cannot be viewed.

## The LogShipJob Stored Procedures

The actual log shipping is handled by the two stored procedures that are executed by a SQL Server agent job every five minutes.

As with the initialization stored procedures, the first stored procedure is created on the warm-standby server; it receives the transaction-log backup. The restore uses the with norecovery option so that the database is left in a state ready to accept additional restores:

```
CREATE PROCEDURE LogShipJobReceive
AS
SET NoCount ON
```

```
RESTORE LOG CHA2
  FROM DISK = '\\Noli\LogShipping\CHA2Job.bak'
  WITH
    FILE = 1,
    NORECOVERY,
    MOVE 'CHA2' TO 'c:\SQL2\CHA2.mdf',
    MOVE 'CHA2_log' TO 'c:\SQL2\CHA2.ldf'
```

**Cross-Reference**  For more details on the transaction log and how it can be restored, refer to Chapter 26, "Recovery Planning."

On the primary server, the following stored procedure performs the transaction-log backup and calls the restore on the warm-standby server:

```
USE CHA2
go
CREATE PROCEDURE LogShipJob
AS
SET NoCount ON
Print 'Log Ship from Primary Server'
BACKUP LOG CHA2
  TO DISK = 'c:\LogShipping\CHA2Job.bak'
  WITH
    NAME = 'CHA2Log',
    INIT
PRINT '----- '
Print 'Receiving Log Ship on Warm Standby Server'
EXEC [NOLI\SQL2].Master.dbo.LogShipJobReceive
```

## Creating a SQL Server Agent Job

To ship the log every *n* minutes, configure a SQL Server Agent job with one step that executes the stored LogShipJob procedure, as shown in Figure 29-4.

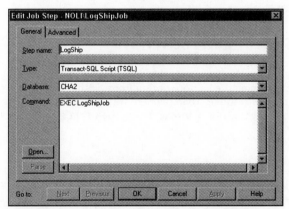

**Figure 29-4:** A SQL Server Agent job executes the LogShipJob stored procedure every five minutes.

While creating SQL Server Agent jobs in Enterprise Manager is definitely easier than using a script, a script has the benefit of being reusable without there being any chance of deviation. The following code also creates the SQL Server Agent job:

```
EXEC msdb.dbo.sp_add_job
  @Job_Name = 'LogShip_CHA2',
  @Enabled = 1,
  @Owner_login_name = 'NOLI\SQL',
  @Description = 'log shipping with stored procedures'

EXEC msdb.dbo.sp_add_jobstep
  @Job_Name = 'LogShip_CHA2',
  @SubSystem = 'TSQL',
  @Step_Name = 'LogShip',
  @Database_Name = 'CHA2',
  @Retry_Attempts = 3,
  @Command = 'EXEC LogShipJob'

EXEC msdb.dbo.sp_add_JobSchedule
  @Job_Name = 'LogShip_CHA2',
  @Name = 'FiveMin',
  @freq_type = 4,    -- Daily
  @freq_interval = 1,
  @freq_subday_type = 0x4,   -- minutes
  @freq_subday_interval = 5 -- every 5 min

EXEC msdb.dbo.sp_add_jobserver
  @Job_Name = 'LogShip_CHA2',
  @server_name = N'(local)'
```

In addition to setting up the SQL Server Agent job, a SQL Server Agent operator should be created so the job can e-mail the operator if the job fails.

**Cross-Reference** For more information on creating SQL Server Agent jobs, see Chapter 25, "Automating Database Maintenance with SQL Server Agent."

## Configuring a Read-Only Standby Query Server

As an additional benefit of using a warm-standby server, the restored data on the server can be configured so that it's available for read-only queries; this enables you to offload some of the work from the primary server. Changing the Restore option from "with no recovery" to "with standby" sets the server to read-only mode. To implement this type of log shipping, the norecovery line in the LogShipJobReceive stored procedure on the warm standby server should be changed to the following:

```
STANDBY = 'c:\SQL2\CHA2.sby',
```

Using the warm-standby server as a query server can be problematic. A restore operation requires exclusive use of the database and both the log-shipping and go-live procedures must execute a restore command. If any users are connected to the warm-standby database (assuming it's being used as a read-only query server) the restore will fail.

If the warm-standby server is used as a query server, the only option is to automatically terminate all user connections prior to the restore command. The following code can be used to kill all non-system spids.

```
create procedure sp_kill_spids
as

set nocount on

create table #connection_processes(
    spid    int           null
, usernm varchar (1000) null
, db      varchar (1000) null
, status varchar (1000) null
, cmd     nchar    (0016) null
)

insert into #connection_processes (spid, usernm, db, status,cmd)
select    p.spid,
          case when p.spid > 6
               then convert(sysname, ISNULL(suser_sname(p.sid),
rtrim(p.nt_domain) + '\' + rtrim(p.nt_username)))
               else 'system'
          end,
          case when p.dbid = 0
               then 'no database context'
               else db_name(p.dbid)
          end,
          p.status,
          cmd
from      master.dbo.sysprocesses p with (NOLOCK)
order by p.spid

declare 'id int, @usernm varchar (1000), @print varchar(1000), @sql
varchar(1000), @cmd nchar(0016)
select 'id = max(spid) from #connection_processes
select @cmd = cmd from #connection_processes where spid = 'id
while 'id is not null
begin
  select @usernm = usernm from #connection_processes where spid = 'id
  if lower(@usernm) <> 'system' -- we ignore all system processes
  OR @cmd not in ('AWAITING COMMAND','CHECKPOINT SLEEP','LAZY
WRITER','LOCK
MONITOR','SELECT','SIGNAL HANDLER')
    begin
     if 'id <> 'id
       begin
        select @sql = 'KILL '+convert(varchar(20), 'id)
        execute(@sql)
       end
    end
  select 'id = max(spid) from #connection_processes where spid < 'id
end
drop table #connection_processes
GO
```

## Shipping the Users

Neither the Log Shipping Wizard nor the stored procedures synchronize the server logins between the primary server and the warm-standby server. If the warm-standby server becomes the current live server, but no one can log in, it will be the same to the users as if the server were down. It's important, therefore, to move the user logins from the primary server to the warm-standby server. The best way to do that is to create a DTS job that connects to each server and transfers the users. If you are routinely adding several users, you may want to schedule this job to run several times per day, otherwise once daily should suffice.

Chapter 19, "Migrating Data with DTS," includes information about creating and scheduling a DTS package.

## Detecting and Handling a Crash

The primary issue with log shipping is that the switch from the primary server to the warm-standby server is normally manually executed by a human DBA. However, if an object is used to manage the connection, the object can serve two vital purposes:

✦ The object can detect a timeout situation on the primary server, attempt to query the server again to be sure, and, if the primary server's database is in fact unavailable, initiate the StandbyGoLive stored procedure.

✦ The object can drop all current connections and redirect all new connections to the warm-standby server.

## Going Live on the Warm-Standby Server

If the primary server goes down, the warm-standby server has to be brought on line. The procedure is the same whether the log was shipped by the Log Shipping Wizard or by SQL Server Agent and stored procedures.

On the warm-standby server, restoring the database with the with recovery option rolls back any uncommitted transactions in the transaction log and makes the database available for data modification.

```
CREATE PROCEDURE StandbyGoLive
AS
RESTORE DATABASE CHA2 WITH RECOVERY
```

On the off chance that the database file is unavailable, but the transaction log is intact, the LogShipJob should run one last time to pick up any last transactions. If the primary server is completely gone, any transactions that were committed after the last LogShipJob was run will be lost.

If the primary server is no longer running, the SQL Server Agent job is probably no longer running as well. It should be disabled. However, any attempt to restore a transaction log to a database that's been restored with the with recovery option will result in an error, so the restore won't harm the warm-standby server's database.

If the database uses full-text searches, the warm-standby server will have to also run a stored procedure after the restore to create and populate a full-text search catalog. Chapter 8, "Searching Full-Text Indexes," includes sample scripts to perform these functions.

## Returning to the Original Primary Server

Once the primary server has been repaired and is ready to return to service, the following steps reinitialize the primary server during a period when users are not connected:

1. Use DTS to move all the user logins from the warm-standby server to the primary server.

2. Transfer the database from the warm-standby server to the primary server using either a full backup and restore or a detach and attach.

# Failover Servers and Clustering

A more sophisticated high-availability recovery method is to implement failover servers and clustering. The cluster allows several servers to appear as a single virtual SQL Server. The user connects to the virtual SQL Server and is unaware of which physical server is processing the request.

A SQL Server cluster is not a Network Load Balancing cluster, which provides scalability for Web servers. SQL Server clusters provide backup availability, not scalability. Clusters do not balance the SQL load.

This method requires Windows 2000 clusters and a shared disk subsystem. Each server requires a connection (usually SCSI or optical) to the shared disk subsystem. Since both servers can see the same disk subsystem, in effect they share the same transaction log and data file. The cluster also uses a high-speed network dedicated to the clustering servers (usually optical), which serves as the heartbeat. Hardware manufacturers make specific models and configurations for clustering, and an OEM (Original Equipment Manufacturer)-specific version of Windows 2000 Server must be purchased with the hardware. Using failover servers and clustering costs several times more than using a warm-standby server.

Each server in the cluster may be active or passive. An active/passive cluster is referred to as a *single-instance cluster*. A cluster with multiple active servers (one database per server) is a *multiple-instance cluster*. If an active server fails, a designated passive server automatically becomes active and takes over from the shared transaction log and data file. From the user's perspective the switch is transparent.

**Best Practice**

If you are planning to implement failover clusters, we recommend the SQL Server 2000 Resource Kit, which contains five chapters on high availability; it's also a good idea to read as many white papers as possible from your hardware vendor. A visit to an IT shop running clustering using the proposed equipment would be time well spent. If your hardware vendor won't supply a list of suitable referral sites, keep shopping.

# Summary

Availability is paramount to the success of most database projects. Log shipping and failover clusters are both high-end techniques to provide a stable database environment for the users.

Log shipping backs up the log every few minutes and restores it on the warm-standby server with a no restore option so the warm-standby server is ready to go live at a moment's notice.

Failover clusters configure multiple servers that share a single disk subsystem into a single virtual server to provide a seamless switch from one physical server to another in case of a server fault.

A cousin to availability is scalability—the ability of a server to handle increasing numbers of users and data. The next chapter provides a framework for understanding scalability and practical techniques to improve the scalability of your projects.

✦     ✦     ✦

# Advanced Scalability

Scalability is related to performance, but specifically scalability refers to the database's ability to survive increasing capacity. Most (but not all) databases will perform well with a handful of users accessing a mere 50MB of data within a database. If the database still performs well with hundreds of users accessing 100GB of data, it is beginning to scale well.

Scalability is a team concept. Even if the database is developed to scale, if the connection object, front-end application, network infrastructure, or reporting application fails to scale, the entire project will fail to scale.

If the database is expected to scale, the optimization guidelines presented in Chapter 28, "Advanced Performance," should already be in place. Beyond the database-optimization methods, SQL Server provides a few high-end techniques specifically intended to improve the scalability of a database. Assuming that the optimization techniques are already in place, this chapter focuses on advanced scalability, concluding with the pinnacle of scalability — federated databases.

## De-normalization Indexes

A popular technique to woo performance out of a database is to make a *de-normalized* copy of some of the data, in which data that's stored in five large tables, for example, is extracted and stored in a single wide table for faster reads. We did some extreme de-normalization on a project, replacing a query that had a couple of dozen joins with a single table, and reduced the search time from a couple of minutes to about a second. It was OK for that project because the data was read-only. When the queries go against live data, de-normalization can be a source of data-integrity problems.

Microsoft provides an alternate to de-normalizing the actual data. SQL Server's *indexed views* are actually clustered indexes storing a de-normalized set of data, as illustrated in Figure 30-1.

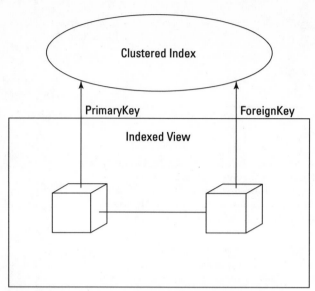

**Figure 30-1:** Indexed views create a bridge between two tables that might actuality be a dozen joins apart.

Instead of building tables to denormalize a join, a view can be created that can select the two primary keys from the joined tables. A clustered index created on the view stores the valid data from the primary-key and foreign-key pairs.

While a normal view only stores the SQL `select` statement and the data isn't materialized until the view is called, an indexed view stores a copy of the data in a clustered index. Clustered indexes merge the data page and the b-tree index leaf to store the actual data in the physical order of the index. The clustered index uses a view as a framework to define the columns to be stored.

Numerous restrictions on indexed views exist. Here are a few:

✦ The ANSI null and quoted identifier must be enabled when the view is created, and when any connection attempts to modify any data in the base tables.

✦ The index must be a unique clustered index; therefore, the view must produce a unique set of rows without using `distinct`. This can be a problem because situations that need de-normalizing include most many-to-many relationships, which tend to produce duplicate rows in the result set. For this reason, most indexed views only span one-to-many relationships.

✦ The tables in the view must be tables (not nested views) in the local database and must be referenced by means of the two-part name (*owner.table*).

✦ The view must be created with the option `with schema binding`.

As an example of an indexed view being used to de-normalize a large query, the following view selects data from the contact to product tables in the OBX Kites database:

```
USE OBXKites

SET ANSI_Nulls ON
SET ANSI_Padding ON
SET ANSI_Warnings ON
SET ArithAbort ON
SET Concat_Null_Yields_Null ON
SET Quoted_Identifier ON
SET Numeric_RoundAbort OFF

GO

CREATE VIEW vContactOrder
WITH SCHEMABINDING
AS
SELECT c.ContactID, o.OrderID
  FROM dbo.Contact as c
    JOIN dbo.[Order] as o
      ON c.ContactID = o.ContactID
  GO

CREATE UNIQUE CLUSTERED INDEX ivContactOrder ON vContactOrder
  (ContactID, OrderID)
```

## Indexed Views and Queries

When SQL Server's Query Optimizer develops the execution plan for a query, it includes the indexed view's clustered index as one of the indexes it can use for the query, even if the query doesn't explicitly reference the view.

This means that the indexed view's clustered index can serve as a covering index to speed queries. When the Query Optimizer selects the indexed view's clustered index, the query-execution plan indicates it with an index scan, as illustrated in Figure 30-2. The following query selects the same data as the Indexed view:

```
SELECT  Contact.ContactID, OrderID
  FROM dbo.Contact
    JOIN dbo.[Order]
      ON Contact.ContactID = [Order].ContactID
```

**Best Practice**

Just adding indexed views without fully analyzing how the queries use them will likely hurt performance more than it helps. Updating indexed views entails a serious performance hit, so avoid them for transactional databases. Carefully add them to databases used primarily for reporting, OLAP, or querying, by identifying specific joins that are impeding frequent queries and surgically inserting an indexed-view cluster index.

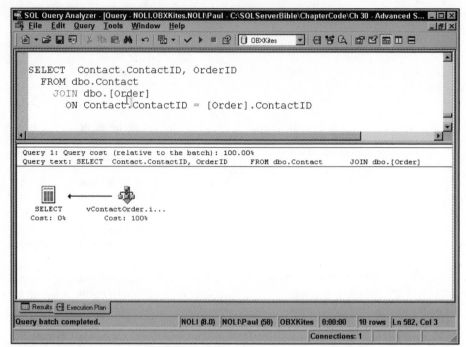

**Figure 30-2:** The query-execution plan performs a clustered index scan to retrieve the data instead of accessing the base tables.

### Updating Indexed Views

As with any de-normalized copy of the data, the difficulty is keeping the data current. Indexed views have the same issue. As data in the underlying base tables is updated, the indexed view must be keep in sync. This process is completely transparent to the user and is more of a performance consideration than a programmatic issue.

## Partitioned Tables

To *partition* a table is to split the table into two or more smaller segments based on a partition key. The partitions are most effective when the partition key is a column often used to select a range of data, so that a query has a good chance of addressing only one of the segments. For example,

✦ A company manages sales from five distinct sales offices; splitting the order table by sales region will enable each sales region's queries to likely access only that region's partition.

✦ A manufacturing company partitions a large activity-tracking table into several smaller tables, one for each department, knowing that each of the production applications tends to query a single department's data.

✦ A financial company has several hundred gigabytes of historical data and must be able to easily query across current and historical data. However, the majority of current activity deals with only the current data. Segmenting the data by era enables the current-activity queries to access a much smaller table.

In the access of data, the greatest bottleneck is reading the data from the drive. The primary benefit of partitioning tables is that a smaller partitioned table will have a greater percentage of the table cached in memory.

**Best Practice**

Very large, frequently accessed tables, with data that can logically be divided horizontally for the most common queries, are the best candidates for partitioning. If the table doesn't meet this criteria, don't partition the table.

With the data split into several partition tables, of course, it may be accessed by means of querying a single partition table. A more sophisticated and flexible approach is to access the whole set of data by querying a view that unites all the partition tables.

The SQL Server query processor is designed specifically to handle such a partitioned view. If a query accesses the union of all the partition tables, the query processor will only retrieve data from the required partition tables.

Data can be inserted directly into each individual partition table, rather than dealing with each partition as if it were one database. With SQL Server you also have the option of inserting the data into the correct partition table by passing the `insert` through a properly configured view that unites all the partition tables.

SQL Server supports two types of partition views: local and distributed. A *local-partition view* unites data from multiple local-partition tables. A *distributed-partition view*, also known as a *federated database*, spreads the partition tables across multiple servers and connects them using linked servers, and views that include distributed queries.

## Local-Partition Views

For a local-partition view to be configured, the following elements must be in place:

✦ The data must be segmented into multiple tables according to a single column, known as the *partition key*.

✦ Each partition table must have a check constraint restricting the partition-key data to a single value. SQL Server uses the check constraint to determine which tables are required by a query.

✦ The partition key must be part of the primary key.

✦ The partition view must include a union statement that pulls together data from all the partition tables.

### Segmenting the Data

To implement a partitioned-view design for a database and segment the data in a logical fashion, the first step is to move the data into the partitioned tables.

As an example, the `Order` and `OrderDetail` tables in the OBXKites sample database can be partitioned by sales location. In the sample database, the data breaks down as follows:

```
SELECT LocationCode, Count(OrderNumber) AS Count
  FROM Location
    JOIN [Order]
      ON [Order].LocationID = Location.LocationID
    GROUP BY LocationCode
```

Result:

```
LocationCode      Count
----------------- ---------
CH                6
JR                2
KH                2
```

To partition the sales data, the `Order` and `OrderDetail` tables will be split into a table for each location. The first portion of the script creates the partition tables. They differ from the original tables only in the primary-key definition, which becomes a composite primary key consisting of the original primary key and the `LocationCode`. In the `OrderDetail` table the `LocationCode` column is added so it can serve as the partition key, and the `OrderID` column foreign-key constraint points to the partition table.

The script then progresses to populating the tables from the non-partitioned tables. To select the correct `OrderDetail` rows, the table needs to be joined with the `OrderCH` table.

For brevity's sake, only the Cape Hatteras (CH) location is shown here, and is included on the book's CD. The script includes similar code for the Jockey Ridge and Kill Devil Hills locations. The differences between the partition table and the original tables, and the code that differs among the various partitions, are boldfaced:

```
--Order Table
CREATE TABLE dbo.OrderCH (
  LocationCode CHAR(5) NOT NULL,
  OrderID UNIQUEIDENTIFIER NOT NULL   -- Not PK
    ROWGUIDCOL DEFAULT (NEWID()),
  OrderNumber INT NOT NULL,
  ContactID UNIQUEIDENTIFIER NULL
    FOREIGN KEY REFERENCES dbo.Contact,
  OrderPriorityID UNIQUEIDENTIFIER NULL
    FOREIGN KEY REFERENCES dbo.OrderPriority,
  EmployeeID UNIQUEIDENTIFIER NULL
    FOREIGN KEY REFERENCES dbo.Contact,
  LocationID UNIQUEIDENTIFIER NOT NULL
    FOREIGN KEY REFERENCES dbo.Location,
  OrderDate DATETIME NOT NULL DEFAULT (GETDATE()),
  Closed BIT NOT NULL DEFAULT (0) -- set to true when Closed
    )
  ON [Primary]
go

  -- PK
```

```
ALTER TABLE dbo.OrderCH
  ADD CONSTRAINT
    PK_OrderCH PRIMARY KEY NONCLUSTERED
      (LocationCode, OrderID)

-- Check Constraint
ALTER TABLE dbo.OrderCH
  ADD CONSTRAINT
    OrderCH_PartitionCheck CHECK (LocationCode = 'CH')

go
-- Order Detail Table
CREATE TABLE dbo.OrderDetailCH (
  LocationCode CHAR(5) NOT NULL,
  OrderDetailID UNIQUEIDENTIFIER NOT NULL -- Not PK
    ROWGUIDCOL DEFAULT (NEWID()),
  OrderID UNIQUEIDENTIFIER NOT NULL, -- Not FK
  ProductID UNIQUEIDENTIFIER NULL
    FOREIGN KEY REFERENCES dbo.Product,
  NonStockProduct NVARCHAR(256),
  Quantity NUMERIC(7,2) NOT NULL,
  UnitPrice MONEY NOT NULL,
  ExtendedPrice AS Quantity * UnitPrice,
  ShipRequestDate DATETIME,
  ShipDate DATETIME,
  ShipComment NVARCHAR(256)
  )
  ON [Primary]
go

ALTER TABLE dbo.OrderDetailCH
  ADD CONSTRAINT
    FK_OrderDetailCH_Order
      FOREIGN KEY (LocationCode,OrderID)
      REFERENCES dbo.OrderCH(LocationCode,OrderID)

ALTER TABLE dbo.OrderDetailCH
  ADD CONSTRAINT
    PK_OrderDetailCH PRIMARY KEY NONCLUSTERED
      (LocationCode, OrderDetailID)

ALTER TABLE dbo.OrderDetailCH
  ADD CONSTRAINT
    OrderDetailCH_PartitionCheck CHECK (LocationCode = 'CH')

go

-- move the data
INSERT dbo.OrderCH (LocationCode,
    OrderID, OrderNumber, ContactID, OrderPriorityID,
    EmployeeID, LocationID, OrderDate, Closed)
```

```
SELECT
    'CH',
    OrderID, OrderNumber, ContactID, OrderPriorityID,
    EmployeeID, [Order].LocationID, OrderDate, Closed
  FROM [Order]
    JOIN Location
      ON [Order].LocationID = Location.LocationID
    WHERE LocationCode = 'CH'

INSERT dbo.OrderDetailCH (
    LocationCode, OrderDetailID, OrderID, ProductID,
    NonStockProduct, Quantity, UnitPrice, ShipRequestDate,
    ShipDate, ShipComment)
  SELECT 'CH',
    OrderDetailID, OrderDetail.OrderID,
    ProductID, NonStockProduct, Quantity, UnitPrice,
    ShipRequestDate, ShipDate, ShipComment
  FROM OrderDetail
    JOIN OrderCH
    ON OrderDetail.OrderID = OrderCH.OrderID
```

## Creating the Partition View

With the data split into valid partition tables that include the correct primary keys and constraints, SQL Server can access the correct partition table through a partition view. The OrderAll view uses a union all to vertically merge data from all three partition tables:

```
CREATE VIEW OrderAll
AS
  SELECT
      LocationCode,
      OrderID, OrderNumber, ContactID, OrderPriorityID,
      EmployeeID, LocationID, OrderDate, Closed
    FROM OrderCH
UNION ALL
  SELECT
      LocationCode,
      OrderID, OrderNumber, ContactID, OrderPriorityID,
      EmployeeID, LocationID, OrderDate, Closed
    FROM OrderJR
UNION ALL
  SELECT
      LocationCode,
      OrderID, OrderNumber, ContactID, OrderPriorityID,
      EmployeeID, LocationID, OrderDate, Closed
    FROM OrderKDH
```

## Selecting Through the Partition View

When all the data is selected from the OrderAll partition view, the query plan, shown in Figure 30-3, includes all three partition tables as expected:

```
SELECT LocationCode, OrderNumber
  FROM OrderAll
```

Result (abridged):

```
LocationCode OrderNumber
------------ -----------
CH           1
...
JR           4
JR           7
KDH          9
KDH          10
```

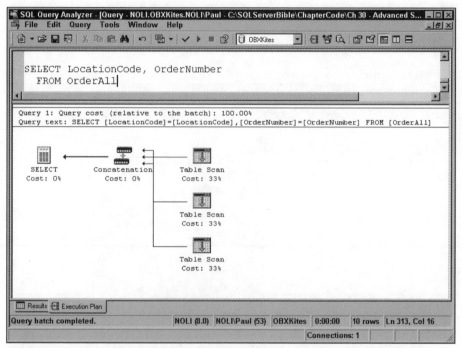

**Figure 30-3:** The partition table's query plan, when run without a where clause r
estriction, includes all the partition tables as a standard union query.

What makes partition views useful for advanced scalability is that the SQL Server query processor will use the partition tables' check constraints to access only the required tables if the
partition key is included in the where clause of the query calling the partition view.

The following query selects on the Kill Devil Hills orders from the partition view. The
LocationCode column is the partition key, so this query will be optimized for scalability.
Even though the view's union includes all three partition tables, the query-execution plan,
shown in Figure 30-4, reveals that the query processor accesses only the OrderCH
partition table:

```
SELECT OrderNumber
  FROM OrderAll
  WHERE LocationCode = 'KDH'
```

Result:

```
OrderNumber
-----------
9
10
```

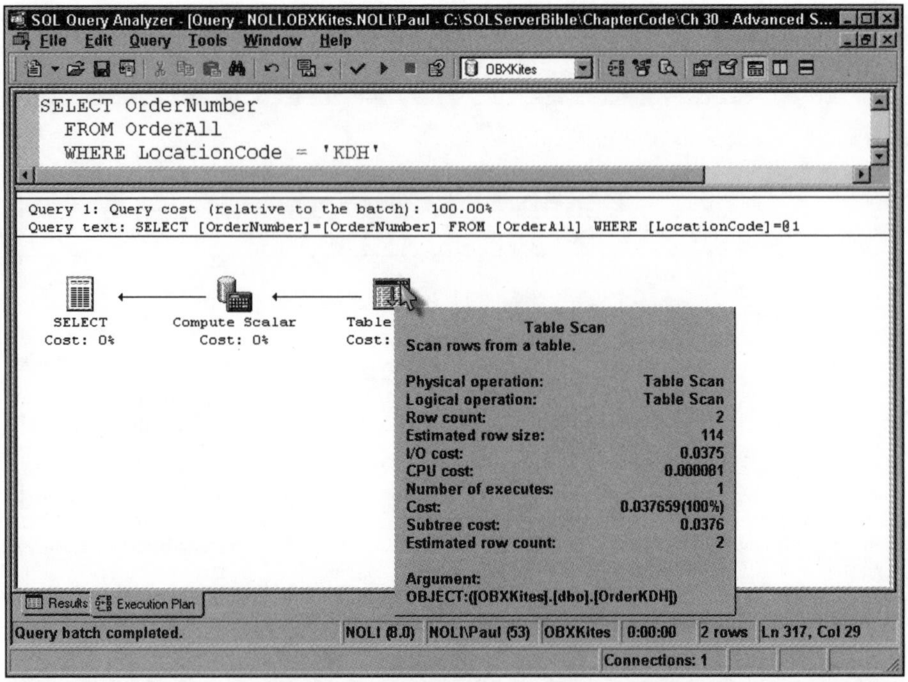

**Figure 30-4:** When a query with a where-clause restriction that includes the partition key retrieves data through the partition view, SQL Server's query processor accesses only the required tables.

## Updating Through the Partition View

Union queries are typically not updateable. Yet, the partition tables' check constraints enable a partition view based on a union query to be updated, as long as a few conditions are met:

✦ The partition view must include all the columns from the partition tables.

✦ The primary key must include the partition key.

✦ Partition-table columns, including the primary key, must be identical.

✦ Columns and tables must not be duplicated within the partition view.

The following `update` query demonstrates updating through the `OrderAll` view:

```
UPDATE OrderAll
  SET Closed = 0
  WHERE LocationCode = 'KDH'
```

Unfortunately, an `update` does not benefit from query optimization to the extent that a `select` does. For heavy transactional processing at the stored-procedure level, the code should access the correct partition table.

## Moving Data

An issue with local-partition views is that data is not easily moved from one partition table to another partition table. An `update` query that attempts to update the partition key violates the check constraint:

```
UPDATE OrderAll
  SET Locationcode = 'JR'
  WHERE OrderNumber = 9
```

Result:

```
Server: Msg 547, Level 16, State 1, Line 1
UPDATE statement conflicted with TABLE REFERENCE constraint
  'FK_OrderDetailKDH_Order'. The conflict occurred in
    database 'OBXKites', table 'OrderDetailKDH'.
The statement has been terminated.
```

For implementations that partition by region or department, moving data may not be an issue, but for partition schemes that divide the data into current and archive partitions, it is.

The only possible workaround is to write a stored procedure that inserts the rows to be moved into the new partition and then deletes them from the old partition. To complicate matters further, a query that inserts into the partition view cannot reference a partition table in the query, so an `insert..select` query won't work. A temporary table is required to facilitate the move:

```
CREATE PROCEDURE OrderMovePartition (
  @OrderNumber INT,
  @NewLocationCode CHAR(5) )
AS
SET NoCount ON

DECLARE @OldLocationCode CHAR(5)

SELECT @OldLocationCode = LocationCode
  FROM OrderAll
  WHERE OrderNumber = @OrderNumber

-- Insert New Order
  SELECT DISTINCT
      OrderID, OrderNumber, ContactID, OrderPriorityID,
      EmployeeID, LocationID, OrderDate, Closed
    INTO #OrderTemp
```

```
   FROM OrderAll
   WHERE OrderNumber = @OrderNumber
     AND LocationCode = @OldLocationCode

INSERT dbo.OrderAll (LocationCode,
    OrderID, OrderNumber, ContactID, OrderPriorityID,
    EmployeeID, LocationID, OrderDate, Closed)
  SELECT
      @NewLocationCode,
      OrderID, OrderNumber, ContactID, OrderPriorityID,
      EmployeeID, LocationID, OrderDate, Closed
    FROM #OrderTemp

-- Insert the New OrderDetail
  SELECT DISTINCT
      OrderDetailID, OrderDetailAll.OrderID,
      ProductID, NonStockProduct, Quantity, UnitPrice,
      ShipRequestDate, ShipDate, ShipComment
    INTO #TempOrderDetail
    FROM OrderDetailALL
      JOIN OrderALL
      ON OrderDetailALL.OrderID = OrderALL.OrderID
    WHERE OrderNumber = @OrderNumber

Select * from #TempOrderDetail

INSERT dbo.OrderDetailAll (
    LocationCode, OrderDetailID, OrderID, ProductID,
    NonStockProduct, Quantity, UnitPrice, ShipRequestDate,
    ShipDate, ShipComment)
  SELECT @NewLocationCode,
      OrderDetailID, OrderID,
      ProductID, NonStockProduct, Quantity, UnitPrice,
      ShipRequestDate, ShipDate, ShipComment
    FROM #TempOrderDetail

-- Delete the Old OrderDetail
DELETE FROM OrderDetailAll
  FROM OrderDetailAll
    JOIN OrderALL
      ON OrderAll.OrderID = OrderDetailAll.OrderID
    WHERE OrderNumber = @OrderNumber
      AND OrderDetailAll.LocationCode = @OldLocationCode

-- Delete the Old Order
DELETE FROM OrderALL
  WHERE OrderNumber = @OrderNumber
    AND LocationCode = @OldLocationCode
```

To test the stored procedure, the following batch moves order number 9 from the Kill Devils Hill store to the Jockey's Ridge location:

```
EXEC OrderMovePartition 9, 'JR'
```

To see the move, the following query reports the `LocationCode` from both the `OrderAll` and the `OrderDetailAll` tables:

```
Select
    OrderAll.OrderNumber,
    OrderALL.LocationCode as OrderL,
    OrderDetailALL.LocationCode AS DetailL
  FROM OrderDetailAll
    JOIN OrderAll
      ON OrderAll.OrderID = OrderDetailAll.OrderID
  WHERE OrderNumber = 9
```

Result:

```
OrderNumber OrderL DetailL
----------- ------ -------
9             JR     JR
9             JR     JR
9             JR     JR
```

## Distributed-Partition Views

Since partition views often segment data along natural geographic lines, it logically follows that a partition view that spans multiple servers is very useful. Distributed-partition views build upon local-partition views to unite data from segmented tables located on different servers. This technique is also referred to as a *federated-database configuration* because multiple individual components cooperate to complete the whole. This is how Microsoft gains those incredible performance benchmarks.

The basic concept is the same as that of a local-partition view, with a few differences:

✦ The participating servers must be configured as linked servers with each other.

✦ The distributed-partition view on each server is a little different from those of the other servers, because it must use distributed queries to access the other servers.

✦ Each server must be configured for lazy schema validation to prevent repeated requests for metadata information about the databases.

**Note** Turning on lazy schema validation means that SQL Server will not check remote tables for the proper schema until it has executed a script. This means if a remote table has changed, scripts dependant on that table will error out. Turning this feature on can have certain bad effects on scripts but does help increase performance.

The following script configures a quick distributed-partition view between `Noli` and `Noli\SQL2`. To save space, we list only the `Noli` half of the script. Similar code is also run on the second server to establish the distributed view. The script creates a database with a single table and inserts a single row. Once a link is established, and lazy schema validation is enabled, the distributed-partition view is created. This partition view is created with a four-part name to access the remote server. Selecting through the distributed-partition view retrieves data from both servers:

```
CREATE DATABASE DistView
go
USE DistView
```

```
CREATE TABLE dbo.Inventory(
  LocationCode CHAR(10) NOT NULL,
  ItemCode INT NOT NULL,
  Quantity INT )
ALTER TABLE dbo.Inventory
  ADD CONSTRAINT PK_Inventory
      PRIMARY KEY NONCLUSTERED(LocationCode, ItemCode)
ALTER TABLE dbo.Inventory
  ADD CONSTRAINT Inventory_PartitionCheck
      CHECK (LocationCode = 'Noli')

INSERT dbo.Inventory
  (LocationCode, ItemCode, Quantity)
  VALUES ('NOLI', 12, 1)

-- Link to the Second Server
EXEC sp_addlinkedserver
  @server = 'Noli\SQL2',
  @srvproduct = 'SQL Server'

EXEC sp_addlinkedsrvlogin
  @rmtsrvname = 'NOLI\SQL2'

-- Lazy Schema Validation
EXEC sp_serveroption 'Noli\SQL2',
  'lazy schema validation', true

-- Create the Distributed Partition View
CREATE VIEW InventoryAll
AS
  SELECT *
    FROM dbo.Inventory
UNION ALL
  SELECT *
    FROM [NOLI\SQL2].DistView.dbo.Inventory

SELECT *
  FROM InventoryAll
```

Result:

```
LocationCode ItemCode    Quantity
------------ ----------- -----------
NOLI         12          1
NOLI\SQL2    14          2
```

## Updating and Moving Data with Distributed-Partition Views

One fact that makes distributed-partition views an improvement over local-partition views is that a distributed-partition view can move data without complication. MS Distributed

Transaction Coordinator must be running and `xact_abort` enabled, because the transaction is a distributed transaction. This update query changes the `LocationCode` of the first server's row to `'Noli\SQL2'`, and effectively moves the row from `Noli` to `Noli\SQL2`:

```
SET XACT_ABORT ON
UPDATE InventoryAll
  SET LocationCode = 'Noli\SQL'
    WHERE Item = 12
```

To show you the effect of the update query, the next query selects from the distributed-partition view and demonstrates that item 14 is now located on `Noli`:

```
SELECT *
  FROM InventoryAll
```

Result:

```
LocationCode ItemCode    Quantity
------------ ----------- -----------
NOLI          12         1
NOLI          14         2
```

## Highly Scalable Distributed-Partition Views

SQL Server's query processor handles distributed-partition views much as it handles local-partition views. Where the local-partition view accesses only the required tables, a distributed-partition view will perform distributed queries and request the required data from the remote servers. Each server executes a portion of the query.

**Best Practice**

For maximum scalability in a multiple-server distributed environment, use a federated-database scheme. To execute an intelligent distributed query that generates smart pass-through queries and shares the query-execution work among multiple servers, be sure to include the partition key in the query's `where` clause.

In the following example, the query is being executed on `Noli`. A remote query request is sent to `Noli\SQL2` and the results are passed back to `Noli`. The query processor knows not to bother looking at the table on `Noli`, as shown in Figure 30-5. Even better, the query passes the row restriction to the remote server as well. `Noli\SQL2` has two rows, but only one is returned.

```
SELECT *
  FROM InventoryAll
    WHERE LocationCode = 'Noli\SQL2'
      AND Item = 14
```

Result:

```
LocationCode ItemCode    Quantity
------------ ----------- -----------
NOLI\SQL2     14         2
```

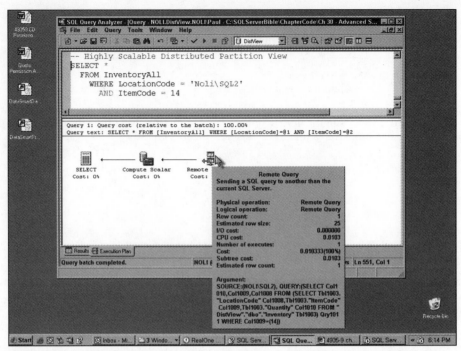

**Figure 30-5:** Noli\SQL2 executes a remote query and returns the requested data to Noli in an intelligent distributed-partition query.

## Summary

Not every database will have to scale to higher magnitudes of capacity, but when a project does grow into the hundreds of gigabytes, SQL Server provides some additional techniques with which to tackle the growth.

High-end scalability techniques are not a substitute for clean design and optimization. Once the database is optimized these techniques can be employed.

Indexed views provide a framework for a clustered index that can de-normalize data and serve as a covering index for queries.

A partition view horizontally segments the data into multiple smaller tables. A partition view is then used to recombine the segments into what appears to be a single table.

The SQL Server Query Optimizer can use the partition tables' check constraints to extract data from only the required tables.

A distributed-partition view, also known as a federated database, spreads the segments among multiple servers. Queries that access the view are transformed into intelligent pass-though queries in which each server performs a piece of the query.

The advanced topic in the next chapter deals with data anomalies — how to identify and track questionable data, and how to measure the data consistency in your database.

✦     ✦     ✦

# Analysis Services

U p to this point, this book has dealt with relational databases in SQL Server 2000. Analysis Services introduces a twist to the standard relational database that we have not yet addressed. While standard databases work well for Online Transaction Processing (OLTP) a standard database is not fast enough to support the types of queries and number crunching for end users that Analysis Services provides.

This chapter covers several terms that are used within Microsoft's Analysis Services. You will learn how to install Analysis Services and create cubes within Analysis Services, and, using Microsoft Excel, how to displays data generated using Analysis Services. While the points covered in this chapter will provide you with enough information to use the most popular features of Analysis Services, it does not cover every detail. For more information check the online documentation included with Analysis Services.

## What's Included with Analysis Services

Analysis Services provides the tools that you will need to generate detailed multidimensional reports. If you are coming from a relational-database background, it might be difficult to think of a report in more than two dimensions, but Analysis Services provides such an environment. Although this may sound rather complex, Microsoft has done a great job of hiding the ugly complexities by means of the wizards and the Analysis Manager MMC snap-in.

The major components of Analysis Services are:

+ *Multidimensional Database Engine* — As mentioned at the beginning of this chapter, a standard relational database does not provide enough flexibility to handle the load required for multidimensional reporting. This database stores data differently from a relational database. Each data item is stored at a coordinate, including data computed ahead of time. The coordinates are usually something more descriptive than the normal $x, y, z$ values — something more specific to the data.

+ *Analysis Manager* — Microsoft has continued using the Microsoft Management Console for systems management and has included a snap-in for Analysis Services. The Analysis Manager snap-in will give you enough flexibility to manage all of the tasks from within a single interface.

+ *Pivot Table Service* — A service that allows external applications to gain access to data stored within the cubes in Analysis Services.

Analysis Services is a product in itself. While it is included with Microsoft's SQL Server 2000, SQL Server is not required to use Analysis Services. Analysis Services will work fine against additional data sources such as Oracle and Access. In fact, the sample application that is installed with Analysis Service, FoodMart, uses Access as its own data source.

That's a look at Analysis Services from a high level. The next section addresses a standard procedure you might follow to actually analyze your data.

# The Process Needed to Analyze Data

Analysis Services functions under the assumption that you have created a data warehouse. Think of a data warehouse as a database that collects data over time. The data warehouse, because it is constantly collecting data over time, will grow even larger than its OLTP counterpart.

Usually the most complicated part of the Online Analytical Processing (OLAP) environment is scrubbing the data from one format in a relational database to the format that the data warehouse requires. Scrubbing data involves combining information from several tables into a single table or combining fields into a single field. This is not a one-time migration, either. To make your OLAP environment most useful this task must be done on an automated and scheduled basis. This is where Microsoft's Data Transformation Services (DTS) helps out.

**Note**    In discussions of data warehousing and Analysis Server, the term OLAP comes up frequently. Analysis Server is Microsoft's answer for Online Analytical Processing and was around long before Analysis Server was even thought of. OLAP databases differ from standard relational databases because they are designed to handle generalized queries looking up summarized data. OLAP databases also precalculate the data before it is requested. This produces fast results to queries.

Once the data has been moved to the data warehouse, Analysis Services can be used to create a cube for reporting. A cube contains precalculated values based on the data from the data warehouse. Analysis Services provides wizards and editors for creating cubes. The whole process is laid out in Figure 31-1.

**Figure 31-1:** The process the data will travel before finally being stored in a cube.

Analysis Services looks to the data warehouse as a data source. In particular, Analysis Services is looking for a fact table. A fact table is a standard table in a database but is made up of both dimensions and members, discussed later in this section. Table 31-1 shows how a fact table based on the Cape Hatteras Adventures database might look.

### Table 31-1: Cape Hatteras Adventures Fact Table

| CustomerID | EventID | Cost | EventDate |
|---|---|---|---|
| 4 | 1 | 365 | 3/19/2003 5:00:00 PM |
| 2 | 4 | 221 | 6/28/2002 6:00:00 AM |
| 1 | 4 | 497 | 1/7/2005 10:00:00 AM |
| 1 | 3 | 187 | 5/2/2002 10:30:00 AM |
| 2 | 2 | 592 | 3/23/2005 10:00:00 AM |
| 3 | 1 | 154 | 7/8/2004 8:30:00 AM |

This fact table represents tours and dates that the company has provided. It indicates which customers attended the tours on which dates and what the costs were. This table will continue to grow over time and would probably be loaded nightly, with the previous day's events. The EventID, CustomerID, and EventDate columns are dimensions. Cost is referred to as a measure. For each of the dimensions included in the fact table a corresponding dimension table will exist, providing additional information about the dimension. The dimension represented as a key is not very descriptive. The measure values are summed to provide additional information. In Table 31-1, Analysis Services could calculate that CustomerID 1 has generated 684 dollars' worth of revenue.

Based on the information in the fact table, Analysis Services can create reports for viewing for several different scenarios. Just based on the small amount of information found in Table 31-1, Analysis Services could break down sales based on customers, events, or even sales for different times of the year. To show what Analysis Manager can provide for a quick report based on a cube generated on data similar to Table 31-1, see Figure 31-2.

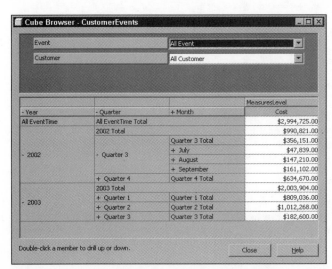

**Figure 31-2:** Analysis Manager provides a simple Cube Browser for looking at the details generated by Analysis Server.

While the topic of Analysis Manager will be covered later in the chapter, usually it's easiest to explain what it can do by showing an image. Figure 31-2 shows some of the detail that Analysis Services will let you drill down to. The formatting and summation that Analysis Services does would be very difficult to draw out of a standard relational database.

This section has covered some of the basics of Analysis Services and has shown you just a little of what it can do. The next section shows what it takes to install it onto your system so you can start generating multidimensional reports.

## Installing Analysis Services

The installation of Analysis Services is relatively easy. To start, you'll need your SQL Server 2000 installation CD handy. After inserting the CD you'll be prompted with the opening screen. If you are not prompted, you'll need to browse the CD and double-click `autorun.exe` at the root of the CD.

From the menu of options, choose to install SQL 2000 Server Components. Then click Install Analysis Services.

Click the Next button on the Welcome screen. This screen indicates that you should close all other open applications and that Analysis Services is protected under copyright law. After clicking Next, you are presented with a license agreement. If you agree with all of the verbiage in text box, click Yes to continue and see the screen shown in Figure 31-3.

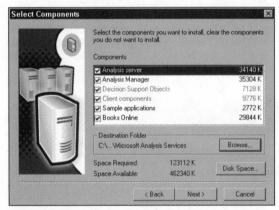

**Figure 31-3:** The Select Components setup screen enables you to select the components that you want installed with Analysis Services.

Check the appropriate boxes in Figure 31-3 to indicate the components you want installed. By default, all the options are checked. Leaving all of the options checked is a good option because the online help provides additional resources and the sample application is a good place to start exploring Analysis Services. Through this screen you are also able to indicate where you want the application installed and see how much disk space is available on the destination disk.

Click Next and you will be prompted with a screen that enables you to indicate where you want the data generated by Analysis Services to be stored.

**Best Practice**

By default, the setup application will install the data on the same physical disk as the application. You may want to consider storing the data on a disk array that may provide better fault tolerance and faster throughput, especially in a production environment. Doing this early on in the process will only help further down the road.

For testing purposes store the data in the default location.

After deciding where you want the data stored, click the Next button. The Select Program Folder setup screen enables you to indicate where in the Start menu you want the shortcut to the applications included with Analysis Services to be located. By default, the setup program places the applications in a folder underneath the Microsoft SQL Server program group.

Click the Next button to complete the installation. Once Analysis Services has been completely installed you should be able to click the Finish button.

After installing Analysis Services you are now ready to start processing cubes and interacting with the Analysis Server. The next section discusses how you can start creating cubes within Analysis Services based on the Cape Hatteras Adventures database.

**Note**

It's always good practice to keep SQL Server 2000 and Analysis Server at the current service packs. The service packs for both of the products can be downloaded at http://www. microsoft.com/sql. There is an issue when installing Analysis Services after installing a SQL Server 2000 service pack; the Microsoft Data Access Components (MDAC) and Analysis Server, for the most part, will stop functioning. To fix this problem you will need to reinstall the service pack after installing the Analysis Server.

# Creating and Browsing Cubes

The installation application for Analysis Services has made some substantial additions to your system. For starters, it has added MSSQLServerOLAPService to the list of available services located in the Control Panel Services applet.

This service is the core of Analysis Services and you interact with it via the Analysis Manager snap-in discussed in the following section.

## The Analysis Manager MMC Snap-in

Analysis Manager, included as the administration tool for Analysis Services, provides a single interface for common tasks pertaining to data processing. Analysis Manager comes in the form of an MMC snap-in just like Enterprise Manager included with Microsoft SQL Server 2000. If you are familiar with the Enterprise Manager snap-in, the Analysis Manager snap-in is easy to adjust to. Figure 31-4 shows what the snap-in looks like.

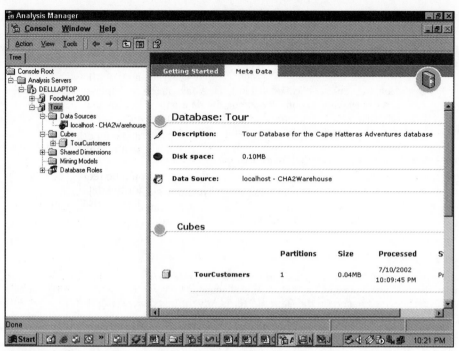

**Figure 31-4:** The Analysis Manager provides a unified interface with which to manage Analysis Services.

Figure 31-4 shows each of the components associated with Analysis Services. The root of the Analysis Manager tree is the Analysis Servers root node. From here you can add additional Analysis Servers, but currently the local server is the only server administered from the Manager. Within Analysis Manager, each of your applications is stored in a database. Figure 31-4 shows two databases: FoodMart 2000, the sample shipped with Analysis Services, and Tour, the example used throughout the rest of this chapter.

If you select a database, such as Tour in Figure 31-4, you can select the Meta Data tab in the details pane. This tab provides information about the Analysis Server database and about the cube data stored within the database. The information includes which data source and cubes are associated with the database, as well as when the cube was last processed and how much space the cube and database are using.

The database contains data sources, cubes, shared dimensions, mining models, and database roles, all discussed in the following sections.

## Data Sources

Analysis Services will look to a data source associated with the database where Analysis Services will draw its information. Usually, as discussed in the beginning of the chapter, the data will be drawn from a data warehouse. The warehouse is usually loaded on a schedule and then imported later into Analysis Services. In Figure 31-4, the data source is located on the local server and has been named CHA2Warehouse. This data source happens to point to a database stored within SQL Server. The data source can use either an OLE-DB provider or an ODBC driver to connect to the data source. The steps involved in creating a data source are detailed later in this chapter under the section titled "Creating your First Cube."

## Cubes

The cube in Analysis Services is where all of the pre-computed values are stored. In Figure 31-4, the cube has been named `TourCustomers`. The cube contains the dimensions and measures defined ahead of time. From within Analysis Manager you can process the cube based on the dimensions and measures specified. The cube can then be queried for values; response times should be very fast.

## Shared Dimensions

The dimensions that you create in the database can be shared among other cubes within the same database. This is convenient and saves you time because it means that it is not necessary to recreate a common dimension for each cube that you create in the database. For example, most cubes will incorporate time in some way. It would be tedious to recreate the same dimension for each cube. All of the shared dimensions for the database appear under Shared Dimensions folder. The topic of shared dimensions is further discussed later in the chapter in the section, "Creating your First Cube."

## Mining Models

As if providing multidimensional analysis weren't enough, Microsoft has also included a way to do predictive analysis. Although not discussed in the book, mining models enable you to perform predictive analysis based on data in the cube. A mining model looks at data in a cube and, based on input from the user, attempts to make assumptions about what the system sees.

## Database Roles

Database roles are the means by which security is implemented in Analysis Services. The permissions associated with roles can be very granular. The permissions are based on a Windows NT or 2000 account pulled from the Active Directory and can include individual users or groups — a big benefit, especially if you have groups predefined in your organization. You can grant them permission to specific cubes or even specific dimensions within the database.

This section has discussed the interface provided in the Analysis Manager. The next section will cover how you can create your own cube and test it to see what types of values you can calculate.

# Creating Your First Cube

As discussed in the previous section, in order to create a cube you need a database to hold all the associated information. For this example you will be creating the Tour database within the Analysis Manager. To get started you need to start up Analysis Manager by selecting it from the Analysis Services menu located under the Microsoft SQL Server menu or in the location that you indicated in the setup process.

Once the application is started you will need to create a database. You can do this by drilling down on the tree presented in the left pane within the MMC. Click the plus sign next to Analysis Services and then click the plus sign next to the Analysis Server running on your local system. You should see the FoodMart 2000 database, which was installed as an example database. For this example you'll be creating a new database called `Tour`. To do this, right-click the local server and select New Database, as shown in Figure 31-5.

**Figure 31-5:** The context menu used to create a new database from within Analysis Manager

After selecting New Database you will be presented with a dialog named Database, which asks you to enter a database name and a description. For this example, type in **Tour** as the database name, and **Tour Database for the Cape Hatteras Adventures Database** as a description. Once you have the values entered, click OK to continue. Analysis Manager has now created your Tour database and is ready to accept information for your first cube. By clicking on the plus symbol next to the Tour database you can see the five default objects within the database—the same five discussed in the previous section.

The next step would be to associate a data source with this database, but at this point there is no data warehouse to be associated. To fix this problem you'll need to have a basic understanding of schemas and then create your data warehouse within SQL Server.

## Star and Snowflake Schemas

The two major schemas when dealing with OLAP are star and snowflake. As it turns out, the snowflake schema is just a variation of the star schema but with one minor difference. In the next section I will discuss the differences between each of them and provide some best practice information for schema layout.

### Star Schema

A star schema contains a central fact table and the supporting dimension tables. The dimension tables describe the data within the central fact table. Dimension tables in a star schema are not normalized. If the example of regions of a country were used, country, region, state, and city would all be stored in a single table. As you might imagine, the state of California is going to be repeated for every city within California. This method can become expensive when it comes to disk space. When dealing with OLAP however, this is not such a bad scenario. Figure 31-6 shows what this layout might look like.

Star Schema Layout

| Country | Region | State | City |
|---------|--------|-------|------|
| US | West | CA | Los Angeles |
| US | West | CA | San Diego |
| US | West | CA | Sacramento |
| US | West | CA | Fresno |
| US | West | CA | Ventura |

**Figure 31-6:** The layout for a star schema contains information combined into a single table.

In Figure 31-6 all of the information appears to be run together. This data is de-normalized and contains repeating values. Currently Figure 31-6 shows only four cities in California. If all of the cities in the United States were to be included the value of "US" would be included for every one. The snowflake schema attempts to resolve this redundancy.

## Snowflake Schema

The snowflake schema differs from the star schema in one major area; it relies more heavily on relationships, much like a standard normalized database. In the previous example country, region, state and city would have all been stored in the same table. Because of this there will be duplication of data. To avoid this you could break the information out into individual tables, just like a standard relational database. Figure 31-7 shows what this layout might look like.

Snowflake Schema Layout

| Country | Region |
|---------|--------|
| US | North |
| US | South |
| US | East |
| US | West |

| Region | State |
|--------|-------|
| North | IN |
| South | TX |
| East | NY |
| West | CA |

| State | City |
|-------|------|
| CA | Los Angeles |
| CA | San Diego |
| CA | Sacramento |
| CA | Fresno |
| CA | Ventura |

**Figure 31-7:** The layout for a snowflake schema breaks the information into multiple tables for more efficient storage.

The layout in Figure 31-7 includes just three tables. The Country Region table contains all of the records needed to represent all four regions of the United States. The Region State table would include a total of 50 records for the entire United States. Finally the State City table would include all of the cities in the United States with its associated state. The State City table will include quite a bit less data than the star schema because it does not include repeating data. The tables would also include associated identity columns and would probably not repeat the actual values, but the identity values themselves.

**Best Practice**

In almost every case you will want to use the star schema. The star schema is easier to maintain and easier for Analysis Services to work with. The star schema has fewer links to navigate which means it will perform faster than the snowflake schema. The only reason that star schema may become a problem is if size becomes an issue. The amount of data that needs to be stored when using a star schema is considerably greater than that of the snowflake schema.

The rest of the chapter will concentrate on the star schema. In the next section you will actually create the data warehouse to store the data.

## Creating the Data Warehouse

For the next example, the database named CHA2Warehouse will include a total of three tables. The layout for the database is shown in Figure 31-8.

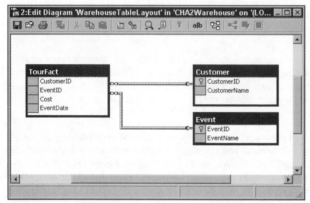

**Figure 31-8:** The layout of the data warehouse, which the data source from within the Tour database will point to.

**On the CD-ROM**

The script for creating the data warehouse in this chapter is on the CD and called CHA2Warehouse.sql. This script will create the three tables from Figure 31-11. You can also load data with scripts included on the CD. To load seven customers you can use the Customer.sql script. You can add 4 events by running the Event.sql script. Finally, you can load 15,000 events into the fact table by running the TourFactLoad.sql script. You can run these scripts from within SQL Query Analyzer.

As indicated at the beginning of this chapter, the fact table for this database is TourFact. Customer and Event are the dimension tables. The dimensions in the fact table are CustomerID, EventID, and EventDate. The single measure in the fact table is the Cost. The dimension tables provide additional information beyond the identity value. If you look at Figure 31-9 of the OLTP database you can see, with some data scrubbing, how the data would get from the OLTP database to the data warehouse.

The only piece of data that is missing from the database diagram in Figure 31-9 is the Cost. This piece of data we fabricated for the purpose of the example, but it would be a relatively easy piece of data to include in the layout of the OLTP database.

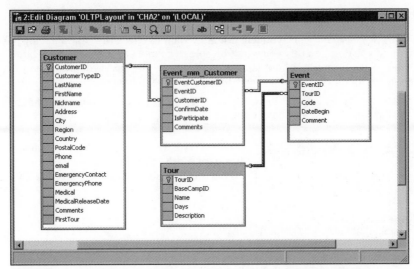

**Figure 31-9:** The layout for part of the Cape Hatteras Adventures OLTP database.

To get the data from the OLTP database to the data warehouse, the `FirstName` and `LastName` fields are merged into one and placed, along with the `CustomerID`, in the `Customer` dimension table. DTS would assist in migrating the data from the OLTP database, but in this example the data is already merged where it needs to be. Next, the `EventName` is actually pulled from the `Tour` table using the `Name` field. The `EventID` from the `Event` table in the OLTP database is also added to the `Event` table in the warehouse. These two tables make up the dimension tables in the data warehouse. The fact table is made up of both the `EventID` and the `CustomerID` and also gets the `EventDate` from the `Event` table in the OLTP database. Finally, the measure `Cost` could have been drawn from either the `Tour` or the `Event` table.

In a production environment DTS and SQL Server Agent working together could automate this process of data migration each night. This process would provide new data each day by using an additional field to keep track of when data was inserted. For the purposes of this example you can run the sample script, which will add 15,000 records to the table for processing in the cube.

Now that the data warehouse has been created, you can set the data source property in the Analysis Server database.

## Creating the Data Source

Microsoft has incorporated the Data Link Properties dialog into the Analysis Management MMC for configuring your data sources. This dialog box is shown in Figure 31-10.

The first tab in the dialog, called Provider, just requires that you select the appropriate OLE-DB Provider for the data source where your warehouse is located. You are not limited to only OLE-DB providers, because Microsoft supplies the OLE-DB provider for ODBC drivers. Using the OLE-DB provider for ODBC drivers, however, is a little slower than just using the native OLE-DB Provider, but sometimes a provider does not exist for your data source. For this example choose the Microsoft OLE-DB Provider for SQL Server. On the Connection tab, set the server name of your SQL Server, a user name, and a password (if you are not using Integrated Security). Also, indicate that you want to connect to the CHA2WareHouse database. If you are using SQL Server logins, you will probably want to check the "Allow saving password" option. (If you don't do this you won't be able to connect to the warehouse later in the example.) You will be prompted about storing an unencrypted password in the Analysis Services repository. After these values have been set, click OK to continue.

Now that the data source for the Tour database is set up, you can continue creating the cube based on the data warehouse you have created.

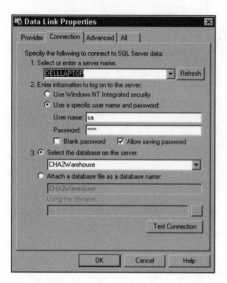

**Figure 31-10:** The Data Link Properties dialog box with which to configure the data source within the Analysis Services database.

## Creating the Cube and Shared Dimensions

This section shows you how to create a cube and the dimension inside the cube. Both are included in this section because Analysis Manager provides wizards to create both the cube and the dimensions.

To start the process you will need to right-click the Cubes folder within Analysis Manager under the Tour database and select New Cube ➪ Wizard. Microsoft also provides a manual cube editor, but the wizard will provide sufficient options for the purpose of this example.

The first screen of the wizard can be disregarded (you can even select the "Skip this screen in the future" option if you don't want to see it again). After clicking the Next button on the opening screen you will see the dialog box shown in Figure 31-11.

Analysis Manager has used the information from the data source to show the tables available in the warehouse. At this point the wizard wants to know which of the tables is the fact table. The fact table is the one titled TourFact. After you select TourFact the wizard displays all the fields within that table in the Details column on the right-hand side of the screen. At this point you can also browse the data within the table by clicking the Browse Data button. If you loaded the data using the scripts from earlier in the chapter, the Browse Data button will display the first 1,000 records. Click Next to continue.

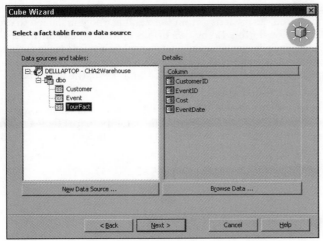

**Figure 31-11:** The first screen for setting up the cube for the Tour database under Analysis Manager.

Next, the wizard will want to know which of the fields from the fact table are the numeric measures. Note that the wizard only displays `CustomerID`, `EventID`, and `Cost`. The wizard knows that `EventDate` is a `datetime` data type and that it will be used later in the wizard. For this example use the `Cost` field as the numeric measure. Add it to the Cube Measure list box by clicking the > button. After the measure has been added the Cube Wizard should look like what is shown in Figure 31-12.

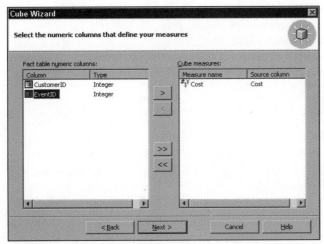

**Figure 31-12:** The Cube Wizard displays the measures that you have selected for the cube from the fact table.

After you click the Next button the Cube Wizard will want to create the dimensions for the cube. Currently there are no shared dimensions within the database so you'll need to create them by clicking the New Dimension button. Doing this brings up the Dimension Wizard. You can ignore the first screen and click the Next button. The wizard now wants to know how to create your dimension. Several options are available, including star shema, snowflake schema, parent-child, virtual model, and mining model. The simplest of the group is star schema, which you can select for this example. Click Next.

The wizard will now ask you which table is the dimension table for the dimension you are creating. Again the wizard is looking at your data source for the list of potential tables to draw from. In this step you can select the Customer dimension table, as shown in Figure 31-13.

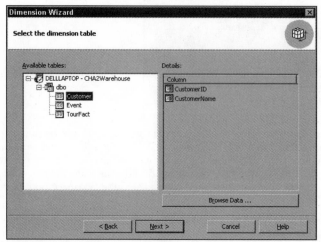

**Figure 31-13:** The Dimension Wizard wants to know which of the tables is a dimension table.

You are also able to view the data for the dimension table by clicking the Browse Data button. The wizard now wants to know about the dimensions within the dimension table. For this example there is only one dimension, CustomerName. In other scenarios you can add additional levels. Doing this would be especially useful if your levels broke down into, for example, region, state, and city, which would enable you to drill down and sort information based on any one of the three groups. If you eventually do add additional levels, you need to sort them from the most broad to the most granular: region, state, and city. Click Next.

The wizard will want to know which of the columns in the dimension table is the key column. You can use the dropdown menu to change the value from "dbo"."Customer". "CustomerName" to "dbo"."Customer"."CustomerID". Click Next two more times to skip the advanced options, and you should be ready to name the shared dimension (Figure 31-14).

The dialog box shown in Figure 31-14 enables you to browse the values of the new dimension and also to name the dimension. You can name the dimension Customer. The final step also enables you to share the dimension with other cubes within the database. (This option is selected by default and, as mentioned before, is a good option to have.) After you click Finish the dimension will be stored in the Shared Dimension folder in the Analysis Manger tree. Once you click Finish you are dropped back into the Cube Wizard. You can now add the Event dimension on your own, following the steps that you went through to create the Customer dimension. Use the EventName as the only level for the dimension and use "dbo"."Event"."EventID" as the member-key column. Finally, name the dimension Event in the last step of the wizard. After you click Finish you are placed back in the Cube Wizard again.

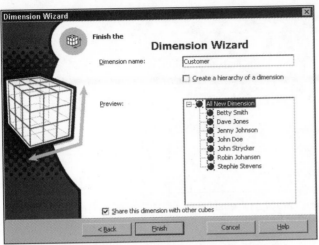

**Figure 31-14:** The final screen in the Dimension Wizard, in which it requests the name of the new dimension and displays the data from the newly created dimension.

This takes care of the two standard dimensions in the cube, but now you need to create a special dimension for time. Analysis Services provides special features for time, which makes it easy for you to break the levels down into years, quarters, months, days, and so forth. To add the Time dimension to the cube, click the New Dimension button, which will bring up the Dimension Wizard again. Skip the first screen and indicate that you want to create another star schema. Click Next and this time select the TourFact table as the dimension table. After you have selected the table the wizard will show the fields contained in the table and enable you to browse the data if you want. Once you click Next you will see a dialog that is a little different from the dialog used to create the previous two dimensions. Figure 31-15 shows that the wizard presents you with a different option.

After you select the Time dimension option, the only value you can select from the dropdown is EventDate. Click Next to continue. The next dialog box in the Dimension Wizard will enable you to specify how granular you want the data. The default selection is year, quarter, month, day, which is fine for this example. (You can experiment with different values if you wish.) This screen also enables you to decide when the year begins and provides an example of the dimension structure based on the type of level you have selected. Click Next twice to move beyond the advanced options onto the dialog that enables you to save your new dimension. Name your new dimension EventTime and click Finish. Once again you will be dropped back into the Cube Wizard; you have now defined all three of the dimensions for your new cube.

Click Next and you should be prompted with the Fact Table Row Count message box. This message box is indicating that the system will now count the rows in the fact table and that this might take some time. Click Yes and let it count them (it should not take very long). This is the last step in specifying the information that Analysis Services will need to create your cube. After the rows in the fact table have been counted you will see the last dialog of the Cube Wizard, which will ask you to name your cube and will display a summary of the data that you have provided in the Cube Wizard process. Name the cube CustomerEvents and click Finish.

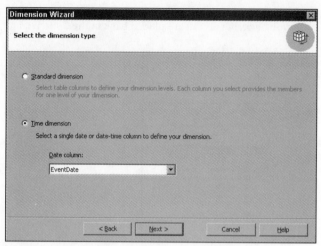

**Figure 31-15:** The Dimension Wizard now enables you to select a Time dimension because the dimension table has a data type of datetime.

This process has provided enough information for a cube to be built. The cube has not actually been processed, and you still have not indicated what type of storage you want to use. The wizard has now left you in the Cube Editor within the Analysis Manager. The Cube Editor is shown in Figure 31-16.

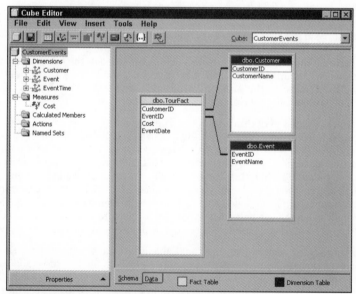

**Figure 31-16:** The Cube Editor provides an interface built by the values that you specify through the Cube Wizard. You can manually create cubes using the Cube Editor.

From here you can save the cube data by clicking the floppy-disk icon in the toolbar. Exit the Cube Editor by selecting Exit from the File menu. While trying to exit you will be prompted to design storage for the cube, which you must do before it can be queried. You can disregard this prompt by clicking No, and design storage from within the Analysis Manager.

After clicking the No button you will be dropped back into Analysis Manager with the new CustomerEvents cube. To use the cube you need to design the storage for it just as the Cube Editor was encouraging you to do when you exited the application. As you might expect, storage of the cube data plays an important part in the performance of the cube. The different types of storage and the process of setting the storage for your cube are discussed in the next section.

## Cube Storage

Three types of storage for your cube are available with Analysis Services: multidimensional OLAP, relational OLAP, and hybrid OLAP. The list below discusses the benefits and drawbacks of each of the storage types.

✦ *Multidimensional OLAP (MOLAP)* — Usually the best fit for most situations. The data is stored in the OLAP multidimensional database. This option provides good performance when compared to the other two storage options but does require more storage space.

✦ *Relational OLAP (ROLAP)* — The data is stored outside the OLAP database. This may degrade performance if the data is stored in the OLTP system for users interacting with the system while other users are running reports.

✦ *Hybrid OLAP (HOLAP)* — A combination of both MOLAP and ROLAP. The data is stored in the relational database, but the aggregations for the cubes are stored within the OLAP database.

In most cases it is best to use MOLAP for storage structure as long as disk space does not become a constraint.

To set the storage for the cube that you have created just right-click the CustomerEvents cube from within Analysis Manager and select Design Storage from the context menu. This will bring up the Storage Design Wizard. You can disregard the first dialog in the wizard by clicking Next. The Storage Design Wizard will now show you a simple screen, which will enable you to choose which storage type you want. For this example select MOLAP, the first option.

After you click Next, the wizard will ask how you want the aggregations calculated. You have three options here: One based on disk space available, one based on performance gains, and one for just stopping the process once you feel it has completed enough. For this example not many aggregations need to be calculated, so you can just leave the default selected. Click Start. The process should not take much time at all, possibly less than a second. Figure 31-17 shows the result of processing the aggregations.

Click Next and the wizard will enable you to process the cube. Select Process and click Finish. The Process dialog shown in Figure 31-18 shows the interaction between Analysis Services and the data warehouse.

After the cube has been processed, click Close. Your cube is finally ready to be queried.

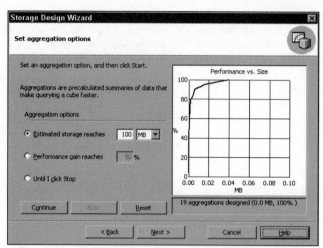

**Figure 31-17:** The aggregations are calculated and provide different storage and performance options.

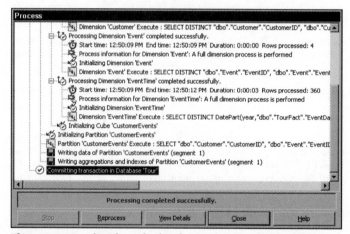

**Figure 31-18:** After the cube has been processed, this dialog enables you to double-click any of the events in order to pull up additional details.

## Querying the Cube from Analysis Manager

Analysis Manager provides a simple interface for retrieving information from the cubes that you have created. You can open the Cube Browser by right-clicking the cube you want to browse and selecting Browse Data from the context menu. The Cube Browser will enable you to see what is stored within the cube and what type of aggregations are able to be computed. Figure 31-19 shows what the Cube Browser sees when looking at the cube created earlier in the chapter.

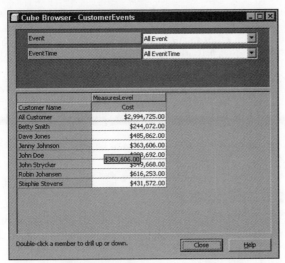

**Figure 31-19:** The Cube Browser presents different scenarios for you to work with.

The Cube Browser can render the data in several different ways. In Figure 31-19, the upper portion of the window where both `Event` and `EventTime` are located is referred to as the *data-slicing pane*. The grid in the lower half of the window where the customers are currently located is referred to as the *data-viewing pane*. Within the Cube Browser you can move the data items around. The default layout is good if you want to know about each of the customers. If your goal is to find out more about the different quarters or months of the year, you can drag the `EventTime` dimension down to the data-viewing pane and move the `Customers` dimension up to the data-slicing pane. This type of interface is shown in Figure 31-20.

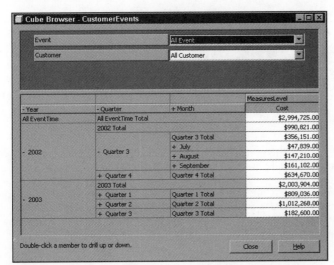

**Figure 31-20:** If you want to view the data based on time, use this interface.

You can now drill down on individual years, quarters, months, and even days. You can also try selecting different dimensions from the data-slicing pane. If you select a different customer the data-viewing pane only shows data that pertains to that customer. Additionally, you can select a single event that the customer attended to see how much was spent at different times in the year.

If you want to you can also drag the remaining dimensions from the data-slicing pane down to the data-viewing pane. The Cube Browser breaks the data down into tiers. Based on some of the numbers from the Cube Browser, it looks as if Cape Hatteras Adventures is doing very well with just a few customers and a limited number of events.

While the Cube Browser is a powerful tool, most users are not going to have access to it. The next section covers the topic of accessing cubes from Microsoft Excel.

## Using Cubes from Microsoft Excel

Microsoft Excel is a perfect match for OLAP cubes. There is a great deal of similarity between the Cube Browser within Analysis Manager and an Excel spreadsheet. In this section you'll see how Microsoft Excel can interact with the Tour cube created earlier in the chapter.

Once you have the data connected to the Excel PivotTable, the interface is similar to that of the Cube Browser. To get started you will need to start Microsoft Excel and select Data ➪ PivotTable and PivotChart. This will launch the PivotChart and PivotTable Wizard shown in Figure 31-21.

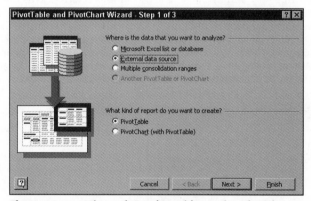

**Figure 31-21:** Microsoft Excel provides an interface for linking to OLAP cubes for data viewing.

In Figure 31-21, the default option is to use a Microsoft Excel list or database. Change this option so that Excel uses the External data source, and click Next. The wizard will ask you to specify where you will be drawing the data for the pivot table. Click the Get Data button to open the Choose Data Source dialog. Continue by clicking the OLAP Cube tab. This will show all the available data sources for OLAP cubes on your system. If <New Data Source> is selected, click OK to create a new data source. Fill out the information for the Create New Data Source dialog, as shown in Figure 31-22.

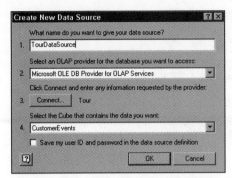

**Figure 31-22:** Excel will get its information for the PivotTable from this dialog.

For the first field shown in Figure 31-22 you just need to enter a data source name. In the second field you need to specify the appropriate provider for the database you are retrieving data from. For this example, you should choose the Microsoft OLE DB Provider for OLAP Services. After clicking Connect, indicate on the Multi-Dimensional Connection screen that you will be connecting to an OLAP server, and then specify the server name. For this example, use the localhost server, the one that runs on your local system. After clicking the Next button, specify which database under Analysis Services you want to work with. Select the Tour database—the one that was created earlier in the chapter—and then click Finish.

After you have indicated where the data is, select the cube you want Excel to use. Do this by checking the combo box shown in Figure 31-22. You can select CustomerEvents from the dropdown box. Click OK once to close the Create New Data Source dialog and then click it again once TourDataSource is selected. You have now entered enough information for the PivotTable to be created. After returning to the PivotTable and PivotChart Wizard, click Next and use the default location of =$A$3 to insert the PivotTable. After clicking Finish, the PivotTable will be inserted and the PivotTable toolbar available for you to use.

Measures will go into the section labeled "Drop Data Items Here," which is similar to the data-viewing pane in the Cube Browser. You can drag the Cost measure from the PivotTable toolbar to the Data Item area within the PivotTable. Next, you can drag different dimensions to different locations within the PivotTable. You can drag dimensions to either the space labeled "Drop Row Fields Here" or the space labeled "Drop Column Fields Here." Figure 31-23 shows a completed PivotTable similar to the one that was created earlier with the Cube Browser from Analysis Manager.

The previous example showed the true power of Analysis Services. Not only can you create cubes from within Analysis Manager, but the cubes can then be used by common client applications like Microsoft Excel. Without Analysis Services a lot of development time would be required to create the basic functionality that Analysis Services provides out of the box. Analysis Services provides both the speed and flexibility required for OLAP.

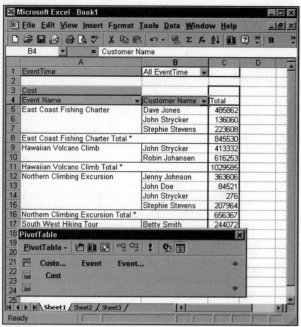

**Figure 31-23:** Microsoft Excel provides an attractive interface with which the end user can look at information within an OLAP cube.

## Summary

This chapter has covered the basics of Analysis Services. You have learned what dimensions, measures, and cubes are, and how Analysis Services uses them. You have learned how to create a cube based on fact and dimension tables and how to browse the cubes using the Cube Browser included with Analysis Manager. Finally, you stepped beyond the Cube Browser and used Microsoft Excel to interact with the cube you created using a PivotTable.

✦    ✦    ✦

# Advanced Portability

T-SQL is a superset of ANSI SQL-92, and it makes a few significant deviations from the ANSI standard. For the most part, these changes make coding easier, although a few minutes saved now may cost hours a few years later as the code is slowly scrubbed of operators that do not comply with ANSI SQL.

I haven't always paid attention to portability.

A while back, someone in the SQLBeginner Yahoo Group asked a question about updating rows based on values in another table using SQL Server. I sent back a quick reply with the `update table set columns from tables` syntax. A frequenter of the group then sent a private message to me stressing the need for code portability. His point was that the cost of database maintenance and porting databases to future platforms, and not the cost of the initial development, is the largest cost of a database.

I've come to agree with notion; I've seen organizations that seemed dead set on a strategy make 180-degree turns without warning.

Even if all indications are that the current database will stay in Microsoft SQL Server for the next 15 years, you can never know for sure. By developing code that's as portable as possible, and clearly commenting code that isn't portable, you're serving your organization well and doing another database developer a favor.

But there's more to the portability problem than just declaring a moratorium on non-portable code. Portability sometimes comes at the cost of proprietary optimizations and enhancements. Microsoft's non-ANSI SQL extensions add significant performance enhancements, add functionality, and make complex programming easier. The question on whether to use non-portable extensions as opposed to straight ANSI SQL pits today's deadline and specifications against tomorrow's conversion project.

## Detecting Non-ANSI Standard Code

The FIPS flagger is a feature in most databases that warns of code that does not meet the Federal Information Processing Standard 127-2, as defined by the National Institute of Standards and Technology and based on ANSI SQL-92 and ISO/IEC SQL-92.

By default, SQL Server's FIPS flagger is off. If you wish to see the warnings as the code is parsed, set the following connection setting:

```
SET FIPS_FLAGGER 'Entry'
```

The FIPS flagger accepts four levels of SQL-92 compliance; off, entry, intermediate, and full.

# Developing Portable Code

Of the non-portable SQL extensions, some are easy to avoid or rewrite later while others would require a major overhaul during the conversion project. Correcting non-portable code can be frustrating because non-portable code tends to have a ripple effect within the database. To that point, a non-portable extension that calculates critical figures in your database could be replaced with code that actually conforms to ANSI standards. In doing so, the output of the modified ANSI compliant code may yield results slightly different and need a larger column in the database, for example. You are then forced to update all tables where these results are stored. This kind of operation can have a negative impact on a DBMS that needs to operate around the clock.

When writing SQL it may prove useful to fully investigate all extensions to determine their portability. If certain non-portable extensions are used throughout your code, it will give you some idea of just how much effort will be involved should the need arise to rewrite everything to conform to ANSI standards.

While it's impossible to develop a 100 percent portable database, some proprietary commands and techniques are best avoided.

## The update...from Command

The update command, by definition, updates a single table. If the criterion to select the correct rows requires an additional table, SQL Server includes the optional, non-ANSI standard, from clause:

```
UPDATE Table
  SET Col = Expression
  FROM table
    JOIN table ...
```

An ANSI-standard version of the same code uses a subquery to locate the correct rows for updating:

```
UPDATE Table
  Set Col = Expression
    WHERE Col IN
      (SELECT Col FROM OtherTable WHERE Col = x)
```

## The delete...from Command

Much like the update...from syntax, the syntax of the delete... from command also uses an extra from clause to specify additional tables used for the where clause:

```
DELETE FROM Table
From
```

As with the `update...from` command, the ANSI-standard method uses a subquery:

```
DELETE FROM Table
  WHERE col1 IN
    (SELECT col1 FROM OtherTable WHERE Col = x)
```

## The top Command

The `top` command returns a limited number of rows from a `select` statement. While it's useful, `top` is specific to Microsoft SQL Server and Access:

```
SELECT TOP 10 WITH TIES ProductName
  FROM Product
  ORDER BY Name
```

The ANSI equivalent of using `top` is actually non-existent and thus a prime example of code that will require a rewrite should you move it to a different database. As you can see in the following table, returning a predetermined number of rows varies among databases.

**Table 32-1: Methods of Limiting the Number of Returned Rows Vary Widely among Various Databases**

| Database | SQL Syntax |
| --- | --- |
| DB2 | select * from table fetch first 10 rows only |
| Informix | select first 10 * from table |
| Microsoft SQL Server and Access | select top 10 * from table |
| MySQL and PostgreSQL | select * from table limit 10 |
| Oracle | select * from (select * from table) where rownum <= 10 |

## User-Defined Functions

When I first got into SQL Server 2000, I was excited about user-defined functions. They combine the benefits of stored procedures with the flexible usage of views. However, user-defined functions are doubly non-portable:

✦ The user-defined functions themselves must be rewritten. Inline user-defined table-valued functions can be rewritten as views. Multi-line table-valued functions can be rewritten as stored procedures. Scalar user-defined functions have no equivalent component.

✦ User-defined functions can supply data to a SQL statement within the `from` clause, meaning that every SQL statement that references the user-defined function will have to be overhauled.

## Partition Views

SQL Server's local- and distributed-partition views add significant scalability. While they are not portable, partition views are easily converted to single tables.

## The set Command

The set command is used to adjust connection-specific properties. Every use of the set command, or any other database- or server-configuration command, is Microsoft-specific and will require redevelopment in a ported environment.

## Logic Programming Flow

T-SQL's programmatic flow-of-control statements, such as if and while, will need to be redeveloped in the language of the new database product. By definition, therefore, most stored procedures and triggers will require modification. However, most programmatic extensions are straightforward and completely unavoidable.

## System Tables

Any reference to SQL Server's system table won't port to another database product, and there's no guarantee that the reference will work in the next version of SQL Server. The safest development plan is to reference the ANSI-standard information-schema views.

## Instead of Triggers on Non-Updateable Views

SQL Server 2000's instead of triggers can be created on views, which converts a normally non-updateable view into a view that is programmatically updateable. The instead of trigger isn't portable, so any code that depends on the view being updateable will have to be redeveloped.

## View with order by

ANSI SQL views do not include an order by clause; however, Microsoft SQL Server will allow an order by clause if the view also includes a top 100 percent predicate.

The order by clause is non-portable, and any SQL DML statements that call the view will require modification.

# Summary

Developing portable code takes more effort than using the SQL Server T-SQL extensions. A few update and delete statements will require a subquery in lieu of a from clause. But in the long term, valuing code portability saves money and extends respect to future developers.

✦　　✦　　✦

# Resources

**T**he following is a collection of resources I have found useful as a
SQL Server developer and DBA.

## Books

✦ Celko, Joe, *SQL for Smarties, Advanced SQL Programming*. This
   is *the* guidebook for using SQL.

✦ Date, Chris J., *A Introduction to Database Systems, 7th Edition*.
   The standard reference work for all things database.

✦ Delaney, Kalen, *Inside SQL Server 2000*. The best source for
   details and insight into the database engine.

✦ Henderson, Ken, *The Guru's Guide to Transact-SQL*. Incredible
   details. One of the best T-SQL books available, but it's for SQL 7.

✦ McCarthy, Jim, *Dynamics of Software Development*. Fifty-three
   rules for delivering great software on time. Written in story
   format.

## Publications

✦ Server Magazine

   http://www.SQLMag.com

✦ SQL Server Professional Newsletter

   http://www.pinpub.com/sq

## Web Pages

✦ The author's Web site:

   http://www.IsNotNull.com

✦ SQL Server and Oracle feature comparison:

   http://www.bristle.com/Tips/SQL.htm

✦ MaraTrane Solutions SQL Server Links:

   http://www.MaraTrane.com/SQLServerLinks.asp

+ SQL Server Performance:

    http://www.sql-server-performance.com/

+ SQL Beginners and SQL Server Yahoo Groups (Search for SQL Server):

    http://groups.yahoo.com/

+ SQL Server Central:

    http://www.sqlservercentral.com/

+ Database Journal:

    http://www.databasejournal.com/

+ SQL DTS–devoted Web site:

    http://www.sqldts.com/

+ SQLDTS.com — Data Transformation Services on the Web:

    http://www.sqldts.com/

+ Planet Source Code's SQL page:

    http://www.planetsourcecode.com/xq/ASP/lngWId.5/qx/vb/default.htm

+ XML info:

    http://www.w3.org
    msdn.microsoft.com/xml

+ XML DTD tools:

    http://www.tibco.com

# Third-Party Products

+ Log Explorer by Lumigent Technologies

    http://www.lumigent.com

+ Total SQL Analyzer by FMS

    http://www.fmsinc.com/products/sqlanalyzer/index.html

# Organizations

+ Professional Association for SQL Server

    http://www.sqlpass.org

+   +   +

# Sample Databases

◆    ◆    ◆    ◆

**In This Appendix**

The filelist, background, requirements, diagrams, and descriptions for the five sample databases.

◆    ◆    ◆    ◆

This book draws examples from the following five sample databases, each designed to illustrate a particular design concept or development style:

♦ *Cape Hatteras Adventures* is actually two sample databases that together demonstrate upsizing to a relational SQL Server database. Version 1 consists of a simple Access database and an Excel spreadsheet — neither of which is very sophisticated. Version 2 is a typical small- to mid-sized SQL Server database employing identity columns and views. It uses an Access project as a front end and publishes data to the Web using the SQL Server Web Publishing Wizard and stored procedures.

♦ The *OBXKites* database tracks inventory, customers, and sales for a fictitious kite retailer with four stores in North Carolina's Outer Banks. This database is designed for robust scalability. It employs GUIDs for replicationand Unicode for international sales. In various chapters in the book, partitioned views, full auditing features, and Analysis Services cubes are added to the OBXKites database.

♦ The *Family* database stores family tree history. While the database has only two tables, `person` and `marriage`, it sports the complexities of a many-to-many self-join and extraction of hierarchical data.

♦ Twenty-five of *Aesop's Fables* provide the text for Chapter 8, "Searching Full-Text Indexes."

♦ The *Material Specification* database demonstrates a dynamic/relational database design and stores an unlimted number of properties for materials organized by type.

This Appendix documents required files (Table B-1) and the database schemas for the sample databases.

## The Sample Database Files

The sample files should be installed into the `C:\SQLServerBible` directory. The SQL Server sample Web applications are coded to look for template files in a certain directory structure. The DTS packages and distributed queries also assume that the Access and Excel files are in that directory.

## Table B-1: Sample Database Files

### *Cape Hatteras Adventures Version 2*

`C:\SQLServerBible\Sample Databases\CapeHatterasAdventures`

| | |
|---|---|
| `CHA2_Create.sql` | Script that generates the database for Cape Hatteras Adventures Version 2, including tables, constraints, indexes, views, stored procedures, and user security. |
| `CHA_Convert.sql` | Distributed queries that convert data from Access and Excel into the Cape Hatteras Adventures Version 2 database. This script mirrors the DTS package and assumes that the Access and Excel source files are in the `C:\SQLServerBible` directory. |
| `CHA_Conversion.dts` | DTS package that converts data from Access and Excel into the Cape Hatteras Adventures Version 2 database. For more information about how the DTS package works, refer to Chapter 19, "Migrating Data with DTS." |
| `CHA1_Customers.mdb` | Access database of customer list, used prior to SQL Server conversion. Data is imported from this file into the `CHA1` SQL Server database. |
| `CHA1_Schdule.xls` | Excel spreadsheet of events, tours, and guides, used prior to SQL Server conversion. Data is imported from this file into the `CHA1` SQL Server database. |
| `CHA2_Events.xml` | Sample XML file. |
| `CHA2_Events.dtd` | Sample XML Data Type Definition file. |
| `CHA2.adp` | Sample Access front end to the `CHA2` database. |

### *OBX Kites*

`C:\SQLServerBible\Sample Databases\OBXKites`

| | |
|---|---|
| `OBXKites_Create.sql` | Script that generates the database for the `OBXKites` database, including tables, views, stored procedures, and functions. |
| `OBXKites_Populate.sql` | Script that populates the database for the `OBXKites` database with sample data by calling the stored procedures. |
| `OBXKites_Query.sql` | A series of sample test queries with which to test the population of the `OBXKites` database. |

### *The Family*

`C:\SQLServerBible\Sample Databases\Family`

| | |
|---|---|
| `Family_Create.sql` | Script that creates the `Family` database tables and stored procedures, and populates the database with sample data. |
| `Family_Queries.sql` | A set of sample queries against the `Family` database. |

| *Aesop's Fables* | |
| --- | --- |
| `C:\SQLServerBible\Sample Databases\Aesop` | |
| `Aesop_Create.sql` | Script that creates the `Aesop` database and `Fable` table and populates the database with 25 of Aesop's fables. This sample database is used with full-text search. |
| `Aesop.adp` | Access front end for browsing the fables. |

| *Material Specifications* | |
| --- | --- |
| `C:\SQLServerBible\Sample Databases\MaterialSpec` | |
| `MS_Create.sql` | Script to create the Material Specification database. |
| `MS_Populate.sql` | Script to populate the Material Specification database with sample data from a computer-clone store. |

To create one of the sample databases, run the `create` script within Query Analyzer. The script will drop the database if it exists. These scripts make it easy to rebuild the database, so if you want to experiment, go ahead. Because the script drops the database, no connections to the database can exist when the script is run. Enterprise Manager will often keep the connection even if another database is selected. If you encounter an error, chances are that Enterprise Manager, or a second connection in Query Analyzer, is holding an open connection.

# Cape Hatteras Adventures Version 2

The fictitious Cape Hatteras Adventures (CHA) is named for the Cape Hatteras lighthouse in North Carolina, one of the most famous lighthouses and life-saving companies in America. Cape Hatteras is the easternmost point of North Carolina's Outer Banks, known for incredible empty beaches and the graveyard of the Atlantic.

Cape Hatteras Adventures leads wild and sometimes exotic adventures for the rich and famous. From excursions down the gnarly Gauley River in West Virginia to diving for sunken treasure off the Outer Banks to chopping through the Amazon jungle, Cape Hatteras Adventures gets its guests there and brings them back, often alive and well.

The staff and management of CHA are outdoors folks and their inclination to avoid the indoors shows in the effort that's been put into IT. The customer/prospect list is maintained in Access 2000 in a single-table database. It's used primarily for mailings. The real workhorse is an Excel spreadsheet that tracks events, tours, and tour guides in a single flat-file format. In the same page, a second list tracks customers for each event. Although the spreadsheet is not a proper normalized database, it does contain the necessary information to run the business.

QuickBooks handles all financial and billing activities and both the company president and the bookkeeper are very satisfied with that setup. They foresee no need to improve the financial or billing software.

# Application Requirements

CHA has grown to the point that it realizes the need for a better scheduling application; however, it desires to "keep the tough work in the rapids and not in the computer." CHA has contracted for the development and maintenance of the database.

All scheduling and booking of tours takes place at the main office in Cape Hatteras, North Carolina. CHA launches tours from multiple sites, or base camps, throughout the world. The base camps generally have no computer access and sometimes no electricity. A guide or guides are dispatched to the base camp with a printed guest list. If it's determined in the future that a base camp may need to be staffed and to have access to the schedule on line, a Web page will be developed at that time.

Each base camp may be responsible for multiple tours. A tour is a prearranged, repeatable experience. Each time the tour is offered, it's referred to as an event. An event will have one lead guide, who is responsible for the safety and enjoyment of the guests. Other guides may also come along as needed.

As CHA brings on more guides with broader skills, the database must track the guides and the tours each is qualified to lead.

# Database Design

The database design uses typical one-to-many relationships between customer type and customer, and from guide to base camp to tour to event. Many-to-many relationships exist between customer and event, guide and tour, and guide and event, as shown in Figure B-1.

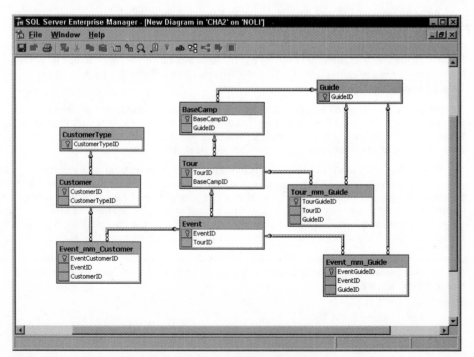

**Figure B-1:** The Cape Hatteras Adventures database schema

Concerning the development style, there is at the moment no need for multiple database sites, so identity columns will be used for simplicity of design. The primary access means that access to the data is through views and direct `select` statements.

### Data Conversion

The `CHA2_Create.sql` script creates an empty database. The data resides in the Access and Excel spreadsheets. Both the `CHA_Conversion` DTS package and the `CHA_Convert.sql` script can extract the data from Access and Excel and load it into SQL Server.

### CHA2.adp Front End

Because the Cape Hatteras Adventures staff is comfortable with Access forms and does not require the robustness of a full Visual Basic or .Net application, a simple front end has been developed using Access .adp project technology.

# OBX Kites

OBX Kites is a high-quality kite retailer serving kite enthusiasts and vacationers around the Outer Banks, where the winds are so steady the Wright brothers chose the area (Kill Devil Hills) for their historic glider flights and their first powered flights. OBX Kites operates a main store/warehouse and four remote retail locations, and is planning to launch an e-commerce Web site.

## Application Requirements

OBX Kites needs a solid and useful order/inventory/PO system with a middle-of-the-road set of features. For simplicity, all contacts are merged into a single table and the contact type is signified by flags. A contact can be a customer, employee, or vendor. Customers have a lookup for customer type, which is referenced in determining the discount. Full details are maintained on customers, with a summer location and the home location. The product/inventory system must handle multiple suppliers per product, price history, multiple inventory items per product, multiple locations, and inventory transactions to track the inventory movement.

## Database Design

The database design uses standard one-to-many relationships throughout.

The database construction must support replication and Unicode for international customers. For performance and flexibility, the database implements with two filegroups — one for heavy transactions and the other for static read-mostly data.

The database design (Figure B-2) is a standard inventory, order-processing database.

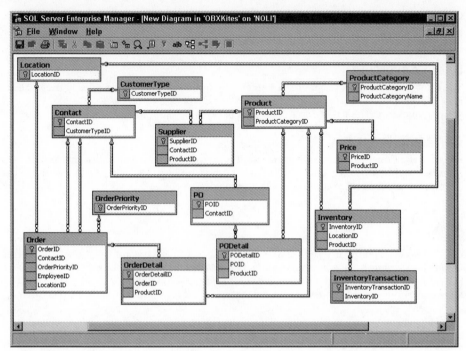

**Figure B-2:** The OBXKites sample database schema, as shown in Enterprise Manager's Database Diagrammer

# The Family

This small database demonstrates multiple hierarchical reflexive relationships for interesting queries and both cursors and queries to navigate the genealogical hierarchy.

## Application Requirements

The family database must store every person in the family, along with genealogical information, including both biological and marital relationships. The database is populated with five generations of a fictitious family for query purposes.

## Database Design

The Family database consists of two tables and three relationships, as configured in the Database Designer in Figure B-3. Each person has an optional reflexive MotherID and FatherID foreign key back to the PersonID. The marriage table has a foreign key to the PersonID for the husband and the wife. The primary keys are integer columns for simplicity.

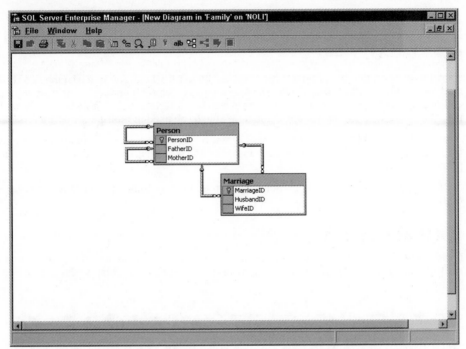

**Figure B-3:** The Family sample database schema as shown in Enterprise Manager's Database Diagrammer

# Aesop's Fables

Aesop's collection of fables is an excellent test bed for string searches and full-text search. The fables are relatively short and familiar, and they're in the public domain.

## Application Requirements

The primary purpose of this database is to enable you to experience SQL Server's full-text search. Therefore the database must include a few character columns, a BLOB or image column, and a BLOB-type column.

## Database Design

The database design is very simple — a single table with one fable per row.

# Material Specifications

The `Material Specifications` database is an example of a data-driven dynamic relational database design.

## Application Requirements

The goal of the material-specification system is to identify any number of material properties for any number of materials.

Materials are grouped by material type and then by material state. A material may go through multiple versions of development, so the specifications for each version must be maintained and readily comparable. The bill of materials for any material must be able to include multiple other materials, and any material must be able to be used in multiple other materials.

A property may apply to multiple material types, but must be limited to materials of those material types. For each version or each material, the system must maintain the spec value for each material.

All this must be dynamic and constant change must be easy to handle without any database or programming changes.

## Database Design

Beginning with the material table, each material belongs to a single material type; the material types are grouped by material state in traditional one-to-many relationships, as shown in Figure B-4

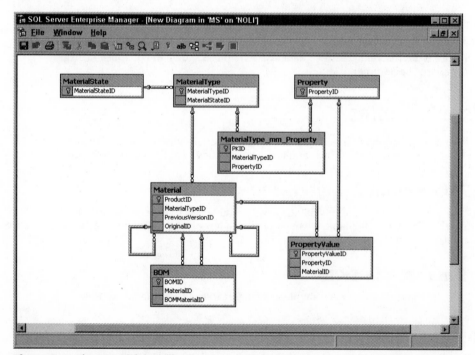

**Figure B-4:** The Material Specification sample database schema as shown in Enterprise Manager's Database Diagrammer

There's a many-to-many relationship between material type and property, so that each material type may have multiple properties and each property may apply to multiple material types. The property value contains the actual material-specification value for each many-to-many combination of material and property.

Materials have two direct reflexive relationships: Each material points back both to the original version of that material and to the previous version.

The bill of materials is actually a multiple reflexive relationship among any material and multiple other materials, with additional data describing the reflexive relationship.

Because the database design is complex, identity columns are used for simplicity.

✦　　✦　　✦

# SQL Server 2000
# Specifications

## Table C-1: SQL Server Specifications

| Feature | SQL Server 6.5 | SQL Server 7.0 | SQL Server 2000 |
|---|---|---|---|
| **Server Features** | | | |
| Automatic Configuration | No | Yes | Yes |
| Page Size | 2KB | 8KB | 8KB |
| Max Row Size | 1,962 bytes | 8,060 bytes | 8,060 bytes |
| Page-Level Locking | Yes | Yes | Yes |
| Row-Level Locking | Insert only | Yes | Yes |
| Files Located | Devices | Files and filegroups | Files and filegroups |
| Kerberos and Security Delegation | No | No | Yes |
| C2 Security Certification | No | No | Yes |
| Bytes Per Character Column | 255 | 8,000 | 8,000 |
| Automatic Log Shipping | No | No | Yes |
| Index-Computed Column | No | No | Yes |
| Max Batch Size | 128KB | 65,536 * network packet–size bytes | 65,536 * network packet–size bytes |
| Bytes Per Text/Image | 2GB | 2GB | 2GB |
| Objects in Database | 2 billion | 2,147,483,647 | 2,147,483,647 |
| Parameters Per Stored Procedure | 255 | 1,024 | 1,024 |
| References Per Table | 31 | 253 | 253 |
| Rows Per Table | Limited by available storage | Limited by available storage | Limited by available storage |
| Table Per Database | 2 billion | Limited by available storage | Limited by available storage |
| Table Per select Statement | 16 | 256 | 256 |
| Triggers Per Table | 3 | Limited by number of objects in database | Limited by number of objects in database |
| Bytes Per Key (Index, Foreign, or Primary) | 900 | 900 | 900 |
| Bytes Per Group by or Order by | 900 | 8,060 | 8,060 |
| Bytes Per Row | 900 | 8,060 | 8,060 |
| Bytes of Source Text Per Stored Procedure | 65,025 | Batch size or 250MB, whichever is less | Batch size or 250MB, whichever is less |

| Feature | SQL Server 6.5 | SQL Server 7.0 | SQL Server 2000 |
|---|---|---|---|
| **Server Features** | | | |
| Columns Per Key (Index, Foreign, or Primary) | 16 | 16 | 16 |
| Columns in Group by or Order by | 16 | Limited by bytes | Unspecified |
| Columns Per Table | 255 | 1,024 | 1,024 |
| Columns Per select Statement | 4,096 | 4,096 | 4,096 |
| Columns Per insert Statement | 250 | 1,024 | 1,024 |
| Database Size | 1TB | 1,048,516TB | 1,048,516TB |
| Databases Per Server | 32,767 | 32,767 | 32,767 (per instance) |
| File Groups Per Database | – | 256 | 256 |
| Files Per Database | 32 | 32,767 | 32,767 |
| Data-File Size | 32GB | 32TB | 32TB |
| Log-File Size | 32GB | 4TB | 32TB |
| Foreign-Key References Per Table | 16 | 253 | 253 |
| Identifier Length (Table, Column Names, Etc.) | 30 | 128 | 128 |
| Instances Per Computer | 1 | 1 | 16 |
| Locks Per Instance | 2,147,483,647 | 2,147,483,647 or 40 percent of SQL Server memory | 2,147,483,647 or 40percent of SQL Server memory |
| Parallel Query Execution | No | Yes | Yes |
| Federated Databases | No | No | Yes |
| Indexes Per Table Used in Query Execution | 1 | Multiple | Multiple |
| **Administration Features** | | | |
| Automatic-Data and Log-File Growth | No | Yes | Yes |
| Automatic Index Statistics | No | Yes | Yes |
| Profiler Tied to Optimizer Events | No | Yes | Yes |
| Alert on Performance Conditions | No | Yes | Yes |
| Conditional Multistep Agent Jobs | No | Yes | Yes |

*Continued*

**Table C-1** *(continued)*

| Feature | SQL Server 6.5 | SQL Server 7.0 | SQL Server 2000 |
|---|---|---|---|
| **Programming Features** | | | |
| Recursive Triggers | no | Yes | Yes |
| Multiple Triggers Per Table Event | No | Yes | Yes |
| instead of Triggers | No | No | Yes |
| Unicode Character Support | No | Yes | Yes |
| User-Defined Function | No | No | Yes |
| Indexed Views | No | No | Yes |
| Cascading DRI Deletes And Updates | No | No | Yes |
| Collation Level | Server | Server | Server, database, table, query |
| Nested Stored-Procedure Levels | 16 | 32 | 32 |
| Nested Subqueries | 16 | 32 | 32 |
| Nested Trigger Levels | 16 | 32 | 32 |
| XML Support | No | No | Yes |
| **Replication Features** | | | |
| Snapshot Replication | Yes | Yes | Yes |
| Transactional Replication | Yes | Yes | Yes |
| Merge Replication with Conflict Resolution | No | Yes | Yes |
| **Enterprise Manager Features** | | | |
| Database Diagram | No | Yes | Yes |
| Graphical Table Creation | Yes | Yes | Yes |
| Database Designer | No | Yes | Yes |
| Query Designer | No | Yes | Yes |

✦　　✦　　✦

# What's on the CD?

Several goodies have been gathered for the book's CD and are organized into the following directories:

+ \ChapterCode — The complete code from this book, organized by chapter.

+ \Chapters — An electronic copy of this book in PDF format.

+ \ProductEvals — Trial editions of the following SQL Server utilities and related products:

  • FMS Total SQL Analyzer Pro, Trial Edition

  • Lumigent's Log Explorer 3.0, Trial Edition

  • RAC 2.0, Trial Edition

  • XML Spy, Trial Edition

  • SQL Expert, Trial Edition

  • Adobe Acrobat Reader (freeware)

+ \SampleDatabase — Six sample databases in the form of DDL scripts to create the databases and scripts to populate the database with sample data. The following sample databases support the code demonstrated within this book:

  • Aesop's Fables (Aesop)

  • Cape Hatteras Adventures (CHA2)

  • Family Tree (Family)

  • Material Specifications (MaterialSpec)

  • Outer Banks Kite Store (OBXKites)

  • Object-Oriented Database (OODBMS)

+ \Utilites — Various useful SQL Server–related scripts.

To use the CD, copy all the files to the \SQLServerBible directory on your C: drive. If you use a different directory, some of the distributed query files may need to be edited.

Check with www.sqlserverbible.com for any code updates, additional links, errata, or additional utilities.

✦  ✦  ✦

# Index

## SYMBOLS AND NUMERICS

*Continued*

*Continued*

*Continued*

# Wiley Publishing, Inc.
# End-User License Agreement

**READ THIS.** You should carefully read these terms and conditions before opening the software packet(s) included with this book "Book". This is a license agreement "Agreement" between you and Wiley Publishing, Inc."WPI". By opening the accompanying software packet(s), you acknowledge that you have read and accept the following terms and conditions. If you do not agree and do not want to be bound by such terms and conditions, promptly return the Book and the unopened software packet(s) to the place you obtained them for a full refund.

1. **License Grant.** WPI grants to you (either an individual or entity) a nonexclusive license to use one copy of the enclosed software program(s) (collectively, the "Software" solely for your own personal or business purposes on a single computer (whether a standard computer or a workstation component of a multi-user network). The Software is in use on a computer when it is loaded into temporary memory (RAM) or installed into permanent memory (hard disk, CD-ROM, or other storage device). WPI reserves all rights not expressly granted herein.

2. **Ownership.** WPI is the owner of all right, title, and interest, including copyright, in and to the compilation of the Software recorded on the disk(s) or CD-ROM "Software Media". Copyright to the individual programs recorded on the Software Media is owned by the author or other authorized copyright owner of each program. Ownership of the Software and all proprietary rights relating thereto remain with WPI and its licensers.

3. **Restrictions On Use and Transfer.**

   (a) You may only (i) make one copy of the Software for backup or archival purposes, or (ii) transfer the Software to a single hard disk, provided that you keep the original for backup or archival purposes. You may not (i) rent or lease the Software, (ii) copy or reproduce the Software through a LAN or other network system or through any computer subscriber system or bulletin- board system, or (iii) modify, adapt, or create derivative works based on the Software.

   (b) You may not reverse engineer, decompile, or disassemble the Software. You may transfer the Software and user documentation on a permanent basis, provided that the transferee agrees to accept the terms and conditions of this Agreement and you retain no copies. If the Software is an update or has been updated, any transfer must include the most recent update and all prior versions.

4. **Restrictions on Use of Individual Programs.** You must follow the individual requirements and restrictions detailed for each individual program in the About the CD-ROM appendix of this Book. These limitations are also contained in the individual license agreements recorded on the Software Media. These limitations may include a requirement that after using the program for a specified period of time, the user must pay a registration fee or discontinue use. By opening the Software packet(s), you will be agreeing to abide by the licenses and restrictions for these individual programs that are detailed in the About the CD-ROM appendix and on the Software Media. None of the material on this Software Media or listed in this Book may ever be redistributed, in original or modified form, for commercial purposes.